WOMEN

AT

WORK

Edited by
Flavia Frigeri, Georgia Atienza
and Constantia Nicolaides

WOMEN

AT

WORK

1900 TO NOW

ME LOOKING AT YOU,
LOOKING AT ME
By Flavia Frigeri
131

THE CHANGING
ICONOGRAPHY OF THE
WOMAN WRITER
By Alison Smith
161

HIDDEN HEROINES OF
DESIGN
By Alice Rawsthorn
179

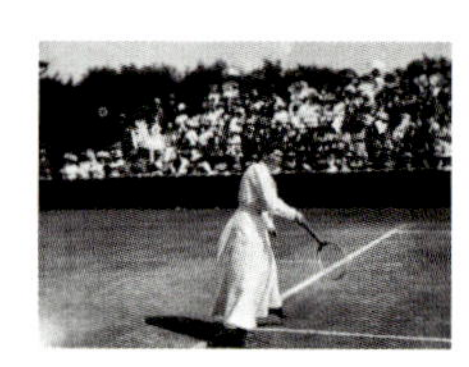
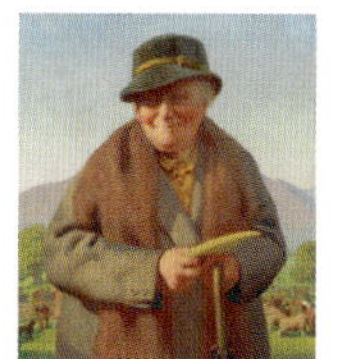
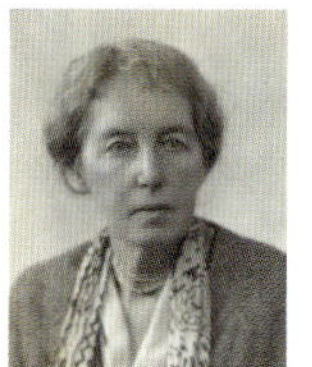
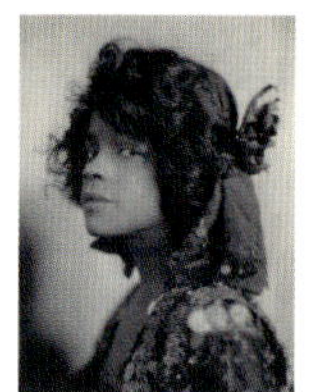
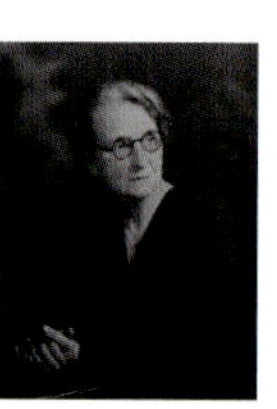
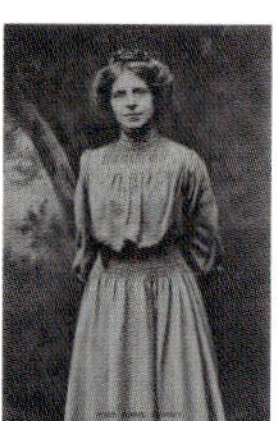
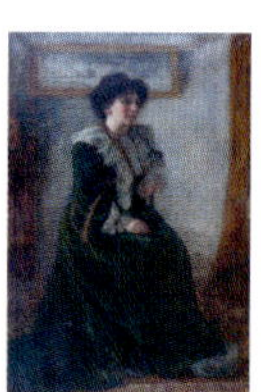
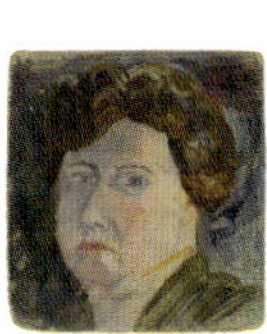
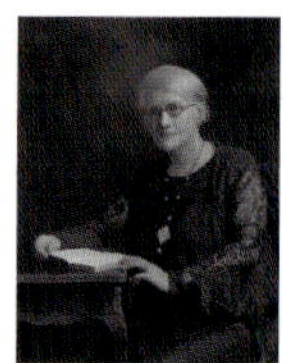
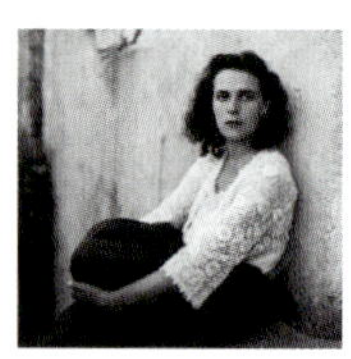
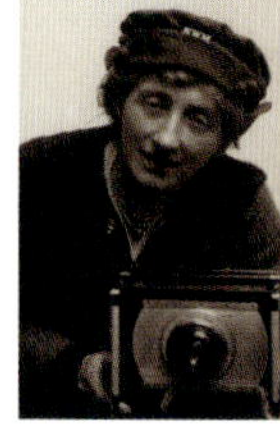
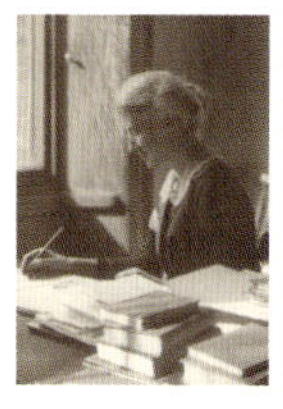
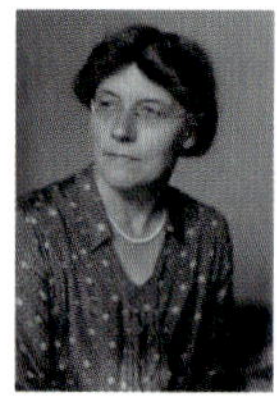
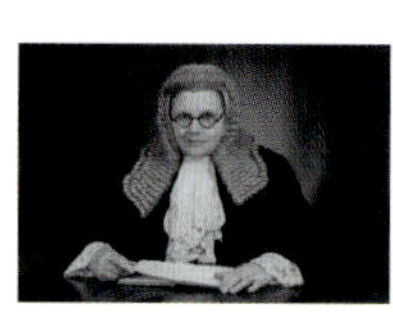
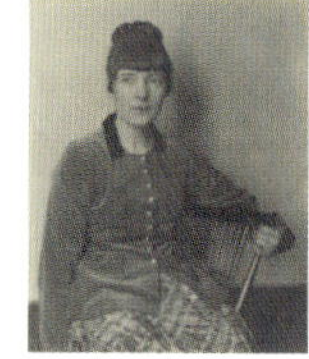
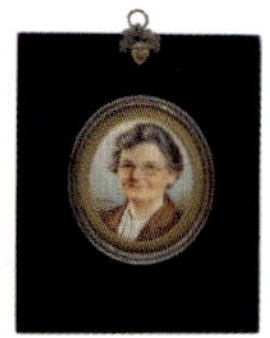
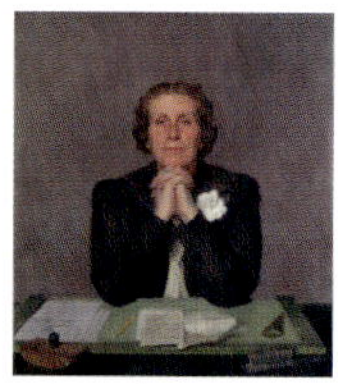
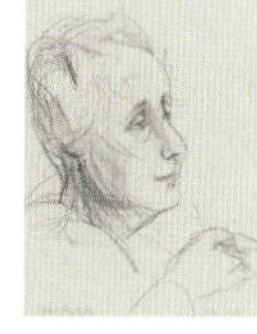
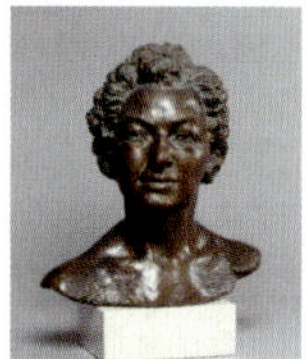
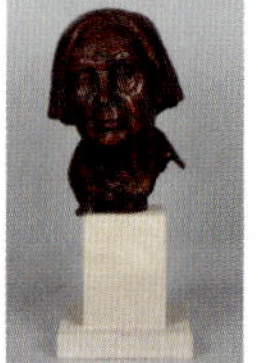
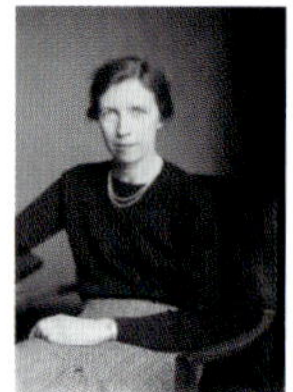
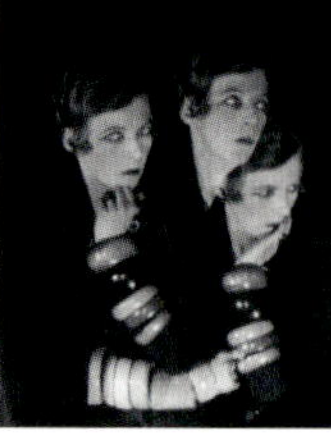
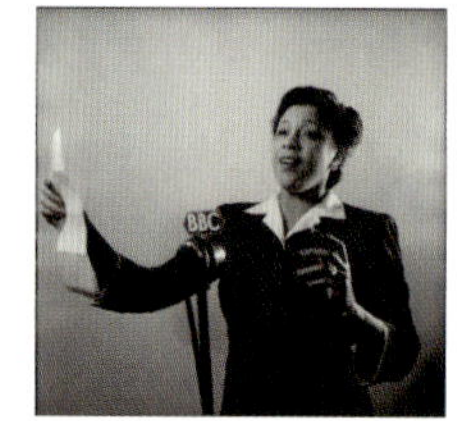
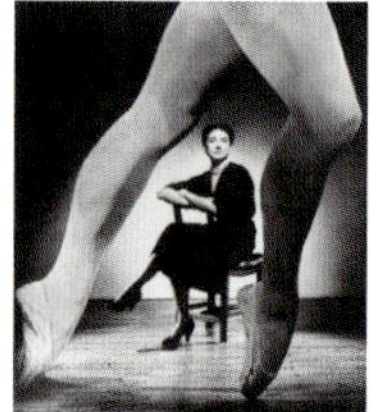
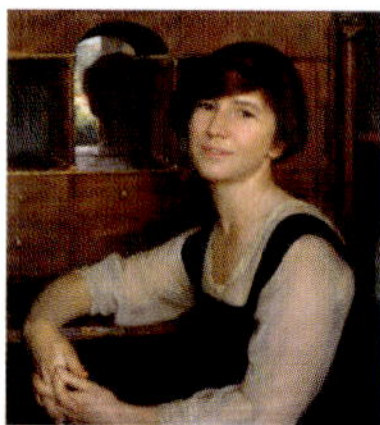
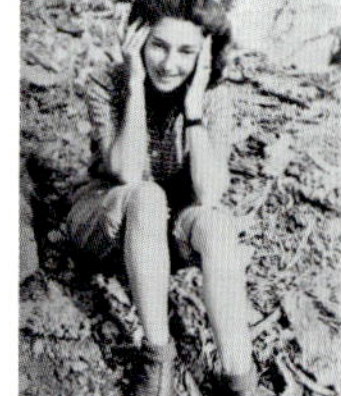
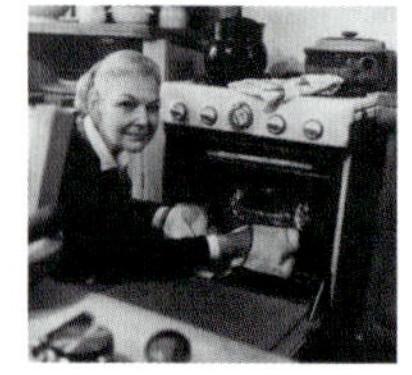

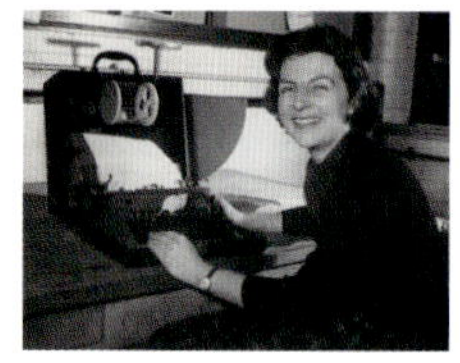
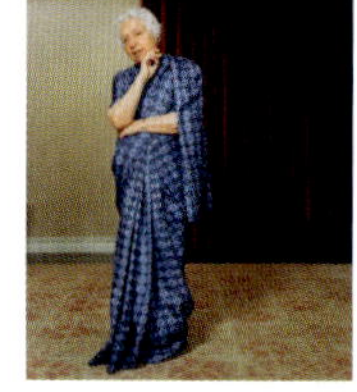
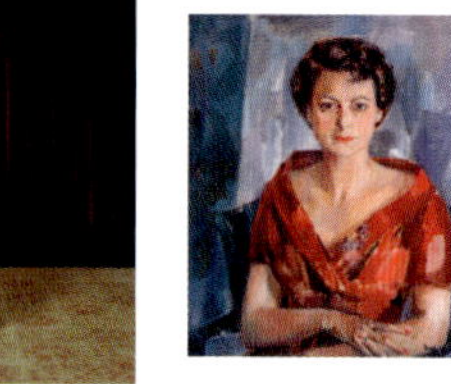
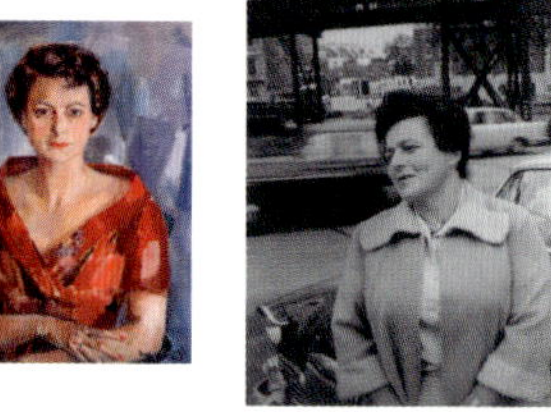
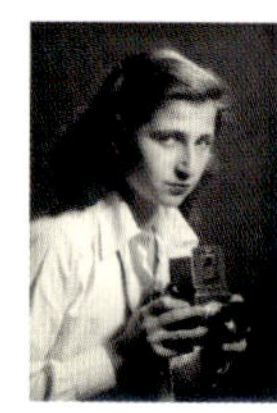
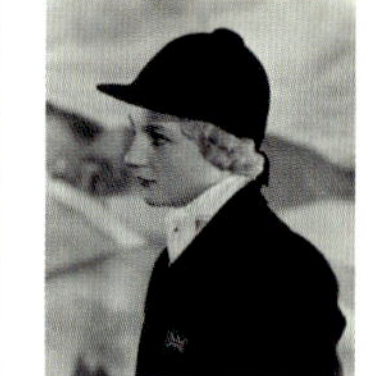
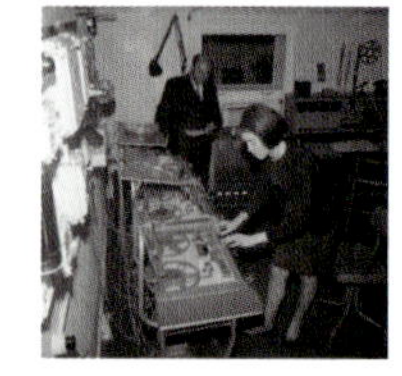
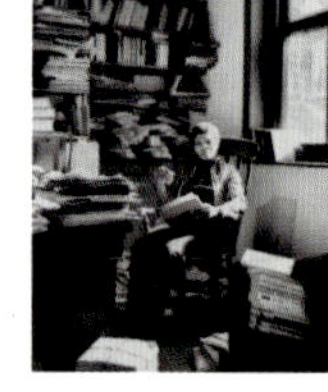
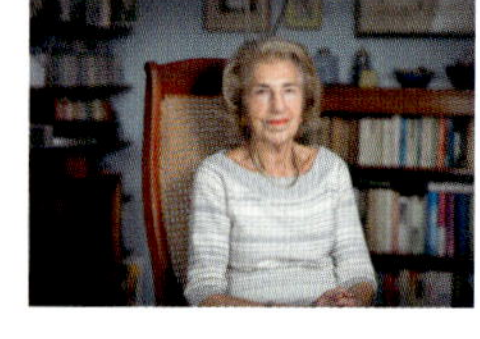
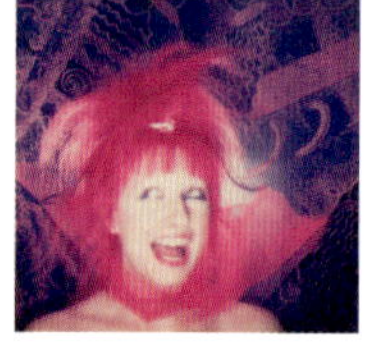
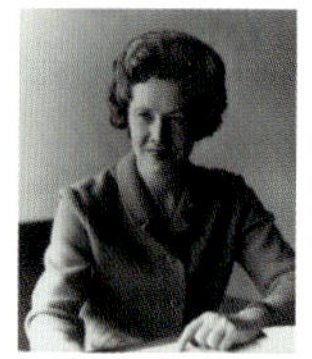
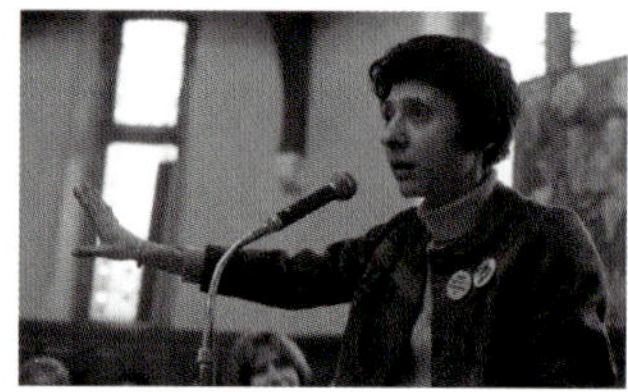
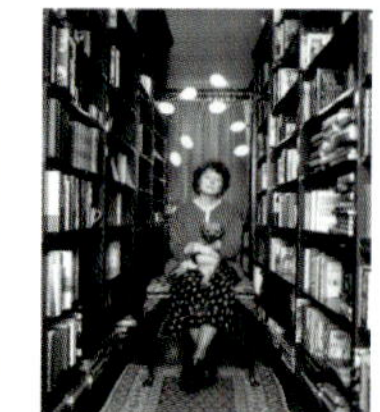
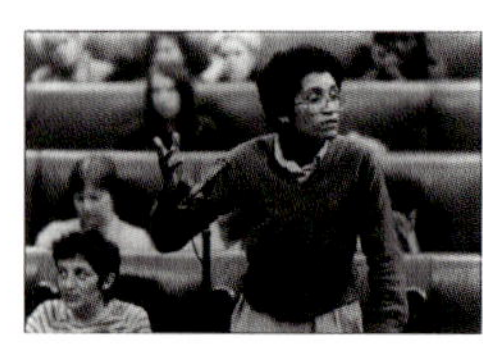
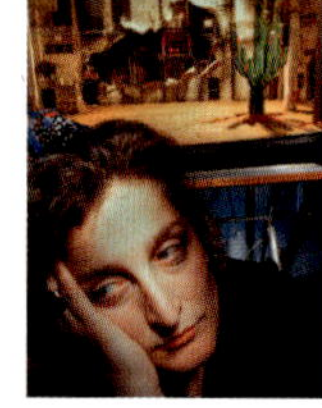
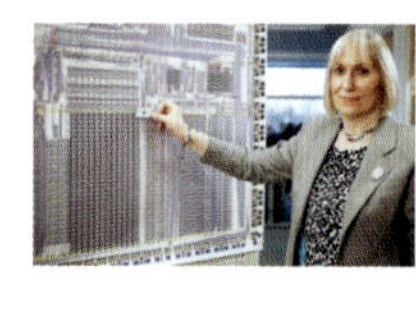
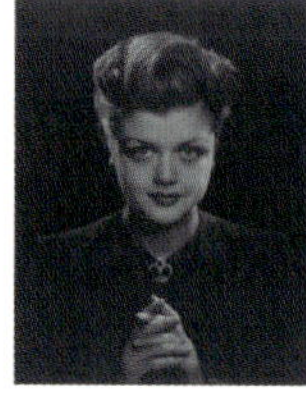
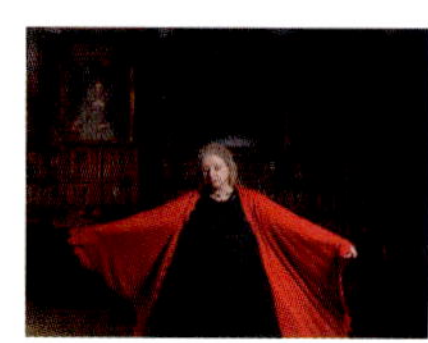
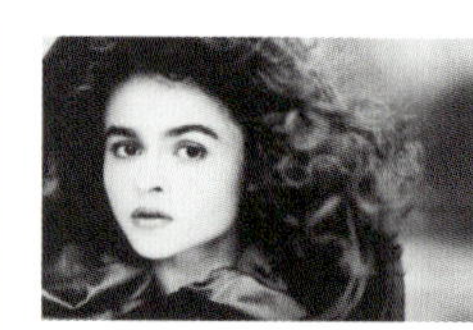
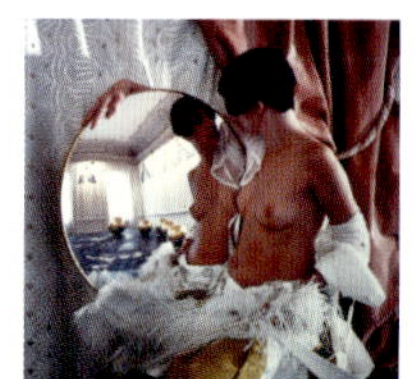
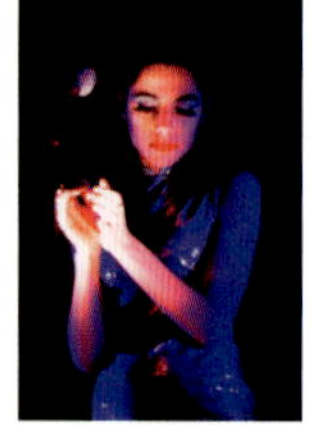
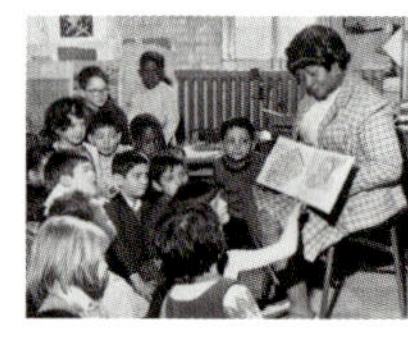
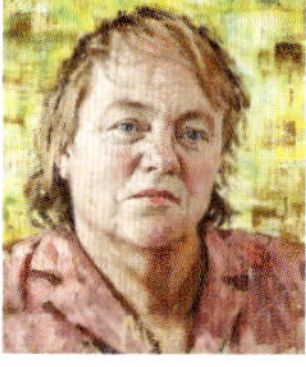
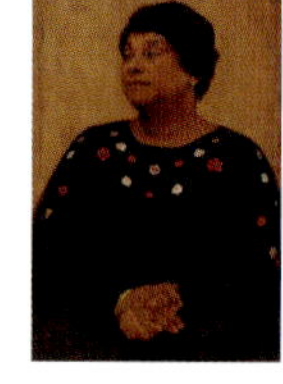
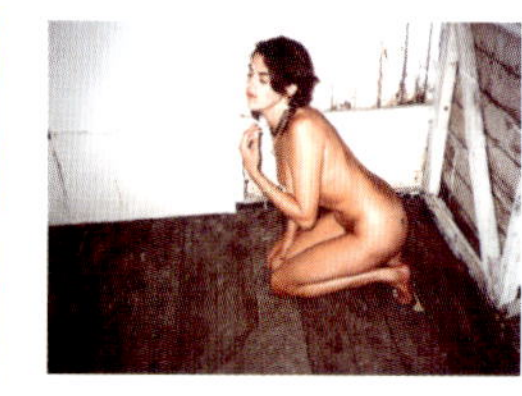
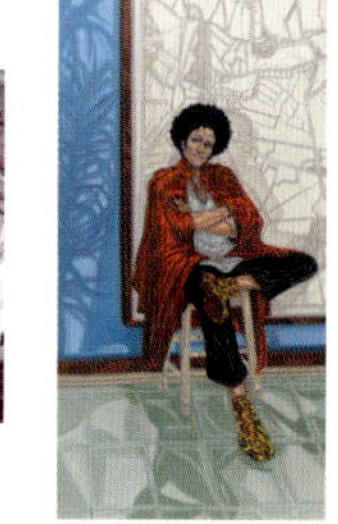
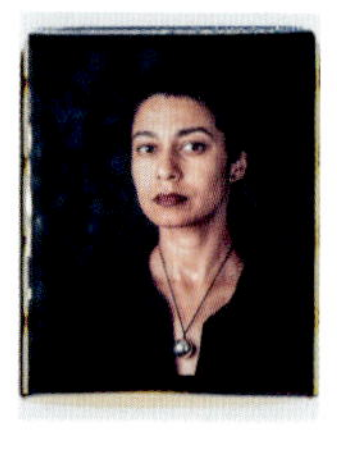
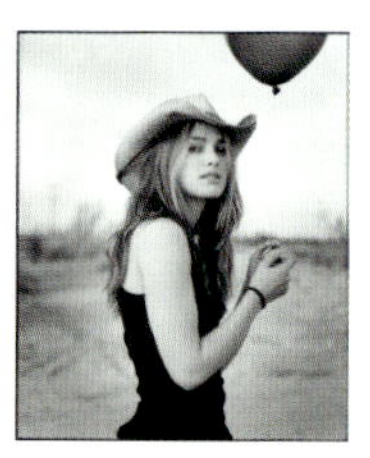
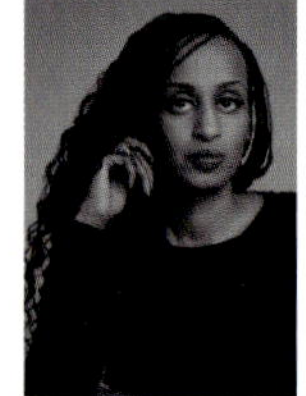
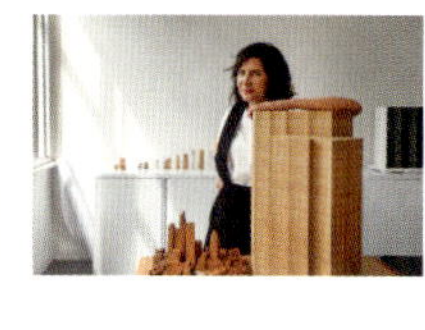
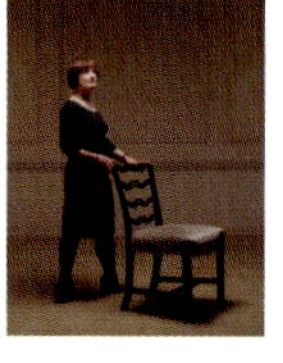
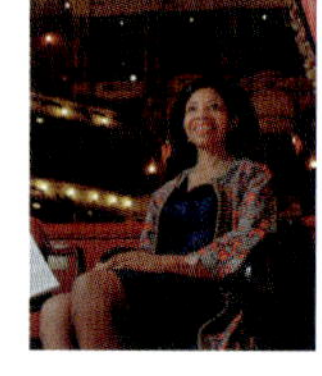
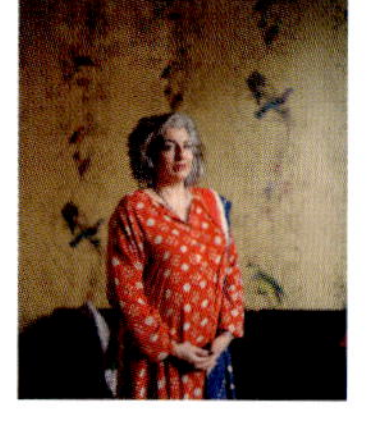
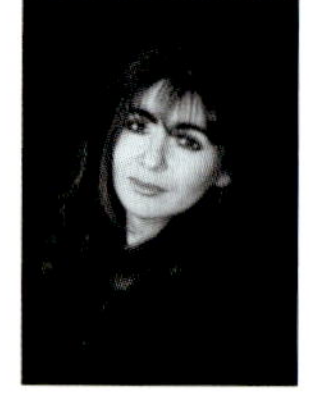
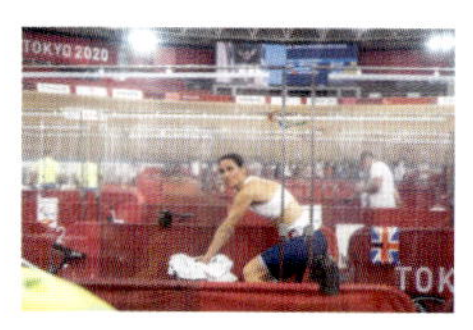
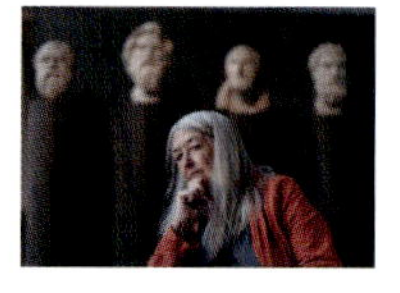

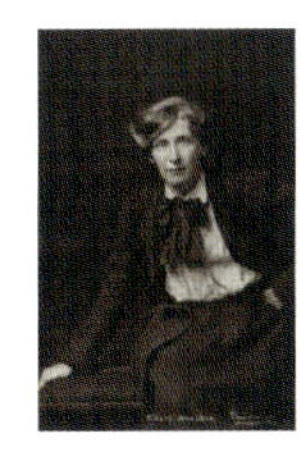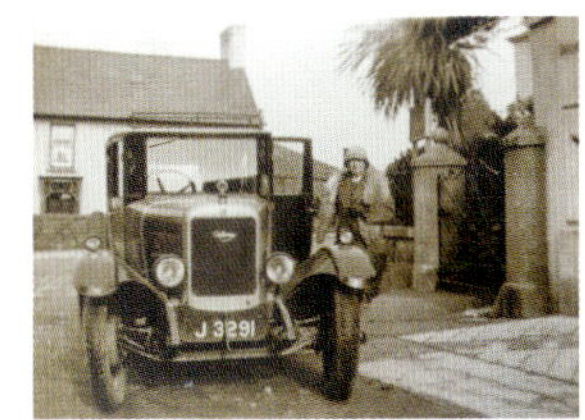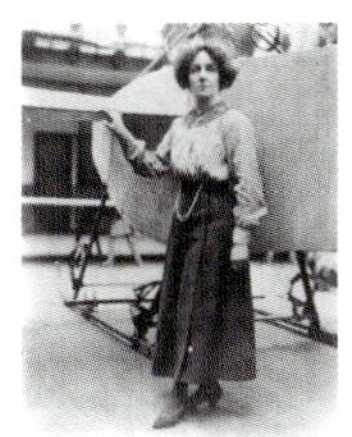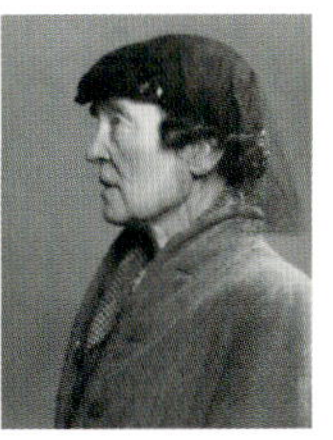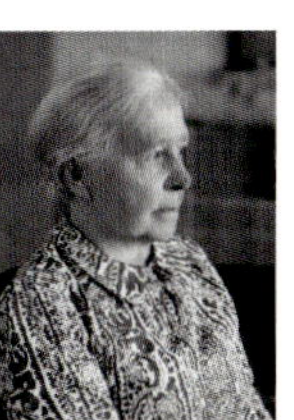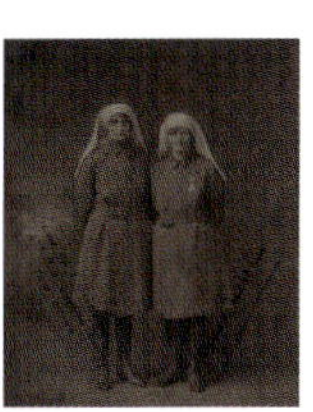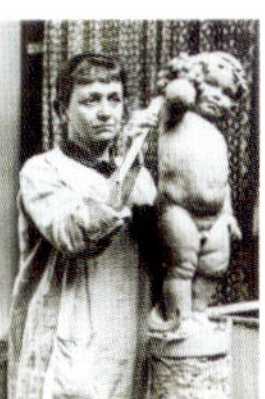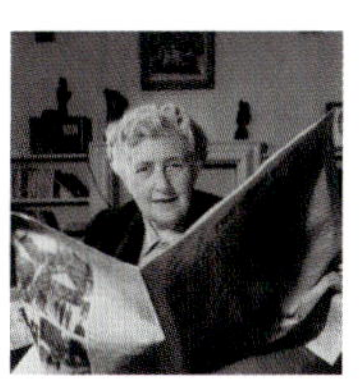
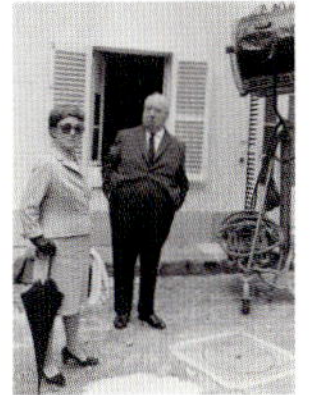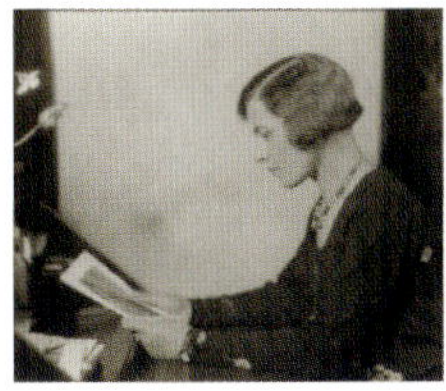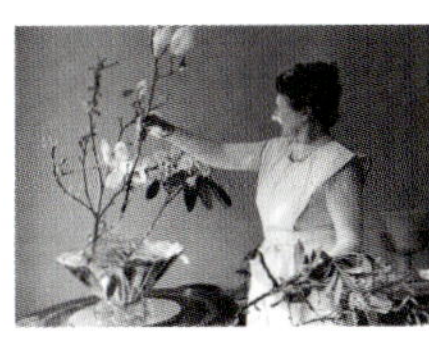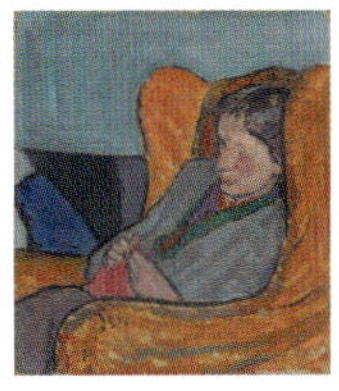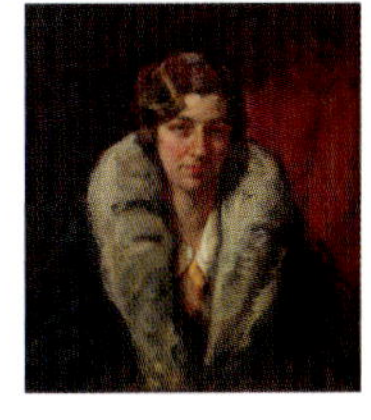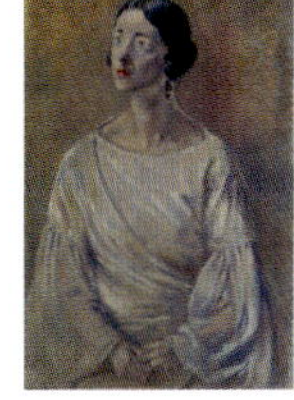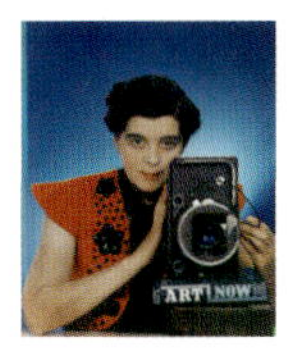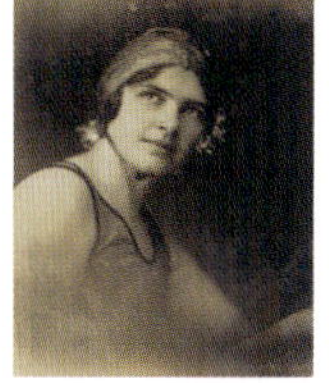
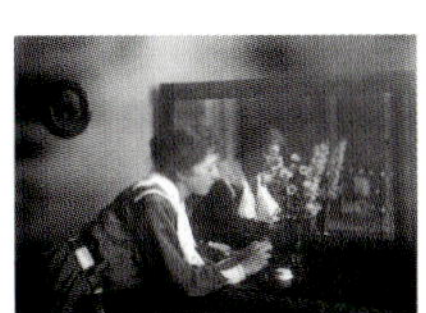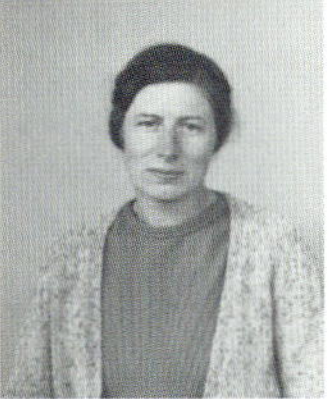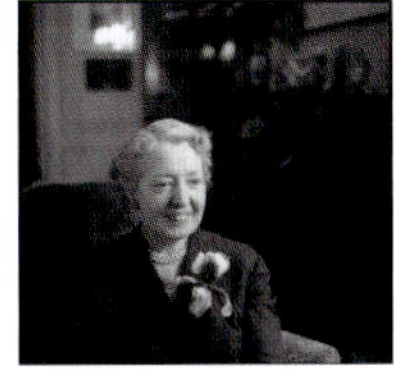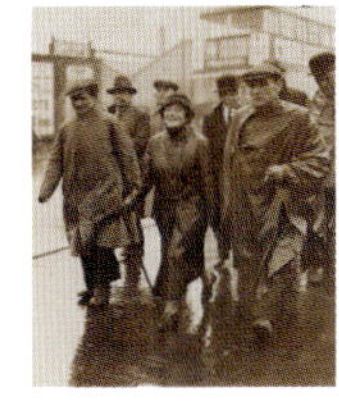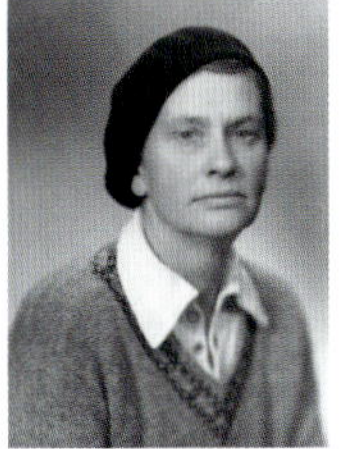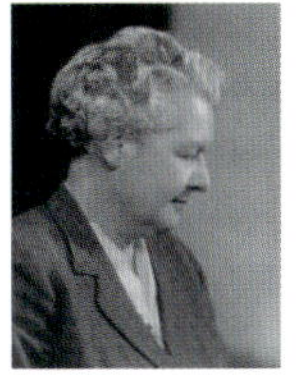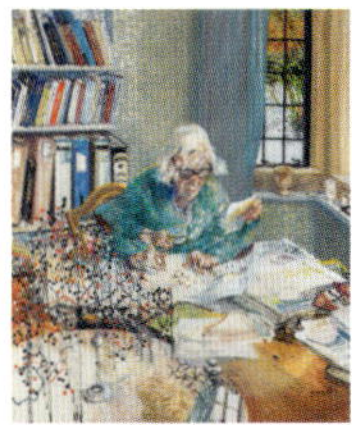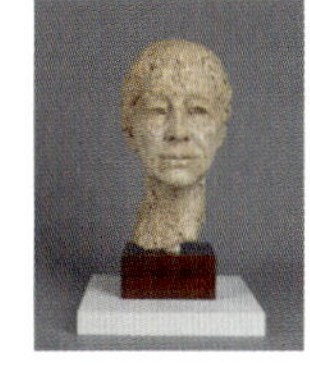
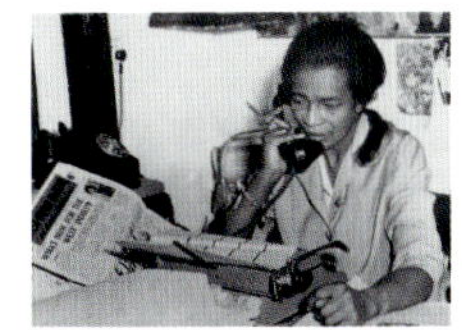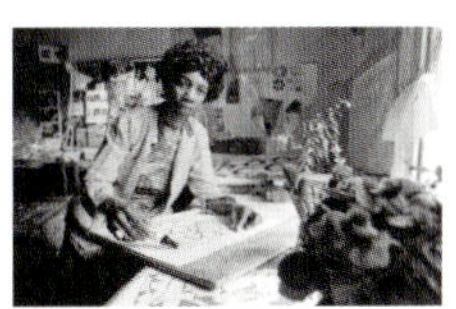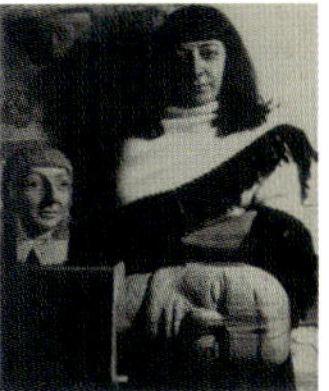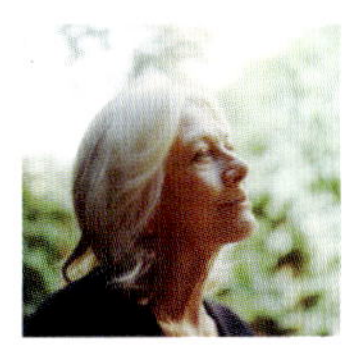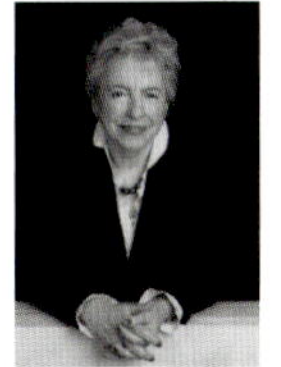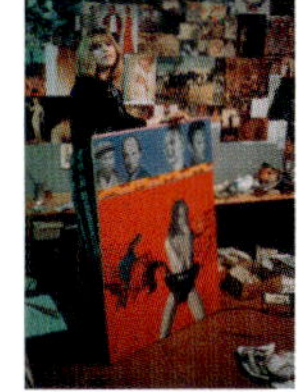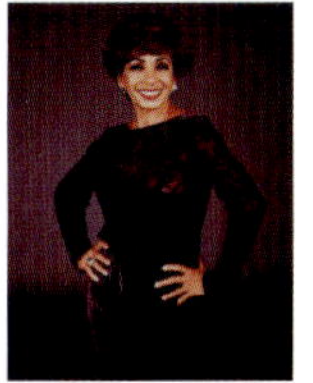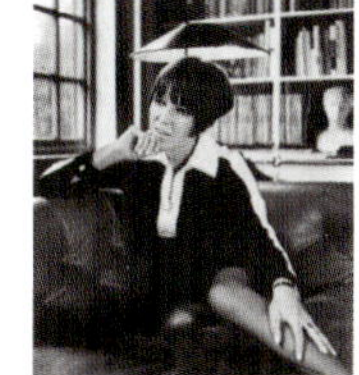
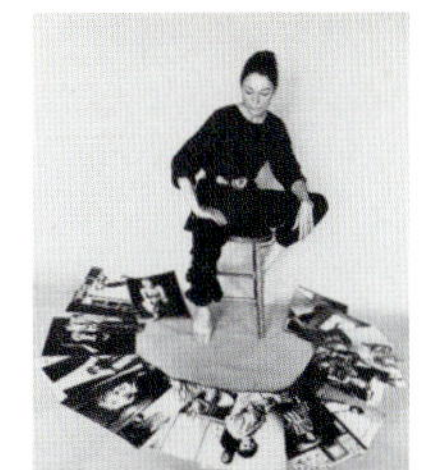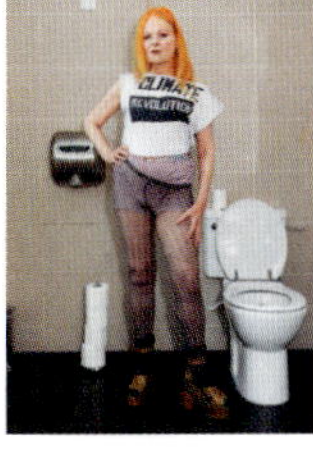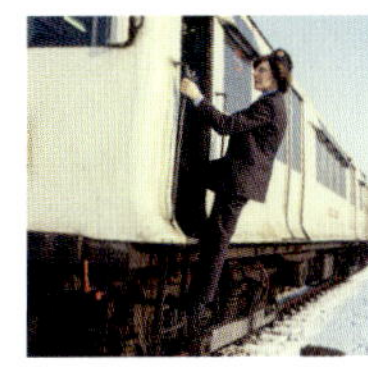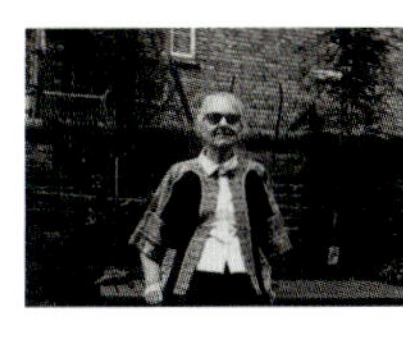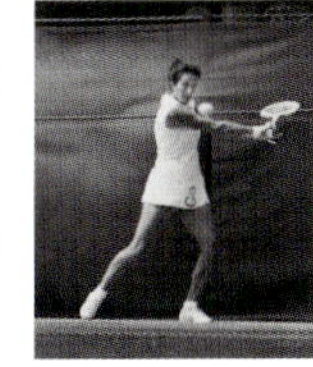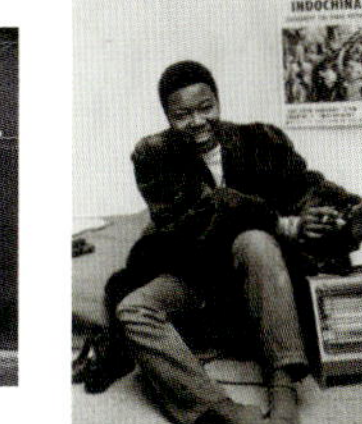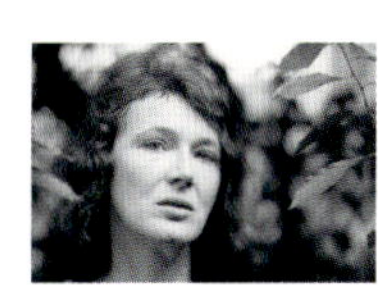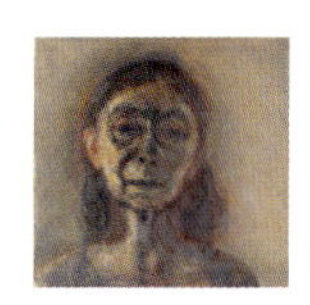
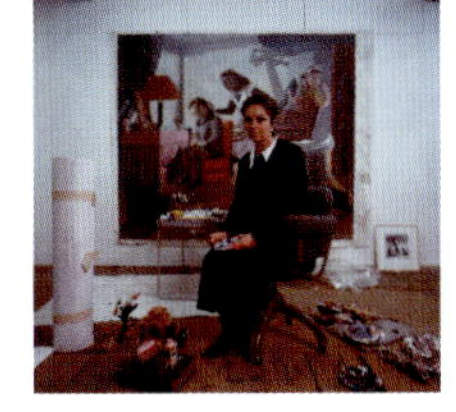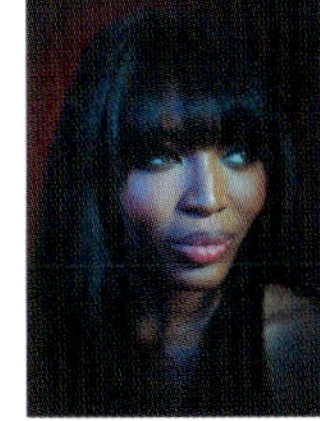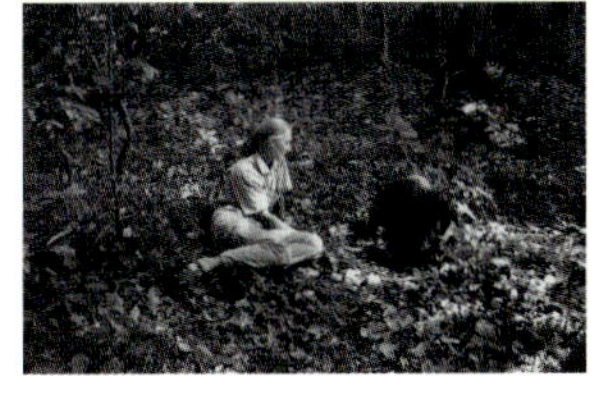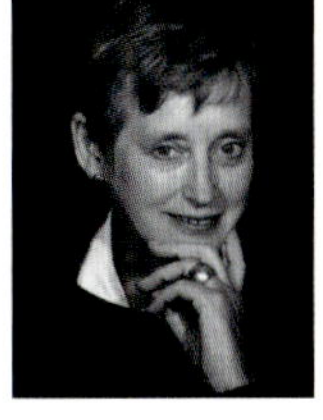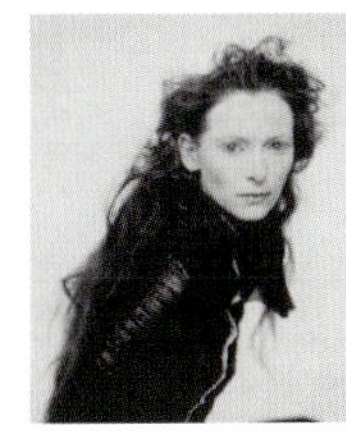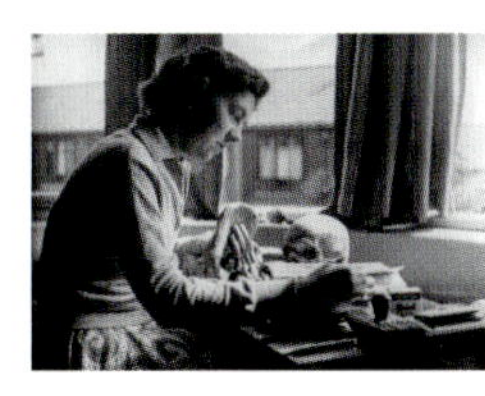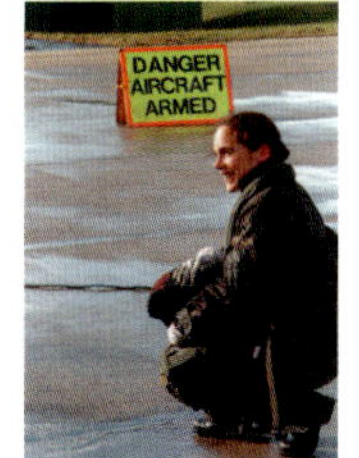
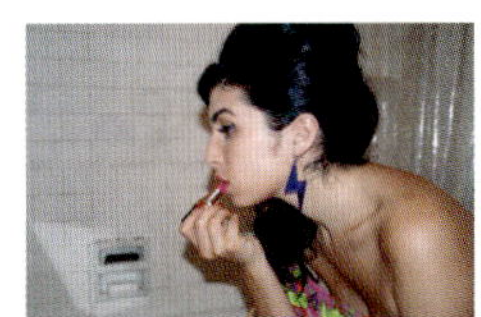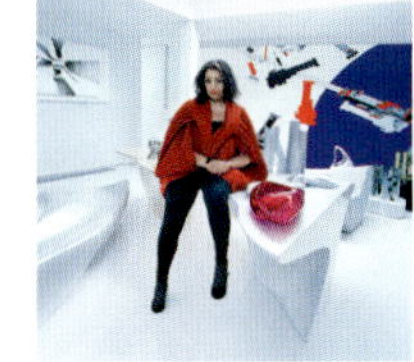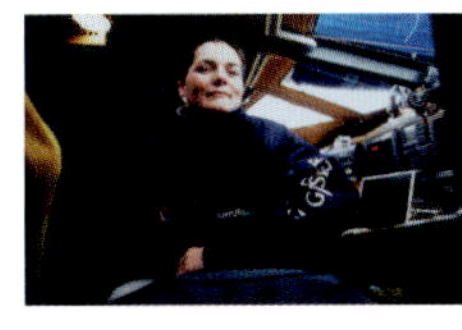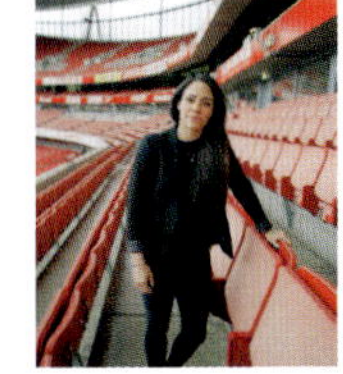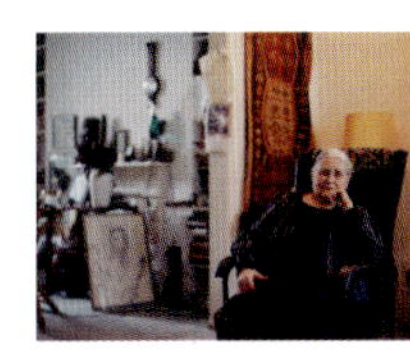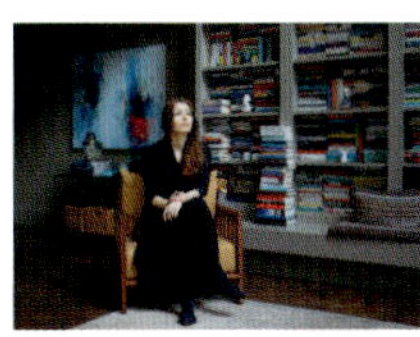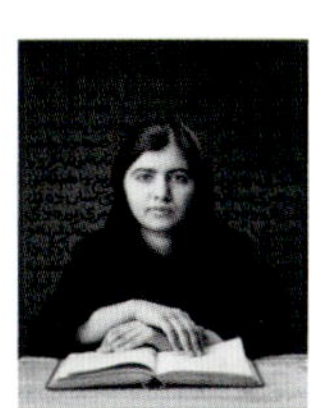
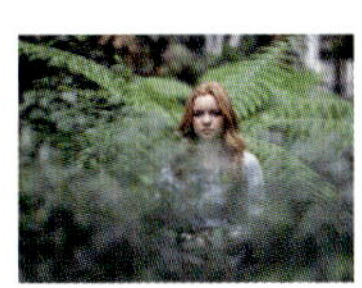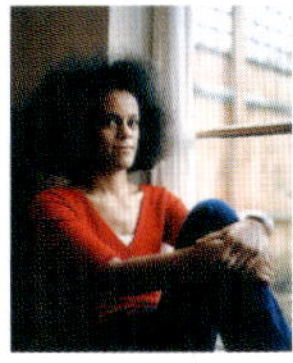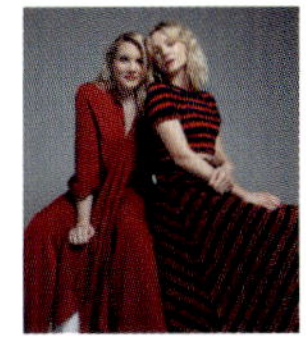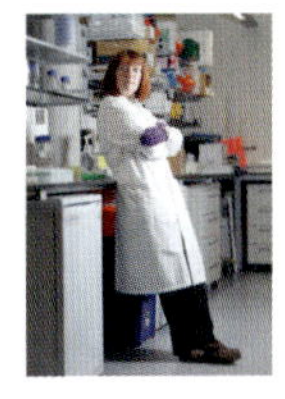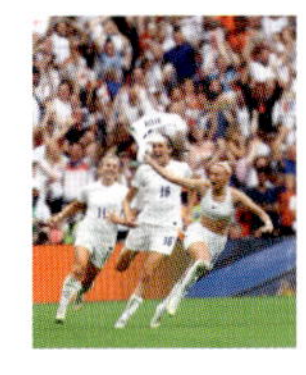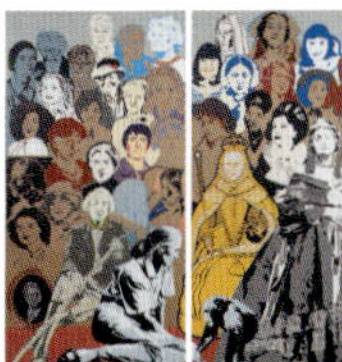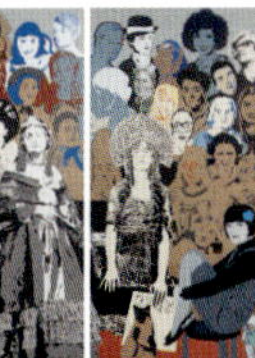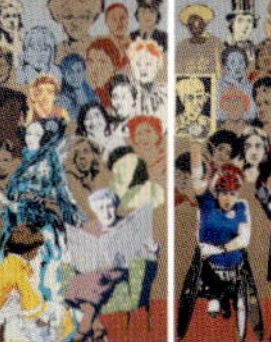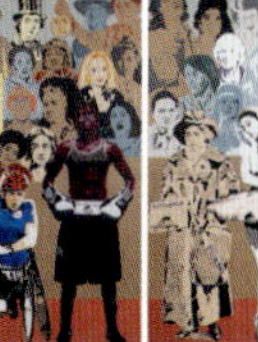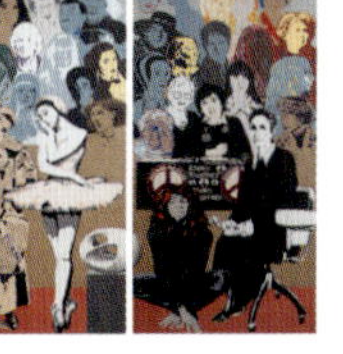

Director's Foreword

For the National Portrait Gallery's founding fathers in the mid-Victorian period the recognition of individual achievement was one of the Gallery's principal objectives. Through portraiture, the inspirational stories of those who 'contributed to British history and culture' were brought to life. The Prime Minister, Lord Palmerston, who had supported the Gallery's foundation in 1856, stated that it would be 'a great gratification to see the likeness of men whose actions have excited our admiration'. Men, as suggested by this statement, took centre stage in the Gallery's early days. Women at the time did not have the right to vote and could not stand for office. A married woman's property belonged to her husband and every divorce required an Act of Parliament. The combination of these factors made women unlikely candidates for the type of broad recognition offered by the Gallery. With this context in mind, it is perhaps unsurprising that the first portrait of a woman to enter the Collection was of the Restoration courtier Elizabeth Hamilton, Countess of Gramont, most notable for her wit and beauty.

Today women are at the forefront of public life. They make their mark in a wide range of areas: from politics to medicine, science to the arts, commerce to sport. Portraiture is uniquely placed to hold these achievements for posterity; the women of the past are role models for those of the present and the future. In keeping with this belief, the Gallery's ongoing mission is to redress the gender imbalance within the Collection by enhancing the representation of women. This ambitious and long-term project can be undertaken only with the support of a partner who shares the Gallery's values around women's excellence, and the CHANEL Culture Fund have proved to be the most wonderful allies in the advancement of this mission.

In 2020 the Gallery, with support from the CHANEL Culture Fund, established the three-year project 'Reframing Narratives: Women in Portraiture', focused on enhancing the representation of both women sitters and women artists by adding to the number of portraits in the Gallery's Collection through acquisitions and commissions. These were complemented by activities including displays, online resources and publications, as well as the cataloguing and digitisation of a major archive of negatives by pioneering colour photographer Yevonde. My wonderful colleague Flavia Frigeri, CHANEL Curator for the Collection, has worked tirelessly to realise this project alongside Assistant Curators Georgia Atienza and Constantia Nicolaides. My sincere thanks to them all for creating something with such vision and openness to the future, which is reflected in this book. My thanks go to Alice Rawsthorn, Emma Chapman, Alison Smith and Magdalene Keaney for their perceptive essays. At CHANEL my heartfelt thanks go to Yana Peel, Global Head of Arts and Culture, for taking on such a special project with vision, energy and insight.

Nicholas Cullinan
Director
National Portrait Gallery

A Note from CHANEL

Gabrielle Chanel was a woman who understood the freedom to be found in work. 'Nothing relaxes me so much as work, and nothing tires me so much as doing nothing. The more I work, the more I want to work,' she said.

Now, more than a century after the founding of the House of CHANEL, we are thrilled to support the landmark book *Women at Work*.

This groundbreaking initiative represents a new approach to history by the National Portrait Gallery, enriching and deepening our understanding of the role of so many trailblazing women whose contributions were previously dismissed or overlooked.

Women at Work places women at the centre of the Gallery's Collection rather than at its margins. Expertly edited by the inaugural CHANEL Curator for the National Portrait Gallery Collection, Dr Flavia Frigeri, this profound research project inspires us to channel these women's legacies into bold new futures.

The book marks the culmination of a broader partnership, 'Reframing Narratives: Women in Portraiture'. Forged between the National Portrait Gallery and the CHANEL Culture Fund in 2020, this is a long-term project that has readdressed historic gender imbalances and doubled the number of women displayed in the twentieth- and twenty-first-century galleries. Following the museum's historic reopening, 48 per cent of portraits on display are now of women, advancing the positive impact that gender equality brings to the world. But there is so much work yet to do.

The research uncovered through *Women at Work* charts the uneven evolution of equality. Consider the radical author Mary Wollstonecraft, who wrote *A Vindication of the Rights of Woman* in 1792 – and yet whose portrait is believed to have been conceived as a marriage portrait, rather than an homage to her brilliant mind.

Today, we see so many more women in the Gallery's Collection publicly recognised for their work. Many of these portraits have been painted by other women – for instance, the author Zadie Smith by artist Toyin Ojih Odutola – revealing two remarkable creatives.

To further support the growth and depth of the Collection, the CHANEL Culture Fund has helped with a number of meaningful acquisitions of portraits of women as seen through their own eyes. These include self-portraits by Chila Kumari Singh Burman, Susan Hiller, Rose Finn- Kelcey, Everlyn Nicodemus and Celia Paul. An important new group portrait co-created by artists Jann Haworth and Liberty Blake has also been commissioned, aptly named *Work in Progress* (2021–2), depicting 130 women who have had a significant impact on British history and culture, from Boudicca to Mary Beard.

The women in *Women at Work* excelled, despite the forces of opposition. It is in celebration of their spirit of persistent innovation that the CHANEL Culture Fund is proud to partner with the National Portrait Gallery during such an important moment for culture in the United Kingdom. The Gallery is pioneering new approaches to our future by reconsidering our past and the people who have made – and are making – British history and culture so vital.

Yana Peel
Global Head of Arts and Culture
CHANEL

PORTRAYING

WOMEN AT WORK

By

Flavia Frigeri

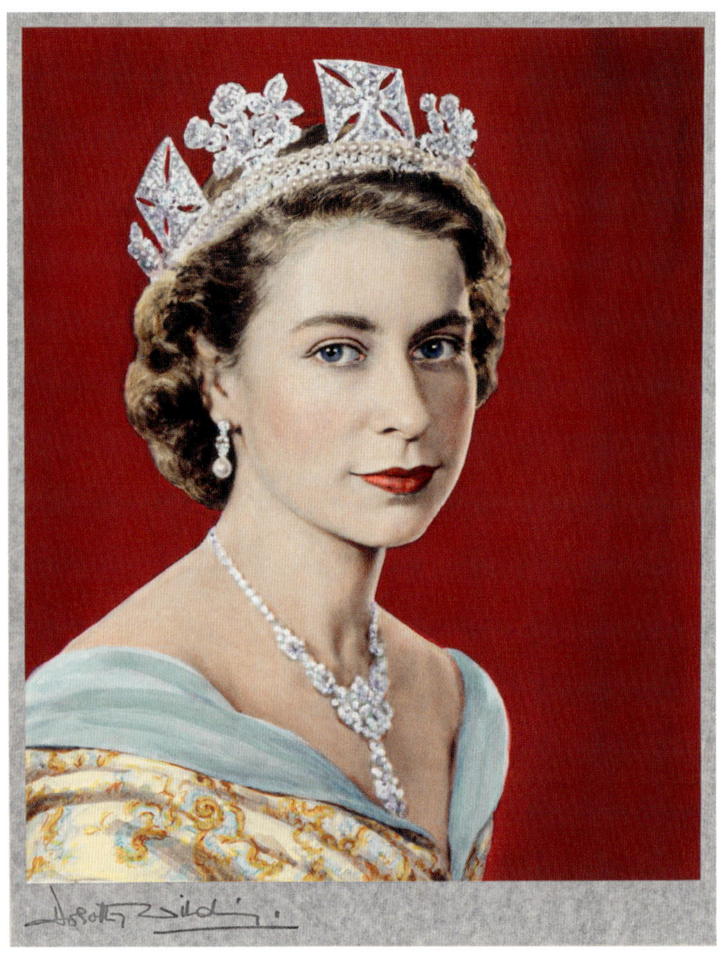

Fig.1: Queen Elizabeth II by Dorothy Wilding

'Representation of the world, like the world itself, is the work of men; they describe it from their own point of view, which they confuse with the absolute truth.' So wrote Simone de Beauvoir in *The Second Sex* (1949), a landmark text addressing human history and the oppression of women within it. Famously, de Beauvoir stipulated that, 'humanity is male and man defines woman not in herself, but as relative to him; she is not regarded as an autonomous being ... He is the Subject, he is the Absolute – She is the Other.' De Beauvoir's statement exposed why and how women throughout history have been largely cast by men as secondary and relational creatures: the 'other' against which men could assert the centrality of their being.

The struggle against oppression has long been at the forefront of many women's lives as they have fought for recognition and equality in a male-dominated world. This book celebrates the professional accomplishments of women who have made their mark on history because of their determination, talent and unique approach to life. Starting in 1900, the year in which tennis player Charlotte Cooper became the first individual woman to win an Olympic gold medal, and ending in 2023 with a collective tribute to trailblazing women led by artists Jann Haworth and Liberty Blake, the book follows a chronological structure, highlighting not only well-known pioneers, but also women whose stories have remained largely untold. The text alongside each featured portrait outlines the key achievements of each sitter in fields as diverse as politics, law, science, business, medicine and the arts.

'YOU ARE NOT LIKE OTHER LADIES. YOU ARE MORE LIKE A WORKING WOMAN ...'

Eglantyne Jebb (p.55), founder of Save the Children, was described by her eight-year-old nephew David thus: 'You are not like other ladies. You are more like a working woman – a sort of "garden" lady. You haven't a hat all on one side and your face isn't so dreadfully clean. And you walk quite differently. Men look nicer than women. You look more like a man.' With these words young David was tentatively sketching the portrait of a working woman. But was this a naïve description, a veiled compliment or a chauvinist remark? David, like many others living at the start of the twentieth century, lacked the frame of reference for a working woman; the role model for a working individual was invariably male. A woman was, by and large, the angel of the hearth, relegated to the home and entrusted with its care and that of those who resided in it. To succeed outside of this claustrophobic realm, a woman had to adopt masculine traits or, as David suggests, 'not [be] like other ladies'. Unladylike (in the eyes of some) women who carved out their own destinies are the subject of this book.

The permanent Collection of the National Portrait Gallery comprises 18,049 women, compared to 54,234 men, and represents a variety of diverse backgrounds and professions, across 500 years of history. Artists, actors, athletes, dancers, doctors, explorers, law-makers, monarchs, philanthropists, politicians, social workers, suffragettes and writers are among the many roles in which women have excelled, both now and in the past, and yet how visible are these women? The simple answer is that only a handful have benefitted from steady recognition and ongoing visibility. Prime amongst them is Queen Elizabeth II (fig.1), the late monarch and the most portrayed sitter in the National Portrait Gallery's Collection, with an astonishing 964 portraits. Under-represented numerically, and yet instantly recognisable for their achievements, are the writers Jane Austen, the Brontë sisters and Virginia Woolf; the architect Zaha Hadid; the artist and founding member of the Royal Academy of Arts Angelica Kauffmann; the nurses Florence Nightingale and Mary Seacole (fig.2); the dancer Josephine Baker and the women's rights advocate and author Mary Wollstonecraft.

Others could certainly be added to this list, and yet the vast majority of women, who in different capacities have actively shaped British history (and beyond), remain invisible, despite the outstanding nature of their contributions. In 2020 the National Portrait Gallery, in partnership with the CHANEL Culture Fund, established 'Reframing Narratives: Women in Portraiture' – a three-year project aimed at enhancing the representation of women in the National Portrait Gallery's Collection and highlighting the often overlooked stories of individual

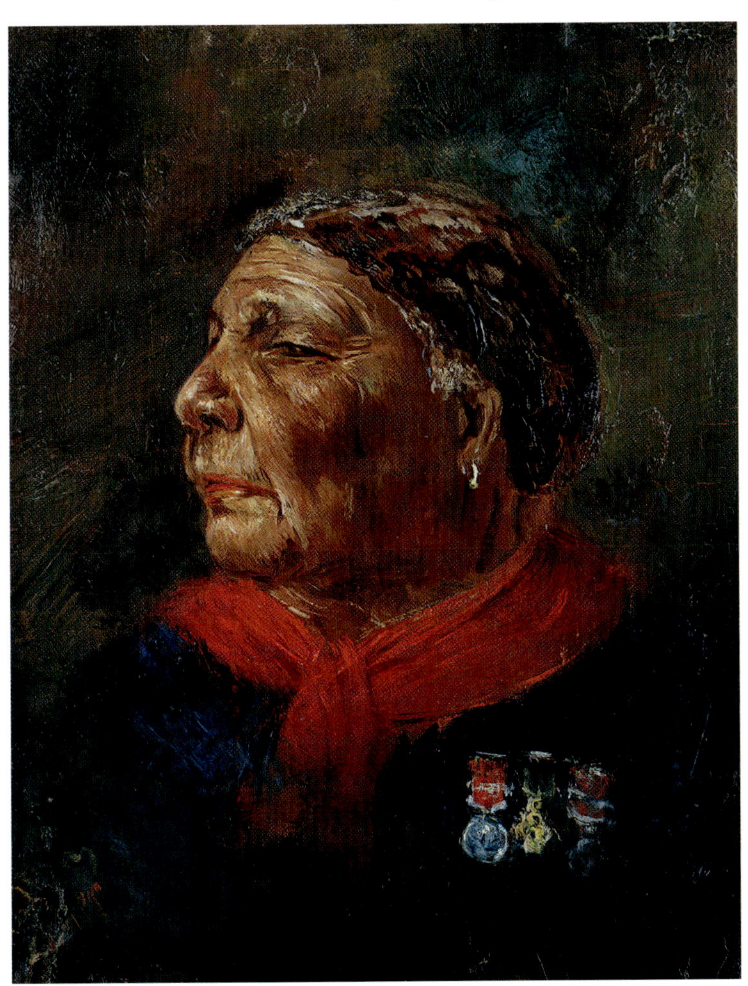
Fig.2: Mary Seacole by Albert Charles Challen

women who have shaped British history and culture. This book brings together findings of that project, as well as new leads for research. Above all, however, *Women at Work* challenges the foundation of how we think about women's careers by uncovering alternative networks of exchange and probing the cultural, institutional, social and political factors that have traditionally shaped the mainstream narrative and defined difference.

PORTRAYING WOMEN

In surveying female achievement through the vehicle of portraiture, one is confronted with the question: what does a working woman look like? Traditionally, it has been difficult to identify a woman as a professional from her portrait. Biographical sketches provide insight into individual

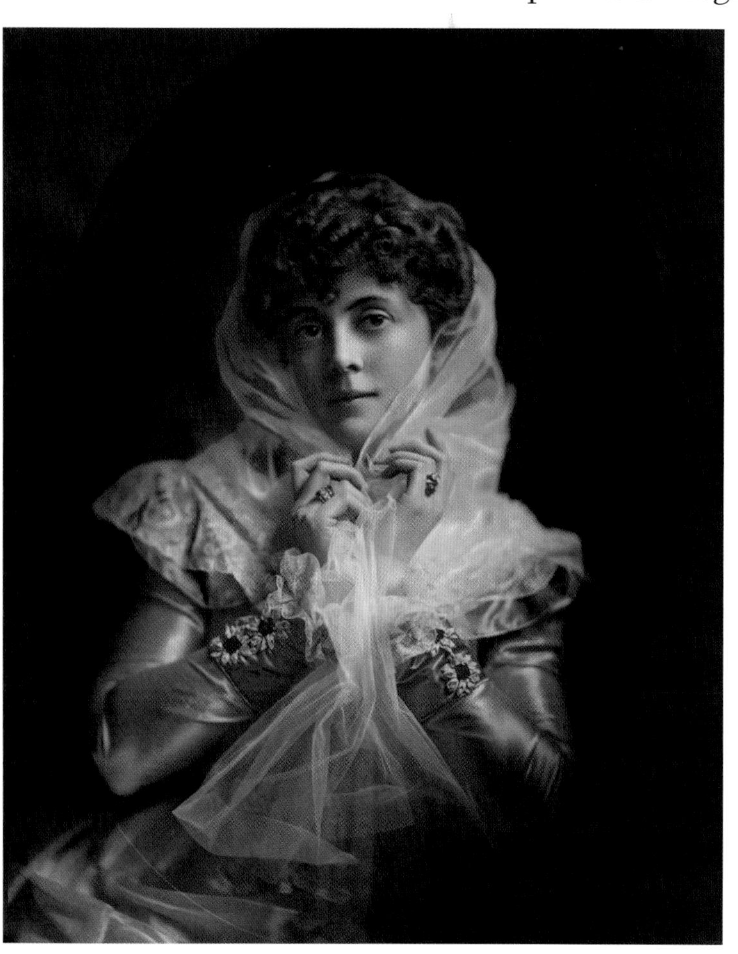
Fig.3: Lady Sarah Wilson by H. Walter Barnett

histories, but the images themselves are often difficult to interpret. Men are still far more likely to be recognised for their professional successes because artists and photographers have a rich iconographic tradition to draw on when representing male figures – typically white and middle- or upper-class. For instance, a portrait of a man riding a horse immediately conjures ideas of power and political achievement. By contrast, portraits of women are frequently warped by a mix of feminine propriety, idealised beauty and subdued countenance – all male constructs that have shaped art-historical narratives for centuries.

Take Lady Sarah Wilson (fig.3), for example. The nine portraits of her that sit in the Collection of the National Portrait Gallery are stylised artifices that adhere to contemporary notions of femininity and the beautiful. A leap of imagination is required to read these portraits as a mirror of her professional achievements: Lady Sarah Wilson acted as one the first female war correspondents, reporting from the besieged town of Mafeking (now Mahikeng) during the Second Boer War. Another portrait of a female pioneer that eschews immediate legibility is that of radical thinker Mary Wollstonecraft (fig.4), whose *A Vindication of the Rights of Woman* (1792) challenged the assumption that women are naturally inferior to men and advocated for equal access to education as a fundamental step in the achievement of a fairer social order.

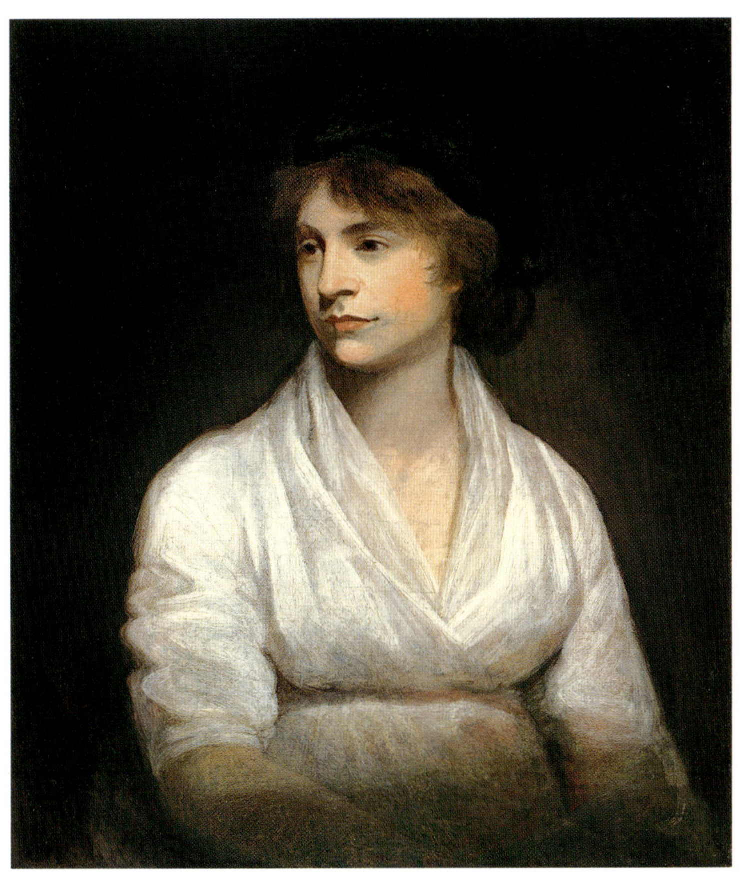

Fig.4: Mary Wollstonecraft by John Opie

The woman who claimed 'It is time to effect a revolution in female manners – time to restore [women] their lost dignity' is portrayed for perpetuity as a 'relative creature' – dependent on an entrenched patriarchal structure that places men at the top.[1] The portrait of Wollstonecraft was, in fact, likely to have been conceived as a marriage portrait, reinforcing the arbitrary division of the world into 'private' and 'public', which saw women firmly relegated to the former. At a stretch, Wollstonecraft's portrait can be read as a mirror of her rather reluctant concession that 'the mighty business of female life is to please'.

When women took the matter of representation into their own hands the emphasis shifted. Long before Laura Mulvey coined the phrase the 'male gaze' in the 1970s, pioneers of painting and photography were redefining how women were portrayed. In doing so, they challenged the complex relationship between masculine agency and feminine passivity that exists in canonical portraiture. Early on, women artists turned to self-portraiture as a vehicle for analysis, self-expression and personal transformation, a stance which has carried through well into the twentieth and twenty-first centuries, when women have gone on to subvert the structures of gender by exploding its theatrics and stereotypes across the visual arts. This shift in gears is made manifest in a series of new acquisitions supported by the CHANEL Culture Fund, which include self-portraits of and by Chila Kumari Singh Burman, Susan Hiller, Rose Finn-Kelcey, Everlyn Nicodemus (fig.5) and Celia Paul.

While painting as a medium carries the historical baggage of heavily invested male egos, the emergence of photography in the nineteenth century offered a more flexible alternative to women. Pioneers of photography such as Julia Margaret Cameron were fully aware of what it meant to author one's own image, while also establishing a name for oneself. Photography granted women a newfound social and political mobility. Alice Hughes opened a photographic portrait studio in London and at one time employed 60 women. Inspired by the success of Hughes, Lallie Charles and Rita Martin became the most successful women portraitists of the first decade of the 1900s. And, after them, Dorothy Wilding and Yevonde Middleton went on to establish thriving portrait studios,

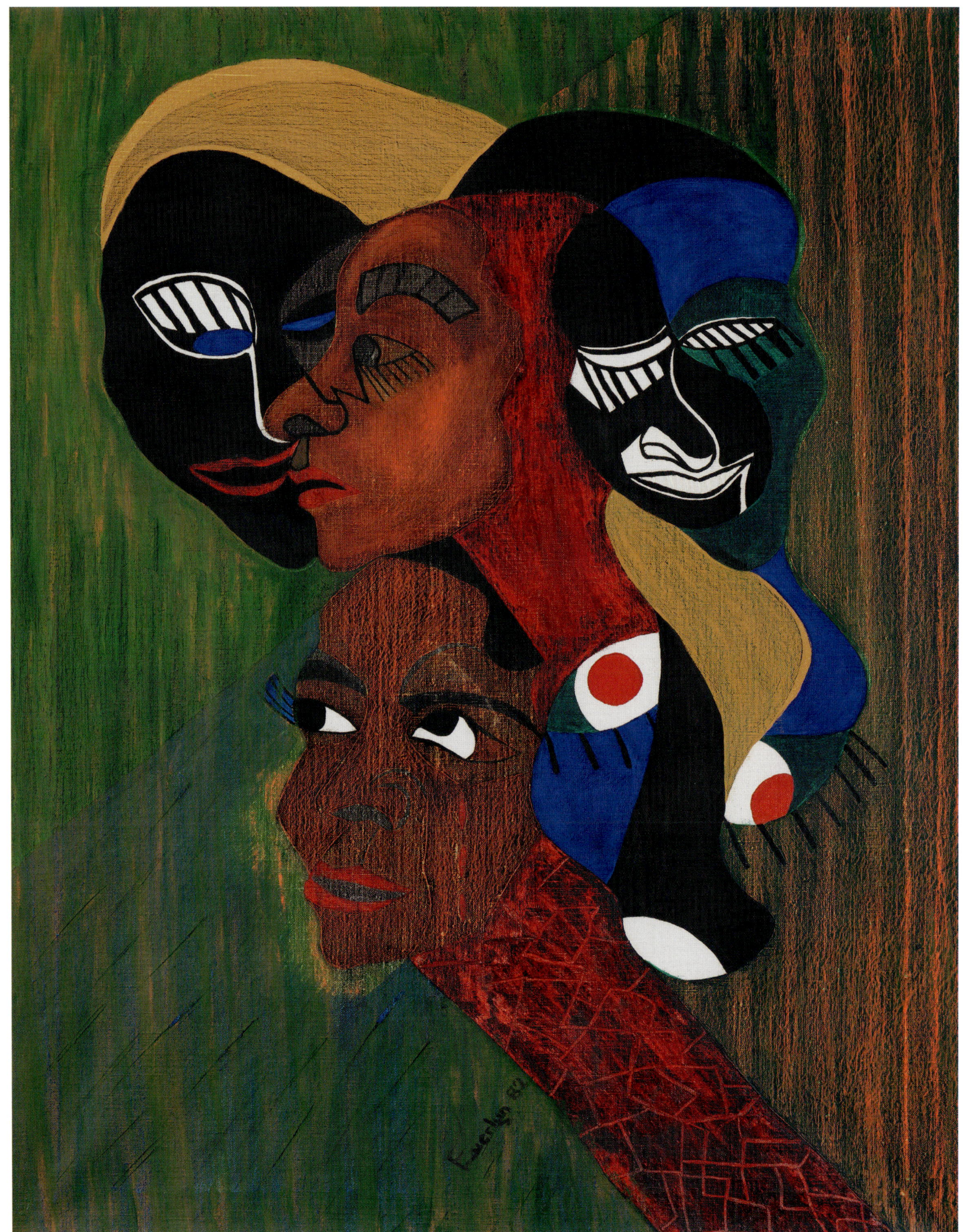

Fig.5: Self-portrait by Everlyn Nicodemus

where a new image of the modern woman could be forged, alongside more conventional portrait imagery. During and after the First and Second World Wars photography allowed women to travel and to work around the world, producing reportages for illustrated magazines, responding to social and political upheavals, recording their immediate milieu and experiencing emigration and exile.

Above all, the birth of photography represented a landmark moment in the history of portraiture as many more people could now afford to have their physical likeness fixed for posterity. Historically, portraiture had been accessible only to those of sufficient means; to commission a painted portrait was a luxury that not many could afford. Thanks to the advent of photography, individuals from a greater variety of backgrounds could secure a record of a life lived, a proof of existence. This applied to women too, and especially to those making waves outside of the household.

As many of the illustrations in this book demonstrate, in the twentieth century female trailblazers could count on photographic portraits as a means to record their likenesses, and were portrayed at various points in their lives. The closer we get to the present, the more photographic records there are available. Where possible, we have privileged images showing women at work. However, these are few and far between, especially in the National Portrait Gallery's Collection, which has traditionally favoured generic representation over professional records. As a result, we have supplemented images from the Collection with those from other sources.

Important to note too are the portraits of women by other women. Embedded within the book is a rich constellation of portraits made by women artists and photographers of their peers. These encompass the sculpted bust of writer Pamela Lyndon Travers by Gertrude Hermes, painted portraits of pianist Harriet Cohen by Clara Klinghoffer, scientist Dorothy Crowfoot Hodgkin by Maggi Hambling and writer Zadie Smith by Toyin Ojih Odutola, and many photographic portraits, including the joint portrait of actor Carey Mulligan and screenwriter Emerald Fennell by Violeta Sofia. Most recently, in partnership with Magnum Photos, the National Portrait Gallery has commissioned a series of photographic portraits of leading contemporary women. Magnum photographers Olivia Arthur, Cristina de Middel and Susan Meiselas have taken on the baton of this commission, resulting in newly acquired portraits of Rose Ayling-Ellis, Mary Beard, Caroline Criado Perez, Amika George, Bella Lack, Elif Shafak and Farhana Yamin.

The links between gender and representational strategies have been the source of extensive art-historical scrutiny in recent decades. It is beyond the scope of this book to rehearse these important ideas, but suffice to say that by entrusting women with the representation

of other women the long-held stereotype of the male artistic genius
and the female muse has been exploded. Nowadays, female artists and
photographers have achieved a new level of outspokenness, allowing
them to address on their own terms complex themes such as gender,
race, sexuality, pain and the inner workings of womanhood.

WOMEN AT WORK

At the turn of the twentieth century, award-winning British engineer
Hertha Ayrton (p.36) painfully reckoned with the fact that while
errors overall are 'notoriously hard to kill ... an error that ascribes to
a man what was actually the work of a woman has more lives than
a cat.' A whole culture is contained in Ayrton's words. For centuries
it was not thought seemly for a woman to put herself forward, let
alone to compete or excel. It was a man's world and women were
chiefly framed as relational creatures, a notion formalised by the laws
around marriage, property and rights. From the moment they were
born, women were trained to put themselves second and to be diligent
daughters, sisters, wives and mothers. They served their families
and, if they had a husband, they were always second to him. Those
who broke free from this pre-established mould were thought to be
unladylike. As the historian Laurel Thatcher Ulrich famously put it,
'well-behaved women seldom make history'.
     Luckily for us, the women documented in this book chose
the untrodden path of misbehaviour over the well-trodden route of
conformity. Many factors were at stake in this choice and context
played no small role in allowing women to break free from the chains
of relationality. On some of the women explored in this book, freedom
from familial ties was unwillingly bestowed upon them, and society
did little to support these women. For instance, in Victorian England
it was estimated that more than one million women were in domestic
service; the alternative to a life of domestic drudgery was prostitution,
especially for those raised in institutions without family support.
On the whole, women of means were better off, but still they were
politically disenfranchised, refused property rights, their access
to higher education was limited and opportunities outside the home
were even fewer. It took guts and a whole lot of imagination for women
to define themselves as professionals in a world that historically
offered few role models.
     The long march in the name of true equality between men and
women, like all struggles, has been, and continues to be, fraught, non-
linear and at times deeply flawed. All those who challenged the wrongs
faced by women have approached it in ways shaped by their own
historical moment and set of beliefs. Feminism, in its different waves

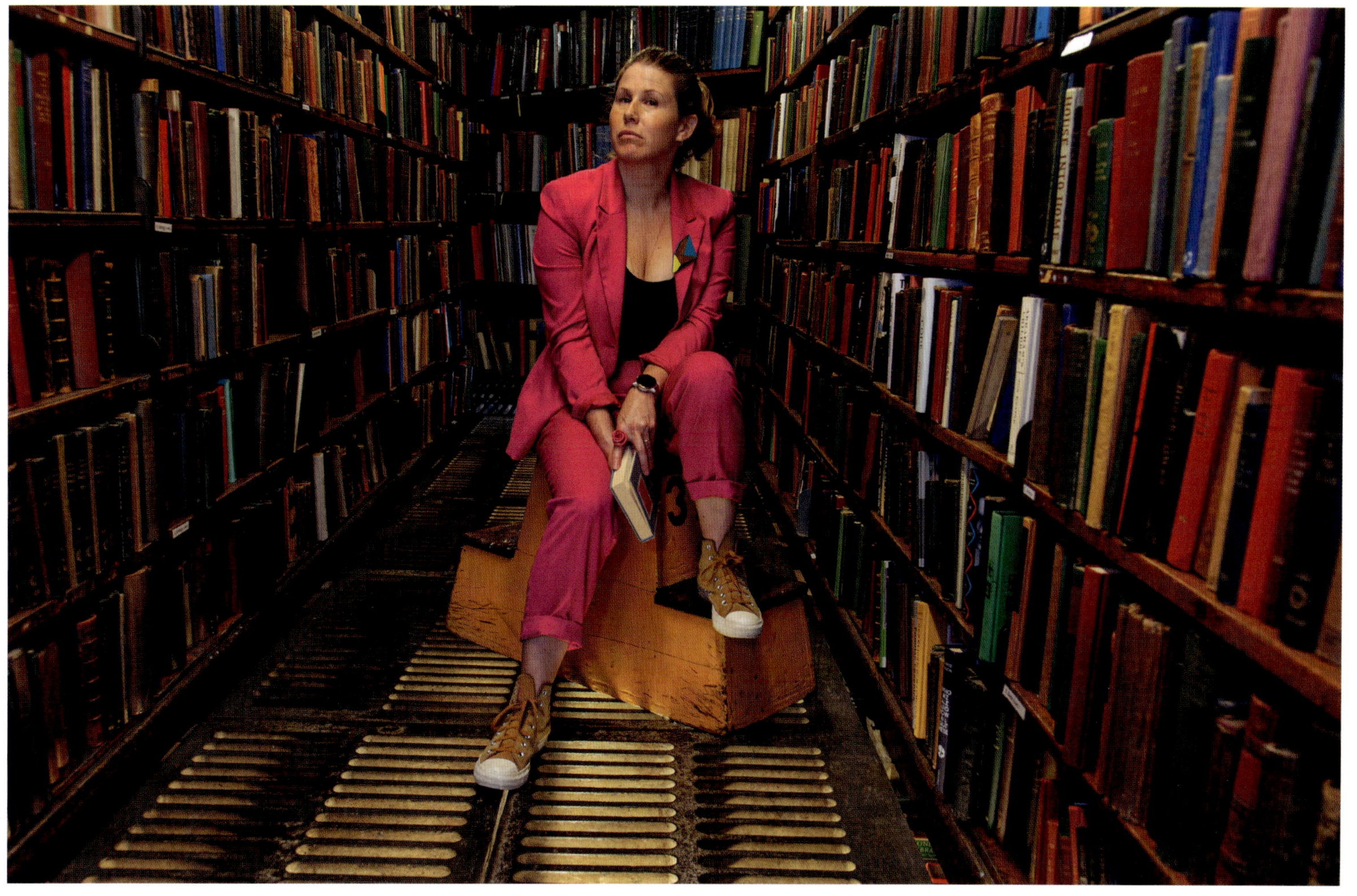

Fig.6: Caroline Criado Perez by Susan Meiselas

and forms, played a substantial role in the struggle for emancipation.
However, it would be incorrect to classify all those who engendered
a profound transformation of how women thought about their lives and
bodies as a feminist. Many women have actively rejected this label –
on the grounds that it was exclusive, limiting and problematic – while
others rode its waves with undivided resolve. Over time, the aspirations
and demands of feminist movements have changed dramatically.
Today, the feminist landscape counts not just one singular hegemonic
feminism, but multiple feminisms, in recognition of the mobility of the
term and its shifting meaning.

It is safe to assume that a number of milestone events applied to
feminists and non-feminists alike, determining their increased freedom
from patriarchal hegemony. These underpin many of the stories told
in this book and have undoubtedly contributed to the progressive
inclusion of women in British public life.

A century ago, women protested for the right to vote. Today,
women are political and business leaders. But the struggle endures.
In her book *Invisible Women: Exposing Data Bias in a World Designed
for Men* (2019), activist and writer Caroline Criado Perez (fig.6) has

demonstrated how female-specific concerns are not factored in when designing a world meant for all but de facto catering to white, able-bodied men. Data, or lack thereof, supports Criado Perez's theory in a wide variety of areas – from public transport to politics, public toilet provisions to medical research. Further ongoing concerns include – but are not limited to – abortion, education, domestic violence, wages for housework and childcare, and equal pay for equal work.

While there is clearly still a long way to go, this book takes a rear view at the past 124 years, charting the achievements of women who have excelled, even when they were told they could not. This is, inevitably, an incomplete history or, to put it in Haworth's and Blake's words, it is a 'work in progress'. This is to say that there are many other women worthy of inclusion in a survey of this kind but who for reasons of space could not be featured. Our encouragement is to find out about them, research them and celebrate them. Each field of achievement is made of not one pioneer, but many. In carrying out the research that fed into this volume we have uncovered many networks of exchange between professional women, as well as rare, but significant, male allies who have supported women in their ambitious endeavours. They too ought to be celebrated because in an ideal world the struggle for equality should have no gender.

Current debates about the porousness and flexibility of gender identities point us to a fundamental notion that the category of 'woman' has never been singular or stable. This book is well aligned with this concept and at no point does it infer the existence of a singular notion of what a woman is or ought to be. This is a story of individuals and each woman is treated singularly to account for her specificities. As part of this, we have deliberately chosen to move away from the customary biographical approach, which has framed a woman's professional achievement vis-à-vis her personal life. Customarily, a biographical introduction to a woman's life always nods to her marital status, number of children and family provenance. It is as if a woman cannot stand on her own feet, as the compulsion to make her a relational creature always seem to prevail. The same cannot be said of men, who instead are for the most part viewed independently of their personal circumstances. In a reversal of this approach, the focus in this book is on professional achievement alone, as all traces of relationality are omitted.

While a deliberate choice has been made to focus on women who have increasingly joined the paid labour force, this is in no way meant to disavow the work that women do within the household. It is a well-known fact that women still shoulder the majority of unpaid domestic labour, irrespective of how much they earn and how demanding their paid job is. While not delving into this issue specifically, we remain sensitive to it and can only hope that a future of truly shared responsibilities between men and women lies ahead.

In keeping with the focus of the National Portrait Gallery Collection, the women portrayed here maintain a clear connection to the United Kingdom. Many were born in this country, while others came to it seeking refuge – especially during and in the aftermath of the Second World War. Despite the national focus, this book sets out a picture of achievement whose effects are felt on the international stage. Above all, this book is about role models – their genesis and ongoing legacy. By looking back, we encourage viewers to look forward and take the cue from Hilary Mantel: 'The pen is in our hands. A happy ending is ours to write.'

Fig.1
Queen Elizabeth II (1926–2022)
By Dorothy Wilding and hand-coloured
by Beatrice Johnson, 1952
Gelatin silver print, 316 × 248mm
National Portrait Gallery, London, x125105

Fig.2
Mary Seacole (1805–1881)
By Albert Charles Challen, 1869
Oil on panel, 240 × 180mm
National Portrait Gallery, London, 6856

Fig.3
Lady Sarah Wilson (1865–1929)
By H. Walter Barnett, c.1900
Whole-plate glass negative
National Portrait Gallery, London, x76621

Fig.4
Mary Wollstonecraft (1759–1797)
By John Opie, c.1797
Oil on canvas, 768 × 641mm
National Portrait Gallery, London, 1237

Fig.5
'Självporträtt, Åkersberga'
Everlyn Nicodemus (b.1954)
Self-portrait, 1982
Oil on canvas, 820 × 620mm
National Portrait Gallery, London, 7130

Fig.6
Caroline Criado Perez (b.1984)
By Susan Meiselas, 2022
Chromogenic print, 340 × 510mm
National Portrait Gallery, London, x202538

Charlotte Cooper

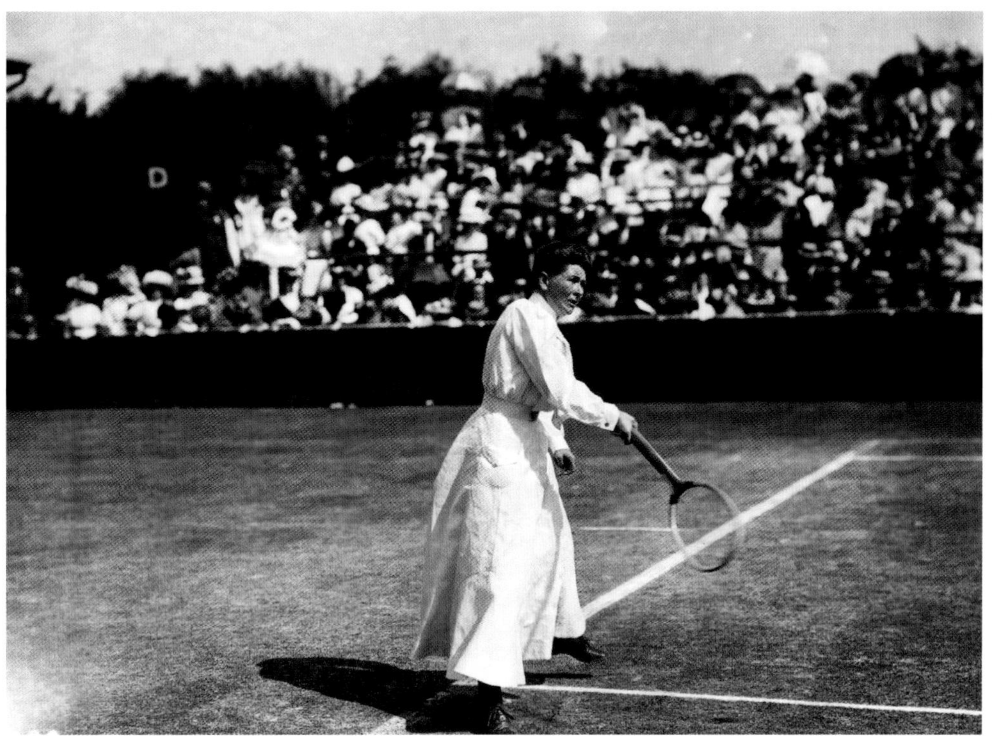

Charlotte Cooper was a record breaker. In winning the women's tennis singles title at the 1900 Paris Olympic Games she became the first woman to earn an Olympic gold medal in an individual event. Fit, active and ready to give it her all, Cooper took to the tennis court wearing a dress that covered her ankles, in keeping with contemporary fashion. Cooper's kit was minimal, consisting of just two rackets: one for rainy days and one for dry ones.

Cooper's tennis journey started at the Ealing Lawn Tennis Club in London, where she developed a strong physical and mental game. Most female top players at that time served underhand, whereas Cooper distinguished herself by serving overhead from the outset. In addition to this distinctive trait, Cooper's game benefitted from a combination of great tactical ability and unflappable determination.

In 1895 Cooper won the first of five singles titles at Wimbledon. That year was also the last time she could hear the balls bouncing off the racket and touching the court floor. At the age of just 26 she was diagnosed as completely deaf. She succeeded in winning many more championships and challenge cups. In recognition of Cooper's determination, the International Tennis Hall of Fame stated: 'In a sport where the sound of a ball coming off the strings is such an integral part of playing, Cooper captured all but one of her [Wimbledon] titles without the benefit of sound, paramount in recognising the pace of an opponent shot.'

Journalists commenting on Cooper's technique often remarked that it was better than many of her male contemporaries'. To her credit, Cooper practised constantly, setting the bar high for a younger generation of players. Later, as a mother of two, she returned to the lawn and succeeded in winning her fifth championship at Wimbledon in 1908. Cooper remains one of only four women to have ever won a Wimbledon title after giving birth. FF

Charlotte Cooper (1870–1966)
By an unknown photographer, 1908
Hulton-Deutsch Collection

Beatrix Potter

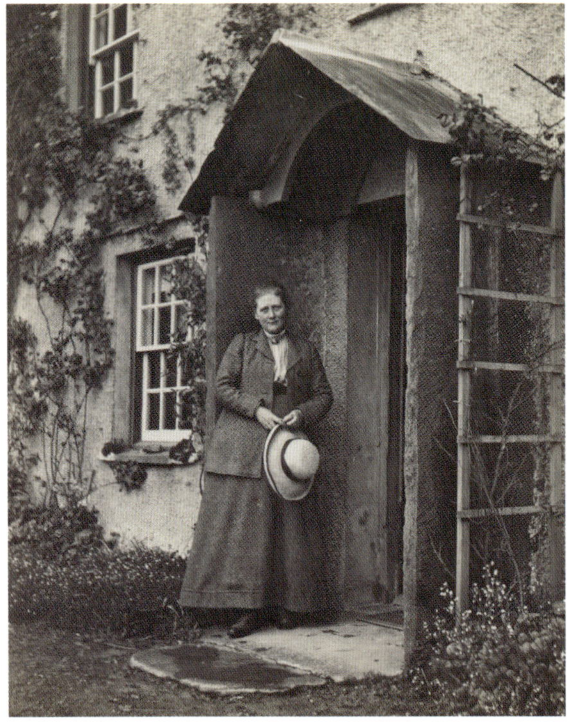

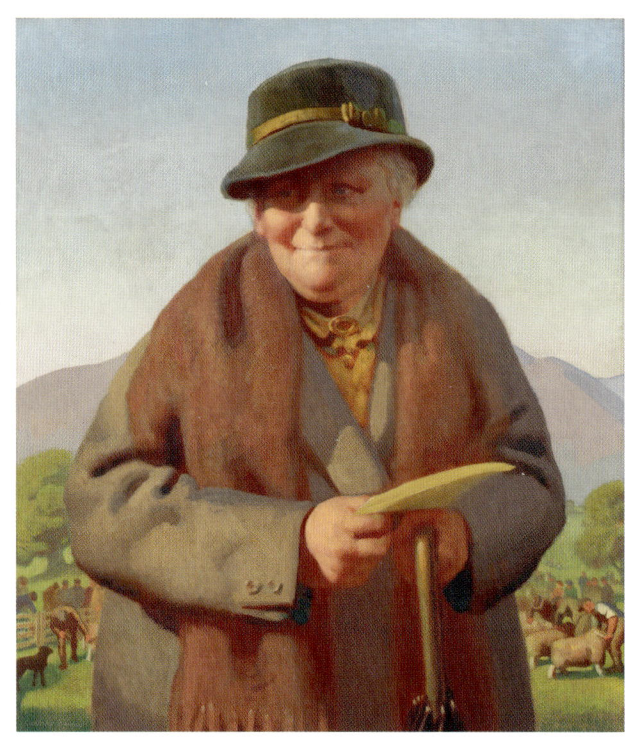

Once upon a time there were four little Rabbits, and their names were – Flopsy, Mopsy, Cotton-tail, and Peter.

So begins *The Tale of Peter Rabbit*, introducing one of the most famous and adored rabbits in children's literature: Peter Rabbit, along with his siblings. An imaginative writer and talented illustrator, Beatrix Potter first invented the characters in 1893, when they featured in a letter to the young son of her former governess. Potter's inspiration came from family trips to Scotland and the Lake District, where her close study of and fascination with nature developed. This she combined with her observations of the various pets she and her brother had kept as children. After extending the text and adding new illustrations, Potter approached publishers with the completed manuscript. But with no offers to publish her work she took matters into her own hands.

In December 1901, using her own funds, Potter privately printed 200 copies of *The Tale of Peter Rabbit*. Proving popular with family and friends, a second edition followed two months later. Soon able to convince Frederick Warne & Co. to publish her book, an initial print run of 8,000 copies immediately sold out, resulting in 20,000 more printed by the end of 1902. Brimming with ideas for many more animal characters, Potter produced two more tales the next year and by 1930 she had published all 23 of her popular children's books.

Potter's success as a full-time children's writer and illustrator ensured her financial independence, and she supplemented this income by developing merchandise based on her stories from as early as 1903. By 1905 she was able to purchase Hill Top Farm in the Lake District, where Charles G.Y. King later photographed her as the proud owner. Passionate about preserving the natural landscape and traditional farming methods, she acquired more neighbouring farms over the subsequent decades, gradually shifting her energies from writing to immersing herself in countryside life. She became a prize-winning breeder of the indigenous Herdwick sheep and a judge at agricultural shows, roles that the Lake District artist Delmar Banner depicts her enjoying happily. Potter's gift of around 4,000 acres of land, including 15 farms and her herds of sheep and Galloway cattle, to the National Trust upon her death has greatly contributed to the area's conservation.

More than a century on, Potter's books are still in print around the world and continue to captivate children and adults alike. Her stories, characters and illustrations have inspired animations, films, stage shows, further publications and toys, ensuring the names of Peter Rabbit and his animal friends remain familiar and popular among subsequent generations. CN

Beatrix Potter (1866–1943)
By Charles G.Y. King, May 1913
Gelatin silver snapshot print, 113 × 87mm
National Portrait Gallery, London, P1825

Beatrix Potter
By Delmar Banner, 1938
Oil on canvas, 749 × 622mm
National Portrait Gallery, London, 3635

Fanny Wilkinson

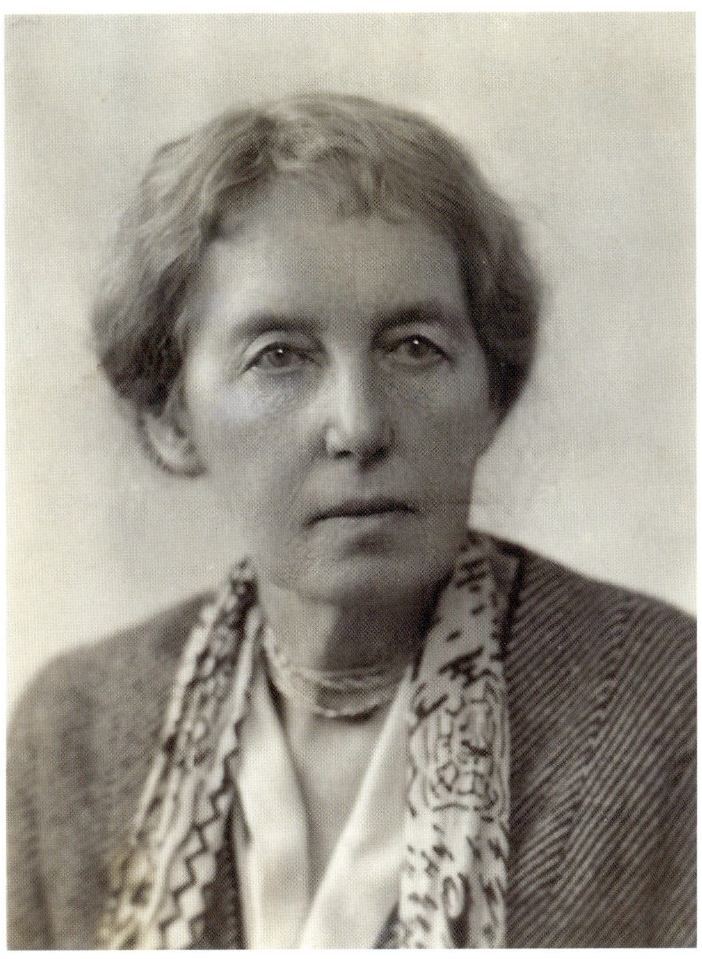

Within a month of opening its doors to male students in 1889, Swanley Horticultural College in Kent received its first enquiry from a woman, asking 'whether ladies are admitted to its benefits'. The question was not without context. Amid national debates regarding how to alleviate the ongoing agricultural depression, careers in horticulture and agriculture were increasingly being proposed as suitable for unmarried women of the middle and upper classes by advocates for women's employment. Offering science-based training, the college's curriculum departed from the traditional apprenticeship-led entry into such work, where women were shunned, and circumvented the common belief that the work was too physically demanding for women. As Britain's first female professional landscape gardener, Fanny Wilkinson was involved in the establishment of a 'Ladies' Branch' at the college in 1891, and the number of enrolments by women was soon surpassing those by men. In 1902, Swanley was turned into a women-only institution, with Wilkinson appointed its Principal that same year.

Wilkinson was well versed in the challenges women encountered in entering the horticultural sector, having overcome the difficulties involved in securing her place as the first woman student at the Crystal Palace School of Landscape Gardening and Practical Horticulture, where she completed her training in 1883. By early 1884, she had succeeded in finding work with the Kyrle Society (begun by Miranda Hill and supported by her sister Octavia Hill, who later co-founded the National Trust) and the recently established Metropolitan Public Gardens, Boulevard and Playground Association, both of which championed access to open spaces for improving the urban public's well-being. It was with the latter organization that Wilkinson contributed extensively to reshaping the London landscape, laying out more than 75 public gardens over 19 years, ranging from the vast Meath Gardens in Bethnal Green to the smaller Goldsmith's Square in Hackney.

Involved in every aspect of the process, including producing designs, ordering materials, supervising teams and engaging in physical landscaping, Wilkinson insisted on receiving proper acknowledgement and payment for her work, asserting: 'I know my profession and charge accordingly, as all women should do.'

Even before joining Swanley, Wilkinson showed her willingness to help other women into the industry, taking on numerous female pupils as assistants. In 1899, she became a founding member of the Women's Agricultural and Horticultural International Union (later the Women's Farm and Garden Union), uniting female land workers and aiming to influence public opinion surrounding their work. The union established the Women's National Land Service Corps, a precursor to the Women's Land Army during the First World War. Serving as Principal at Swanley until 1916 (and again in 1920–21), Wilkinson was directly involved with the drive to train wartime land girls. CN

Fanny Wilkinson (1855–1951)
By an unknown photographer, 1935
Gelatin silver print, 55 × 75mm
From a private collection

1903 Aida Overton Walker

The musical *In Dahomey* was first staged on Broadway in February 1903. Following its success, the production was transferred to the Shaftesbury Theatre in London, opening on 16 May of the same year. It was the first time that a British audience had seen a musical with an all-black cast, and it was a triumph. Its run in London included a performance for King Edward VII's birthday at Buckingham Palace as well as a national tour.

In Dahomey was genuinely groundbreaking and featured a cakewalk finale (a dance that first originated among enslaved black people as a satire on the elegance of white ballroom dances), as well as spawning several hit songs. During their stay in London the cast posed for photographer Cavendish Morton, whose portraits were circulated in the press at the time alongside praise for the performers' virtuoso dance routines.

Aida Overton Walker choreographed the show and played Rosetta Lightfoot, dazzling audiences with her original dance moves. Known as 'the queen of the cakewalk', she starred in *In Dahomey* alongside her husband, George Walker, and their creative partner, Bert Williams. Their vaudeville team, known as Williams and Walker, was led by Overton Walker, who was the company's main actor, principal choreographer and creative director.

Arguably, the most famous black woman performer of the early twentieth century and one of the first choreographers, modern dance pioneer Overton Walker went on to lead her own vaudeville company, and throughout her career she strove for better conditions and to expand roles for black women on the stage by challenging stereotypes of class, race and gender.

Commenting on Overton Walker's life and legacy, historian Veronica Jackson explains:

From the beginning of her onstage career in 1897 – just 32 years after the end of slavery – to her premature death in 1914, Overton Walker was a vaudeville performer engaged in a campaign to restructure and re-present how African Americans, particularly black women in popular theatre, were perceived by both black and white society.[2]
GA

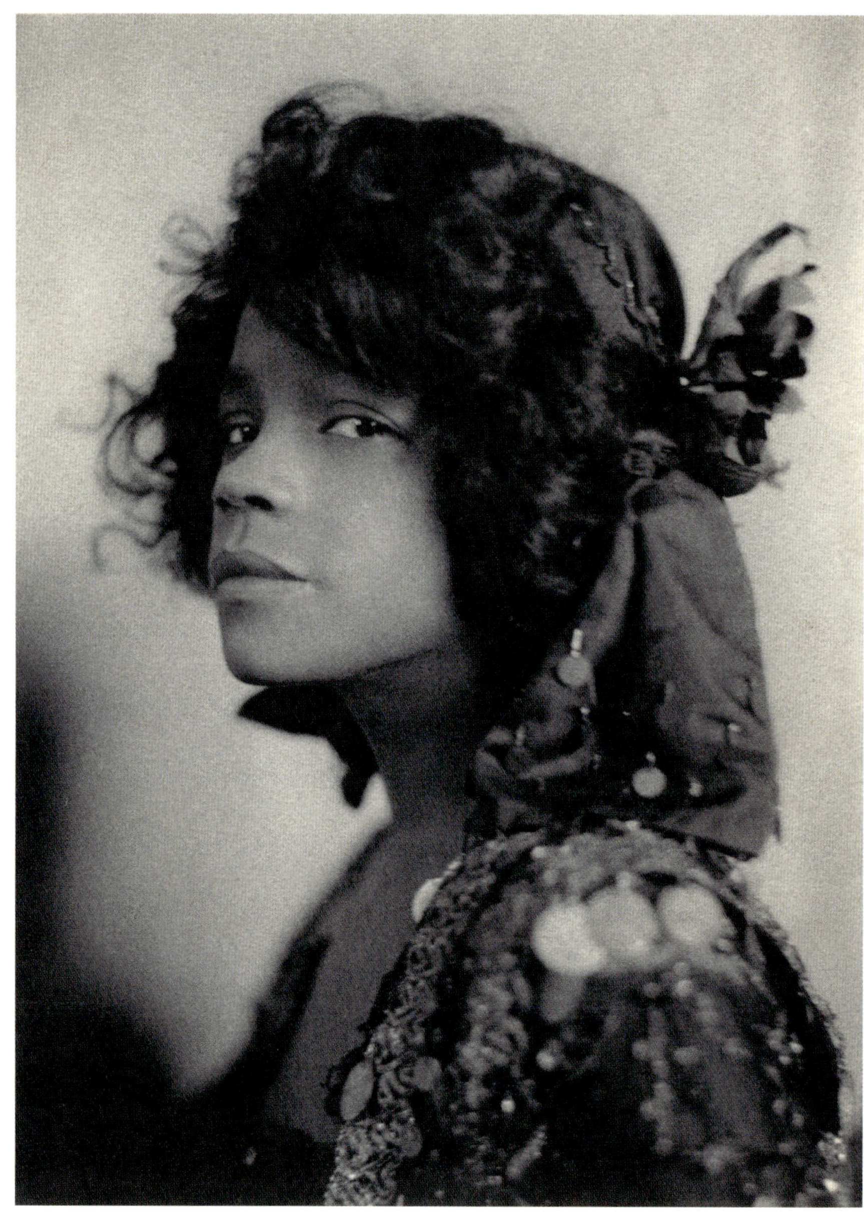

 Aida Overton Walker (1880–1914)
By Cavendish Morton, 1903
Platinum print, 151 × 106mm
National Portrait Gallery, London, x46664

Martha Whiteley

Martha Annie Whiteley was a pioneer chemist and a campaigner for the empowerment of women in science. In 1904 she joined forces with 18 women chemists petitioning for women to be admitted to the Chemical Society (later the Royal Society of Chemistry). The Society's council objected and they were refused admission. The same happened four years later when Whiteley and her peers produced another request to change the men-only admission policy. In 1920 they succeeded and women were finally admitted to the Society. Throughout her career Whiteley would continue to support women in various capacities, and was considered a role model by those seeking to pursue professions in the sciences. She went to great lengths to provide pastoral care to women scientists at undergraduate and graduate level.

In a concrete effort to enhance their careers, Whiteley founded the Imperial College Women's Association in 1912 and served as its president for two decades.

Alongside her advocacy, Whiteley was an accomplished chemist and university lecturer. In 1904 she joined the chemistry department at the Royal College of Science (which, from 1907, became part of Imperial College) and quickly rose through its ranks. By 1920 she was made assistant professor, becoming one of the first women to hold a full-time position in a chemistry department at a British institution.

As a chemist, Whiteley first specialised in the organic chemistry of barbituric compounds, a subject she explored in her doctorate. During the First World War she worked alongside the renowned chemist Sir Jocelyn Field Thorpe, developing drugs to treat soldiers and on the production of lachrymatory gases for military use. For these services, she was officially recorded as a volunteer in support of the war effort and in 1920 she was awarded an OBE.

In addition to her many achievements, Whiteley also co-authored with Thorpe *A Students' Manual of Organic Chemical Analysis: Qualitative and Quantitative* (1925). This comprehensive and accessible guide was based on the knowledge of organic chemistry acquired by Whiteley in her many years of lecturing and researching. Over almost four decades Whiteley made contributions and edited several editions of *Thorpe's Dictionary of Applied Chemistry* – she saw the last revision through completion just before her ninetieth birthday. FF

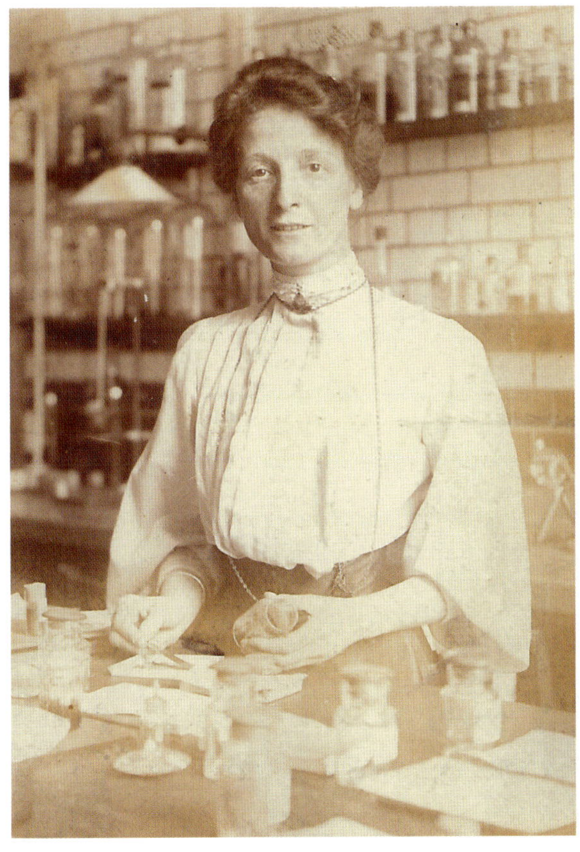

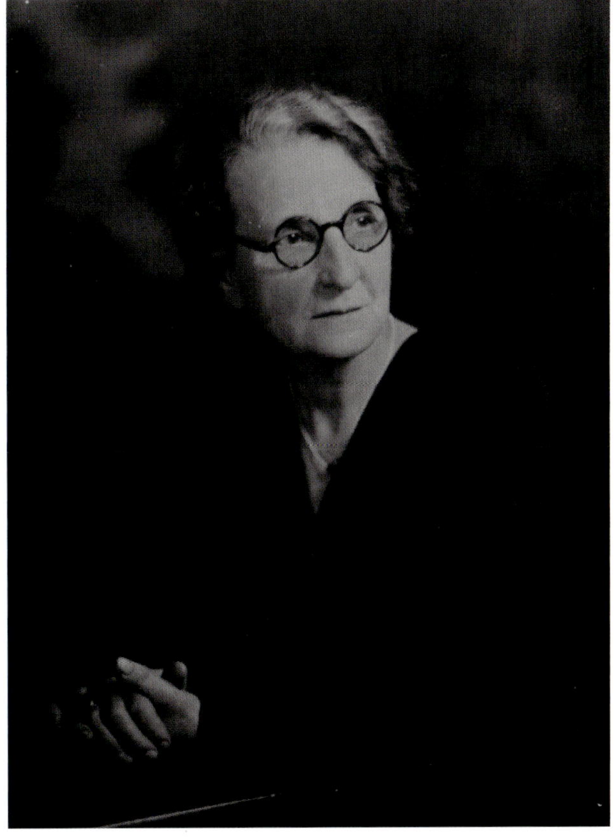

Martha Annie Whiteley (1866–1956)
By Edward Cahen, 1907
Archives, Imperial College, London

Martha Annie Whiteley
By Elliott & Fry, 1946
Gelatin silver print, 148 × 105mm
National Portrait Gallery, London, x91765

Annie Kenney

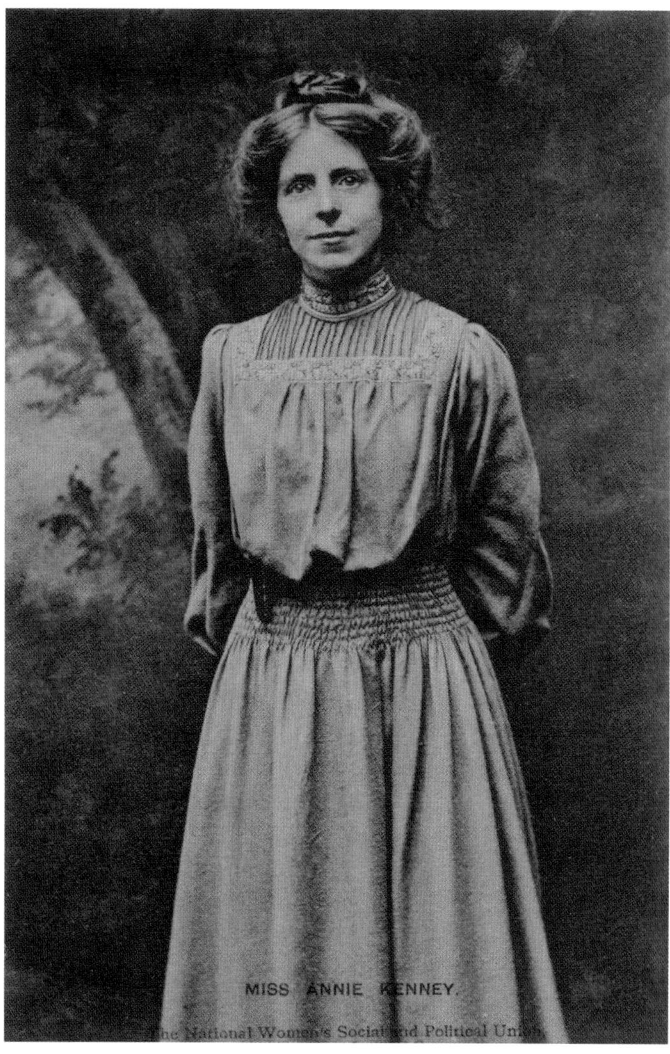

inoffensive protest ... was in itself a sign that astute parliamentarians realized that we knew what we were about.

Dedicated to the cause, Kenney was imprisoned 12 more times following numerous daring stunts. Police brutality, hunger strikes and force feedings weakened her health, which was aggravated further through the tactics of the 1913 Prisoners (Temporary Discharge for Ill Health) Act, nicknamed the 'Cat and Mouse Act'.

Lancashire-born Kenney had begun working part-time in a textile mill on her tenth birthday, leaving school aged 13 for full-time employment. Working long hours and suffering a severed finger from a whirling bobbin, Kenney knew well the difficulties that working-class women faced. In 1905 she joined the WSPU, where leading members recognised the value of Kenney's working-class background for broadening the organization's appeal. She was soon thrust into a central role, opening the WSPU's first London branch in Canning Town and speaking charismatically at gatherings nationwide. The reproduction of her photograph on postcards furthered her public reputation among supporters.

By 1912 Kenney was leading the WSPU under Christabel Pankhurst's instruction, after the latter fled to Paris. She toured America giving lectures and encouraged women into war work when the WSPU's focus shifted at the outbreak of the First World War. In 1918, 'exhausted to death', Kenney stepped back from the WSPU and concentrated on family life. Alongside her autobiography, Kenney's articles for the Scottish *Sunday Post* newspaper in 1921 have allowed us to understand her key contribution to the fight for women's votes. CN

On 13 October 1905, suffragettes Annie Kenney and Christabel Pankhurst attended the Liberals' election rally at Manchester's Free Trade Hall. At the end, Kenney bravely stood and asked the speakers, if elected to government, would they give women the right to vote. Kenney was immediately shouted down, a flag bearing the words 'Votes for Women' was unfurled, and 'disgraceful scenes' ensued. Forcibly ejected, Pankhurst spat at a policeman, while Kenney attempted to gather a crowd outside in protest. The two women were fined for disorderly conduct and causing an obstruction, but refusing to pay,

Kenney was imprisoned for three days and Pankhurst for one week.

This widely reported incident is now regarded as a turning point in the struggle for women's suffrage towards the use of high-profile, militant action by the Women's Social and Political Union (WSPU), following two years of unsuccessful campaigning. In her autobiography, *Memories of a Militant* (1924), Kenney reflected:

The bait had been strong enough; the Press had bitten; the night's catch was rich in the extreme. The very extremity of abuse, criticism, and condemnation hurled at us by the morning Press for such an

Annie Kenney (1879–1953)
Published by Sandle Brothers, *c.*1907
Halftone postcard, 138 × 90mm
National Portrait Gallery, London, x200692

RISING UP:

UNCOVERING WOMEN'S ACTIVISM

By

Constantia Nicolaides

So much has changed in the lives of women since 1900. In the last century and a quarter, we have witnessed the expansion of women's rights and opportunities, as well as a significant shift in the perceptions of both the position and role of women in society. Much of this has been driven by the sustained efforts of determined women activists, who have bravely challenged power and the status quo to raise awareness and bring about changes in legislation and societal attitudes. These women have confronted discrimination and overcome limitations in order to improve their own lives and also the lives of others.

Of course activism by women is not unique to the twentieth and twenty-first centuries. We need only look at etchings depicting the Peterloo Massacre in 1819, where women are seen among the protesters attacked by the cavalry while demanding voting rights for all men, or at the few bonneted heads in Benjamin Robert Haydon's painting of the 1840 convention of the British and Foreign Anti-Slavery Society, to find earlier examples. Yet as women's voices have gained more force over time, so too has their activism, along with its effectiveness and visibility, developed in ever increasing directions. From Margaret Bondfield's social investigations into working conditions and pay to Vijaya Lakshmi Pandit's anti-colonial campaigning, and from Jane Goodall's environmental concerns to Barbara Lisicki's disability rights activism, the reasons for women's activism are wide and varied. Whether they define themselves as activists or not, engage with one issue, or dedicate their lives to multiple concerns, countless individuals and groups of women, often working alongside like-minded men, have taken part in demonstrations, marches, sit-ins, boycotts, letter writing, petitions, the distribution of pamphlets, or acts of civil disobedience in the name of their respective causes. However, not all have gained the same level of recognition for their efforts, as some of the portraits showing women activists in the National Portrait Gallery's Collection reveal.

One of the most prominent and well-documented campaigns by women was the struggle for women's suffrage during the earliest part of the twentieth century. In 1905, Emmeline Pankhurst's Women's Social and Political Union (WSPU) turned from peaceful campaigning to militant action, widely considered to have been initiated by Annie Kenney and Christabel Pankhurst's disturbance at a Liberal election rally that year. The WSPU's law-breaking and often violent activities, which included arson and the smashing of windows, immediately grabbed the attention of the press, who mockingly dubbed Union members 'suffragettes' (though the women would go on to embrace this term). The suffragettes' high-profile and disruptive activities ensured that their names were frequently published and their photographs – such as those of Emmeline Pankhurst being arrested and carried away against her will by police officers – were widely circulated.

In 1913 the suffragettes' activities extended to targeting and defacing artworks in public galleries and museums. As a result, a memorandum was issued in April 1914 to numerous cultural institutions, including the National Portrait Gallery, from the Criminal Record Office at Scotland Yard. Drawing special attention to known perpetrators of such 'outrages', it featured the identity photographs of 18 suffragettes, mainly taken covertly in the exercise yards of Manchester and Holloway prisons while the women served sentences for their actions (fig.1). Having resisted the taking of 'mugshots' upon their incarceration, Scotland Yard had gone to new lengths to document the women's appearances in the interests of security, using a specially purchased camera and lens to surreptitiously

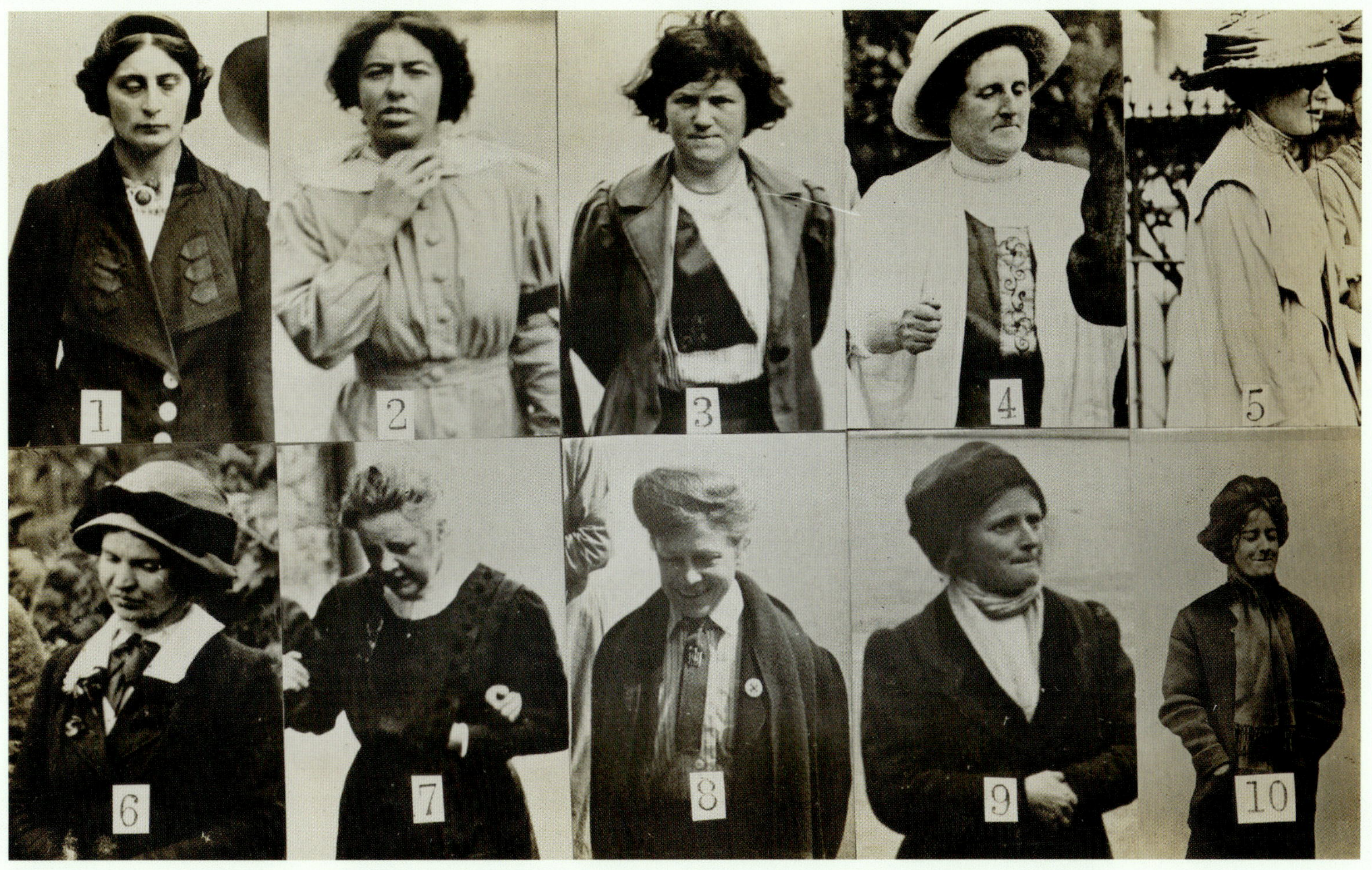
Fig.1: 10 Surveillance photographs of suffragettes by the Criminal Record Office

photograph the women from a distance. The suffragettes countered this visual presentation of them as criminals by employing the talents of professional photographers affiliated with the suffrage campaign, such as Lena Connell and Lallie Charles, to create images that provided an antidote to those showing them as dishevelled or distressed. The resulting feminine, elegant and demure portraits of leading suffragettes, taken in the controlled setting of the photographic studio, were mass-produced and sold as collectable postcards to raise funds for campaigns and to inspire loyalty among members to their leaders. Such postcards, like that depicting Annie Kenney (p.28), have also left us with an extensive visual record of the movement's key figures long after the end of their campaign.

Although the Scotland Yard images were destined for the National Portrait Gallery's files, it was not long before a more legitimate position within the Gallery's Collection was gained for these women. The Representation of the People Act in 1918 gave the parliamentary vote to all women aged 30 and over who met a minimum property qualification. Further legislation in 1928 extended this right to all women from 21 years of age. With the latter passed into law less than three weeks after Emmeline Pankhurst's death, a group of former suffragettes – including Kitty Marshall, Flora Drummond and Margaret Haig Thomas, 2nd Viscountess Rhondda – swiftly established a memorial committee and fund to secure their past leader's legacy in the most prominent ways they could conceive. These consisted of a headstone for Pankhurst's grave in Brompton Cemetery, a bronze statue that was unveiled in 1930 in close proximity to the Houses of Parliament (the site for many

With this close connection to her subjects, Fraser created a body of images that captured all aspects of the conference's atmosphere. Her photographs depict impassioned speakers as well as close-ups of women listening intently or amusing their young children, who accompanied them or attended the makeshift crèche run by fathers. Also included are images showing the busts of distinguished men found within the hall, subversively covered with scarves or banana skins. Filmmaker Sue Crockford was also present, recording footage for her film *A Woman's Place* (1971, fig.3). Recalling the need to ask the plenary sessions for permission to film, she remarked, 'it was the only way that this was going to get reported accurately.'

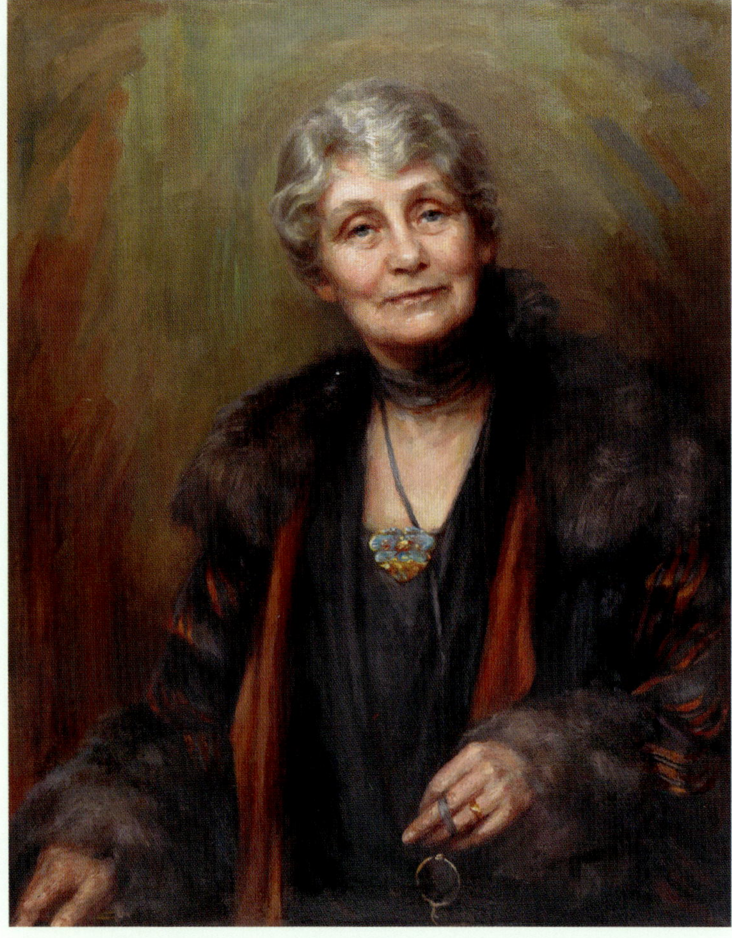

Fig.2: Emmeline Pankhurst by Georgina Brackenbury

of the suffrage movement's protests), and the donation of a very respectable-looking portrait by Georgina Brackenbury to the National Portrait Gallery in 1929 (fig.2). Adept propagandists during the height of their campaign, the suffragettes were now directing their representation in the history books. Moreover, their example strikingly underlines how public perceptions of activists can shift dramatically over time.

Decades on, the second-wave feminists, like their suffragette predecessors, understood the need to influence their public portrayal. Aware of the potential for their ridicule in the media, they banned the press from the first national Women's Liberation Conference at Ruskin College, Oxford in 1970. Activist-photographer Chandan Fraser (then known as Sally) documented the historic event and recalled:

Yet not all activists have enjoyed this kind of widespread or enduring visibility; much grassroots activism has been marginalised from the mainstream press. Such was the case for Olive Morris (p.128), a Jamaican-born, London-based feminist and communist campaigner, who was active in numerous black women's and anti-racist organizations during the 1970s. She was almost all but written out of history, until recent research brought her vital contributions back into the light. While delving in the files at Peckham Library in south-east London in 2006, the artist and writer Ana Laura López de la Torre became intrigued by a photograph from a Black Panther demonstration in Brixton in 1969, where an unidentified, barefoot woman holding a commanding placard reading 'Black Sufferer Fight Police Pig Brutality' stood amongst the

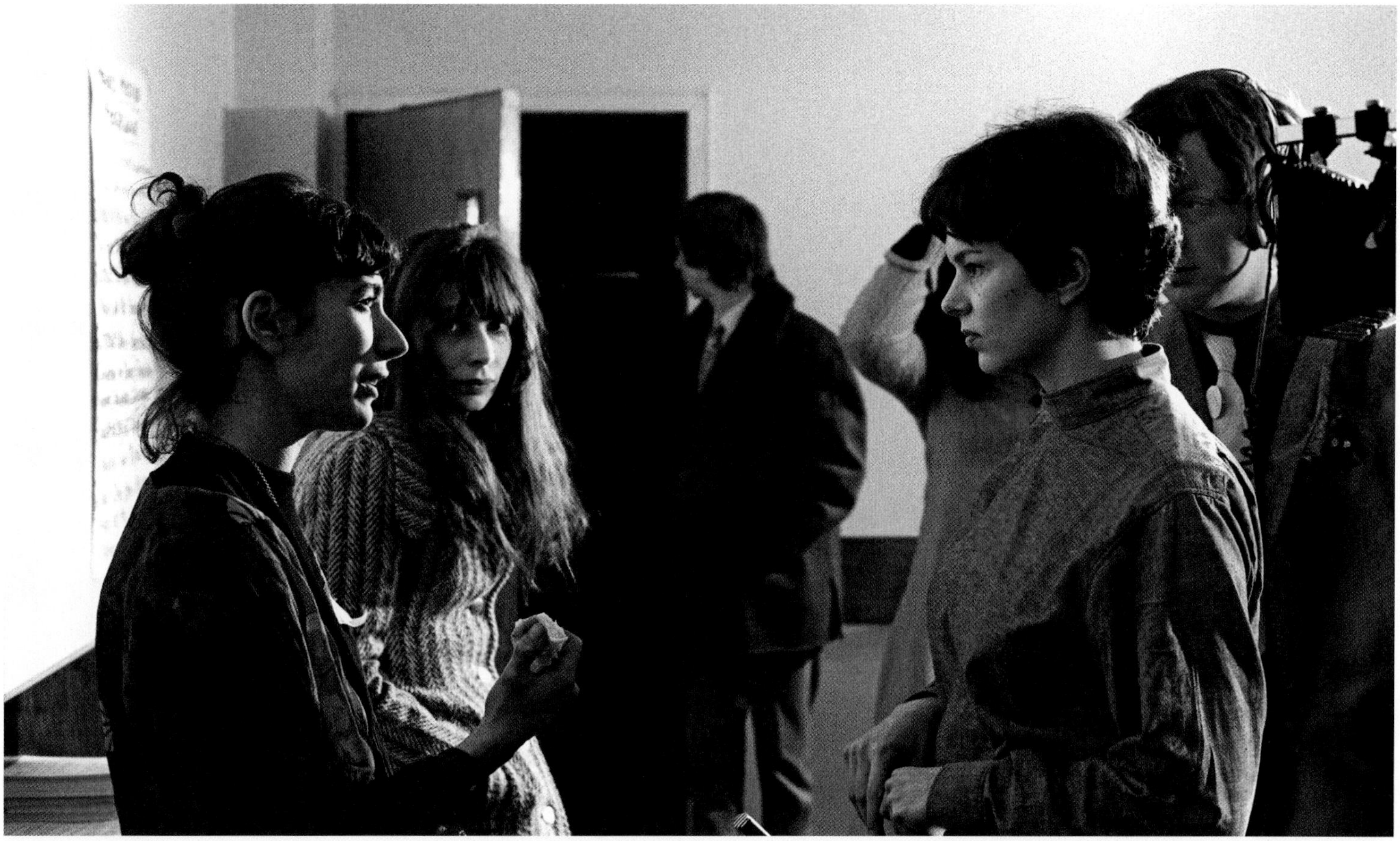

Fig.3: The first Women's Liberation Conference by Sally Fraser

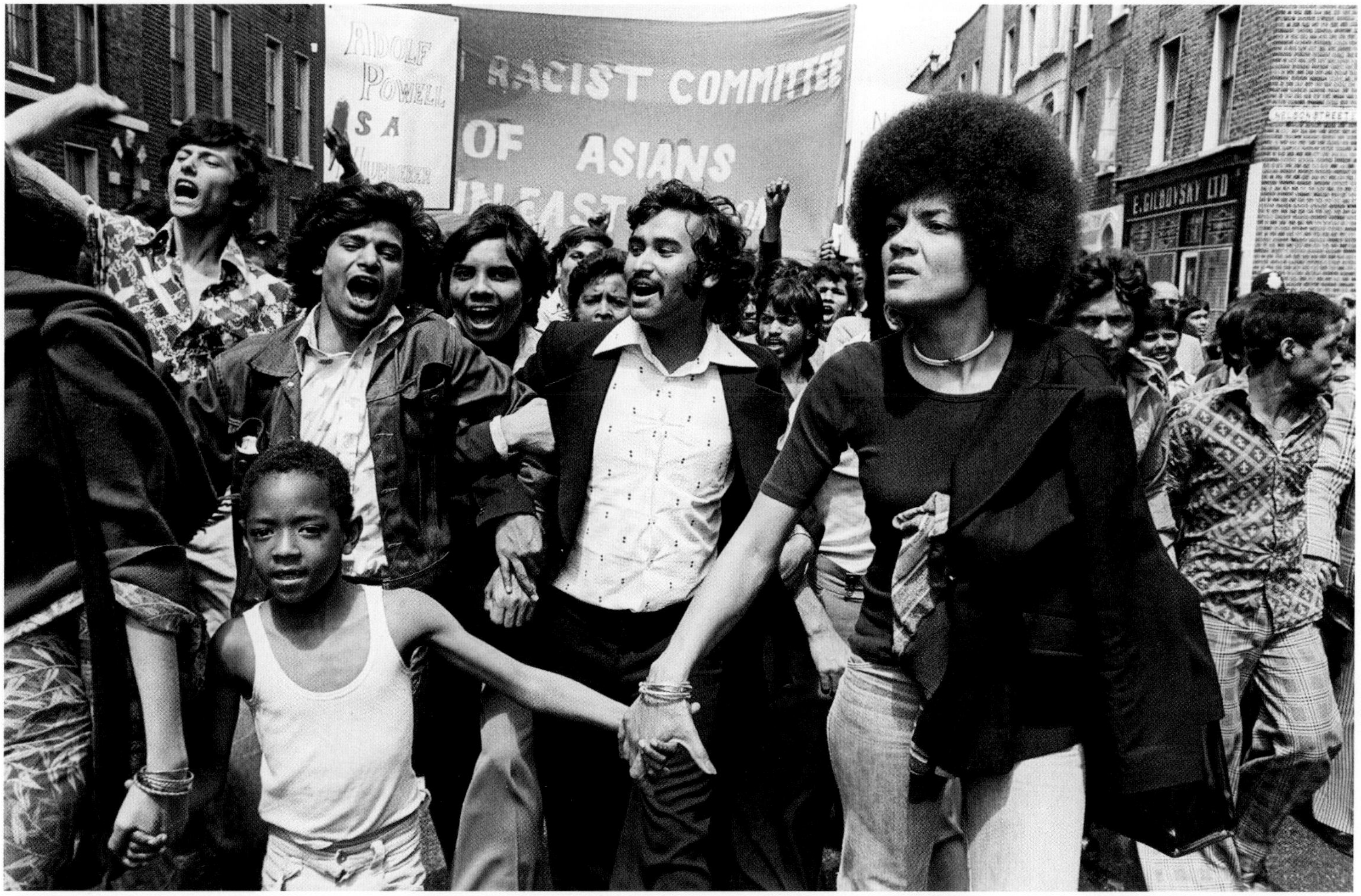

Fig.4: Anti-racism demonstration, Brick Lane by Paul Trevor

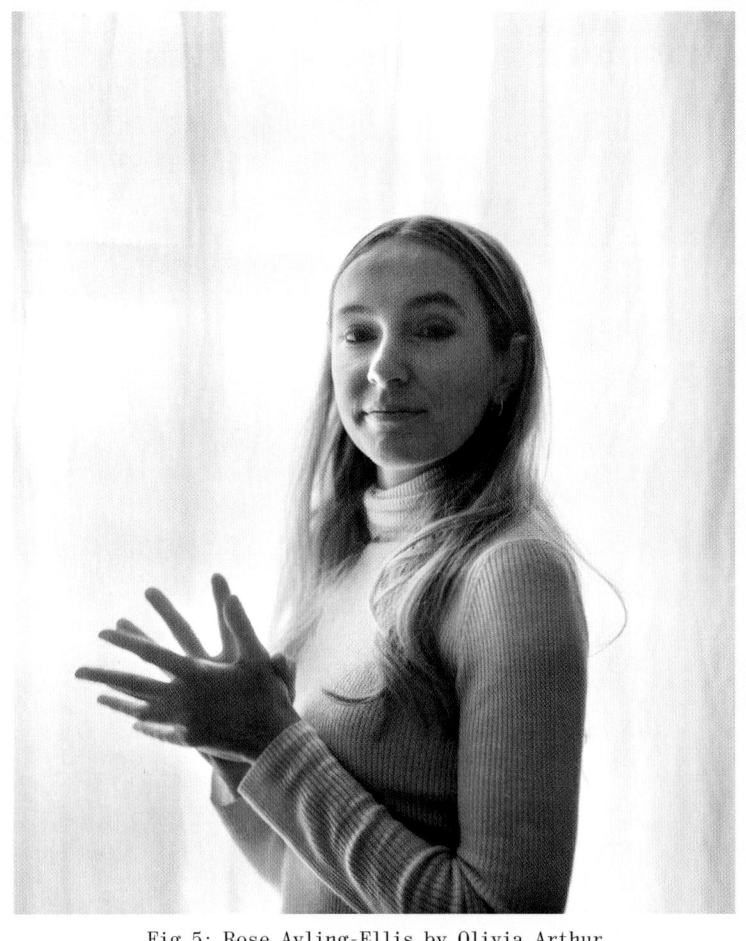

Fig.5: Rose Ayling-Ellis by Olivia Arthur

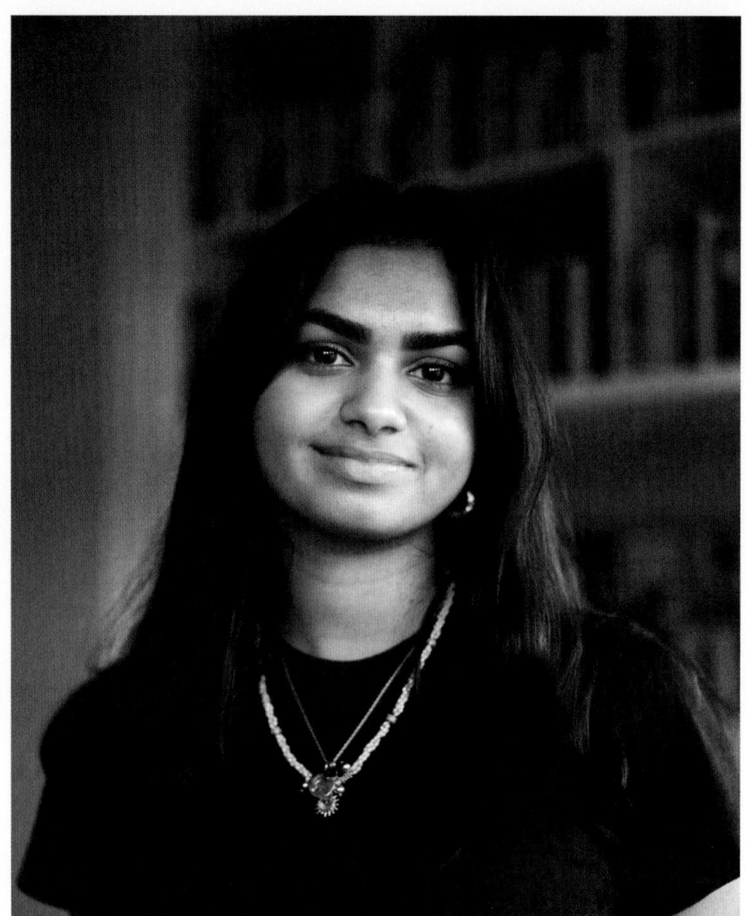

Fig.6: Amika George by Olivia Arthur

men present. Determined to find out more, López de la Torre eventually made contact with Liz Obi, a fellow activist and close friend of Morris, and by 2008 the two women had co-founded the Remembering Olive Collective as a means of gathering information from those who knew Morris during her short life. Beginning with no public records in existence, by the following year, López de la Torre and Obi were able to deposit the Olive Morris Collection at Lambeth Archives, containing oral histories, photographs and ephemera relating to Morris and her activism. López de la Torre reflected: 'I think it's interesting how histories have been deactivated and have to be started all over again.'

While the often collective and sometimes ephemeral nature of activism means that there are many campaigners whose names we will never know, this impulse to pinpoint faces in a crowd and uncover individual biographies

and contributions remains an important way of recovering the histories of overlooked activists. Echoing López de la Torre's story, when a project began in 2019 to research photographer Paul Trevor's vast archive of images documenting the east London Bengali community's anti-fascist campaigns during the 1970s, the photographs of previously unknown women at the head of the marching male crowds were immediately conspicuous. In one photograph, the Bengali-Indian activist Mala Sen – responsible for the Bengali Housing Action Group that helped to establish London's Brick Lane area as the centre of the British Bangladeshi community – was identified, while Barbara Beese (fig.4) – one of the Mangrove Nine group of black activists acquitted in a groundbreaking trial in 1970 in which police racism was foregrounded – was named in another. The women were both involved in the Race Today Collective and the images highlight the alliances formed between African Caribbean and other ethnic minority communities in their efforts to fight widespread discrimination.

This interest in gaining a window into individuals' contributions and achievements through their likenesses also lies at the core of the National Portrait Gallery's collecting. Commissions at the Gallery in recent years have sought to celebrate the contributions of contemporary women activists as well as those re-emerging through the efforts of historical research and recovery. These have included education activist Malala Yousafzai by Shirin Neshat (p.176) and anti-racism campaigner Doreen Lawrence by Thomas Ganter (p.158). A commission in partnership with Magnum Photos between 2022 and 2023 created a series of photographic portraits of contemporary women. Although not intended to focus on campaigners, many of the selected sitters have been involved with activism on different issues and to varying

degrees. These individuals and the images of them provide just a snapshot of the various ways in which women are involved in activism today: actor Rose Ayling-Ellis, who has raised awareness of deaf people's rights (fig.5); classicist Mary Beard, whose *Women & Power: A Manifesto* (2017) looked to history to underline the need to redefine the structures of power in society; writer Caroline Criado Perez, whose campaigns for recognising historical female achievements led to the inclusion of Jane Austen on the £10 note and a statue of suffragist leader Millicent Fawcett being erected in Parliament Square; period poverty campaigner Amika George (fig.6); conservationist Bella Lack; and lawyer Farhana Yamin (p.187), who is a long-standing climate activist. Portraits from across the Collection reveal how pervasive activism by women is in our lives, although these just scratch the surface as more portraits emerge and new research seeks to uncover the lost faces of women activists.

1906   Hertha Ayrton

In 1906, electrical engineer Hertha Ayrton became the first woman recipient of the Royal Society's distinguished Hughes Medal 'for her experimental investigations on the electric arc, and also on sand ripples'. This acknowledgment was especially notable given that four years earlier her nomination for a Fellowship with the same institution was rejected because as a married woman she had no legal standing. Ayrton would find herself constantly battling such inequalities and inconsistencies throughout her career.

Educated at Girton College, Cambridge, in 1884 Ayrton went on to attend evening classes on electricity at north London's Finsbury Technical College, taught by the physicist and electrical engineer William Edward Ayrton. By 1885 they were married and Ayrton began assisting in her husband's experiments, although he also supported her personal scientific ambitions. She asserted: 'He has never joined with me in any bit of work just because he knew that it would all be ascribed to him, and he wanted me to get the full kudos for all I did.' Passionate that women should be properly credited for their work, she registered 26 patents for her inventions and argued publicly for recognition of her friend Marie Curie as radium's true discoverer: 'an error that ascribes to a man what was actually the work of a woman has more lives than a cat.'

Through her work on the electric arc (widely used in nineteenth-century public lighting) and her solution to its problematic flickering and hissing, Ayrton also secured her election as the Institute of Electrical Engineers' first woman member in 1899. Meanwhile, the application of her studies on the formation of sand ripples by oscillations of water to the movement of air led to her developing the 'Ayrton Fan' during the First World War, designed to dispel poisonous gases, widely used in chemical warfare from 1915, from the frontline trenches. Initially dismissed by the War Office, Ayrton fought for the fan's acceptance, with over 100,000 of her life-saving devices eventually deployed.

Ayrton's dedication to women's rights also meant she became closely involved with the campaign for women's suffrage. She was among the leading suffragettes who marched to the Houses of Parliament during the infamous 'Black Friday' on 18 November 1910 and in 1919 she co-founded the International Federation of University Women. CN

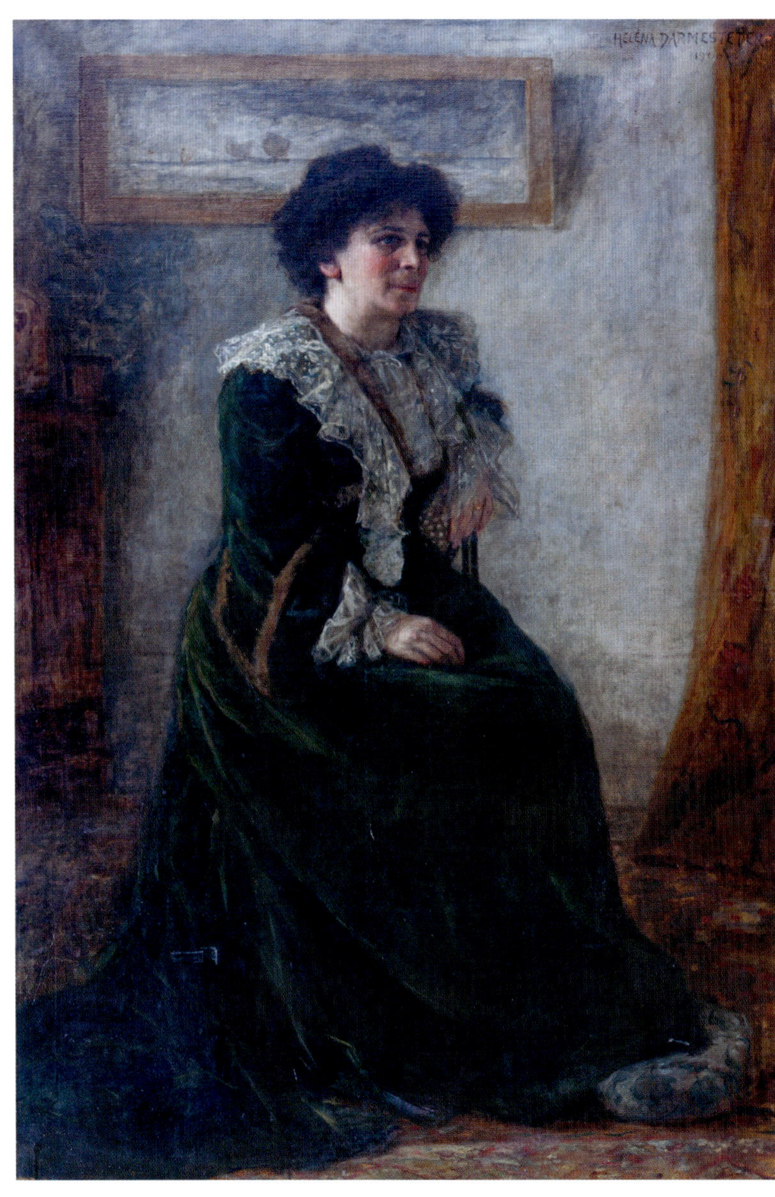

Hertha Ayrton (1854–1923)
By Helena Arsène Darmesteter, 1906
Oil on canvas, 1590 × 990mm
Girton College, University of Cambridge

Ray Strachey

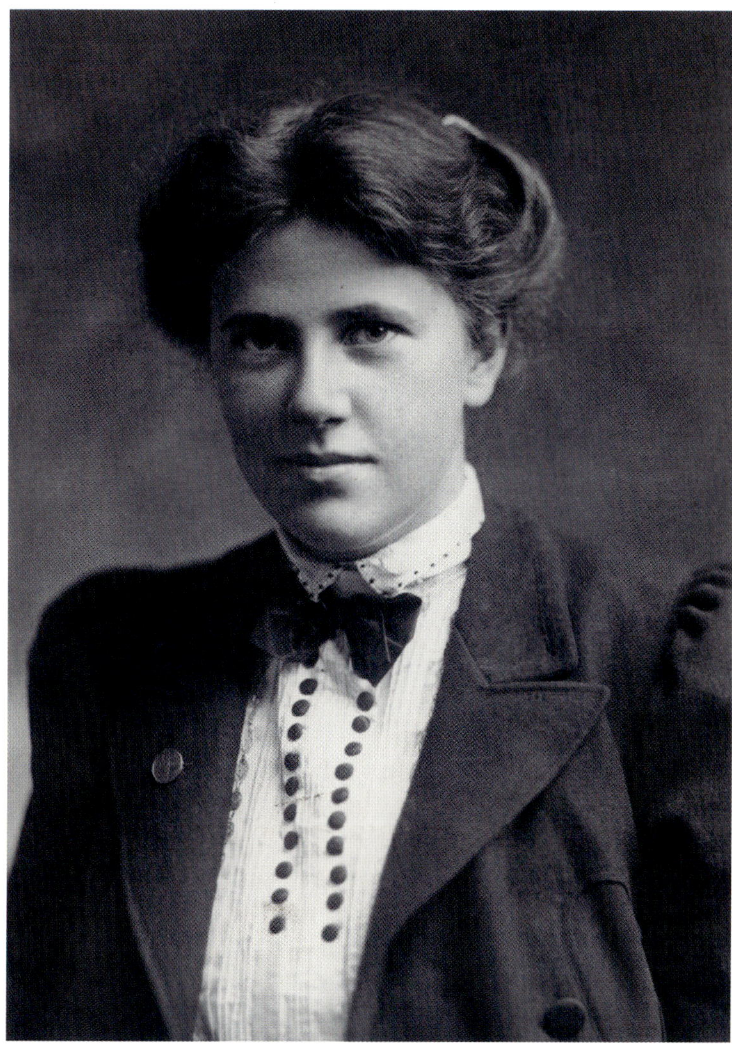

With education, enfranchisement, and legal equality all conceded, the future of women lies in their own hands.[4]

Ray Strachey was one of the leading feminists of the inter-war years. An activist, artist and writer, she was deeply committed to gender equality, women's suffrage and women's employment issues. She established her reputation with her history of the women's movement, *The Cause* (1928), and as the biographer of feminist politician Millicent Garrett Fawcett.

Born Rachel Pearsall Conn Costelloe, she was brought up by her Quaker grandmother, Hannah Whitall Smith, and her aunt, Alys Russell, both supporters of women's right to vote. Ray, as she was known from birth, read mathematics at Newnham College, soon joining the Cambridge University Women's Suffrage Society with her close friend Ellie Rendel, the granddaughter of Sir Richard and Lady Jane Strachey.

On 9 February 1907, Ray took part in a marching procession through London, later known as the 'Mud March' due to the bad weather conditions. Over 3,000 women set off from Hyde Park to Exeter Hall on the Strand. The event was a great success, with women from all backgrounds demonstrating peacefully for the right to vote. Organized by Pippa Strachey – a friend and later sister-in-law of Ray – it was the largest public demonstration staged to that date. Soon afterwards, Ray found herself in high demand to speak at suffrage meetings, and by 1913 she became the Chair of the London Society for Women's Suffrage.

From 1916 until 1921, she was honorary Parliamentary Secretary to the National Union of Women's Suffrage Societies (NUWSS), having a major input in the negotiations for the passage of the 1918 suffrage bill. She was also one of the first woman parliamentary candidates, standing as an Independent in the elections of 1918, 1920 and 1922, although she was unsuccessful. During the inter-war period, she continued her work towards extending and improving employment opportunities for women, alongside her personal commitments as a working mother with connections to the Bloomsbury Set. In 1931 she became Parliamentary Secretary to Nancy Astor, the first serving British woman Member of Parliament.

Today, Strachey is celebrated on the plinth of Gillian Wearing's statue of Millicent Garrett Fawcett in Parliament Square. GA

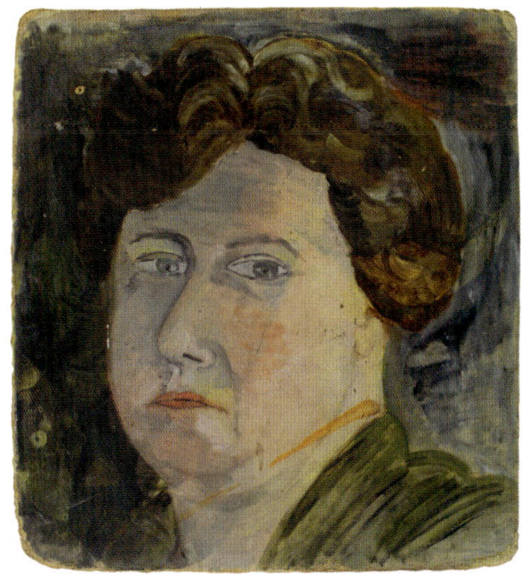

Ray Strachey (1887–1940)
By an unknown photographer, 1908
Gelatin silver print, 134 × 93mm
National Portrait Gallery, London, Ax160792

Ray Strachey
Self-portrait, *c*.1926
Oil on board, 445 x 394mm
National Portrait Gallery, London, D240

Annie S.D. Maunder

It is like a silver mist, it is like ivory gauze, it is like the wings of an angel, it is like the petals of the lilies of heaven. Its form takes on here and there the shape of a flower-leaf, and when I saw the sun's eclipse in 1898 it seemed to me as if a child had been playing the game of 'Loves me, loves me not,' until but three or four of the sunflower's petals had been left on the red-rimmed, black-hearted stalk.

This charming description of a solar eclipse from *The Heavens and their Story* perfectly illustrates Annie Scott Dill Maunder's passion for astronomy, as well as her desire to make it accessible and appealing to as wide an audience as possible. The book was published jointly in 1908 with her husband and lifelong collaborator, E. Walter Maunder, though he acknowledged it in the preface as 'almost wholly the work of my wife'. Praised in reviews for its lucid writing and careful composition, it introduced the sun, moon, stars and planets, approaching each as a 'story' with further poetic analogies, in the hope of inspiring beginners.

Maunder's own interest in astronomy had emerged while studying mathematics at Cambridge University. In 1891, she eagerly took one of the few roles available to her, as a 'Lady Computer' at Greenwich's Royal Observatory. Though the work was mostly tedious, routine and poorly paid, she also gained experience in using telescopes and taking daily photographs of the sun to track sunspots. It was there that she met Walter and left shortly before their wedding in 1895, owing to prohibitive rules regarding the employment of married women. Yet, it was far from the end of her career in astronomy.

The following year, Maunder's outstanding talents were recognised when she was awarded the inaugural Pfeiffer Research Student Fellowship, allowing her to undertake a photographic study of the Milky Way. Further opportunities came through the inclusive British Astronomical Association (a Fellowship with the Royal Astronomical Society eventually came in 1916, after its admission policy changed to permit women), including as editor of its journal. With this continued access to a professional and amateur network, Maunder visited solar eclipse sites around the world where she continued to practise her skills as an astrophotographer. This included India where, in 1898, she captured the longest coronal streamer recorded at that time, using a camera she had adapted herself.

Maunder's adept observations and shrewd analysis over many years contributed numerous original findings to astronomy, although not all were widely recognised during her lifetime within the male-dominated field. Her determination to popularise the subject continued, including through a regular column for the *Daily News* (1928–30). CN

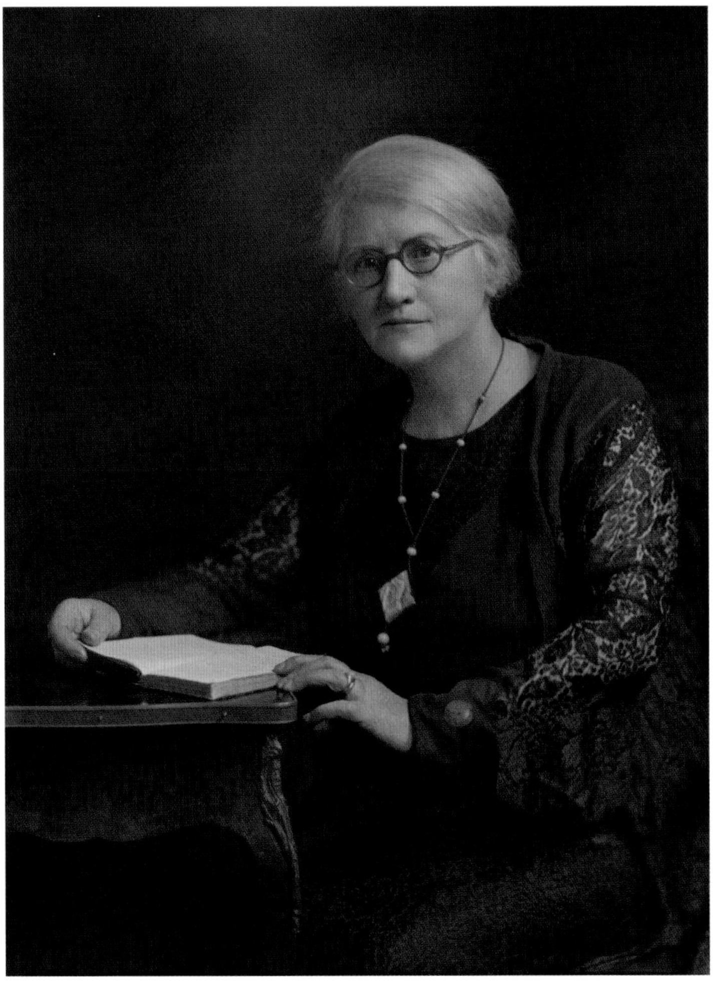

Annie S.D. Maunder (1868–1947)
By Lafayette, 7 December 1931
Half-plate nitrate negative
National Portrait Gallery, London, x47933

First staged at London's Scala Theatre on 10 November 1909, Cicely Hamilton's suffrage play, *A Pageant of Great Women*, opened with the character 'Woman' pleading with 'Justice' for the freedom to determine her own life. Pursued by the production's singular male character, 'Prejudice', who embodies man's oppression and criticises women as desiring nothing more than 'a man's arm round her waist', 'Woman' responds:

… Oh, think you well
What you have done to make it hard for her
To dream, to write, to paint, to build, to learn –
Oh, think you well! And wonder at the line
Of those who knew that life was more than love
And fought their way to achievement
and to fame!

Thus, she introduces 44 historical women from six categories – learned women, artists, saintly women, heroic women, rulers and warriors – to demonstrate otherwise. The distinguished individuals, including Jane Austen, Boudicca and Florence Nightingale, were performed by a cast also featuring leading actresses of the day. This dignified and empowering gathering of figures, presented during the height of the suffrage campaign, countered more controversial militant tactics and was intended to contradict anti-suffrage claims that women were incapable of voting as they lacked experience in contributing valuably to public life. The hugely popular play, serving as an artistic propaganda tool, toured nationwide and was published in 1910 to raise funds. It has also been compared to modern feminist attempts to highlight the often overlooked stories of women in history.

A former actress, Hamilton's reputation as a playwright had been established a year earlier with *Diana of Dobson's* (1908), which exposed the plight of exploited women shop assistants. Her subsequent works

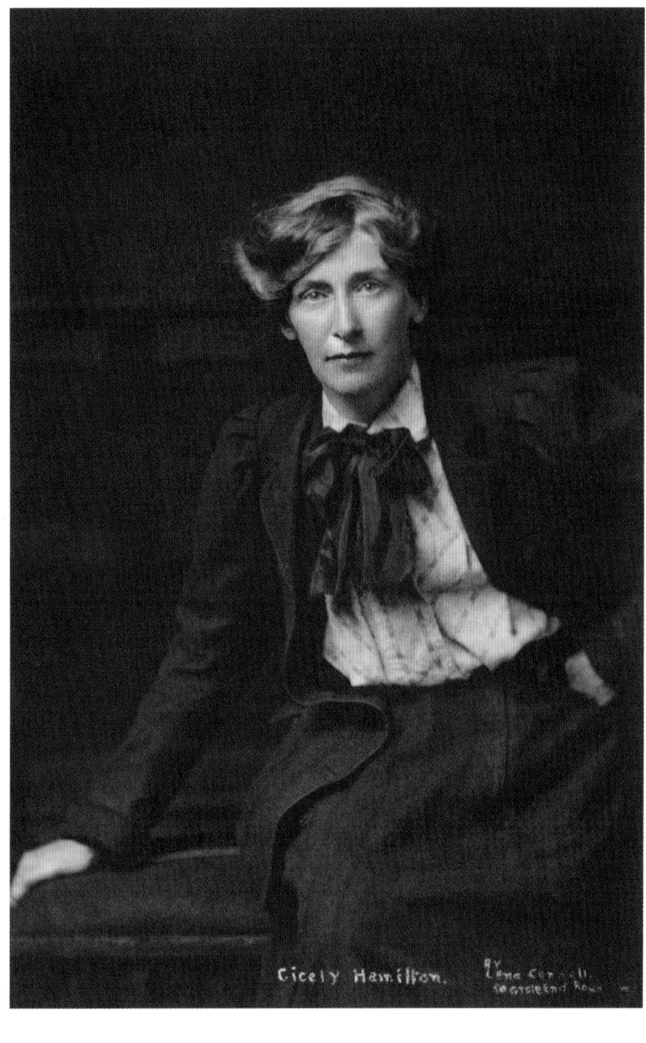

also encompassed feminist themes. Earlier in 1909, she had co-authored the one-act comedy, *How the Vote was Won*, which also ridiculed anti-suffrage arguments and English laws that maintained wives' and unmarried women's economic dependence on their husbands or nearest male relatives. *Marriage as a Trade* (also from 1909) was described in the press as 'the most revolutionary book of the age'; it attacked the gender stereotyping that limited women's prospects and measured their success by their ability to become wives and mothers. Notably, Hamilton never married and supported herself financially throughout her adult life.

In 1910, Hamilton supplied the rousing lyrics to the Women's Social and Political Union's anthem, 'The March of the Women'. However, she later criticised the organization and identified herself as a 'feminist rather than suffragist' in her autobiography, *Life Errant* (1935). Her writing also encompassed several novels and journalism, which included her contributions to *Time and Tide*, the journal for the feminist Six Point Group with whom she was active from the 1920s until the 1940s. CN

Cicely Hamilton (1872–1952)
By Lena Connell, 1910s
Sepia-toned gelatin silver postcard, 135 × 84mm
National Portrait Gallery, London, x17331

1910 Dorothée Pullinger

Automobile engineer Dorothée Pullinger began her career in 1910 as a junior draughtswoman at the Arrol-Johnston car factory in Scotland. Her father, Thomas Pullinger, managed the plant in Paisley and, although he considered engineering to be an unsuitable interest for a girl, she convinced him to give her a chance. Aged 16, having just left school, Pullinger eagerly gained extensive knowledge of the manufacturing process, alongside supervising experience while acting as forewoman of the core shop. As a result, Pullinger was asked to manage 7,000 new women employees making high explosive shells during the First World War. In 1920 she received an MBE for this work.

After the war, Pullinger re-joined her father at the Galloway Engineering Company's recently built factory, near Kirkcudbright, but this time as a director and manager. Fully converted to the possibility of women as engineers, Thomas had offered a structured apprenticeship to his wartime female workforce, declaring his enthusiasm in an article in the *Gentlewoman* in 1917: 'There is no finality in engineering, and the trained woman engineer has come to stay.' Pullinger, who became a founder member of the newly formed Women's Engineering Society in 1919, was also keen that this training and employment should continue, particularly while many women were losing their jobs to returning soldiers.

The factory switched from wartime production to car manufacturing, and the Pullingers pioneered 'a car made by ladies for others of their sex', as *The Light Car and Cyclecar* magazine described it. Women had long been interested

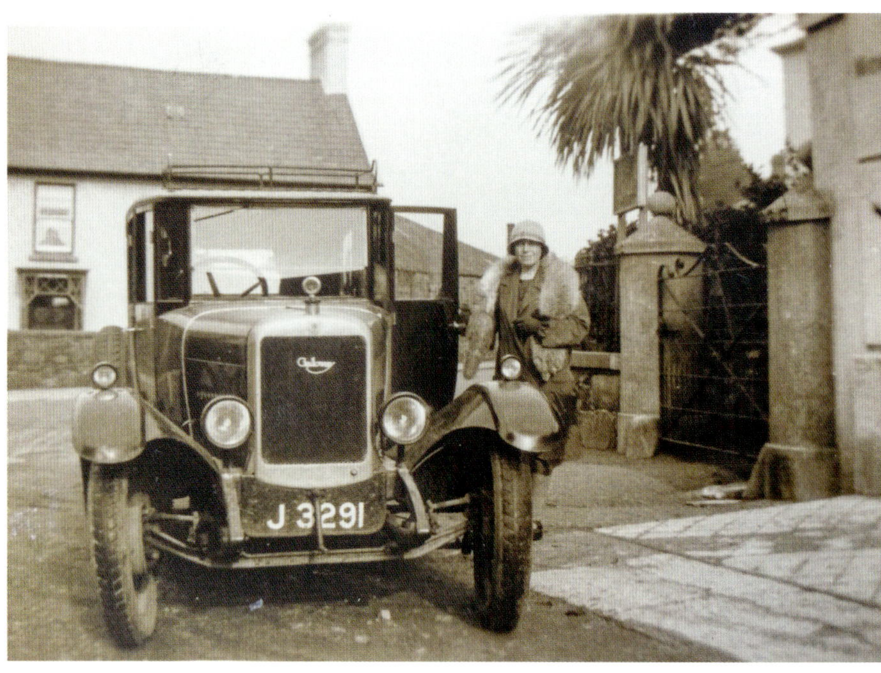

in motoring and, with more learning to drive to fulfil wartime roles, the unsuitability of existing models was clear. Smaller and lighter, the Galloway 10/20 was launched in 1920 and featured a raised seat and lowered dashboard to give women drivers better sight-lines. The cars included a rear-view mirror as standard and a handbrake repositioned beside the driver's seat – innovations that remain today.

While Pullinger's achievements led to her eventual acceptance as the first woman member of the Institution of Automobile Engineers in 1921, she faced hostility for remaining in the industry after the war and soon left. A resolute entrepreneur, she set up a thriving commercial laundry service with the latest steam-laundry equipment, arguing: 'I thought washing should not be doing men out of a job.' Her skills in business and manufacturing were prized during the

Second World War, when she served as a government adviser.

Pullinger finally settled in Guernsey, where she opened another laundry company and is said to have spent her last years speeding around the local roads in her Galloway car. CN

Dorothée Pullinger (1894–1986) with a Galloway car
By an unknown photographer, *c*.1926
Le Couvey-Martin Family Archives

Hilda Hewlett

In this unassuming sketch, the soon-to-be pioneer aviator and businesswoman Hilda Hewlett sits huddled alongside her husband – the novelist Maurice Hewlett – and the artist's wife, Caterina Kerr-Lawson, as they dry themselves after a wild, stormy drive in the Italian Apennines. The scene captures Hilda's daring, adventurous spirit and points to her avid interest in the new world of motoring, which led her to enter competitions and to journey with Muriel Hind in her Singer tricar along the length of Britain. This fascination with motoring would shortly be supplanted by one with aviation.

In October 1909, after watching planes taking off at Britain's first air show in Blackpool, Hewlett felt instantly exhilarated and entranced: 'I was rooted to the spot in thick mud and wonder and did not want to move. I wanted to feel that power under my own hand and understand about why and how.'[5] Determined to fly, on 29 August 1911 she received the Royal Aero Club's Aviator Certificate no. 122, becoming Britain's first woman to gain a pilot's licence.

Hewlett was one of countless individuals who were eager to take

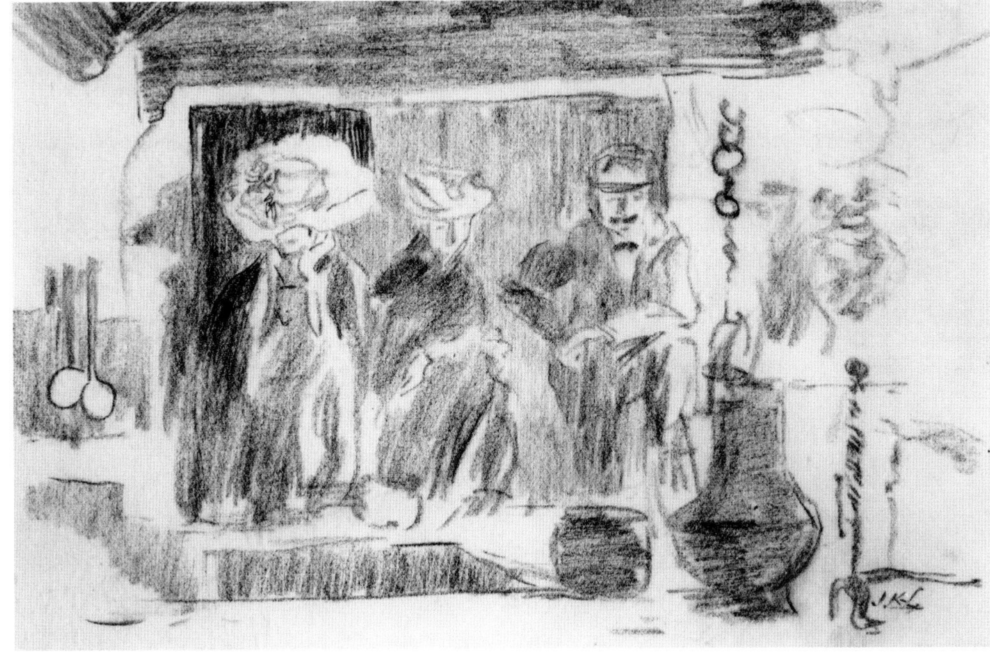

to the skies during the 1910s, which saw many new aviation records set. However, she distinguished herself further with her entrepreneurialism. Having bought a plane to qualify for flying lessons, in September 1910 she opened a flying school with the French pilot and engineer Gustav Blondeau at Brooklands airfield in Surrey. Hewlett proved to be practical and versatile as she managed the flourishing business and assisted with aircraft maintenance and construction, while Blondeau conducted lessons.

For their next venture, in 1912 Hewlett and Blondeau opened a factory, Omnia Works in Clapham, and soon needed larger premises for their expanding company. An ardent advocate for the development of the aeronautics industry in Britain, Hewlett invested in the elaborate, expensive machinery required to make this possible.

By the outbreak of the First World War, Omnia Works was undertaking commissions for the Admiralty and the War Office that 'proved perfect at the first trial' and, in June 1915, the factory

was placed under government control, obliging them to employ women in skilled roles.[6] Despite initial resistance from male staff, Hewlett believed in the opportunities the fledgling aeronautics industry could offer women, identifying it as 'delicate and exacting work for which they are quite fitted'. She established a training school for women in aircraft construction, which became an official centre under the Ministry of Munitions for women employed around the country. With the post-war decline in demand for planes, the factory closed in 1920 and Hewlett's desire to travel returned. She came to settle in Tauranga, New Zealand, where she continued to organize the local flying community and wrote an unpublished memoir. CN

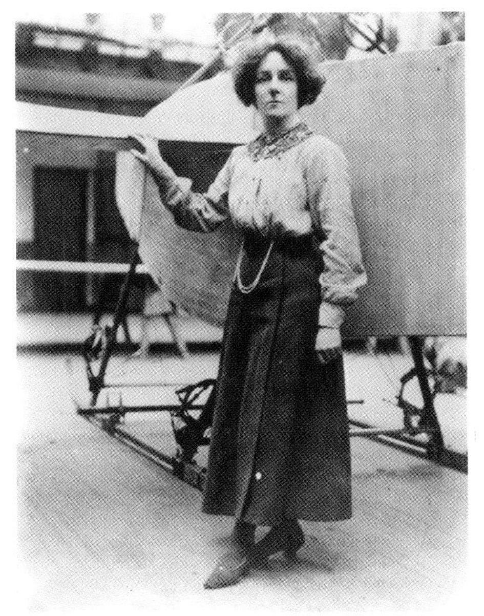

Hilda Hewlett (1864–1943) standing by
a Hanriot plane at Omnia Works, Battersea
By an unknown photographer, *c*.1911–13
Hewlett Family via Brooklands Museum, Weybridge

Hilda Hewlett, Caterina Kerr-Lawson
and Maurice Hewlett
By James Kerr-Lawson, *c*.1904
Pencil drawing, 194 × 254mm
National Portrait Gallery, London, 3264

1912 Louisa Garrett Anderson

In a modest cottage at 688 Harrow Road, near Kensal Green in west London, 'a small revolution', as the *Standard* newspaper described it, was taking place. This is where medical pioneers Louisa Garrett Anderson and Flora Murray – whose lifelong partnership was both professional and personal – founded the Women's Hospital for Children in February 1912, the first of its kind in Britain to be established, staffed and managed entirely by women.

Founded at a time when medical services for infants and children were scant and female medics encountered severely limited opportunities (often attributed to the perceived impropriety of their treating male patients), the hospital proved vital for not just the community it served, but also for women doctors to gain experience in paediatrics. Situated in a deprived and populous neighbourhood, demand was immediate and overwhelming and the premises soon expanded to two adjoining cottages with an in-patients' ward added. The women worked indefatigably to treat the scores of patients, amounting to over 7,000 within the first 18 months, and created an atmosphere likened by the *Daily Herald* to 'a friendly home rather than that of a public institution', well stocked with toys and brightly coloured bed linen.

Anderson had entered the world of medicine having experienced the ideal role model in her mother, Elizabeth Garrett Anderson. Elizabeth was Britain's first qualified female doctor and co-founded the London School of Medicine for Women, where Louisa completed her undergraduate studies. Acutely aware that 'a woman's difficulties begin after she qualifies', Anderson was committed to providing openings for employment and actively supported the campaign for female suffrage. She adopted the Women's Social and Political Union's slogan, 'Deeds not Words', for the hospital's motto, and was briefly imprisoned for her suffragette activities a month after it opened.

When war was declared in 1914, Anderson and Murray were able to build on the experiences they had gained with the children's hospital. They wasted no time in forming the Women's Hospital Corps and established two military hospitals in France. Treating male soldiers as chief surgeon and chief physician respectively, they dismantled the existing barriers surrounding their work and, as a result of their success, were invited to set up a similar facility in London. The extraordinary, entirely female-run Endell Street Military Hospital in Covent Garden helped almost 50,000 soldiers between May 1915 and September 1919, with most of the 7,000 operations performed there by Anderson herself.

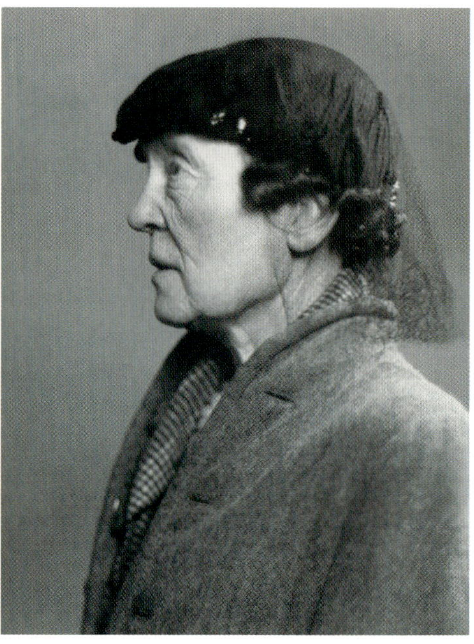

While Anderson and Murray were made CBE in 1917 for their groundbreaking work, post-war prospects for women in medicine were bleak, as was the case in many other professions. Meanwhile, fundraising for a more adequate site and to continue the work of the children's hospital (renamed the Roll of Honour Hospital) remained challenging. The hospital closed in 1921, having helped over half a million children during the decade of its existence. CN

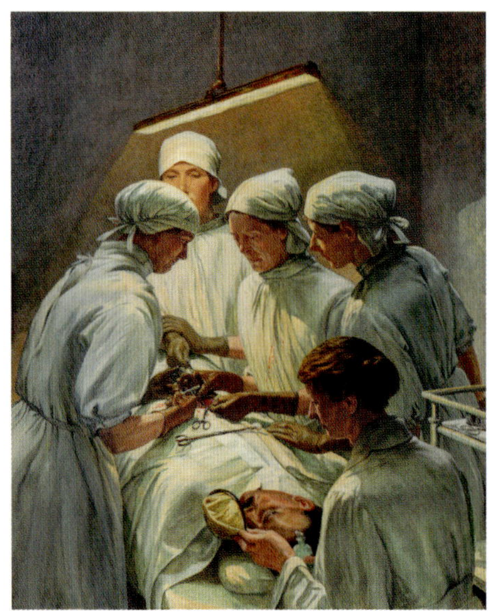

'An Operation at the Military Hospital, Endell Street' (Louisa Garrett Anderson, centre)
By Francis Dodd, 1920–1
Oil on canvas, 1219 × 965mm
Imperial War Museum, Art.IWM ART 4084

Louisa Garrett Anderson (1873–1943)
By Elliott & Fry, 1943
Gelatin silver print, 140 × 110mm
National Portrait Gallery, London, x86169

Margaret Murray

My first experience of field archaeology was in the winter of 1902–3. I had already a fairly good knowledge of Egyptology by books and museum specimens, and had written a few articles, but had not done any field work. Therefore when Petrie suggested that I should go out to his camp and share a dig with Mrs. Petrie and I also copy the Coptic inscription on the walls of the Setekhy's temple, I was delighted.[7]

The archaeologist and Egyptologist Margaret Murray began studying at University College London in 1894. There she met the famous Egyptologist W. Flinders Petrie, who would become a lifelong mentor and colleague. In collaboration with Petrie, Murray carried out fieldwork in Egypt; she assisted in his excavations at Abydos in 1902 and 1903 and then at Saqqara in 1903 to 1904.

Alongside her fieldwork, Murray developed an outstanding career as a lecturer, researcher and writer. At a time when women were still struggling to be taken seriously outside of the home, let alone in the academic world, Murray rose through the ranks at her alma mater, UCL. She joined the

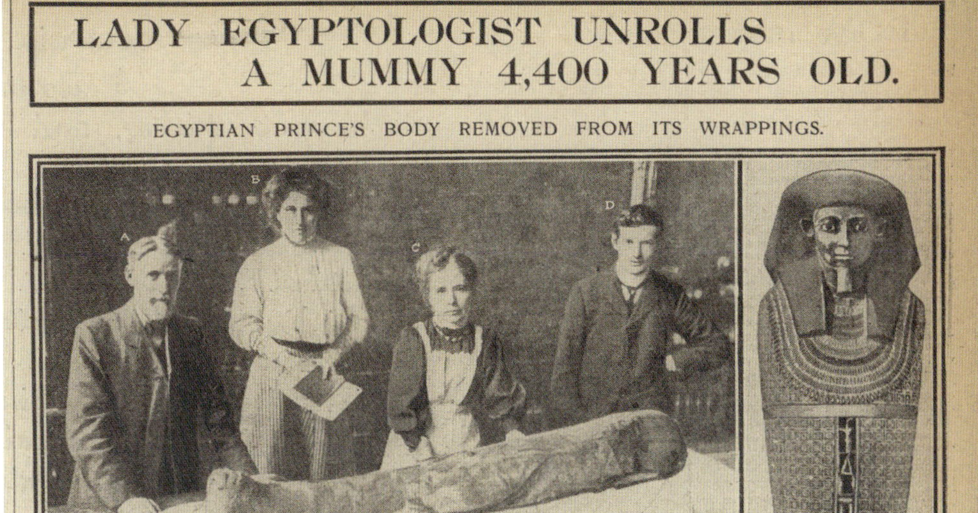

LADY EGYPTOLOGIST UNROLLS
A MUMMY 4,400 YEARS OLD.

EGYPTIAN PRINCE'S BODY REMOVED FROM ITS WRAPPINGS.

faculty as a junior college lecturer in 1899 and by 1924 was made assistant professor. Teaching took up most of Murray's time, especially since she was covering for Petrie, who was absent for much of the year on excavations. Mindful of her own experience as a student, Murray was particularly supportive of women and was closely involved with the suffrage movement.

In spite of the heavy teaching workload, Murray was an accomplished writer and published more than a hundred books and articles reflecting the breadth of her interests. As she wrote in her autobiography, published when she was 100: 'one of my chief pleasures in my work has been making discoveries and recording them.' She wrote on folklore and the history of witchcraft, as well as on the various aspects of Egyptian life and culture. In 1913 Murray published *Ancient Egyptian Legends* – a compilation of Egyptian mythological tales preserved through stone or papyrus scripts.

As the 1913 book amply demonstrates, Murray's legacy is closely associated with her fieldwork and extensive study of the ancient world. FF

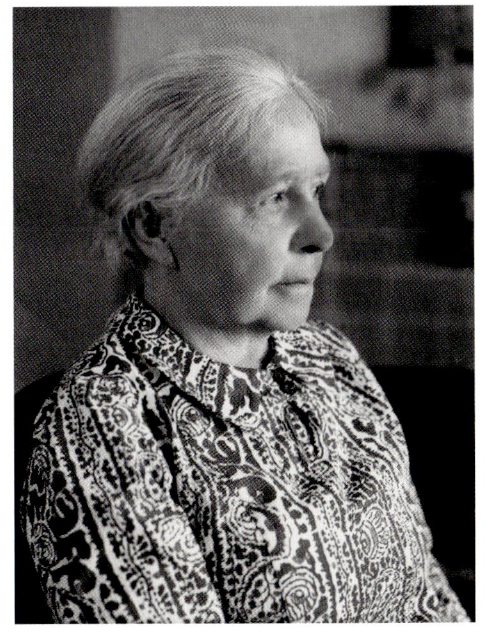

Margaret Murray (1863–1963)
By Bassano Ltd, 26 August 1938
Half-plate nitrate negative
National Portrait Gallery, London, x155707

Margaret Murray (third from left)
Detail from the *Daily Mirror*, 8 May 1908, p.9
By an unknown photographer

Mairi Chisholm and Elsie Knocker

Elsie Knocker wrote with anticipation and uncertainty in her diary on 24 September 1914:

I am now prepared to go to bed, my last night in England for how long nobody can tell. It seems funny to think that this time tomorrow night I shall be in Belgium – in the midst of all the terrors of war.

The next day, she and Mairi Chisholm departed on a ship to Belgium as part of the volunteer Flying Ambulance Column. The First World War had been declared four weeks earlier and, like many, they were eager to do their bit. The women had become friends over a shared enthusiasm for motoring, taking part in trials and rallies, so upon hearing the news, Knocker told Chisholm there was 'work to be done' and they immediately headed for London on their motorcycles. Initially serving as dispatch riders for the Women's Emergency Corps, they soon joined the Flying Ambulance Column on the basis of their motoring skills and Knocker's prior nursing experience.

Soon after their arrival in Belgium, they settled in Furnes, near Dunkirk, where, amid the 'most hideous sights imaginable', Chisholm and Knocker began transporting casualties to the field hospital.[8] In an ambulance with no windscreen, they risked their lives driving along treacherous routes in the pitch dark, wind and rain, often while under fire. Knocker quickly realized that many soldiers were dying before receiving treatment owing to complications from clinical shock, so the women left the corps and independently established their own dressing station in an abandoned cellar in the town of Pervyse, just 90 metres from the

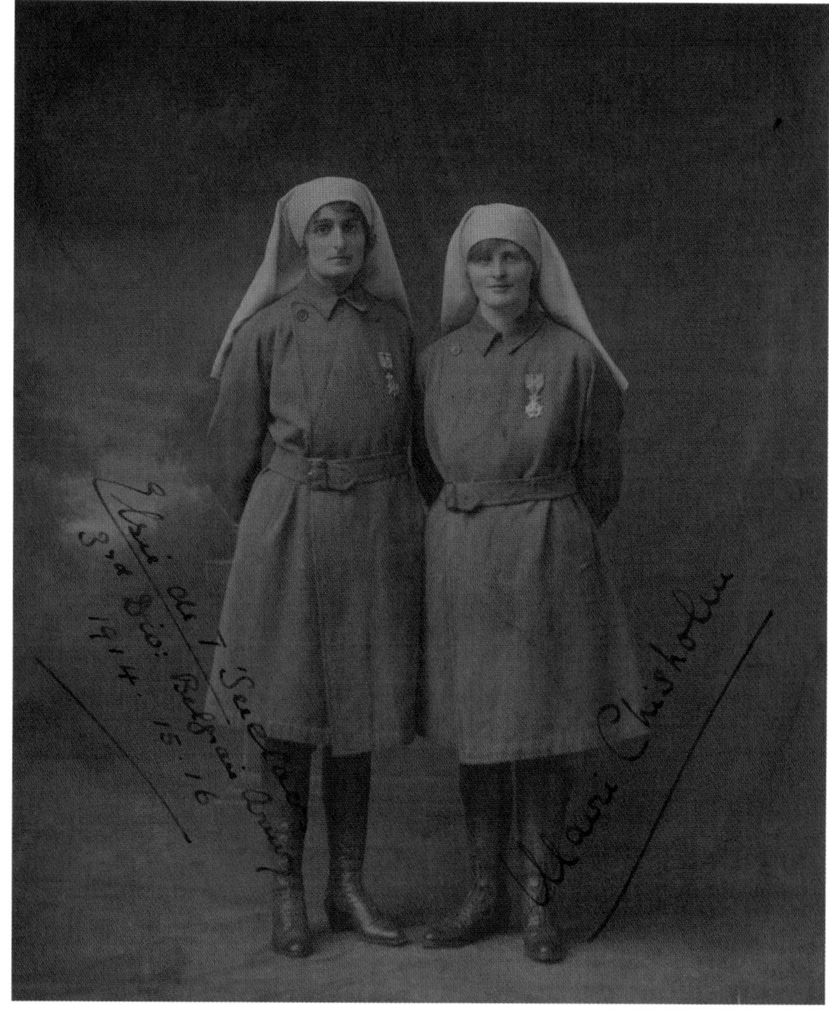

trenches. Living and working tirelessly among the ruins, and sleeping in their clothes, they were unflinching while administering first aid to an overwhelming number of men with wide-ranging injuries and ailments, and driving the wounded to a base hospital 24 kilometres (15 miles) away.

The two women continued in this way for three and a half years – publicizing their work during trips home to raise funds for running their post – until a gas attack in March 1918 caused them to be invalided home. Chisholm returned to Pervyse briefly, but was gassed again, and both women ended the war as part of the newly created Women's Royal Air Force. Celebrated in the press as the 'Madonnas of Pervyse', their medals for courage included the Military Cross and the Belgian Order of Léopold II.

Although they went their separate ways after the war, their story remains as a remarkable example of the women who willingly served beyond the home front at a time when they were still prohibited from active service. CN

Elsie Knocker (1884–1978)
and Mairi Chisholm (1896–1981)
By S.A. Chandler, *c.*1917
Gelatin silver print, 276 × 223mm
National Portrait Gallery, London, x87250

1915   Anne Acheson

In 1915, like many women wishing to support the war effort, Anne Acheson joined the Surgical Requisites Association (SRA) – an organization set up to provide surgical dressings for wounded soldiers. Little did the SRA know, but Acheson's contribution to the cause would prove transformative and have a legacy that extended beyond the First World War. During her time at the SRA Acheson made a pioneering invention: the plaster cast, still used to treat broken bones today.

Before volunteering with the SRA, Acheson had dedicated herself to art. She studied sculpture at the Royal College of Art, specialising in bespoke sculptures for country houses and gardens. Gender had an impact on Acheson's sculptural practice. Unlike her male peers, who often counted on the help of a team of assistants, Acheson worked alone. This determined the scale of her works, which were often relatively small in comparison to the monumental works produced by her male contemporaries. Acheson nonetheless succeeded in exhibiting at the Royal Academy, as well as internationally.

Thanks to her background in sculpture, Acheson had an excellent understanding of human anatomy. She knew how the body moved and cleverly deployed this knowledge in bettering the lives of the wounded when she joined the SRA. Originally tasked with making bandages and antiseptic swabs, Acheson teamed up with fellow sculptor Elinor Hallé, and together they designed a cradle to support broken arms. Papier mâché, a material which Acheson knew well from her sculpture days, proved useful in creating a lightweight and stable support, which in turn ensured the correct healing of broken limbs. Always striving to better her creation, Acheson worked tirelessly on improvements to the original cradle.

While the legacy of Acheson's invention is undoubtedly far-reaching, her sculptural achievements also remain worthy of notice. Acheson was the first female Fellow of the Royal Society of Sculptors – an honour she received in 1938. FF

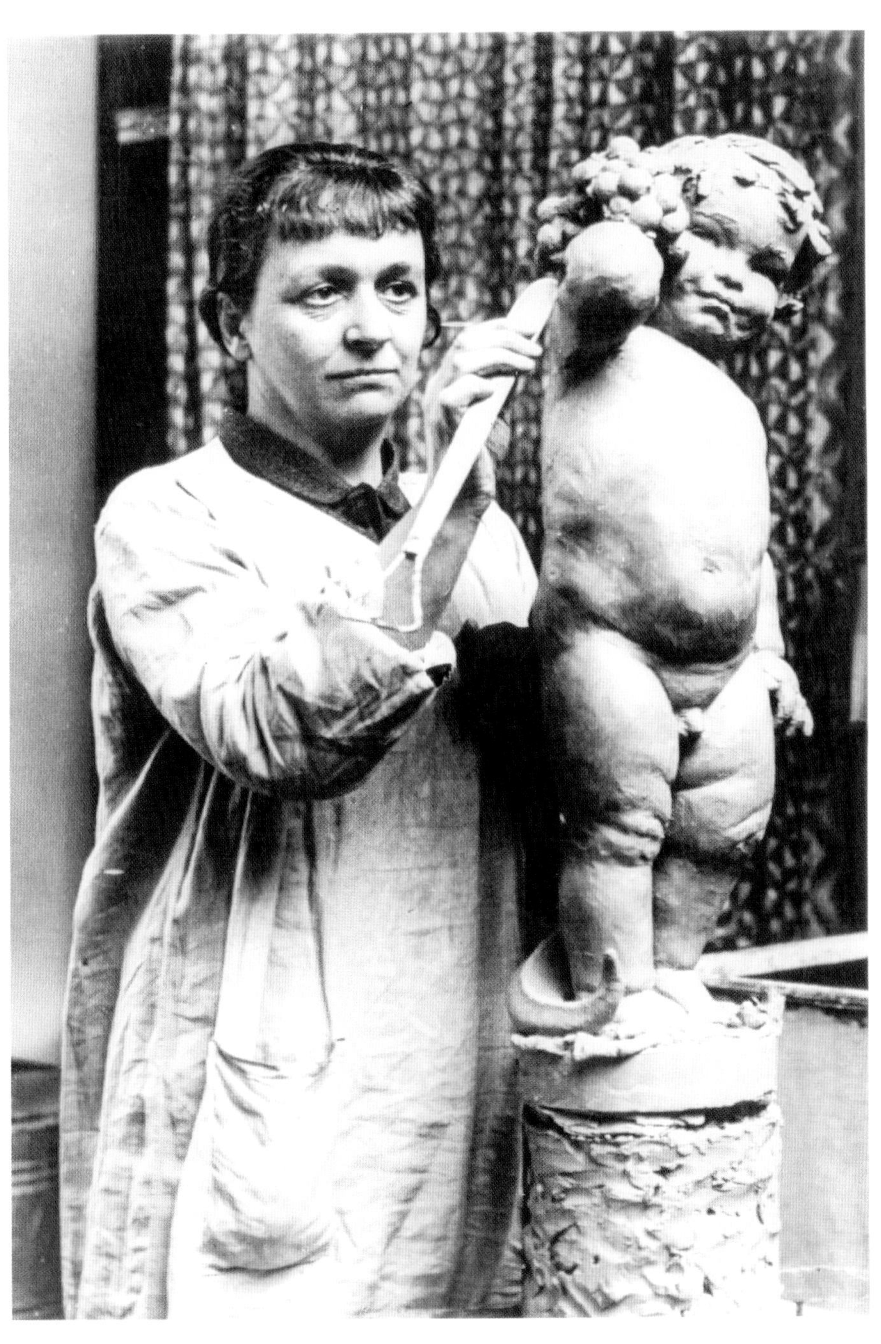

Anne Acheson (1882–1962)
By an unknown photographer, late 1920s
Gelatin silver print, 205 × 134mm
Royal Society of Sculptors

Agatha Christie

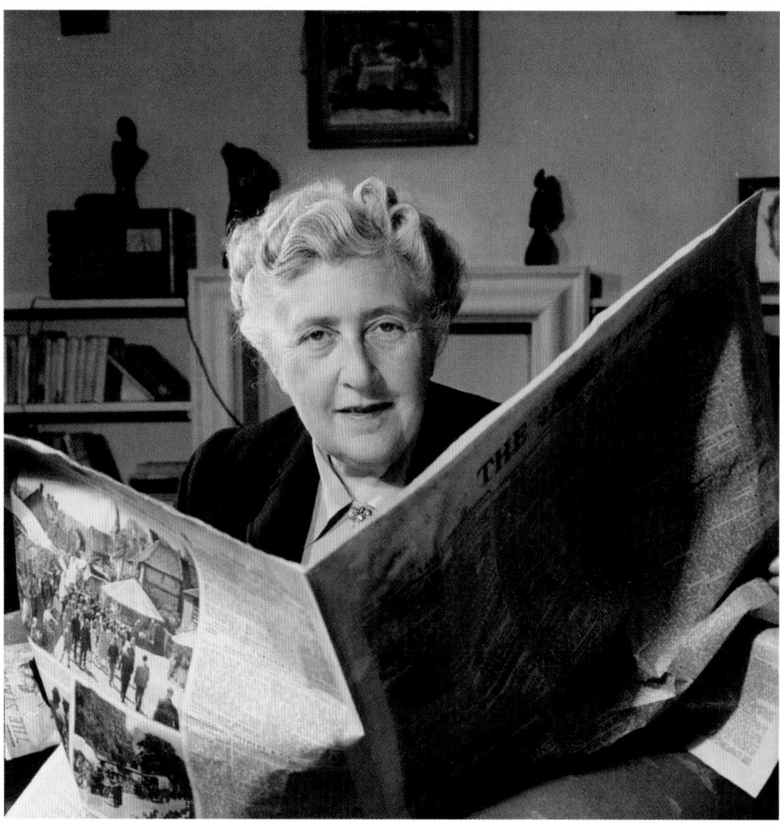

Agatha Christie, the First Lady of Crime, remains the bestselling author of all time – outsold only by the Bible and Shakespeare. From book to book, Christie conjured intriguing puzzles made up of unexpected twists, false identities and tricks of all kinds. Timing, structure and carefully crafted clues all contribute to the intricate choreography of Christie's mysteries, which feature a set of recurring characters – the most famous being Hercule Poirot and Miss Jane Marple.

The creation of Poirot marked the emergence of Christie the mystery novelist. When the First World War broke out in 1914, Christie initially worked with the Voluntary Aid Detachment in a local hospital and then in a Red Cross dispensary. The latter proved to be a dull but particularly formative experience. For a start, it gave Christie a deep understanding of poisons that would be crucial in the unfolding of many of her mysteries. Secondly, the monotony of dispensary work jump-started her first book, *The Mysterious Affair at Styles* – published in 1920 but written around 1916. Challenged by her sister to create a detective outside of the Sherlock Holmes pattern, Christie settled on a Belgian detective called Hercule Poirot. In her autobiography Christie provides a lively account of Poirot's genesis:

I allowed him slowly to grow into his part. He should have been an inspector, so that he would have a certain knowledge of crime. He would be very meticulous, very tidy ... And he should be very brainy – he should have little grey cells of the mind – that was a good phrase: I must remember that ...

Christie's characteristic wit emerges in this loose sketch of Poirot. *Styles* would be the first of many novels where Poirot's mental acuity would lead to the unravelling of page-turning mysteries.

Curious-minded and adventurous, Christie drew inspiration for her novels from her real-life experiences. In 1922, she joined her first husband, Archibald Christie, on a ten-month overseas mission in the British colonies. Christie later accompanied her second husband – the archaeologist Max Mallowan, whom she married in 1930 – on expeditions in the Near East. While helping Mallowan with the recording and photographing of archaeological findings, she also conjured plots for some of her most successful books, including *Murder on the Orient Express* (1934) and *Death on the Nile* (1937). Christie's popularity remains unrivalled and film adaptations of her novels continue to be must-sees. Among numerous honours, she was awarded a Damehood in 1971. FF

Agatha Christie (1890–1976)
By John Gay, published in
The Strand Magazine, February 1949
Gelatin silver print, 259 × 212mm
National Portrait Gallery, London, x126501

1917 Leonora Carrington

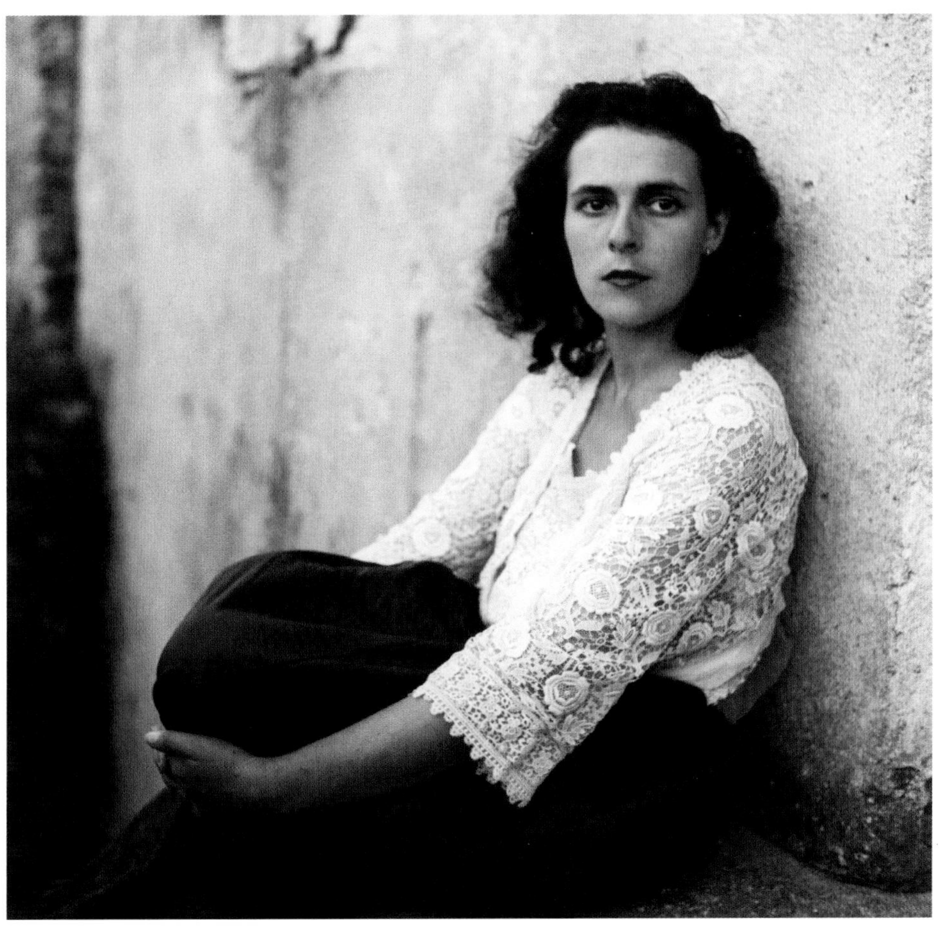

The birth of artist Leonora Carrington in 1917 coincided with the birth of surrealism – a revolutionary art movement that aspired towards the liberation of the mind through the unconscious and dreams. Carrington, who was born into a privileged Lancashire family, defied convention to become a member of the surrealist movement in the 1930s. Her paintings and sculptures are now on display in some of the most prestigious art galleries in the world and she is regarded as one of surrealism's leading exponents.

Carrington's encounter with surrealism was both seismic and serendipitous. From a young age, Carrington was drawn to art, but despite her unruly spirit she bowed to her family's expectations. In 1935 she was persuaded by her parents to become a debutante and had a ball thrown for her at the Ritz. The experience proved gruelling for Carrington, who recounted it in surrealist terms in one of her written and illustrated stories, *The Debutante* (1938).

1936 marked a turning point in Carrington's life and career. That year, the International Surrealist Exhibition was held in London and Carrington became enthralled with one of its most prominent participants, the artist Max Ernst. At 26 years her senior, Ernst did not meet her parents' approval. Carrington defied them by eloping with Ernst to France, where the couple led a bohemian lifestyle and she became closely involved with surrealism. The outbreak of the Second World War ended Carrington and Ernst's idyll, and by 1942 the two had parted ways. The separation was to some extent responsible for triggering a terrible breakdown, which forced Carrington to spend time in a Spanish asylum. Eventually she moved to Mexico City, where she joined a community of artists and writers who had fled Europe. This is where her artistic language reached new heights: the product of half-real and half-imaginary worlds, her paintings contain references to Celtic legends and traditional Mexican imagery and are inhabited by hybrid creatures, often in thrall to occult forces.

Despite being associated with surrealism, Carrington claimed late in her life: 'I have never read the Surrealist Manifesto.' In such a statement one can detect Carrington's opposition to a conventional reading of surrealism, which portrays women as the muses and handmaidens of their male peers. Through her art Carrington countered this male-dominated narrative and went where imagination and passion called her, pushing against the grain of artistic and social mores. FF

Leonora Carrington (1917–2011)
By Lee Miller, 1939
Modern gelatin silver print, 253 × 255mm
National Portrait Gallery, London, P1075

1918   Olive Edis

Pioneering photographer Olive Edis was one of the most successful portraitists of her day. In 1905 she set up a studio in Sheringham, Norfolk, together with her sister Katharine. She later went on to open studios in London, Cromer and Farnham. Over the course of her career, her naturally lit portraits featured a diverse portfolio of sitters ranging from local fishermen to suffragettes, authors, politicians and royalty. Edis was also a leader in new photographic techniques and from 1912 she was one of the first women photographers to specialise in colour, producing autochromes and going on to design and patent her own autochrome viewer.

In 1918, during the First World War, Edis was commissioned by the Imperial War Museum's Women's Work Committee to photograph British women serving in France and Flanders (although permission to visit the Western Front was only granted after the Armistice). Agnes Conway and Lady Priscilla Norman, Secretary and Chair of the Women's War Work Subcommittee respectively, set about organizing the tour. Edis responded to their invitation enthusiastically:

Your letter asking me to go to France with Lady Norman and yourself to photograph the British Women's Services arrived this morning. The idea attracts me so much. It would be a most interesting trip ... I would be very pleased to give my services [unpaid] as it is for a national collection, not as an operator pure and simple.[9]

As a result of this appointment, Edis became the first official woman war photographer, albeit during the aftermath of the war. Accepting the post, which was expenses-only, Edis noted in her journal:

The Imperial War Museum thought that a woman photographer, living among the girls in their camps, was likely to

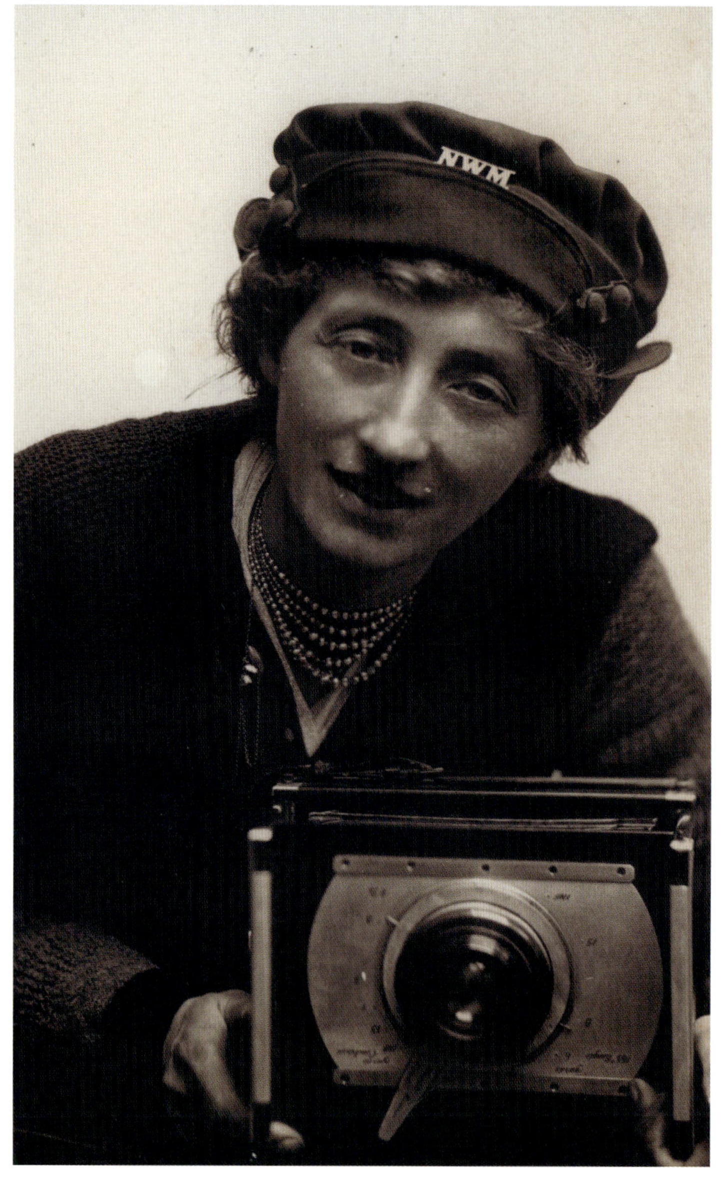

achieve more intimate pictures, more descriptive of their everyday life, than a man press photographer.

In her self-portrait Edis is holding one of the cameras used on her trip. She specifically requested the badge worn on her cap in order to signify her status as an official war photographer; it was one of the last to bear the initials of the National War Museum, which had by then been renamed the Imperial War Museum.

The assignment lasted four weeks. Equipped with three cameras and at times developing glass plates in makeshift darkrooms in hospital X-ray units, Edis produced a remarkable document of service women. She photographed women in the auxiliary services, nurses, ambulance drivers, engineers, telegraphists and surgeons, creating a powerful portrait of their achievements and their commitment to the war effort. GA

Olive Edis (1876–1955)
Self-portrait, 1918
Sepia-toned gelatin silver print, 133 × 79mm
National Portrait Gallery, London, x7960

PHOTOGRAPHY IN THE

HANDS OF WOMEN

By

Georgia Atienza

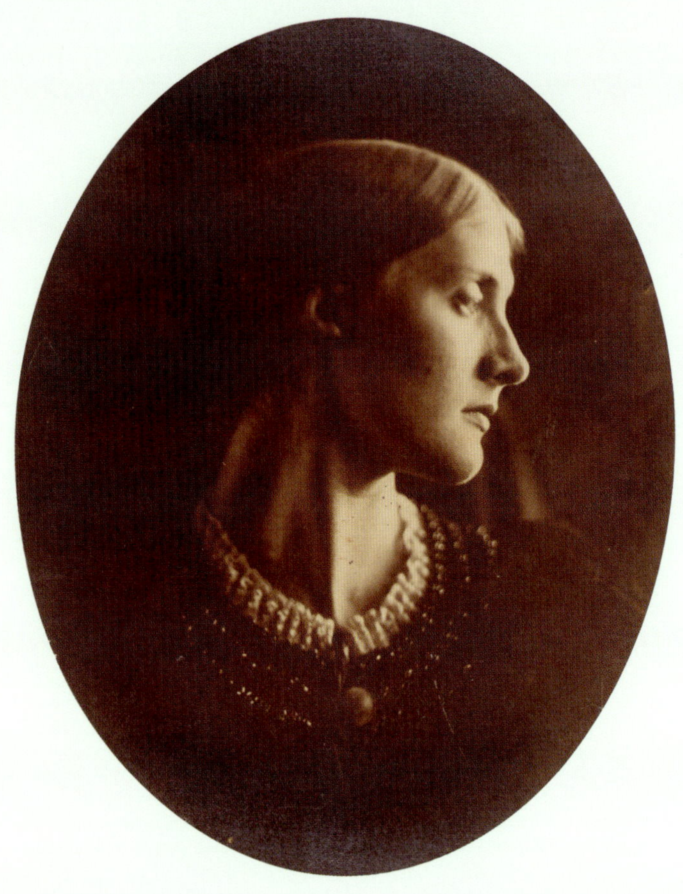

Fig.1: Julia Stephen by Julia Margaret Cameron

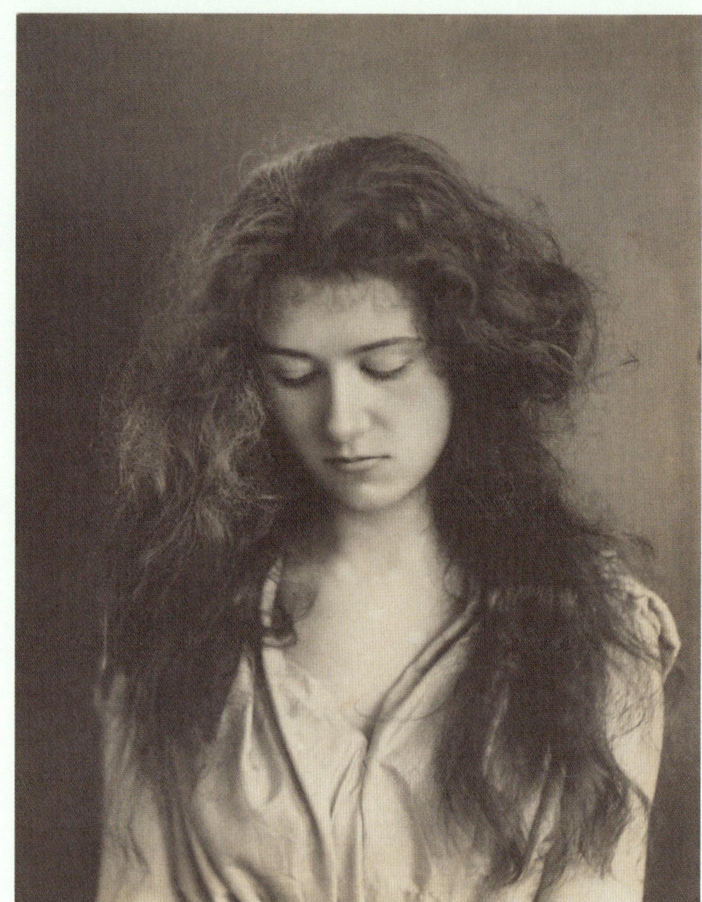

Fig.2: Adelaide Passingham by Eveleen Myers

Women have played an active role in photography since its inception, both as early practitioners and in the study and dissemination of photographs. Thus photography has been a powerful tool in the emancipation of women, with the camera offering artistic and professional outlets. It has allowed women to entrench egalitarian views by running their own businesses and making a living alongside their male counterparts. Likewise, photography played a key role in the fight for equal rights, from the suffrage campaigns to the growth of feminism. More broadly, since its introduction photography has provided a space in which women could play with new identities and personas.

One of the earliest women to own a commercial studio was Jane Wigley. She practised in Newcastle upon Tyne and subsequently in London, producing daguerreotype portraits from 1845 onwards, having purchased a licence from the patent holder Richard Beard. A few decades later, pioneering art photographer Julia Margaret Cameron – one of the most notable practitioners of the nineteenth century working exclusively on portraiture – became a model for future women photographers, proving that it was possible to succeed in a male-dominated profession (fig.1). Although she never ran a commercial studio, Cameron exhibited widely, sold her work and copyrighted her images.

During the nineteenth and twentieth centuries, facilitated by technical improvements and innovations, commercial studios run by women flourished. Photography was increasingly perceived to be a suitable career for a woman as the studio was conceptually associated with domesticity. Furthermore, to enter the profession one did not require an official qualification. Thanks to the introduction of the Kodak hand-held camera in 1888 by the George Eastman Company, launched with the slogan: 'You press the button – we do the rest', photography was democratised. The simple box camera came loaded with a 100-exposure roll of film that could be sent off for processing and printing. Advertisements for Kodak cameras targeted women as both the makers and consumers of photography. Amateur photography became particularly popular with women, with many subsequently setting up their own studios, aided by efficient new technologies such as the dry-plate process. Inspired by Cameron, Eveleen Myers started making portraits of her children. Her status as an amateur allowed for greater freedom and she soon built an impressive portfolio of famous Victorians, with photography regarded as an acceptable outlet outside of her more traditional role as a mother and wife (fig.2).

Women practitioners were also encouraged by the press, with articles describing the profession of photographer as being particularly suitable and profitable for a woman wishing to be financially independent. Alice Hughes, who built her reputation as an exclusive photographer of women and children, became a reference for early studio portraitists such as Lallie Charles (fig.3) and her sister Rita Martin, whose business in Regent's Park was inspired by Hughes's success. Charles's studio centred on the portrayal of women and, with her idealised likenesses, she became the most commercially successful photographer of the Edwardian period. As her business grew, Charles employed only women; one of her apprentices, Yevonde Cumbers, later Yevonde (p.68), described the experience in her autobiography as her 'first step towards independence'.

In 1914, having taken just one photograph under her mentor's supervision, Yevonde opened her own studio, becoming one of the most successful commercial photographers of the twentieth century and a pioneer of colour. In 1921, she accepted an invitation to speak at the Professional Photographers' Association, becoming the first woman to do so. Her subject, 'Photographic Portraiture from a Woman's Point of View', celebrated the growing number of women photographers who owned successful studios. These included Lena Connell, Yvonne Gregory, Alice Hughes, Florence Vandamm, Maud Basil, Dorothy Wilding, Marion Neilson, Dora Head, Madame Pestel and Genia Reinberg.

During the suffrage campaigns of the early twentieth century, photography became instrumental. Women photographers used the suffrage press to advertise positions, create networks and discuss equal pay, highlighting the economic, social and political disadvantages borne by women at this time. Lizzie Caswall Smith (who made her name photographing stage performers) and Lena Connell were some of the studio

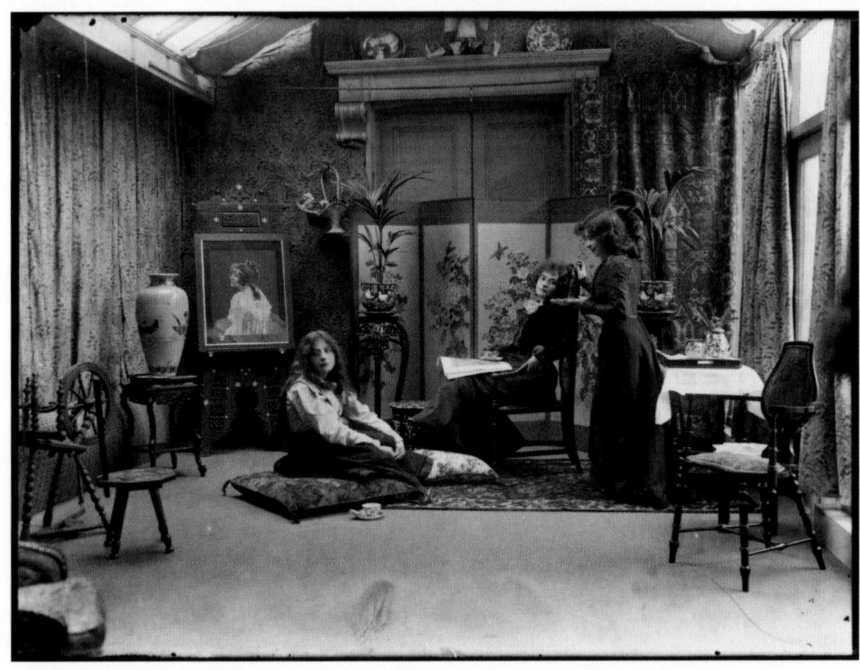
Fig.3: Lallie Charles and her sisters Isabella and Rita

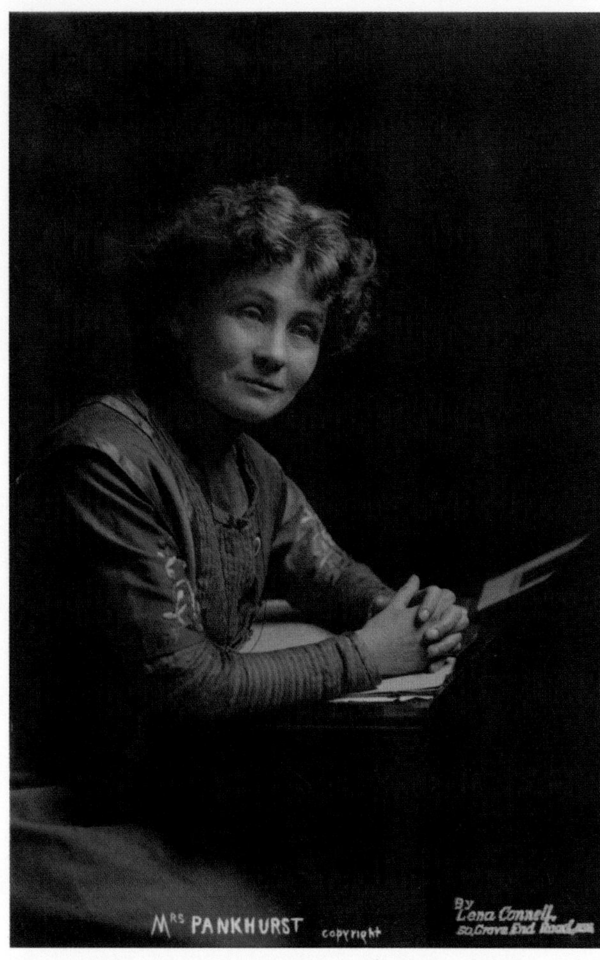

Fig.4: Emmeline Pankhurst by Lena Connell

photographers working for the campaign. Their portraits were key in shaping the image of the leaders of the movement and projecting ideas of social and civic advancement (fig.4). Trailblazing press photographer Christina Broom worked on the street rather than in the studio. She took up photography late in life to support her family. Equipped with her camera, a tripod and glass plates, she documented life on the streets of London. Assisted by her daughter Winifred, she built a remarkable career photographing the suffrage movement as well as capturing royal, military and sporting events. Her photographs were self-published as picture postcards at the height of the medium's popularity, and Broom was able to create a stable income from her business.

Photography also played a key role in the fight towards gender equality in the workplace. Famed as a studio portraitist, Olive Edis (p.48) also documented service women and the role they played on the Western Front shortly after the Armistice in 1918. Photographing them in occupations usually reserved for men, her photographs served as an account of women's achievements and their determination not to be confined to the domestic sphere. Prior to this important documentary series, Edis contributed to a careers handbook for young women wishing to enter the photographic profession.

Former apprentice to photographer Marion Neilson, Dorothy Wilding established her practice just before the outbreak of the First World War, when she was aged just 21. She went on to become one of the most fashionable photographers of her time, with studios in London and New York. Her clients included royalty and film stars; she was active for several decades and was constantly innovating. Joan Craven trained under Wilding and in 1926 opened her own studio at the smart address of New Bond Street, building an impressive portfolio of cultural figures.

The booming illustrated press generated a constant demand for pictures and this in turn assisted in the rise to prominence of these new photographic businesses, with the number of studios run by women steadily rising. Photography's rapid expansion required a new workforce and women were able to enter the profession, often starting as studio assistants and re-touchers before going on to become operators. Consequently, the studio became a key space for women's photographic practice. Dress, makeup, props and background, as well as lighting arrangements, could all be choreographed, setting the mood before the camera. Studios were equipped with darkrooms for the preparation of the negatives as well as with printing facilities. Hand-colouring, retouching and the mounting of the photographs were key to the finished portrait (fig.5).

Throughout the inter-war years, social and technological shifts changed the shape of metropolitan life, with growing numbers of women taking on new roles. Photography offered a way into these new social and artistic spheres and was increasingly a viable career option beyond marriage and motherhood. Pioneering photographers who moved away from the artifice of society portraiture during the 1930s include innovative practitioners such as Barbara Ker-Seymer, who took over the studio of Olivia Wyndham, later opening her own premises. Under the influence of the avant-garde, the camera offered a new way of seeing and women photographers experimented with multiple exposures, distorting reflections and solarisation, challenging conventional ideals of beauty and femininity. Within the National Portrait Gallery's Collection there are examples such as Helen Muspratt's photograph of mime artists Mary and Hilda Spencer Watson (fig.6) as well as works by Ramsey & Muspratt, the joint studio of photographers Lettice Ramsey and Helen Muspratt, which opened in Cambridge in 1932.

During this period, émigré women photographers fleeing Nazi persecution made careers in photography in Britain. Some were already skilled practitioners, while others trained and went on to run studios, photography becoming a vehicle to rebuild their professional lives and assert their social and political outlook. The fields in which these remarkable women practised were wide-ranging and included fashion photography, portraiture and documentary photography. Lucia Moholy worked as a portraitist (fig.7) alongside lecturing and teaching, while her pupil Elsbeth Juda specialised in fashion photography. Edith Tudor-Hart and Gertie Deutsch most notably produced photo essays for *Picture Post*, a popular weekly magazine that addressed the concerns of the day in a

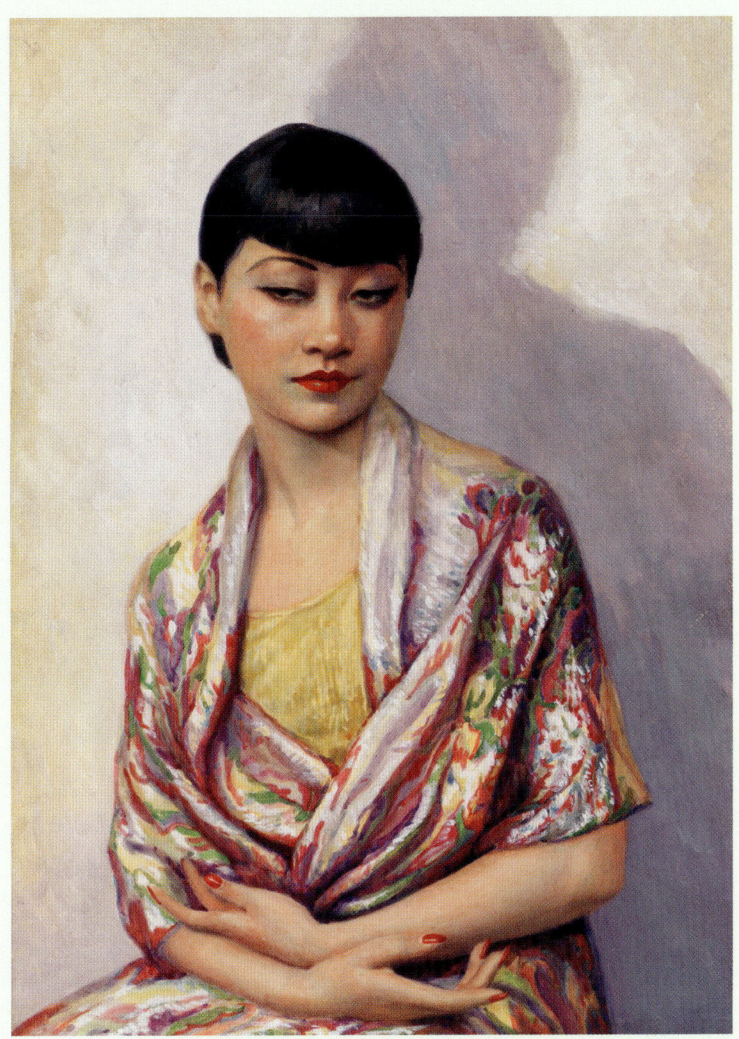

Fig.5: Anna May Wong by Dorothy Wilding

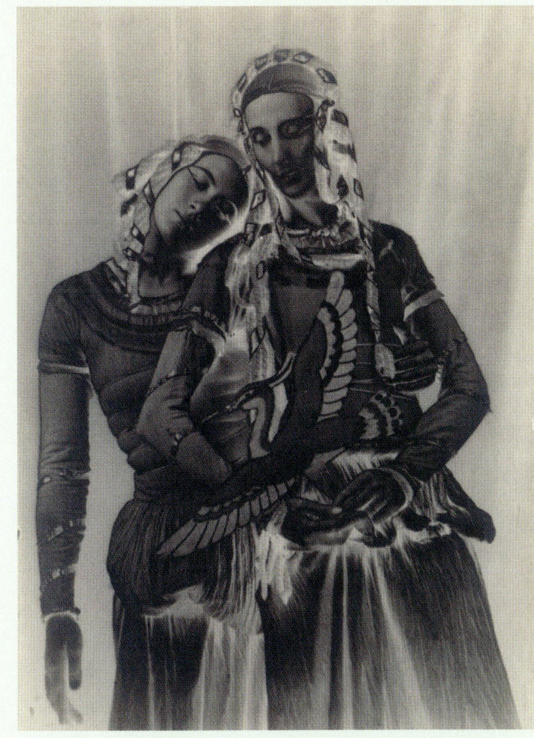

Fig.6: Mary and Hilda Spencer Watson by Helen Muspratt

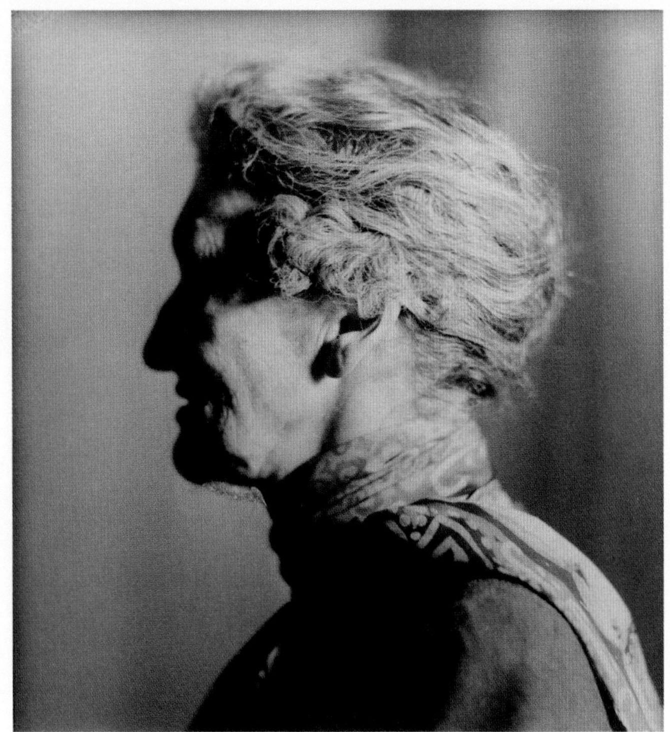

Fig.7: Margot Asquith by Lucia Moholy

new and radical way. The impact of the Second World War expanded women's photographic practice as they found themselves driven by a sense of justice and freedom. Photographers such as Germaine Kanova (who inspired Dorothy Bohm to take up photography, see p.106), ran a commercial studio in London in the early 1940s photographing politicians, actors and writers, and also acted as a war photographer, for which she was later awarded the Croix de Guerre by the French government. Commissioned by British *Vogue*, Lee Miller produced important bodies of work documenting the atrocities of the war in Europe as well as a series illustrating the contribution of women at work to the war effort.

The early twentieth century saw a growth in the number of entrepreneurial studio photographers, with photography enabling women to become financially self-sufficient. The camera opened up new possibilities with new-found freedoms and opportunities. Women photographers used the medium as a mode of self-expression as well as a means of documenting the changing world around them. Turning the camera on one's self also allowed for a statement of independence and self-confidence, challenging identity and gender roles. Under the influence of modernism women were no longer models of beauty, but creators in their own right, paving the way for the feminist activism of the early 1970s when the Women's Liberation Movement came to prominence.

Fig.1
Julia Stephen (1846–1895)
By Julia Margaret Cameron, 1867
Albumen print, 344 × 263mm
National Portrait Gallery, London, x18018

Fig.2
Adelaide Passingham (1867–1954)
By Eveleen Myers, 1889
Platinum print, 293 × 222mm
National Portrait Gallery, London, Ax36315

Fig.3
Lallie Charles (1869–1919) and her sisters Isabella and Rita Martin, both assistants in her studio
By Lallie Charles, *c.*1899
Whole-plate glass negative
National Portrait Gallery, London, x68949

Fig.4
Emmeline Pankhurst (1858–1928)
By Lena Connell, *c.*1907
Sepia-toned gelatin silver postcard, 135 × 85mm
National Portrait Gallery, London, x136722

Fig.5
Anna May Wong (1905–1961)
By Dorothy Wilding and hand-coloured by Beatrice Johnson, 1929
Gelatin silver print, 435 × 310mm
National Portrait Gallery, London, x44636

Fig.6
'Mary and Hilda Spencer Watson as Jacob and Esau'
Mary Spencer Watson (1913–2006) and Hilda Spencer Watson (1879–1952)
By Helen Muspratt, 1935
Solarised gelatin silver print, 364 × 259mm
National Portrait Gallery, London, x134874

Fig.7
Margot Asquith (1864–1945)
By Lucia Moholy, 1935
Gelatin silver print, 165 × 147mm
National Portrait Gallery, London, x76368

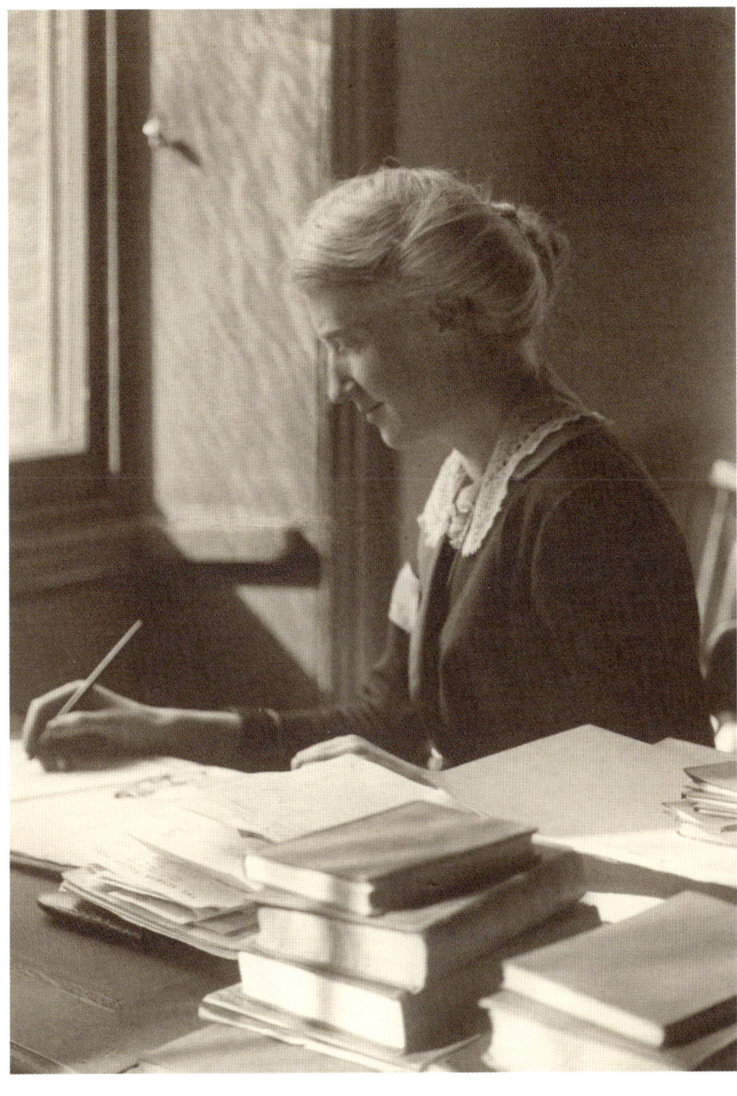

In 1919, in the aftermath of the First World War, Eglantyne Jebb and her sister Dorothy Buxton founded the Save the Children Fund (SCF), an emergency relief fund for child victims of the war. In May 1919 Jebb was arrested for distributing uncensored SCF leaflets in Trafalgar Square. She later told a reporter for the *Daily Mail* that, 'if publicity surrounding her arrest provided food for one starving child, then the five-pound fine was the "equivalent to victory".' Such an assertive statement proves Jebb's deep commitment to children and their welfare, a cause to which she would dedicate the rest of her life. Today, the International Save the Children Alliance is one of the world's most impactful organizations for children.

With compelling emotion, Jebb delivered many public speeches to raise awareness of the plight of children irrespective of their nationality; in war-torn Europe this was a particularly ambitious feat. Many doubted that Jebb could secure the necessary funds, but a combination of sheer determination, flair for publicity and astute political and diplomatic skills saw her succeed in this quasi-impossible mission. She directed her pleas to men and women alike and frequently lent to her discourses a maternal-feminist slant. On one occasion she called on the compassion of her British female peers by stating:

I appeal to my fellow country women to help me lift the whole question of the saving of the child life of Europe out of the political region altogether. Let the women of this country take the lead in a work which the men, in their political groupings, seem powerless to carry forward.

Jebb's vision transcended political loyalties and national borders; she liked to describe it as 'supranational'.

In March 1922 she started working on a document 'defining the duties of adults towards children, which each country should recognise either by means of State intervention or by private action.' The 'Children's Charter', as it was known, went through several iterations – causing Jebb great distress. However, the final draft – 'Declaration of the Rights of the Child' – incorporated Jebb's original principles. It was ratified by the League of Nations in 1924 and its principles are now enshrined in the United Nations Convention on the Rights of the Child.

For a woman who spent her whole life fighting for the well-being of children it is perhaps surprising to learn that she was not particularly fond of the 'little wretches', as she used to call them. Ever conscious of social duty, Jebb embraced the cause of children to quench her need to rectify what she felt was a grave injustice. At a time when career opportunities for educated women were meagre, Jebb's yearning for independence went hand in hand with a cause that saved the lives of millions of children worldwide and continues to do so today. FF

Eglantyne Jebb (1876–1928)
By Lafayette, mid-1920s
Sepia-toned gelatin silver print, 146 × 98mm
National Portrait Gallery, London, x200862

1920 Winifred Brenchley

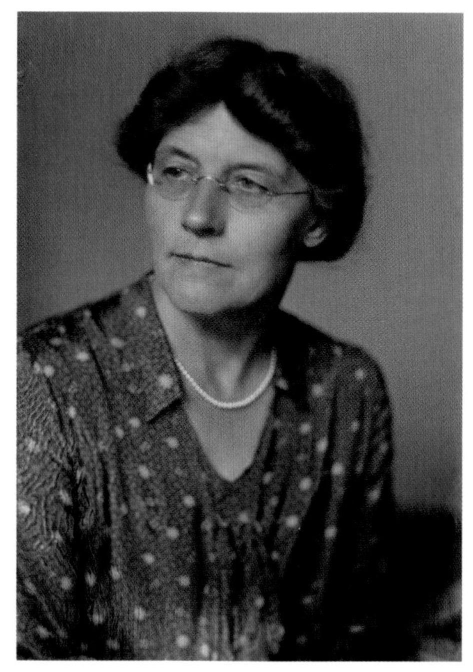

Everyone who cultivates the soil, whether on the farm or garden, is perforce interested in weeds, for their absence or presence amongst the crops has much to do in determining the relative success or failure of the undertaking.

With these words, the agricultural botanist Winifred Brenchley introduced readers to the first comprehensive study of weeds in the United Kingdom. In *Weeds of Farmland,* published in 1920, Brenchley related weed distribution to soil type and classified weeds according to their temperaments – 'Arable Weeds,' 'Parasitic Weeds,' and 'Poisonous and Injurious Weeds', among others.

The work that Brenchley did was pioneering as it gave cultivators the tools to better understand how to enhance the growth of crops. In her earlier studies she had also investigated the growth of plants in water culture and came close to discovering the role that copper and zinc played in aiding plant nutrition. Brenchley's findings on the subject were substantial for the time and were included in her book *Inorganic Plant Poisons and Stimulants* (1914, revised 1927).

While Brenchley's study of weeds made her an authority on the subject, her work at the leading agricultural institution Rothamsted Experimental Station (now Rothamsted Research) broke new ground in the field for aspiring women agricultural scientists. Brenchley's arrival at Rothamsted in 1906 was dictated by the meagre funding available to the institution. The proposed salary for what would become Brenchley's post was deemed inadequate for a man and so the decision was made that a woman would be invited to join. It was out of necessity, rather than vision, that Rothamsted was pushed to change its male-only policy and many viewed this shift in workforce make-up with great scepticism. Within a year, however, Brenchley proved her worth and by 1907 was made head of the botanical section at Rothamsted – a post she held until she retired in 1948. That same year she received an OBE. FF

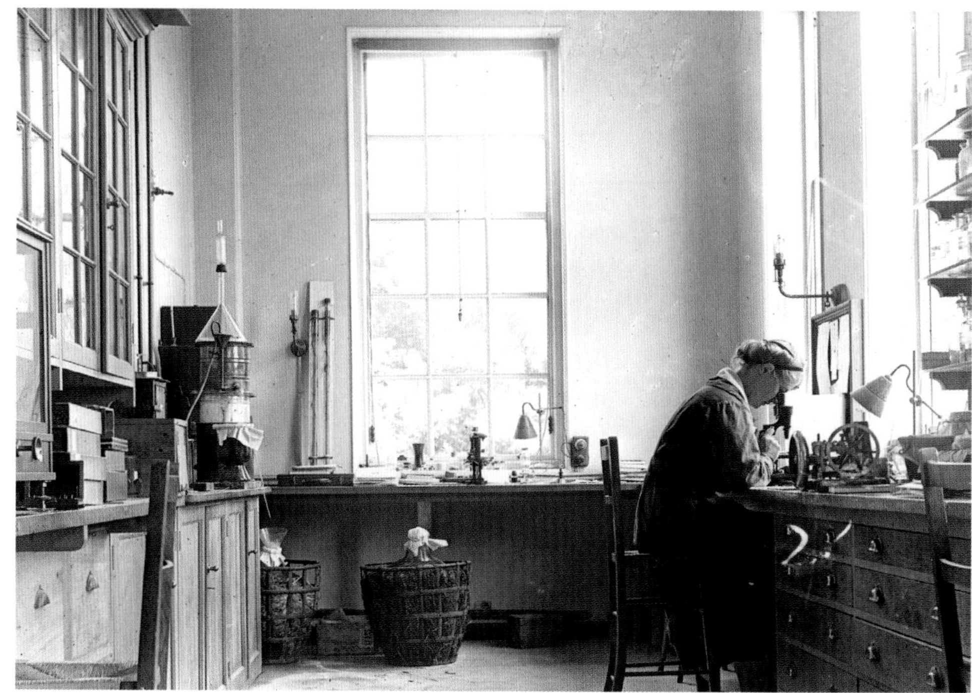

Winifred Brenchley (1883–1953)
By Elliott & Fry, 1940s
Gelatin silver print, 159 × 110mm
National Portrait Gallery, London, x86482

Winifred Brenchley working in her laboratory at Rothamsted Experimental Station
By an unknown photographer, 1920s
Rothamsted Research Ltd

Helena Normanton

1919 saw the passing of the Sex Disqualification (Removal) Act, which allowed women entry into the legal profession. Helena Normanton was one of the first to benefit from this change to the law and made history on 24 December 1919 by becoming the first woman to join an Inns of Court, Middle Temple, the day after the Act was passed. Normanton had spent almost two years tirelessly lobbying to join an institution of the legal profession and had been repeatedly turned down. The Act made it possible for her to fulfil the professional ambition she had nurtured since childhood: to become a lawyer.

At the age of 12, in 1894, Normanton had accompanied her single mother on a visit to a solicitor's office and helped her navigate the legal advice that she was given in relation to a mortgage application. This led the attendant solicitor to compliment young Normanton on her legal intuition and affirmed in her the desire to become a lawyer when she grew up. Law, like many other professions,

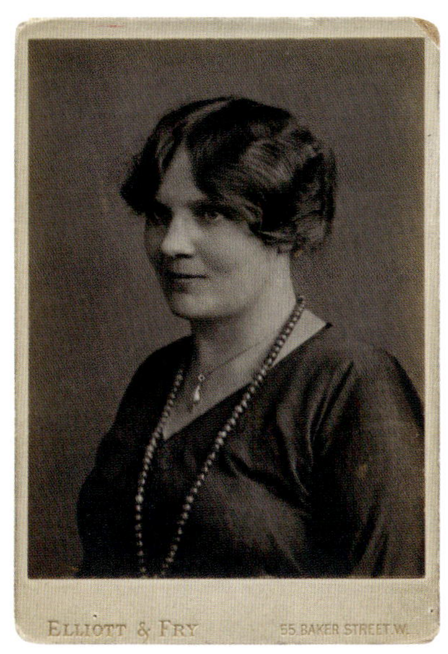

did not offer a clear career path for women, who were kept on the margins. Normanton began as a history lecturer and, while teaching, she developed an interest in feminist issues. In 1914 she published a pamphlet called *Sex Differentiation in Salary* advocating for equal pay for equal work, a topic still relevant today in the form of the gender pay gap. Normanton continued to advance the fight for women's rights through writing and public speaking throughout her life. She urged 'to press forward to open the Church, the Stock Exchange, the House of Lords, the Diplomatic and Consular Services, the Press Gallery in the House of Commons, and the Overseas Civil Services to women'. Normanton was prepared to change the professional landscape for women.

After being called to the Bar on 17 November 1922, Normanton became a woman of many firsts. In 1925, she was the first woman to conduct a case

in the United States and in 1948 she was the first woman to both obtain a divorce for a client and lead the prosecution in a murder trial in an English court. Normanton also became the first woman in Britain to hold a passport in her maiden name.

On 26 October 1921, Normanton married Gavin Bowman Watson Clark and attracted considerable attention for choosing to retain her maiden name after her marriage. She believed that surrendering her surname was deplorable both personally and professionally. While respectful of her marriage, she wished to retain continuity of identity in her professional career. She would reaffirm the importance of her choice in an ironic remark published in the *Yorkshire Post* in 1954: 'Anne Boleyn did not change her name even though she married the King. He at least had the decency to leave her with her own name even though he took her head.' FF

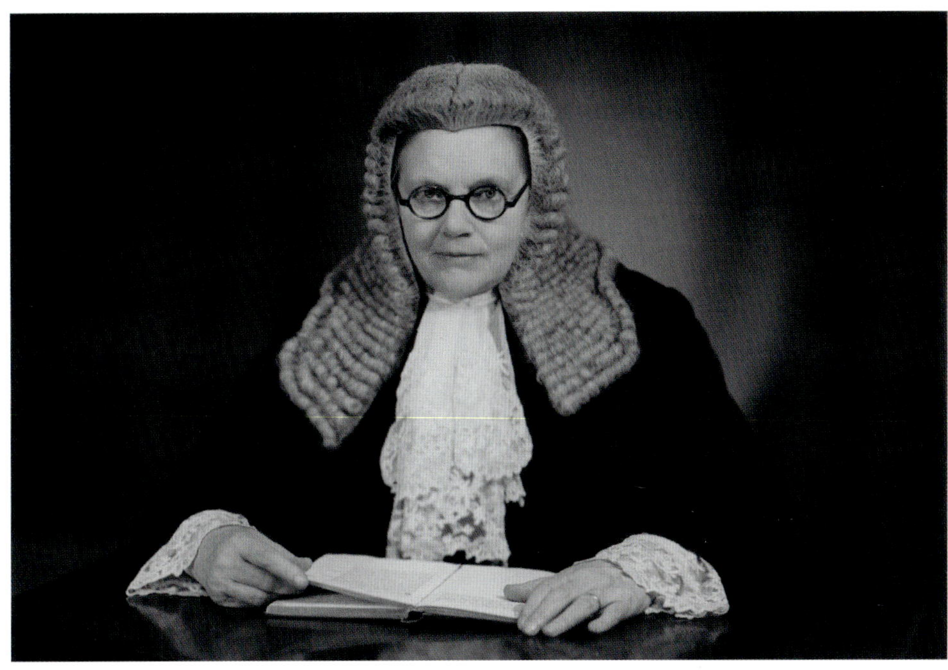

Helena Normanton (1882–1957)
By Elliott & Fry, *c*.1921
Cabinet card, 161 × 107mm
National Portrait Gallery, London, x138955

Helena Normanton
By Elliott & Fry, 4 September 1950
Gelatin silver print, 120 × 168mm
National Portrait Gallery, London, x90837

1922 Katherine Mansfield

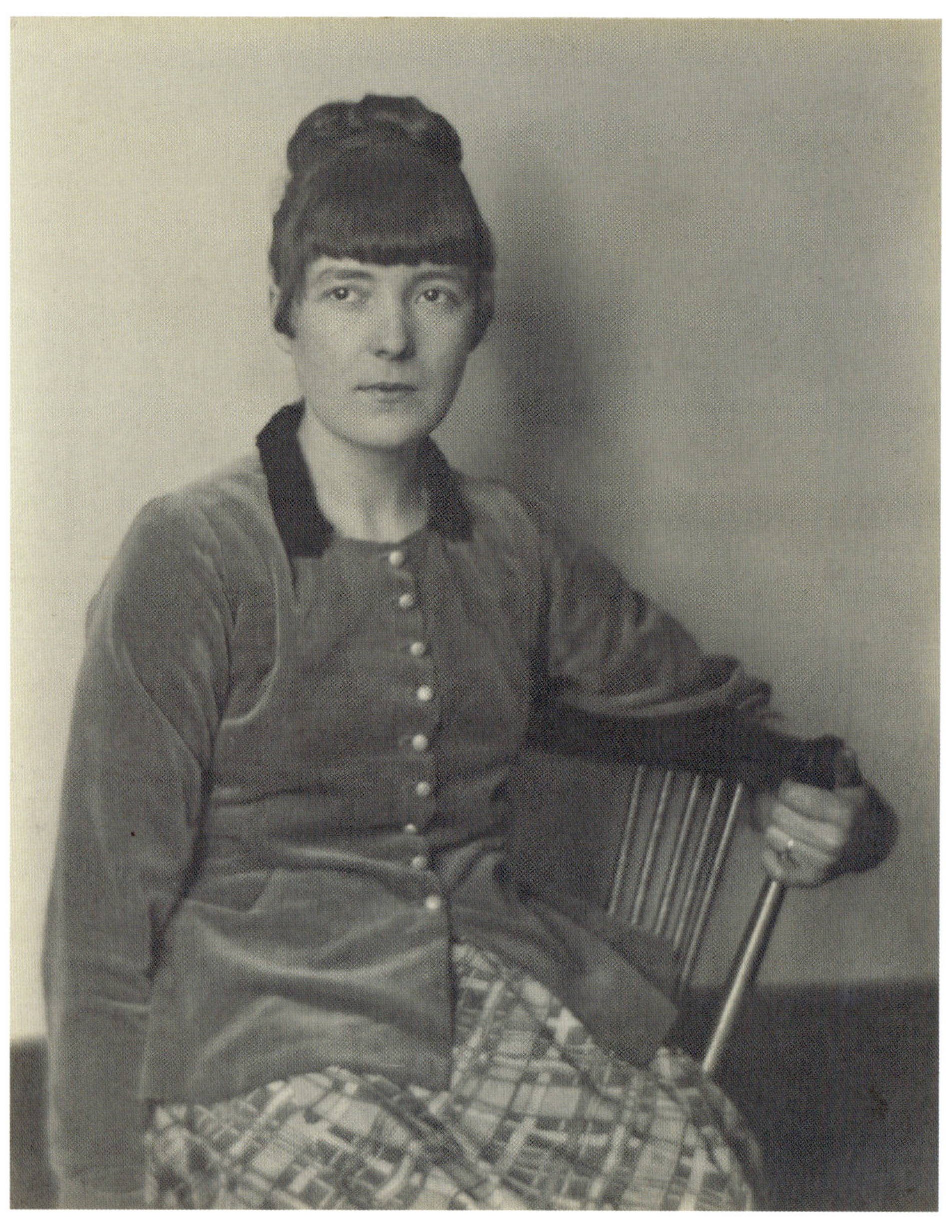

In 1922, a year before her untimely death from tuberculosis, author Katherine Mansfield published her third collection of short stories, *The Garden Party and Other Stories*. Mansfield explained that what she 'tried to convey' in *The Garden Party* was 'the diversity of life and how we try to fit in everything. Death included.' Indeed, through the story's protagonist, Laura Sheridan, we are transported into a richly textured narrative, at once emotionally intense and psychologically laden.

Today, Mansfield is credited for her contribution to literary modernism, but for a long time her reputation lagged behind that of her more prolific contemporary, Virginia Woolf (p.65). Yet Mansfield's prose is scrupulously choreographed and each sentence carefully pondered. As the author noted in a letter, 'there mustn't be one single word out of place, or one word that can be taken out.' Precision, experimentation and innovation set Mansfield's work apart from that of her contemporaries.

Born into a bourgeois family, Mansfield rejected middle-class values, which saw women bound to familial duty. In 1908 she left New Zealand, where she was born, to settle in London, where she embraced a bohemian lifestyle and connected with avant-garde literary circles. Frequently moving between the United Kingdom, France and Switzerland, Mansfield led a peripatetic life. She took both male and female lovers and married twice.

Impressions of her own life experience made it into her bold short stories, many of which are still hailed for their portrayal of gender roles and insightful understanding of self. During her lifetime, Mansfield published the collections *In a German Pension* (1911), *Prelude* (1918), *Bliss* (1920) and *The Garden Party and Other Stories* – the latter won her great and deserved acclaim. After her death, Mansfield's second husband John Middleton Murry took charge of her estate. He edited and published her journal, as well as stories, poems and letters. Later generations of women writers and readers would recognise Mansfield as an iconic figure and credited her with expressing deep existential concerns in her writings. FF

Katherine Mansfield (1888–1923)
By Walter Benington, 1916
Gelatin silver print, 198 × 153mm
National Portrait Gallery, London, x201364

Margaret Bondfield

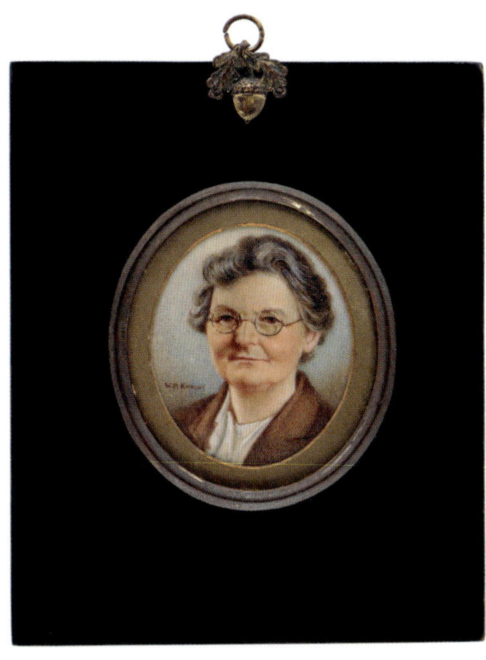

[S]uch a very large number of citizens are already converted to the belief that women are as necessary in legislative and administrative bodies as are men. There is hardly a subject now which can honestly be described as having no bearing on the lives of women …

This was the answer the prominent trade unionist Margaret Bondfield provided when asked in 1920 by *The Vote* newspaper if women Members of Parliament were necessary. Women had partially gained the vote two years earlier, along with the right to stand as parliamentary candidates, though by 1920 Nancy Astor remained the only woman in Parliament, with Margaret Wintringham joining a year later. This was soon set to change. In the 1923 General Election, Bondfield became one of six newly elected female politicians as Labour's MP for Northampton, marking another step forward in the representation of women's voices and their active participation in British politics. It was one half of what the

Daily Mirror dubbed Bondfield's 'double triumph'. Just three months earlier, she had been appointed the first woman Chair of the Trade Union Congress's General Council, 'the supreme position in the industrial wing of Labour', as she called it.

Throughout her career, Bondfield would achieve such 'female firsts', while persistently championing women's and workers' rights. Her union involvement and commitment to socialism had been initiated through her encounters with the harsh 'living-in' system while working as a shop assistant in her youth. Bondfield soon became active in numerous women's organizations, including as co-founder of the National Federation of Women Workers, and campaigned on issues including maternity and child welfare, married women's employment and minimum wage rates for women.

After losing her parliamentary seat in 1924, Bondfield returned in 1926 as MP for Wallsend and in 1929 became the first woman cabinet member as Minister of Labour. Coinciding with the global economic fallout of the Wall Street Crash, her post was doomed from the outset. As unemployment soared, she found herself forced to consider restricting benefits to curb state spending. The dilemma split the cabinet and the government ultimately resigned in 1931.

Bondfield subsequently returned to trade union work and investigated public welfare during the 1940s, where her findings prepared the ground for many post-Second World War social reforms. Although her political career was short-lived, in her autobiography Bondfield reflected on the importance of her contribution, which 'touched much more than merely my own self – it was part of the great revolution in the position of women which had taken place in my lifetime and which I had done something to help forward.' CN

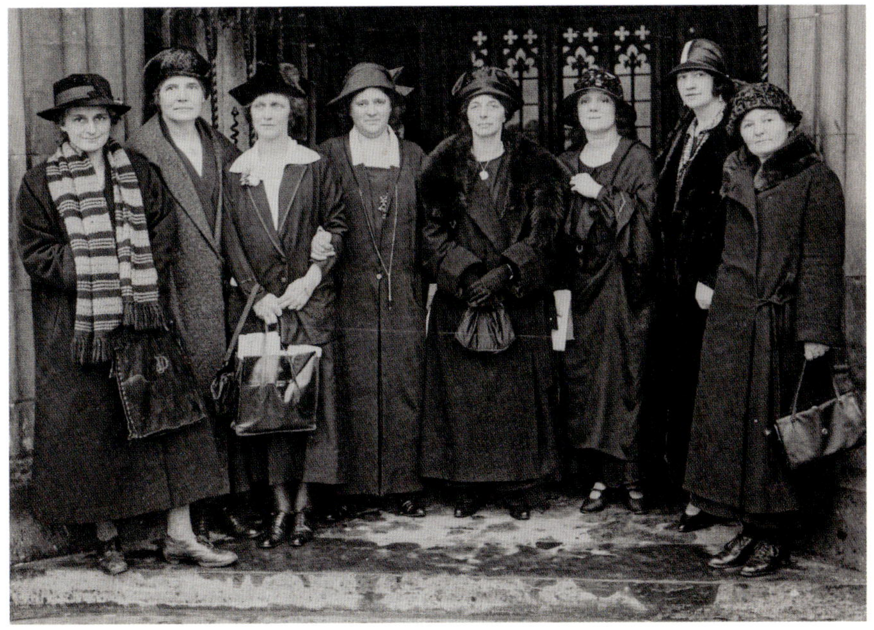

Margaret Bondfield (1873–1953)
By W. Milner Knight, 1937
Watercolour on ivory, 76 × 60mm
National Portrait Gallery, London, 3966

'The eight women Members of Parliament'
Margaret Bondfield (far right)
By an unknown photographer, 1924
Gelatin silver press print, 177 × 237mm
National Portrait Gallery, London, x196075

Caroline Haslett

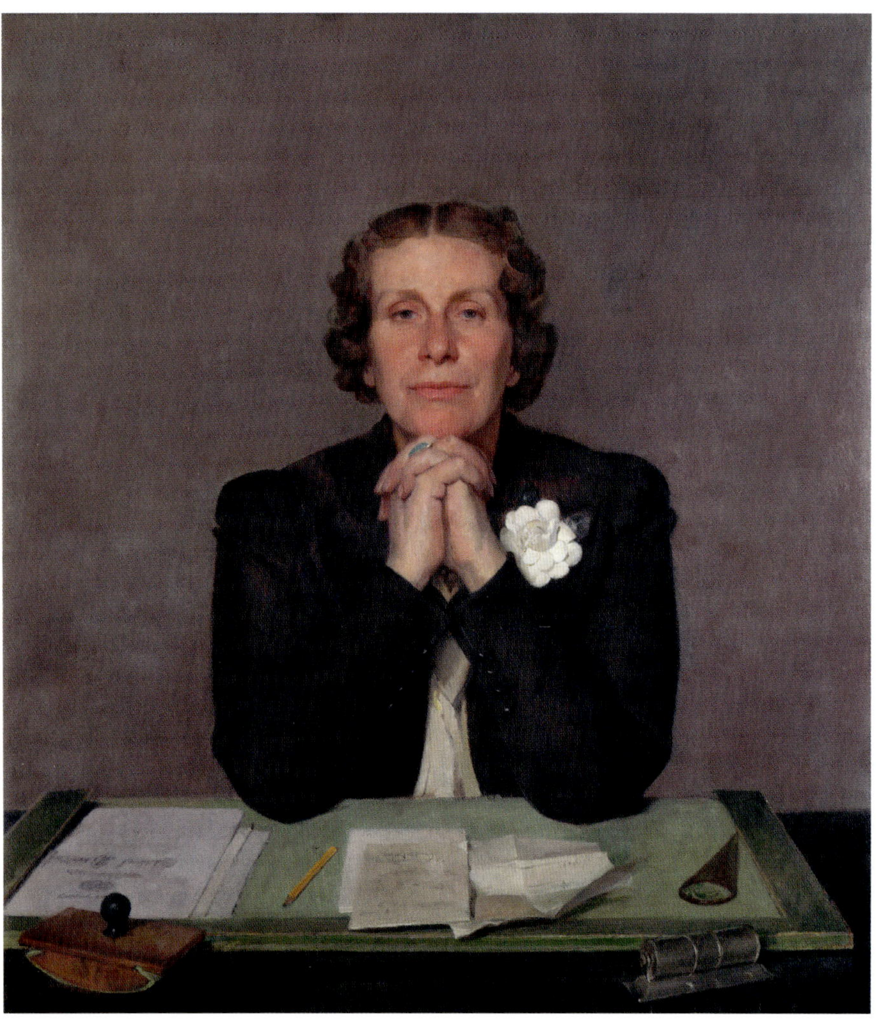

Way is being made by Electricity for a higher order of women – women set free from drudgery, who have time for reflection, for self-respect.[10]

A trailblazing electrical engineer and electrical industry administrator, Caroline Haslett realized early on that she was disinterested in the conventional occupations available to women. Initially employed as a secretary for the Cochran Boiler Company in 1914, she swiftly transferred to their factory during the First World War and gained practical engineering experience. Yet her prospects remained limited and the Restoration of Pre-War Practices Act in 1919 meant women were being pushed out of their wartime industrial roles to make way for returning soldiers. In this context, the Women's Engineering Society was founded and as their first secretary Haslett was a committed, effective, dynamic and visionary administrator. She launched and edited the Society's journal, and showed flair in organizing publicity tours and high-profile conferences.

In 1924, when Mabel Lucy Matthews approached the Society about popularising electricity for domestic use and establishing a women's electrical association, Haslett enthusiastically took it forward. At the time, few British homes had access to electricity, but Haslett immediately recognised its potential for streamlining domestic chores, allowing women the time to pursue opportunities outside the home and thus raise their social status. With this ambition, Haslett co-founded the Electrical Association for Women (EAW) that year and became its first director. For over 30 years, she edited its journal and also the *Electrical Handbook for Women* (1934), published in numerous editions until the 1980s. Other EAW initiatives included campaigning for more plug sockets in homes, improving electrical safety, influencing commercial product designs, organizing demonstrations at their showrooms, and running courses for women including to teach them basic electrical skills, such as how to change a fuse. When Haslett resigned the directorship in 1956, the EAW had 14,000 members across 160 branches, mostly domestic science teachers, educationists and housewives, demonstrating its broad appeal.

Beyond the EAW, Haslett held many public and honorary posts. She consistently championed women's rights, joining the feminist campaigning Six Point Group and advising the government during the Second World War on women's work. As an advocate for female professionals, Haslett was President of the British Federation of Business and Professional Women (and President of its international equivalent). Within the electrical industry, her most prestigious appointment was as the first female member of the British Electricity Authority, which oversaw Britain's nationalised electrical operations. Sir Gerald Kelly's painting of Haslett, seated before some papers, only subtly hints at her reputation as Britain's 'busiest woman'. Haslett was made a Dame in 1947. She died ten years later and fittingly requested to be cremated by electricity. CN

Caroline Haslett (1895–1957)
By Sir Gerald Kelly, *c.*1949
Oil on canvas, 888 × 780mm
Lent by the Royal Society of Arts, L217

Melanie Klein

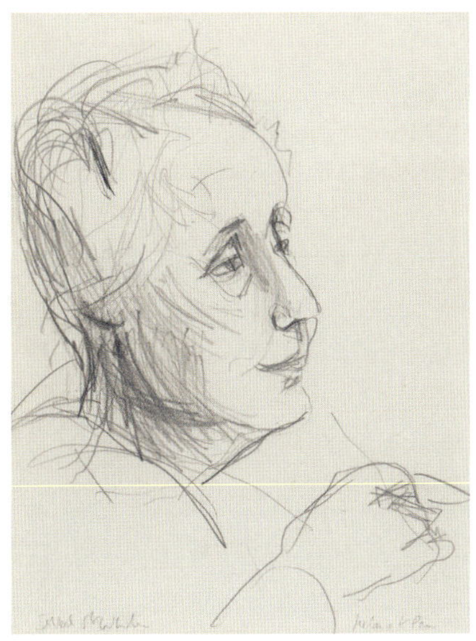

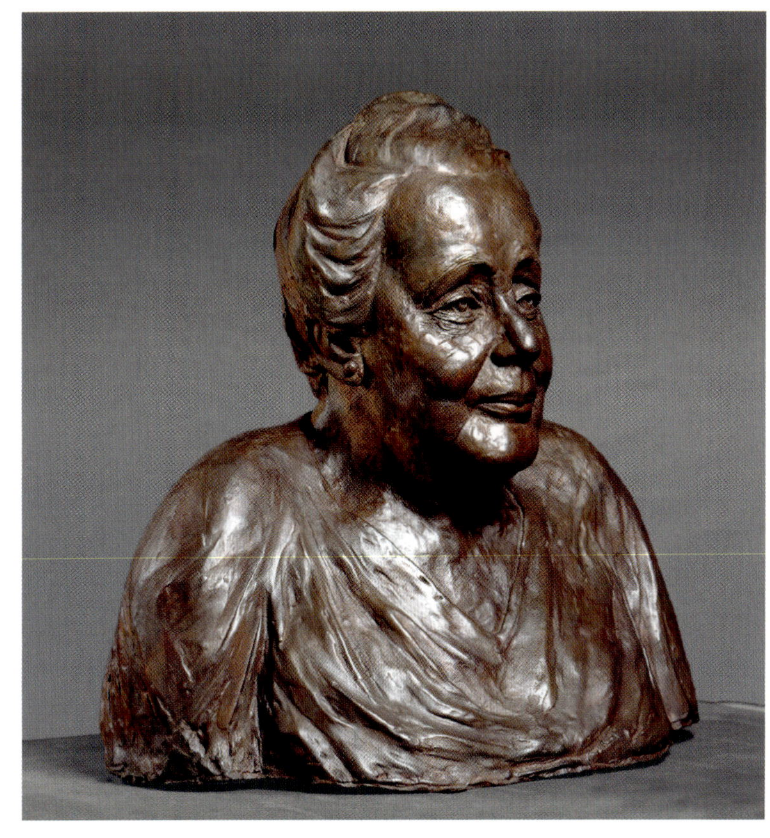

A pioneer in the psychoanalysis of young children, Melanie Klein's therapeutic techniques still influence child analysis today.

Born in Vienna, she became interested in psychoanalysis in Budapest while undergoing therapy herself. Her initial observations were on her own children, which led her to write her first paper. Inspired by Sigmund Freud, she was one of the first to use psychoanalysis on children by encouraging and observing free play. Klein explained that the resulting drawings or play scenarios offered clues about children's anxieties:

I have often been asked how it was that I tackled the children in the way I did, which was entirely unorthodox and, in many cases, in contrast to the rules laid down for the analysis of adults. I still cannot answer what made me feel that it was anxiety that I should touch and

why I proceed in this way, but experience confirmed that I was right and, to some extent, the beginning of my play technique goes back to my first case.

In 1921 she left Budapest for Berlin, the centre of psychoanalytic activity, and joined the Berlin Psychoanalytic Institute. Her theories were radical; she recognised the importance of childhood experiences and their influence in the formation of the adult emotional world.

Encouraged by Alix and James Strachey, Freud's English translators, and the British psychoanalyst and neurologist Ernest Jones, in 1925 Klein was invited to London to give a series of landmark lectures on child analysis that provoked a great interest among members of the British Psychoanalytical Society. These six lectures formed the basis of the initial part of *The Psycho-Analysis of Children*, her first book, published in 1932.

In 1927 Klein moved permanently to England, becoming a member of the British Psychoanalytical Society. She continued her clinical research, developing new theories, however, in the 1940s Klein's ideas on the psychoanalysis of children led to a heated disagreement with Freud's daughter Anna, also a child analyst, and between their respective followers. Klein's ideas were seen as unorthodox, but though their differences were never fully resolved, a split within the British Psychoanalytical Society was averted.

A collection of Klein's published works appeared in 1975, *The Writings of Melanie Klein*; it includes two books, 37 papers, and five short contributions. Clinicians and psychoanalysts practising today continue to explore and develop Klein's ideas. GA

Melanie Klein (1882–1960)
By Ishbel McWhirter, 1950s
Pencil drawing, 352 × 254mm
National Portrait Gallery, London, 5108

Melanie Klein
By Eileen Klein, *c*.1968
Resin plaster bust, 545 × 540mm
National Portrait Gallery, London, 6484

1926   Alma Reville

'Miss Reville?' inquired a formal male voice. 'This is Alfred Hitchcock. I am assistant director for a new film', the voice went on stiffly. 'I wonder if you would accept a position as a cutter [editor] *on the picture.'*[11]

With this momentous phone call the renowned director Alfred Hitchcock changed the course of his life and film career. In 1921 he had briefly crossed paths with a young and well-respected film editor called Alma Reville.

The daughter of Matthew Edward Reville – a lace warehouseman who worked in the costume department at Twickenham Studios in St Margaret's – Alma knew how to navigate the film industry from a young age. Aged 16 she was already working on set, making tea. Within a few years she had risen through the ranks, working as an editor, script editor and eventually as a director's assistant. By 1923, when Hitchcock approached Reville to offer her 'a position as a cutter' on the film *Woman to Woman* (directed by Graham Cutts) she was more established within the British film industry than he was. Soon to become the power couple of the film world, this was to be the first of many joint endeavours.

In 1926, the year Hitchcock directed his first feature film, *The Pleasure Garden*, he and Reville were married. The previous year he had proposed to Reville on the voyage back to Britain from Germany, where they had been working on *The Blackguard* – another film directed by Graham Cutts. The proposal had been rather theatrical, with Reville struggling from seasickness and Hitchcock seizing this moment of weakness to set in stone their partnership. From then on, Reville would become Hitchcock's most trusted advisor. Over the years she supported him with script material, casting and all aspects of production. Her tasks would vary according to the project and often her

work went uncredited, leaving Reville in the shadow of Hitchcock's growing popularity. In 1925, however, *Picturegoer* magazine recognised Reville's pioneering role in the burgeoning film industry. The feature was significantly titled 'Alma in Wonderland: Proving a Woman's Place is Not Always in the Home', and it shed light on her role as an editor with the sharpest eye for

detail. Word has it that it was thanks to this eye for detail that *Psycho* (1960) enjoys such flawless editing. As the film critic Charles Champlin later noted, 'The Hitchcock touch had four hands and two were Alma's.' FF

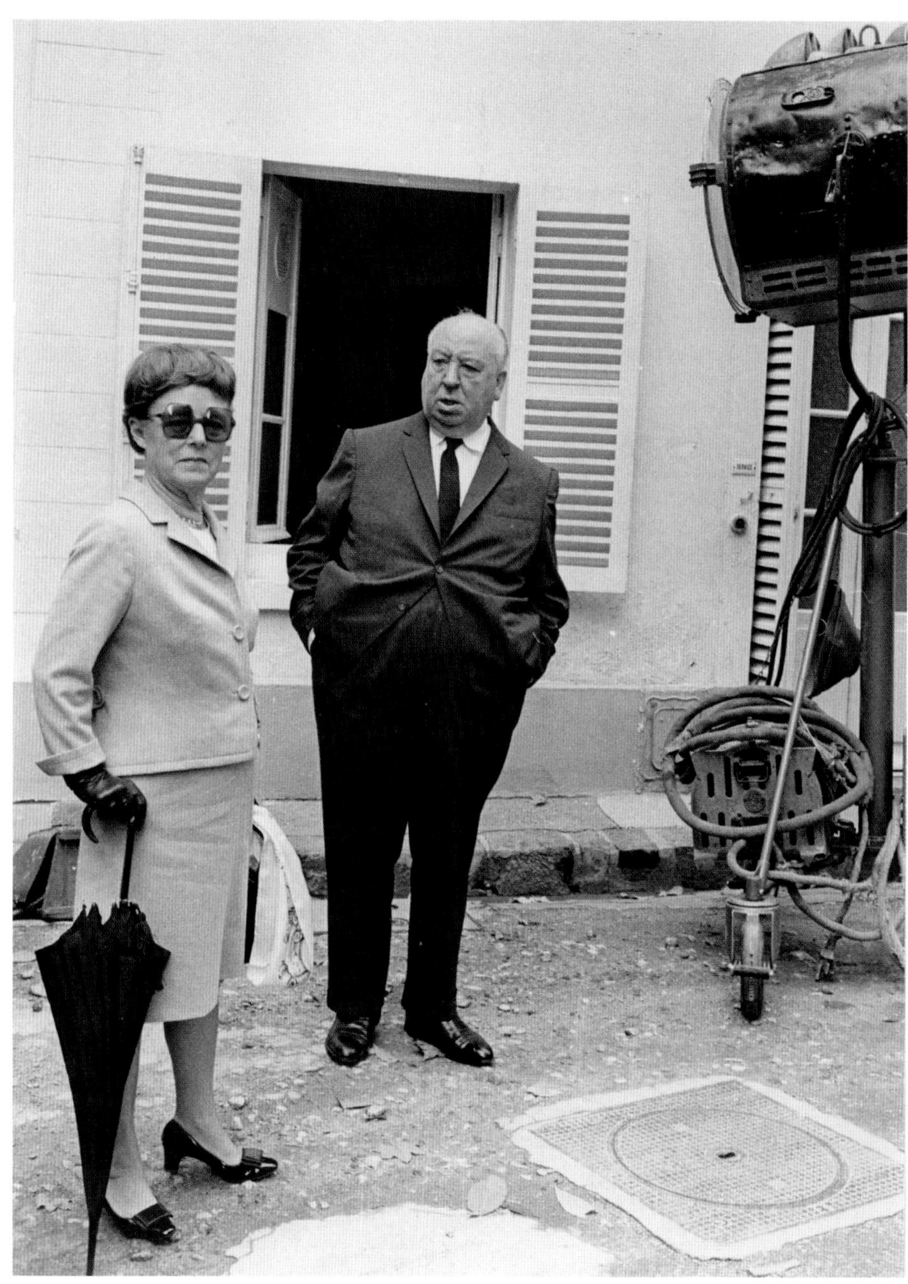

Alma Reville (1899–1982) and Alfred Hitchcock inspecting a location set for *Topaz*
By Roland Schoor for Pix Publishing Inc., 1969
Gelatin silver press print, 273 × 193mm
National Portrait Gallery, London, x201543

Hilda Matheson

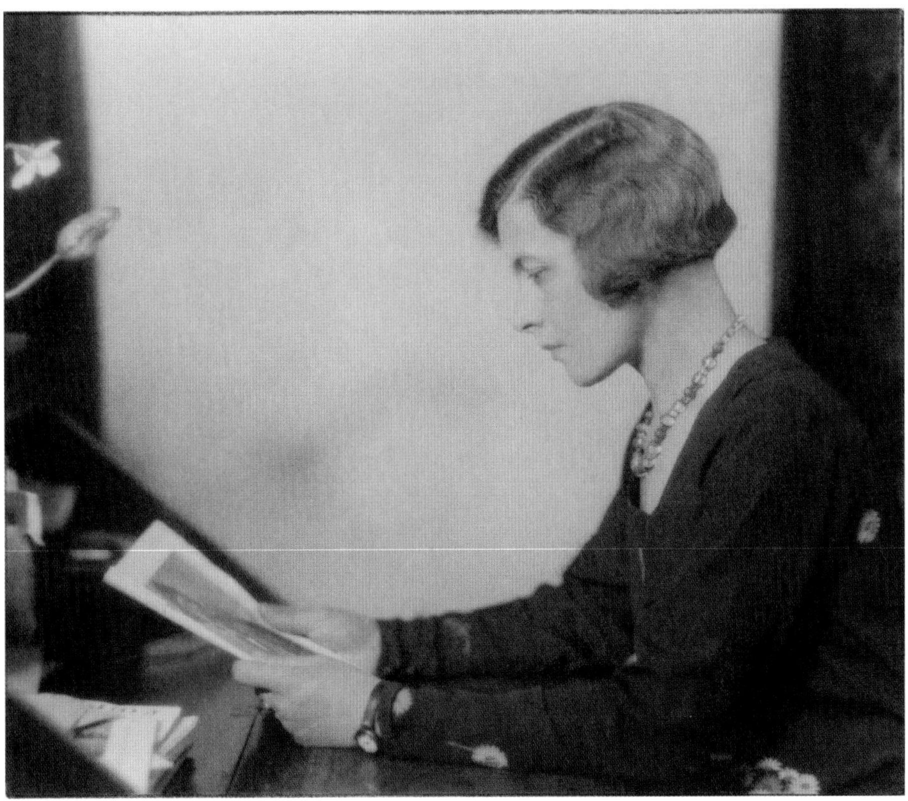

In so far as broadcasting merely adds to the general welter, it may fill us with foreboding; in so far as it helps us to coordinate, to select, to apply scales of value, to give us time to think, it may relieve some of our present perplexities. It is worth remembering ... that broadcasting seemed to one great poet, fastidious scholar and uncompromising critic, a possible vehicle for truth and beauty.

With these closing remarks, broadcaster and producer Hilda Matheson wrapped up her 1933 book *Broadcasting*, a volume that would prove to be a work of reference for many well into the 1960s. In *Broadcasting*, Matheson addressed both the technological and semantic meaning of the medium, then in its heyday. She introduced readers to the inner workings of the airwaves and allayed the fears of those who were sceptical of this new technology.

In 1926, Matheson was offered a senior position in the fledgling British Broadcasting Company, nominally to support the education department. Within a year, she became the first Director of Talks and established the first news section. In 1927, for a woman to be in charge of a major provider of news was revolutionary and Matheson was well-equipped to lead this progressive shift. By then, the Company had changed its name to the British Broadcasting Corporation, also known as the BBC. Matheson, who had previously worked as political secretary to Lady Nancy Astor (the first serving female Member of Parliament), was known for her keen eye for experimentation. As Director of Talks this meant revolutionising the way the news was presented, and bringing to the wireless leading figures of the day, such as H.G. Wells, George Bernard Shaw and Winston Churchill, among many others.

At this time, all broadcast talks were scripted, and Matheson taught broadcasters how to 'write for the ear', a skill she had earned through practice. Matheson knew that the microphone was one of the most powerful instruments of communication, capable of swaying public opinion like no other. With that in mind, every word had to be carefully chosen and scripts were extensively rehearsed; the spoken word on air had to be perfect.

In 1931, growing tensions between Matheson and the BBC led to her resignation. She went on to become the radio critic for the *Observer* and wrote a column for the *Week-End Review*. By 1939, Matheson's skills had been put to use by military intelligence. She was tasked with setting up the joint broadcasting committee, responsible for the broadcasting of British information and opinions by foreign radio stations. FF

Hilda Matheson (1888–1940)
By Douglas Ltd, late 1920s
Gelatin silver print, 144 × 163mm
National Portrait Gallery, London, P1386

Constance Spry

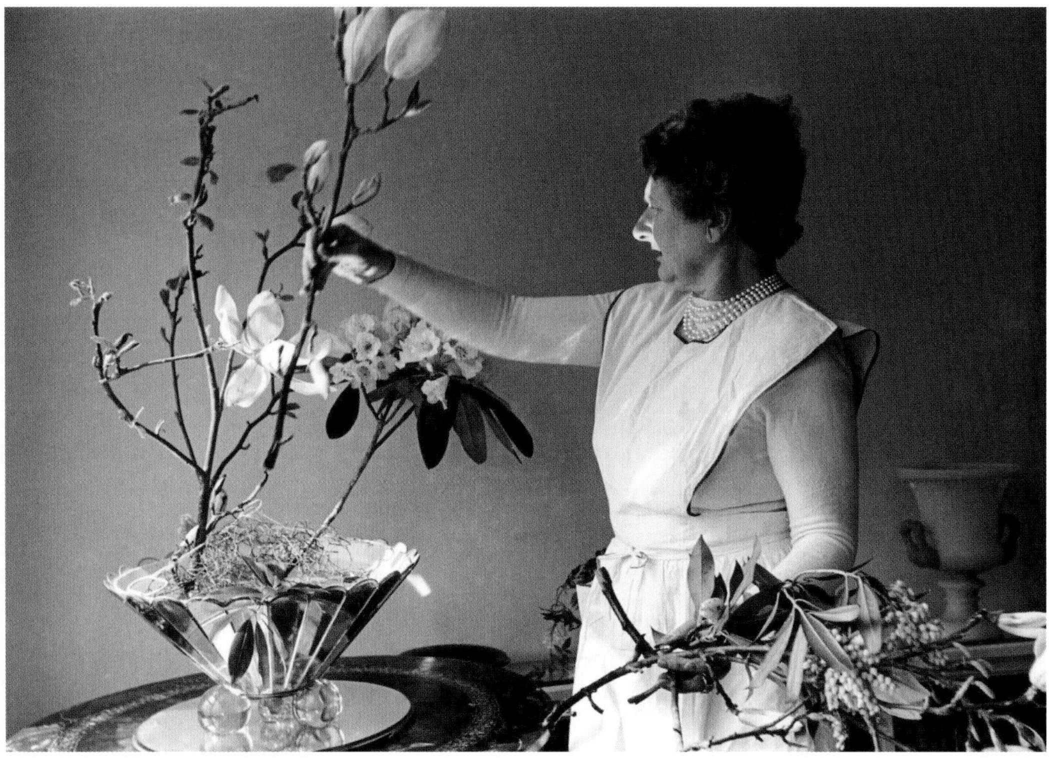

Constance Spry was a woman who caused a 'storm in a flower vase'.[12] In 1928, the then 42-year-old Spry gave up her work in social reform and education to revolutionise the art of flower arranging. She went on to instil in people from all backgrounds the freedom to create beauty through flowers. Spry turned outdated arrangements into theatrical masterpieces, inspired by an eclectic range of sources including sixteenth- and seventeenth-century Dutch and Flemish still lifes. She combined sophisticated and commonplace flowers with foliage, seeds, berries, fruits and vegetables. Spry described the dynamic process and highlighted the importance of improvisation:

One arranges flowers as the spirit moves you; to obey some inner prompting to put this colour with that, to have brilliance here, line there, a sense of opulence in this place or sparseness in that; to suit your surroundings, your mood, the weather and the occasion. In a word, to do as you please, just as, if you could, you might paint a picture.

Spry's achievements were not limited to flower arrangement. After the war, together with Rosemary Hume, she established the Cordon Bleu Cookery School and co-authored with Hume *The Constance Spry Cookery Book* (1956), which quickly became a bestseller. She also established a college at Winkfield Place, near Windsor, where she taught cookery, housekeeping and the art of making things beautiful. These endeavours, together with her flower shops, point to Spry's entrepreneurial spirit. Unfortunately, her ambition was not always matched by sound business acumen, meaning that Spry never acquired much wealth despite being the most sought-after floral artist of her time.

For Spry, flower arrangement was an art and as such she liked to be described as a horticulturalist rather than a florist. At first, she took on commissions for dinner tables and parties for friends and acquaintances, but she was quickly enlisted by Granada Cinemas and Atkinsons perfumery on Old Bond Street to take care of their flower arrangements. Her client list grew to include the wealthiest and most fashionable London homes, as well as the trendiest members of the fashion, interior and design worlds. Notably, Spry was entrusted with the flowers in Westminster Abbey for the marriage of Princess Elizabeth and Prince Philip in 1947, and later for the 1953 Coronation of Queen Elizabeth II. She was awarded an OBE in the Coronation Honours.

While in recent years Spry has been widely celebrated for her aesthetic approach, her legacy extends beyond flower arrangement to also encompass a pioneering stance towards education. FF

Constance Spry (1886–1960)
By Paul Popper/Popperfoto, 1953
Getty Images

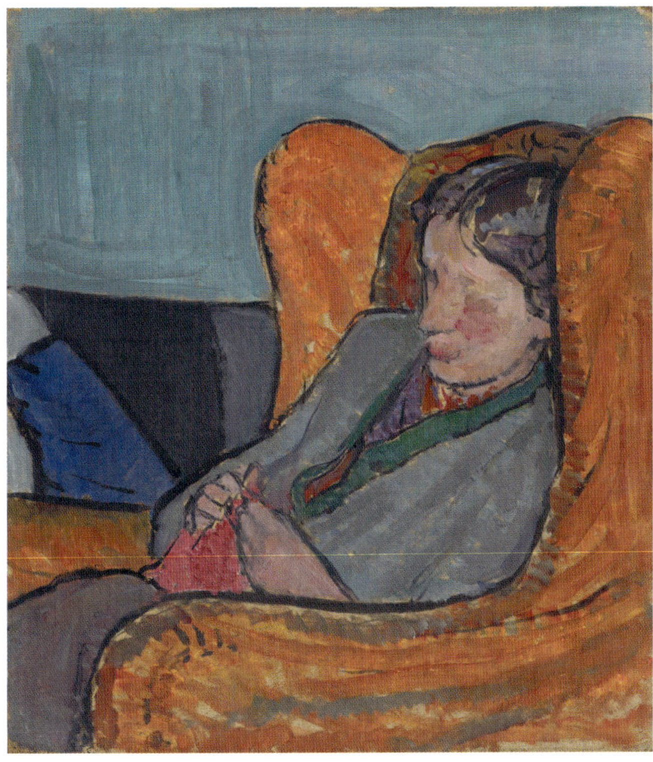

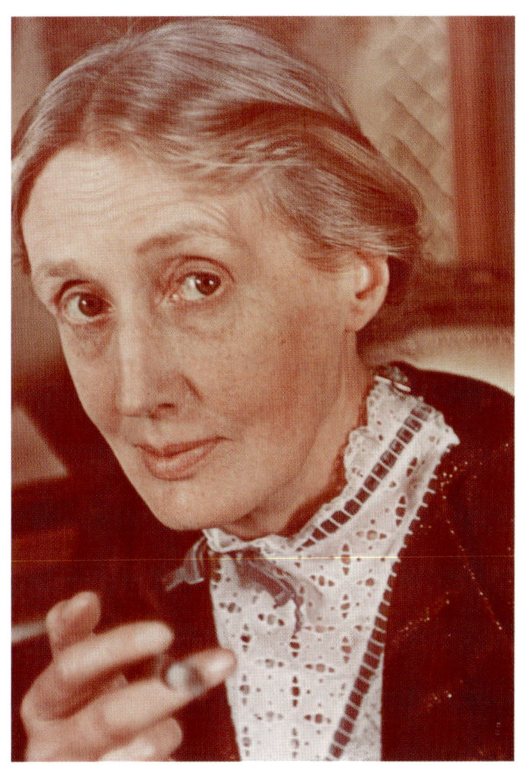

All I could do was to offer you an opinion upon one minor point – a woman must have money and a room of her own if she is to write fiction.

With these words Virginia Woolf coined one of the most oft-cited feminist beliefs of all time – the inextricable link between financial independence and creative freedom. For Woolf this was the central tenet of her celebrated essay *A Room of One's Own*, published in 1929, in which she argued that the limiting factor for creative output by women was lack of opportunity rather than an absence of ability.

A central figure in the Bloomsbury group of writers, artists and intellectuals, Woolf pioneered the use of interior monologue as a literary device. This innovative strategy was deployed in many of her novels, including *Night and Day* (1919), *Jacob's Room* (1922), *Mrs Dalloway* (1925), *To the Lighthouse* (1927) and *The Waves* (1931). In *A Room of One's Own*, Woolf uses the same lively and descriptive prose found in her novels to confront a tangible problem: the educational and financial disadvantages that women have faced throughout history. Through the fictionalised character of Judith Shakespeare – a gifted but uneducated sister of William Shakespeare – she imagines what kind of life Judith would have lived when compared to that of her famous brother. The comparison reveals a disheartening disparity between female and male genius; the latter has access to everything while the former is constrained by a society that expects women to marry and spend time housekeeping and childrearing. Woolf ends Judith's short cautionary tale with the words:

… what is true in it, so it seemed to me, reviewing the story of Shakespeare's sister as I had made it, is that any woman born with a great gift in the sixteenth century would certainly have gone crazed, shot herself, or ended her days in some lonely cottage outside the village, half witch, half wizard, feared and mocked at.

In examining the marginalisation of women in history, Woolf observes that history itself is a male construct and that women are not by nature inferior writers or subjects, they simply have not been given the same opportunities as their male counterparts. They were not allowed to attend school or university and women's material circumstances were extremely limited.

Ingrained value judgement is another strong suit of Woolf's argument. She observes: 'This is an important book, the critic assumes, because it deals with war. This is an insignificant book because it deals with the feelings of women in a drawing-room.' While masculine values had long prevailed, Woolf makes a point of discarding these in favour of a liberated space for women to create to the fullest of their potential. FF

Virginia Woolf (1882–1941)
By Vanessa Bell, 1912
Oil on board, 400 × 340mm
National Portrait Gallery, London, 5933

Virginia Woolf
By Gisèle Freund, 1939
Colour dye transfer print, 299 × 200mm
National Portrait Gallery, London, P440

Amy Johnson

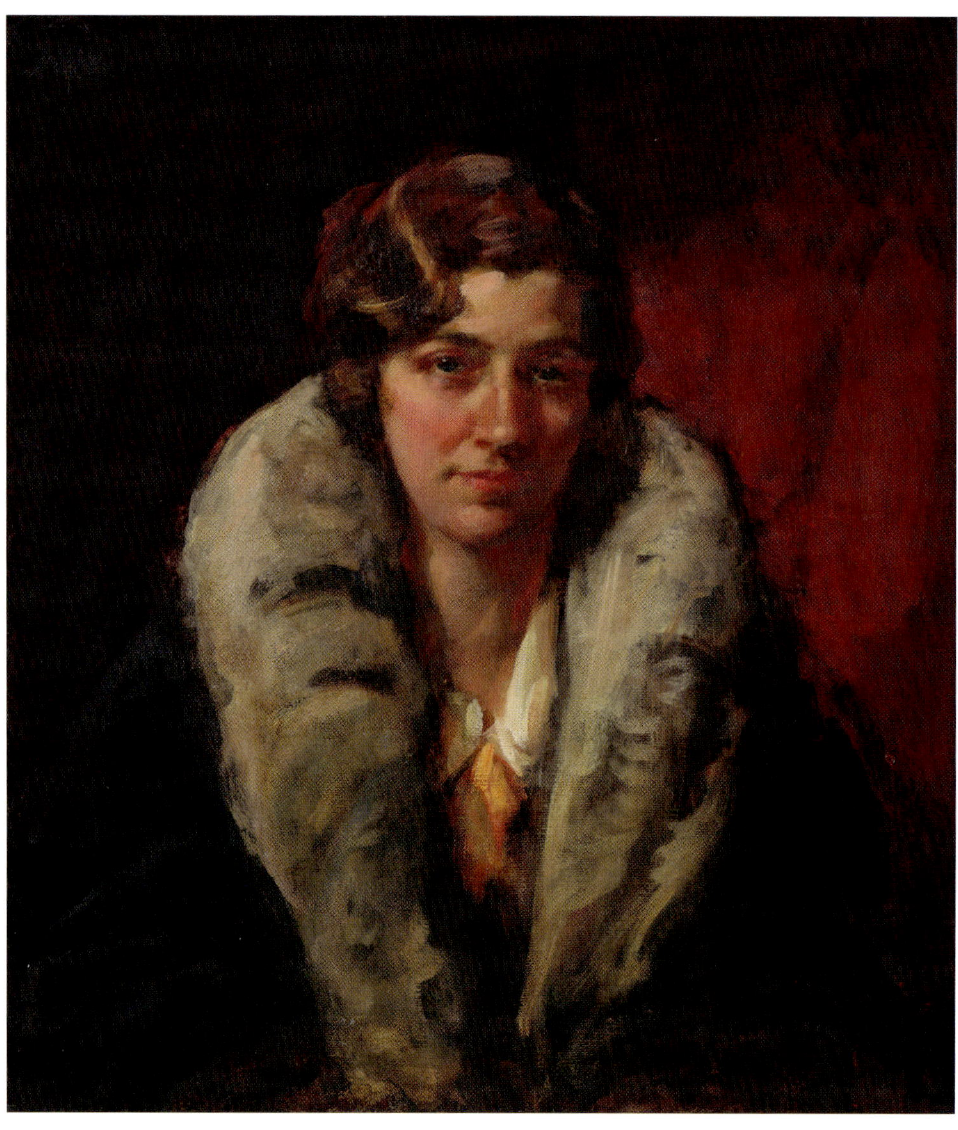

Originally from Hull, Amy Johnson discovered her passion for flying during the late 1920s, after having moved to London to work as a secretary. At this time, the newspapers brimmed with the flying feats of audacious aviators and soon Johnson too would be the subject of their news. Within months of gaining her pilot's 'A' licence in July 1929, Johnson became Britain's first woman to earn a Ground Engineer's 'C' licence and, as her unusual achievement made the front pages in January 1930, she declared to one reporter:

I am awfully pleased about getting the certificate, which means that now, as I am a fully qualified pilot, I can pass out my own machine as being airworthy without recourse to anyone else.

This assertion of independence and expertise would prove essential for her next striking endeavour: to become the first woman to fly solo from England to Australia.

Daring, confident and adventurous, Johnson was undaunted by her less than 100 hours of flying experience when she departed from Croydon Aerodrome in her second-hand Gipsy Moth light biplane – named 'Jason' and painted a 'lucky' green – on 5 May 1930. Following a route mapped out using a straight line, Johnson's physical and mental endurance, skill and courage were tested as she flew over challenging and sometimes uncharted terrain, and battled extreme weather conditions in her open cockpit, before making planned stops for rest, refuelling and repairs. The media enthusiastically reported the daily highs and lows of her ambitious 11,000-mile journey, so that upon arriving in Port Darwin 19 and a half days later to eagerly waiting crowds, she was already an international celebrity and Britain's 'darling'. Accolades quickly followed, including a CBE less than a week later.

Johnson's record-breaking flights continued until 1936, and all the while she actively maintained her engineering interests, alongside her dedication to advancing aviation and women's place within it. Her 1931 paper on 'The attention that I gave Jason's engine during my flight' earned Johnson the Society of Engineers' President's Gold Medal. In 1932, she became Vice President, and later President (1934–7), of the Women's Engineering Society, where she established an Aeronautical Section (a predecessor of the British Women Pilots' Association) and a series of aeronautics debates.

Despite being overqualified, Johnson ferried planes across Britain for the Royal Air Force with the newly formed Air Transport Auxiliary during the Second World War's earliest days. On 5 January 1941, she bailed out into the Thames Estuary's icy waters and her body was never recovered. Tributes immediately flowed to the popular but modest 'Queen of the Air', whose pioneering accomplishments in aviation have never ceased to captivate and inspire. CN

Amy Johnson (1903–1941)
By Sir John Longstaff, 1930
Oil on canvas, 692 × 572mm
National Portrait Gallery, London, 4201

Harriet Cohen

*The Bach Book sounds like one
of the Barber's brothers in
Cornelius's opera –
'It's nice and easy'.
I should call the concert Five finger
Exercises for Harriet
by Infatuated Celebrities*

The playwright George Bernard Shaw, who penned these words, was one such infatuated celebrity. The object of his infatuation was the pianist Harriet Cohen.

Cohen was a remarkable pianist, with an intuitive feel for music. She is said to have given more first performances of works than any other pianist of her time. Cohen's immense and ever-increasing repertoire encompassed contemporary music, as well as compositions from the past. She brought back the Elizabethans, Henry Purcell and, most significantly, Johann Sebastian Bach. Cohen's reinterpretation of Bach contributed to her success; in the words of German musicologist Adolf Weissmann: 'So deeply has the Master's spirit entered into her that she has few, if any, equals as a Bach player.' She approached Bach from a contemporary perspective and lent to her interpretations an exuberant vitality which made them compelling in the 1920s and 1930s when Cohen was performing.

Cohen's devotion to Bach was such that, in 1931, 12 composers who admired her were persuaded to contribute new arrangements, which were published as *A Bach Book for Harriet Cohen* the following year. Contributors to this collective effort included Arthur Bliss, Constant Lambert and Arnold Bax – with whom Cohen shared a sentimental relationship for many years. While *A Bach Book* consecrated Cohen's lifelong dedication to the German composer, she also maintained connections to contemporary peers like the Russian ballerina Tamara Karasavina, for whom Cohen first played in 1920. Cohen was notably beautiful, forceful and generous. The National Portrait Gallery holds a rich collection of portraits of Cohen, most of which capture the essence of an artist whose personality spoke through her art. To end on the words of musicologist Alfred Einstein:

'Harriet Cohen must be added to the list of those chosen ones who stand among the elect.' FF

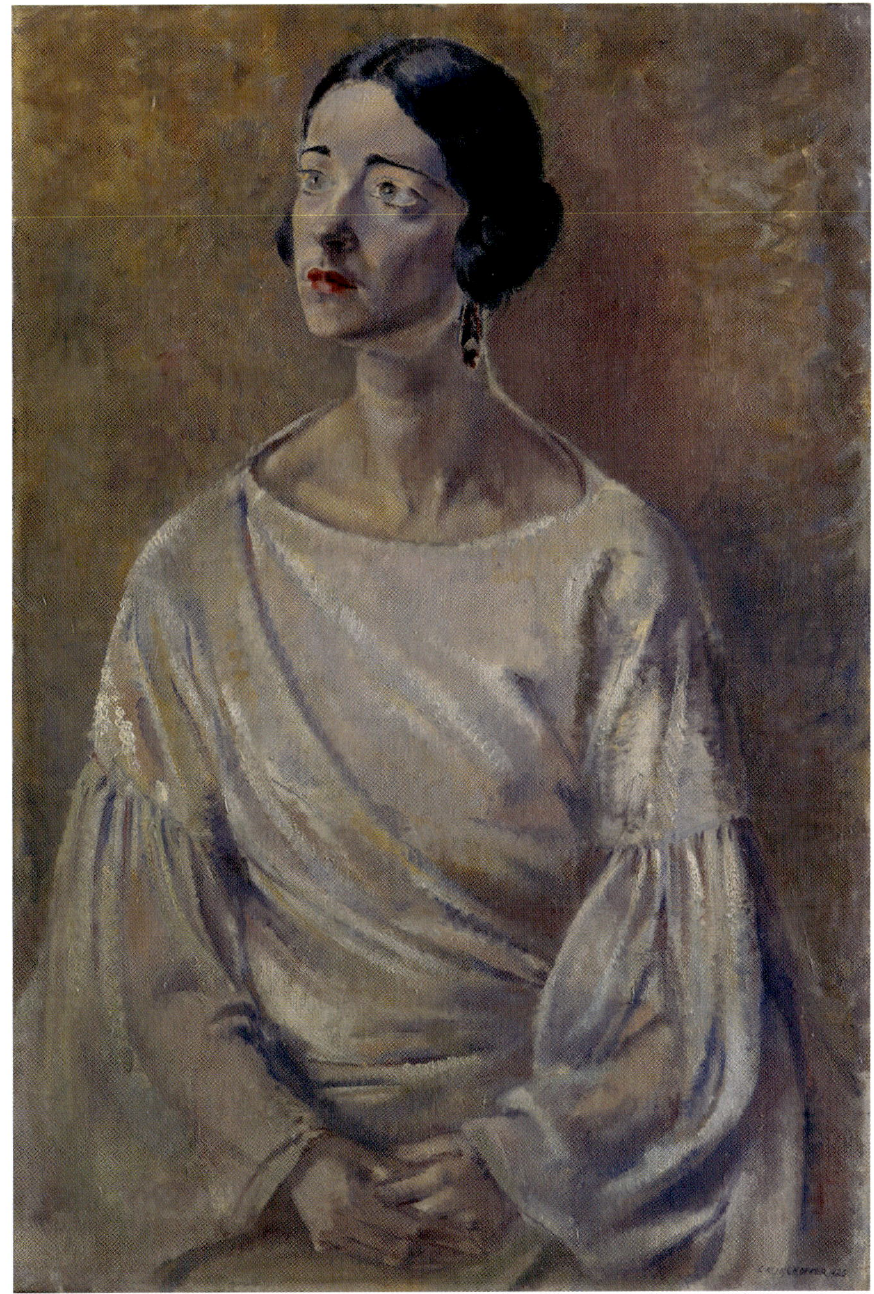

Harriet Cohen (1895–1967)
By Clara Klinghoffer, 1925
Oil on canvas, 920 × 611mm
National Portrait Gallery, London, 5736

Yevonde

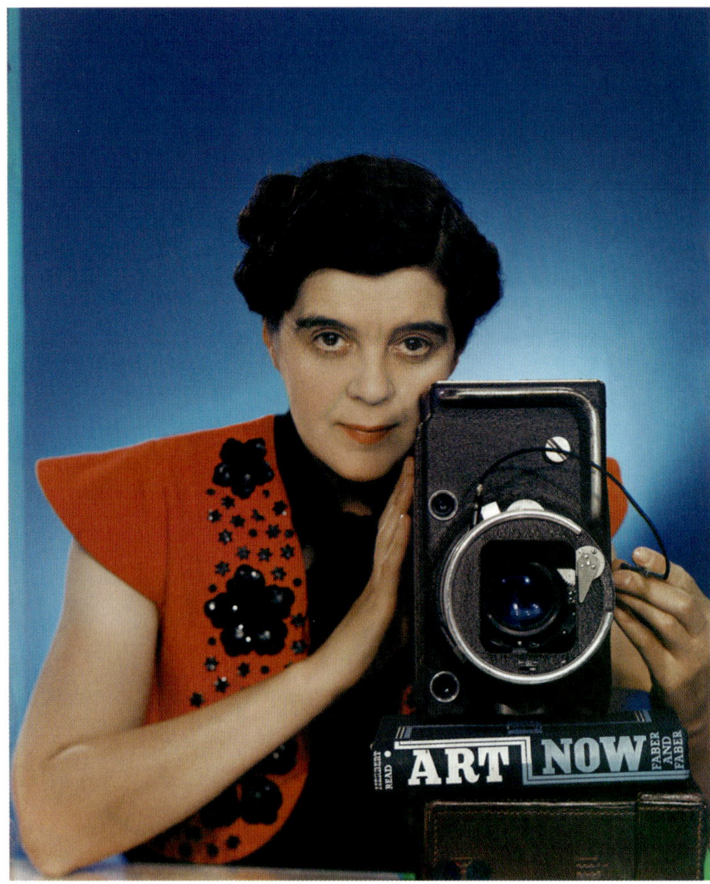

For Yevonde, who had been a suffragette, photography was the key to independence. She opened the door to her first London studio in 1914, but it was the commercialisation of colour in the 1930s that truly enabled the translation of her vivacious personality and creative imagination into enduring works of art.

'Photographs by Yevonde', held at the Albany Gallery, Mayfair in April 1932, was the first solo exhibition of colour photographs in Britain. It was Yevonde's launch into a vibrant decade and the emergence of her advocacy of the medium to the sceptical elite of the photography world and the 'colour-blind' public. Yevonde's 'apologia for the colour photograph, as yet in its infancy' in the exhibition pamphlet declared experimentation as key; 'Colour Photography must develop along photographic lines ... it has no tradition – only a future.'

In her address 'Why Colour?' to the Royal Photographic Society later that year, she explained her use of backgrounds, compositions, make-up and lighting, which conveyed the relative freedoms of women in the inter-war period. Film, advertising and publishing industries joined the push for colour, with Yevonde ahead of the game. Using a cumbersome repeating back or a one-shot camera, Yevonde's exposed tri-colour negatives would be sent off to Colour Photographs Ltd lab for the production of lustrous 15 × 12-inch Vivex prints.

To publicize her new prestigious West End studio, 'Goddesses and Others', a galaxy of Yevonde's best-known creations, was exhibited in 1935. Studio regulars and much-photographed beauties were made up, dressed up, propped and posed in a collaboration with the photographer at the height of her creativity. Inspired by classicism, Yevonde's goddesses are reinvented for the age of modernity. She also brought colour to royal patronage; her robed peers and peeresses for the Coronation of George VI, draped in red velvet and ermine, illuminated tradition for a new age.

She frequently advocated photography as a profession for women and was invited to speak at the Business and Professional Women's Federation conference in 1936. She created covers for *Women & Beauty*, *Eve's Journal* and *Modern Home* that both subverted and enhanced engendered expectations. Spirited, creative and humorous, Yevonde's commercial work evolved into surrealist still life pieces and compositions with models fusing domesticity and allure.

Yevonde's life changed dramatically on the outbreak of the Second World War, which coincided with the death of her husband of 19 years, Edgar Middleton, and the closure of the primary printer of her works, Colour Photographs Ltd. Her creativity had to find new channels of expression. Through montage, solarisation and studio portraits of 'distinguished women', Yevonde's business continued into the 1970s. Reappraisal of Yevonde's place in the canon of history-making photographers has been reinstated since her death in 1975, while the digitisation of her tri-colour negatives continues to evolve our understanding of her brilliance. CF

Yevonde (1893–1975) with Vivex one-shot camera
Self-portrait, 1937
Tri-colour separation negative
National Portrait Gallery, London, x223231

CAMERA LUCIDATA:

WOMEN PHOTOGRAPHERS AND THE CELEBRITY PORTRAIT

By

Magdalene Keaney

When photography came to the attention of the world in 1839, it was the medium itself that was the celebrity. Who, or what, was in the image was something of a second thought. Within a few years, portrait making took hold as one of the most widely practised forms of photography. The celebrity photograph almost immediately provided a popular and enduring anchor within the sea of portraits taken, printed and sold in the last decades of the nineteenth century. More than just the *subject* of a photograph, celebrity, fame and infamy were largely the very *reason* for photography.

The National Portrait Gallery has an enormous collection of early celebrity portraits in a format called *carte-de-visite*. These are small rectangular photographs that were mass produced and collected widely by the 1860s. Popular sitters included prominent public figures such as members of the royal family, politicians, writers, performers, great beauties of the day and even those considered 'curious' in Victorian society. Yet very few of the many thousands of *cartes-de-visite* in the National Portrait Gallery Collection were produced by women photographers or at least women that are named. Women were more often the subject of the celebrity 'carte' and the precedent that was followed in the history of photography has been woman as muse not maker. Approaching the Collection of the National Portrait Gallery with the celebrity portrait in mind reveals a fascinating history of women, not only in front of the camera, but also crucially, and perhaps less well-known, behind the lens.

Julia Margaret Cameron is rightfully renowned as an innovative Victorian photographer who pursued the artistic and expressive potential of the medium. Cameron's project was also embedded in celebrity portraiture and she did things many celebrity photographers continue to do to this day: she sought out the most prominent and renowned artists, writers and thinkers of her time (almost always male sitters) and in photographing them she hoped to convey something of what she considered their 'greatness'. She understood that the Victorian fascination with celebrity offered her commercial, as well creative, opportunities, and she often reproduced the autographs of her famous sitters on her prints to make them even more appealing. Cameron also made portraits of women who were celebrated beauties, and her images of women emphasise physical beauty – the quality that most often made a woman noteworthy in the late nineteenth century (fig.1). She counted on the commercial value of fame and beauty to distribute and sell her pictures and translated her images from exhibition prints into the collectible format of the cabinet card to expand her audiences.

The Royal Family were among the earliest and most consistently photographed 'celebrity' sitters in Britain. Queen Victoria and Prince Albert commissioned numerous

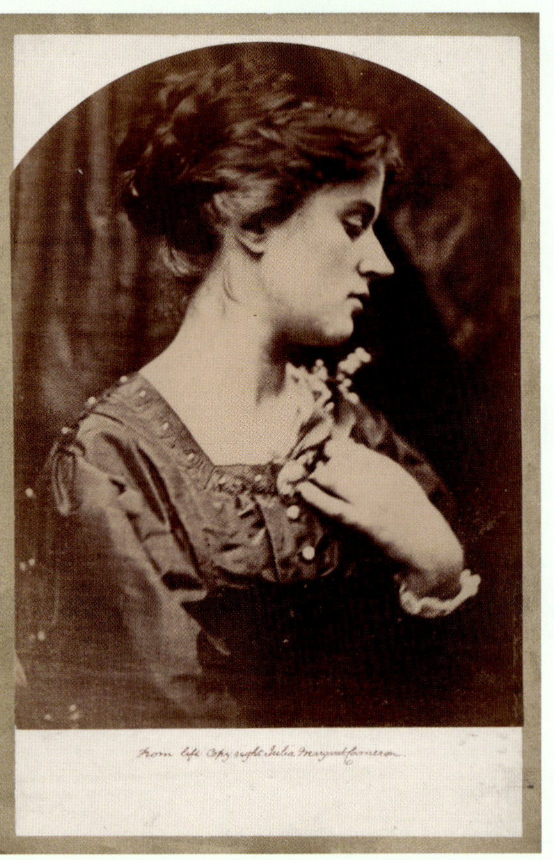

Fig.1: Marie Stillman by Julia Margaret Cameron

photographers to make images intended for wide public circulation, including Frances Sally Day, who was the first woman to photograph the Royal Family. In the twentieth and twenty-first centuries, members of the Royal Family have become celebrities and royal portraits can be official – marking formal and ceremonial events and creating opportunities for 'soft diplomacy', as well as having the status and appeal of popular culture celebrity images. While Queen Victoria ascended to the throne in 1838, the year before the 'invention' of the daguerreotype was announced, the first time the British coronation was a photographic event was for the crowning of Edward VII in 1902. The popularity of the coronation in the print media has been defining in the careers of a number of women photographers, including Dorothy Wilding and Yevonde, and royal portraits by both are represented in the Collection. There is only one image of Diana, Princess of Wales made by a woman photographer in the National Portrait Gallery Collection – a sensitive likeness by British photographer Carole Cutner (fig.2). Made in 1981, the same year as Diana's marriage to the then Prince of Wales, it is a portrait which conveys the 20-year-old sitter's strength and vulnerability in equal measures. Diana was known as the 'people's princess' and she famously captured the hearts and minds of the British public. Her extensive photographic iconography is an example of royal portraits aligning with modern-day celebrity and fashion image making.

At the turn of the century, early fashion photographs were often also celebrity portraits, depicting named actresses or well-known high society ladies, as well as the elegant garments they wore. Since this time, magazines have been so full of photographic likenesses that they have become alternative portrait galleries in their own right. Women fashion and editorial photographers

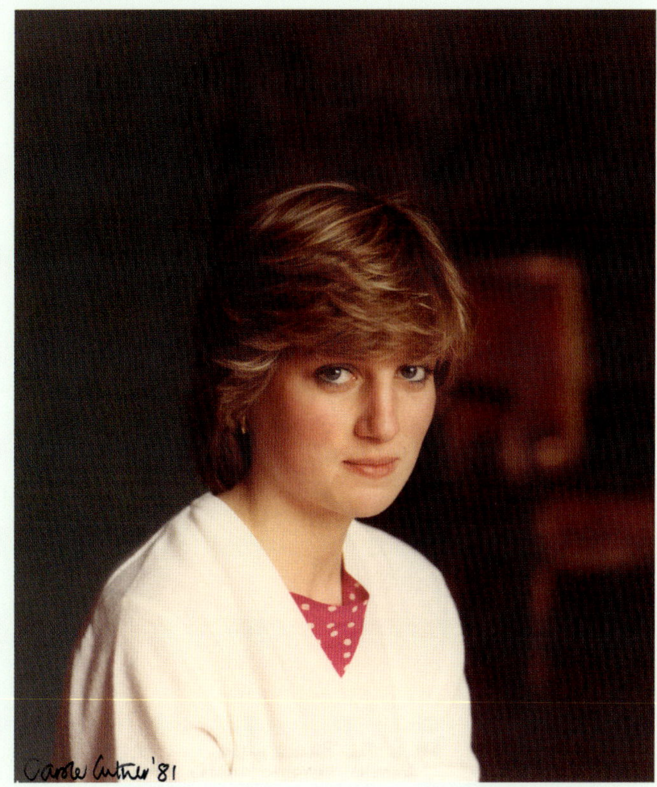

Fig.2: Diana, Princess of Wales by Carole Cutner

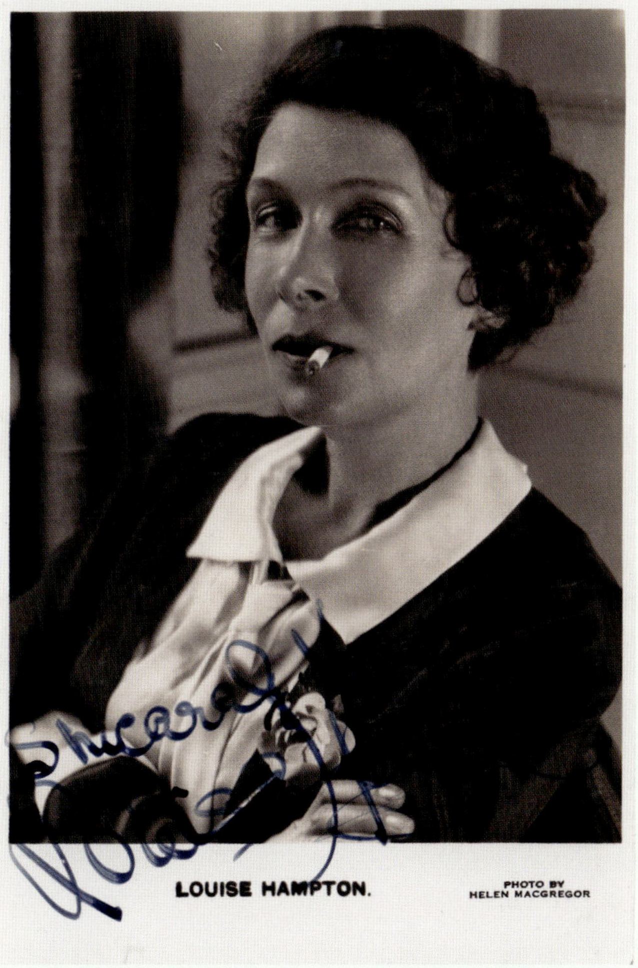

Fig.3: Louise Hampton by Helen Macgregor

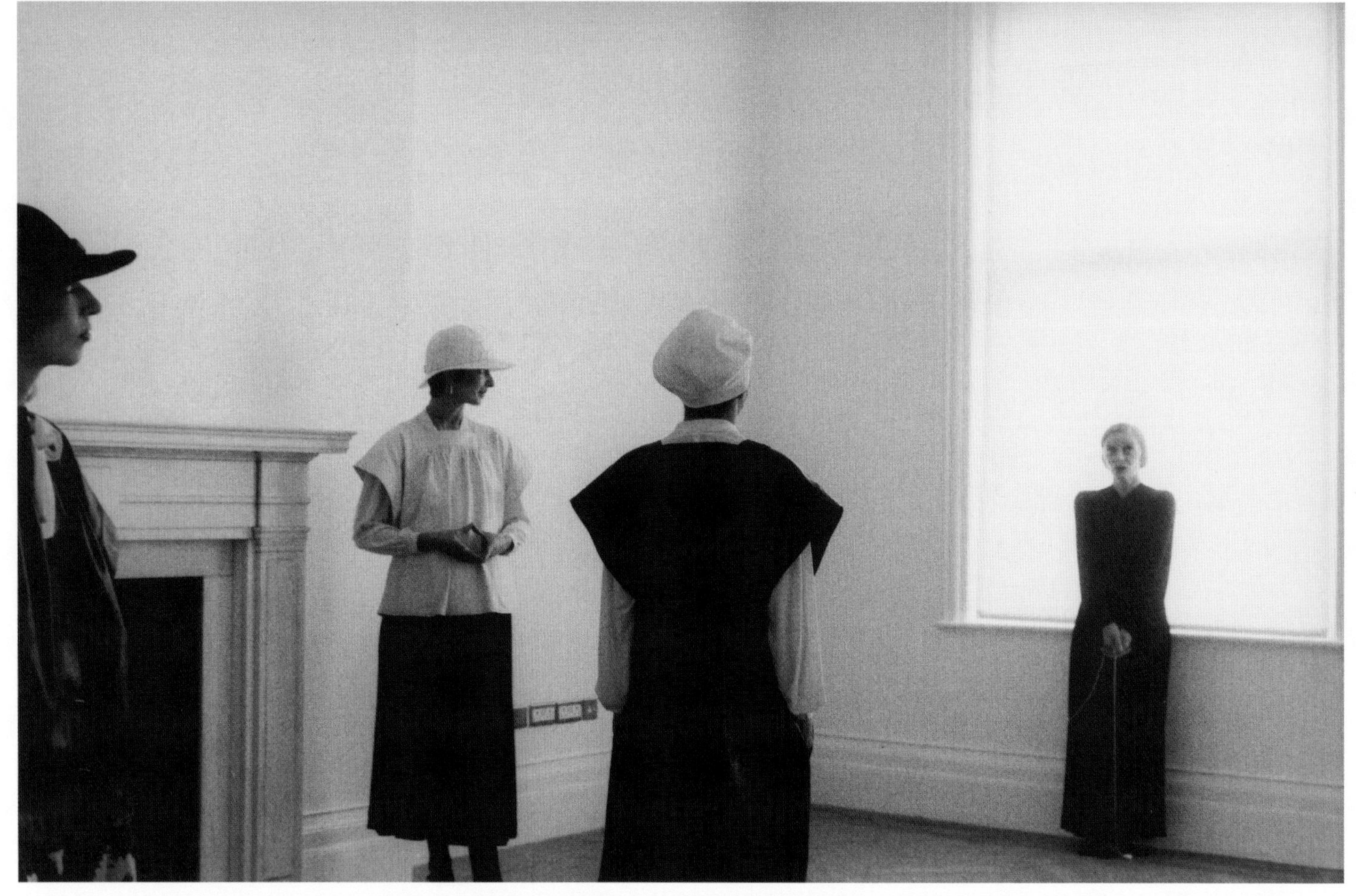

Fig.4: Jean Muir by Deborah Turbeville

sustaining long and visible careers were few and far between up to the early 2000s, but celebrity portraits made by women who ran commercial studios regularly appeared in magazines during the first half of the twentieth century. These chart a shift in the ways in which women were celebrated during these decades, from the demure femininity of Almina Victoria, the Countess of Carnarvon, by Lallie Charles in 1908, to the actress Louise Hampton photographed by Helen Macgregor as the epitome of the 'new woman' in 1930 (fig.3). The acclaimed novelist Ivy Compton-Burnett was photographed by Lee Miller for *Vogue* in 1943, in the magazine's purpose-built studio facilities in London. While portraits of leading women in the arts were frequently published at this time, Miller was one of only a small number of women photographers who regularly worked in *Vogue's* own studios.

Fashion magazines continue to be one of the most prolific commissioners of celebrity portraits from which we expect artistic and psychological complexity and the revelation of the new. When photographer Deborah Turbeville photographed designer Jean Muir for Vogue in 1975, she created a portrait in keeping with her enigmatic fashion tableaux imagery (fig.4). Turbeville's portrait does not focus on Muir's face or physicality, in fact these occupy the furthest space from the camera. Surrounded by friends wearing her designs, Muir is set apart in a dream-like world that she has both created and inhabits. She is presented as an artistic visionary, as statuary, almost votive.

If an image such as Turbeville's extends the familiar format of the famous sitter seen in their environment, Rineke Dijkstra presents Cate Blanchett in a way that refers to the

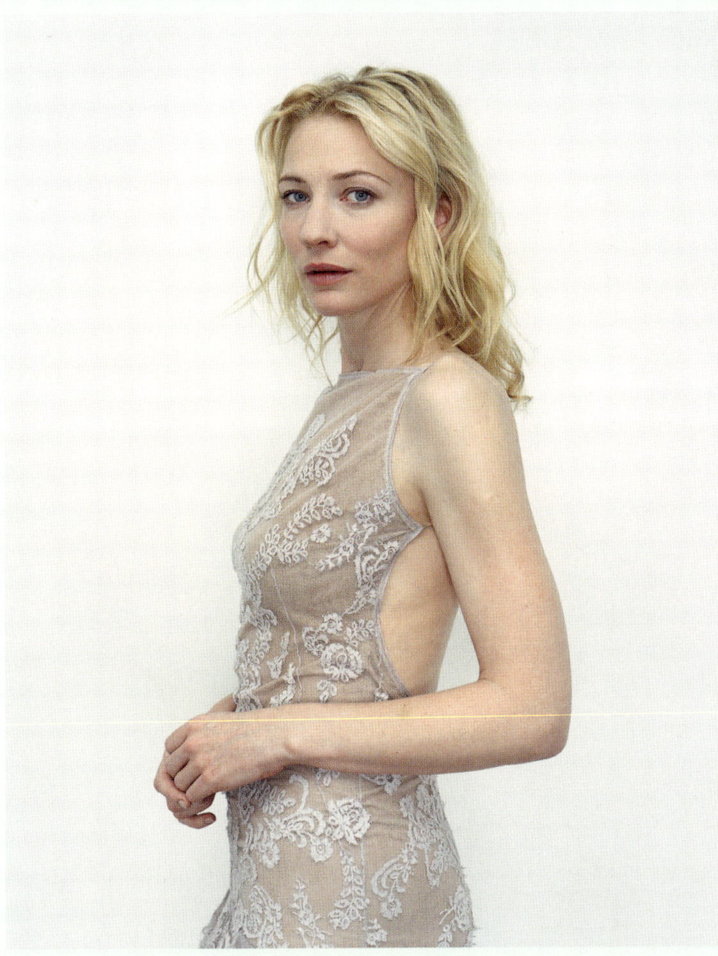

Fig.5: Cate Blanchett by Rineke Dijkstra

tradition of the studio photograph, as well as to her own aesthetic interests in portrait making (fig.5). Commissioned by the *New York Times Magazine* for the 2007 'Academy Awards Portfolio', Dijkstra's photograph marked Blanchett's nomination for best actress in the costume drama *Elizabeth: The Golden Age*. It is striking in its pared back focus on the actress in white space – an apparent neutrality of pose, her understated hair and makeup, belies Blanchett's nuanced control over every aspect of her physicality, gesture and expression in the still image. As is often the case in Dijkstra's work, the sitter – Blanchett – directly engages with the camera and photographer. In its simplicity, the commanding beauty and individuality of the actress emerge forcefully. Both subject and artist were well known at the time of publication. Dijkstra is not a fashion

or celebrity photographer per se, and the pairing of a sought-after contemporary artist with a celebrity subject has been a popular and much-emulated approach for editorial portrait commissions.

The American photographer Annie Leibovitz is probably one of the most famous portrait photographers currently working. For five decades she has made defining images of celebrities, after establishing her reputation as *Rolling Stone* magazine's Chief Photographer in the 1970s. Having a portrait taken by Leibovitz is a unique opportunity for even the biggest stars or most powerful world leaders, who may have been photographed hundreds of times before. Her long-running series of fold-out covers for *Vanity Fair* magazine, shot from 1995, are particularly high profile and eagerly awaited on the news-stands. Leibovitz photographed the British musician Adele in 2015 for the cover of March 2016's British *Vogue* (fig.6). Taken at the historic London hotel Claridge's, Adele appears as both maker and muse. With one hand intuitively placed on the keys, she is observed in profile – listening, introspective, connected to her instrument and absorbed in creative thought. Though Leibovitz is often associated with the use of lavish sets and props to create narrative storytelling in her celebrity portraits, there is an intimacy in this image that is also a hallmark of her work. Leibovitz subverts codes of gender representation in her iconic double portrait of Yoko Ono and John Lennon (fig.7). Here it is Lennon, nude, exposed, defenceless and child-like who surrenders himself to Ono. The artist had been sent to photograph the couple by *Rolling Stone* magazine; only hours after the sitting Lennon had been shot dead. The image is one of the most famous photographs of the twentieth century.

Indeed, many portraits in the National Portrait Gallery Collection made by women are not necessarily what you would expect from

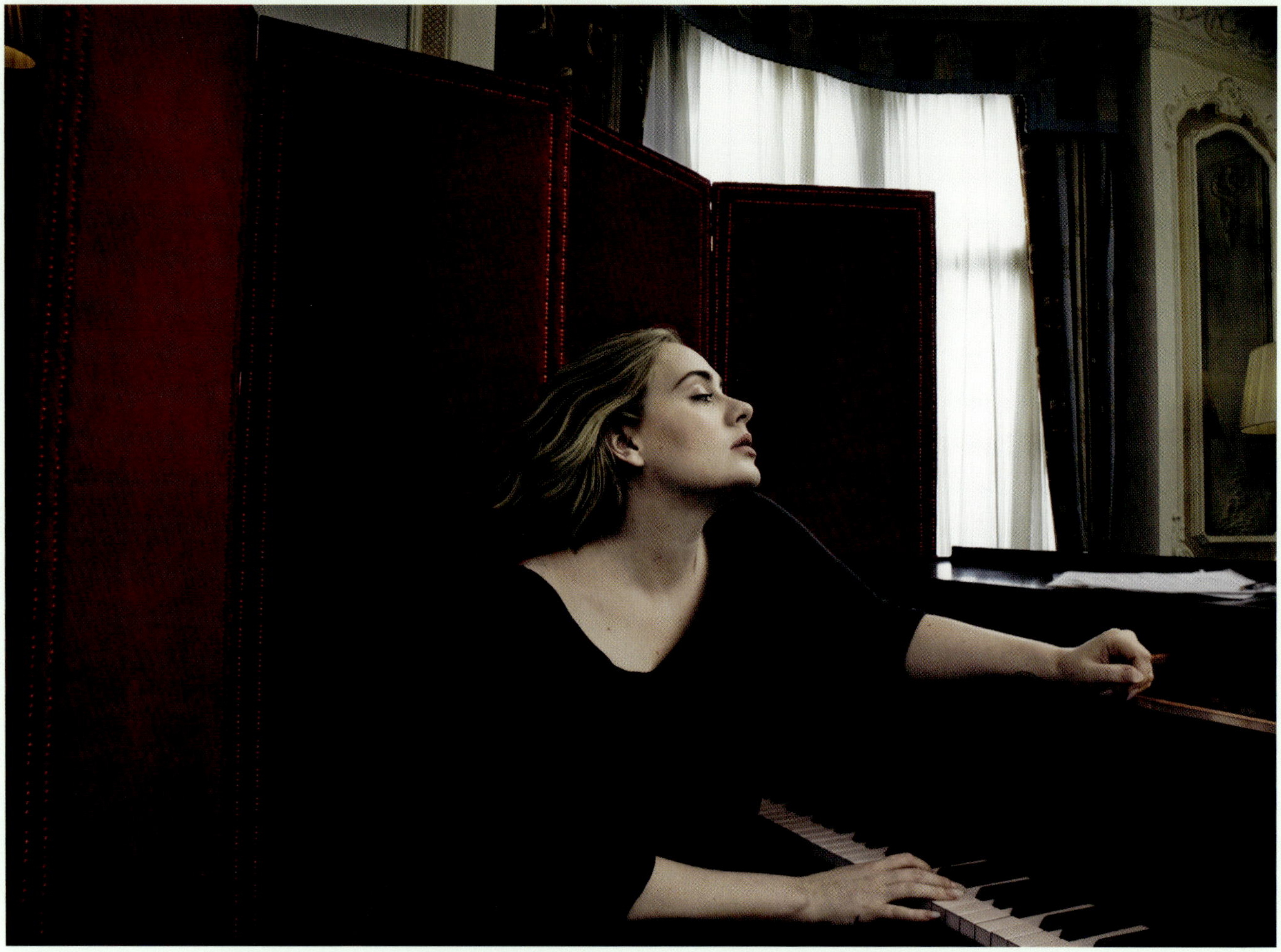

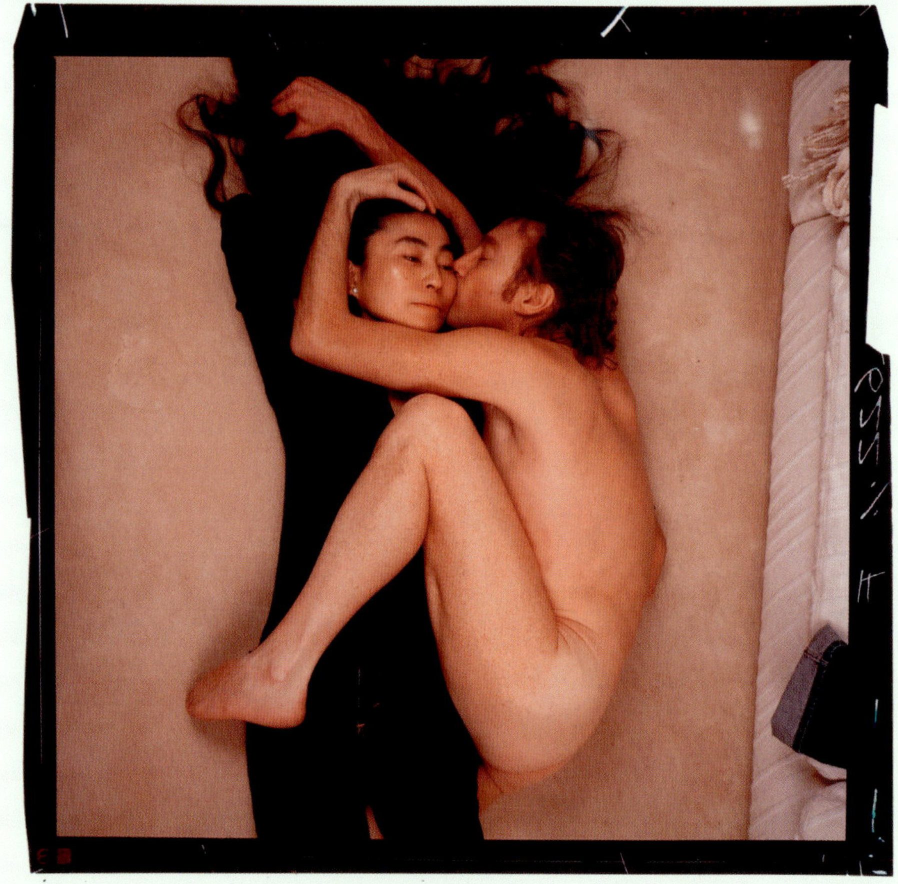

Fig.6: Adele, London by Annie Leibovitz

Fig.7: Yoko Ono and John Lennon by Annie Leibovitz

a celebrity photograph and revel in intimacy
and interiority rather than outward
appearance. In a nude portrait of Sir Paul
McCartney with his new daughter Mary,
photographer Linda McCartney switches
the traditional representation of the 'Mother
(Madonna) and Child', in this case father and
daughter both vulnerable and expectant.
In *David*, a celebrity portrait but also a
commission instigated by the National Portrait
Gallery, Sam Taylor Johnson filmed footballer
David Beckham in a single take sleeping in
a hotel in Madrid. Watching a lover sleep
has inspired poets and artists for centuries,
enticing physical desire and metaphysical
contemplation, yet historically it is most often
women who are observed and represented.
Beckham and Johnson were not romantically
involved and though Beckham is a physically
powerful athlete and a pop culture icon,
Taylor Johnson evokes a gentle and beautiful
masculine muse.

Corinne Day's portrait of Kate Moss
expresses the friendship and intimacy between
two women (fig.8). Moss is one of the most
famous models of all time, yet Day has chosen
to represent her without reference to this
fashion context. Of making the photograph
Day said: 'I suggested to Kate that we have
a conversation about a serious subject.
The subject she chose to talk about revealed
her true feelings and in turn defined her
character.' The commission is a portrait
of Moss in dialogue and acknowledges the
idea of exchange and expression as being
important to women's relationships. When
the National Portrait Gallery commissioned
the work, Day and Moss had been friends for
decades. That Day is frequently credited
with first discovering Moss makes the pairing
even more engaging. The portrait, which is
made up of a series of images, suggests that
Moss is a multi-faceted, thinking person first,
and a public figure or face second.

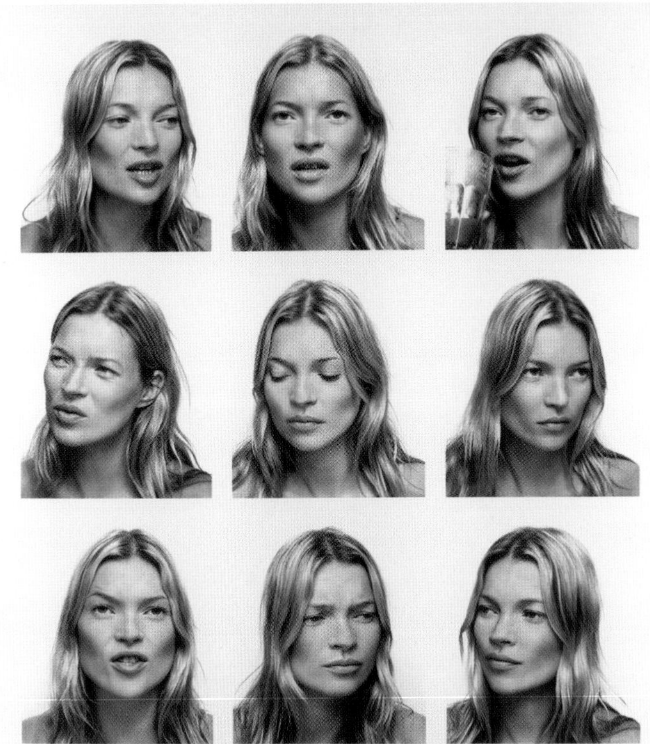

Fig.8: Kate Moss by Corinne Day

Music photography was a popular
phenomenon in the last decades of the
twentieth century when rock, pop and other
forms of youth music and style culture
flourished. A constant stream of the latest
portraits of singers and bands were in demand
for magazines and fanzines, album sleeves,
billboards and posters across the world,
supporting a rising field of photographic
talent. The 1970s and 1980s were a period in
which the industry was particularly dominated
by male photographers, but it was also
the time British documentary photographer
Janette Beckman began work. Based in
London, her first commissions were for
Sounds, an important music weekly, before
working for *Melody Maker* and *The Face*.
In 1982 she relocated to New York and became
one of the most significant women chronicling
the hip hop scene. The National Portrait
Gallery has recently acquired several works
by Beckman from the early 1980s when she
was active in England. Her works of this
period are typically black and white portraits

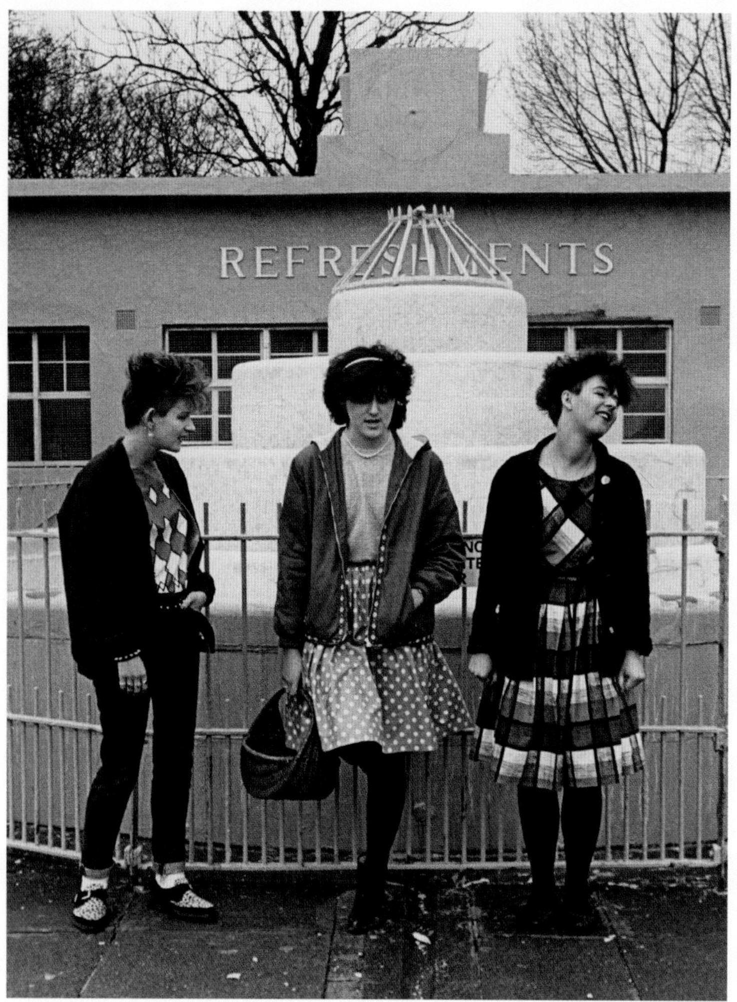

Fig.9: Marine Girls by Janette Beckman

made on location. For example, she shot the all-girl group Marine Girls at Tooting Bec Lido in west London for the cover of *Melody Maker* (fig.9). Beckman chose the location for a light-hearted reference to water given in the band's name. She explained: 'At the time I was living in Streatham and we used to spend our summers there at the pool. I loved that crazy fountain that looked like a giant cake, the pool and changing rooms had a kind of 1950's feel that seemed to work with the Marine Girls style.'

Today the accessibility of digital photography and sharing platforms means that almost anyone with a mobile phone and an internet connection can be a celebrity – perhaps these days for 15 seconds rather than '15 minutes', as Andy Warhol famously quipped. Yet as the Collection of the National Portrait Gallery shows, there is an undeniably important history of celebrity portraiture that exists outside of the digital or social media realm, and women photographers have been stars of this genre in their own right.

Fig.1
Marie Stillman (1844–1927)
By Julia Margaret Cameron, 1868
Albumen cabinet card, 133 × 99mm
National Portrait Gallery, London, x18051

Fig.2
Diana, Princess of Wales (1961–1997)
By Carole Cutner, July 1981
Resin print, 304 × 254mm
National Portrait Gallery, London, x22210

Fig.3
Louise Hampton (*c.*1880–1954)
By Helen Macgregor, 1930s
Gelatin silver postcard, 136 × 89mm
National Portrait Gallery, London, x198117

Fig.4
Jean Muir (1928–1995) and three unknown models
By Deborah Turbeville, 1975
Gelatin silver print, 356 × 508mm
National Portrait Gallery, London, P2033

Fig.5
Cate Blanchett (b.1969)
By Rineke Dijkstra, 2007
Chromogenic print, 1235 × 995mm
National Portrait Gallery, London, P2073

Fig.6
'Adele, London' (b.1988)
By Annie Leibovitz, 2015
Pigment print, 508 × 660mm
National Portrait Gallery, London, P2096

Fig.7
Yoko Ono (b.1933) and John Lennon (1940–1980)
By Annie Leibovitz, 1980
Chromogenic print, 327 × 327mm
National Portrait Gallery, London, P628

Fig.8
Kate Moss (b.1974)
By Corinne Day, 2006
Gelatin silver print, 1510 × 1305mm
National Portrait Gallery, London, P1274

Fig.9
Marine Girls
By Janette Beckman, 1982
Gelatin silver print, 455 × 330mm
National Portrait Gallery, London, x201359

Mercedes Gleitze

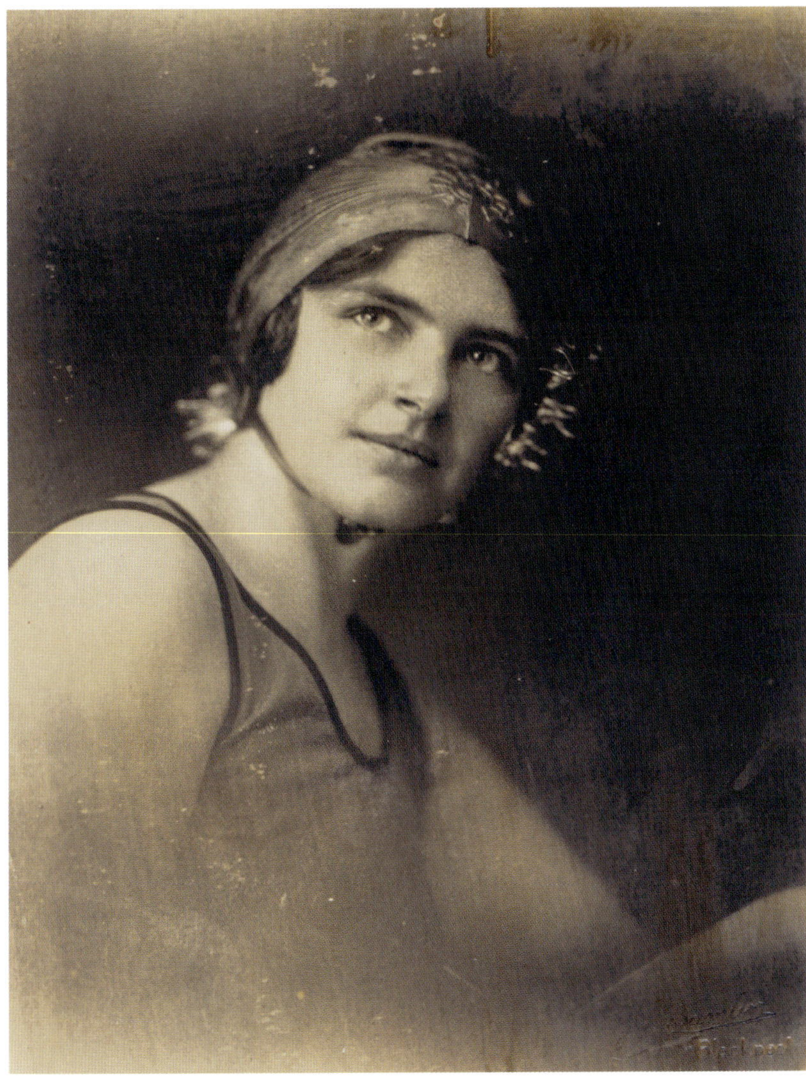

Cheered on by crowds, entertained
with gramophone records and fuelled
with beef tea, coffee, honey, toast and
sweets, Mercedes Gleitze set a new
swimming endurance record on 20
May 1933 of 47 hours at the Worthing
Corporation Baths. It was Gleitze's 27th
swim of this kind, steadily increasing
her time from 26 hours in front of
fee-paying audiences at public baths
around the United Kingdom, Ireland,
New Zealand, Australia and South
Africa. Since her first attempt to cross
the Channel in 1922, Gleitze's self-led
career in endurance and open-water
swimming had taken her around
the world and made her a celebrity,
chronicled closely by the press.

Born just half a mile from the
Brighton coast, Gleitze worked as
a typist in Westminster during her
early twenties and spent her spare
time swimming in the River Thames.
The inter-war period had seen a rise
in competitive attempts to swim the
Channel, which until 1923 had only
been achieved twice and never by
a woman. Funding her training and
the crew needed for the crossing with
savings from her day job, Gleitze
completed several long-distance feats
in between her ten Channel attempts,
including setting the British Ladies'
Record while swimming over 43
kilometres (27 miles) along the Thames
between Putney and Silvertown in 1923.
With each swim she faced numerous
challenges, including aching limbs,
strong tides, cold temperatures,
jellyfish stings and even an attack of
flies and porpoises. She achieved her
ultimate goal on 7 October 1927 as
the first British woman to swim the
Channel, completing this feat in a time
of 15 hours 15 minutes. The following
year, Gleitze also became the first
person to swim the Straits of Gibraltar.

Though another Channel
attempt was planned, the 1933 swim
in Worthing was Gleitze's last public
challenge. Family life took over
following the birth of her first child
seven months earlier. She also began
concentrating her energies, and the
money she had earned through prize
winnings, endurance events and
sales of her photographic portrait
postcards, on setting up the Mercedes
Gleitze Homes for Destitute Men
and Women. Motivated by her own
humble beginnings and a desire to
alleviate poverty, in that same year
she converted a property in Leicester
into flats to temporarily house
unemployed and homeless families.
While the homes were destroyed
during enemy action in 1940, Gleitze's
trust fund survives as the Mercedes
Gleitze Relief in Need Charity, ensuring
the continuation of her charitable
ambitions. CN

Mercedes Gleitze (1900–1981)
By J.P. Bamber Studios of Blackpool, 1928
Sepia-toned gelatin silver print, 146 × 108mm
National Portrait Gallery, London, P872

P.L. Travers

Mary Poppins is both a joy and a curse to me as a writer.[15]

Born in Australia as Helen Lyndon Goff, Pamela Lyndon Travers had her own newspaper column and published poetry before moving to London in 1924 to advance her writing career. Deciding on the pen name P.L. Travers, in 1934 she published *Mary Poppins*, her fictional tale of an extraordinary nanny blowing in on the east wind with her parrot-headed umbrella and magical carpet bag to care for the Banks children. Reflecting her interest in fairy tales, mythology and mysticism, it detailed the characters' fantastical adventures, including a tea party on a ceiling and birthday celebrations hosted by animals at the zoo. The book was an immediate success and the first of seven sequels appeared the following year.

Travers spent the duration of the Second World War within the safety of the US, and it was around this time that the animator Walt Disney made the first of many attempts to acquire the rights for a film adaptation of the popular book. Reluctant to see *Mary Poppins* turned into a cartoon, Travers resisted Disney's attempts over a period of nearly 20 years. Work on the film eventually began after they settled on a live-action format and final script approval for Travers, but she soon found herself frustrated with plans to convert her story into a musical. Nonetheless, the film was completed and released in 1964, starring Julie Andrews as the title character and incorporating animated elements. Travers remained deeply upset by the apparent trivialisation of her book and the elimination of its mythological elements, but it was loved by critics and the public alike. The film gained five Academy Awards from its 13 nominations and brought Travers financial security and renewed interest in her work.

Travers published further novels and essays, and returned to the US during the 1960s and 1970s as a writer-in-residence and lecturer at several prestigious American colleges. Having pursued a number of spiritual movements throughout her life, she edited *Parabola: The Magazine of Myth and Tradition* from 1976 until her death. Myths and fairy tales recurred throughout her later works, including in her novel *Friend Monkey* (1971), based on a Hindu story.

With Mary Poppins established as a classic character of children's literature and film, Travers kept adding to the book series until 1988. The sources for her inspiration have continued to occupy subsequent generations, with Travers adding to the mystery: 'I never for one moment believed that I invented [Mary Poppins]. Perhaps she invented me.' CN

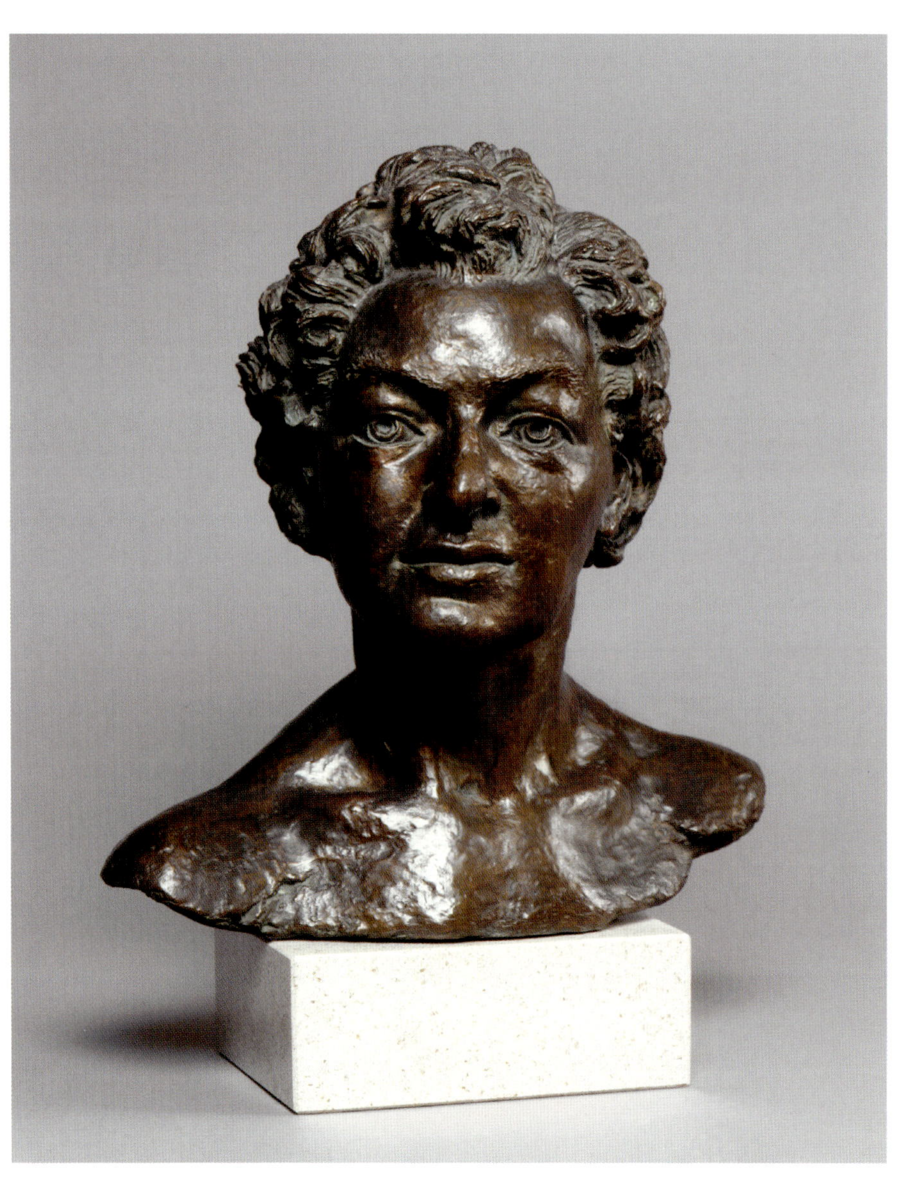

Pamela Lyndon ('P.L.') Travers (1899–1996)
By Gertrude Hermes, *c*.1942
Bronze bust, 460 × 350mm
National Portrait Gallery, London, 5888

Myfanwy Piper

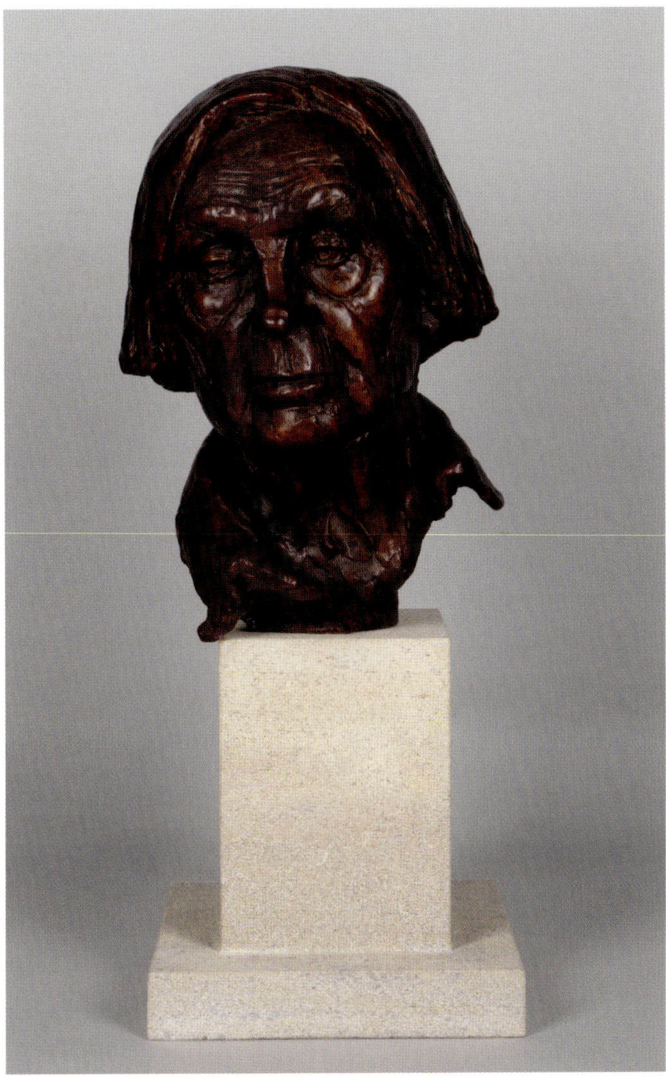

This momentous conversation between French abstract artist Jean Hélion and art historian Myfanwy Piper led to the establishment of *Axis*, a quarterly art magazine. At the time, Paris (where Piper had met Hélion) was still considered the epicentre of modern art. By setting up a magazine focusing on British art, Piper was shifting the axis of influence and consolidating England's role in the dissemination of avant-garde abstract art.

When *Axis: A Quarterly Review of Contemporary 'Abstract' Painting & Sculpture* was announced in January 1935 a healthy audience awaited its publication with great anticipation. This was especially the case for artists who had chosen to work in an abstract idiom, including Ben Nicholson and Barbara Hepworth. The new periodical counted on Myfanwy's editorial lead, while her husband, John Piper, was in charge of the strikingly modern layout. He would also contribute articles and be the subject of other writings during the magazine's short-lived tenure, but it was Myfanwy who firmly held the reins of the project. *Axis* ran its last issue in 1937, by which point the emphasis on abstraction had subsided, giving way to surrealism.

While *Axis* heralded a new age for British and international abstract art, Piper remained ambivalent towards pure abstraction. She would go on to reveal the range of her artistic interests in *The Painter's Object,* an edited book published in 1937 bringing together a mix of articles on abstract and figurative art, as well as surrealism. Piper felt that for 'art to have any importance it must be intimately related to the life of its own time'. This meant that style and form had to adapt to changing circumstances. As an art historian, Piper was also involved in the *Penguin Modern Painters* series and authored a monograph on painter Frances Hodgkins, published in 1948.

In 1952, Piper's career evolved in a new direction. Composer, conductor and pianist Benjamin Britten asked her to write the libretto for his opera *The Turn of the Screw* – based on Henry James's novella of 1898. This marked the start of a creative partnership, with Britten and Piper collaborating on two subsequent operas, *Owen Wingrave* (1970) and *Death in Venice* (1973). For Britten, the relationship between words and music was of primary importance and he encouraged Piper to carefully distil her writing, on the assumption that music would colour her words, bringing them to life. While Piper turned her hand to a variety of literary tasks, she also supported her husband with her 'acute intelligence', as John himself stated late in his life. FF

Myfanwy Piper (1911–1997)
By Clive Duncan, 2022, based on
a portrait made from life in 1995
Bronze head, 530 × 204mm
National Portrait Gallery, London, 7136

Mary Cartwright

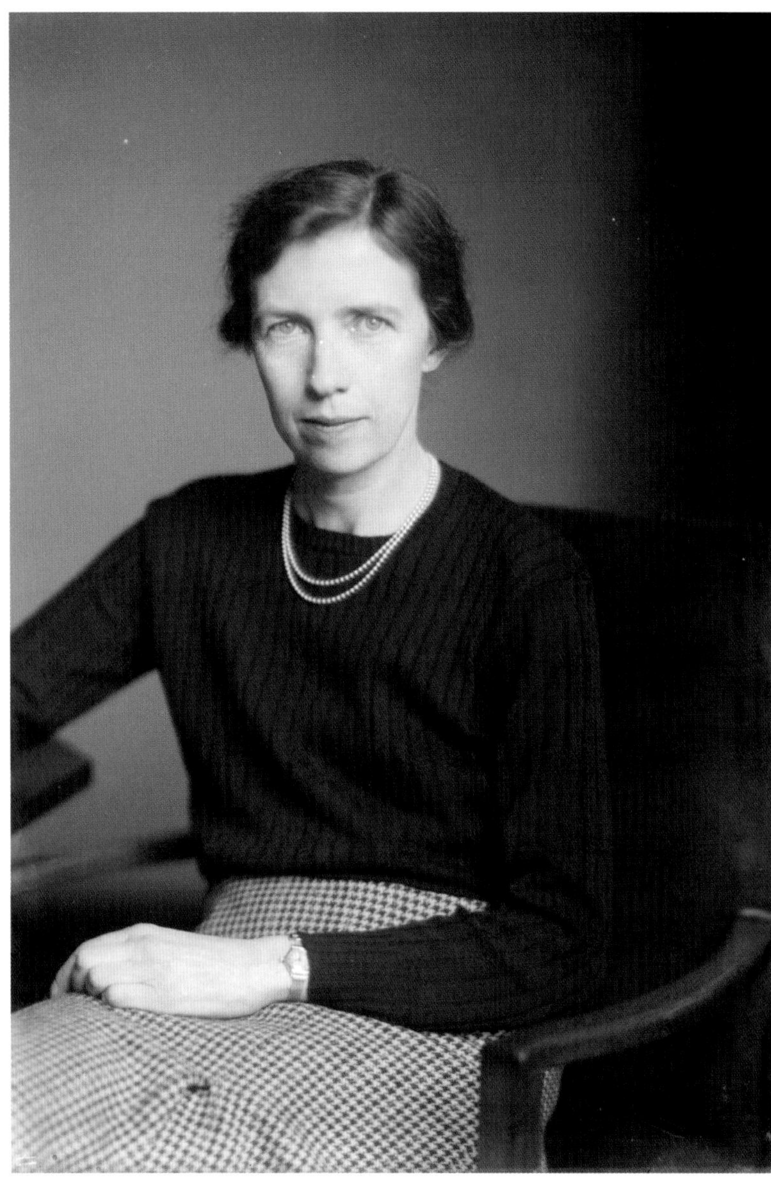

Maths genius Mary Cartwright was one of the early founders of what would later be known as chaos theory. In 1936, she became Director of Studies in mathematics at Girton College, Cambridge, establishing a long association with the institution. A former student there, Dr Kay Barker, fondly remembered her mentor:

Those of us whose studies she directed would probably all wish to say that she was a conscientious supervisor, but that to many of us she was a somewhat awe-inspiring figure. We knew of her as an eminent mathematician and this, together with her shyness and lack of small talk, made her supervision period seem rather daunting. Glimpses of her sense of humour did, however, indicate that behind this serious, scholarly facade was a gentle and kindly human being.

Cartwright was one of the first women to have a professional academic career. Her many achievements include being the first female mathematician elected to the Royal Society in 1947 and the first woman to receive the Society's Sylvester Medal (1964). She was Mistress of Girton from 1949 until 1968, and President of the London Mathematical Society from 1961 to 1963. In 1968 she received the Society's highest honour, the De Morgan Medal, and in 1969 she was made a Dame.

Born in Northamptonshire, Cartwright studied mathematics at St Hugh's College, Oxford, and became the first woman to complete the course, getting a first-class degree in 1923. After a few years as a schoolteacher she returned to academia, studying at Oxford under the leading mathematician G.H. Hardy. She moved to Cambridge in 1930, becoming a research fellow at Girton, which later led to her appointment as Director of Studies.

During the Second World War, Cartwright worked alongside Professor J.E. Littlewood on the mathematical problems that came up in radar and discovered some of the first signs of the complex behaviour known as the 'butterfly effect', which contributed to the wartime defence of Britain against enemy air attack. Although this is widely recognised as the birth of a new branch of mathematics, the significance of this work was overlooked for more than 20 years.

While Mistress at Girton, she continued her lecturing and research and served on many university committees. Cartwright wrote over 90 articles, making important contributions to the theory of functions and differential equations. GA

Mary Cartwright (1900–1998)
By Walter Stoneman, May 1947
Half-plate glass negative
National Portrait Gallery, London, x188708

Nancy Cunard

It is unthinkable for any honest intellectual to be profascist, as it is degenerate to be for Franco, the assassin of the Spanish and Arab people. Spain is not 'politics', but life; its immediate future will affect every human who has a sense of what life and its facts mean, who has respect for himself and humanity. Above all others, the writer, the intellectual, must take sides. His place is with the people against fascism; his duty, to protest against the present degeneration of the democracies.

With these strong words, poet, political activist and journalist Nancy Cunard professed her allegiance to the Spanish people and the republican government in their struggle against General Franco's rebel armies. From the beginning, the Spanish Civil War was of enormous importance to many people outside of Spain itself. It was perceived as a trial in the clash between democratic and dictatorial rule that was raging across Europe. From her first visit in 1936, until the spring of 1939, Cunard wrote impassioned reports from Spain, many of which were published in Sylvia Pankhurst's paper, *New Times*, and the *Manchester Guardian*. Her articles urged Britain, France and the US to intervene in light of Italy and Germany's support for Franco.

In 1937 she instigated a brilliant political strategy addressed to 'Writers and Poets of England, Scotland, Ireland and Wales' and supported by Louis Aragon, W.H. Auden, Pablo Neruda and Stephen Spender, amongst others. In a huge broadsheet, printed in red and black and sent to all the writers and poets that Cunard could think of, she asked: 'Are you for, or against, the legal government and the People of Republican Spain? Are you for, or against, Franco and Fascism? For it is impossible any longer to take no side.' While the vast majority swore their allegiance to the People of Republican Spain, a small minority sided with Franco. The results were published by the *Left Review* as 'Authors Take Sides on the Spanish War'.

Cunard was an eccentric rebel. Born into wealth, she defied social conventions to take up a lifelong battle against social injustice. An icon of the jazz age, she was known for her ravishing looks and seductive powers, which led to romances with many of the great writers of the era. Inspired by her love for the black American jazz pianist Henry Crowder – whom she met in 1927 – Cunard embarked on a mammoth book project in recognition of African culture and the fight for racial justice. FF

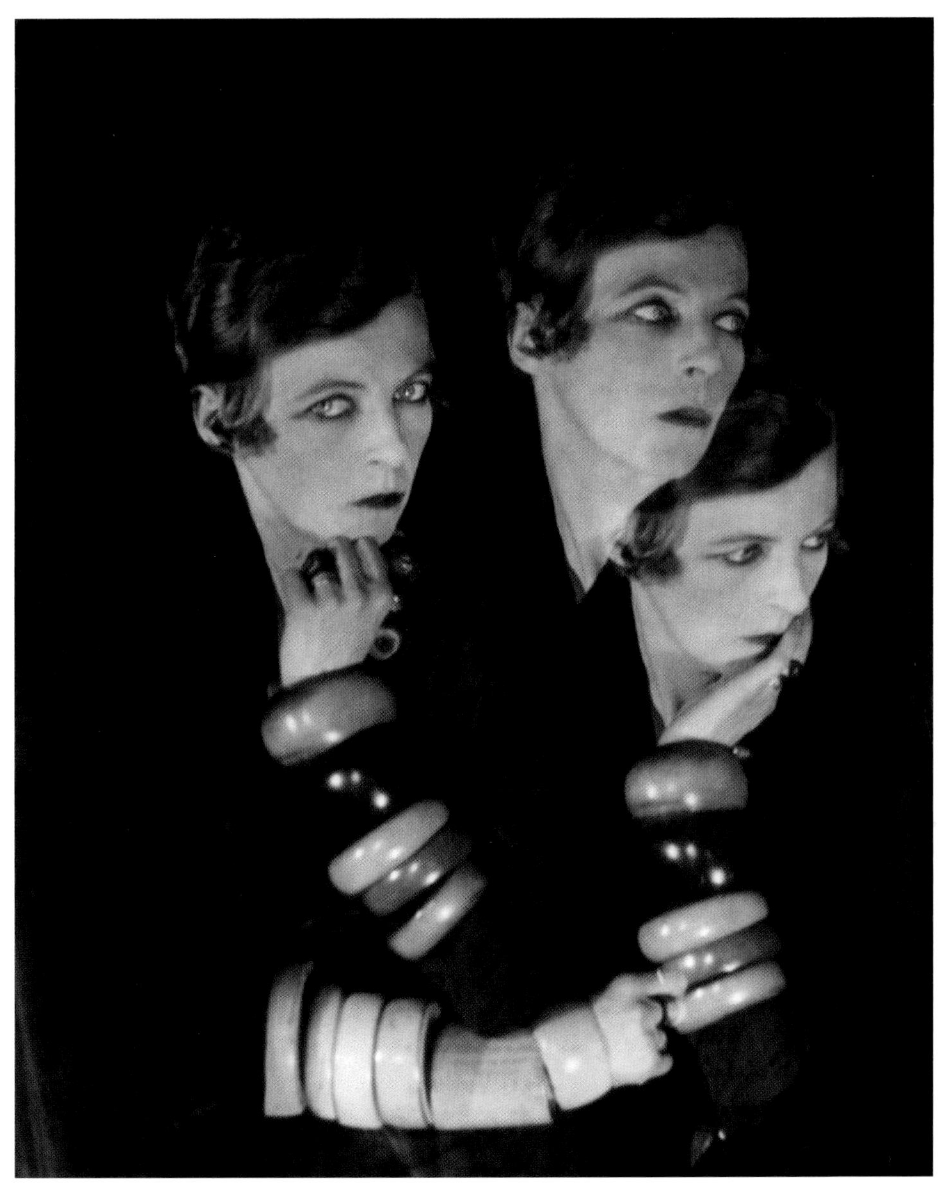

Nancy Cunard (1896–1965)
By Cecil Beaton, 1929
Gelatin silver print, 241 × 188mm
National Portrait Gallery, London x40077

1938 Adelaide Hall

How do you spell success – if you're a variety artist? The answer is with two 'P's, to be Pleasing and to possess Personality. Adelaide Hall … is a definite success. That she Pleases can be seen by the expressions on the faces of her audience, and heard by the applause when she takes her final curtain. That she has Personality is all too obvious directly [when] she smiles.[16]

This *Eastbourne Chronicle* reviewer's enthusiasm following Adelaide Hall's performances in the town in 1946 indicates the great affection with which British audiences received her. A Brooklyn-born singer and cabaret performer, Hall moved to Britain in 1938 with her husband and manager, Bert Hicks, to perform in *The Sun Never Sets* at London's Drury Lane Theatre. Her popularity meant she stayed and in the years after, she charmed audiences with her voice, beauty, elegance and stage presence, as captured in this publicity photograph. By 1941 Hall was Britain's highest paid woman entertainer and two years later she became the first black artist to gain a long-term BBC contract.

Hall's career had begun in the US in the all-black Broadway hit musical revue *Shuffle Along* (1921), widely credited for initiating the Harlem Renaissance. She performed at the legendary Cotton Club and travelled to Europe with shows such as *Blackbirds of 1928*. Her collaboration with Duke Ellington on the song 'Creole Love Call' (1927) – where she used her voice like an instrument in her wordless counter-melody, also known as scat-singing – confirmed her place as a jazz innovator, although her contribution has not always been recognised.

As successful nightclub owners previously in Harlem and Paris, Hall and Hicks took over the Florida Club in Mayfair when they relocated to London. Following its destruction during the Blitz, Hall became a staple performer

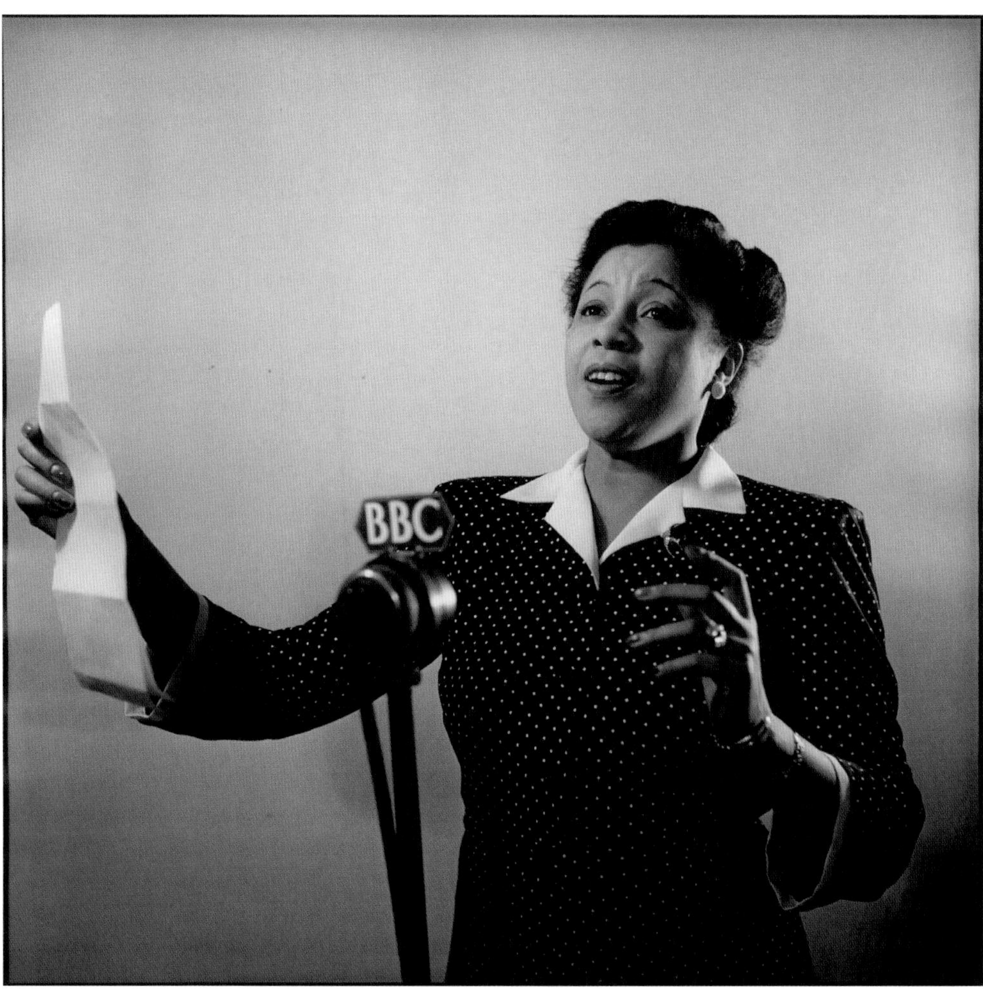

in efforts to boost the country's morale during the Second World War through popular music. She toured Britain's music-halls – bravely singing 54 songs to a trapped audience during an air raid at one show in Lewisham, entertained troops in the United Kingdom and abroad, and hosted her own BBC Radio series, *Wrapped in Velvet*, in 1943, with songs such as 'As Time Goes By' (1943) becoming wartime favourites.

After the war, Hall's performances for the BBC included the live television recording *Variety in Sepia* (1947), dedicated to black talent. The couple opened another club, the Calypso, on London's Regent Street, where Hall is said to have taught the future Queen Elizabeth II how to dance the Charleston, and she made occasional appearances in cabaret and on the West End stage.

The 1980s brought renewed interest in Hall's career and her involvement in the Harlem Renaissance, and she continued to perform and record into her nineties. With material released over eight consecutive decades, she became one of the world's most enduring artists. CN

Adelaide Hall (1901–1993)
By a BBC photographer, 18 August 1945
Modern gelatin silver print, 380 × 377mm
National Portrait Gallery, London, x128772

Margot Fonteyn

Prima ballerina Margot Fonteyn was a remarkable dancer with a career spanning 45 years. A cultural icon, she was celebrated for her grace, lyricism and musicality. According to dance critic John Percival she was more than simply the greatest British dancer, 'she summed up the whole art of ballet, and made its artistry so expressive that to see her was to love her'.

Fonteyn started ballet lessons at the age of four in Ealing with dance teacher Grace Bosustow. By the time she was eight, the family had moved to Shanghai, China, where she continued her training under the former Bolshoi dancer George Goncharow. In 1933, Fonteyn and her mother returned to London where she attended Ninette de Valois' Vic-Wells Ballet School (later Sadler's Wells Ballet and The Royal Ballet). Tenacious and graceful, Fonteyn stood out in class and it is said that she became de Valois' favourite pupil.

Her mother remembers when they first caught a bus to the Vic-Wells Ballet School in Islington and presented themselves at the stage door:

I had not anticipated Peggy being asked to do some dance steps so we had not

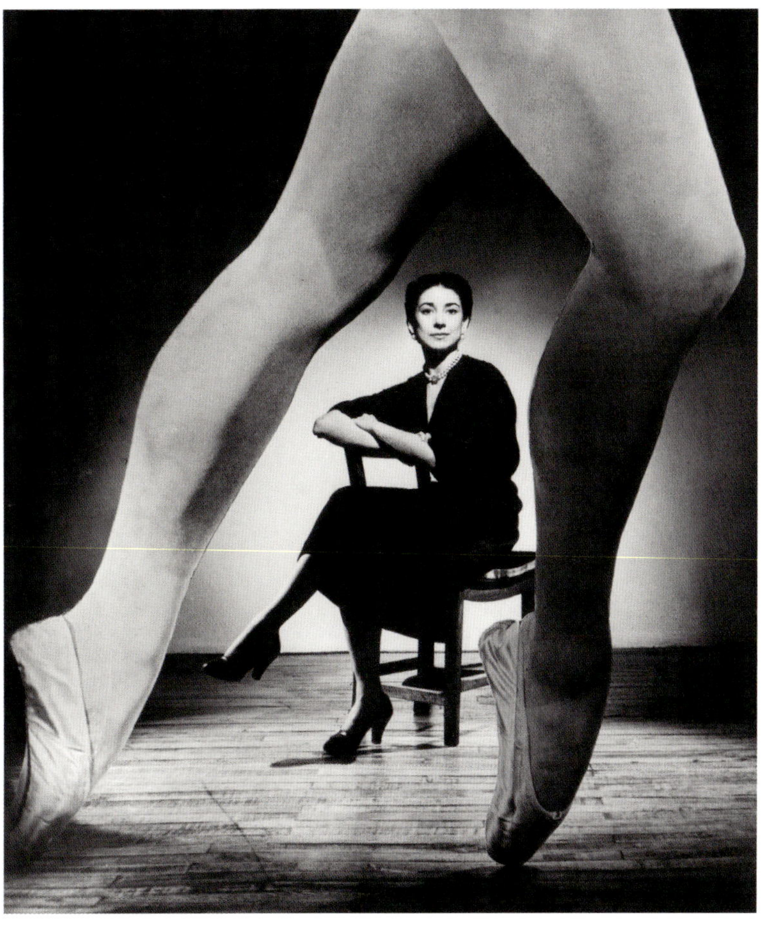

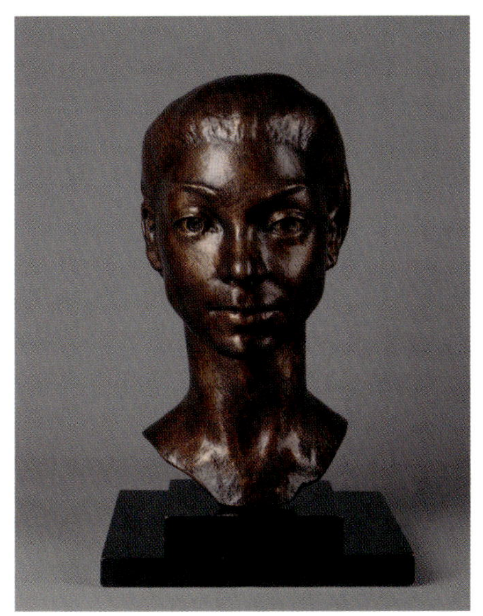

brought along any practice clothes or shoes. Miss [Ursula] Moreton suggested that Peggy take off her street shoes and her dress and stand in first position at the barre.

Thus it was that immaculate Fonteyn was accepted into the famed dance school – in her petticoat.

Born Margaret Hookham, in Reigate, Surrey, 'Peggy' took the stage name of Margot Fonteyn, adapting the surname of her Brazilian grandfather, Fontes, early in her career. She made her stage debut aged just 15 and two years later won ecstatic reviews for her first *Giselle*, rising quickly and becoming the ballet company's principal dancer in 1939. Her effortless artistry in translating music into movement was unique. That same year, she made her debut as Aurora in *The Sleeping Beauty*, a role that would become closely associated with her. During the Second World War, the dancers of the Royal Ballet toured to boost the morale of the nation, with Fonteyn performing tirelessly and growing ever more confident as an artist. Frederick Ashton, the lead choreographer of the company and with whom Fonteyn established a strong rapport, created moving ballets for her. They became an inspiration for each other and together they devised many roles that are still reprised today. Fonteyn was made a Dame in 1956. Late in her already distinguished career, her dance partnership with Rudolf Nureyev was hailed as one of her greatest, dazzling audiences with their chemistry. GA

Margot Fonteyn (1919–1991)
By Maurice Lambert, 1956
Bronze bust, 400 × 170mm
National Portrait Gallery, London, 6033

Margot Fonteyn
By Angus McBean, 1951
Gelatin silver print, 244 × 198mm
National Portrait Gallery, London, P894

1940   Freya Stark

Described by *The Times* as 'the last of the Romantic travellers', Freya Stark was a woman who found in intrepid wandering a professional calling as well as a form of personal propaganda. Audacious in her solo adventures in little-known regions of the Middle East, and adept at capturing these in witty writings, Stark steadfastly fashioned herself as a woman who relished danger in the pursuit of knowledge.

In 1940, the British Foreign Office called on Stark's knowledge of the Middle Eastern region and fluency in Arabic to help with anti-Axis propaganda in hostile northern Yemen. It was a very delicate mission and as Stark later recalled:

The plan was particularly to smuggle in, and to show, a portable cinema – a religiously forbidden object which could at that time make some noticeable difference to opinion. At the beginning of February, in a lorry with cook, servant, three men, and the cinema unmentioned among my suitcases, I made the six-day journey from Aden.

The perilous journey that lay ahead of Stark and her comrades proved successful and thanks to her extensive network – which stretched from Cairo to Baghdad – she averted sabotage actions against the Allies on the Eastern Front. A remarkable achievement for a woman who had been propelled into a life of adventure almost by chance.

A trained historian, Stark took Arabic lessons in order to become a governess in the Middle East. It was an extended stay in Lebanon in 1927 that set her on a different path; her thirst for adventure almost caused an international incident when she crossed a military cordon in the mountains of Lebanon. A few years later, she became ill while searching for a buried Arabian city and had to be airlifted to the nearest hospital by the Royal Air Force.

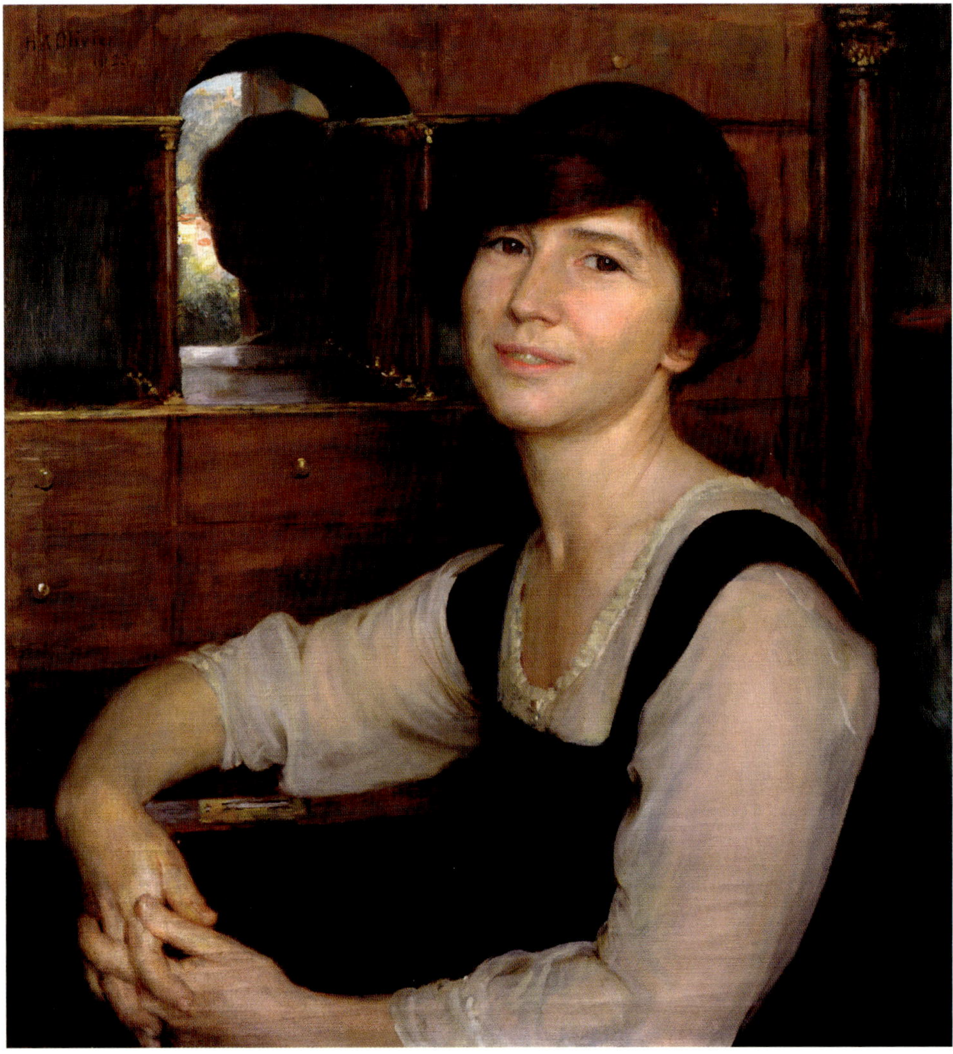

She returned a celebrity and her book, *The Southern Gates of Arabia* (1936), received great praise.

Despite receiving accolades – including a DBE in 1972 – as a pioneering traveller, and being celebrated for her writing (for Stark the most coveted of achievements), she led a complex life. She was afflicted with periodic illnesses, fell victim to an unrequited love and had a penchant for extravagant expenditure that she could not always sustain. Stark wrote 30 books on her adventures and countless letters capturing the nuances of Middle Eastern societies. Enthralled by adventure, Stark lamented that 'One life is an absurdly small allowance.' She lived hers with intrepidness, curiosity and determination to the last. FF

Freya Stark (1893–1993)
By Herbert Olivier, 1923
Oil on canvas, 619 × 555mm
National Portrait Gallery, London, 5465

Christine Granville

The Special Operations Executive (SOE) was formed secretly by the British government in 1940 to 'coordinate, inspire, control and assist the nationals of the oppressed countries'. During the Second World War, a significant number of women worked as SOE agents, trained to conduct espionage, sabotage and reconnaissance and to endure harsh interrogation. Christine Granville was the first woman agent recruited by the SOE and the nation's longest serving wartime woman spy, also becoming the most highly decorated.

Born Krystyna Skarbek in Warsaw, she is celebrated for her brave activities on secret missions in Nazi-occupied Poland and France. According to British Secret Service records, Skarbek was described as 'a flaming Polish patriot, expert skier and great adventuress', and 'absolutely fearless'. Determined to help Poland in their fight against the Nazis, Skarbek yearned for an active role and presented the British Secret Service with a shrewd plan; she would ski into Nazi-occupied Poland and deliver British propaganda.

With this ambition, during the winter of 1939–40 Skarbek became a key part of the Resistance, smuggling intelligence out of Poland to the Allies. In January 1941 she was arrested in Hungary by the Gestapo, together with Andrzej Kowerski, a Polish army officer, fellow SOE agent and her lover and lifelong partner. During her interrogation, Skarbek bit her tongue to fake tuberculosis, prompting their immediate release. Soon after, she was given a British passport and a new name. Skarbek adopted the *nom-de-guerre* Christine Granville, a name she used for the rest of her life. Biographer Clare Mulley explains:

Her service in Nazi-occupied Poland and Eastern Europe included smuggling microfilm, hidden in her gloves, with film evidence of preparations for Operation Barbarossa, the Nazi invasion of the Soviet Union. When this reached Winston Churchill's desk, he reportedly described Christine as his 'favourite spy'.

Granville made her way to Egypt where she was further trained for a parachute drop into occupied France. As well as helping with preparations for D-Day, she secured communications between the French Resistance and the Italian partisans on either side of the Alps. Such were her exploits that she even managed to ensure the defection of an entire German garrison on a key mountain pass, as well as saving the lives of several of her male colleagues.

Having been awarded British citizenship, the OBE in 1947, the George Medal and the French Croix de Guerre, Granville was tragically murdered at a London hotel in June 1952. GA

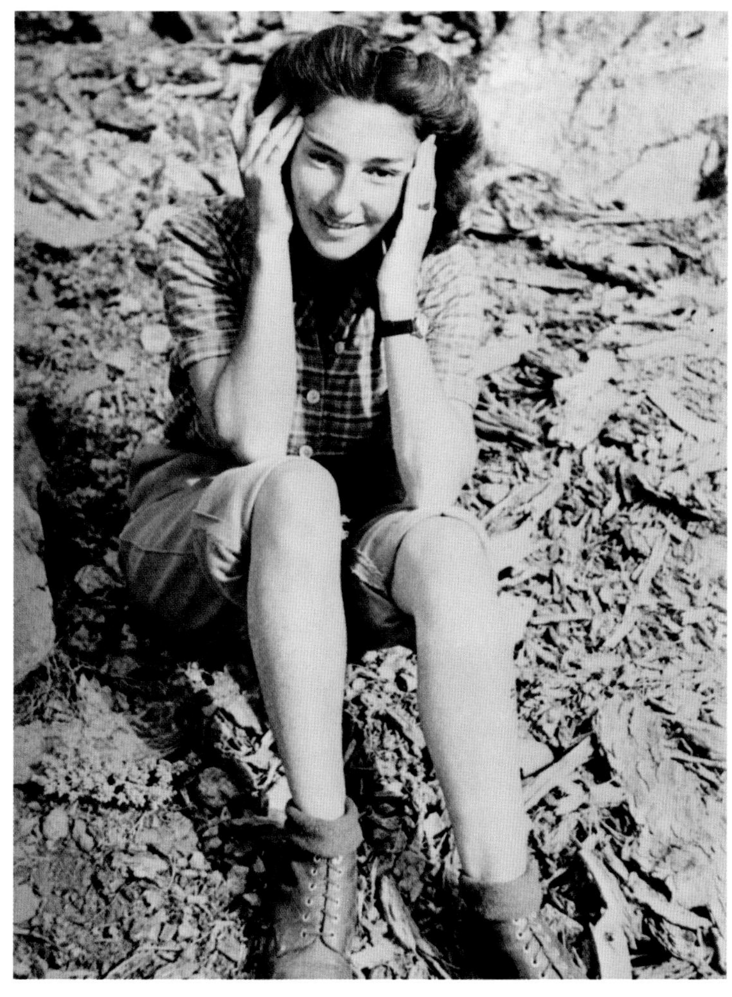

Christine Granville (Krystyna Skarbek) (1908–1952)
By an unknown photographer, *c.*1944
Half-plate glass copy negative
National Portrait Gallery, London, x201396

Maria Pawlikowska-Jasnorzewska

Artist, poet and playwright Maria Pawlikowska-Jasnorzewska once stated: 'I shall go into the horror of experience.' Experience was a multi-faceted beast for Pawlikowska-Jasnorzewska, who first tackled it through art. Born in Poland into a thriving cultural milieu, she started out by making watercolours infused with an art nouveau spirit. As time went by, her work became more intricate and layered. In spite of the challenges faced by many female artists of her generation – who were given limited access to academic training – she persevered and succeeded in developing her own brand of art. Pawlikowska-Jasnorzewska's artistic focus, however, shifted the moment she married her first husband, Wladyslaw Bzowski. She assumed that marriage would bring her freedom, but instead, the union with Bzowski turned out to be a mismatch. Pawlikowska-Jasnorzewska used her art as a platform to reflect on the constraints imposed by her gender.

Her literary interests prevailed over her artistic ones during the inter-war years and coincided with her second marriage to writer and ecological activist Jan Gwalbert Henryk Pawlikowski. During this time, she mostly dedicated herself to poetry writing, winning her the epithets of the Polish Sappho and 'queen of lyrical poetry'. Alongside her poetical output, she also developed a thriving career as a playwright. Her plays, like her art, were meant to challenge gender stereotypes. She confronted taboo issues such as abortion and extra-marital affairs, and undermined

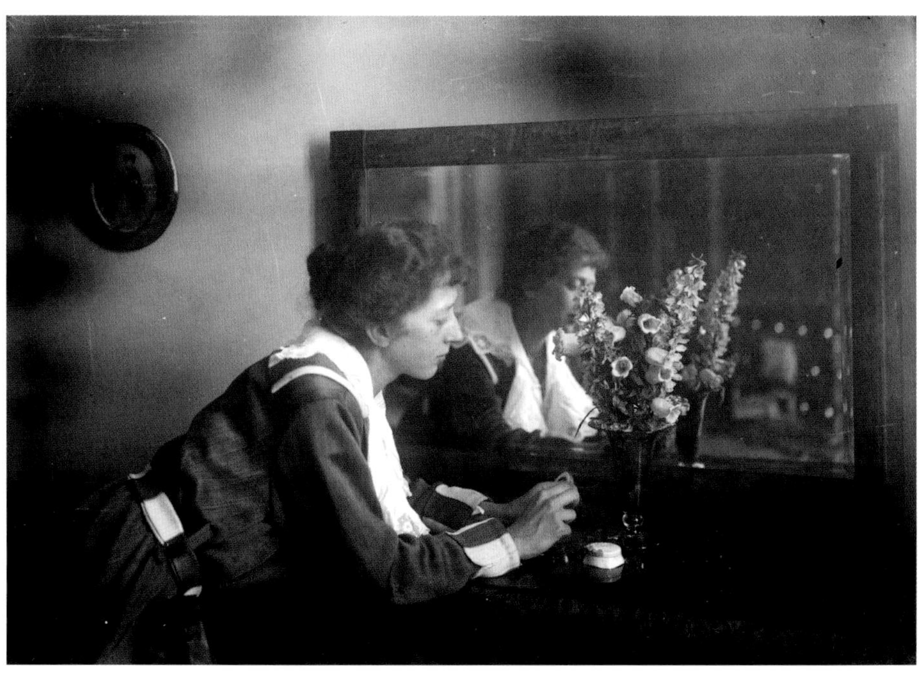

traditional notions attached to motherhood – for Pawlikowska-Jasnorzewska it represented the end of marital complicity and constrained women within the claustrophobic space of domesticity.

Out of all of Pawlikowska-Jasnorzewska's plays, the satirical *Baba-Dziwo* (translated as *A Woman of Wonder*) remains the most radical. Written in 1937, it premiered in Krakow in 1938 and in Warsaw in 1939; the same day that Pawlikowska-Jasnorzewska relocated to England with her third husband, the pilot Stefan Jasnorzewski. By 1942, she was living in Manchester and writing about the effects of the war on English soil.

In *A Woman of Wonder* she reflected on the impact of a repressive dictatorship on gender. In the play,

a ruthless dictator called Valida Vrana rules over Ritonia (a fictional country). In Ritonia, a woman's function is merely procreative and the more children women have, the higher their status in society. The childless couple Petronika and Norman escape this model and after a series of vicissitudes manage to reclaim Ritonia from Vrana. The play is layered with meaning, but ultimately it offers a poignant commentary on societal expectations surrounding gender. For Pawlikowska-Jasnorzewska choice was what made women free and this understanding firmly placed her ahead of her time. FF

Maria Pawlikowska-Jasnorzewska (1891–1945)
By Jan Gwalbert Henryk Pawlikowski, *c*.1918–19
5 × 7 inch glass plate negative
National Portrait Gallery, London, x202552

Eileen Guppy

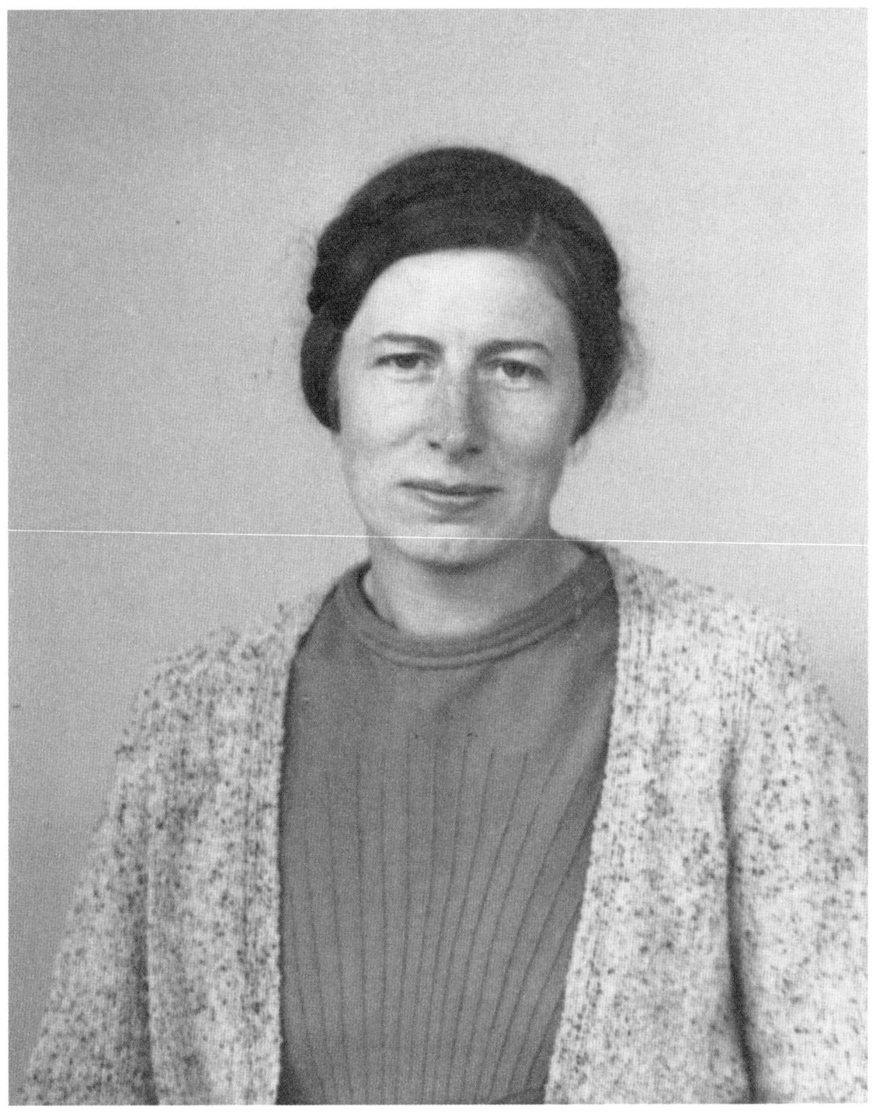

An insightful piece focusing on the composition of an Icelandic dyke, it was the first of Guppy's many publications. Over the years, she authored numerous publications and significantly contributed to *The First Hundred Years of the Geological Survey of Great Britain,* published in 1937.

Geology, like many other professional fields, was depleted of its men during the Second World War, allowing women to take on positions now vacant. After spending many years in subordinate roles, Guppy benefitted from this changing professional landscape and in 1943 she was promoted to the rank of Assistant Geologist, making her the BGS's first female geologist. In other areas women were employed by the BGS to meet the requirements of war. However, by the end of the war the assumption was that women would go back to their lowly pre-war status, as men returned home to resume their old roles. Guppy, like many other women, paid the price of this patriarchal diktat and was demoted to the grade of Senior Experimental Officer in 1945. Guppy's dedication to geology was undefeated and in spite of the challenging circumstances, she carried on working at the BGS, and by the time she retired in 1966 she was one of its longest serving and most dedicated members. FF

In 1835, the British Geological Survey (BGS) was founded. For the first 108 years of its existence, the BGS – and geology more broadly – was, for the most part, a male bastion. Women who aspired to a career in geology were either classed as amateurs or given subordinate roles. No women were recruited by the BGS until the 1920s and even then it was mandated that women be single or widowed to be employed, forcing women to choose between professional and sentimental fulfilment. One of the first women to enter this male realm was Eileen Guppy, who joined the BGS as a Technical Assistant for Petrology in 1927.

Before joining the BGS, Guppy earned a degree in geology from Bedford College – the first higher education college for women in the United Kingdom – and worked as a research assistant to Leonard Hawkes, Head of the Geology Department. During her time at Bedford College, Guppy published her influential paper 'A Composite Dyke from Eastern Iceland' in the *Quarterly Journal* of the Geological Society of London.

Eileen Guppy (1903–1980)
By an unknown photographer
Gelatin silver print, 76 × 102mm
British Geological Survey, CP23/024

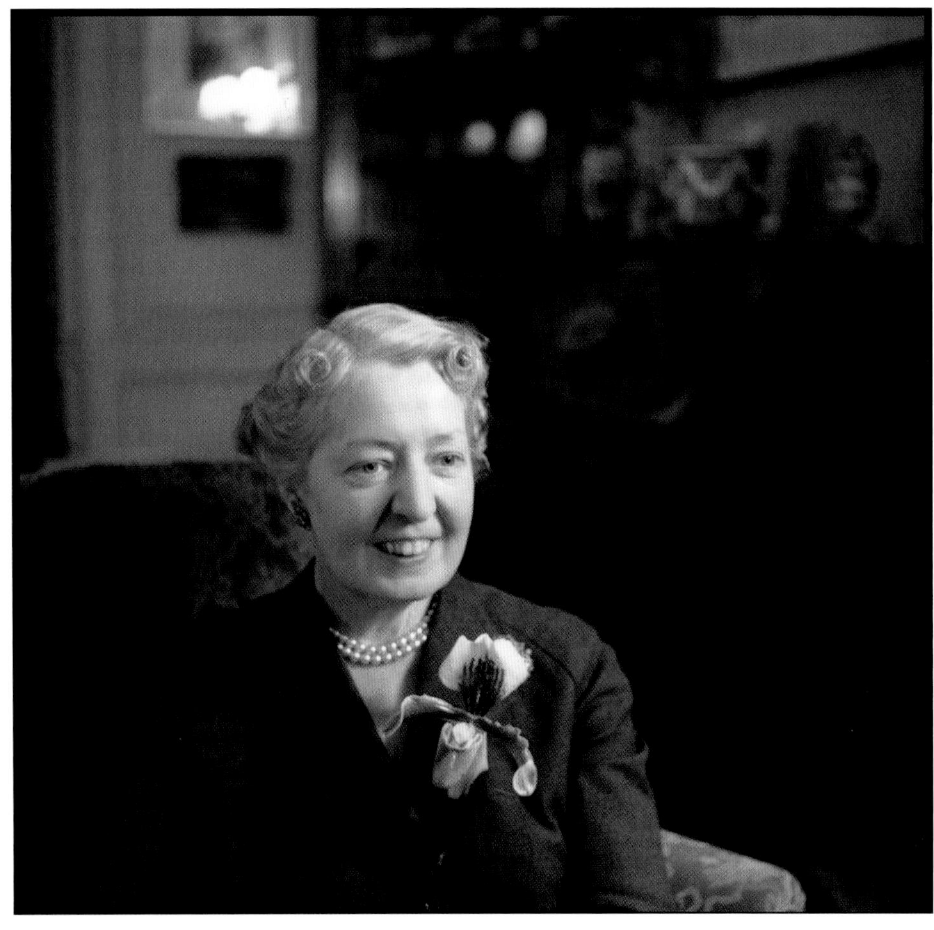

Women in wartime have been marvellous. They have gone everywhere, been an example of energy, enterprise and courage, and I think higher offices should be extended to them.

With these words, spoken in 1944, Brendan Bracken, Minister of Information, celebrated women's contribution to the war effort and laid the ground for post-war emancipation. By then, British *Vogue* editor Audrey Withers had amply demonstrated that women could be leaders at the toughest of times.

As wartime editor of *Vogue*, Withers was determined to show that the magazine had a purpose beyond promulgating fashion. As she once stated, *Vogue* should cover 'every subject in which the intelligent sophisticated woman is currently interested', and its politics 'must be progressive'.

Usually dressed in navy or grey, Withers was not the stereotypically fashionable editor; she was a hard-working and pragmatic woman. Withers joined *Vogue* magazine in 1931 as a sub-editor and was made editor in 1940 – a time when London was contending with the constant menace of bombing. As she later recalled:

I am very well aware that I would not have been an appropriate editor of Vogue *at any other period in its history … I had come up through copy-writing and administration, with no fashion training.*

Withers overcame her lack of fashion training by understanding that if

Vogue was to survive the war, it had to radically rethink its tone and purpose. Over the course of the Second World War, Withers worked with the government to persuade women to adapt to wartime limitations by changing the way they dressed and ate and how they worked. From the pages of *Vogue*, she chartered women through the bleakness of austerity restrictions, and in the July edition of 1942 she invited the *Vogue* reader to apprehend the imposed changes in positive terms:

Fashion is undergoing a compulsory course of slimming and simplification … It is a great opportunity for the couture. They, by sheer skill of cut, sheer interest of fabric, can turn negative restrictions into positive triumphs.

From that point onwards, Withers decided to focus individual issues of *Vogue* on different aspects of wartime life. She notoriously commissioned the American photojournalist Lee Miller to report from the front, taking *Vogue* into the heart of the conflict. After the war, Withers carried her bold vision for the magazine into the post-war moment. She invited the likes of Bertrand Russell, Simone de Beauvoir and Dylan Thomas to contribute to *Vogue*, and engaged some of the most inventive photographers of the day. To this day, Withers is best remembered as the editor who transformed *Vogue* into a progressive fashion magazine. FF

Audrey Withers (1905–2001)
By Lida Moser, 1953
Film negative
National Portrait Gallery, London, x45330

1945　Ellen Wilkinson

Less than two months after the Victory in Europe (VE) Day celebrations on 8 May 1945, Britain turned its attention towards its post-war future. The Labour government won the July 1945 General Election by a landslide to lead on reforms for rebuilding the country, including the introduction of the National Health Service and the welfare state. Politician Ellen Wilkinson was appointed Minister of Education with a responsibility to oversee the expansion of state-funded education. As such, she was the only woman in the new cabinet and the second woman to have held a ministerial position.

Determined to 'improve the lot of underprivileged children and to make secondary education much more than elementary education with frills', Wilkinson focused on implementing the wartime coalition's 1944 Education Act.[17] She attempted to address the inequality of educational opportunity by raising the school leaving age to 15, eradicating secondary school fees, increasing university scholarships and expanding part-time adult education.

Wilkinson was born in Manchester to a working-class family and had been a committed socialist since her youth. She was elected Labour Member of Parliament for Middlesbrough East in 1924, one of only a handful of female MPs at the time, and consequently she pressed on numerous women's issues, including pensions and equal franchise. Equal pay had been a major concern since her days as a trade union organizer during the First World War, when many women joined the workforce. Though Wilkinson succeeded in some negotiations, pay remained a central issue throughout her career.

In 1931, Wilkinson lost her parliamentary seat, but she returned in 1935 to represent another industrial area as MP for Jarrow. Deeply loyal to her working-class constituents, she steadfastly supported the families of miners during the 1926 General Strike, and in 1936 she joined around 200 unemployed men in a 454-km walk from Jarrow to Westminster to urge government intervention in regenerating their region's devastated shipbuilding industry. Whilst it was unsuccessful, the Jarrow Crusade came to symbolise the decade's struggles and laid the foundations for social reform in subsequent years.

Dedicated to her work, Wilkinson neglected her health and died 17 months into her ministerial office. She was criticised for not doing enough to promote comprehensive schooling, but her priority immediately after the war was on reconstruction before reform. The *Times Educational Supplement* reflected:

Had she lived longer, there is little doubt that the children of England and Wales would have had reason to bless her name ... she would have seen to it that in fact, as well as promise, no child would be denied the opportunity that was his due.
CN

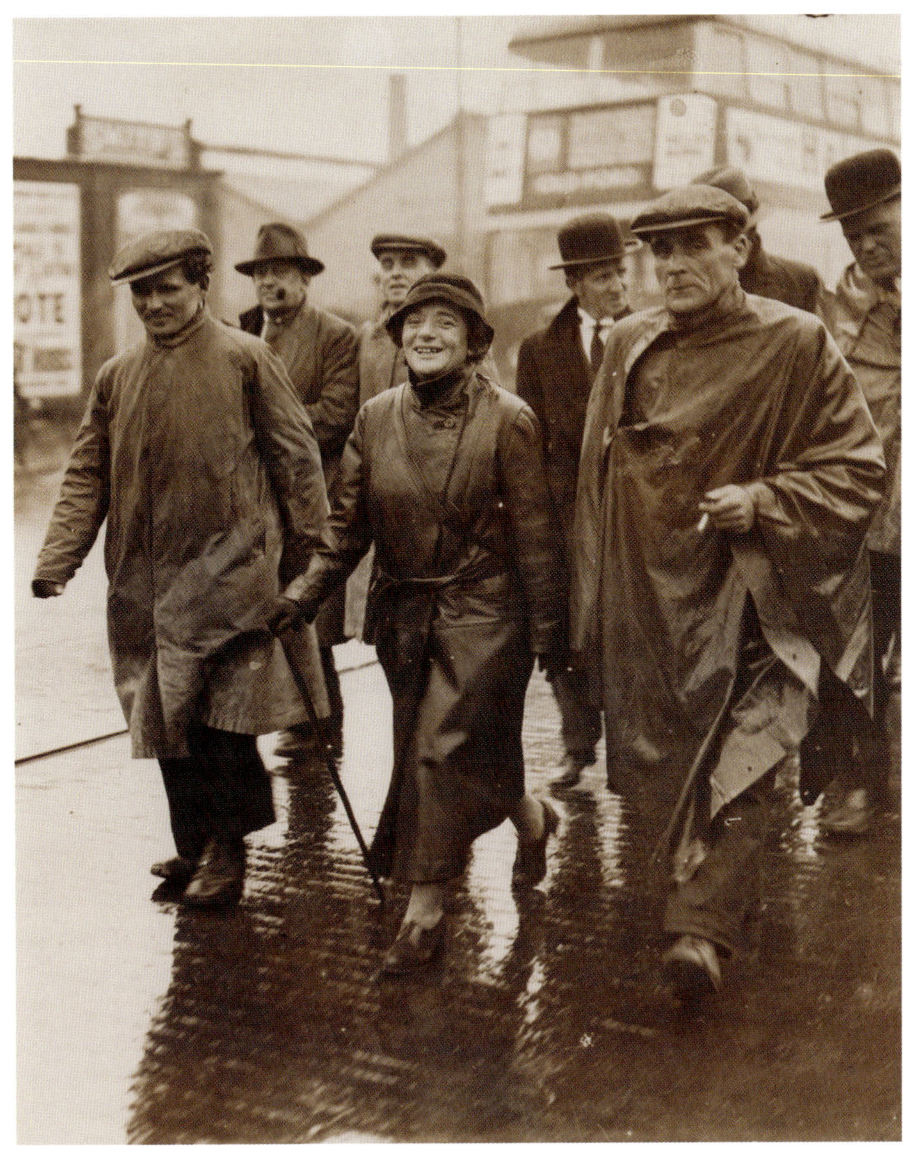

Ellen Wilkinson (1891–1947) leading the
Jarrow marchers
By Fox Photos Ltd, 31 October 1936
Sepia-toned gelatin silver press print, 228 × 178mm
National Portrait Gallery, London, x36118

1946   Eve Balfour

If the nation's health depends on the way its food is grown, then agriculture must be looked upon as one of the health services, in fact the primary health service.[18]

Despite her aristocratic background, Eve Balfour – better known as Lady Eve – always had ambitions to be a farmer. After gaining a university diploma in agriculture in 1917, she took advantage of the opportunities opening up to women during the First World War. Claiming to be older than she was, she secured a role managing a farm in Monmouthshire and overseeing a team of land girls, before buying New Bells Farm in Haughley Green, Suffolk with her sister in 1919. However, the next decade would prove challenging for farmers, with wartime governmental provisions repealed, so that Balfour soon found herself playing saxophone in a band and writing detective novels to make ends meet.

The 1930s brought for Balfour a growing preoccupation with the relationship between human health and methods of soil cultivation, and she began questioning the sustainability of conventional farming. Believing that soil, plants and livestock were interdependent and that farming without artificial fertilisers would produce more nutritious food, Balfour launched the pioneering Haughley Experiment in 1939 to prove her ideas. Dividing the farm into sections, it was the first long-term scientific investigation into chemical-based versus organic techniques, and the benefits of the latter quickly became apparent. Balfour included the initial findings in her popular book, *The Living Soil* (1943). Reprinted in numerous editions, it became a seminal text for the emerging organic movement.

Yet, after the Second World War, Britain continued to embrace intensive farming to tackle the food shortages

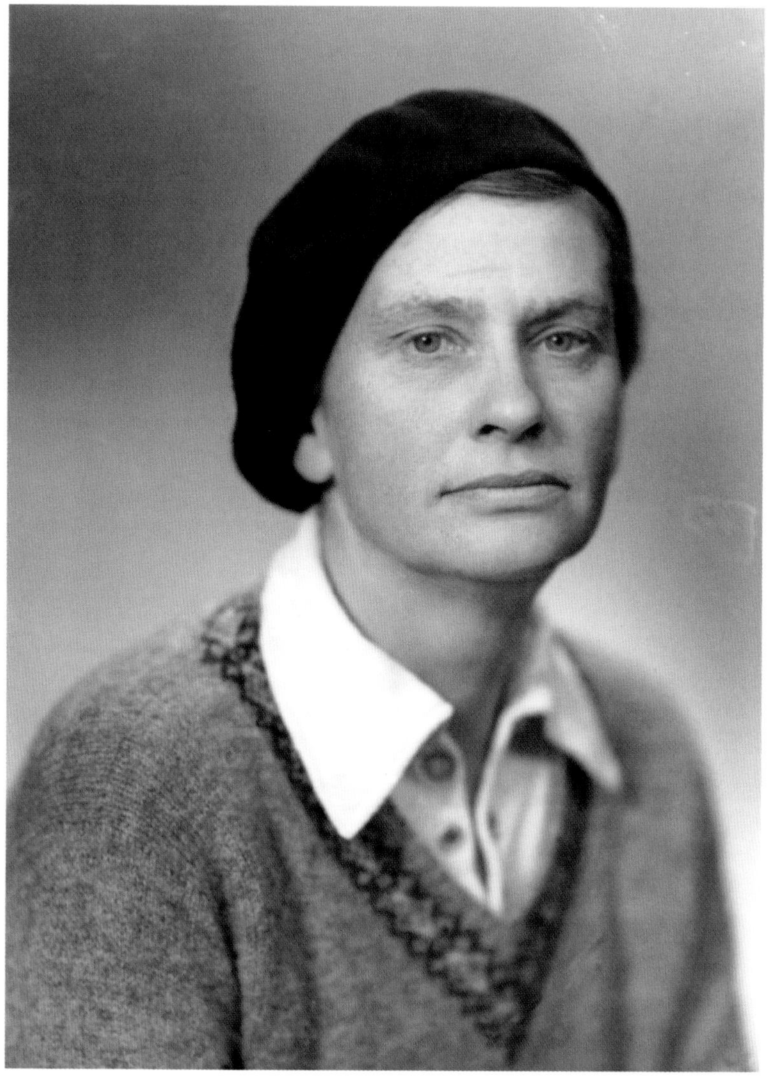

that kept rationing in place until 1953. In 1946, Balfour co-founded the Soil Association to promote sustainable agriculture, and became its first president. Under her leadership, its membership grew, organic food production standards were developed, there were campaigns against the use of harmful pesticides and the respected Soil Association Certification scheme was launched. Still writing and undertaking lecture tours, Balfour spread her message far and wide until her retirement in 1984.

Once deemed eccentric for her progressive views, opinion was shifting towards the end of Balfour's life, as public attention increasingly turned to healthier eating and environmental concerns. She received an OBE shortly before her death in 1990, and the new decade also saw the implementation of state funding for organic farming.

Although organic farming still constitutes a small proportion of the United Kingdom's overall agricultural output, consumer demand for organic products has risen. Meanwhile, the Soil Association continues to campaign for change, support farming innovation and influence government policy on food, farming and land use. CN

Eve Balfour (1898–1990)
By Elliott & Fry, 1943
Gelatin silver print, 168 × 120mm
National Portrait Gallery, London, x86256

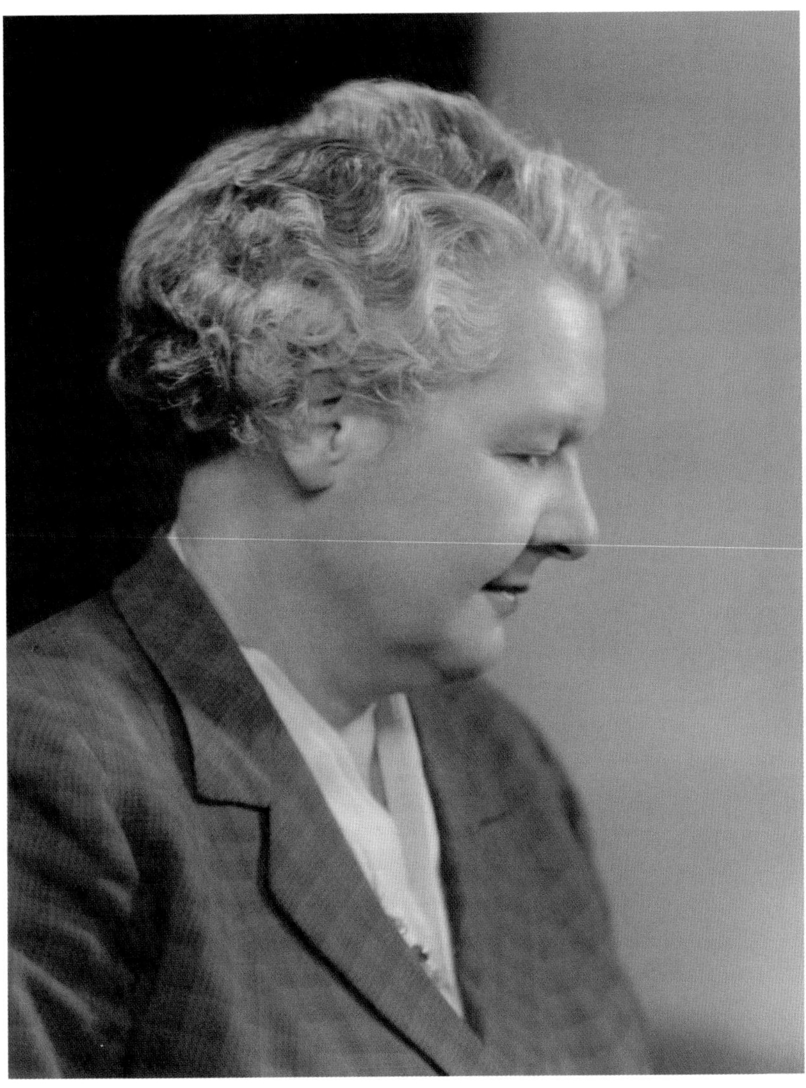

During her time in the Ministry of Health, Winner was also a visiting lecturer at the London School of Economics and later a Linacre fellow at the Royal College of Physicians, being responsible for postgraduate education in medicine.

Later in life, Winner was a key figure in the setting up of the hospice movement and the development of services for the long-term sick. Upon retiring from the Civil Service, she took a clinical refresher course at the age of 60 to help Cicely Saunders in forming the first modern hospice at Christopher's Hospice in Sydenham, London. Winner became its Deputy Medical Director in 1967, helping to establish its clinical and administrative standards.

Winner was appointed OBE in 1945 and was made a Dame in 1967. She was also President of the Medical Women's Federation between 1971 and 1972. Saunders described her friend and fellow doctor with these words, which give an account of the warmth and care that Winner brought to her various roles:

Dame Albertine reckoned that she had enjoyed at least five careers, to all of which she brought her vital interest and concern for people, whether they were patients or fellow workers … Of average height and robust figure, she gave the impression of being larger than she really was but this was offset by her warm smile. From her integrity stemmed her capacity for the attentive and skilful kindness that constitutes the very best moral support, which she gave so generously.[19]
GA

The physician and medical administrator Albertine Winner served in the Ministry of Health from 1947, where she worked for 20 years and rose to become the first woman Deputy Chief Medical Officer in 1962. Winner joined the Ministry of Health with a wealth of administrative experience acquired during her war service. Her appointment coincided with the establishment of the National Health Service (NHS) in 1948, under the premise that everybody should have access to all necessary medical care. With a deep interest in patients' welfare, she was particularly concerned with the development of services for the long-term sick.

Winner was born in London, and after graduating from University College Hospital Medical School, and winning the university gold medal, she practised at the Elizabeth Garrett Anderson Hospital, the Mothers' Hospital in Clapton and Maida Vale Hospital for Nervous Diseases. At the outbreak of the Second World War, she enlisted in the Royal Army Medical Corps and was the Assistant Medical Director-General and the chief woman doctor of the Auxiliary Territorial Service, serving as Lieutenant-Colonel.

Albertine Winner (1907–1988)
By Elliott & Fry, 1950s
Gelatin silver print, 159 × 117mm
National Portrait Gallery, London, x13944

Dorothy Crowfoot Hodgkin

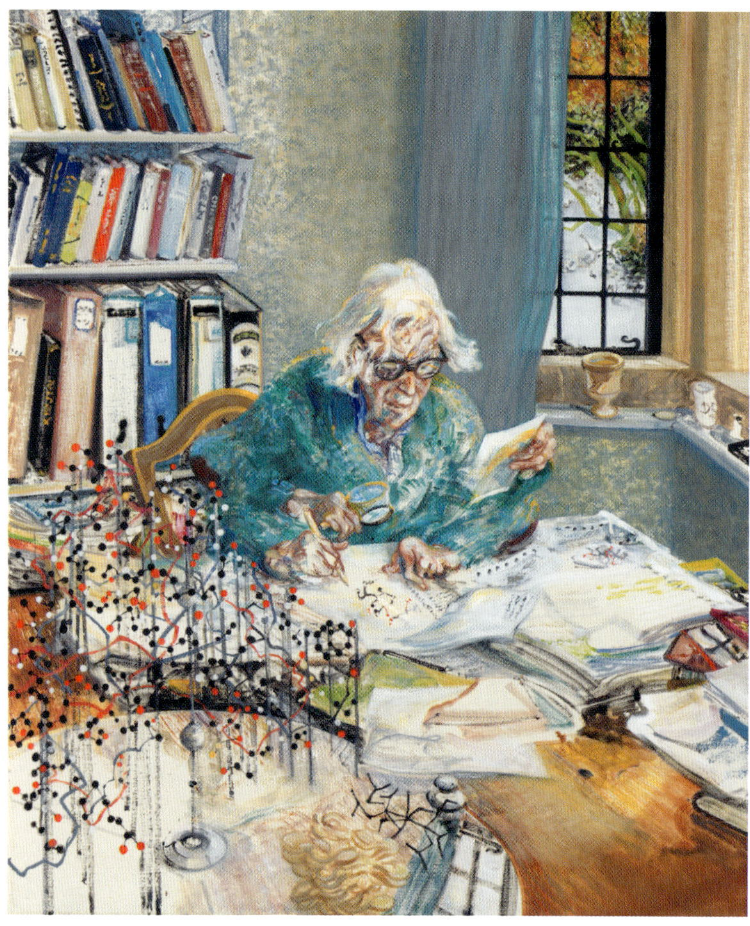

There's the moment when you know you can find out the answer and that's the period you are sleepless before you know what it is. When you've got it and know what it is, then you can rest easy.[20]

Surrounded by papers and with a structural model of insulin in the foreground, the chemist and crystallographer Dorothy Crowfoot Hodgkin is shown in Maggi Hambling's portrait still working hard several years after retiring. The doubling of her hands suggests her continued energy and activity, but also reveals the increasingly painful rheumatoid arthritis by which they were affected.

Hodgkin developed the chronic condition during her twenties, but it did not inhibit her unerring focus and willingness to persist in research that took years, sometimes decades, pushing the boundaries of X-ray crystallography and making crucial discoveries that informed the development of life-saving drugs.

With a passion for chemistry and crystals that emerged during childhood, Hodgkin excelled in her studies at Somerville College at the University of Oxford. It was there in 1934 that she established a laboratory for taking X-ray diffraction photographs of crystals to ascertain their atomic and molecular structures. Initially occupied with investigating insulin, Hodgkin was soon diverted by urgent wartime efforts to better understand penicillin. Within four years, in 1945 she determined its structure, making it far easier for the important antibiotic to be mass manufactured, and enabling scientists to create more potent derivatives for curing bacterial infections.

In 1948, Hodgkin embarked on her next major project, mapping the complex structure of vitamin B12, vital in the treatment of pernicious anaemia, with her growing team of researchers. Using emerging computer technology, the vitamin's structure was uncovered by 1955. Fellow crystallographer Lawrence Bragg declared Hodgkin's breakthrough equivalent to 'breaking the sound barrier' and 'in a class of its own'.

Among the honours she received, Hodgkin was awarded the prestigious Nobel Prize in Chemistry in 1964, but another major scientific achievement was still to come. Returning to her research of insulin (begun in 1934), Hodgkin and her team finally pinned down its elusive structure in 1969, facilitating the large-scale production of insulin for treating diabetes.

Alongside her laboratory work, Hodgkin was an active advocate for peace and disarmament, serving as Director of the Pugwash Conferences on Science and World Affairs from 1976 to 1988. She gave her time generously, frequently travelling to speak at international events, and encouraged scientific dialogue between the West, China and the Soviet Union, despite political tensions. CN

Dorothy Crowfoot Hodgkin (1910–1994)
By Maggi Hambling, 1985
Oil on canvas, 932 × 760mm
National Portrait Gallery, London, 5797

THE

FIRST (WOMAN) SCIENTIST

By

Emma Chapman

Draw a scientist. What do you draw? A mop of grey hair? A white lab coat? A figure clutching a test tube? Before 1985 less than one per cent of children asked to draw a scientist drew a woman in the role. The statistics have improved since then – these days the figure is pushing 25 per cent, though overwhelmingly the majority of these pictures are drawn by girls. In general, if you ask someone to imagine a scientist, they imagine a man. Odd really when you consider that the word 'scientist' was invented for a woman.

Mary Somerville was a Scottish polymath, known as the 'Queen of Science' (fig.1). She translated, and added to, French works on the mathematics of the solar system, and wrote the very first textbook on physical geography, as well as a best-selling exploration of molecular biology. It was hard for the scientific establishment to decide what to call her. The accepted term at the time for someone working in so many fields was a 'man of science'. Clearly this wasn't going to work.

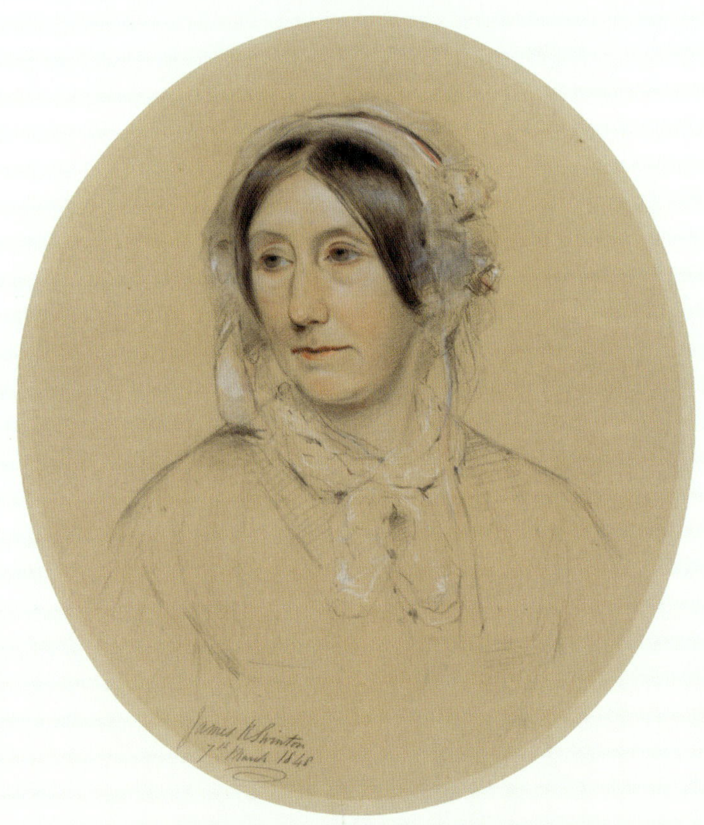
Fig.1: Mary Somerville by James Rannie Swinton

A contemporary of Somerville, the polymath William Whewell, wanting to describe her work, coined a new term: 'scientist'.

Somerville moved in the highest scientific circles and her work was published in the most prestigious journals, but her recognition and reputation were hard-won. She had read Euclid's works by candlelight, hiding from her father, who disapproved of her wild academic ways. Her first husband was no more encouraging. Following his early death, she was able to use the freedom that a widow's inheritance brought her to finally devote her attention to academic study. Her second husband was a fellow of the Royal Society and his support then gave her a platform from which to express her ideas, and the respect that her considerable talents and drive warranted.

Since the very beginning of scientific investigation, women scientists have found themselves at the margins. Somerville is typical of those women who managed to overcome the obstructions set against them. They had both to be exceptional in themselves and in their work, and also exceptionally lucky to have the support of an influential family member or friend. Most women with questions were simply told to be quiet, that their scientific interests were unhealthy and suspect, that science was a male endeavour.

The largest barrier for women wanting to pursue a scientific career was securing access to education. The University of London first accepted women undergraduates in 1868, the first university in Britain to do so. The University of Cambridge established the UK's first residential university college for women the year after, but women still had to seek permission to attend lectures and exams, and the university did not award women degrees until 1948. Cecilia Payne-Gaposchkin (fig.2), who revolutionised astronomy when she discovered that stars have an entirely different

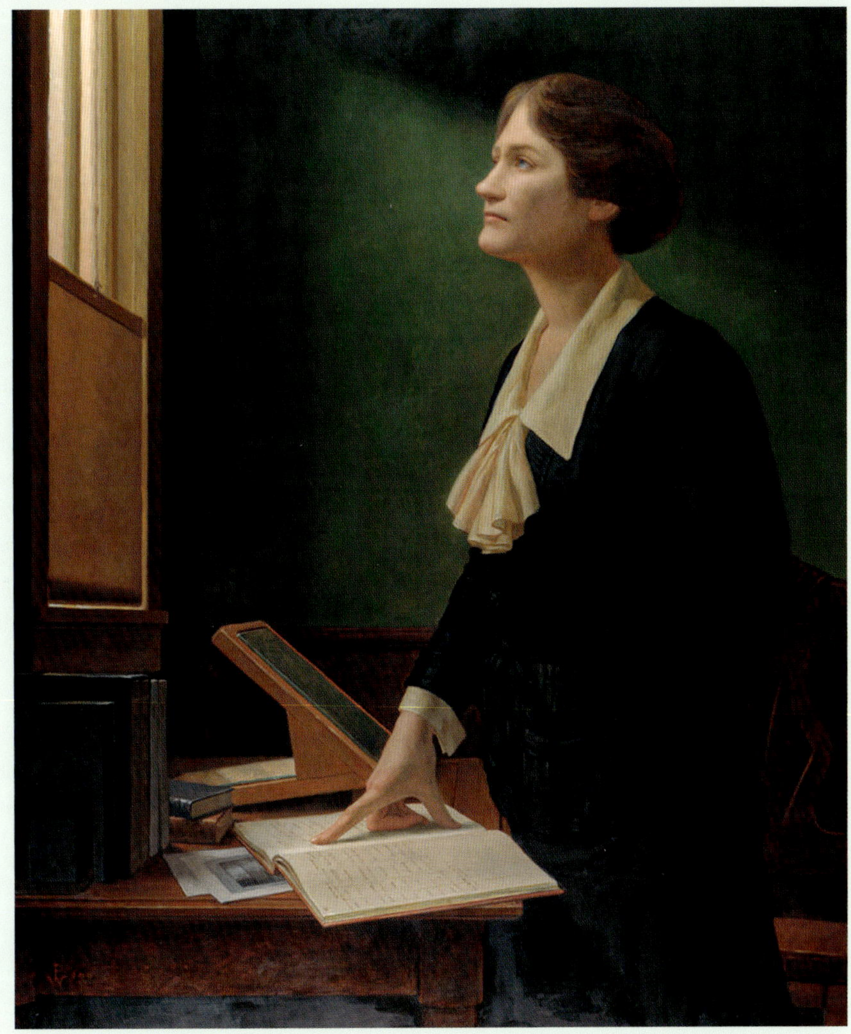

Fig.2: Cecilia Payne-Gaposchkin by Patricia Watwood

composition to planets, attended Cambridge in the 1920s. She had to endure professors remarking that her corsets would interfere with experiments and ignore the stamping feet of male students as she entered each lecture hall. Some 40 years later, things had improved very little. Jocelyn Bell Burnell (fig.3) had to suffer similar disrespect when she attended lectures at the University of Glasgow in the 1960s. Another 40 years later, when I began to attend lectures as a woman in science, I found myself as a minority in every lecture hall and meeting room, but thankfully I have never had to experience the same levels of vocal and public humiliation. Now women make up about one third of the UK undergraduate STEM intake and there are enough of us around to make stamping one's

feet at the sight of a woman less likely to prove a sustainable protest.

Once a woman had managed to gain a scientific training, there was then the question of how she could practise her chosen subject. Family connections could only take you so far in the world of academia, where the presentation and discussion of findings occurred in the halls of the learned societies, or within the pages of their journals. In the early days of organized scientific discussion, membership of a professional body such as the Royal Astronomical Society (RAS), the Chemical Society, or the Royal Society was essential.

Mary Somerville, despite her education and relative fame and respect, still found herself ineligible for membership of the RAS.

95

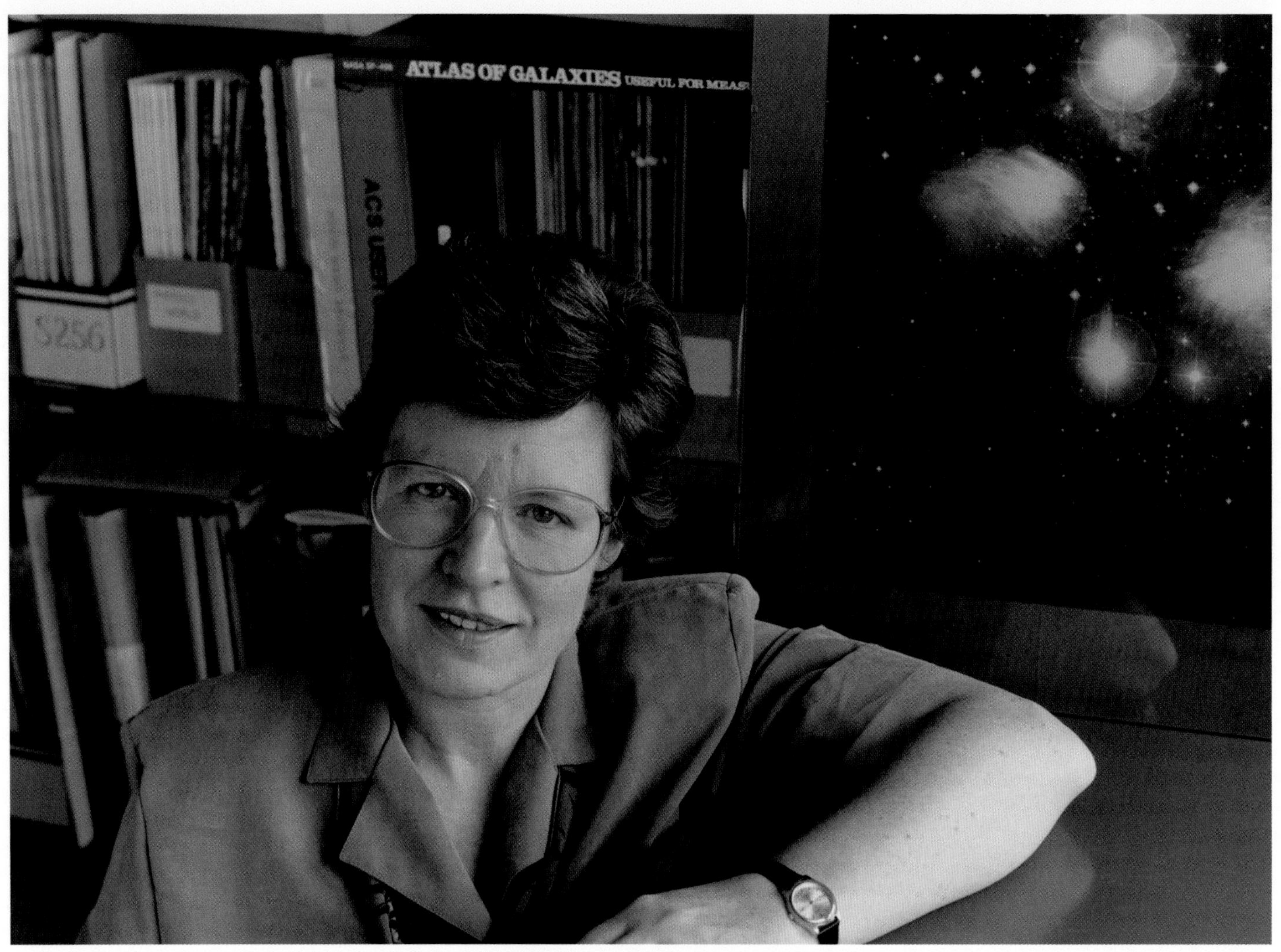

Fig.3: Jocelyn Bell Burnell by Julia Hedgecoe

The Society's charter specifically referred to members using the male pronoun and so, while Mary Somerville was named a member in 1835, the membership was honorary only. A stray pronoun may seem a small matter, but in the right hands it can be weaponised to bestow inertia upon grassroots change. Mary Somerville had achieved much, much more than most of her male contemporaries, but the inflexibility of the policies that determined membership ultimately served the naysayers. The pronoun was later directly referenced as the reason for denying women full membership, alongside a snide comment that if women were allowed in then the RAS might as well get a piano and a fiddle so they could 'dance through most of the papers'. It would take until 1916 for a byelaw to be introduced stating that 'words denoting the masculine gender only shall include the feminine gender also'.[21]

Alongside Somerville, Caroline Herschel (fig.4) also received the consolatory accolade of an honorary membership in 1835. This honorary-only status seems all the odder when you consider that the RAS had previously awarded her the highest honour of the society, the Gold Medal, in 1828. Herschel would stand out at her and her brother's telescope night after night, her skirts freezing to the ground. She penned catalogues of all that she saw and discovered several new comets, alongside her brother William. William, of course, was allowed to present the results. I have had the great honour of handling some of Herschel's original notebooks. What struck me immediately was how the spines of these great tomes had her name written – scrawled – in oversized, block letters along the spine. It felt like she was trying to claim the physical evidence of her own research viscerally and permanently.

The Royal Society, too, treated women with maddening inconsistency. Hertha Ayrton (p.36) was another polymath and inventor, excelling in mathematics, engineering and physics. Her research into the 'electric arc' – artificial lightning then used for public lighting – was recognised internationally, and she registered 26 patents over her lifetime. Despite this, Ayrton had her petition to read a paper before the Society turned down in 1899 because of her sex and instead it had to be read by a male proxy. The science was good enough, you understand, but she was not. Three years later, her bid for membership was unsuccessful too, though this time not because she was a woman, but because as a *married* woman she had no personhood under law. Ayrton received the highest recognition in physics offered by the Society, the Hughes Medal, in 1906, but she never was allowed to be a fellow.

The honours Ayrton and Herschel received were extremely rare, and continue to be. The gender statistics for STEM awards over the past century is pretty dire reading. To take the Hughes medal as an example, Ayrton may have made history as the first woman recipient, but the second medal given to a woman was then not until 2008, over a century later.

My career path has been peppered with the names of the women who forged the way. I chose between Josephine Butler College and Somerville College for my undergraduate studies, won the Jocelyn Bell Burnell physics award and I am a Dorothy Hodgkin fellow. I even studied for my PhD in the Katherine Lonsdale building – the first woman to be elected a fellow of the Royal Society, in 1945. The names of these few women who were allowed a measure of success despite the obstacles presented to them are now liberally used to adorn prizes, job titles and buildings. They are the few who were captured in artistic works and fill the pages of the 'women in science' kids' books I read to my children. For my daughters, there is no question that they can be scientists if they want to be, thanks in part to the visibility of historical figures. The path towards a career in the sciences will be much clearer for them, should they choose to take it. Access to education is equal by law, though we still have to combat outdated ideas that science is somehow a male subject, or simply 'hard' and therefore not for girls, thanks to other societal assumptions. Women now have the right to membership of

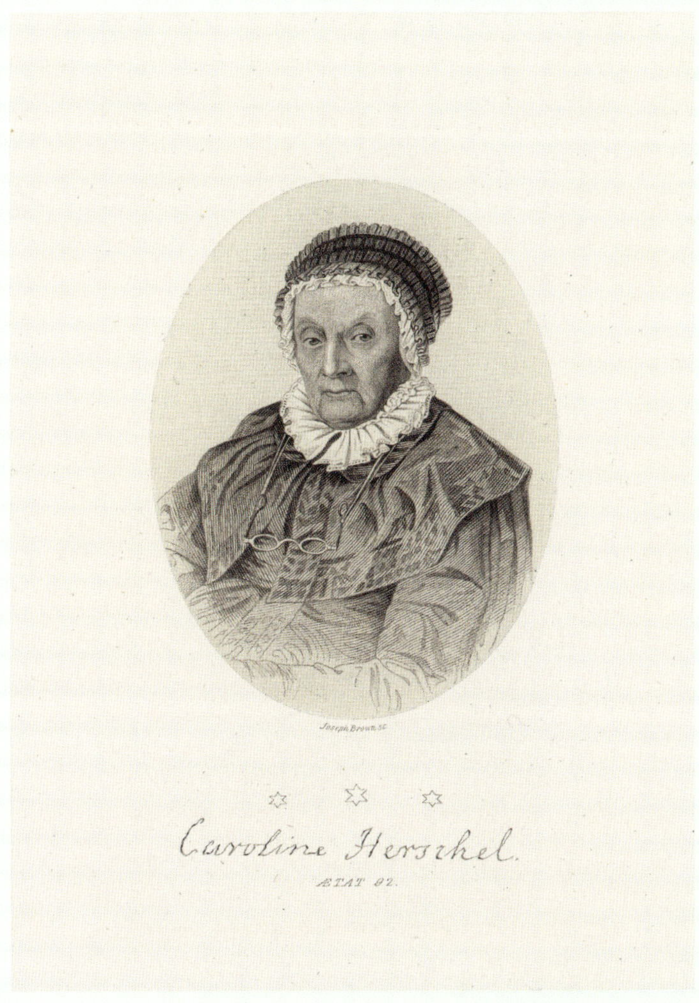

Fig.4: Caroline Herschel by Joseph Brown

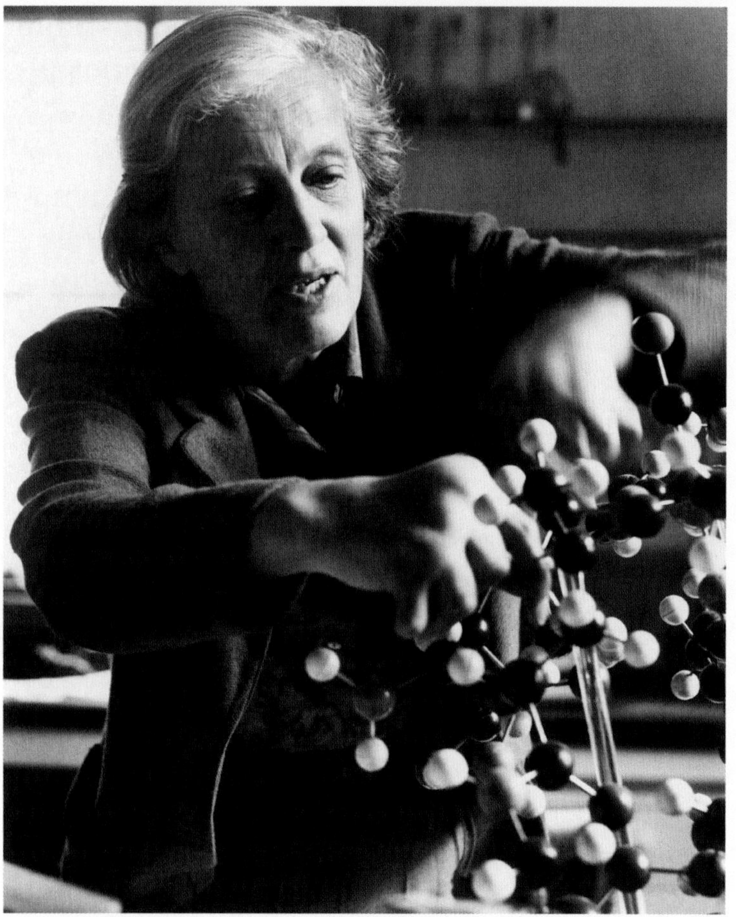

Fig.5: Dorothy Crowfoot Hodgkin by Jorge Lewinski

scientific societies, the right to submit papers and the right to speak at conferences. The equality and diversity teams now standard within the learned societies mentioned here contain some of the most passionate and hardworking campaigners out there. Far from closing off the entrance, institutions and societies now pour time, money and attention into numerous initiatives encouraging girls through their doors and into a scientific career. When we look at the numbers of women achieving the top career positions and the highest honours, though, it is clear that we have much more work to do to ensure these women have supportive environments in which to thrive. Women now have every right to wonder and question and be recognised for their insights. They have every right to be scientists. After all, the word was made for them.

Fig.1
Mary Somerville (1780–1872)
By James Rannie Swinton, 1848
Chalk drawing, 692 × 607mm
National Portrait Gallery, London, 690

Fig.2
Cecilia Payne-Gaposchkin (1900–1979)
By Patricia Watwood, 2001
Oil on canvas, 1197 × 967mm
Harvard University Portrait Collection, H743

Fig.3
Jocelyn Bell Burnell (b.1943)
By Julia Hedgecoe, 1997
Gelatin silver print, 293 × 391mm
National Portrait Gallery, London, P751(3)

Fig.4
Caroline Herschel (1750–1848)
By Joseph Brown, after George Müller, 1840s
Stipple engraving, 203 × 145mm
National Portrait Gallery, London, D9005

Fig.5
Dorothy Crowfoot Hodgkin (1910–1994)
By Jorge Lewinski, 1967
Gelatin silver print, 379 × 300mm
National Portrait Gallery, London, x13727

Dorothy Stuart Russell

As far as possible the facts have been allowed to speak for themselves and the theories have been allowed to drop into the background … the immense variety of pathological lesions have this single feature in common: all create an obstruction in some point in the pathway of the cerebrospinal fluid.

These words are drawn from pathologist Dorothy Stuart Russell's important work *Observations on the Pathology of Hydrocephalus*, published by the Medical Research Council (MRC) in 1949. Russell was the first woman to be appointed a pathology chair in Western Europe and was known for her scrupulous analysis and clear expression. Unlike many of her contemporaries, she avoided scientific jargon and lent her writings a simple but penetrating thrust.

From a young age, Russell 'was determined to be a doctor – not a practising doctor, but a research doctor.' She accomplished this through rigorous training, first at Girton College, Cambridge and then at the London Hospital Medical College. In 1919, the London allowed Russell and 30 other women to enter its medical ranks.

She studied morbid anatomy under the direction of the pathologist Professor Hubert Turnball, a leading authority in the field. In 1922, she qualified and entered the Institute of Pathology after working in various clinical roles. Around this time Russell met Hugh Cairns – one of the founders of neurosurgery in Britain – and the two would go on to collaborate for many years. Cairns understood how crucial neuropathology was to neurosurgery and encouraged Russell into this specialism – she was to follow it for the rest of her career.

In 1939, the day before the Second World War was declared, Russell moved to Oxford, where she joined the Military Hospital for Head Injuries – a unit commanded by Cairns, who was by then Nuffield Professor of Surgery in Oxford. Russell's wartime period at Oxford was one of intensive and highly productive work; she conducted necropsies and brain cuts for the hospital; undertook extensive research; experimented with new techniques of staining with metallic impregnations; and started work on *Observations on the Pathology of Hydrocephalus*. In 1944 she returned to the London Hospital and in 1946 she succeeded Turnball as Professor of Morbid Anatomy and Director of the Bernhard Baron Institute of Pathology, where she remained until her retirement in 1960.

Described as a complex and fascinating character by those who knew her, Russell was authoritative in public and reserved in private. In the words of one of her acquaintances: '[she] seemed at first forbidding, but at heart very kind.'[22] FF

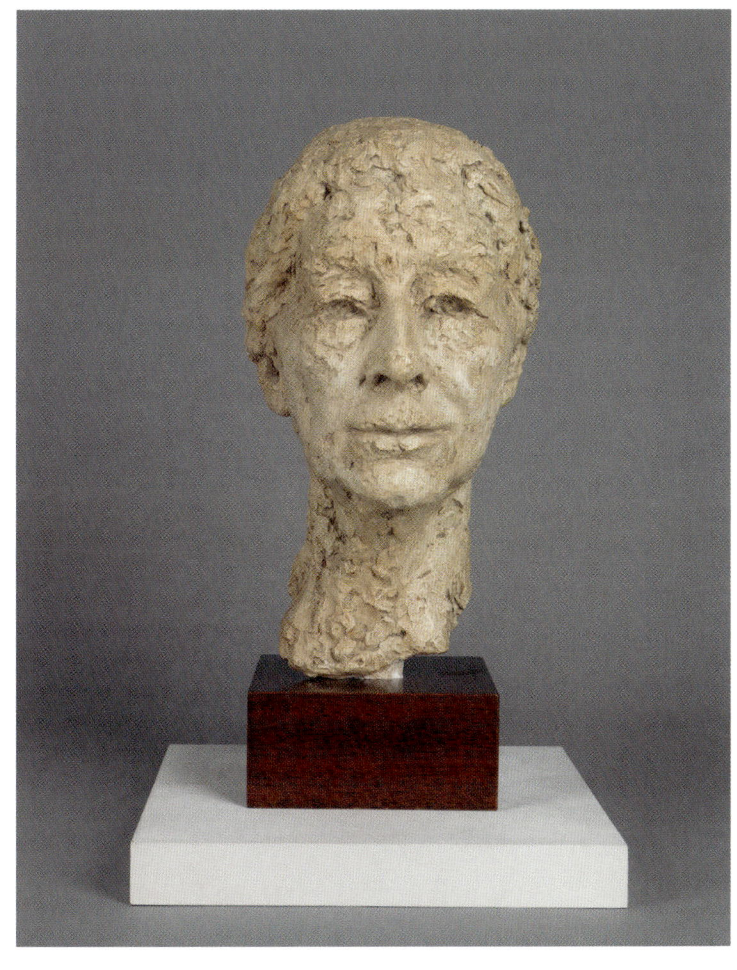

Dorothy Stuart Russell (1895–1983)
By Ismond Rosen, 1960
Plaster bust, 433 × 190mm
National Portrait Gallery, London, 6604

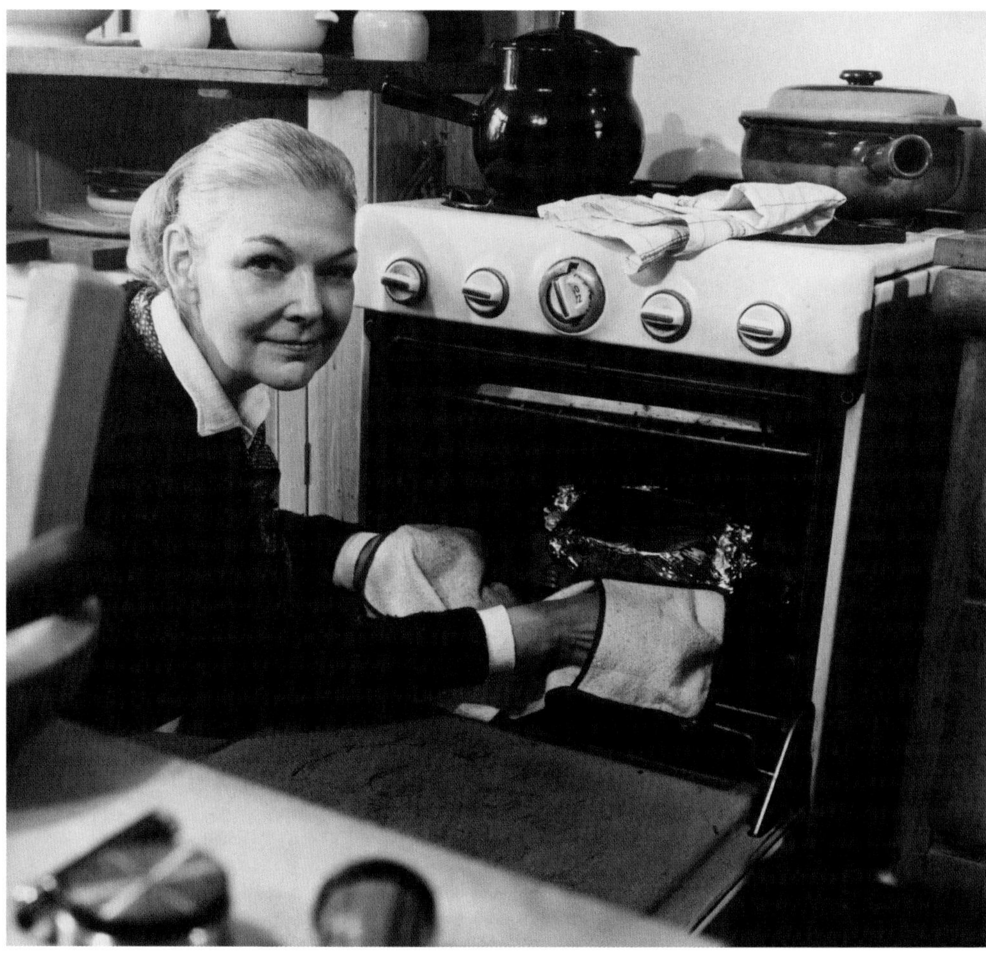

... the oil, the saffron, the garlic, the pungent local wines; the aromatic perfume of rosemary, wild marjoram and basil ... the brilliance of the market stalls piled high with pimentos, aubergines, tomatoes, olives, melons, figs ... the great heaps of shiny fish, silver, vermilion, or tiger-striped, and those long needle fish whose bones mysteriously turn green when they are cooked. There are, too, all manner of unfamiliar cheeses made from sheep or goat's milk ...[23]

In the aftermath of the Second World War, cookery writer extraordinaire Elizabeth David taught her English readers how to make rich and colourful dishes while also taking them on a journey:

From Gibraltar to the Bosphorus, down the Rhône Valley, through the great sea ports of Marseilles, Barcelona, and Genoa, across to Tunis and Alexandria, embracing all the Mediterranean islands, Corsica, Sicily, Sardinia, Crete, the Cyclades, Cyprus ... to the mainland of Greece and the much-disputed territories of Syria, Lebanon, Constantinople.

David developed an interest in cooking whilst studying in Paris and subsequently while travelling during the Second World War. On returning to England in 1946 she began to write about cookery, yearning for the food she had grown to love in France, Greece and Egypt. In 1949 she was asked to write a cooking column for *Harper's Bazaar* and by the end of the year David had put together a coherent collection of recipes. In 1950, she approached John Lehmann, publisher of the prestigious Penguin New Writing, with her manuscript. Lehmann was sceptical at first, and later admitted that David's was the untidiest typescript he had ever laid eyes on; she had been using it to cook from. The recipe for Turkish Stuffing for a Whole Roast Sheep, finally won Lehmann over and he agreed to publish the manuscript with the title of *A Book of Mediterranean Food*.

After years of wartime rationing, the Mediterranean escapism of David's book proved an immediate hit. She inspired thousands of domestic cooks with her soup Basque, iced beetroot soup, Avgolémono, soup au Pistou, moules marinières, kokoretsi, paella Valenciana, bouillabaisse and many more original recipes. Even though aubergines, lemons and olive oil were almost unobtainable in the immediate post-war years, David inspired people with her compelling prose. 'I think,' she wrote, 'that the ideal cookery writer is one who makes his readers *want* to cook as well as telling them how it is done; he should also leave something, not too much perhaps, but a little, unsaid; people must make their own discoveries, use their own intelligence, otherwise they will be deprived of part of the fun.' FF

Elizabeth David (1913–1992)
By Cecil Beaton, 1970
Gelatin silver print, 187 × 191mm
National Portrait Gallery, London, P869(8)

1951 Elizabeth Friedländer

Born in Berlin, Friedländer studied with influential typographer Emil Rudolph Weiss at the Academy of Berlin's Museum of Decorative Arts. Through Weiss she was introduced to Georg Hartmann, who ran the Bauer Type Foundry. In 1927 they commissioned Friedländer to design a typeface, making her one of the first women to undertake such a task. Unlike her male peers who bestowed their surnames on their typefaces, Friedländer's was commonly known by her first name only, a discrimination based entirely on gender.

By the time that the Elizabeth typeface had been cut and its form had entered the graphic realm, Friedländer was forced to leave Germany due to the mounting anti-Semitic laws. She relocated to Milan in 1936 and then to London in 1939. During her time in Milan, Friedländer had worked as a designer for the publishers Mondadori and Editoriale Domus. On her arrival in London, she became involved with Britain's Political Warfare Executive at Bush House and was employed as Head of Design, focusing on black propaganda – this entailed forging Nazi rubber stamps, amongst other disruptive strategies.

With the end of the Second World War, Friedländer veered her professional interests towards the publishing world and in particular she began a long-standing collaboration with Penguin, which extended well into the 1950s. At Penguin she was responsible for many book covers. A series of drawings made in the early 1950s show Friedländer trialling and testing different types of penguins – all drawn using black ink on a plain white sheet of paper.

Alongside her work for Penguin, Friedländer was also involved in the advertising industry. She worked on the branding and packaging of cosmetic products, and also involved herself in the design of instruction sheets to accompany the various products; a drawing for the mechanism of a lipstick stands testament to her scrupulous work. Friedländer's career path is remarkable for its variety. She not only pioneered the Elizabeth typeface but went on to establish what by today standards would be described as a graphic design studio, working on branding and identity for different clients. FF

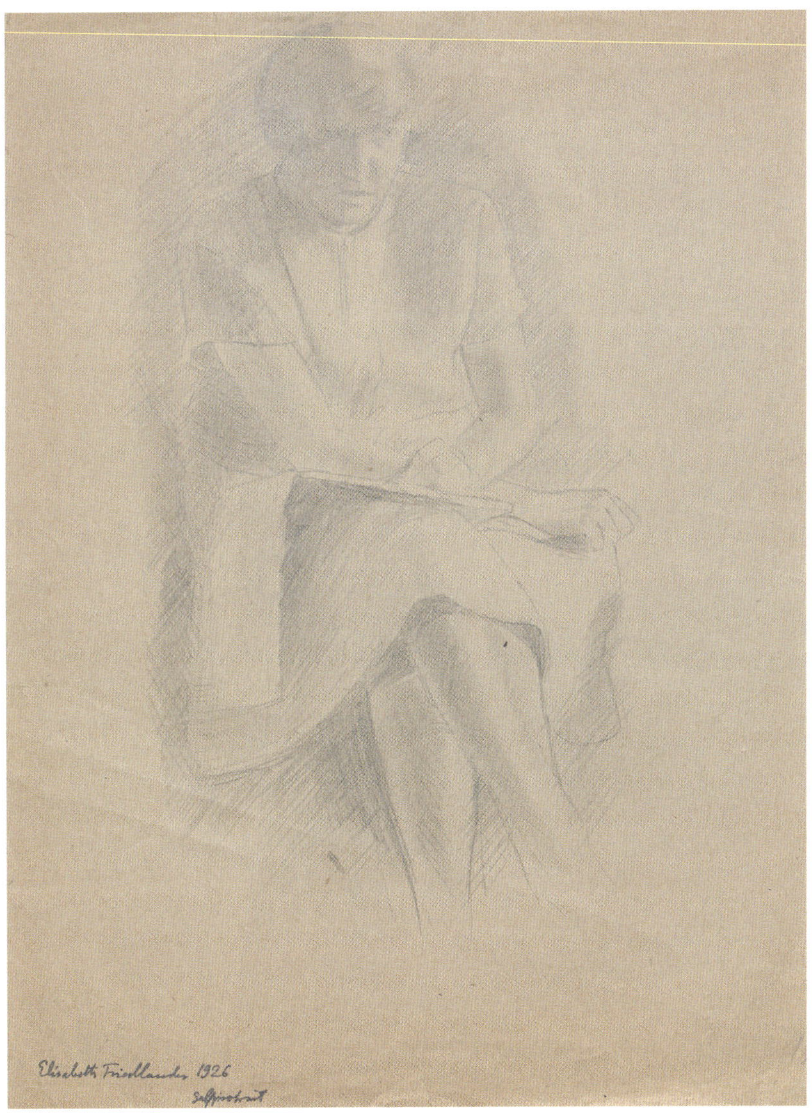

Elizabeth Friedländer (1903–1984)
Self-portrait, 1926
Pencil on paper, 208 × 192mm
University College Cork

Anne McLaren

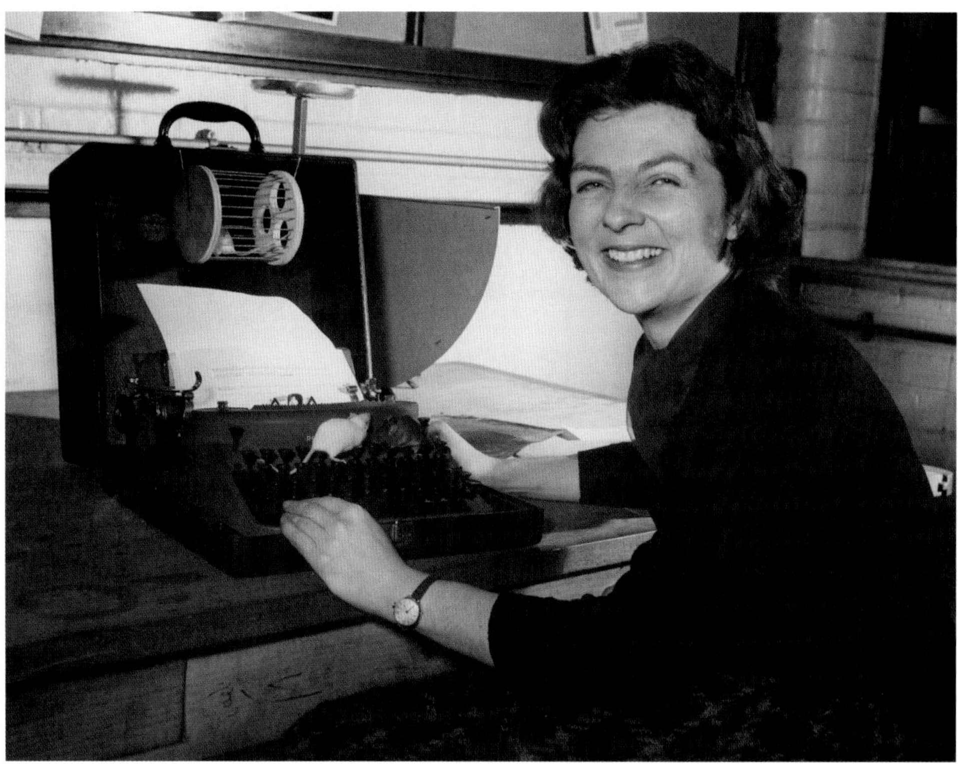

In 1952, reproductive and developmental biologist Anne McLaren completed her doctorate and commenced her influential studies on the reproductive biology of mice at University College London. In collaboration with Donald Michie (to whom she was also married between 1952 and 1959), McLaren explored the effects of the mouse's uterine environment on the development of the spinal column, leading her to advance superovulation and embryo transfer techniques. Emerging from this, and alongside John Biggers, McLaren successfully developed mice embryos in test tubes before implanting them in surrogates until birth. Their report on this groundbreaking work, published in *Nature* in 1958, has been described as 'one of the most significant papers in the history of reproductive biology and medicine', and laid the foundations for human in vitro fertilisation (IVF), a transformative treatment for many struggling with infertility.

Following a move to Edinburgh's Institute of Animal Genetics in 1959, McLaren continued to expand her innovative research on subjects relating to mammalian fertility and embryonic development, or, as she succinctly described it, 'everything involved in getting from one generation to the next'. At the Medical Research Council's new Mammalian Development Unit at University College London and at Cambridge's Gurdon Institute, she furthered her interest in the formation of primordial germ cells into sperms or eggs, and how these converted into stem cells with the potential for treating illness and injuries. This extensive work resulted in over 300 scientific papers published during her lifetime, alongside her classic texts on *Mammalian Chimaeras* (1976) and *Germ Cells and Soma* (1981).

Aware of the major ethical implications these areas of study raised, McLaren participated widely in debates with a commitment to finding resolutions and increasing public understanding. She notably served on the Warnock Committee, whose report influenced legislation, and the Human Fertilisation and Embryology Authority for regulating infertility services and the use of embryos.

McLaren's achievements resulted in many honours, including a DBE in 1993 and the Royal Society's highest award – the Royal Medal, where she was made Fellow in 1975. She also broke new ground within the scientific establishment as the Society's Foreign Secretary (1991–6) – becoming the first woman to hold office in its more than 300-year history – and as its Vice President (1992–6). In these roles she endeavoured to promote scientific careers and equal opportunities for women, though she professed to not having felt disadvantaged, stating 'I never thought of myself as a woman scientist, just as a scientist, and as a woman.' CN

Anne McLaren (1927–2007)
By an unknown photographer, 1958
Gelatin silver print, 199 × 248mm
National Portrait Gallery, London, x202504

1953

Vijaya Lakshmi Pandit

Somewhere, way back in my genealogical line there must have existed an ancestor (or was it perhaps an ancestress!) who loved a fight, and this fighting blood has been transmitted to me and rejoices whenever there is a chance to prove its mettle.

This statement by Vijaya Lakshmi Pandit from her book *So I Became a Minister* (1939) articulates well the tenacity that she showed throughout her long involvement with Indian politics and international diplomacy. Born in Allahabad in India, Pandit was an ardent nationalist campaigner for many years preceding India's independence from British rule in 1947. Like her father, husband and brother (Jawaharlal Nehru, later India's first Prime Minister), who were also prominent nationalists, she was imprisoned several times for her non-violent activism. Pandit was elected to the United Provinces Legislative Assembly and served from 1937 to 1938 and again from 1946 to 1947. She also became India's first woman cabinet member as Minister for Local Self-Government and Public Health, proving highly effective and popular in this role despite her inexperience.

Pandit's emergence on the global stage came between 1944 and 1945 during a visit to the US, where she captivated audiences and attracted media attention with her pro-nationalist and anti-imperialist arguments, and established herself as a charismatic 'diplomatic celebrity'. This included her conspicuous unofficial attendance at the San Francisco Conference, where delegates of the newly formed United Nations (UN) gathered to draft the organization's Charter.

Although women held few and limited roles during the UN's earliest days, Pandit returned in 1946, and several times thereafter, as leader of the Indian delegation, where her presence challenged Western expectations of Indian womanhood. She gained a reputation for her persistence, persuasiveness, democratic nature and informality, before rising to one of the highest positions the UN could offer. Pandit's election in 1953 as the first female and first Asian President of the UN's General Assembly (its policy-making body) was welcomed with such great hope and optimism that 'the UN Secretariat had to engage nine secretaries to deal with her mail'.[24] In the context of the Cold War and an increasing number of colonised nations seeking independence, her appointment was seen to represent an 'awareness of the shifts and changes which have been going on in global politics'.[25]

At the end of this eminent year-long role, Pandit was made India's High Commissioner in London (1954–61), the most important of the numerous diplomatic positions she occupied, where she navigated the changed post-colonial relationship between India and Britain. In her later years, Pandit returned to the Indian government, notably as Governor of Maharastra (1962–4). Other books by her also provide great insight into her experiences, including *Prison Days* (1945) and her memoir, *The Scope of Happiness* (1979). CN

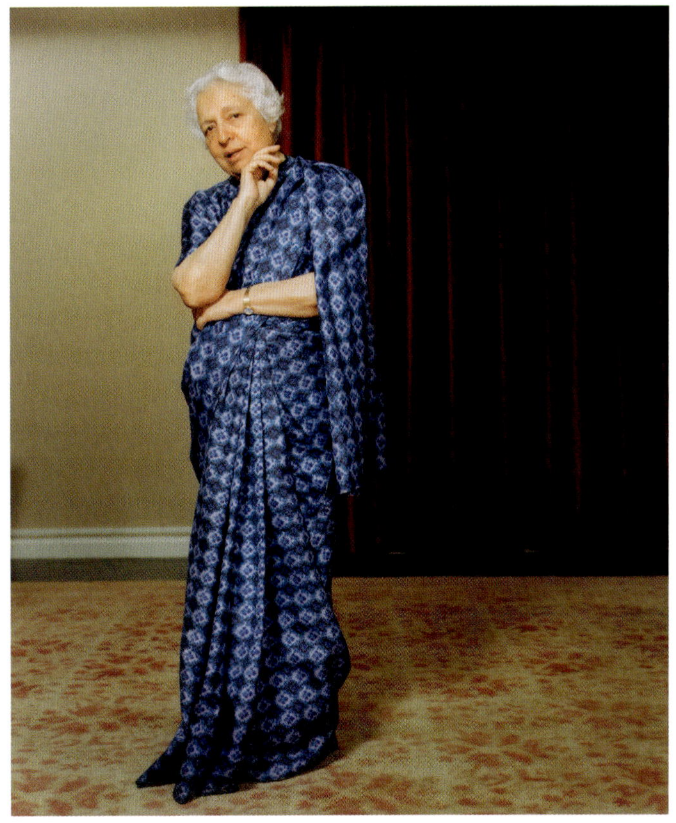

Vijaya Lakshmi Pandit (1900–1990)
By Bern Schwartz, 27 March 1978
Dye transfer print, 251 × 200mm
National Portrait Gallery, London, P1231

Rika Markus

In 1954, before the European Championship, I took part in the International Bridge Festival at Monte Carlo, always a pleasant place to play and now a major fixture of the bridge year. I was captain of the team … and to everyone's surprise, even our own, we emerged the clear winners of this team event … I felt that in women's bridge I had reached the zenith – three European Championships for Austria and two for Britain – and it was a natural ambition to play in the Open Championship.

Writing here Rika – also known as Rixi – Markus is triumphant in her tone, as well she might be. Fresh from a hard-earned victory in Monte Carlo, Markus is looking ahead to future challenges. Her hopes are high and the expectation to be enlisted as the sixth member of the British Open team for the European Championship at Montreaux in a few months' time seems a concrete reality. However, to Markus's great disappointment, the call to join the team did not

materialise. This setback represented only a small glitch in an otherwise stellar 60-year career. Markus was, in fact, the first Woman World Grand Master within the World Bridge Federation, winning seven European and four world titles for Britain.

Despite her own successes, Markus held the controversial view that women were less adept at bridge than men. She believed that women lacked the power of concentration, could not count as quickly or as accurately as men and could not plan ahead. Markus herself was living proof that women were far from being less capable and that these perceived disadvantages were part of a broader societal attitude that tended to undermine women's abilities.

Markus not only had a triumphant career playing bridge, starting in 1955 she was also bridge correspondent for the *Guardian*, a role which spanned 37 years. Looking back on this experience she wrote: 'It is naturally tempting to write mainly about hands one has played oneself, but too much of that makes the column look like an exercise in egotism, so friends have been a great boon with their suggestions and anecdotes.' The popularity of her column led Markus to develop some of her short pieces into fully fledged books, making her a published author, as well as a bridge champion. The accessible nature of these publications is captured by their snappy titles, which include *Bid Boldly, Play Safe* (1966), *Aces and Places: The International Bridge Circuit* (1972) and *More Deadly than the Male: First Lady of Bridge* (1984). The last title, in particular, suggests that Markus came to recognise the power of her female hands, which were as competitive, if not more, than those of her male peers. FF

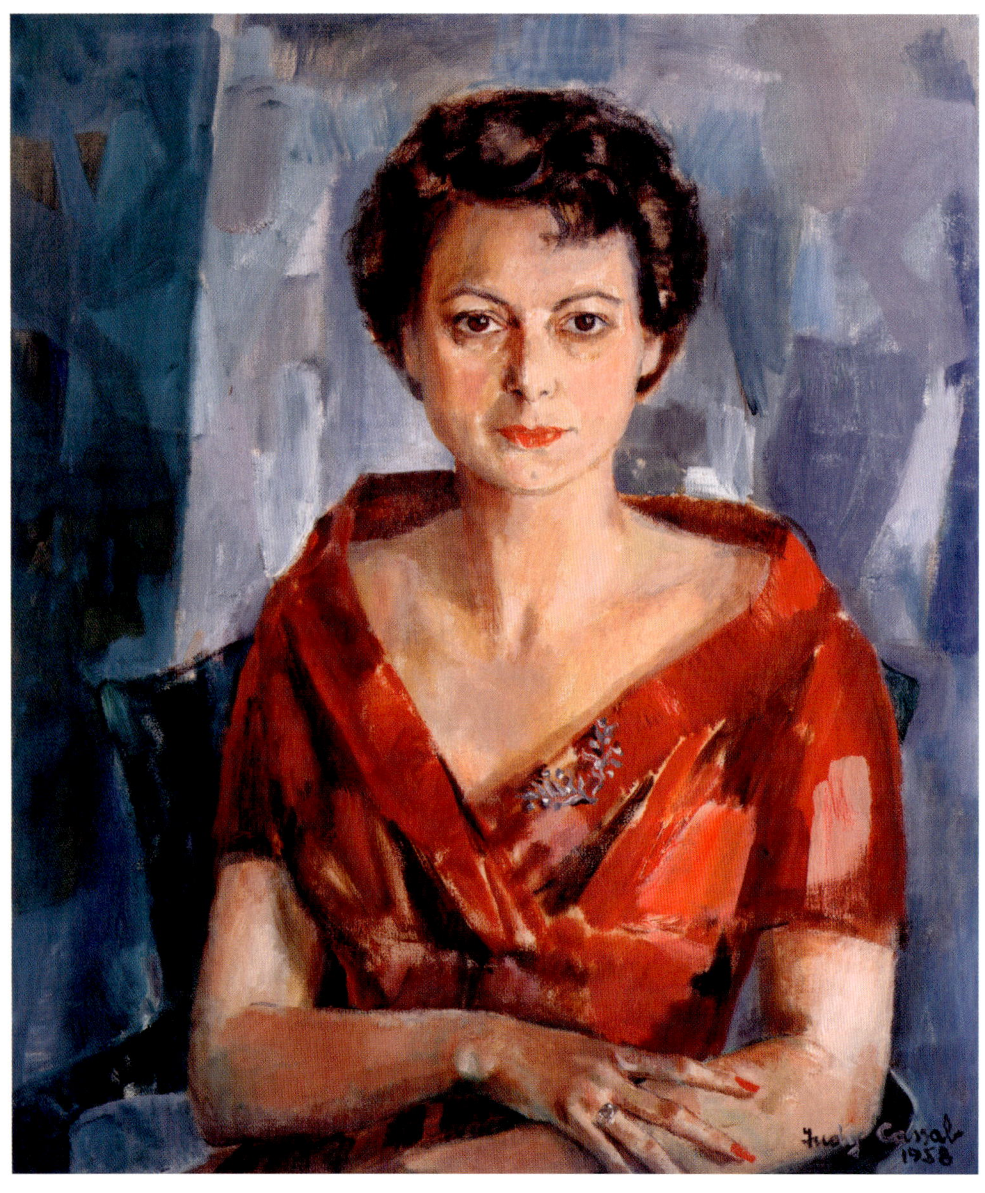

Rika ('Rixi') Markus (1910–1992)
By Judy Cassab, 1958
Oil on canvas, 762 × 634mm
National Portrait Gallery, London, 6199

Sheila van Damm

Sheila van Damm was a leading rally-car driver and a theatre manager. In 1955, she won the Coupe des Dames in the Monte Carlo Rally, the highest award for women. Van Damm had competed in the Rally every year since 1951, becoming the first British driver to win it since 1932.

Van Damm tended to downplay her talent. An interview after her 1955 win stated:

'I'm very careful of my neck' says Sheila van Damm, women's European touring car champion and winner of the women's section of the hazardous Monte Carlo rally. 'I don't intend to break it if I can help it, although I'm a great fatalist ... I never had what you might call real driving ability', she said in an interview outlining her trail to the top in a sport that takes contestants over icy roads, up mountains and down rainy valleys for days and nights at a time. 'The test,' she says, 'is endurance, driving ability and leaving nothing to chance. Every step must be carefully planned, maps and watches checked and the whole thing gone over thoroughly. And of course a bit of luck always helps.'

The daughter of a London theatre impresario, van Damm's first taste for motoring was supporting the war effort as a driver in the Women's Auxiliary Air Force. She subsequently trained as a pilot and joined the Royal Air Force Volunteer Reserve, where she learnt acrobatics and formation flying – but in the late 1940s there was no place for a woman in civil aviation. It was as a publicity stunt for the Windmill Theatre in 1950, organized by her father, that she took part in her first motor racing event, the *Daily Express* Rally, with her sister Nona as co-driver. Their Sunbeam Talbot car had 'Windmill Girl' painted on the side. Van Damm's performance was so impressive, winning third prize in the women's section, that she was offered

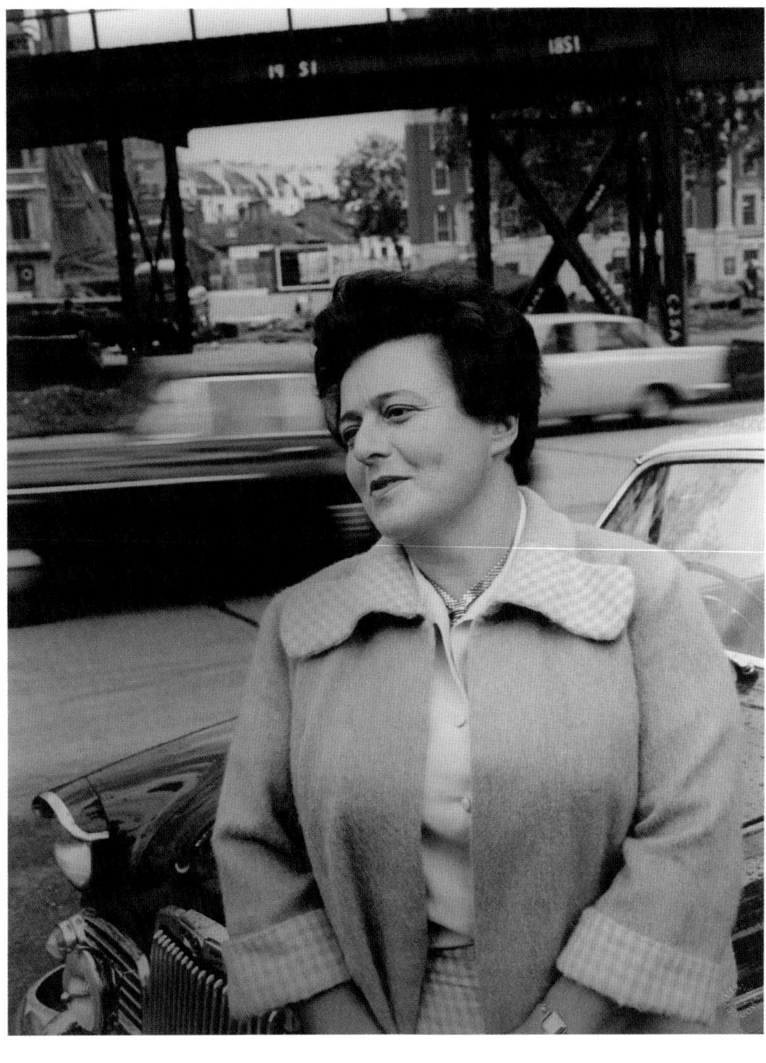

a seat for the following season. She came fifth in the 1951 Monte Carlo Rally before her first major success in the 1952 Motor Cycling Club Rally, winning the top prize in another Sunbeam Talbot. In 1953 she was officially known as 'the fastest woman in Europe' after winning the Coupe des Dames in the Alpine Rally and a Coupe des Alpes with her co-driver Anne Hall. They went on to win the Women's European Touring Championship in 1954 and in 1955.

Her heart however, had always been at the Windmill, where she had begun working aged 16, and in between the rallies she helped her father run the theatre until she officially retired from motor racing. In 1957 she published her autobiography, *No Excuses*. Van Damm inherited the Windmill when her father died in 1960. It was famous for remaining open at the height of the Blitz, as she noted in her later memoir, *We Never Closed. The Windmill Story* (1967). She eventually retired to Sussex where she ran a farm and 'confined her driving to country lanes'.[26] GA

Sheila van Damm (1922–1987)
By Lewis Morley, 1962
Resin print, 401 × 297mm
National Portrait Gallery, London, x76644

1956   Dorothy Bohm

*Dorothy Bohm knows that her camera
does not only see, it also feels.*[27]

Trailblazing photographer Dorothy
Bohm lived in Hampstead from 1956.
She travelled the world, photographing
life as she saw it, but this area of
north-west London where she lived
was also a constant source of
inspiration. Focusing entirely on
observational, unmanipulated
photography, Bohm's work shows her
fascination with ordinary people and
the world of fleeting appearances.
Her career, spanning eight decades,
included portraiture, still life,
landscape and social documentary,
in black and white and, from the mid-
1980s, in colour. Reflecting on her
work, Bohm explained:

*I have spent my lifetime taking
photographs. The photograph fulfils
my deep need to stop things from
disappearing. It makes transience less
painful and retains some of the special
magic, which I have looked for and found.
I have tried to create order out of chaos,
to find stability in flux and beauty in
the most unlikely places.*

Bohm was born Dorothea Israelit
in Königsberg, Germany (now
Kaliningrad, Russia). In 1932, her
Jewish family moved to Memel
(now Klaipeda, Lithuania) but aged 14,
just before the outbreak of the Second
World War, Bohm was sent to the
safety of England. Upon departure, her
father gifted her his Leica camera.

Inspired by a visit to the Baker
Street studio of émigré photographer
Germaine Kanova in 1940, Bohm
decided to study photography at
Manchester College of Technology.
After graduating, she worked as a
studio assistant before setting up
her own portrait business, 'Studio
Alexander', on Manchester's Market
Street. A wife and mother, she became
the breadwinner while her husband

completed his PhD. In the late 1940s,
she began taking pictures outdoors,
travelling widely and photographing
the world around her, establishing
herself as a prominent humanist
photographer. Her images capture
moments in time, life as it happens,
and reveal her profound interest
in people as well as an instinct for an
aesthetically satisfying composition.
Bohm's images portray her subjects
with great sensitivity, empathy and
occasionally humour. In the late 1960s
and 1970s, she created an important
body of work depicting street life
in London and revealing a wide range
of human sentiment and incident.

Bohm was part of a remarkable
generation of women émigré

photographers who fled Nazi
persecution and helped shape post-
war British visual culture. Her first
solo exhibition was in 1969 at the
Institute of Contemporary Arts,
London, and her first book was
published in 1970. In 1971, she was
closely involved in the founding of
The Photographers' Gallery, and was
its Associate Director for the next 15
years. Bohm was elected an Honorary
Fellow of the Royal Photographic
Society in 2009. She continued making
pictures into her nineties, remaining
closely engaged with her photography.
GA

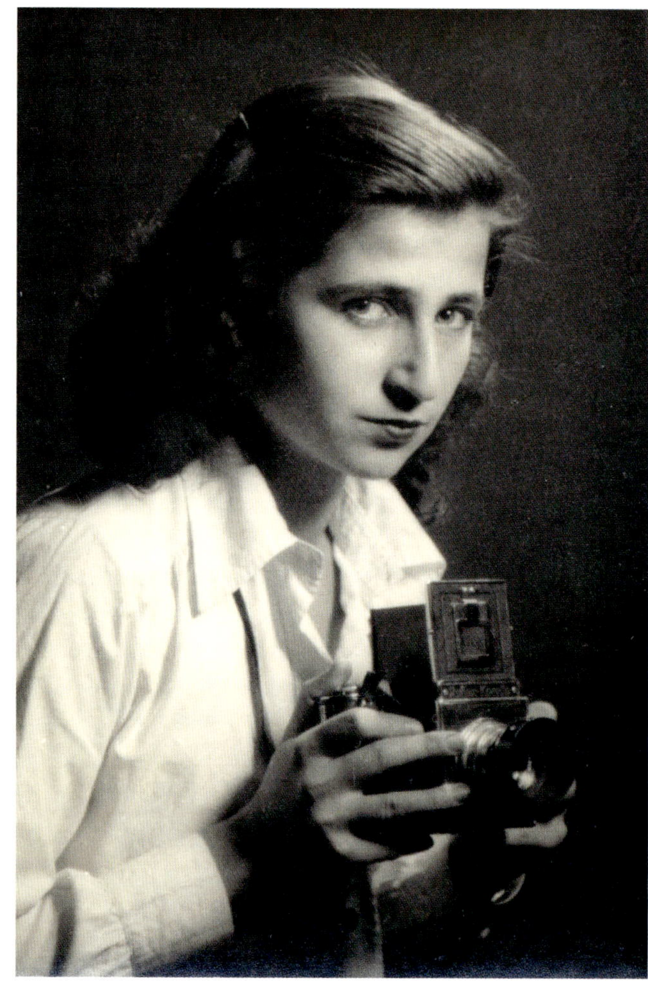

Dorothy Bohm (1924–2023)
Self-portrait, 1942
Gelatin silver print
Dorothy Bohm Archives

1957   Sheila Willcox

At the end of the second day at the Badminton Horse Trials in 1957, eventer Sheila Willcox belatedly celebrated her twenty-first birthday with a cake decorated with a castle, streams and undulating terrain, plus 21 fences with 'a little model of Chips and me leaping safely over the last one'.[28] This vision of her succeeding would swiftly translate into reality. The competition is one of the most prestigious in the international equestrian calendar and Willcox was already leading in the initial dressage and cross-country phases with her horse High and Mighty, whom she nicknamed Chips. Despite her late night, the next day she rode a clear round in the third and final show-jumping phase and won the title. Months later in October, Willcox added to this victory as the first woman to secure team and individual gold medals at the European Championships.

Willcox had shown her instinctive ability to prepare horses for success from a young age. Aged ten, she sufficiently trained her first young, unbroken pony, Folly, within six months for entry into a local agricultural show. Willcox revelled in the competitive atmosphere: 'to wear a number, to be called by name into the ring and walk, trot and canter round with the other ponies – this was halcyon bliss', and she went home with a rosette. Eight years later, Willcox decided to devote herself to eventing, feeling 'most attracted to a competition demanding talent in three distinct directions'.

Hardworking and single-minded, Willcox was disciplined and had a strong desire to win, leading her to secure more national and international titles, including two further Badminton victories in 1958 and 1959 (becoming the only rider to achieve three consecutive wins in this challenging event), another European team gold in 1959 and first place at the Burghley Horse Trials in 1968.

These accomplishments should have qualified Willcox for the British Olympic team, but eventing was still an exclusively male sport within the Games. Nonetheless, Willcox paved the way for future generations of female eventers by dismantling preconceptions that the sport was too challenging for women. Eventing is now one of the few Olympic sports where men and women compete alongside one another.

A fall at the Tidworth Horse Trials in 1971 left Willcox paralysed in one leg, but did not inhibit her equestrian ambitions, and she switched her focus from eventing to Grand Prix dressage. Drawing on her extensive experience, she went into coaching and published *The Event Horse* in 1973 – a comprehensive and influential training guide, which was the first of its kind for eventers. She also produced two autobiographies, one of which was released posthumously. CN

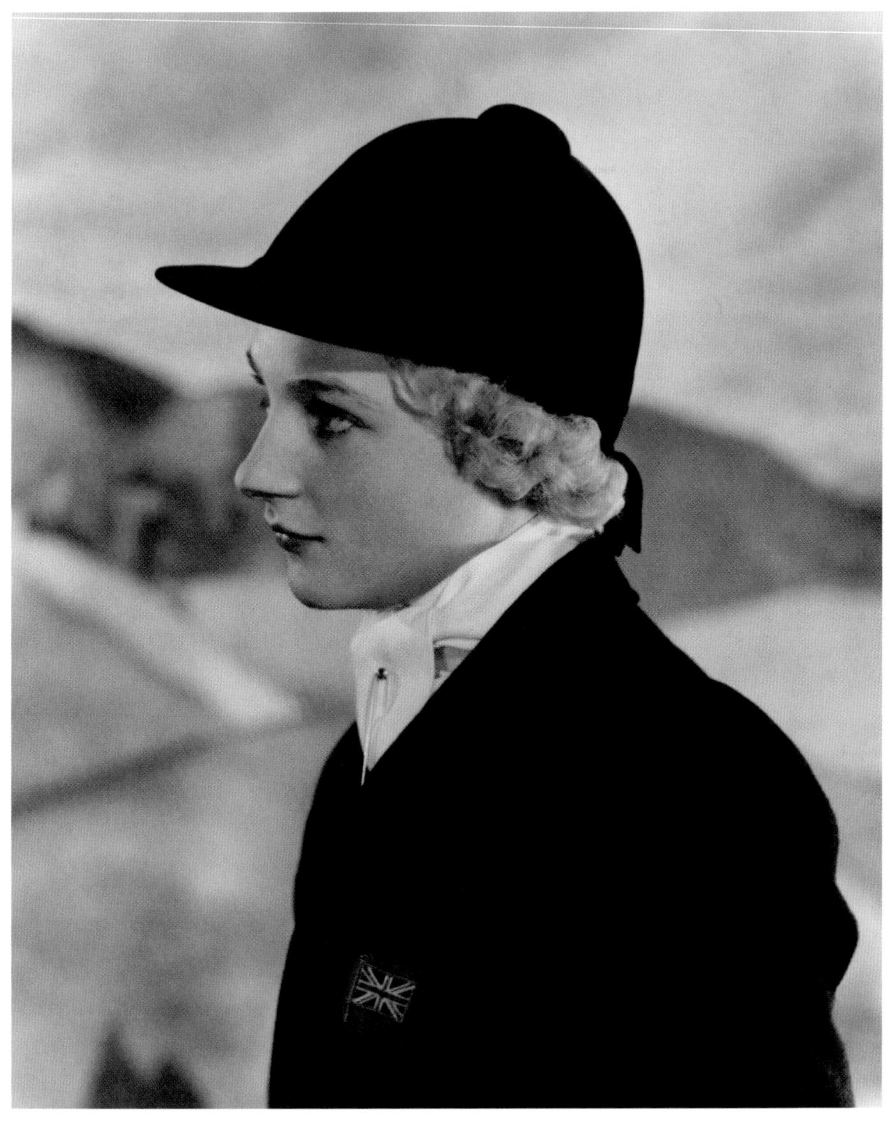

Sheila Willcox (1936–2017)
By Yevonde, 1956
Gelatin silver print, 358 × 278mm
National Portrait Gallery, London, x29858

Claudia Jones

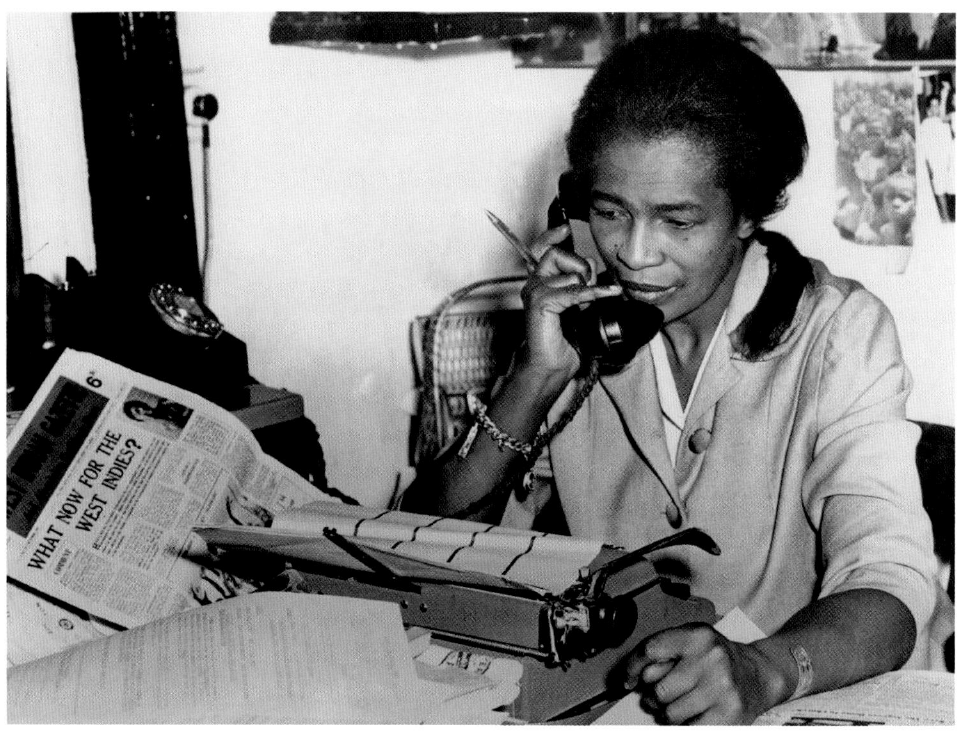

Seated in the offices of the *West Indian
Gazette and Afro-Asian Caribbean
News* in Brixton, south-west London,
the political activist and journalist
Claudia Jones is shown entirely
absorbed in her work as founding
editor of what is considered Britain's
first major black newspaper.

Jones had arrived in Britain
just 27 months before publishing the
West Indian Gazette's inaugural issue
in March 1958. Born in Trinidad and
raised in Harlem, New York, Jones
became politically motivated through
her experiences of the adversity the
black community faced and emerging
anti-racist movements. As a communist
and feminist, she gained journalistic
experience at the American *Daily
Worker* newspaper, and explored the
'super-exploitation' of black women in
her theoretical writings. This activity
inevitably alerted the authorities
during the height of the McCarthy-era
'Red Scare', and Jones was imprisoned
on numerous occasions before her
deportation to England in December
1955, where she remained.

Once in London, Jones found
many West Indians who had emigrated
in the years following the Second World
War and encountered widespread
prejudice upon their arrival. The
monthly *West Indian Gazette* attempted
to foster a shared cultural identity
among this developing community, and
strived to raise political consciousness
with its reports on local cases
of racial discrimination, alongside
stories detailing African struggles
for independence and the US Civil
Rights Movement. Mixed with arts
reviews, poems, short stories and
beauty articles, the paper aimed to
appeal to the widest possible audience,
and by 1959 its total circulation was
around 10,000. Although the paper
was constantly in debt (and closed
eight months after Jones's death), her
belief in its importance for the black
community was unflagging.

Jones was also a dynamic and
charismatic leader, arranging political
rallies and events, which became
important meeting places for the
black community. On 30 January 1959,
to counteract the negative impact of
racially motivated attacks and riots
in Nottingham and Notting Hill over
the summer of 1958, she organized
the first annual Caribbean Carnival
at St Pancras Town Hall, to revitalise
the black community. Sponsored by
the *West Indian Gazette* and televised
by the BBC, the carnival was a vibrant
expression and celebration of West
Indian culture, epitomising Jones's
belief that 'a people's art is the genesis
of their freedom'. Proceeds went to
funding community projects, and the
event is considered to be a forerunner
to the Notting Hill Carnival, which,
since 1966, has become one of the
world's largest and most renowned
street festivals. CN

Claudia Jones (1915–1964)
By FGP/Archive Photos, attributed
to Getty Images Hulton Archive, 1962
Modern gelatin silver print, 270 × 372mm
National Portrait Gallery, London, x200196

1959   Althea McNish

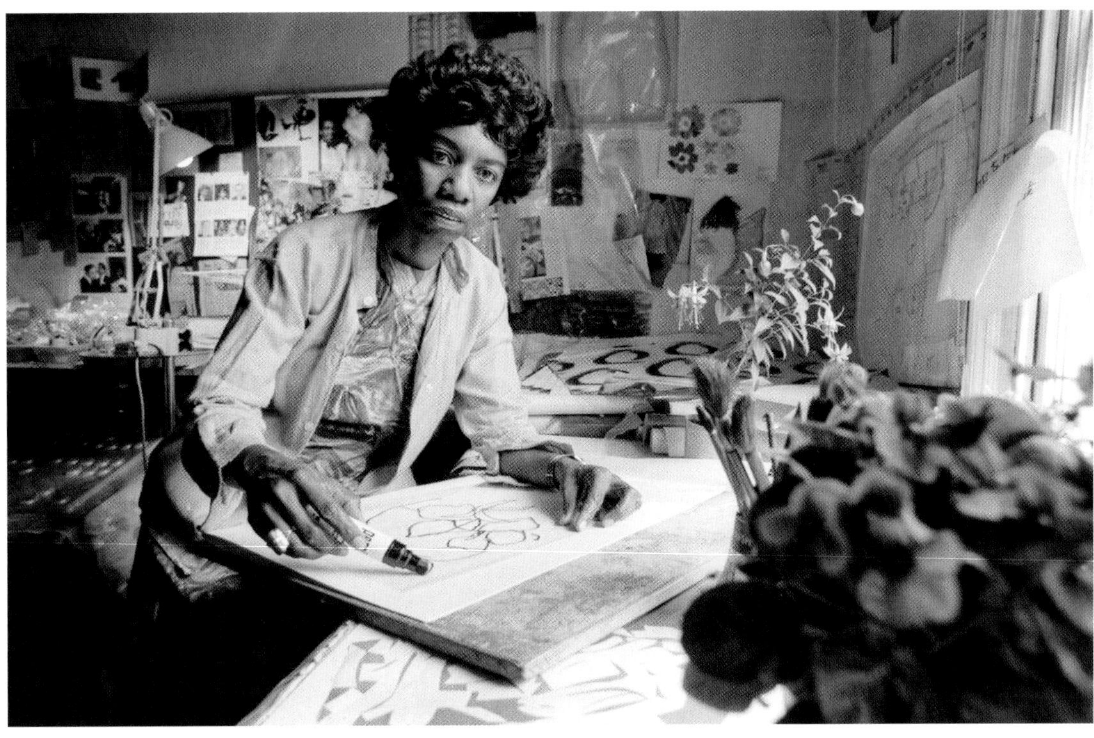

In this black and white portrait we see textile designer Althea McNish surrounded by her drawings for fabrics. Trinidad-born McNish migrated to the United Kingdom in 1951, becoming one of the first textile designers of African-Caribbean descent to achieve international recognition. Legend has it that the day after graduating from the Royal College of Art, she was approached by the chairman of London's Liberty department store to design fashion and furnishings fabrics for them. Her breakthrough moment, however, came in 1959 when she created one of her most famous patterns, 'Golden Harvest' for Hull Traders. Inspiration for this arose from a walk in the Essex countryside where McNish stumbled upon a wheat field, which serendipitously reminded her of the sugar cane plantations in Trinidad. Like many of her future designs, 'Golden Harvest' was imbued with a joyful tropical spirit, which epitomises McNish's belief that 'Everything I did, I saw it through a tropical eye.'

McNish's choice of bright colours and innovative motifs made her designs stand out in the immediate post-war years. Tropical flora and fauna, as well as lively abstract patterns, characterised the furnishing and fashion fabrics that she designed over the years for Liberty, Heal's and Hull Traders. Drawing on her background as an artist, she always strived to make 'the impossible become possible', as she would say. Among her clients was Zika Ascher – co-founder of a textile manufacturing company known for its collaborations with leading contemporary artists, including Henri Matisse and Henry Moore. For Ascher, McNish produced designs printed in silk that were chosen by couture clients such as Christian Dior.

1966 was a momentous year for McNish, who was entrusted with the fabrics for Queen Elizabeth II's wardrobe for the royal tour of Trinidad and the Caribbean. That same year, she was invited to design and decorate the 'Bachelor Girl's Room' for London's popular Ideal Home Show. McNish envisioned this setting as a pad for a creative young woman like herself. Filled to the brim with mood boards and swatches, the space oozed creativity and promoted the image of an emancipated woman: resonant with 1960s counterculture and the exuberant vibe of Swinging London. Alongside her design practice, she also taught, painted and was an active member of the Caribbean Artists Movement (CAM), founded in London in 1966 with the aim of celebrating a shared sense of Caribbean 'nationhood'. FF

Althea McNish (1924–2020)
By an *Evening Standard* photographer, 1973
Evening Standard/Hulton Archive/Getty Images

1960 Ida Kar

This is photography at its best and portraiture at its most human.[30]

It was in the spring of 1960 that Ida Kar's retrospective opened at one of Britain's most bold and prestigious art galleries, making her the first photographer to receive a retrospective at such an institution. Kar presented her portraits of artists and writers as high-contrast, board-mounted, impactful prints on the Whitechapel Gallery's walls – as Colin MacInnes wrote for her catalogue, 'her subjects stand revealed … and she tells us … indirectly, quite a lot about herself.'

Kar was born in 1908 to Armenian parents and spent her childhood in Armenia, Russia and Iran, until the family moved to Alexandria, Egypt, in 1921, where she attended the Lycée Français. Kar produced her first experimental photographs in the heady atmosphere of 1920s Paris, while there studying piano. Back in Egypt, she worked as a photographer's assistant, before collaborating with her first husband Edmond Belali as 'Idabel' and exhibiting with the surrealist Art and Liberty Group, who aligned themselves with revolutionary independence.

Following her divorce from Belali, Kar married Victor Musgrave, a writer-artist and advocate of the avant-garde who had been drafted to Cairo during the war. Together they established an artistic circle, which they then gradually reinvented on their relocation to London in 1945.

By 1949 they were installed at 1 Litchfield Street off Charing Cross Road, with Kar's studio at the top and, by 1953, Musgrave's Gallery One below. It was the following year that visits to Parisian ateliers and London studios resulted in Kar's photographic series *Forty Artists from London and Paris*. In 1956 the gallery moved to Soho, the bohemian centre of London, and John Kasmin began assisting, gaining commissions from the *Tatler*, which

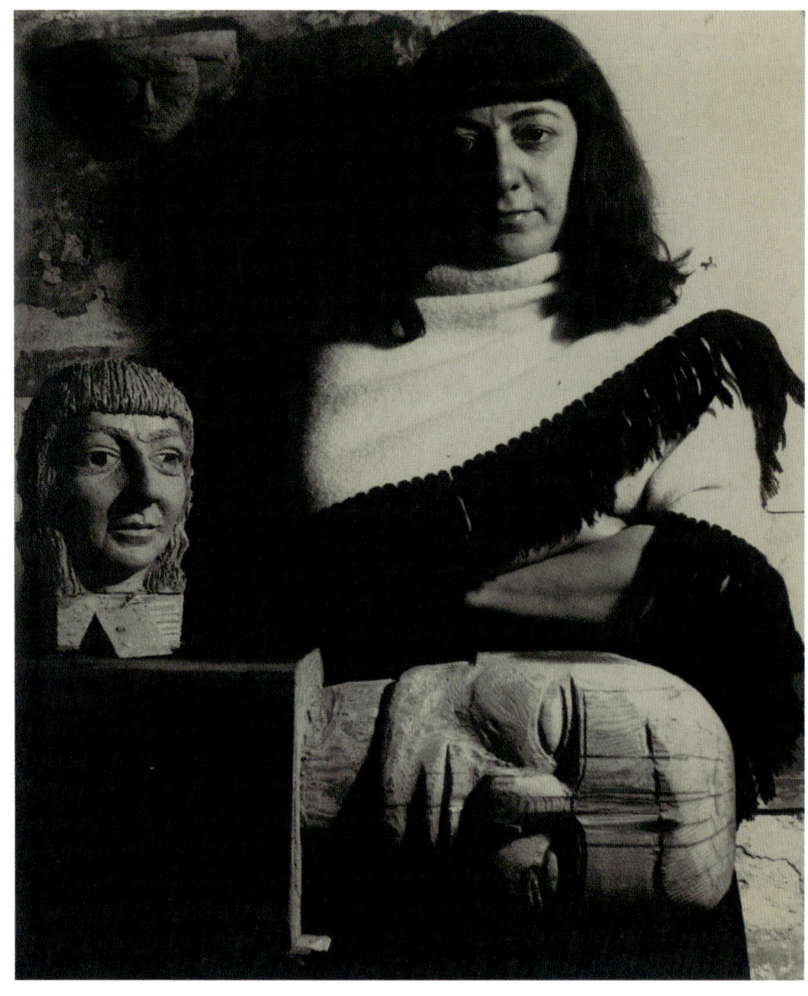

published 'Return to Armenia' in 1958. Kar's heritage was of deep importance to her, as was photography as her means of expression and income. In 1959 she travelled again to Armenia, documented residents of East Germany and exhibited in Moscow.

By now in her early fifties, Kar's exhibition at the Whitechapel was the pinnacle of her career as a photographer. Working with her Rolleiflex, shooting 6 to 36 frames, Kar connected with her artistic subjects as she positioned them with all the accoutrements of their trade, letting daylight sculpt their forms.

After the closure of Gallery One in 1963, Kar photographed creatives in Havana following the Cuban revolution – her shift towards reportage was applauded. She went on innovating, forming KarSEC with three young photographers – John Cousins, Les Smithers and Lawrence Ellar – and photographed a series of nudes shortly before her death in 1974. The National Portrait Gallery acquired Kar's archive in 1999 and held a major exhibition of her work in 2011.

Collectively, the portraits shown at the Whitechapel Gallery in 1960 along with her wider archive describe the life and soul of artistic post-war London. Kar's portraits rendered visual the bohemian spirit of Soho, where anyone could belong. CF

Ida Kar (1908–1974)
Self-portrait, 1955
Gelatin silver print, 242 × 195mm
National Portrait Gallery, London, x133217

1961 Vanessa Redgrave

'Tonight a great actress was born',
announced Laurence Olivier during
a 1937 performance of *Hamlet* at The
Old Vic theatre in London. This was
in reference to his co-star's newborn
child, Vanessa Redgrave. Born into
a family of professional actors, she
was the daughter of Michael Redgrave
and Rachel Kempson. Redgrave's
sister Lynn and brother Corin,
as well as her daughters Natasha
and Joely, continued the Redgrave
acting tradition.

In 1961, Redgrave rose to
prominence with her portrayal of
Rosalind in *As You Like It* with the
Royal Shakespeare Company. She
was just 24 when she played the
Shakespearean heroine and her
performance drew widespread acclaim,
praised for the naturalness and
depth of her acting. The production
transferred to London's Aldwych
Theatre in 1962, and the following year
an adapted version aired on the BBC.
Since then, Redgrave has appeared in
myriad productions in London's West
End and on Broadway. Playwrights
Arthur Miller and Tennessee Williams
declared her 'the greatest actress
of our time'.

Redgrave's film career has
included roles in new wave films
such as *Morgan – A Suitable Case for
Treatment* and *Blow-Up*, both in 1966.
She was also in *Camelot* (1967), *Isadora*
(1968) and avant-garde films such as
The Devils (1971), before winning an
Oscar in 1977 for *Julia*. Throughout
her career, she has appeared on
stage, screen and television, winning
numerous accolades, including
two Emmys, a Tony, an Olivier, two
Golden Globes, the BAFTA Fellowship
Award and the Golden Lion Honorary
Award. Her reputation has been further
cemented over the years with onscreen
credits including *Agatha* (1979),
Howards End (1992), *Mission: Impossible*
(1996) and *Atonement* (2007).

Redgrave published her
autobiography in 1993. Throughout
her life she has also been a vocal
political activist; her directorial debut
in 2017 was a documentary about
Syrian refugees, *Sea Sorrow*.

She was made a Dame for
services to drama in 2022, having
previously turned down the honour. GA

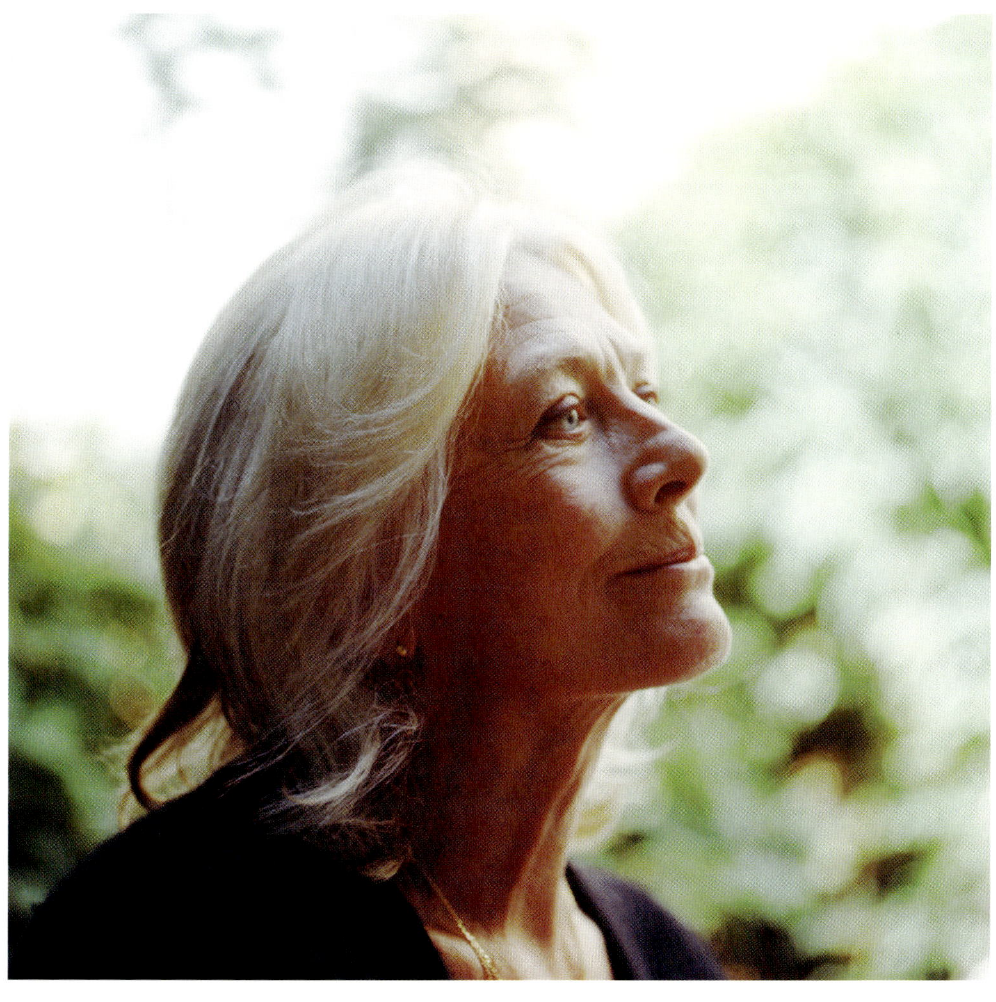

Vanessa Redgrave (b.1937)
By Jillian Edelstein, 2008
Chromogenic print, 455 × 455mm
National Portrait Gallery, London, x135423

1962 Stephanie Shirley

Ambition, determination and resilience made Stephanie Shirley one of the most remarkable women of her generation. Shirley was just five years old when in 1939 she boarded the Kindertransport train for child refugees from Vienna to London. Little did she know that she would go on to become a groundbreaking entrepreneur and one of the most successful businesswomen in British history.

In the early 1960s Shirley was frustrated by the sexism and inequality faced by women trying to build a career in a man's world. Undeterred by these obstacles and filled with ambition, she decided to start her own company, selling software. This was 1962, and Shirley had '£6 of capital, a dining room table, a telephone,' and, as she went on to explain, 'one other mad idea: those who worked for me would all be women, employed on a freelance basis and working from home.' Every aspect of Shirley's plan was revolutionary. For a start, the world of computer technology was still in its infancy and to set up in 1962 what today would be described as a start-up was exceptionally forward-thinking. Making it even more astounding was Shirley's decision to 'offer opportunities to the kind of women whom traditional male-dominated companies considered unemployable.' These were wives, mothers and carers for elderly relations or disabled partners.

Shirley's company was called Freelance Programmers and it offered to write computer programmes on behalf of clients. Finding clients, however, proved to be a struggle at first. Through contacts Shirley was able to secure some initial jobs, but many of the potential customers that she approached by letter failed to respond. Given the sexist climate, it quickly became apparent that companies were refusing to take Shirley's proposals seriously because she was a woman. At her husband's suggestion, she swapped Stephanie for Steve, and positive responses started to trickle in. Customers included Tate & Lyle, Mars and British Railways. Over the decades, the business flourished and by the year 2000 – the same year Shirley was awarded a DBE – it was valued at $3 billion. Thanks to the co-ownership structure she had set up, over 70 of her employees became millionaires. The impact of Shirley's vision has extended beyond business to encompass a wide range of philanthropic projects, including work in the field of autism inspired by her late son Giles. FF

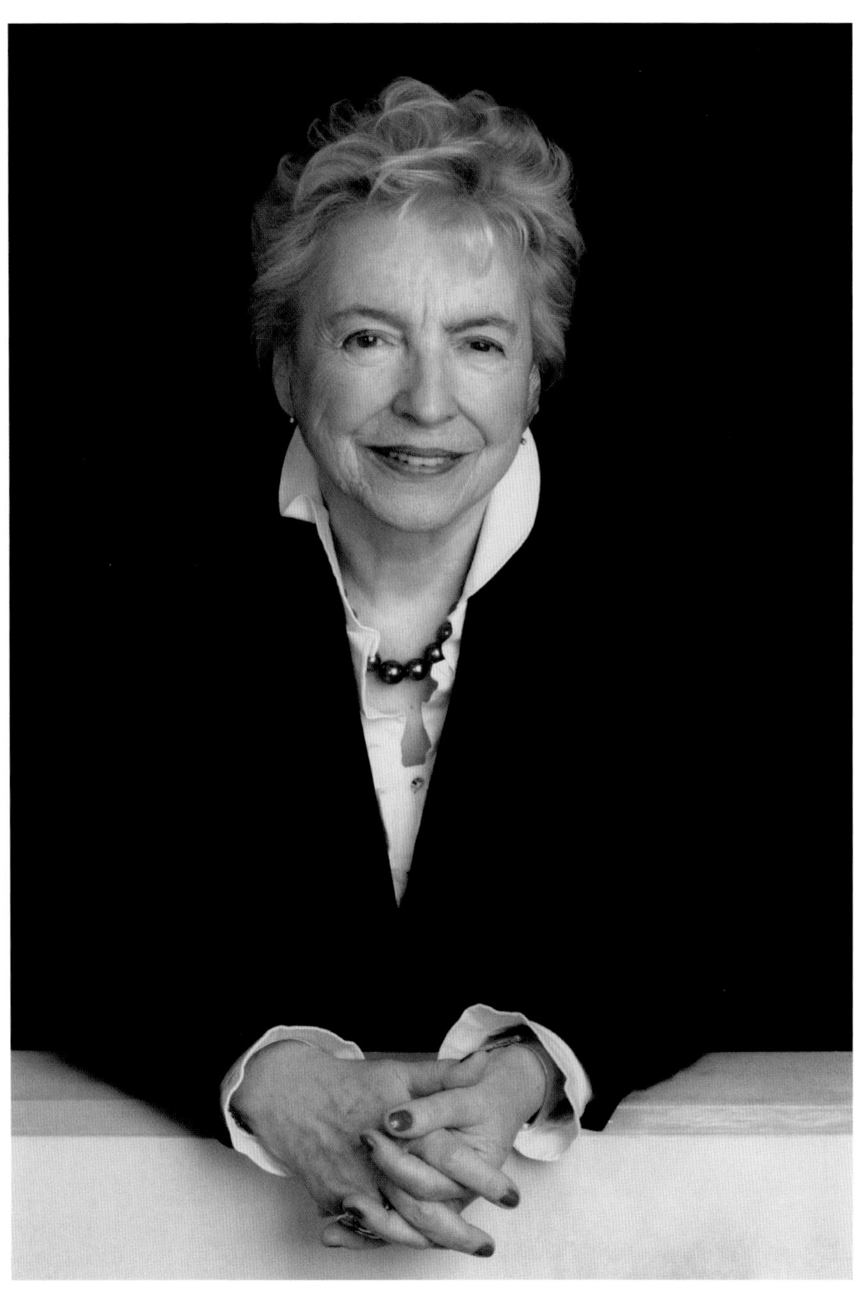

Stephanie ('Steve') Shirley (b.1933)
By Robert Taylor, September 2008
Pigment print, 406 × 269mm
National Portrait Gallery, London, x133001

Pauline Boty

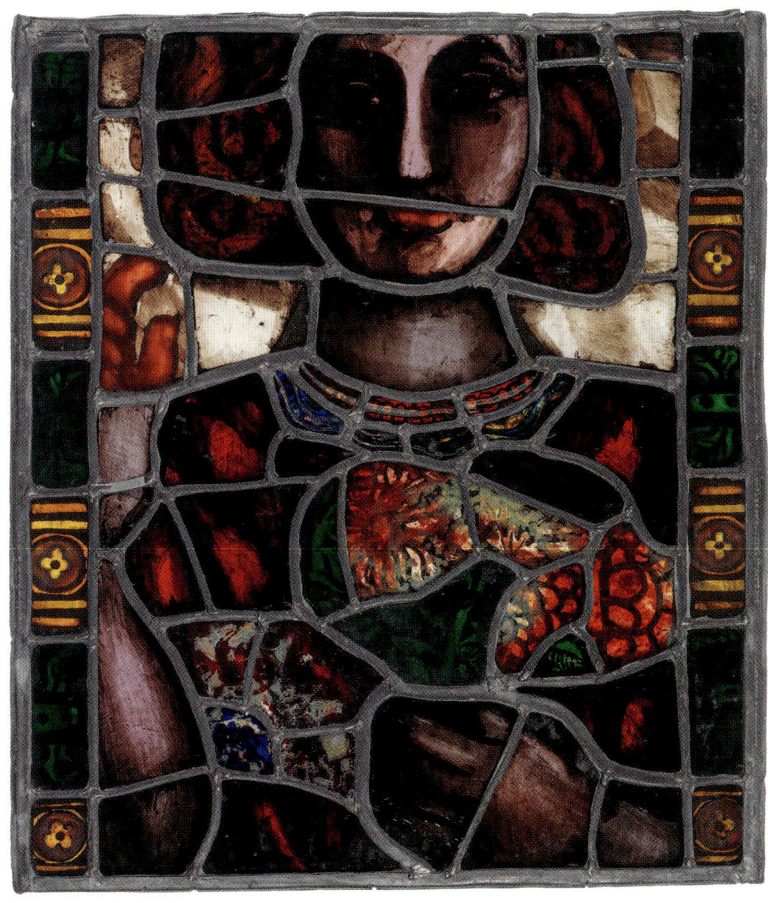

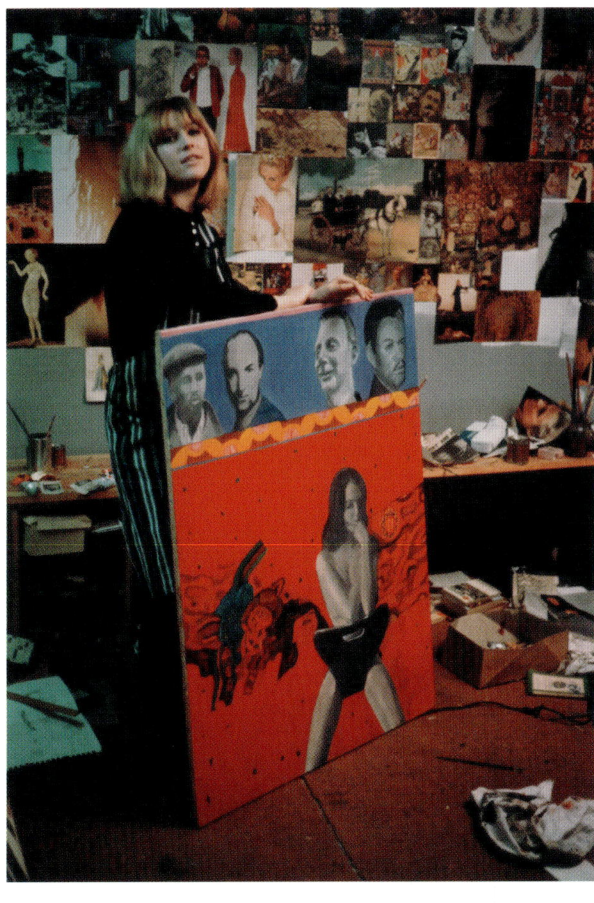

Artist Pauline Boty quickly established herself as an icon of glamour in 1960s 'Swinging' London. Her work was largely associated with the British pop art movement, then on the rise. Boty's contribution to pop was confirmed by her appearance in Ken Russell's BBC television documentary on the London pop scene, *Pop Goes the Easel* (1962). By 1963, the year of her first solo exhibition at Grabowski Gallery in London, she was going from strength to strength. Yet in spite of her growing recognition as an artist, the world continued to value her primarily for her looks.

Boty attended Wimbledon School of Art (1954–8) before studying stained glass at the Royal College of Art (1958–61). The rare stained-glass self-portrait in the National Portrait Gallery's Collection was made during Boty's student days and displays a mix of classical technique and innovative approach. Boty subsequently turned her attention to painting, and by 1963 was making some of her most recognisable works. Her pop vocabulary utilised images culled from mass media. These included portraits of celebrities like Elvis Presley, Marilyn Monroe and Brigitte Bardot, among others. Through her work, Boty strived to undermine gender stereotypes, some of which reverberated within pop art itself. Most male pop artists were making works in which women appeared as mere sexual objects, intended to satisfy the male gaze. Boty was critical of these sexist and demeaning attitudes towards women and used her painting as a way to challenge them.

In a photograph from 1964, Michael Ward portrays Boty in her studio holding the painting *Scandal 63* (now lost). The work is one of Boty's more explicitly political pieces. In it, she refers to the affair between John Profumo, a British cabinet minister and Secretary of State for War, and Christine Keeler, a model and showgirl, who also had personal relations with Yevgeny Ivanov, an attaché at the Russian Embassy. When the affair was revealed, Keeler ended up being the scapegoat in the ensuing political fallout. For the portrait of Keeler, Boty used a photograph by Lewis Morley that presents the showgirl in an over-sexualised pose. Boty's intention here was to undermine the sexual objectification to which Keeler had fallen prey. FF

Pauline Boty (1938–1966)
Self-portrait, *c*.1958
Stained glass, 500 × 430mm
National Portrait Gallery, London, 7030

Pauline Boty
By Michael Ward, 13 January 1964
Chromogenic print, 330 x 220mm
National Portrait Gallery, London, x125839

Shirley Bassey

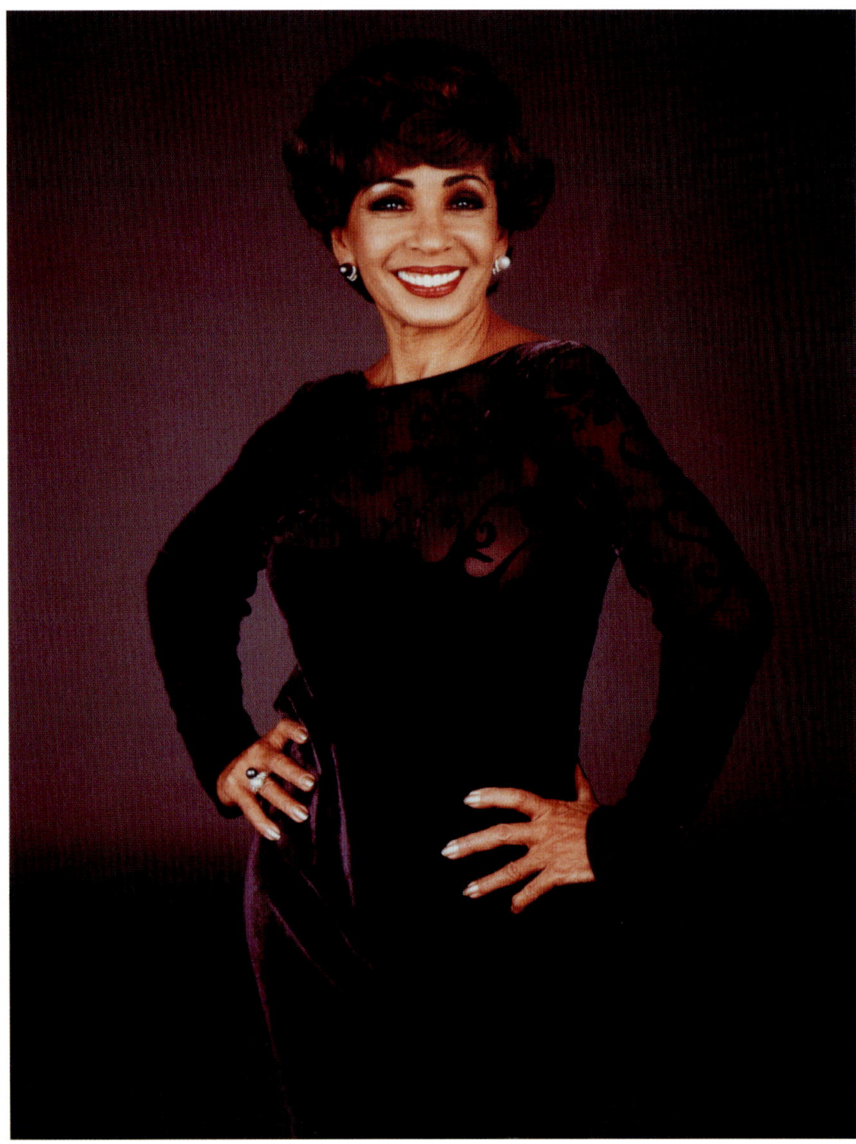

Goldfinger
He's the man, the man with the
Midas touch ...

Following a flamboyant trumpet opening, these are the first words, sung in Shirley Bassey's powerful voice, of the title song for *Goldfinger* (1964), the third film in the now hugely successful James Bond franchise. Bassey recalled that the lyrics were not yet written, but 'the moment [John Barry, the composer] played the music to me, I got goose pimples, and I told him, "I don't

care what the words are. I'll do it".' Barry remarked:

Shirley was great casting for 'Goldfinger.' Nobody could have sung it like her. She had that great dramatic sense. When it came to the studio, she didn't know what the hell the song was about, but she sang it with such total conviction that she convinced the rest of the world.

The single reached the top ten internationally and led to her recording two further Bond songs, 'Diamonds Are

Forever' (1971) and 'Moonraker' (1979). 'Goldfinger' has since become Bassey's most recognisable song, and a classic of twentieth-century popular music; it was inducted into the Grammy Hall of Fame in 2008.

Though 'Goldfinger' made Bassey into a global star, she was already established as a singer in Britain, renowned for her impressive vocal range and on-stage charisma. Her characteristic glamour was a significant departure from her poor upbringing in Cardiff, where she sang in local pubs and working men's clubs before gaining contracts to perform in musicals. Wider success then came quickly, with her first single recorded in 1956 while she was still in her teens. Bassey gained her first UK number one single, 'As I Love You', in 1959, and further top ten hits followed.

After a lull during the latter part of the 1960s, the next decade brought renewed success for Bassey. A hardworking performer, she released 15 albums in the 1970s alone, and demonstrated her versatility and appeal through sold-out shows at prestigious venues such as New York's Carnegie Hall and as the host of her own eponymous television show. Although her output decreased in subsequent decades, performances at Glastonbury Festival in 2007 'to an ecstatic, enraptured audience – most of whom were probably not even born when Dame Shirley began her musical career'[32] – and at the BBC Electric Proms in 2009 proved her enduring popularity. With *I Owe It All To You* in 2020, Bassey achieved album chart success in seven consecutive decades. Since winning Best Female Singer at the NME Awards at the beginning of her career in 1959, Bassey has received numerous honours and awards, including a Damehood in 1999. CN

Shirley Bassey (b.1937)
By Mike Owen, 1997
Chromogenic print, 242 × 195mm
National Portrait Gallery, London, x128532

Mary Quant

In post-war Britain, fashion designer Mary Quant revolutionised the way women dressed. From the 1950s, her distinctive look expressed a new attitude to fashion which epitomised the vibrant lifestyle and optimistic spirit that a whole generation wanted to experience.

With the opening of the boutique Bazaar on London's King's Road in 1955, Quant and her eponymous brand harnessed the boom in high-street consumerism. For Quant, it was key to 'make fashionable clothes available to everyone' and as an astute communicator she made use of the media – photography, graphics, journalism and advertising – to promote her lifestyle brand. Quant's clothes represented an innovative identity for post-war Britain; witty and playful, her miniskirts quickly became the ultimate symbol of the Swinging Sixties.

Quant's knee-skimming skirts made an appearance in the press at the start of the 1960s, but only became a widespread phenomenon from 1966. Quant designed the miniskirt to be worn with flat shoes and liberate women from the constraints of high-heeled outfits of the 1950s. As she later recalled, 'short, short skirts [were] the most self-indulgent, optimistic "look at me, isn't life wonderful" fashion ever devised … [marking] the beginning of women's lib' and anticipating the 'fashion freedom of the early twenty-first century'.

While Quant never associated herself with the burgeoning feminist movement, her designs eloquently spoke to a new wave of emancipated women. As a successful businesswoman she also proved a powerful role model. The face of her fashion label, Quant was the quintessential Swinging Sixties woman, modelling her own designs as effectively as a professional model. Quant ensured that all media opportunities were optimised to transform young women, just like herself, into the new style mavens.

In 1965 Quant started working on her autobiography *Quant by Quant*, published in 1966. In it, she recounted how she managed to 'catch the spirit of the day and interpret it in clothes before other designers'. As she went on to explain: 'The clothes I made just happened to fit in exactly with the teenage trend, with pop records and espresso bars and jazz clubs.' Quant – who was made a DBE in 2015 – remains a powerful symbol for the transformation of Britain from Second World War austerity to an outward-looking global trendsetter – a concept captured effectively by the Swinging Sixties. FF

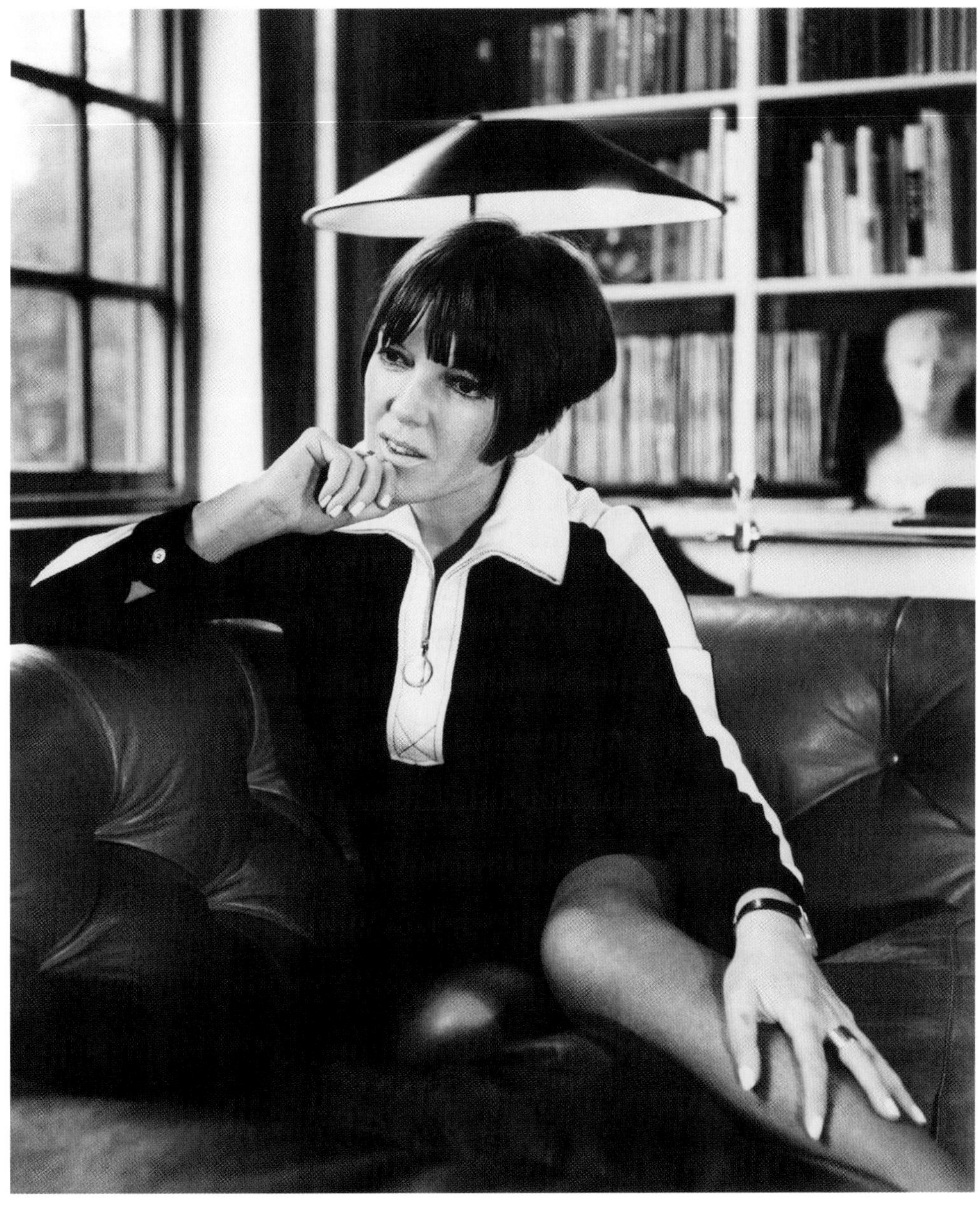

Mary Quant (1930–2023)
By Jorge Lewinski, June 1996
Gelatin silver print, 427 × 343mm
National Portrait Gallery, London, P1056

Delia Derbyshire

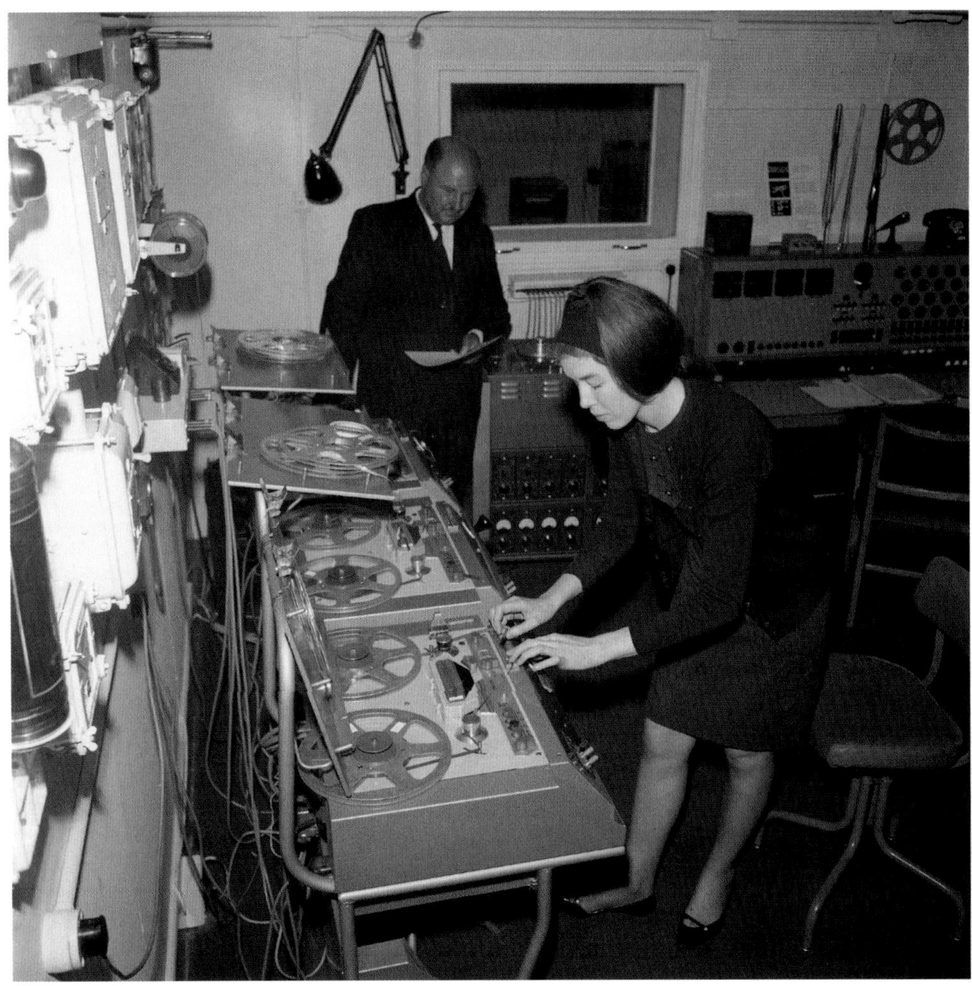

Delia Derbyshire was a pioneering musician and composer of electronic music, most celebrated for her arrangement of the *Doctor Who* theme tune. However, there is more to Delia Derbyshire's creative activity than just *Doctor Who*. In 1966, she was instrumental in the establishment of Unit Delta Plus, Kaleidophon and Electrophon, private electronic music studios where she collaborated with composer and inventor Peter Zinovieff, amongst others. Visionary endeavours that captured the 1960s psychedelic mood in music, the studios acted as experimental platforms, paving the way for original collaborations across disciplines, including film, theatre and so-called 'happenings' (then on the

rise), and introducing electronic music events to a British audience.

For Derbyshire, sound and cerebral perception were strictly entwined and took precedence over any formulaic conception of sound. In other words, the way the ear and the brain perceived sound was more important than the mathematical principle that underpinned it. Drawing on her extensive knowledge of music and mathematics, Derbyshire struck a fine balance between the two fields in her electronic music. She was also keen on integrating sounds from her own personal vocabulary into her compositions. For instance, in 1968 for the opening theme music of the television series *The World About Us*

(focusing on people journeying across the Sahara) she combined the sound of her metal lampshade and that of her own voice to give an impression of camels crossing through a scorching hot desert.

Like many women, Derbyshire was discriminated against at the start of her career. In 1959, she approached Decca records, and was told that women were not employed in their studio. Undefeated, she went on to knock on the BBC's door, who proved to be far more welcoming. She joined as an Assistant Studio Manager and, in 1962, transferred to the BBC Radiophonic Workshop, where she would remain until 1973. During her time at the BBC she created title themes for various shows, the one for *Doctor Who* having a lasting impact in raising people's awareness of electronic music. Alongside her work at the BBC, she established a flourishing freelance practice, collaborating with many leading artists of the day, including Yoko Ono; she provided the score for Ono's 'Wrapping Event' at the City of London Festival. By 1973, she had grown disillusioned with the BBC, feeling that the increasing commercialisation was curtailing her creative freedom, and decided to leave. Some 50 years later, Derbyshire is widely celebrated for her groundbreaking electronic arrangements. The city of Coventry, where she was born, posthumously bestowed on her the title of 'Sculptress of Sound'. FF

Delia Derbyshire (1937–2011)
By an unknown photographer, 1965
BBC Photo Archive

Margaret Busby

[A]lthough being the first at something can be seen as an achievement, it has always been more important to me not to remain 'the only', so I am always happy to encourage others to enter the industry. I would like as many people to dream of being publishers as of being writers.[33]

Still in her early twenties, in 1967 Margaret Busby became Britain's first black woman (as well as youngest) publisher when she founded Allison & Busby with Clive Allison. Busby had been leading the publishing house for a decade, doing 'most of the editorial heavy lifting', when Mayotte Magnus photographed her at her Soho office surrounded by her work.[34] She continued to run the company until 1987, publishing an eclectic range of authors including Michael Horovitz, Hunter S. Thompson, the sonnets of Michelangelo and Jill Murphy's popular *The Worst Witch* series. She also championed many black authors such as C.L.R. James, George Lamming, Buchi Emecheta and Nobel nominee Nuruddin Farah.

Busby's commitment to increasing the representation of black authors in published literature led to her compiling the landmark anthology *Daughters of Africa* (1992), early in her freelance career. Groundbreaking in its ambition and scope, it illuminated over 200 examples of writing by women of African descent from ancient Egypt to the present, in various genres, across 1,089 pages. *New Daughters of Africa* followed in 2019, adding 200 more examples, including writers who had been inspired by the first volume and 'come of age' during the 27 years that had elapsed since its publication. The launch of the New Daughters of Africa student scholarship to support emerging African women writers in London sought to extend this impact further.

Among her persistent efforts to address the lack of black and Asian staff within the publishing industry, Busby co-founded Greater Access to Publishing (GAP) in 1987 and was patron of the trade association Independent Black Publishers. However, with a lack of cultural and racial diversity remaining an issue within the sector, Busby has noted that more needs to be done to create sustained change: 'We don't need to keep doing the same survey; we need to think what are we going to do about it.'

Nonetheless, Busby's importance as a role model and mentor continues to make an impact and to be acknowledged. A recipient of the Royal Society of Literature's Benson Medal and the Royal African Society's inaugural Lifetime Achievement in African Literature award, she was also awarded an OBE in 2021. Editor Ellah Wakatama Allfrey celebrated Busby as 'somebody who makes culture', while writer Zadie Smith (p.160) has asserted: 'She helped change the landscape of both UK publishing and arts coverage and so many Black British artists owe her a debt. I know I do.' CN

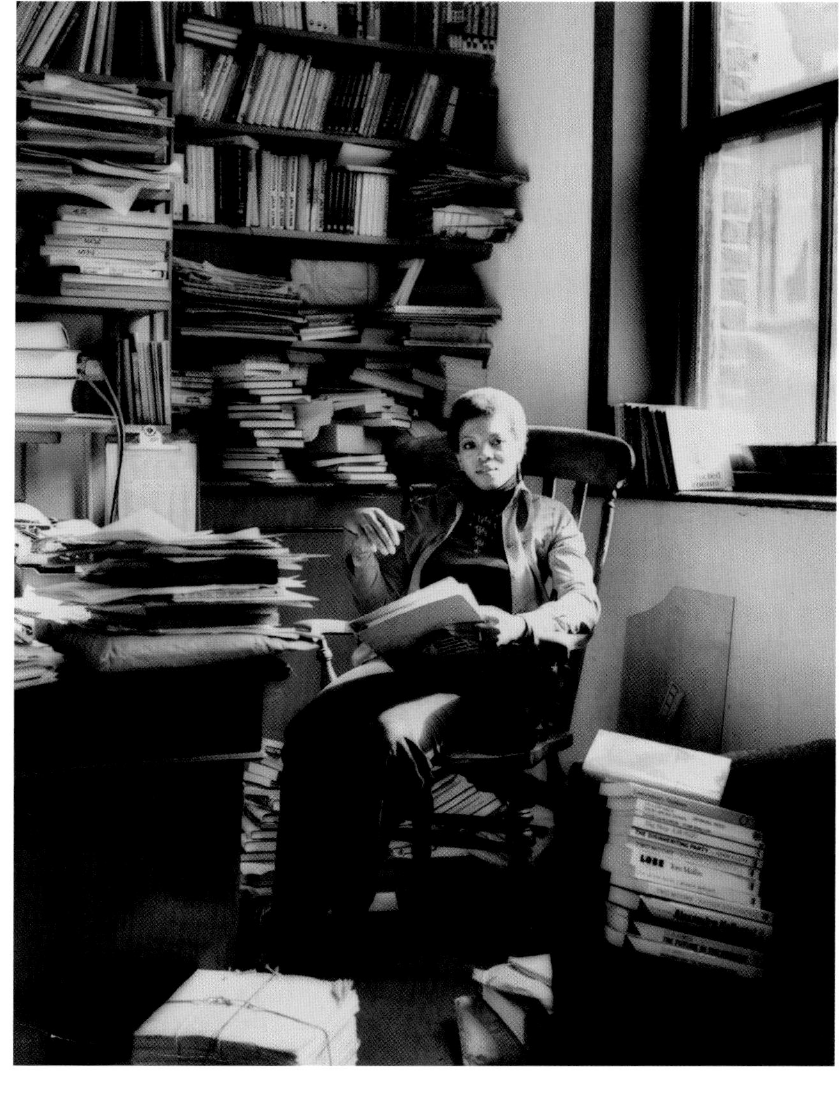

Margaret Busby (b.1944)
By Mayotte Magnus, October 1977
Gelatin silver print, 401 × 305mm
National Portrait Gallery, London, x18607

Hella Pick

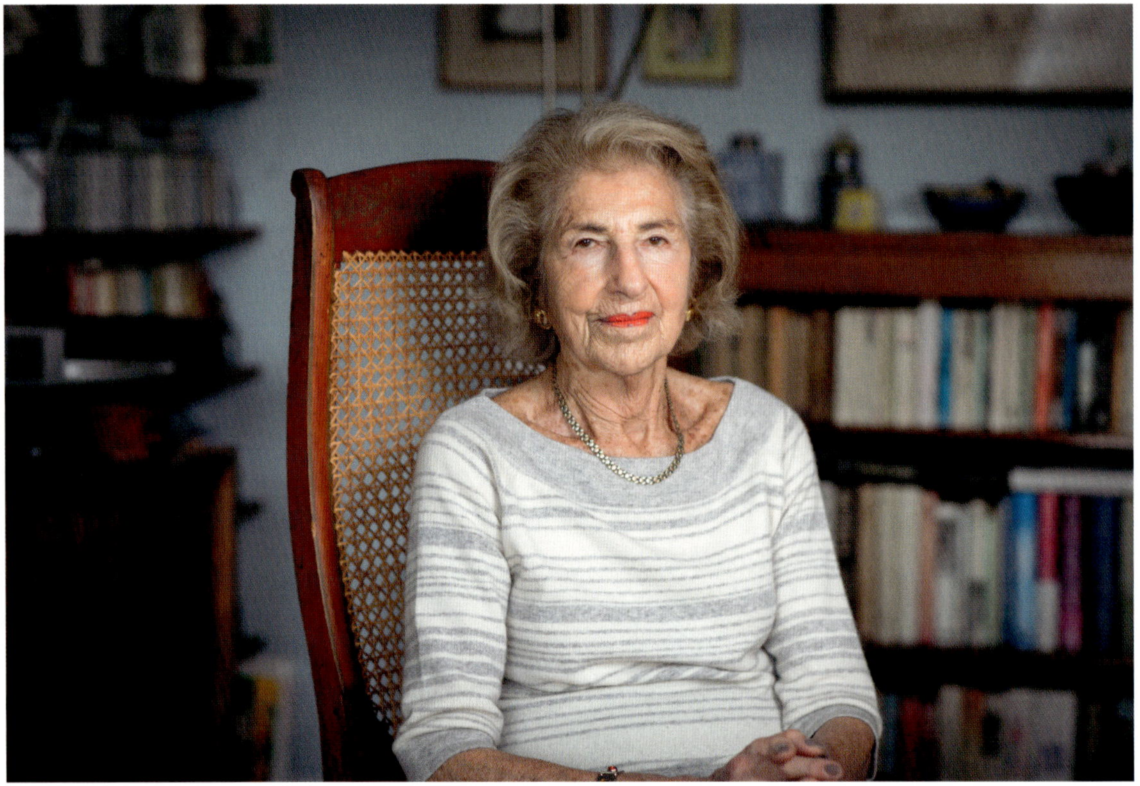

That night of bloody riots I was out and about, a witness to the street battles. I was simultaneously enthused by the students' actions, horrified by the aggressiveness of the riot police and all the time deeply fearful of getting into harm's way ...[35]

The night in question was 11 May 1968, and the location was Paris. Hella Pick, the *Guardian*'s correspondent at the United Nations, witnessed a student revolt that had taken to the streets of the French capital. Pick had come to Paris at the start of May to report on the opening of peace negotiations between the US and North Vietnam; it would take five more years and dozens more meetings before a ceasefire was implemented. While Pick had originally planned to stay just a few days, she soon found herself trapped in France. Workers were on strike and all transport was at a standstill. Alongside her daily news reports on the Vietnam talks, she took it upon herself to also cover the French Revolution of May 1968, a civic upheaval that would profoundly change France and have ripple effects around the world.

Pick was physically and emotionally drained by the Parisian events and yet she was no novice when it came to challenging situations. On 15 March 1939 Pick arrived in London at Liverpool Street Station as a child refugee on a Kindertransport from Vienna; she had been assigned the number 4,672 as a form of identification.

The journey that brought her to British shores was one of many that she would undertake during her lifetime. In her 35 years with the *Guardian* she witnessed and reported on the end of the British Empire in West Africa, the Cuban Missile Crisis and the Kennedy assassination, the building of the Berlin Wall and the collapse of Communism in the Soviet Union and Eastern Europe. Prior to the internet this meant being on the ground, working to fixed deadlines, and dictating articles over the phone to copy-takers. As one of the few female journalists writing about foreign affairs in the post-war era, Pick was a true trailblazer. In her own words:

The small handfuls of women in the media were by and large confined to covering domestic and social issues written for 'women's pages' – a category slow to be dropped even by progressive media. Women covering foreign affairs were generally considered an exotic and far-from-welcome intrusion into an entrenched breed of males enjoying their well-tried mix of camaraderie and fierce competition.

Through her dedication and hard work, Pick succeeded in becoming one of the most well-respected journalists of her generation. FF

Hella Pick (b.1929)
By David Levene, 2017
Digital photograph

Zandra Rhodes

Pioneering textile and fashion designer Zandra Rhodes is best known for her dazzling colours and exuberant couture. She has dressed celebrities from rockstars to royalty and has created costumes for opera. A trailblazer throughout her career, Rhodes's unconventional hand-drawn prints and embellishments, combined with a daring use of colour, have become a statement of her personal style as much as her neon-pink hair.

Rhodes began her career by selling her striking prints to fashion designers, before opening the Fulham Road Clothes Shop in 1967 with Sylvia Ayton. Her breakthrough moment, however, came in 1969 with the launch of her first collection designed under her own label, Knitted Circle. Drawing inspiration from her mother's sewing books and from knitting with friends, Rhodes made the garments using hand-printed silks featuring motifs inspired by embroidery and knitting stitches. She said, 'I made swirling, dramatic shapes with no concessions to the saleable, the acceptable or the ordinary. The true Rhodes style came into being.' She took her chiffons to New York, where influential editor Diana Vreeland featured Rhodes's debut collection in American *Vogue*. Soon afterwards the department store Henri Bendel bought her designs. In London, Fortnum & Mason sold her dresses, as championed by Beatrix Miller at British *Vogue*, and Rhodes quickly established herself as one of the most prominent designers of the 1970s and 80s.

Rhodes was born in Chatham, Kent. Her mother was a fitter at the House of Worth, a French fashion house, and subsequently taught fashion at Medway College of Art where Rhodes trained, initially thinking of becoming an illustrator. Encouraged by her teacher Barbara Brown, who was an important fabrics designer, she went on to study textile design at the Royal College of Art (RCA) and specialised in dress fabrics. Working directly from her prints, she learnt the process of silk-screen printing. During this time, the RCA was at the centre of contemporary art; pop art was providing a new visual language and Rhodes became part of the early Swinging Sixties youth culture. After graduating, she set up her own printing studio in west London alongside her then boyfriend, Alex Macintyre. She recalled:

In those days people would say 'You're a textile designer, you can't design dresses' but there wasn't much choice, because no one was going to buy my prints, so I wanted to make them into the sorts of dresses that people might believe in. When I look back, I think, I don't know how I did it!

In 1972 she was named Designer of the Year. Rhodes was made a Dame in 2014. She celebrated her fiftieth year in fashion in 2019 with an exhibition at the Fashion and Textile Museum, which was founded by Rhodes herself in 2003. She continues to thrive as a designer, revered by the fashion world. GA

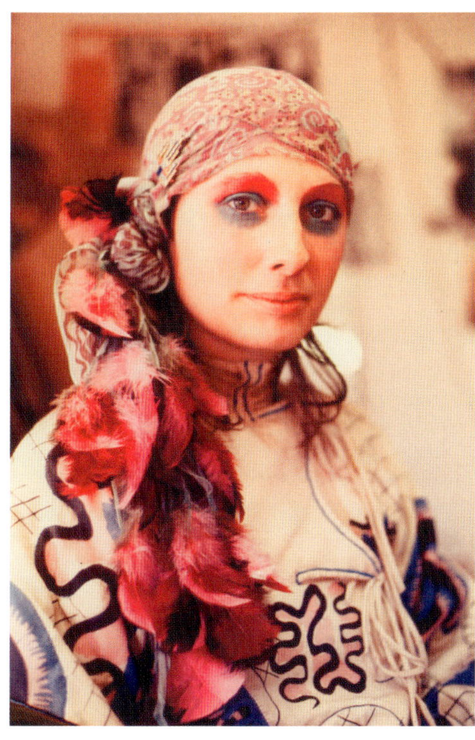

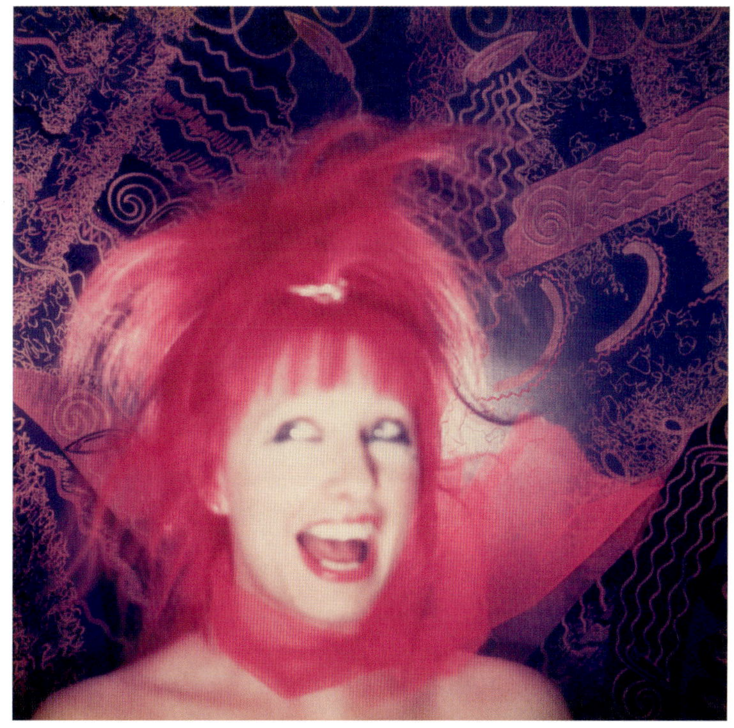

Zandra Rhodes (b.1940)
By Bruno Karlson, late 1960s
Pigment print, 490 × 319mm
National Portrait Gallery, London, x201367

Zandra Rhodes
By Norman Parkinson, 1981
Chromogenic print, 368 × 368mm
National Portrait Gallery, London, P850

1970   Barbara Castle

In the summer of 1968, production at the Ford Motor Company plant in Dagenham halted. The women machinists who sewed the car seat covers had all walked out regarding a pay dispute, and after seven hours of negotiations with Labour politician Barbara Castle on 28 June, the much-publicized three-week strike ended. A pay increase for the women followed, but more significantly it triggered the implementation of the 1970 Equal Pay Act, overseen by Castle in her role as Secretary of State for Employment and Productivity. Presenting the bill to the House of Commons, she declared:

While other people have talked – lots of people have talked – we intend to make equal pay for equal work a reality, and, in doing so, to take women workers progressively out of the sweated labour class.

The legislation, which came into effect on 29 December 1975, made separate rates of pay for men and women illegal, representing a historic development in the fight for gender equality after generations of women had campaigned for the right to equal pay for equal work.

It was also a defining moment in Castle's political career, which began following her election as Member of Parliament for Blackburn in 1945. Appointed to several ministerial positions, Castle oversaw changes that made marked differences to countless lives, particularly to those of women. After briefly serving as Minister for Overseas Development in 1964, she was made Minister for Transport in 1965 and increased road safety by introducing the breathalyser, making the 70 mile per hour maximum speed limit permanent and ensuring all new cars had seat belts. As Secretary of State for Health and Social Services (1974–6), she reformed benefits for carers and disabled persons and replaced Family Allowance with Child Benefit, paying it directly to mothers to boost their independence. Castle also occupied one of Parliament's most senior roles as the only woman to have been appointed First Secretary of State (1968–70).

Castle's career was not without controversy, however. Her contentious proposals for curbing the power of trade unions in her white paper 'In Place of Strife' (1969) threatened to divide the Labour Party. Returning to the backbenches in 1976, she resigned in 1979 as one of the longest-serving women MPs in British history.

She continued in politics as a Member of the European Parliament and in the House of Lords after being made a life peer in 1990.

In 2021, a bronze statue of Castle was unveiled in Blackburn, her constituency for 34 years. The dynamic depiction captures the 'Red Queen's' energy and determination, as she appears striding and holding a copy of the Equal Pay Act, her most enduring legacy. Decades on, while a gender pay gap still exists, this momentous legislation was an important step in the right direction. CN

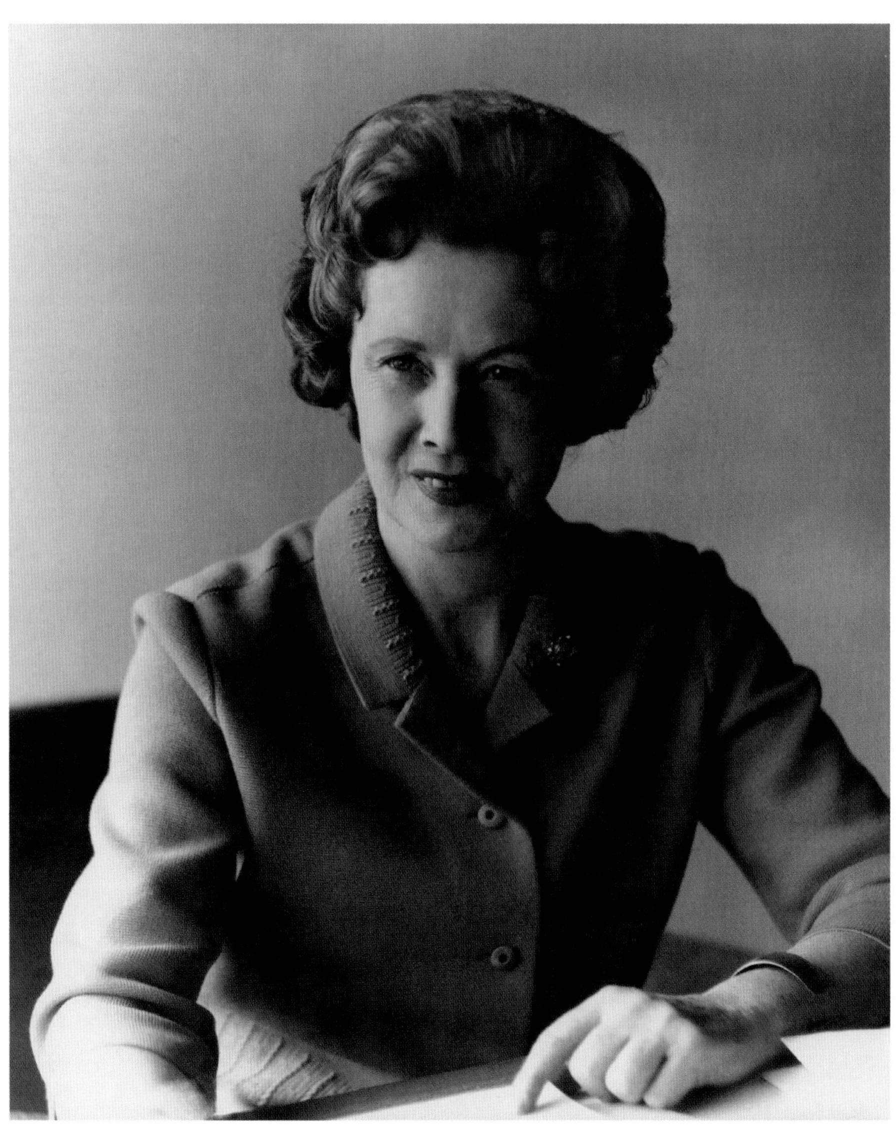

Barbara Castle (1910–2002)
By Yevonde, 1967
Gelatin silver print, 364 × 290mm
National Portrait Gallery, London, x11642

Selma James

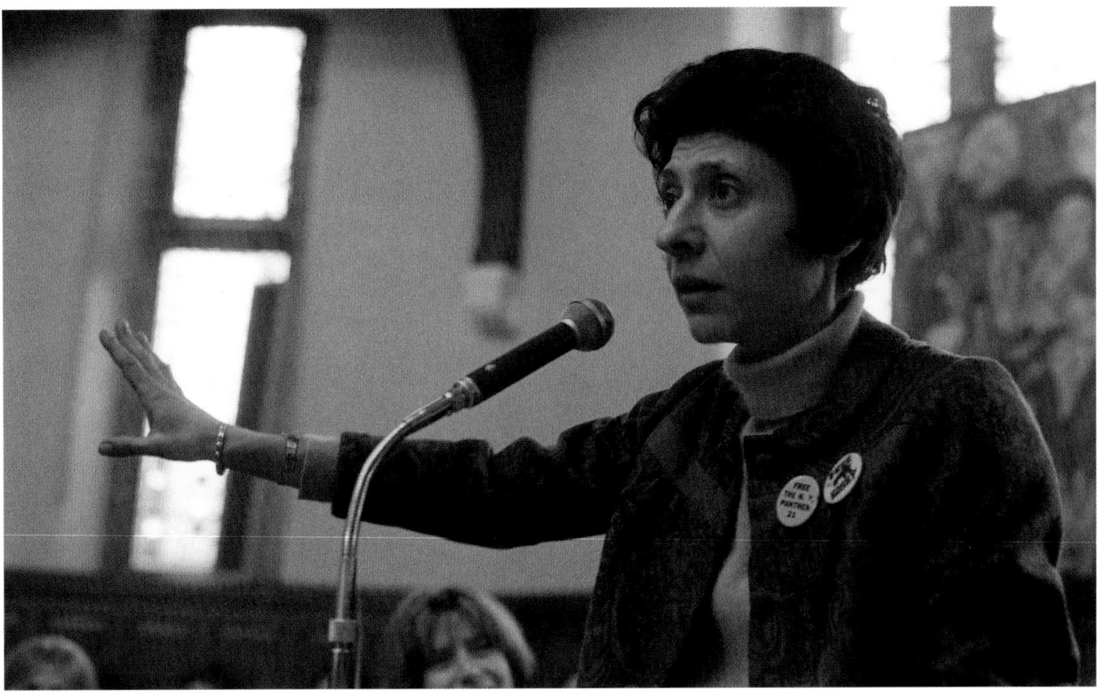

Who am I? Like millions of women everywhere, I'm a typist. I'm a housewife, a mother and I've been a factory worker. For 25 years I've been involved in revolutionary politics, concentrating on the liberation of women in the US where I grew up and later in the West Indies and England. I am one of those people who have always listened to women assuming that what they are is not necessarily what they can be.

With this introduction, socialist and feminist activist Selma James opened the television programme *Our Time is Coming Now*, made as part of the *People for Tomorrow* series and broadcast on 21 January 1971 by the BBC. The programme examined the oppression of women in contemporary society and featured interviews with both full-time housewives and working women who also had to bear sole responsibility for domestic chores and childcare, challenging the feminist view that employment emancipated women. Young women were also shown expressing their dissatisfaction and

desire for change, while footage from women's liberation meetings gave a glimpse into the issues being debated by second-wave feminists at a time when the movement was gaining momentum in Britain, but also faced ridicule in the mainstream press. In a reaffirmation of the programme's optimistic title, James appealed to her viewers: 'We've always been told nothing can be done. We won't accept that ... We've got to use [our] energies to create a new society.'

Motivated by her own experiences, New York-born James had begun discussing the daily frustrations experienced by women in their roles as housewives, mothers and workers two decades earlier in her pamphlet *A Woman's Place* (1952), written when the image of the happy housewife was still prevalent. Together with her second husband, C.L.R. James, she campaigned against racism and for West Indian independence and federation in Trinidad and Tobago, before eventually settling in Britain in 1962. She joined the women's liberation

movement in 1970, speaking at the historic first Women's Liberation Conference at Ruskin College, Oxford that year, where she was photographed by Sally Fraser.

In 1972 James collaborated with Mariarosa Dalla Costa to produce the feminist classic *The Power of Women and the Subversion of the Community*, which developed the idea that women's unwaged labour fundamentally underpins the capitalist economy. That same year, James co-founded the International Wages for Housework Campaign and she continues to argue for the valuing of unpaid domestic and caring responsibilities. Although feminists have been divided on the impact of doing so, the fact that the United Nations resolution in 1995 declared that women's unpaid labour should be officially recognised in national statistics reveals a shifting attitude. James also helped found the Crossroads Women's Centre in London in 1975 and campaigns through the Global Women's Strike. CN

Selma James (b.1930)
By Sally Fraser (Chandan Fraser), 1970
Modern gelatin silver print
National Portrait Gallery, London, x202545

Carmen Callil

I started Virago to publish books which celebrated women and women's lives, and which would, by so doing, spread the message of women's liberation to the whole population and knock on the head forever the idea that it was anything to do with burning bras or hating men.[36]

Inspired by Marsha Rowe and Rosie Boycott's setting up of the feminist magazine *Spare Rib* in 1972, as well as by second-wave feminism's call to rethink culture, Australian-born Carmen Callil was driven to achieve the same in publishing. That same year, Callil established Spare Rib Books with Rowe and Boycott (her former colleagues at the counterculture newspaper *Ink*), although by June 1973 the name had permanently changed to Virago – the Latin word for 'female warrior'. Callil remembered: 'We chose it for this heroic meaning: a strong, courageous, outspoken woman, a battler.' With its entirely female staff,

Virago was a trailblazer in the then male-dominated publishing sector, in which women routinely held the lowest-paid roles, and began championing frequently overlooked women's writing in its quest to cater for the '52 per cent of the population – women' who were thus far being underserved.[37]

Callil initially partly funded the London-based publishing house with earnings from her book publicity company – also begun in 1972 – balancing her energies between the two businesses. Support also came from an overdraft guaranteed by two men, as women could not yet independently apply for credit. By 1978, Harriet Spicer, Ursula Owen, Alexandra Pringle and Lennie Goodings had joined Callil in leading Virago, and the women worked tirelessly to ensure the company's success. Callil's next innovation also came that year when she launched the pivotal, green-spined (because it was neither 'boy blue' nor

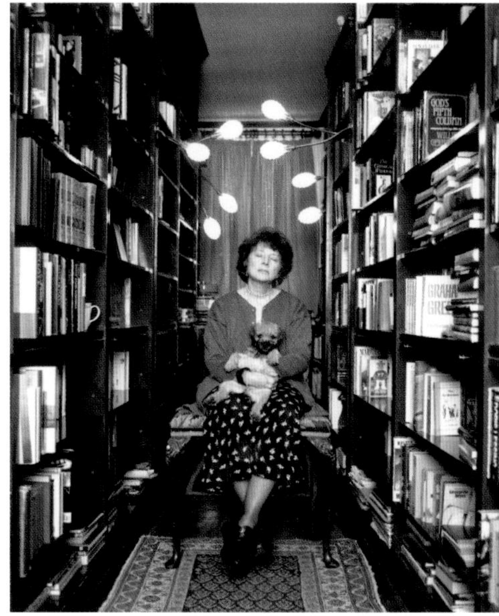

'girl pink') Virago Modern Classics series to illuminate women's literary history by reprinting and celebrating past writing by women. These books were published alongside titles by contemporary authors that included Angela Carter, Margaret Atwood, Maya Angelou and Sarah Waters.

Callil firmly believed: 'It is our duty not to go bust. Virago must be here for future generations, ensuring that women writers are not forgotten again', and so took Virago with her when she moved to Chatto & Windus in 1982, remaining as Virago's chairman until 1995. One of the success stories of the feminist publishing houses that opened during that era, Virago survives now as an imprint, still headed by Goodings, who hailed Callil as 'a powerhouse who changed the publishing world for the better'. Callil's important contribution was widely recognised during her lifetime, including with the Benson Medal from the Royal Society of Literature and a Damehood, both received in 2017. CN

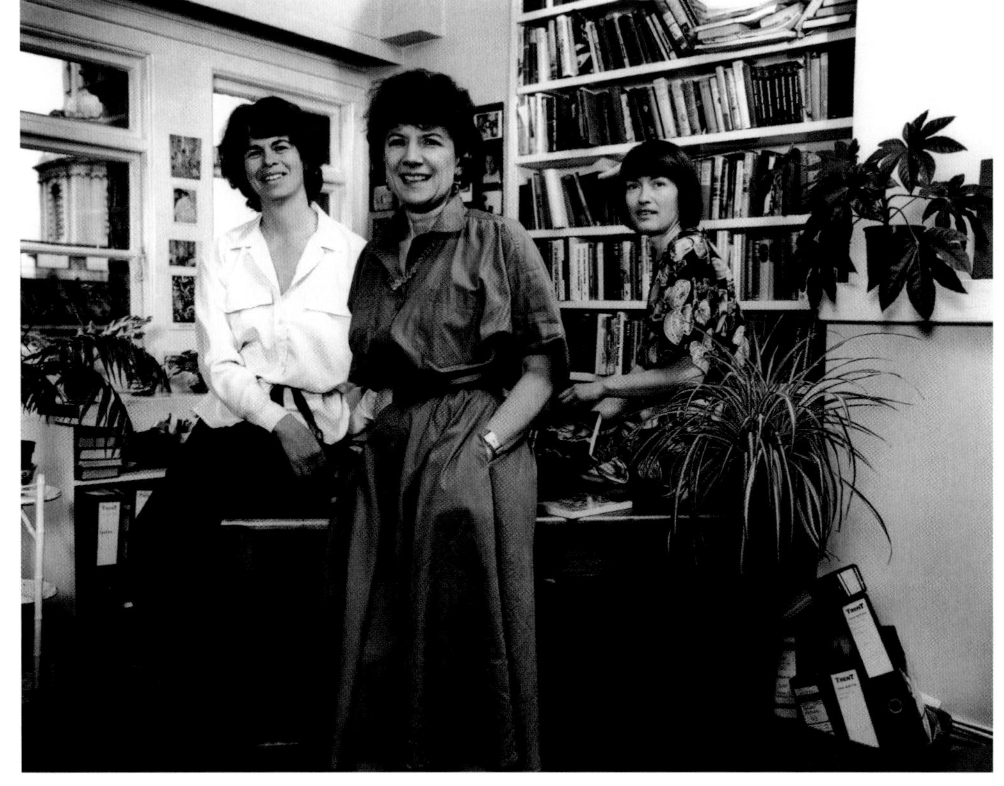

Ursula Owen, Carmen Callil and Harriet Spicer
By Raissa Page for Format Photographers, early 1980s
Modern gelatin silver print, 280 × 346mm
National Portrait Gallery, London, x133134

Carmen Callil (1938–2022)
By Polly Borland, October 1999
Gelatin silver print, 495 × 392mm
National Portrait Gallery, London, x88450

1973 Mayotte Magnus

In 1973 Mayotte Magnus was awarded a Fellowship from the Royal Photographic Society. The 1970s would be for her a decade of liberation through – and recognition in – her chosen field. It was also the decade in which photography gained wider admission to museums and the art market.

Born in Algiers in 1934 and raised in Paris, Magnus practised ballet, choreography, classical guitar and painting before arriving at photography as a profession. In 1971 Australian advertising photographer Bruce Pinkard guided her initial experiments and taught her darkroom techniques. Soon after she won the ILFORD international photographic competition.

In 1977 the National Portrait Gallery staged a landmark exhibition, 'Mayotte Magnus: Photographs of Women', featuring nearly 90 of her portraits of eminent women. Commissioned by Colin Ford, Keeper of Film and Photography at the National Portrait Gallery, it was the first photographic exhibition in the Gallery's history to focus exclusively on the achievement of women. Studies of contemporaries including Margaret Drabble, Glenda Jackson and Nadine Gordimer reflect Magnus's deep interest in people, the arts and global affairs. The exhibition was shown in Parliament in 1978 and toured the United Kingdom. It celebrated 50 years of equal voting rights for women and chimed with second-wave feminism. A further selection was shown as the exhibition 'Illuminating Women' at the Gallery in 2018.

Magnus worked alongside her second husband, the photographer Jorge Lewinski, whom she met in 1972, making insightful portraits of artists and writers. Described as 'image-building', she researched her subjects intensely and often included pertinent visual symbols to complete the composition. Her work was included in the celebrated exhibition 'Women's Images of Men' at the Institute of Contemporary Arts in 1981. As well as commissions from magazines including *Harpers & Queen*, *Fortune* and *Point de Vue*, Magnus established a photography school with Lewinski, which they ran from their home in south London from 1983 to 1997. Books published with Lewinski, including *Venice Preserved* (1986), *The Royal Warrant* (1989) and *A Writer's France* (1989), demonstrate her skill across photographic genres as well as her broad interests.

Since 1998 Magnus has been restoring the Palais des Evêques de Comminges in Alan, near Toulouse, which she has also opened to the public as an arts centre. A revisited photography project, 'The Eye of Proust', has recently been exhibited across France and further illustrates literary inspiration for Magnus's photographic portrayals. CF

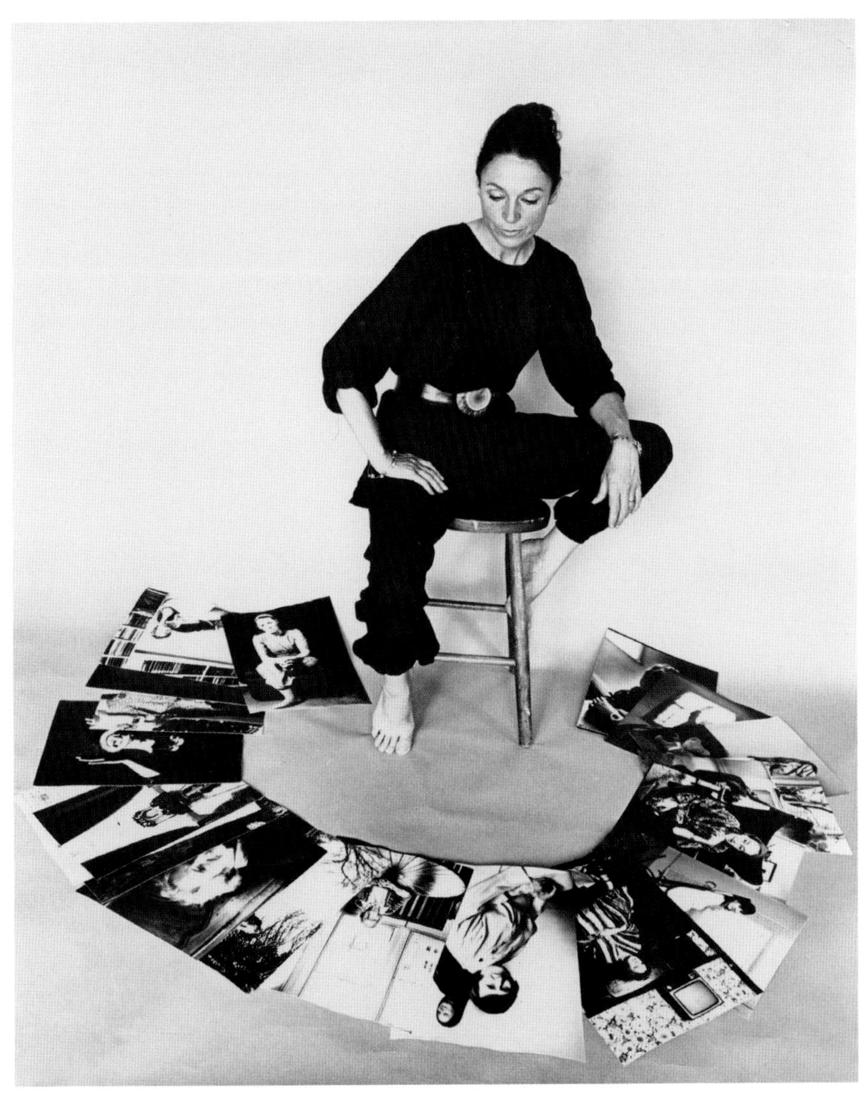

Mayotte Magnus (b.1934)
By Jorge Lewinski, 1977
Gelatin silver print, 305 × 240mm
National Portrait Gallery, London, x200185

1974 Vivienne Westwood

Craft must have clothes but Truth loves to go naked.

This aphorism, borrowed from seventeenth-century historian Thomas Fuller, adorned the entrance to Vivienne Westwood's shop, 'SEX', which opened in 1974 at 430 King's Road, London. In the early 1970s Westwood and her then husband and collaborator Malcolm Edwards (known as McLaren) were experimenting with biker gear. As Westwood recalled: 'We began sticking studs on the back of jackets and printing glitter on to clothes … we wanted to cross the biker look with the feel of witch-doctors or black magic.' The outcome was, to Westwood's and McLaren's own admission, surreal – a crossbreed between biker look and fetish wear. This deviant aesthetic was what Westwood was aiming for: 'The only reason I'm in fashion is to destroy the word "conformity". Nothing's interesting to me unless it's got that element.'

SEX embodied the spirit of Westwood's provocative and politicised fashion and quickly established itself as a destination for all those who wished to defy convention; the clientele included voyeurs, prostitutes, Japanese tourists, rock stars and young proto-punks. The name SEX was spelt out above the door in large, pink, PVC letters. A pile of naked and headless mannequins stood in the window of the shop. The interior was sprayed with pornographic graffiti and hung with rubber curtains. SEX's slogan was 'Rubber wear for the office' and the stock was intentionally shocking – leather miniskirts, chains, fishnets, stilettos and leather underwear were among the items on sale.

SEX helped set the scene for the phenomenon known as punk rock.

Over the next few years Westwood's fashion followed suit. By the start of the 1980s however, her focus had shifted and Westwood began to look at history for ideas and techniques, reviving silhouettes, heritage fabrics and colours. In her words: 'The way ahead is to go into the past. I would describe it really as nostalgia for a better future. Something like that.'

Westwood – who was made a Dame in 2006 – has been widely acknowledged as one of Britain's most important fashion designers. She was the first to bring British street-style to the catwalk and her experimental designs have had a lasting influence on her peers and customers. Underpinning all of Westwood's work was her ethos: 'Fashion is very important. It is life-enhancing and, like everything that gives pleasure, it is worth doing well.' FF

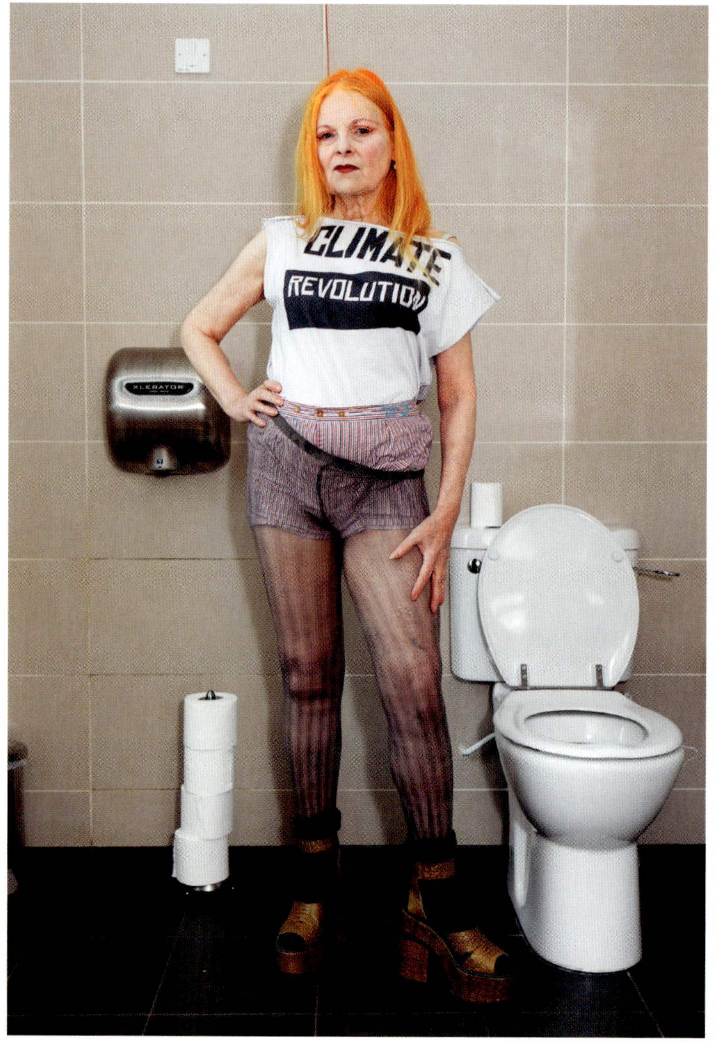

Vivienne Westwood (1941–2022)
By Martin Parr, 2012
Pigment print, 1528 × 1052mm
National Portrait Gallery, London, P2089

Hannah Dadds

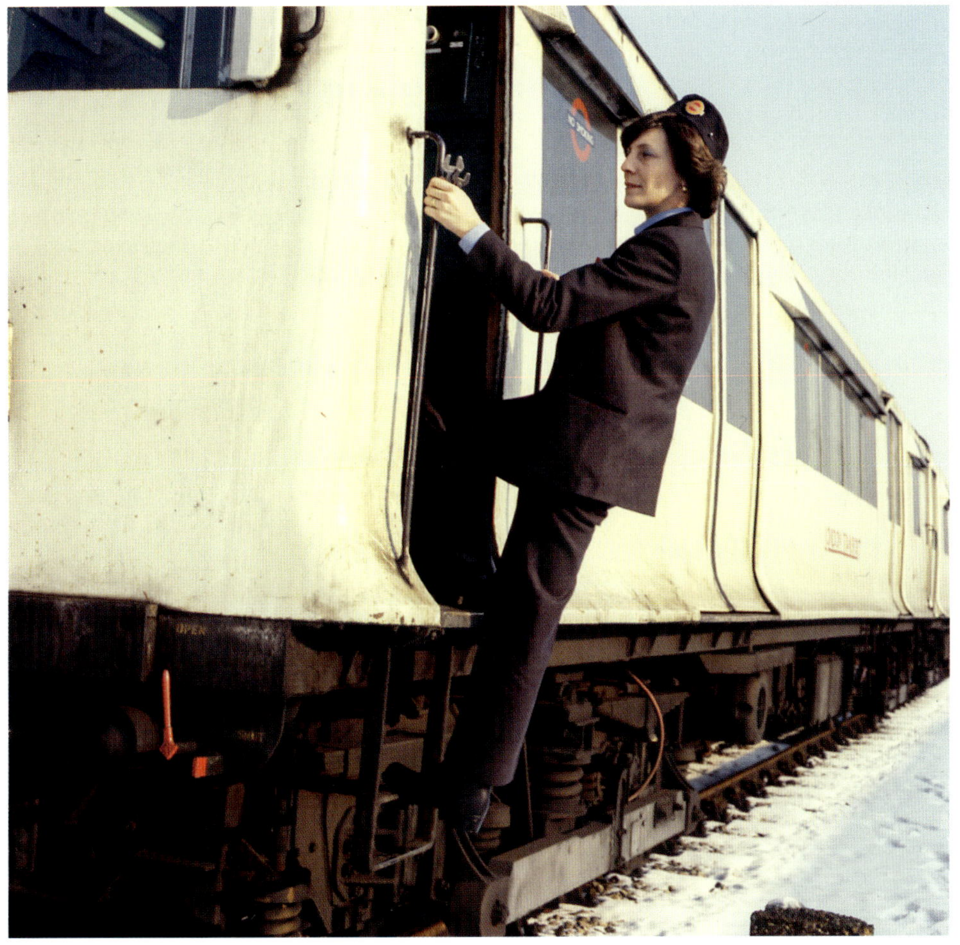

as a train driver. Male colleagues were startled and mostly unsympathetic, leaving Dadds and other female trainees to contend with verbal abuse and harassment during their training. Undeterred, Dadds completed her training in October 1978 and went on to become the first female Tube driver. She was assigned to the District line first and later was responsible for trains on the Bakerloo and Jubilee lines.

To celebrate the start of Dadds' role as a train driver the London Underground arranged a press conference, which was attended by a wide spectrum of media, all keen to speak to the woman of the hour. As she recalled: 'I did all the press and the television, and anyone else from radio. There were loads of them! And I drove a train out of Acton, drove it from there to Ealing Broadway. And then I had a lot of them [pictures] taken there, and then I had to fetch it back in again. And then we went to the pub.' While Dadds paved the way for other women to enter the profession, the number of women drivers lagged far behind that of men. This still remains the case today. FF

An Act to render unlawful certain kinds of sex discrimination and discrimination on the ground of marriage, and establish a Commission with the function of working towards the elimination of such discrimination and promoting equality of opportunity between men and women generally; and for related purposes.

Cited above is the opening statement of the Sex Discrimination Act, passed by the British Parliament on 12 November 1975. The Act protected men and women from discrimination on the grounds of sex or marital status and was instrumental in helping women enter the workforce on an equal footing with their male counterparts. Hannah Dadds was one of the many women who took advantage of this piece of legislation to reach the professional goal she had set for herself.

In 1969, Dadds joined the London Underground, working as a 'station woman' at Upton Park station. She worked her way up, first as a ticket collector and later as a train guard. However, Dadds' ultimate aspiration was to become a Tube train driver – a role deemed unsuitable for women up until the passing of the Sex Discrimination Act. Once this gender barrier was removed, Dadds was one of the first women to apply to become a driver. She was moved by the firm conviction that 'Women have been held back too long. If they can do a job, they should be allowed to.'

In August 1978, Dadds started a seven-week training course to qualify

Hannah Dadds (1941–2011)
By an unknown photographer, 1978
Colour transparency
Transport for London Archive, W/200A/D/4346

Shirley Ardener

An anthropologist by training, Shirley Ardener pioneered the field of women's studies before the subject was open to academic enquiry. The 1970s was a particularly fertile decade for Ardener, who wrote seminal texts on feminist anthropology and was the founding director of the Centre for Cross-Cultural Research on Women (CCCRW) (now the International Gender Studies Centre) at Lady Margret Hall, Oxford.

The CCCRW was formally established in 1983, but its activities date back to 1972 when a group of academics, mainly female anthropologists, created a seminar series dedicated to women and their place and role in society. It was felt that mainstream anthropology missed this area of enquiry. Women researchers like Ardener were thus keen to carve out a space for discussion where research findings could be presented and notes compared – ultimately, to extend the anthropological frontiers. The emergence of the CCCRW network was particularly welcomed by those who were involved with the feminist movement, which was extremely active at this time. Feminist anthropology was in fact at the crossroads of anthropology and feminist studies and contributed to a radical rethinking of anthropology itself.

Ardener identified feminist anthropology as an approach, rather than a field of study. She outlined this concept in 'The Social Anthropology of Women and Feminist Anthropology', a seminal essay written in 1985. By this point in her career Ardener had authored a number of important publications including *Perceiving Women* (1975) and *Defining Females* (1978). In the opening paragraphs of her 1985 essay, Ardener drew attention to a series of remarks indicative of the context in which she was working. Of *Perceiving Women*, a male colleague remarked in a puzzled manner, 'I want to read it, but I can't bring myself to do so.' Meanwhile, a visiting scholar 'patiently and earnestly warned me of the dangers of studying women and becoming thereby too "narrow". Knowingly, I fear, I enquired of his own field: it was Japan; moreover it was restricted to Buddhism in Japan. He seemed unsure of how to respond to my amusement.'

Ardener's studies proved to be anything but narrow. She played an instrumental role in challenging historical gendered structures and making people think about the role that gender plays in the formation of power imbalances within society. FF

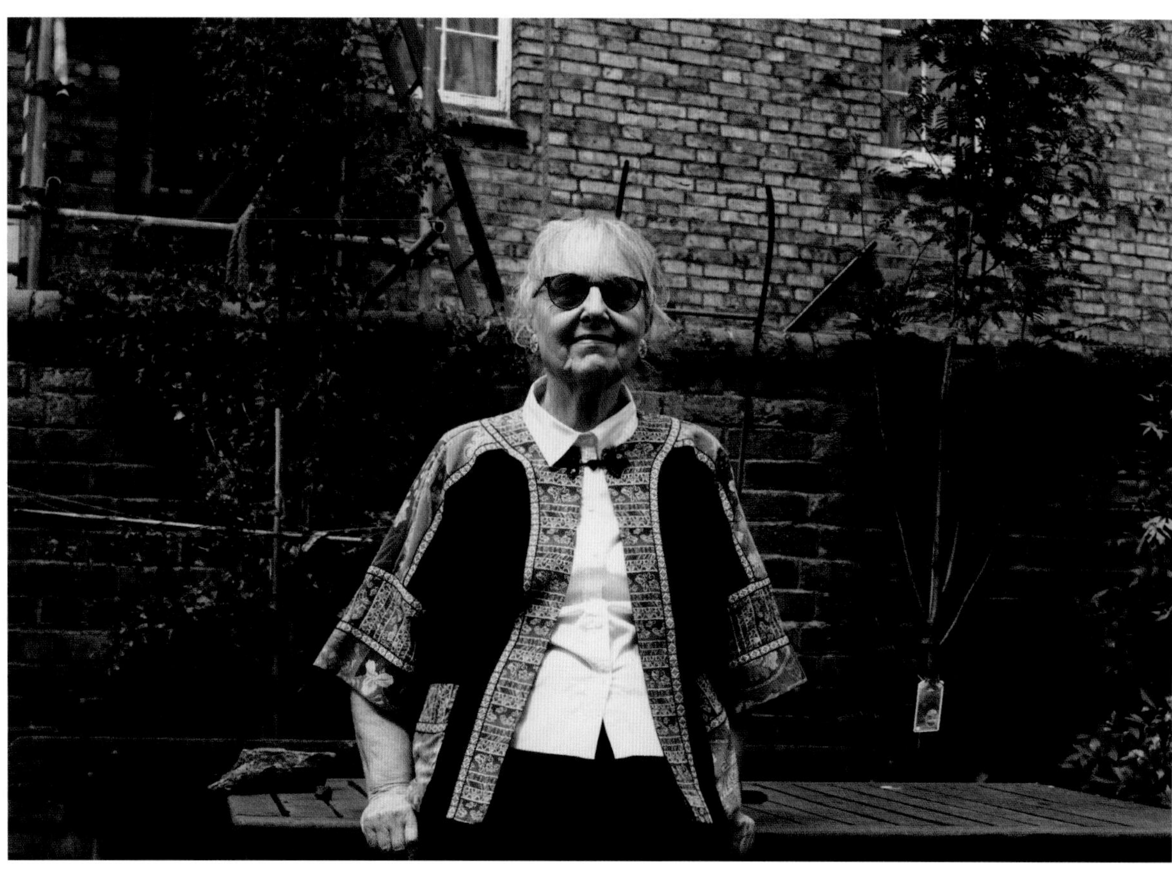

Shirley Ardener
By Samuel Finlak and Joseph Chila, June 2005
Gelatin silver print, 279 × 380mm
National Portrait Gallery, London, x128891

1977 Virginia Wade

In 1977, tennis player Virginia Wade beat Betty Stöve of the Netherlands 4-6, 6-3, 6-1 winning the Wimbledon women's singles title. She remains the most recent British woman to win it. 1977 was an historic year as it was the tournament's centenary and Queen Elizabeth II's Silver Jubilee. In preparation for Wimbledon, Wade trained with coaches for the first time. She improved her serve and went on to play some of the best tennis of her career at the tournament. Athletic and aggressive, and having learned to control her temperament and game, Wade took to Centre Court with self-assurance and maturity.

A press article about Wade's historic win described the atmosphere on Centre Court as like that of the Last Night of the Proms, with the crowd singing 'Land of Hope and Glory': 'At the end the cheers were loud and deafening.' A Wimbledon champion at last, Wade agreed: 'It was like a fairy-tale, with everyone cheering for the Queen and cheering for me.' The Queen presented Wade with the trophy. Wade remembers thinking before entering the tournament, 'Well, if she [Queen Elizabeth II] is going to be there,

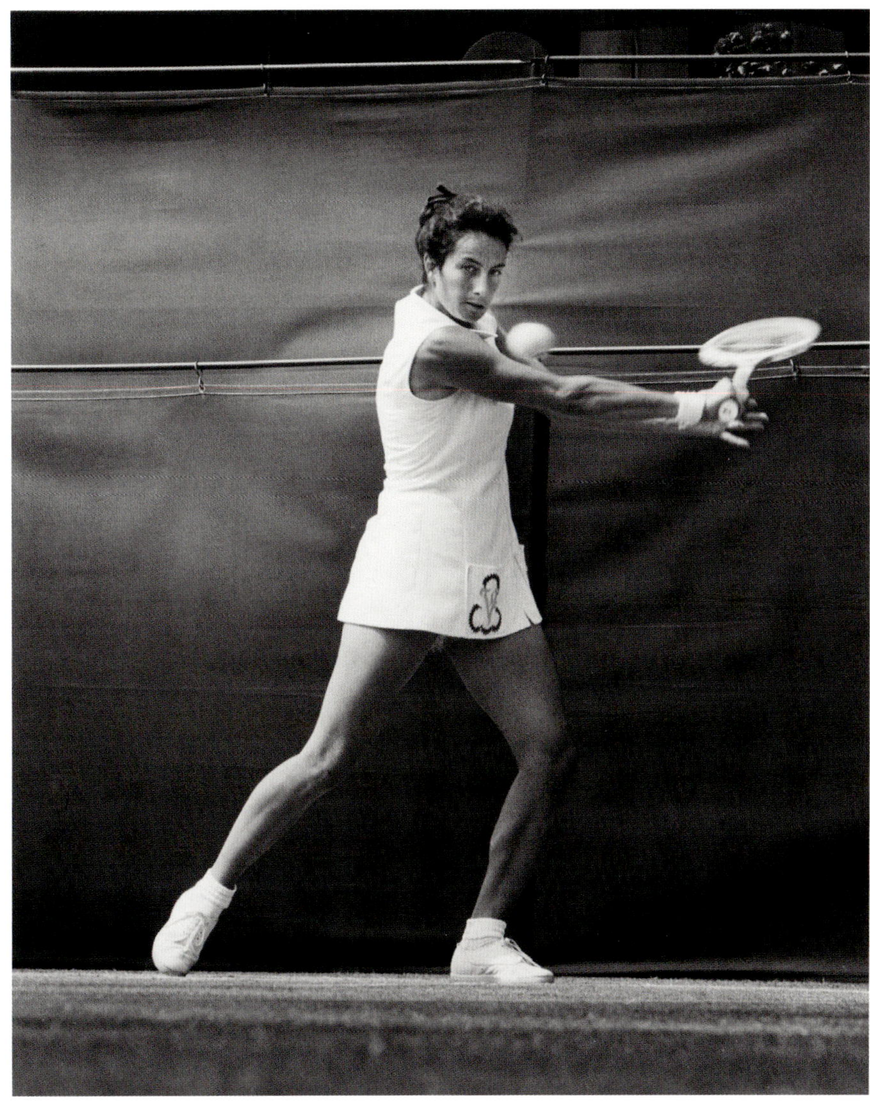

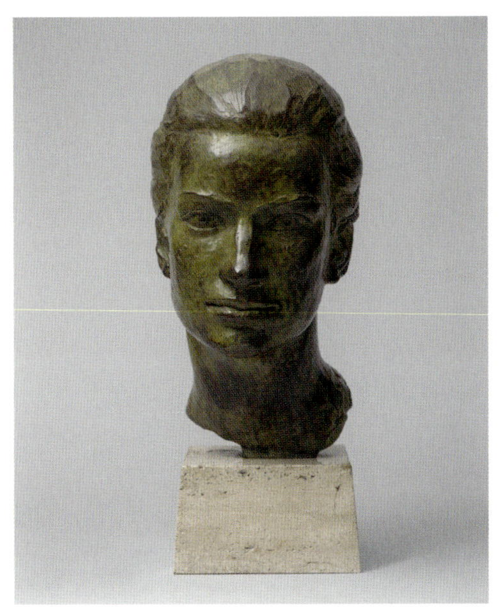

I better be there. And if I am there I better win.'

Born in Bournemouth, Wade grew up in South Africa. She learnt to play tennis there and continued to play successfully when she returned to England in 1960 aged 15. Whilst studying at Sussex University, from which she graduated with a degree in maths and physics, she travelled to the Queen's Club in London three times a week to practise her tennis. She won the first Open tournament in Bournemouth as an amateur in 1968 before defeating Billie Jean King

at the final of the US Open that same year. She later won the Australian Open in 1972.

During her 26-year career, Wade secured 55 singles titles, most significantly the Wimbledon Singles in 1977. She is the only British woman in history to have won titles at all four majors: three singles titles and four in doubles. Wade published her autobiography, *Courting Triumph*, in 1978. She received an OBE in 1986 and, following her retirement, she has remained active in tennis as a television commentator. GA

Virginia Wade (b.1945)
By David Wynne, 1972
Bronze head, 435 × 170mm
National Portrait Gallery, London, 7009

Virginia Wade
By Jorge Lewinski, June 1962
Gelatin silver print, 413 × 323mm
National Portrait Gallery, London, P1067

Olive Morris

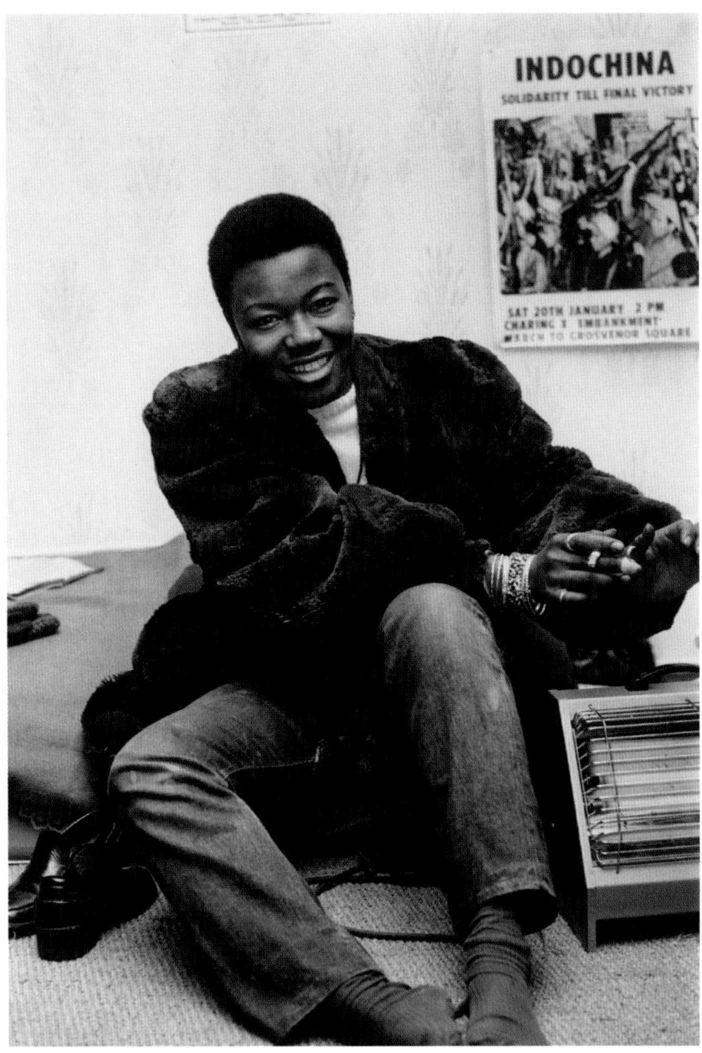

The founding of the Organisation for Women of African and Asian Descent (OWAAD) in 1978 by radical activist Olive Morris – alongside Stella Dadzie, Gail Lewis and others – is regarded as a 'watershed in the history of black women's rights activism'.[39] Until 1982, OWAAD provided a supportive, non-hierarchical network for groups representing black and Asian women to coordinate campaigns on issues such as immigration, school exclusions, criminal justice and healthcare, not prioritised by the white-majority feminist movement or by male-driven racial equality organizations. The attendance of around 250 women from across the country at its first annual conference in Brixton signalled an eagerness to organize and press for change.

Before then, Morris had already proved herself as a capable and tireless leader in grassroots community groups, fighting against racism, sexism and classism. Born in Jamaica, Morris became politicised by her experience of the racial discrimination faced by the African-Caribbean community during her youth in south London. After being brutally assaulted and arrested at the age of 17 for her involvement in an altercation between police and a Nigerian diplomat who was questioned under the controversial 'sus' laws (a stop and search power), Morris became driven to campaign against police harassment.

She joined the revolutionary socialist British Black Panthers and helped to establish the Brixton Black Women's Group in 1973, developing its socialist, feminist ideology and contributing to its newsletter, *Speak Out*. Neil Kenlock, the British Black Panthers' official photographer, photographed Morris that same year, warming herself by a heater at 121 Railton Road in Brixton, where she squatted with friends and which later emerged as a cultural and political hub for the black community. At a time when thousands of black and Asian people struggled to gain adequate housing, Morris was dedicated to promoting housing for all and was active in local squatter campaigns. Morris continued her activism as a student in Manchester and upon returning to London she became involved in scrapping the 'sus' laws while working at the Brixton Community Law Centre's juvenile unit.

Later in 1978 Morris was diagnosed with non-Hodgkin lymphoma and died the following July, aged just 27. An obituary in *Speak Out* summarised Morris's influence during her short life: 'For Olive it was not simply "doing things" for those who could not do it for themselves, it was her way of getting people involved in the struggle, showing by example the will to resist and to challenge.'

Campaigning by the Remembering Olive Collective since 2008 has brought Morris's long-overlooked efforts to empower the black community to the fore, and the Olive Morris Memorial Award, launched in 2011 to support young women activists of African or Asian descent, also ensures that her legacy survives. CN

Olive Morris (1952–1979)
By Neil Kenlock, January 1973
Modern gelatin silver print, 381 × 254mm
National Portrait Gallery, London, x199645

1979   Angela Carter

The short story is not minimalist, it is rococo. I feel in absolute control. It is like writing chamber music rather than symphonies.[40]

Angela Carter is considered one of the most original and daring literary voices of the twentieth century. In her novels and short stories, Carter engaged with the genres of gothic horror, science fiction and fairy tales from a distinctly feminist perspective, often challenging taboos.

Carter's *The Bloody Chamber*, published in 1979, was one of her most successful books, winning the Cheltenham Festival Literary Prize, with Carter establishing herself as a rising literary genius. The book is a collection of her versions of European folk and fairy tales. Carter made it clear that her intention was 'to extract the latent content of those traditional stories and to use [that content] as the beginnings of new stories'. *The Bloody Chamber* includes her take on stories she first heard from her grandmother, such as *Little Red Riding Hood*, *Beauty and the Beast*, *Puss in Boots* and the title story, which is a version of *Bluebeard*. The stories, written from a woman's perspective, with a radical intent and brimming with sex and violence, were created when Carter was a Fellow in Creative Writing at the University of Sheffield between 1976 and 1978. She was inspired to write these tales after translating the work of seventeenth-century writer Charles Perrault, a French collector and author of fairy tales. The ten stories in the collection consider the topics of femininity and gender roles using a rich metaphorical language. In 1984, she worked with director Neil Jordan to develop some of these stories into a horror film, *The Company of Wolves*. Alongside *The Bloody Chamber,* Carter published *The Sadeian Woman and the Ideology of Pornography* (1978), in which she reinterprets the works of the Marquis de Sade to reflect on sexuality and oppression within contemporary culture.

Carter read English at Bristol University, specialising in mediaeval literature, and published her first book, *Shadow Dance* (1966), when she was 26. *The Magic Toyshop* (1967) and *Several Perceptions* (1968) followed and, with the latter, she won the Somerset Maugham Award. She used the prize money to travel to Tokyo and later she settled there for two years, returning to England in 1972. As well as writing fiction, she also contributed essays to the *Guardian* and *New Society* and was associated with the feminist publisher Virago (p.122). During the late 1970s and 80s she taught at several universities. She died aged 51 whilst still at the peak of her career as a writer. GA

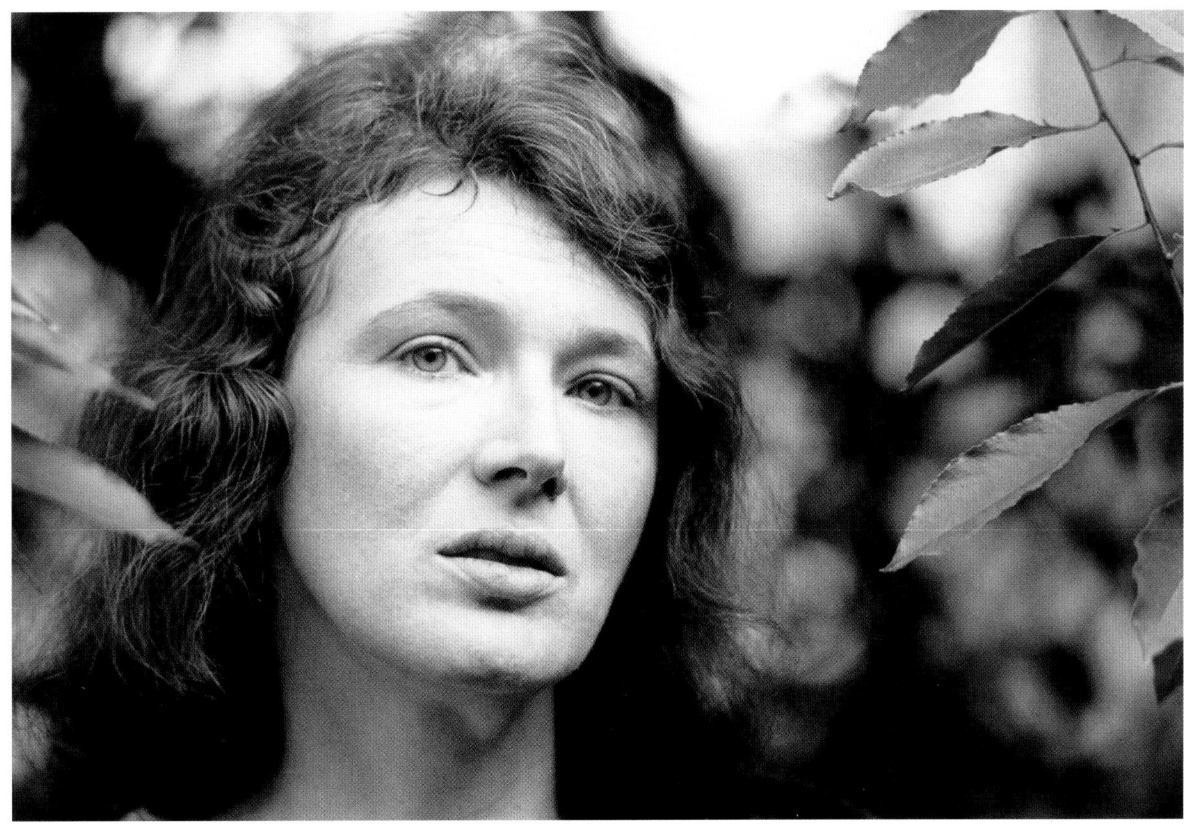

Angela Carter (1940–1992)
By Fay Godwin, 1976
Gelatin silver print, 178 × 125mm
National Portrait Gallery, London, x68245

Celia Paul

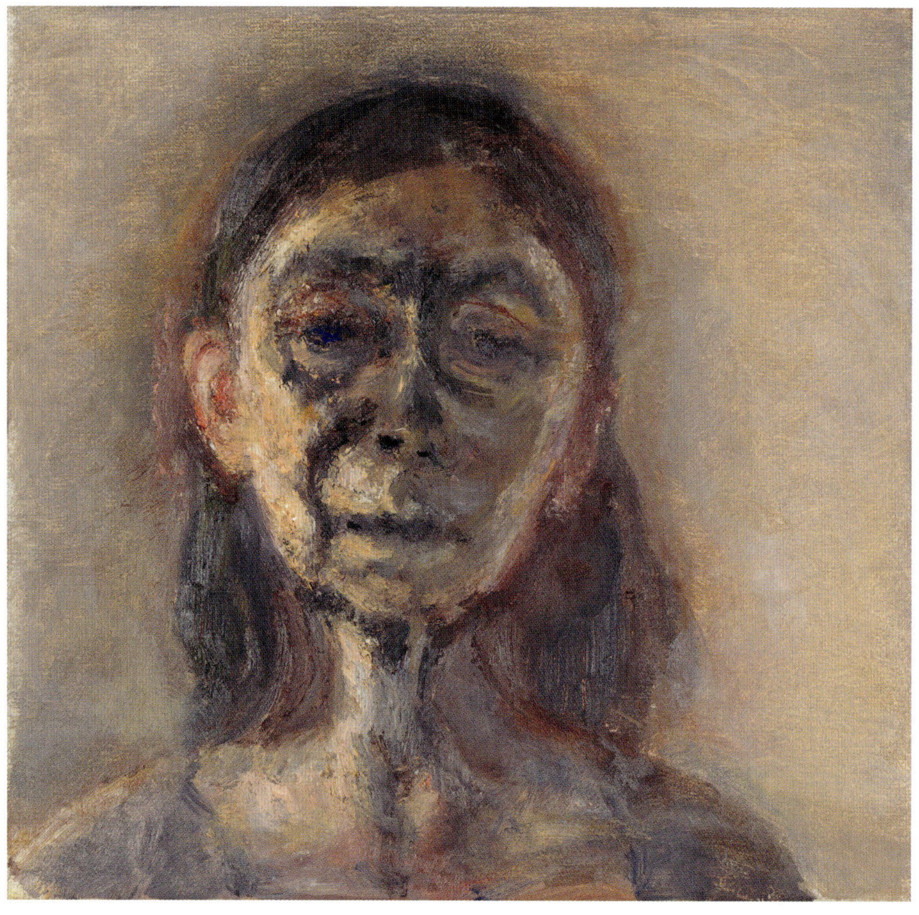

In 2022, artist Celia Paul wrote a book called *Letters to Gwen John*, which centres on a series of letters addressed to the painter Gwen John, who has long been a tutelary spirit for Paul. Both John and Paul studied at The Slade School of Fine Art in London. While Paul was enrolled in the 1980s, John was a student at the end of the nineteenth century. The two never met, and yet Paul feels a close kinship to John. As the younger artist noted in one of her first letters to John:

… I do feel a mysterious connection to you … We both came to study at The Slade School of Fine Art from our homes in the West Country; we both had passionate relationships with much older and more famous male artists, whom we also modelled for; we were driven to find our true creativity by leading interior, solitary lives; we both became interested in the idea of abstraction (and the idea of God) later in life. … We both work from women.

Both women entertained intense and complicated relationships with notorious artists – in Paul's case it was Lucian Freud and in John's it was Auguste Rodin. As the author Zadie Smith eloquently contended: Paul has long been classed as 'a muse who later became a painter,' when in fact, she is a 'painter who, for ten years of her early life, found herself mistaken for a muse.' The extent of the exchange between Paul and John goes beyond the fraught nature of the artist-muse dichotomy. It extends to broader questions around art-making and what it means to have dedicated a lifetime to painting.

Paul's paintings are unique in their ability to capture human emotions and the intimacy of a glance. Over the years, Paul has repeatedly painted herself, her close relatives and landscapes with a deep personal connection. Painting the same person over and over again allows Paul to get closer to her subjects, and at the same time it enables her to focus on the very materiality of painting – tone, form and structure. Every brushstroke in Paul's work is carefully pondered, as nothing is left to chance. Her portraits are gentle but powerful reminders that seeing someone for who they truly are means going beyond the surface of appearance. FF

'Portrait, Eyes Lowered'
Celia Paul (b.1959)
Self-portrait, 2019
Oil on canvas, 254 × 254mm
National Portrait Gallery, London, 7124

ME LOOKING AT YOU, LOOKING AT ME

By

Flavia Frigeri

All self-portraits are records of identity. Yet the extent to which an artist has chosen to reveal their personality, artistry and aspirations within their self-portraits has varied enormously over the centuries, and remains in flux to this day. In a world in which image making is a universally accessible endeavour, the creation of self-portraits is available to all through the now omnipresent selfie. But long before the selfie made waves, self-portraiture acted as the primary vehicle for self-analysis and self-representation for many artists.

On a very basic level, the self-portrait responds to a primal urge for humans to leave a record of their existence. But it would be reductive to think of self-portraits in these terms alone. No self-portrait simply mimics external appearance; there is always more than meets the eye. Like prisms, self-portraits capture many concerns at once; these range from self-promotion to proof of existence, and may also encompass role-play, technical skill, stylistic affirmation and vanity. By portraying themselves, artists not only document their existence at a particular point in time, but they set up a dialogue with those who will look at their self-portraits in the future. The feeling of being in the presence of the artist is, in fact, one of self-portraiture's most powerful tropes, and arguably it is what lends a self-portrait much of its enduring appeal. The gaze filtered through the mirror – a key tool in the making of most self-portraits – is often directed at the viewer, forcing the artist and the onlooker into a direct exchange.

The rise of the self-portrait in the fifteenth century coincided with the rise of the professional artist. By then, the status of the artist in society was changing. Long deemed mere artisans, artists were emancipating themselves from this narrow perspective and asserting their role as artistic personalities. The self-portrait played an important part in this shifting landscape and artists

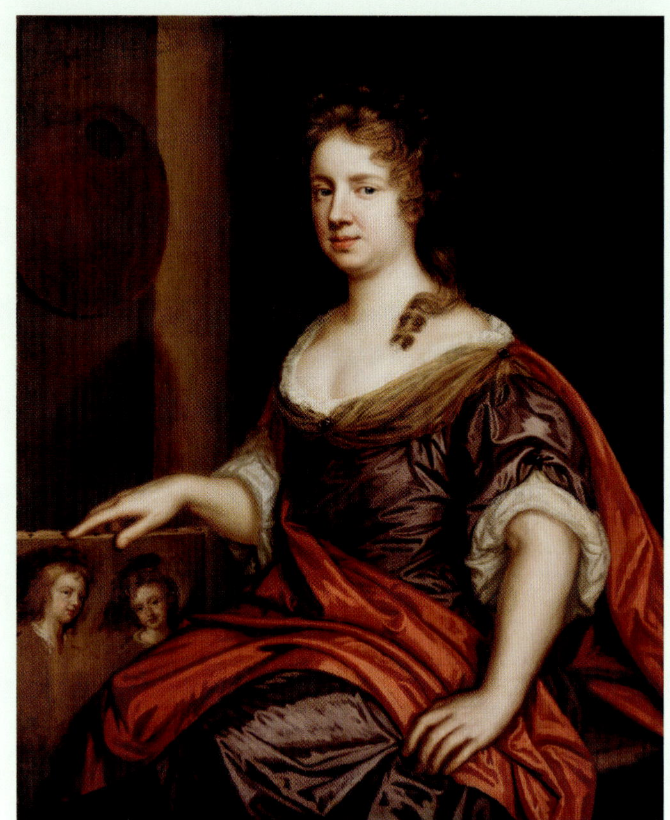
Fig.1: Mary Beale

turned to it in their search for a heightened self-awareness. More so than their male counterparts, female artists have historically tended to deploy the self-portrait as a means of legitimising their professional activities. For centuries women were exceptions in a male profession. As such, their self-portraits offered an opportunity to explore their subjectivity, lived experience and subvert patriarchal viewing positions. No longer just an object of male reverie, women were taking charge by their own hand as both subjects and creators.

In the words of the late art historian Lucy Lippard: 'Of course art has no gender, but artists do.' In keeping with Lippard's landmark statement, a fundamental distinction is made here between male and female self-portraiture. The basic premise of which is that every woman who paints, sculpts, draws, performs or photographs herself challenges the art-historical hierarchy which has traditionally placed men at the top and women at the bottom.

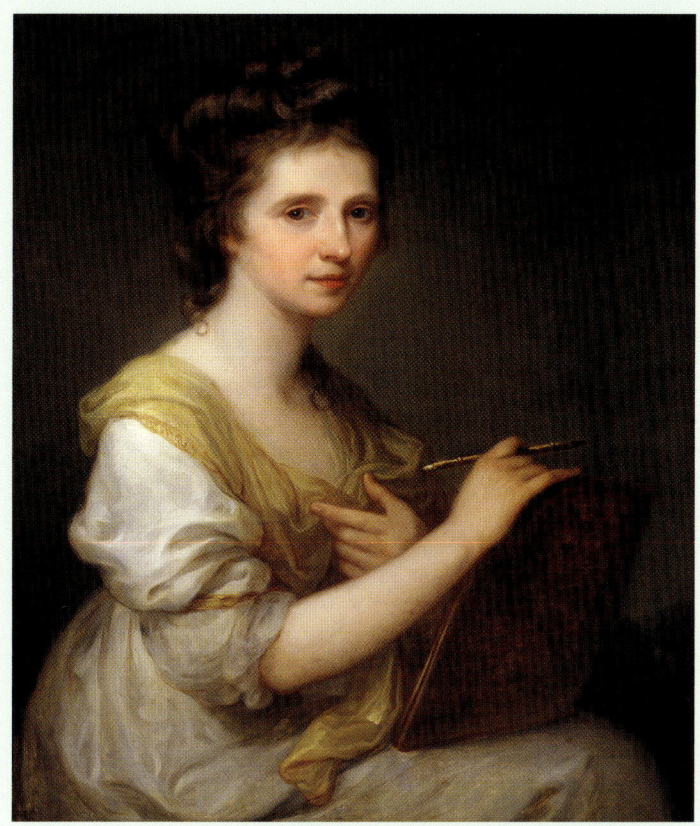

Fig.2: Angelica Kauffmann

WHY PAINT SELF-PORTRAITS?

Classed as muses, or at best amateurs, women had little stake in a world that longed for the uniquely gifted male genius. Often relegated to the periphery of art-making, female artists found in self-portraiture a powerful ally; in one stroke they empowered themselves and their art. Mary Beale (fig.1), one of the very few women artists working in England during the seventeenth century, recognised the importance of self-portraiture in the promotion of her career. In an imposing self-portrait of around 1665 Beale produces an image of professional distinction. She strikes a balance here between idealised femininity – detectable in her outfit and posture – and her role as a successful portrait painter. Beale's right hand rests on a canvas portraying her two sons, a joint testament to her pictorial skill and motherly love, while the palette hanging on the wall behind Beale serves as an attribute clearly indicating her trade.

The artist at work, or in close proximity to their easel, palette or brushes, is a common motif in the history of self-portraiture, of all genders. However, when it comes to women the use of such a motif takes on a charged quality that goes beyond mere illustration. An artist at work is a professional figure whose essence is determined by their art. Angelica Kauffmann, one of the two founding female members of the Royal Academy of Arts in London in 1768, shows off her skill by portraying herself holding a drawing book under her right hand (fig.2). Poised to draw, Kauffmann is inviting us to acknowledge her profession, something she reaffirms by pointing her finger at her chest. She presents us with the image of a woman artist who can combine feminine charm with academic achievement – no mean feat in the eighteenth century.

By the start of the twentieth century, women were increasingly achieving greater independence and, unlike their foremothers, they were gradually being granted access to the same educational opportunities as their male peers. Nonetheless, there was still a compulsion to reassert their role as artists by including the tools of their trade in their self-portraits. Exemplary is Anna Zinkeisen's self-portrait of around 1944 (fig.3), where she is shown clasping a bunch of brushes. Her carefully coiffed hair and perfectly set make-up are meant to enhance her feminine beauty, while her blue working robe enhances the impression of a confident working woman. Zinkeisen is thought to have painted this self-portrait in a disused operating theatre at St Mary's Hospital, Paddington, where in the mornings she worked as an auxiliary nurse in the casualty department. Zinkeisen, like many others, was supporting the war effort and she seems keen for this self-portrait to capture her two hats: painter and auxiliary nurse. As a reinforcement of this latter connection, Zinkeisen shows off a bracelet bearing the

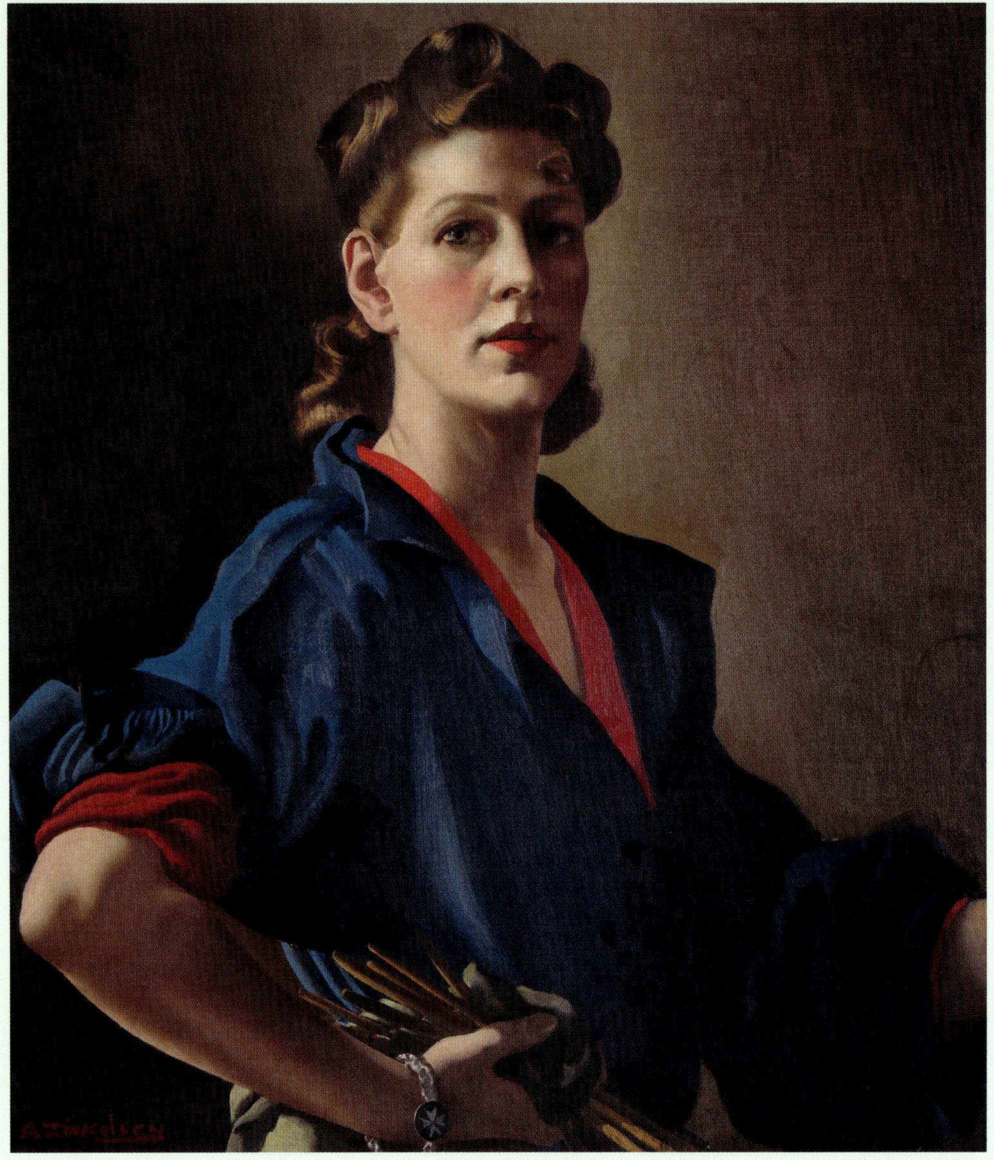

Fig.3: Anna Zinkeisen

insignia of the St John's Ambulance Brigade with which she was associated during the Second World War. The war effort chimes here with the artistic one, enhancing Zinkeisen's appearance as a modern woman.

Around 1958 Maeve Gilmore also chose to present herself as a working artist (fig.4). In her case, she holds a charcoal stick and looks out straight at us, as if to invite us into her world. Her world, however, is not as straightforward as the charcoal stick alone would suggest. As a mother and wife, Gilmore, like many women, was having to negotiate her various roles all at once, and art-making could have fallen to the wayside if it was not

for the artist's sheer determination to carve out a space of her own. This self-portrait exudes self-empowerment and the small piece of charcoal is there to remind us that we are looking at an artist first, and a woman next.

The easel is also part and parcel of this recurring trope of the artist at work. Both Bess Norris and Milein Cosman chose to portray themselves at work on easels. The invitation here is to join in on the creative moment. Dividing their attention between the work in progress and the viewer in their role as 'sitter', the two artists make eye contact and gazes are exchanged, implying a degree of complicity between maker and viewer.

A sense of the theatrical permeates Laura Knight's ambitious self-portrait of 1913 (fig.5), set in her studio and featuring a posed, naked, female model. Both artist and model give their backs to the viewer, a visual tactic that makes the onlooker feel part of the scene. A game of looking is at stake here, as we observe Knight dividing her attention between the model and the canvas; we look at Knight, who looks at her model, Ella Naper, who in turn gives her back to us. This exquisitely choreographed scene speaks to Knight's pictorial bravura, whilst acknowledging her pioneering role in depicting a nude figure. The female nude, long treated as the sole preserve of male painters, is now the subject of an artwork by a woman, and it is she who takes charge of who looks at what and how.

Equally theatrical, but with a different framework in mind, are the many self-portraits taken by female photographers breaking new ground during the first half of the twentieth century. Photography offered women an alternative outside of the traditional male-dominated medium of painting. Society portraitist Dorothy Wilding recorded her exuberant personality alongside her huge stand camera, while savvy businesswoman and innovator Yevonde – whose mantra was 'Be original or die!' – appears miniscule next to her over-life-size camera (p.68). A reversal of roles is happening here as the medium seems to be taking over the maker. Yevonde, like Wilding, turned her self-portraits into a not-too-veiled celebration of photography, a medium largely conceived of as more democratic than painting.

Through performing the self, artists have also promoted their artistic vision. Ithell Colquhoun imbues her self-portrait with a feeling of ambiguity resonant with her spiritualist outlook and reliance on the unconscious as a source of inspiration. Like Colquhoun, Eileen Agar came to be

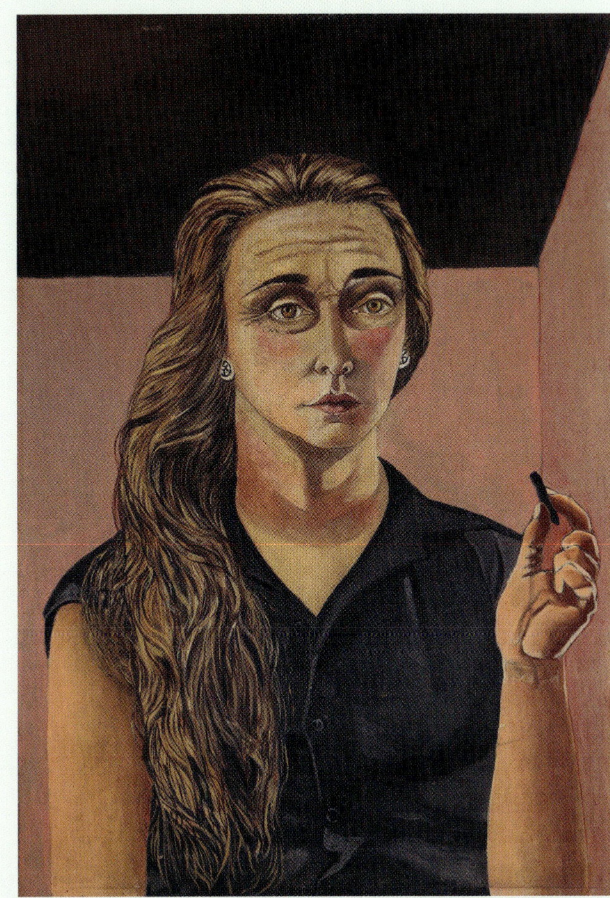

Fig.4: Maeve Gilmore

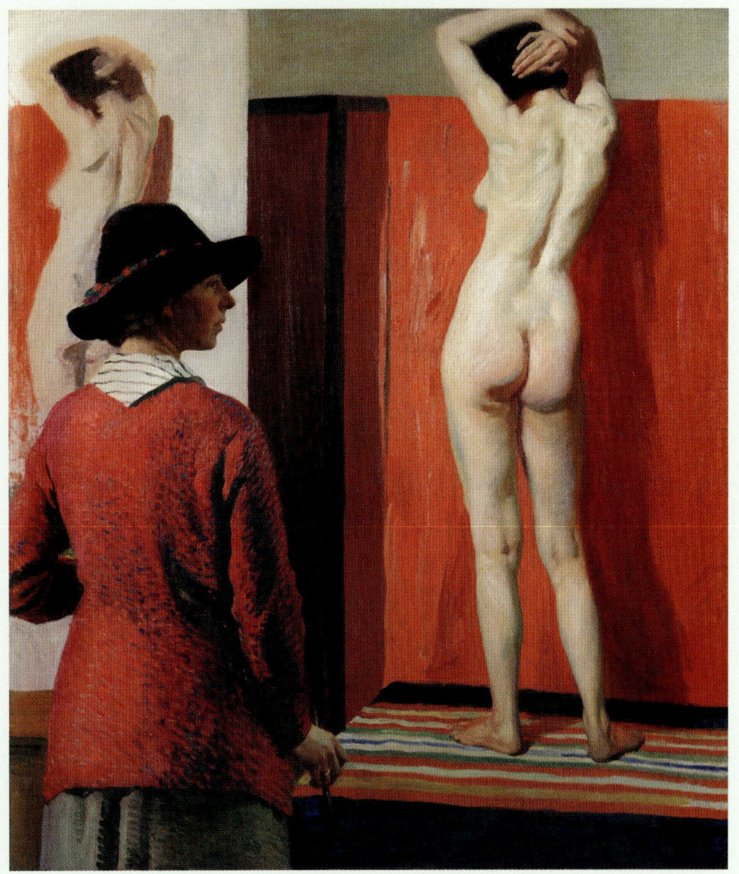

Fig.5: Laura Knight

associated with surrealism. But the self-portrait painted by Agar in 1927 is reminiscent of a loose post-impressionist style suggesting that the artist was still searching for her own visual lexicon when she painted this image. The strong three-quarter pose speaks more eloquently to the confidence of youth, rather than suggesting a particular form of art-making. More programmatic is Paule Vézelay's self-portrait entitled *Harmony* (fig.6). In it, Vézelay nods to her turn to abstract forms, suggested here by the interlocking shapes defined by the muted colours.

In the twentieth century there was an expansion in the meaning and function of self-portraiture. Unlike previous centuries, a greater emphasis was placed on the workings of women's inner life. Marie-Louise von Motesiczky's *Self-portrait in Black* of 1959 bears witness to a feeling of unease, conveyed by her melancholic expression. By contrast, Gwen John's portrait (fig.7), painted at the start of her career around 1900, oozes confidence and self-assurance. With her entire life stretching in front of her, John presented an image of herself that was purposeful and determined. Life events would dampen John's vision, as her career and personal life failed to follow the clear trajectory that this early self-portrait might imply.

Contemporary artist Celia Paul is reported to have felt a close kinship with John, despite not having known her personally. As demonstrated by *Portrait, Eyes Lowered* (p.130), Paul's self-portraits are acutely intimate and reflective. The eyes lowered and the sombre palette reinforce the emotional intensity of the work and infuse it with an ethereal aura, while the intimate scale of the work draws the viewer into Paul's profoundly meditative work.

Numerous artists have deployed self-portraiture to reject a unified image of the self. For Everlyn Nicodemus (p.16), self-portraiture is a site of self-discovery. As she explained: 'I exhibited myself as a subject, showing every part of myself, my problems, my hopes, my conflicts – my whole life … It was a form of psychological survival.' Through the layering of multiple faces, Nicodemus contemplates herself from co-existing perspectives and visualises what it means to be an artist, a mother, a wife and a lover, all at once. Nicodemus marries society's expectations with her own perception of self – plurality is part and parcel of her being, as it is for each and every one of us.

Chila Kumari Singh Burman has also dismantled static notions of selfhood in her self-portrait, *Reaching*

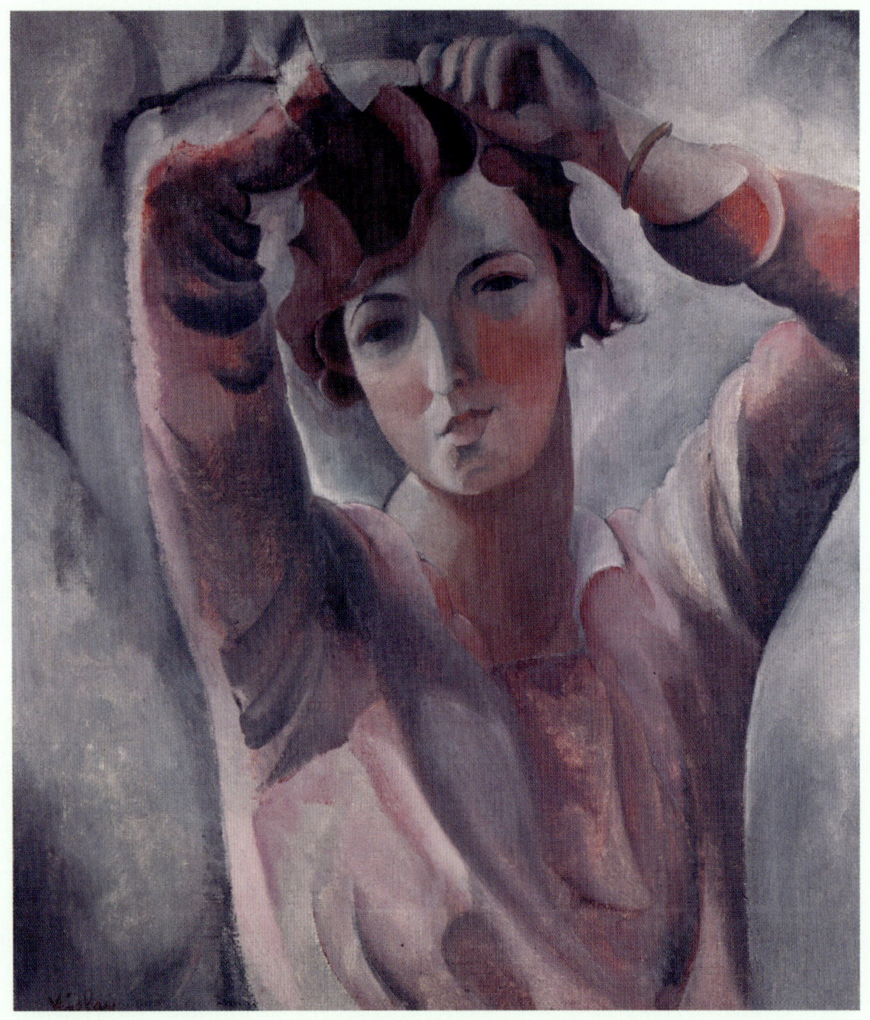

Fig.6: Paule Vézelay

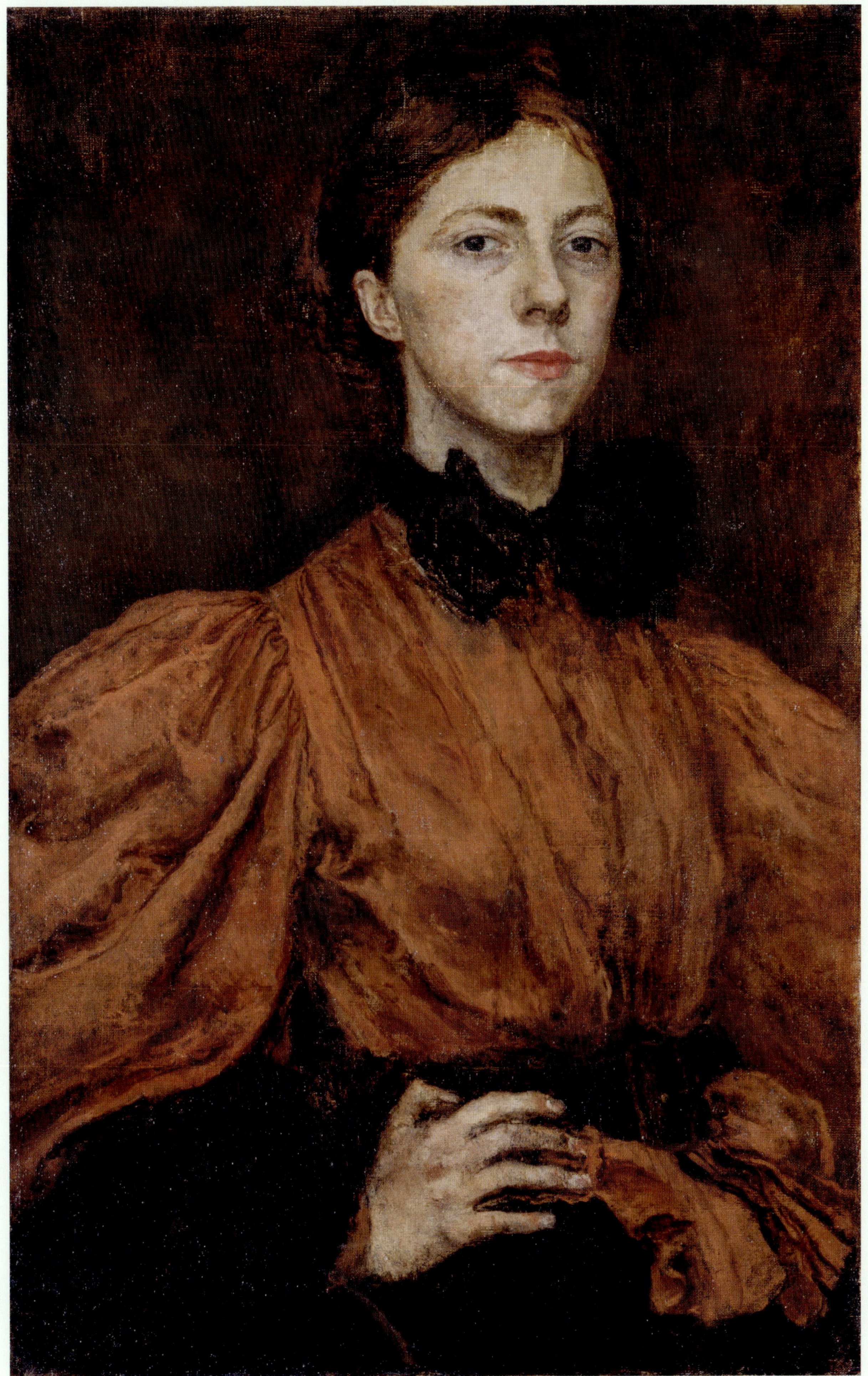

Fig.7: Gwen John

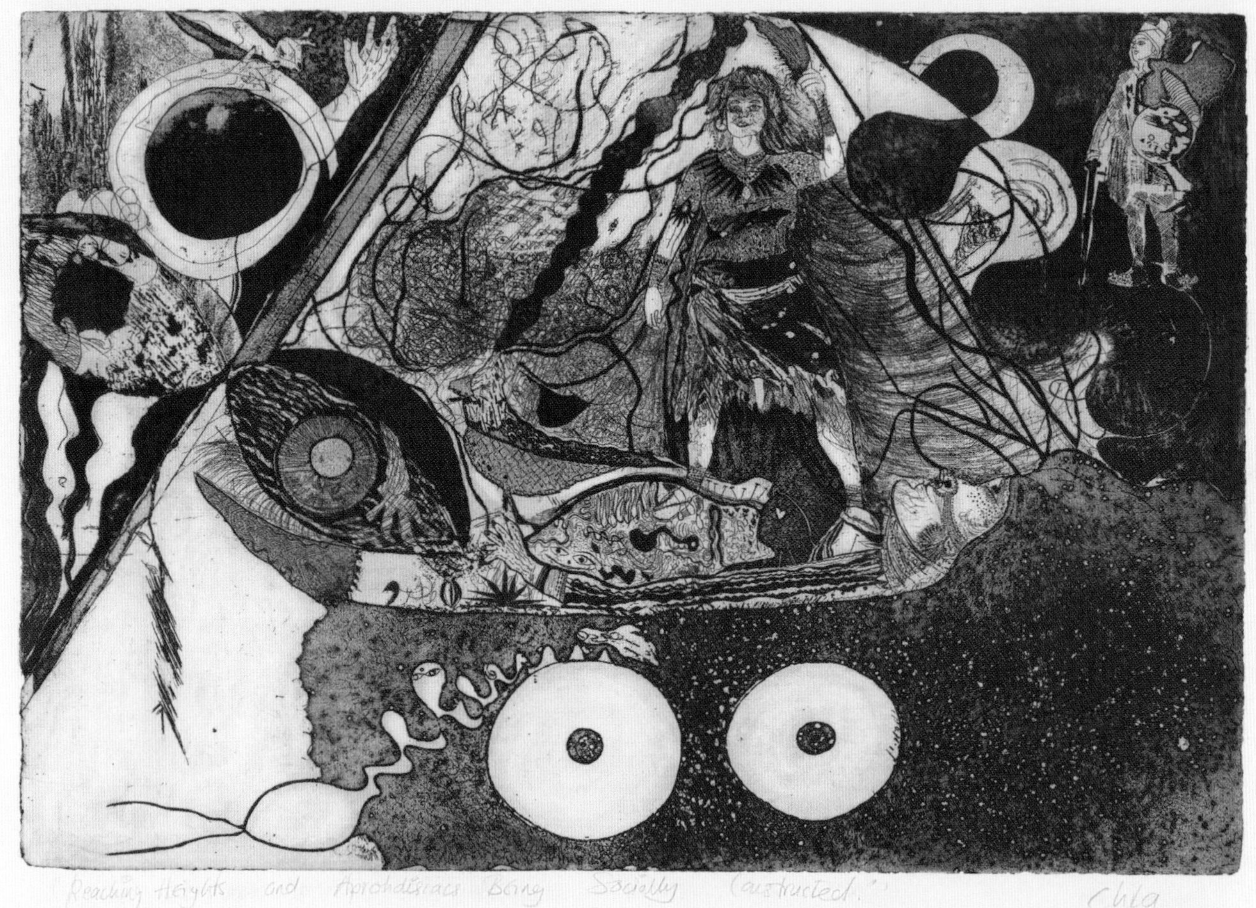

Fig.8: Chila Kumari Singh Burman

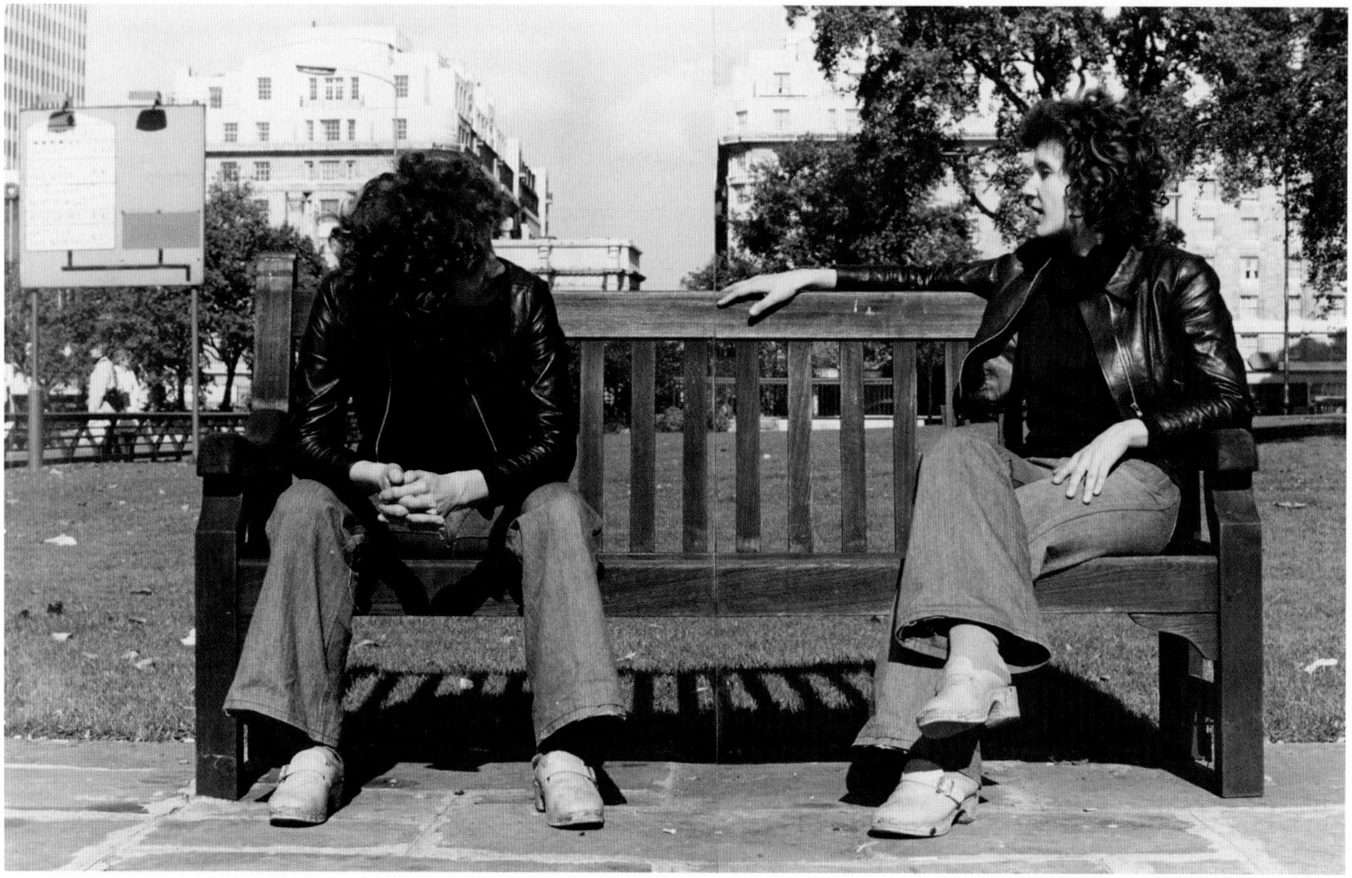

Fig.9: Rose Finn-Kelcey

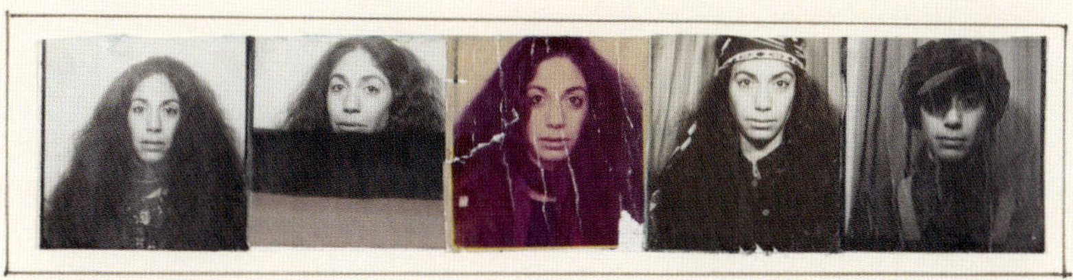

Fig.10: Susan Hiller

Heights and Aphrodisiacs Being Socially Constructed (fig.8). In an arresting combination of multiple visual references, Burman's self-portrait reveals a determined artist and a young woman ready to escape the social constructions attached to womanhood. A complex matrix of personal histories, as well as collective mythologies, informs her self-representation.

Rose Finn-Kelcey stages different versions of the 'I' that make up the self, by appearing in one of her self-portraits as a double presence (fig.9). This self-portrait shows the artist seated on a bench at Speaker's Corner in Hyde Park in London. Since the mid-nineteenth century, Speaker's Corner has been the site for public speeches and debate, hosting figures such as Karl Marx, Vladimir Lenin and George Orwell. Finn-Kelcey built on this tradition of public speaking, but to highlight how women's voices have traditionally gone unheard. By staging a conversation between her two selves she furthers this point to suggest that

being ignored meant that women had only themselves to talk to.

Susan Hiller also turns to the photographic medium but with the intention of subverting its canonical use (fig.10). All the images present in *ACE (retrieved)* from 'The Photomat Portrait' series were done using a photo-booth machine – a key tool in the mass production of identity images. A sense of 'active co-operation', as Hiller described it, is entertained here between the artist and the machine, making the critical investigation of self through automated means apparent. By combining an arrangement of self-portraits, each taken at a different point in time, Hiller visualises the individuality of each machine, as well as her changing self.

As one of the first openly transsexual British artists, Erica Rutherford spent many years questioning the nature of gender. In her autobiography, *Nine Lives* (1993), she recalled never having related to the male gender assigned to her at birth. Made in 1970, a few years before Rutherford had gender

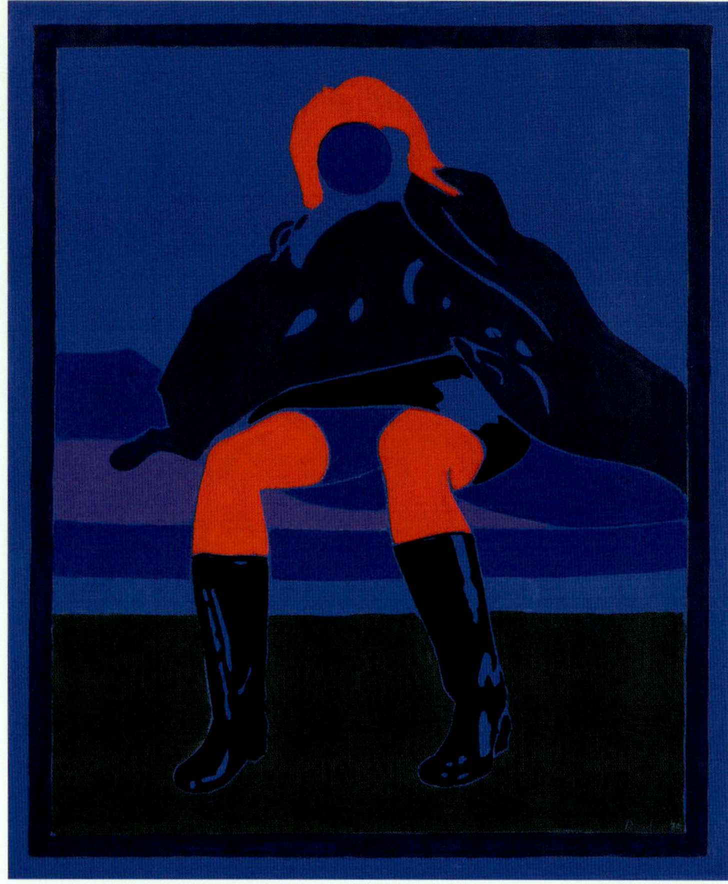

Fig.11: Erica Rutherford

reassignment surgery (at the age of 53), this is one of a handful of self-portraits showing her in mid-transition (fig.11). It shows a confident figure dressed in knee-high boots and brightly coloured stockings – a style reminiscent of 1960s Swinging London and the pop craze that held sway at the time. Rutherford's self-portrait is concerned with becoming, reminding us that notions of selfhood are porous and prone to change.

The self is always divided, oscillating between conscious and unconscious processes, suspended between a quest for authenticity and the inevitable pressure of conventions in the way we see and publicly present ourselves. With their steady gazes, the self-portraits in the National Portrait Gallery look at us and invite us to look back. In this exchange, we acknowledge the women who across a dazzling range of presentations have lent authority to themselves, their gaze and their art.

Fig.1
Mary Beale (1633–1699)
Self-portrait, *c*.1666
Oil on canvas, 1092 × 876mm
National Portrait Gallery, London, 1687

Fig.2
Angelica Kauffmann (1741–1807)
Self-portrait, *c*.1770–5
Oil on canvas, 737 × 610mm
National Portrait Gallery, London, 430

Fig.3
Anna Zinkeisen (1901–1976)
Self-portrait, *c*.1944
Oil on canvas, 752 × 625mm
National Portrait Gallery, London, 5884

Fig.4
'Self-Portrait with Charcoal'
Maeve Gilmore (1917–1983)
Self-portrait, *c*.1958
Oil on canvas, 760 × 508mm
National Portrait Gallery, London, 7138

Fig.5
Laura Knight (1877–1970) with model Ella Louise Naper
Self-portrait, 1913
Oil on canvas, 1524 × 1276mm
National Portrait Gallery, London, 4839

Fig.6
Paule Vézelay (1892–1984)
Self-portrait, *c*.1927–9
Oil on canvas, 651 × 543mm
National Portrait Gallery, London, 6003

Fig.7
Gwen John (1876–1939)
Self-portrait, *c*.1900
Oil on canvas, 610 × 378mm
National Portrait Gallery, London, 4439

Fig.8
'Reaching Heights and Aphrodisiacs Being Socially Constructed'
Chila Kumari Singh Burman (b.1957)
Self-portrait, 1988
Etching and aquatint, 560 × 740mm
National Portrait Gallery, London, 7131

Fig.9
Preparatory study for 'Divided Self'
Rose Finn-Kelcey (1945–2014)
Self-portrait, 1974
Gelatin silver prints collaged on board, 390 × 605mm
National Portrait Gallery, London, x201525

Fig.10
'Ace (retrieved)' from 'The Photomat Portrait Series'
Susan Hiller (b.1940)
Self-portrait, 1972–3
Photo booth prints and ink, 210 × 300mm
National Portrait Gallery, London, x201523

Fig.11
'Red Stockings'
Erica Rutherford (1923–2008)
Self-portrait, 1970
Gouache on paper, 600 x 485mm
National Portrait Gallery, London, 7161

Linda Bellos

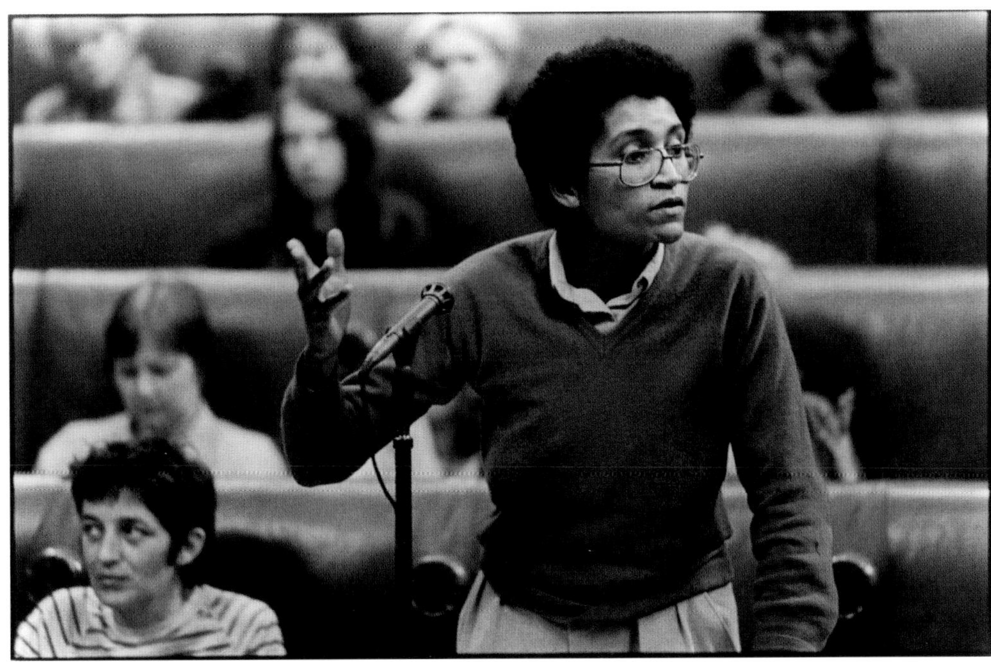

If you're going to talk about the sisterhood being all-powerful, what version are you talking about? ... What unites us is being women. But we bring to being women our class, race, religion ...[41]

In 1981, fresh from completing her politics studies at the University of Sussex, Linda Bellos joined the staff of *Spare Rib*. The now iconic magazine and collective, begun in 1972, had grown out of the Women's Liberation Movement in the early 1970s and became a central outlet for second-wave feminist discussions in Britain until its closure in 1993. Bellos, of Polish Jewish and Nigerian Yoruban heritage, had recently come out as a lesbian and, as *Spare Rib*'s first black member, she questioned the publication's predominantly white, heterosexual, middle-class perspective. She argued for a more inclusive approach on women's issues that encompassed differences in social class, ethnicity, sexuality, disability and religion, rather than treating these as marginal topics. While the collective struggled to accommodate this view,

it reflected wider concerns about how well feminism was serving women from varied backgrounds. It also marked the beginning of Bellos's lifelong efforts to foreground equality and diversity on a wider scale.

In the years that followed, Bellos – who describes herself as a revolutionary feminist and Marxist – campaigned for women's, black and LGBT rights and established herself as a prominent figure in left-wing politics. As Vice Chair of the Labour Party Black Sections, she pushed for more African, Caribbean and Asian parliamentary and council candidates. In 1985, she was elected a Labour councillor for Lambeth London Borough Council, and became its leader from 1986 to 1988. There, she pioneered the 'equality impact assessment' to prioritise the needs of the most disadvantaged in the face of extensive budget cuts. Bellos has also campaigned widely for increased representation of black people in the media. In 1987, during her time as Chair of the London Strategic Policy Unit, she was instrumental in introducing Black History Month in the United Kingdom to celebrate the contributions and achievements of black people in Britain.

Since 2002, Bellos has been a leading consultant to both private and public organizations, including the Metropolitan Police Service and the British Army, advising on how to integrate equality legislation into their practices. Bellos was appointed OBE in 2006 for services to diversity, though she questioned the continuation of the award's outdated use of 'Empire'. Described as one of the 'Loony Left' by the 1980s tabloid press, her initially progressive ideas have now become standard practice, as Bellos herself has noted: 'I believe my politics has stood still and the world has come to meet us. Equality and justice are not special pleading – they are generally understood.' CN

Linda Bellos (b.1950)
By Val Wilmer for Format Photographers, 1985
Modern gelatin silver print, 246 × 371mm
National Portrait Gallery, London, x133133

1982   Maria Björnson

Maria Björnson is the woman who created one of the most memorable and heart-stopping moments in theatrical history: the crash of a chandelier in Andrew Lloyd Webber's sensational musical, *The Phantom of the Opera* (1986). Lloyd Webber entrusted Björnson with the set and costume design of *The Phantom of the Opera*, to which she lent her creative flair. At once lavish and unsettling, the set design was inspired by the decadent glamour of the Paris Opera. 'We used drapes swagging downwards and upwards', she wrote, 'dark Turkish corners leading off to nowhere, and candles rising out of the floor through mist.' The haunted styling conceived by Björnson continues to have a mesmerising effect on audiences worldwide, with contemporary productions still replicating her staging.

Over the years, Björnson contributed set and costume designs to over 120 productions. She worked on plays, musicals and operas, and for each production she would dream up a rich visual world; she reinterpreted the settings of Shakespearean tragedies, as well as the imaginary world of *The Little Prince*. One of the earliest supporters of Björnson's work was Philip Prowse of the Citizens Theatre in Glasgow, where she designed 13 productions, mostly focusing on Brecht. In the 1970s, Björnson was responsible for the Janáček cycle for the Scottish and Welsh National Operas. In the 1980s, her penchant for visual experimentation found a further outlet thanks to a series of ambitious projects. These included a magical *Midsummer Night's Dream* (1981), a sumptuous staging of *The Valkyrie* (1983), where spectacular rings of fire lit the scene, a radical *Carmen* (1986) set in an abandoned car lot and, in 1982, she created a set for *The Tempest* characterised by the skeleton of an abandoned ship where Prospero was stranded.

Björnson's life was one of intense creative fulfilment, but also of loss and resilience. Although born in Paris, Björnson grew up in London where she had relocated with her Romanian-born mother. Carrying the social stigma of illegitimacy, mother and daughter struggled at first to make ends meet. Björnson's mother, undeterred by the polio from which she suffered, managed to establish herself first as a cleaner, and then working for the Romanian department in the BBC's World Service. Mother and daughter were united by a strong bond and only later in her life was Björnson reconciled with her estranged Norwegian father.

Despite the growing recognition and the wealth that came with her successful career, Björnson remained sensitive to the struggles experienced by those in vulnerable situations and provided financial support to numerous charities. Her legacy lives on in the re-staging of her designs, the most iconic of which remains *The Phantom of the Opera*. FF

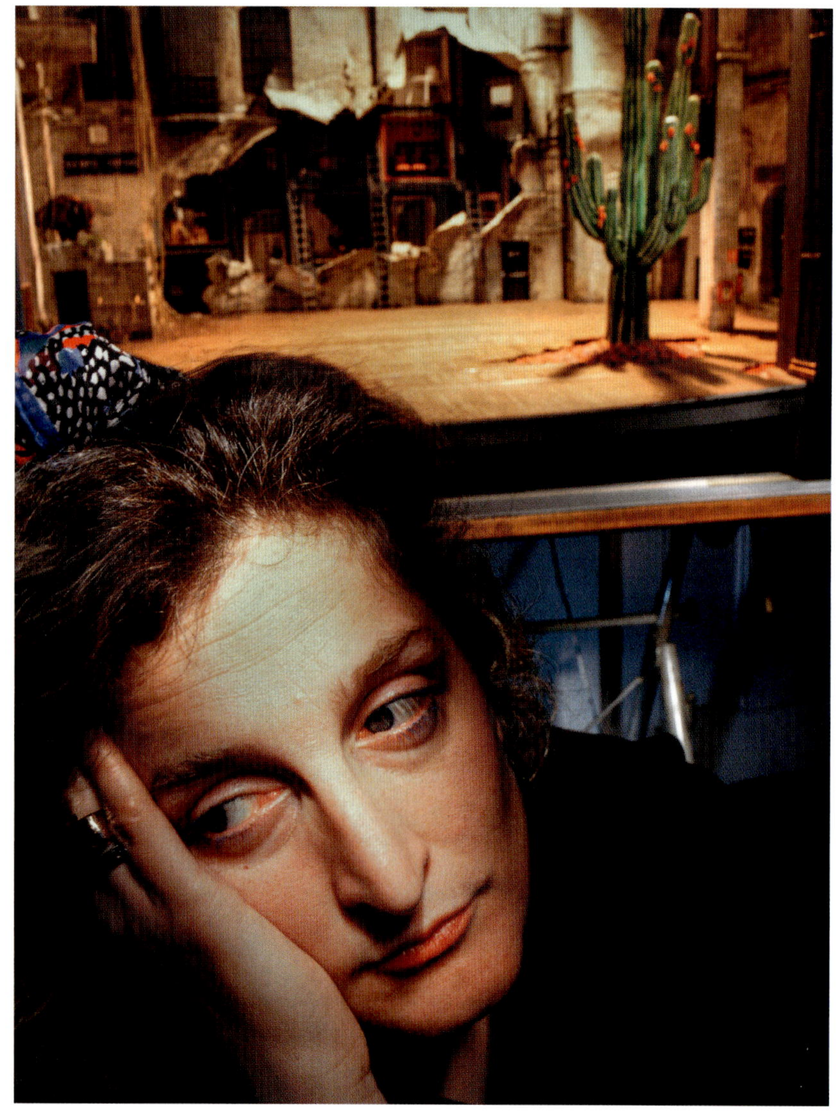

Maria Björnson (1949–2002)
By Steve Speller, 1988
Cibachrome print, 393 × 293mm
National Portrait Gallery, London, x87438

1983   Sophie Wilson

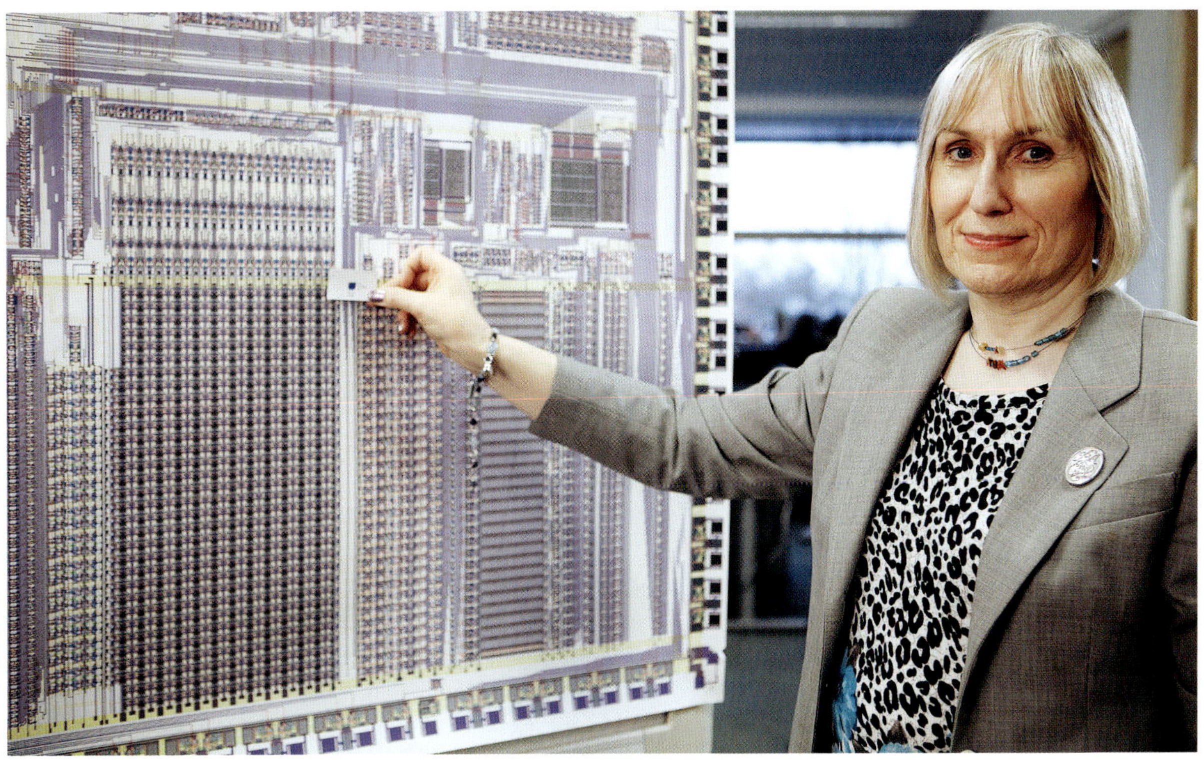

In the 1980s computer scientist Sophie Wilson designed one of the first British home-build microcomputers, known as the Acorn System 1. This, along with other subsequent computer systems developed by her, has contributed to Wilson's recognition in the history of tech.

Wilson's journey started when she was just fifteen years old and began building microprocessors. As a student of computer science at the University of Cambridge in 1975, she developed her first embedded system (a microcomputer that can be contained within everyday objects to perform specific tasks) that allowed farmers to electronically regulate the distribution of cow feed. After graduation she launched the first of her personal computer and microprocessor designs. She designed the Acorn System I, and personally coded the operating system in binary before designing and implementing Acorn Assembler, Acorn BASIC and

Atom BASIC. The latter eventually led to BBC Basic, a milestone in Wilson's career and in the history of tech more generally. Together with Steve Furber she designed and implemented the prototype of the BBC Microcomputer, Acorn. This family of computers was an instant success, beating all sales forecasts. As Wilson later recalled: 'I thought the BBC were crazy and that we'd sell 50,000 of the Proton design, now rechristened the BBC Microcomputer, which we also thought was a little pedestrian, as names went. In the end, we sold 1.25 million of them.'

Following the unprecedented success of the BBC Microcomputer, Wilson began designing the instruction set for one of the first reduced set computer (RISC) processors, the Acorn RISC Machine (ARM), found in over half of the world's consumer electronics. Wilson worked closely with Furber on the development of the ARM processor and recalled with elation the moment that they set their hands

on the finished product: 'We sent ARM off to VLSI Technology to be fabricated. It came back on April 26th, 1985. We plugged it into the ready and waiting second processor board. The Tube operating system booted up. It ran BBC Basic. We said, "PRINT PI", and cracked open the bottles of champagne, because everything worked.' This processor was to become one of the most popular IP-cores and is now used in thousands of different products, from smartphones and tablets to digital televisions and video games. Wilson is a Fellow of the Royal Society, a Fellow of the Royal Academy of Engineering, a Distinguished Fellow of the British Computer Society, a Fellow of the Women's Engineering Society and a CBE. FF

Sophie Wilson (b.1957)
By Heinz Troll, 2014
Digital photograph

Angela Lansbury

The film star Angela Lansbury captured the biggest audience of her career with the television crime series *Murder, She Wrote*. On 30 September 1984 the pilot episode was aired on CBS, introducing audiences for the first time to Jessica Fletcher, a mystery writer and amateur sleuth. A bicycle-riding widow living in a small town in Maine, Fletcher was described as 'Miss Marple meets Mary Poppins'. A comforting presence capable of solving all mysteries, Fletcher proved a huge hit, throwing Lansbury into the realms of international stardom.

Richard Levinson – one of the show's creators – recalled the show's genesis and the shared belief that it would not be a success against more competitive products. In his words: 'we were getting condolences even before we went on air … at best, we hoped that it would be a marginal success.' Lansbury's own agents had advised her against the show, but she pressed full steam ahead nonetheless. The show won international acclaim and continued for 12 years and 9 seasons. Looking back on *Murder, She Wrote* Lansbury commented on her relationship to Fletcher: 'I wanted her to be real. I didn't want to have to put on any kind of veneer for 24 hours a day, which is what a television schedule sometimes feels like. I'm not as smart as Jessica, but I'm intuitive and sensitive the way she is. If you're sensitive, I've found, you can pick up what you need as you go along.'[42] Fletcher's reason and empathy remain a hallmark of the show and have come to inflect the audience's perception of Lansbury more generally.

Beyond *Murder, She Wrote*, Lansbury had a career spanning eight decades, across film, theatre and television. English-born Lansbury fled war-torn London and moved to the United States in 1942. She was first noticed at a party in Hollywood by an MGM executive who cast her as the saucy maid in the 1944 film *Gaslight*, which won her an Oscar nomination for Best Supporting Actress. Over the years, Lansbury starred on Broadway and in many movies, including the Disney musical fantasy *Bedknobs and Broomsticks* (1971) where she played a witch. An indefatigable performer, Lansbury admitted in an interview in 2009: 'I really don't know how to relax to the degree that I could just stop … so when something comes along and is presented to me, and I think "Gee, I could have some fun doing that", or "I think I could bring something to that", I'll just do it.' In 2014 Lansbury was made a Dame for services to drama, charitable work and philanthropy. FF

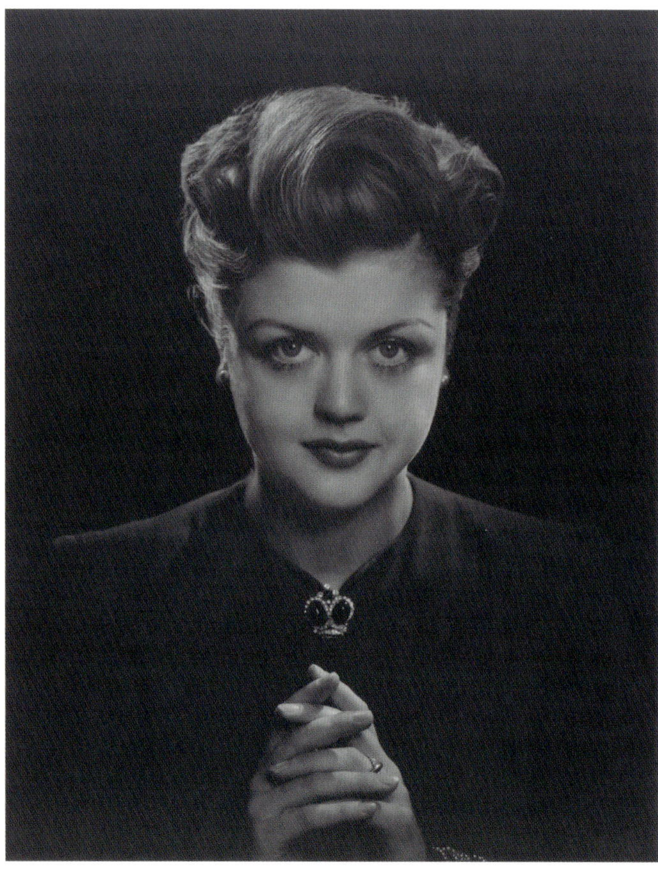

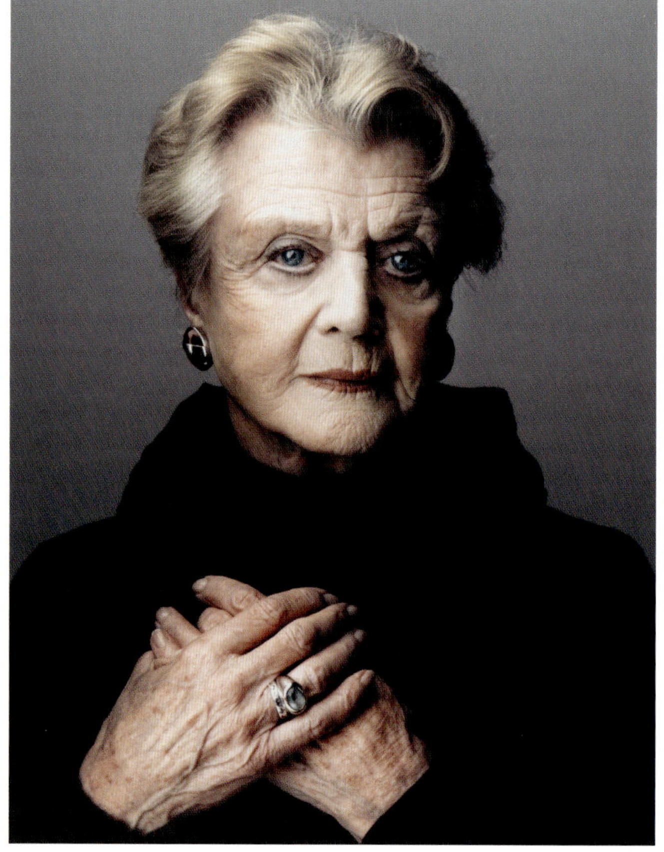

Angela Lansbury (1925–2022)
By Yousuf Karsh, 1946
Gelatin silver print, 498 × 403mm
National Portrait Gallery, London, P490(45)

Angela Lansbury
By Marco Grob, 2009
Inkjet print, 510 × 381mm
National Portrait Gallery, London, x139790

Hilary Mantel

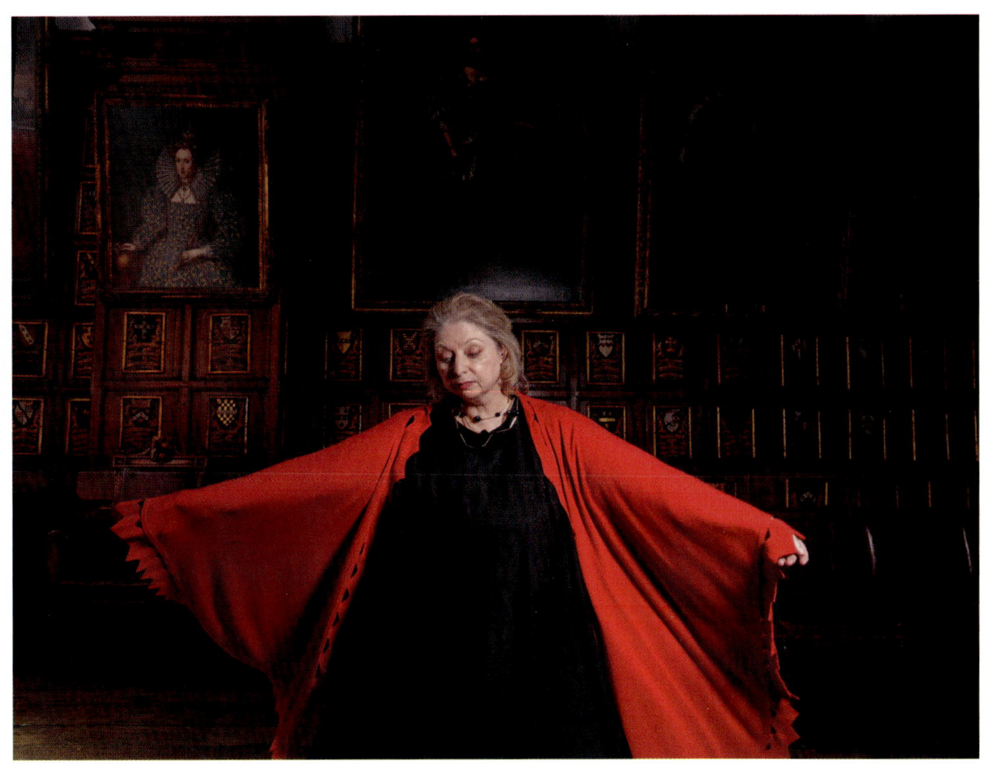

Some writers claim to extrude a book at an even rate like toothpaste from a tube, or to build a story like a wall, so many feet per day. They sit at their desk and knock off their word quota, then frisk into their leisured evening, preening themselves. This is so alien to me that it might be another trade entirely.

Speaking here with blunt honesty about her experience of writing is the author Hilary Mantel. She goes on to say of her own writing process: 'A book grows according to a subtle and deep-laid plan. At the end, I see what the plan was.' Mantel has 'grown' many books according to this organic scheme and today she is widely celebrated for her historical fiction, personal memoirs and short stories.

In 1985, Mantel published her first book, *Every Day is Mother's Day,* partly inspired by her own experience as a social worker at a geriatric hospital. She extended the story of her first book into her second, *Vacant Possession*, published in 1986. Mantel often used material from her own life in her work but without a clear autobiographical intent. For instance, *Eight Months on Ghazzah Street* (1988) drew on her memories of Saudi Arabia, where she lived for four years. In 2003, however, she went on to publish her memoir *Giving up the Ghost,* in which she shared with readers some of her more personal thoughts and memories. Over the years, Mantel also penned many reviews and essays celebrated for their clarity of prose and analysis.

In 2009 she turned her attention to historical fiction with *Wolf Hall* – the first book in a trilogy about Thomas Cromwell. The sequel, *Bring Up the Bodies,* was published in 2012 and the third in the saga, *The Mirror and the Light*, followed in 2020. The first two instalments both won Mantel the Booker Prize and she was also awarded a DBE in 2014. Subsequent screen and stage adaptations of *Wolf Hall* brought her millions of fans around the world. Speaking of Cromwell and historical fiction more generally Mantel explained:

I have to say, I think I've given Thomas Cromwell a better audience, a better airing, a better public than historians have managed to do through the ages … I stick as closely as I can to the historical record. You won't go far wrong if you want to know about Thomas Cromwell by reading those books. It is not a locked box to which only historians have the key. There's a great deal that the record doesn't tell us, that was never on the record or for some reason has been lost and yet there are scenes, conversations that we know were crucial. It is the job of a novelist to work between the lines and I don't think for a moment that anyone is confused between fact and fiction. Every time I say 'he thought', they know I'm making it up, that I do not have access to the inside of a dead man's head.
FF

Hilary Mantel (1952–2022)
By Richard Ansett, 2017
Chromogenic print, 508 × 609mm
National Portrait Gallery, London, x202505

1986   Helena Bonham Carter

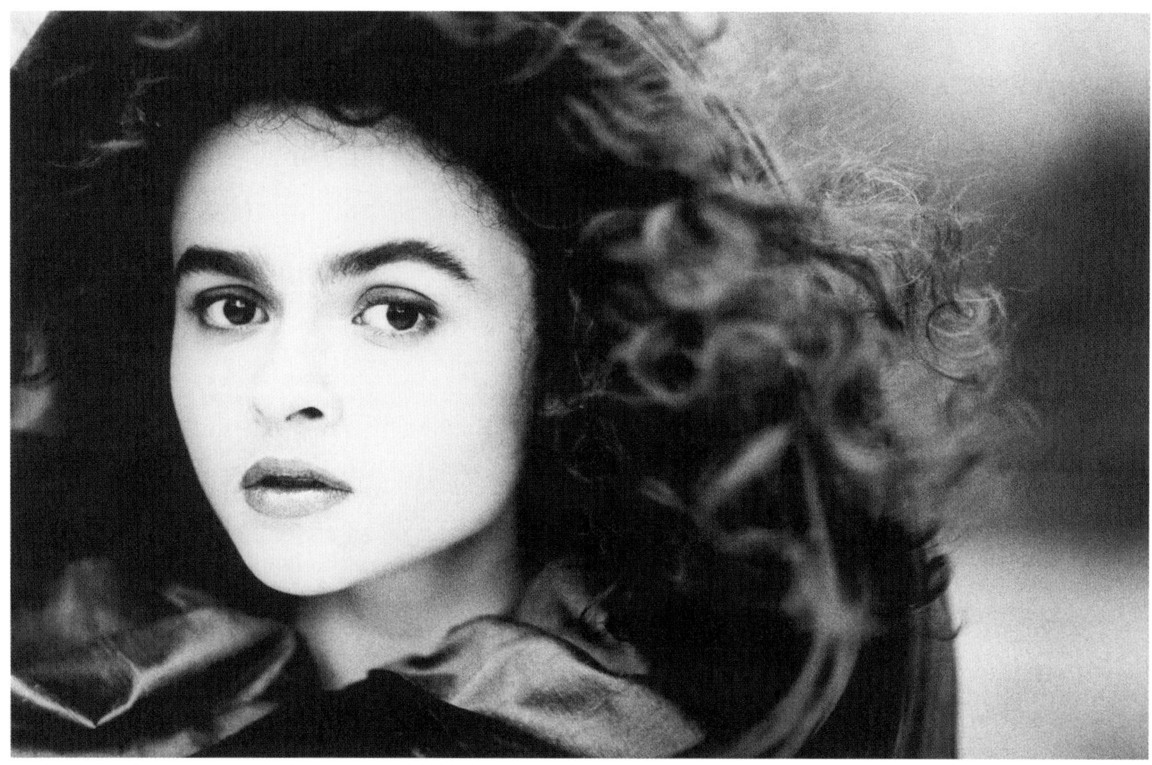

A young Helena Bonham Carter played the role of Lady Jane Grey, the 'nine-day queen', in the costume drama of the same name, directed by Trevor Nunn and released in 1986. The film tells the story of Jane's short reign and that of her marriage to Lord Guilford Dudley in spring 1553. Filmed around the same time, but preceding the release of *Lady Jane* by just a few months, was *A Room with a View* (1985) in which Bonham Carter was cast as the Edwardian heroine Lucy Honeychurch. The film was widely praised, making Bonham Carter an international name for period roles. Typecast as the quintessential 'English Rose' she went on to play Ophelia in *Hamlet* (1990), Helen Schlegel in *Howards End* (1992), Elizabeth in *Frankenstein* (1994) and Kate Croy in *The Wings of the Dove* (1997).

In spite of the fame that period dramas brought her, Bonham Carter was determined to try her hand at different types of characters. The roll call is impressive and speaks to Bonham Carter's chameleonic talent as an actor. She played Marla Singer, a support-group addict in *Fight Club* (1999), Queen Elizabeth in *The King's Speech* (2010), Miss Havisham in a 2012 adaptation of Charles Dickens's *Great Expectations*, the dark witch Bellatrix Lestrange in the final four Harry Potter films (2007–11) and the activist Edith Garrud in *Suffragette* (2015). Amongst Bonham Carter's most memorable roles is the Red Queen in Tim Burton's dark fantasy, *Alice in Wonderland* (2010). As she later commented: 'I was being paid to imagine my way into Wonderland and to do something that I'd done all my life, which was to indulge in all things Alice.' Most recently, Bonham Carter has portrayed Princess Margaret in seasons three and four of the series *The Crown* (2019–20).

Over the years Bonham Carter has been the recipient of many awards, a further testament to the flair she has brought to her wide-ranging roles. Asked about what it feels like to re-watch herself on screen she has confessed: 'I am allergic to watching myself, and I mean that. My inner critic is strong and I am the first person to criticise myself. Everything I've done has been to get away from myself, really.' While acting may have been a form of escape for Bonham Carter, the skill that she brings to each of her roles makes her one of the most remarkable actors of her generation. FF

Helena Bonham Carter (b.1966)
By John Swannell, 1987
Inkjet print, 345 × 520mm
National Portrait Gallery, London, P717(2)

1987   Helen Chadwick

In 1987, Helen Chadwick became one of the first women to be nominated for the Turner Prize – an annual award presented to an outstanding British visual artist. While Chadwick did not go on to win the Prize that year, her nomination nonetheless stands testament to the strength of her art, which explores issues of gender and sexuality, often making use of visceral and abject elements in the presentation of aspects of bodily life. Speaking to this, she remarked: 'Right from early art school, I wanted to use the body to create a sense of inner relationships with the audience.'

Chadwick's *oeuvre* spans a variety of media – sculpture, performance, photography and large-scale installation. The use of photography to record performative actions was especially appealing to women artists of Chadwick's generation, as it enabled them to reject prescribed notions of gender, whilst making their mark in the art world outside of the traditional male-dominated medium of painting. An example of this is Chadwick's performance *In the Kitchen* (1977), which was recorded in a series of photographs. For this, Chadwick wore a series of home electrical appliances, including an oven and a washing machine, made from canvas. These appliances were used to symbolise the shackles of unpaid household labour, which disproportionately affected women over men. Chadwick hoped to raise awareness of the rigid gender-binary system that forced women to relinquish their individuality to become relational creatures.

Another important topic seen in Chadwick's art was the critique of the ideal of beauty. The post-war era saw the ascendancy of the advertising industry which, amongst other things, promoted the expectation that women were supposed to look 'pretty' at all times. In her self-portrait *Vanitas II* (1986) Chadwick tackles this issue head on. Chadwick is portrayed here within her installation *Of Mutability*, presented at the Institute of Contemporary Art in 1986. Like most of Chadwick's installations, *Of Mutability* was an ambitious project, which carried multiple meanings. It referenced the allegory of vanitas – showing the transience of life and the certainty of death. At the same time, it challenged the long tradition of paintings of female nudes, made by male artists for the pleasure of other men. By gazing at herself in a mirror, she disrupts this convention and regains control of female representation, underscoring how women are no longer passive models of beauty but are creators in their own right. Elements of the work were done in collaboration with the National Portrait Gallery. In the summer of 1985 a photobooth machine was installed in the Gallery and Chadwick used it to depict a series of crying heads which were in turn pasted on the walls of *Of Mutability*; a faint glimpse of these can be seen on the walls in the mirror. FF

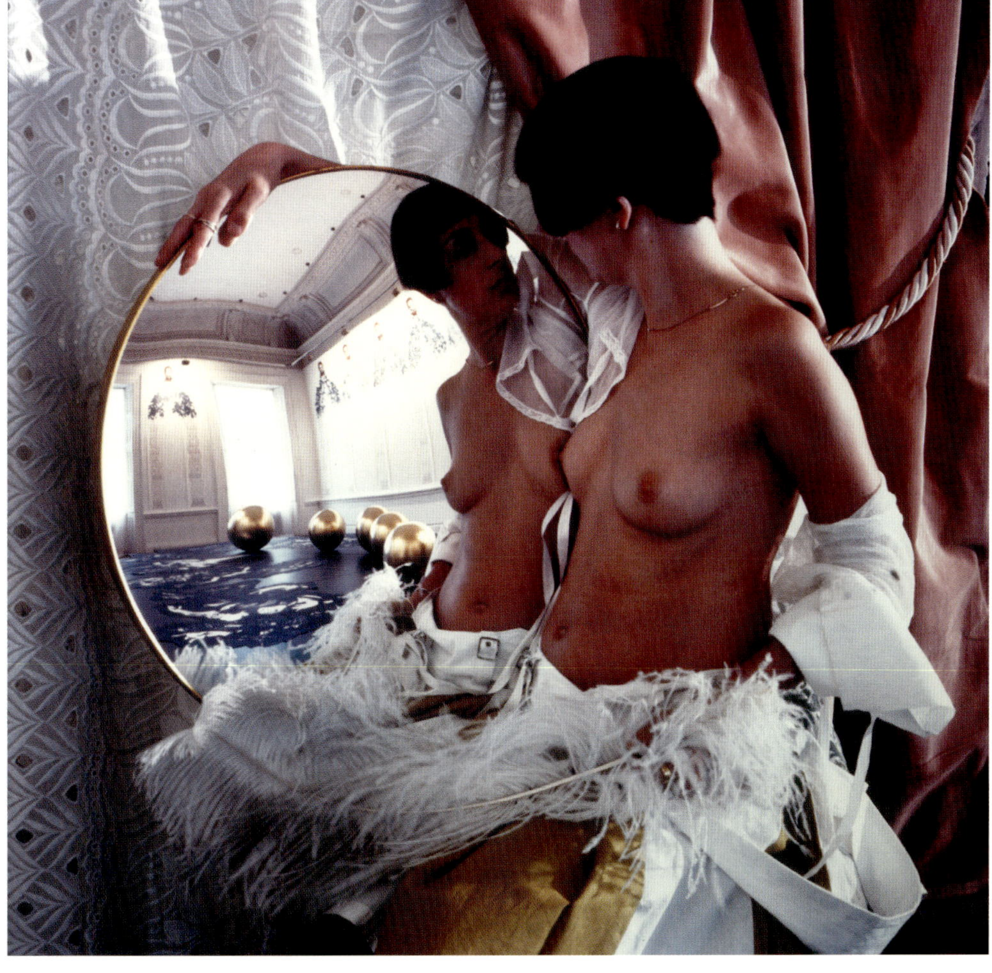

'Vanitas II'
Helen Chadwick (1953–1996)
Self-portrait, 1986
Cibachrome print, 828 × 677mm
National Portrait Gallery, London, P874

1988   Paula Rego

With these words, artist Paula Rego characterised her relationship to image-making. Like many artists, Rego's artistic practice was primarily studio-based. A glimpse of her studio can be seen in this portrait of Rego, taken in 1988 by the photographer Chris Garnham. Rego is depicted surrounded by the tools of her trade: paint tubes, brushes, sticks and a variety of props; a painting from 1987 entitled *The Maids* completes the scene. This painting was inspired by the 1947 play *Les Bonnes*, by French playwright Jean Genet. Both painting and play explore themes of power, domination and female subjugation.

The Maids is imbued with a sense of ambiguity and tension, which characterises much of Rego's pictorial production. Using strategies of parody, theatricality and storytelling, Rego surveys the experiences of women in a startlingly complex world. By resisting dominant ways of representing the female subject, she explores questions of social inequality, violence and power hierarchies. As she once asserted in an interview, 'I paint to give fear a face'. Indeed, in her drawings, etchings and paintings, Rego does not shy away from fear and the undercurrents of love and submission that lie beneath it.

In her paintings she remembers the Portugal in which she was born and grew up, a country defined by years of Catholic power allied with the authoritarian regime of Prime Minister António de Oliveira Salazar. Despite having lived for most of her life in the United Kingdom, Rego maintained a strong connection to her birthplace and took an interest in the plight of Portuguese women, who were confronted with fascist patriarchy and its backward-looking social mores. Even after the demise of Salazar's regime, Rego remarked on Portugal's lack of progressive views. In 1998, after a referendum failed to legalise abortion due to a low turnout, Rego produced a series of works on the topic. These proved instrumental in the lead up to a second referendum, which legalised abortion in 2007.

Rego studied at the Slade School of Fine Art in London from 1952 to 1956. In the career that followed, she made a mark on the British art scene with her imposing figurative paintings. Her 1988 retrospective at the Gulbenkian Foundation in Lisbon and the Serpentine Gallery in London was pivotal in cementing significant recognition for Rego, both in the United Kingdom and internationally. She was made a Dame in 2010. FF

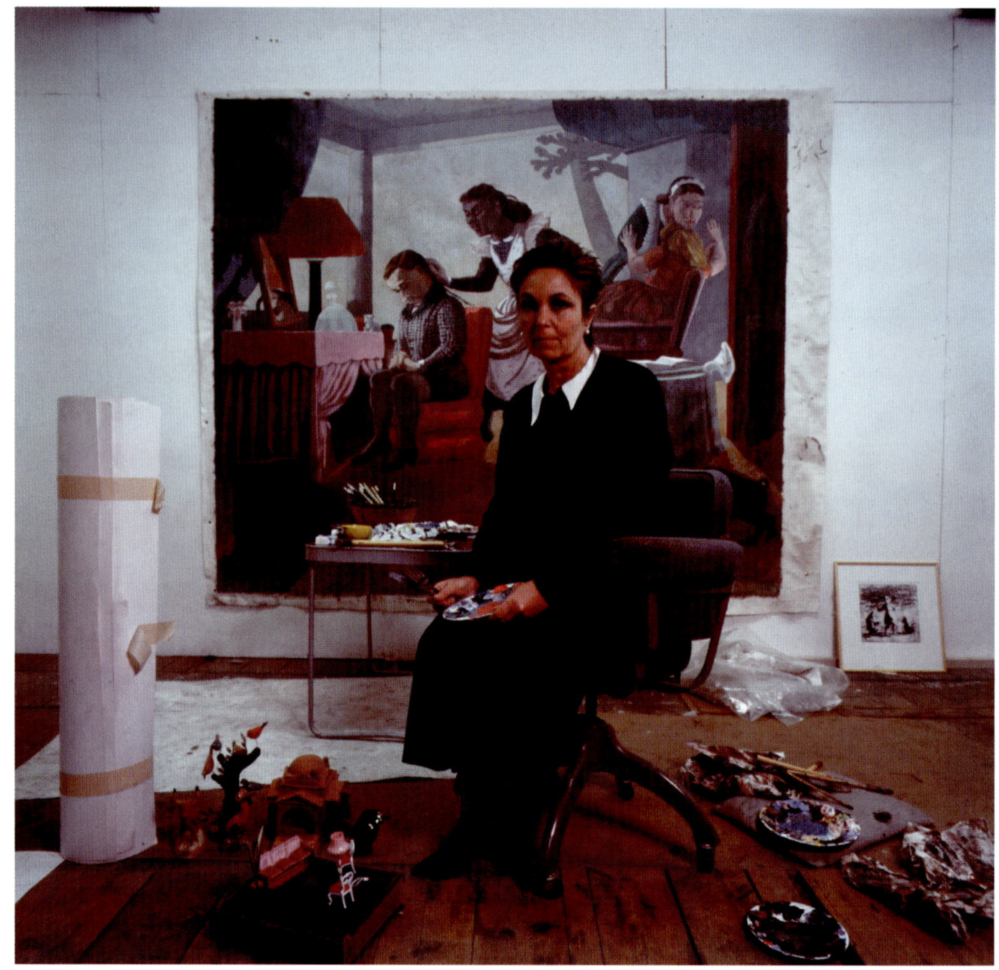

Paula Rego (1935–2022)
By Chris Garnham, February 1988
Cibachrome print, 456 × 460mm
National Portrait Gallery, London, x38120

1989 Naomi Campbell

Naomi Campbell was scouted while window-shopping in Covent Garden, London. Her breakthrough was fast and furious and within a year of being discovered she graced the cover of British *Elle*. Since then, Campbell has appeared on the covers of more than 500 magazines – in many cases setting an important precedent for models of colour. She was the first black model to feature on the cover of *TIME* magazine, French *Vogue* and Russian *Vogue* as well as the first British black model to appear on the cover of British *Vogue*.

Most significantly, Campbell was the first black model to front the September issue of American *Vogue* in 1989. In the world of fashion magazines, the September issue is widely regarded as the most important publication of the year; it sets the tone for what is to come fashion-wise. When Anna Wintour was appointed editor-in-chief of American *Vogue*, she brought to the magazine a fresh and more progressive perspective. From the very get-go Wintour was determined to have Campbell on the cover of her first September issue. As she explained to hesitant top executives: '[Campbell] is a fantastic girl, this is the model of the moment.' Wintour succeeded and the image she chose – a portrait of Campbell shot by fashion photographer Patrick Demarchelier on a beach in the Hamptons – stands testament to Campbell's charisma, both on and off the catwalk.

One of the five original 1990s supermodels, declared as such by the fashion industry and the international press, Campbell has fronted high-profile campaigns for prestige couture houses and stands against racism and for diversity in her industry. In 1997 she stated, 'There is prejudice. It is a problem and I can't go along any more with brushing it under the carpet. This business is about selling, and blonde and blue-eyed girls are what sells.' Campbell has since been active in making the fashion industry a more inclusive place and as part of this effort she has encouraged younger and more vulnerable models to 'not give up or give in'.

In addition to her modelling career, Campbell has embarked on other ventures, including an R&B studio album and several acting appearances in film and television. She is also involved in charity work for various causes, fundraising for the Nelson Mandela Children's Fund and is a spokesperson for Fashion for Relief. FF

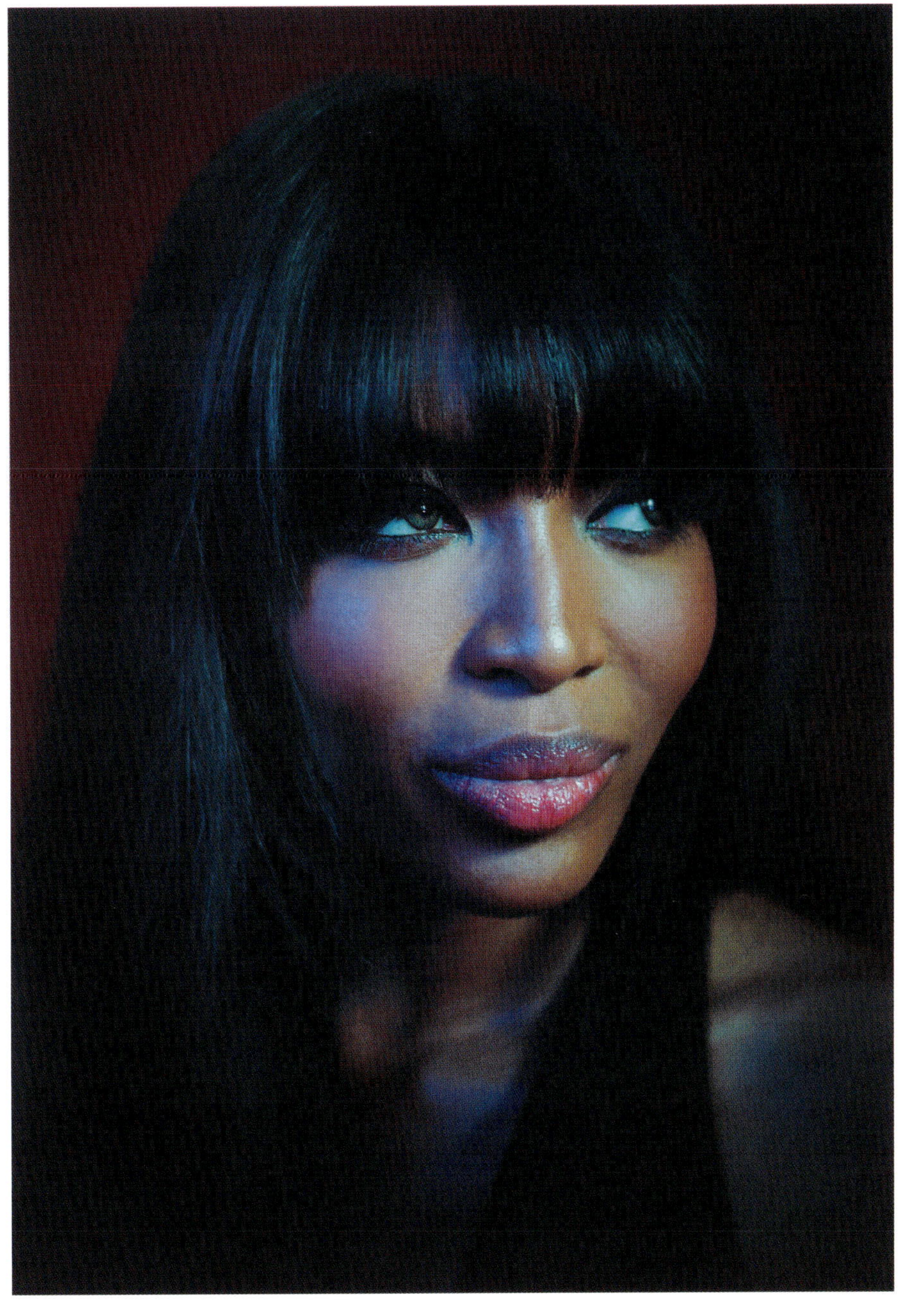

Naomi Campbell (b.1970)
By Simon Frederick, 2016
Inkjet print, 380 × 260mm
National Portrait Gallery, London, P2035

Jane Goodall

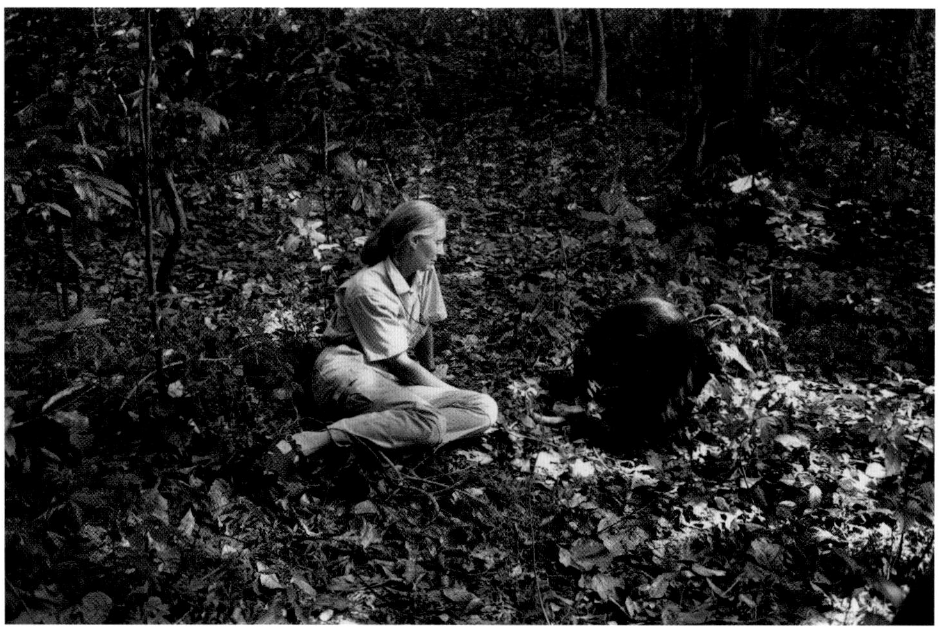

To mark an astonishing three decades of closely observing wild chimpanzees in Tanzania's Gombe Stream National Park, the leading ethologist Jane Goodall published *Through a Window: Thirty Years with the Chimpanzees of Gombe* in 1990. In it, she reflected:

As long as one looks with gentleness, without arrogance, a chimpanzee will understand, and may even return the look. And then – or such is my fantasy – it is as though the eyes are the windows into the mind.

Thus, Goodall foregrounds the respect and empathy with which she treated the animals during her quest – unprecedented in its longevity, pioneering in its methods and groundbreaking in its findings – to better understand humans' closest living relative. Ken Regan's image of Goodall comfortably seated beside a chimpanzee in its natural habitat embodies her unique approach, which revolutionised the study of animal behaviour and captured the public's imagination through literature and documentary films about her work.

More of Regan's photographs appeared in *Through a Window*, which was written in a rich, narrative style, designed for a general audience. This title followed her bestselling books *In the Shadow of Man* (1971) and *The Chimpanzees of Gombe: Patterns of Behaviour* (1986); the latter is considered 'one of the most important books on animal behaviour published in the twentieth century'.[43]

Goodall had begun her study of chimpanzees in Gombe in 1960, having been sent there by the renowned paleoanthropologist Louis Leakey for whom she worked as a secretary. Initially inexperienced and with no academic background (she embarked on her university education in 1962), Goodall broke with the scientific convention of numbering subjects to maintain objectivity by naming the chimpanzees. She allowed herself to bond with them and challenged established beliefs about their capacity for possessing individual personalities and experiencing emotions, complex social interactions and relationships. While her techniques were initially criticised, they facilitated a richer understanding than previously

achieved and influenced modern approaches. Through her daily observations, Goodall witnessed a range of affectionate and aggressive 'human-like' behaviours and gestures, including armed conflict, the use of basic 'tools', and proved that chimpanzees were not vegetarian, as was thought.

In *Through a Window*, Goodall also supplemented these remarkable discoveries with the ethical concerns such an awareness of the 'true nature of non-human animals' raises. Using her high profile, Goodall continues to campaign extensively on wildlife and environmental issues, including deforestation and the treatment of animals in captivity, for medical research and in farming. Through her global charity, the Jane Goodall Institute (founded in 1977), Goodall has not only extended her Gombe research, but has also foregrounded community-centred conservation projects in Africa, and engaged young people through its Roots & Shoots programme. She was made a United Nations Messenger of Peace in 2002 and was appointed DBE in 2004. CN

Jane Goodall (b.1934) with Figan
By Ken Regan, *c*.1989
Gelatin silver print, 230 × 340mm
National Portrait Gallery, London, x136430

Stella Rimington

Far and away the strangest experience of my working life was a visit I paid in December 1991 to Moscow to make our first friendly contact with the KGB … Suddenly everything was turned on its head, nothing seemed fixed and nothing was impossible. It was breathtaking for me, after more than twenty years spent combating the activities of Soviet intelligence, to be setting off to Moscow to meet them for what we hoped would be friendly talks.

In 1991 Stella Rimington, Deputy Director General of MI5, travelled with two colleagues to Moscow to establish a peaceable line of communication with the KGB. As she wrote in her memoirs, this marked a tide change for Rimington, who had been working for the Security Service (MI5) in a variety of roles, including counter-subversion and counter-terrorism against the Soviet security agency, since 1969.

Rimington fell into the world of the Secret Service by chance. Prior to her marriage to John Rimington she had worked as an archivist. In 1965 her husband was posted to India and she followed him there. In Rimington's words: 'I was a diplomat's wife, holding coffee mornings and the like, when I was tapped on the shoulder and offered a job as a typist in the Service. I was grateful for an end to the boredom.' From that moment, Rimington's life accelerated and took an unexpected course. During her many years of service, she would be closely involved in seismic social and political events, such as the rise of terrorism and the end of the Cold War. As part of her role, she also gave profound thought to broader social questions, including the extent to which the state should intrude on the privacy of its citizens and how much should the general population know about the Secret Service and its activities.

Many of these concerns came to the fore in 1992 when Rimington was made Director-General of MI5, a position she held until 1996, when she was also awarded a DCB (Dame Commander of the Order of the Bath). Rimington was the first woman to hold such a role and she was the first Director-General whose name was made public on appointment. This led to a slew of unwelcome public visibility. Gender clearly played a part in many of the comments levelled at Rimington. In her autobiography, *Open Secret* (2001), she countered such comments, writing:

I am not and never was a 'Housewife Superspy', but a twentieth-century woman who by chance found herself at the centre of some great national events and some big social changes. My story illustrates, in a sometimes extreme form, the balancing act that many modern women have to perform between the requirements of home, career and family. Most women don't resolve the conflict to their own satisfaction and neither have I.
FF

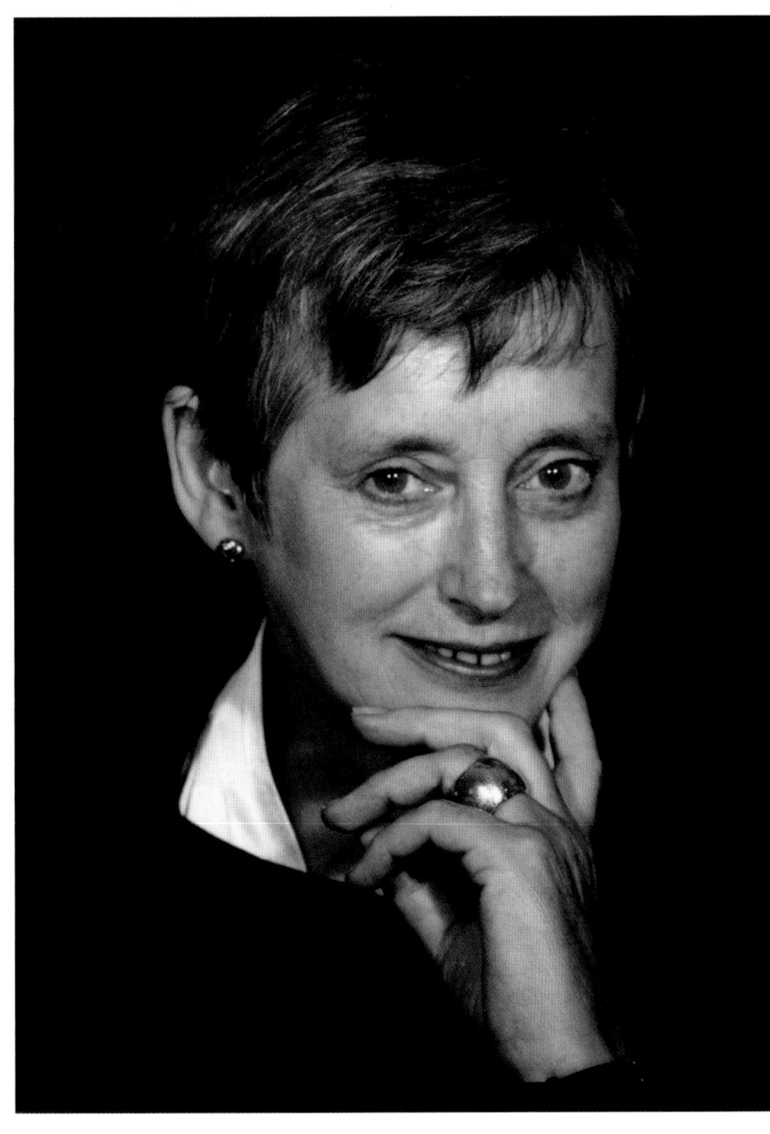

Stella Rimington (b.1935)
By Boo Beaumont, July 1996
Gelatin silver print, 253 × 173mm
National Portrait Gallery, London, x87560

Tilda Swinton

I could see the film, in my mind's eye, completed. Fully formed. I had been able to do so ever since first reading 'Orlando' as an adolescent. It was a book that attempted to exteriorize consciousness. And in addition to the hallucinatory, transcendent imagery, it dispatched gender with élan, mortality with daring, and English history with bitter irony. It was even more revolutionary than it was ever given credit for. It is the work of a female writer [Virginia Woolf] *carving out a huge psychic space, refusing categorization, refusing death.*

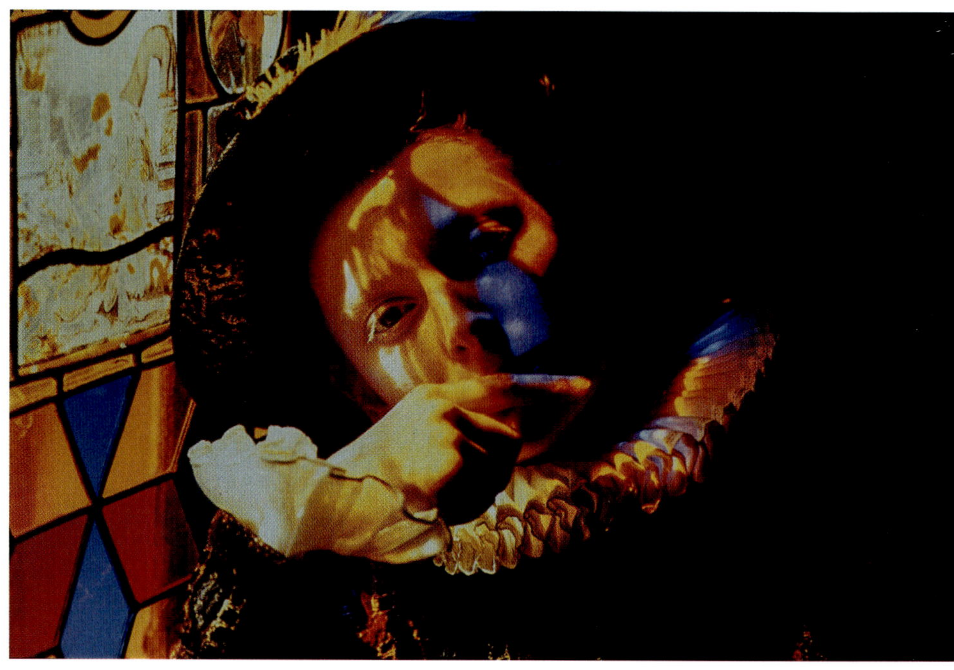

This is film director Sally Potter reflecting on the unfaltering legacy of Virginia Woolf's *Orlando: A Biography* – a novel published in 1928 pushing the boundaries of gender and time. Enthused with *Orlando*'s powerful narrative, Potter set out to adapt Woolf's words for the large screen, but it took her many years to secure funding and find the right actor to play Orlando; 'a man who becomes a woman, who lives for centuries'. Eventually, Potter invited Tilda Swinton to play this complex part, a fortuitous choice that led to one of the most striking visual adaptations

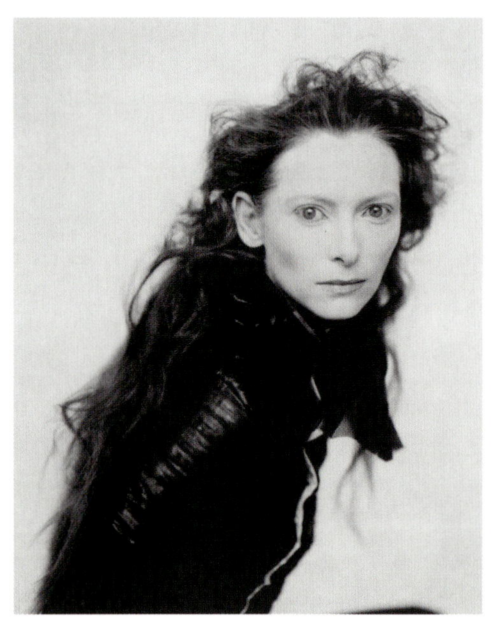

of a literary classic in film history. The movie was released in 1992 and remains exemplary for its performative conception of gender.

In 2019, the photography magazine *Aperture* invited Swinton and a host of other contributors – including Potter – to look back on the impact of *Orlando*. In it, Swinton offers her own account of *Orlando*'s enduring legacy: '*Orlando* is a story about the life and development of a human striving to become liberated entirely from the constructs of prescriptive (tired old binary) gender or social norms of any kind.' He/she is exemplary of what transformation means and how it unfolds over time. In the case of *Orlando,* three centuries go by as he/she takes us on a journey of self-discovery and political awakening, starting with the reign of Elizabeth I and ending in the early twentieth century.

Swinton's film career has been punctuated by a vast range of equally fascinating characters, making her one of the most versatile actors of her generation. She collaborated closely with artist and director Derek Jarman, who cast her in her first film, *Caravaggio* (1986), a take on the life of the Renaissance painter. After that, she appeared in eight more films by Jarman, including *The Last of England* (1988) – a critical commentary on the United Kingdom in the age of Margaret Thatcher. More recently, Swinton has been cast in several of Wes Anderson's movies, including *The Grand Budapest Hotel* (2014) and *The French Dispatch* (2021). FF

Tilda Swinton (b.1960)
By Paolo Roversi, 2005
Pigment print, 240 × 189mm
National Portrait Gallery, London, P1280

Tilda Swinton
By Sally Potter, 1988

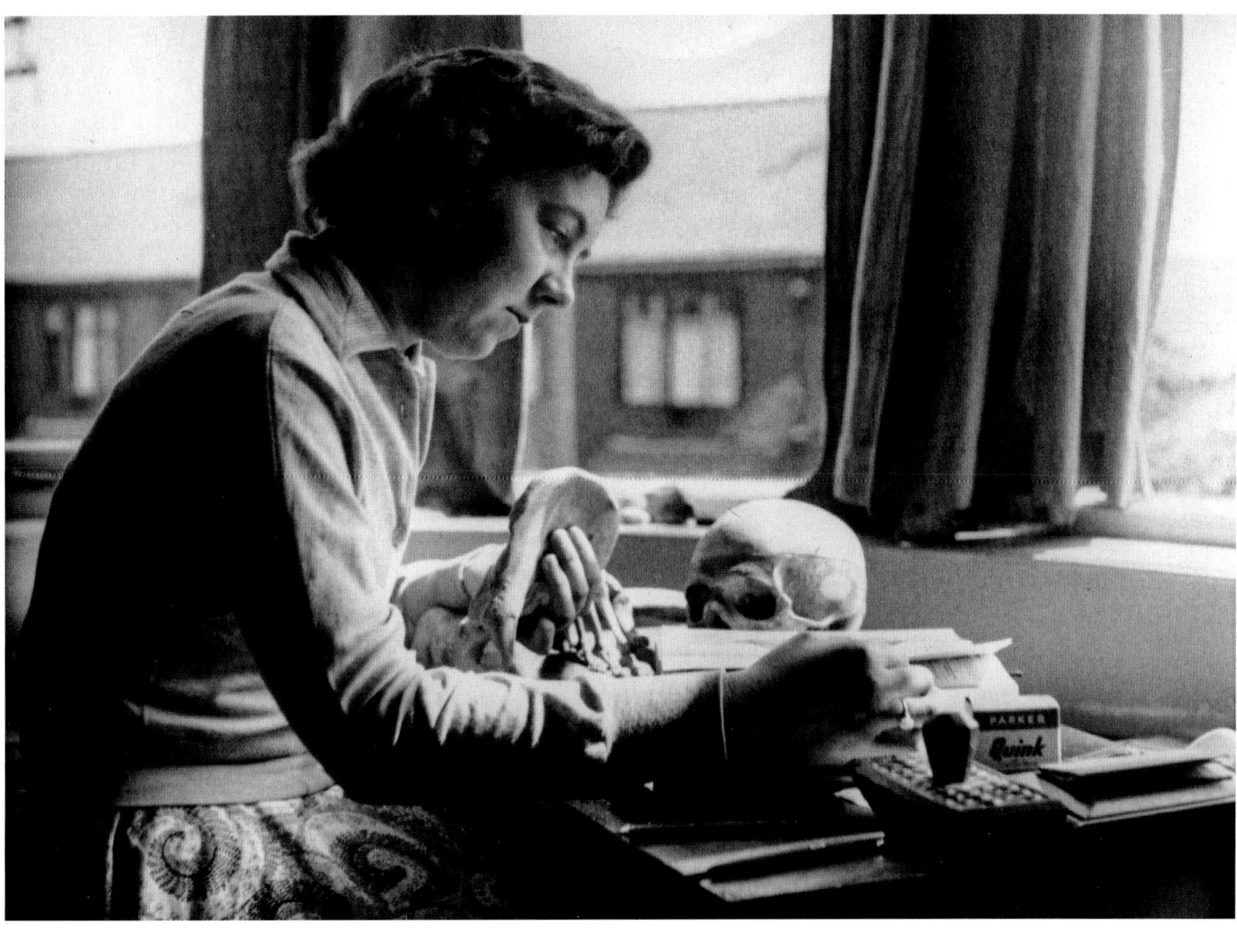

In 1993, I was appointed professor of surgery at St Mary's Hospital and became the UK's first female professor of surgery. Female surgeons were rare throughout much of my career but I found that if you're doing a job and you're doing it well, people are not concerned whether you're a man or a woman.[44]

Averil Mansfield was the first woman in the United Kingdom to become a professor of surgery and enjoyed a distinguished career as the country's leading vascular surgeon. As well as her trailblazing work in the NHS, she also used her profile to inspire more women to join the profession. She started the Women in Surgical Training initiative and was founder of Women in Surgery at the Royal College of Surgeons.

Mansfield knew she wanted to be a surgeon from the age of eight; her interest arose thanks to the books about medicine and the history of surgery she found in her local library. She qualified as a doctor in Liverpool in 1960 and trained as a general surgeon at a time when women surgeons were almost unheard of. She then began her career at the Royal Liverpool University Hospital, and became a consultant vascular surgeon there in 1972 and later a lecturer in surgery at the University of Liverpool. She moved to London in 1980 to work at Hillingdon Hospital before her appointment at St Mary's Hospital in Paddington as a consultant vascular surgeon, where she remained for the rest of her career. Mansfield pioneered surgeries in the field of stroke

prevention which are now available throughout the United Kingdom and have saved thousands of lives. She remains grounded about her job, which she describes as similar to plumbing.

In 1999 she received a CBE for her services to surgery and women in medicine, and in 2018 she was presented with the NHS Lifetime Achievement Award. As well as winning numerous prizes, she has held several eminent appointments, including the presidencies of the Association of Surgeons of Great Britain and Ireland and of The Vascular Surgical Society of Great Britain and Ireland. Her autobiography, *Life in Her Hands: The Pioneering Career of One Female Surgeon,* was published in 2023. GA

Averil Mansfield (b.1937)
By a family member, 1957
From a private collection

1994　Jo Salter

No matter how many times I fly a loop or a barrel roll, it still puts a smile on my face.[45]

For Jo Salter, the biggest challenge of her career was becoming Britain's first woman fast jet pilot in a male-dominated field. Yet while Salter found this a difficult environment to enter, she remained undeterred and, despite the sexism she faced, she became a pioneer, paving the way for gender equality within the Royal Air Force (RAF).

At 18, Salter joined the RAF to study engineering at the Royal Military College of Science (now the Defence College of Management and Technology) in Wiltshire, completing her degree in 1989. Soon after, the government accepted women into flying training, although they were still not permitted to fly fast jets or go to the front line. The Women's Royal Air Force had restarted in 1949, allowing women to have a full professional career for the first time, but the roles available did not include flying, nor could women work in combat positions. It wasn't until 1994 that women were fully integrated into the air force, when the RAF and WRAF merged.

Once the ban on women piloting fast jet planes had been overturned, and just two years after earning her wings, Salter trained in a Panavia Tornado. In 1994, Flight Lieutenant Salter became the first woman operational fast jet pilot. The following year she was the first British woman declared 'combat ready'. Salter remembers thinking, 'I'm good at this. I was good enough to be posted to fast jets, so I started flying them, but I still wasn't allowed to go to the front line. Then the policy changed and I ended up being the first.' Since then, women pilots have flown operationally in various theatres, including Afghanistan and Iraq.

Soon after qualifying, Salter was posted to 617 Squadron (Dambusters) based at RAF Lossiemouth in Scotland and she flew sorties over the no-fly zone in a peacekeeping role in Iraq. During that time, she studied for a Master's in Business Administration with the Open University before leaving the RAF in 2000. She is now an inspirational speaker and was appointed MBE for services to aviation in 2022. GA

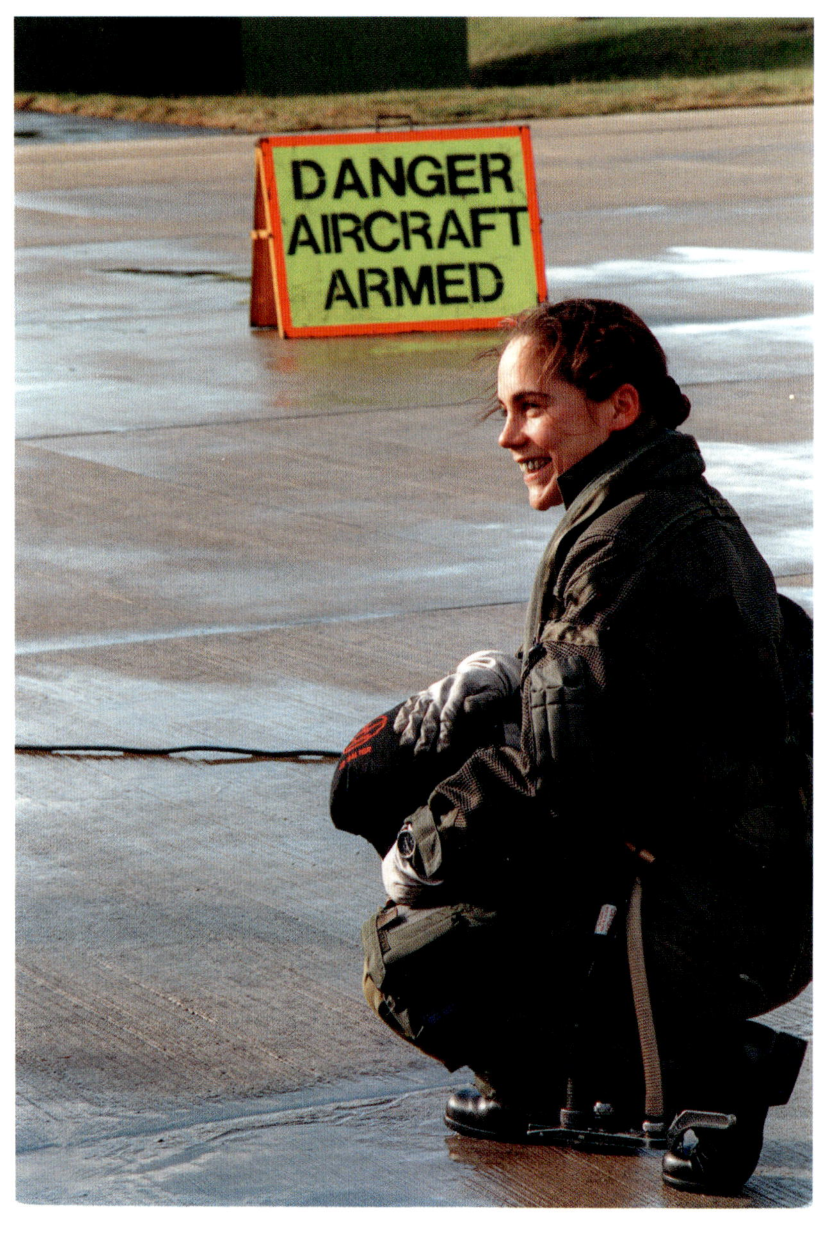

Jo Salter (b.1968)
By Paul Jarrett, 1995
Alamy Stock Photo

1995 PJ Harvey

Polly Jean Harvey, better known as PJ Harvey, released *To Bring You My Love* in 1995. This was her third album, but her debut as a solo artist. Harvey wrote all of the songs for the album from her isolated, countryside home, just outside of Yeovil in Somerset. The songs reference religious imagery and the American blues, while the cover artwork shows Harvey as a heavily made-up Ophelia. *To Bring You My Love* featured her friend John Parish, Bad Seeds member Mick Harvey, and French percussionist Jean-Marc Butty. It was produced by Flood. This album would help to establish a team of collaborators with whom she continued to work. On *To Bring You My Love*, Harvey adopted different personas and varying identities, something that she has continued to do throughout her career. She also experimented with a wider range of instrumentation and sounds, including strings, organs and guitars. A few months after its release she performed on Glastonbury's Pyramid Stage wearing a pink jumpsuit and thick eye makeup, challenging conventions of beauty and singing through the guise of one of her many characters. Regarding her creative process, Harvey explained:

I come from a visual arts background and I would have gone to art school had I not moved into music. So it's very natural for me to think in visual terms. Very often a song will actually begin as something that I can see. It's more as if I can see a scene from a film; I can see the colour, I can see the setting, the light, the character or characters involved, the time of day that it is, and I just describe that picture that I can see. And that picture, that image, would have first been generated by a general train of thought or something I know I want to explore within lyrics, within writing.

Raised in a bohemian household in Dorset, Harvey grew up listening to blues music, Bob Dylan and Captain Beefheart. She began performing as a teenager with the local band Automatic Dlamini, before playing as PJ Harvey in a new trio. Their debut album, *Dry* (1992), received critical acclaim and it was followed by *Rid of Me* (1993) before Harvey went solo. Deeply dedicated to her craft, she has reinvented herself over the years, pushing boundaries with her lyrics, music and stage persona. She is constantly moving into new areas of music, such as scoring for TV and film. In 2022, she wrote and illustrated *Orlam*, a reflective narrative poem set in her home county, inspired by the magical realism of the landscape and her local dialect. This was followed by her tenth studio album, *I Inside the Old Year Dying* (2023). To date, Harvey is the only artist to have won the Mercury Prize twice, for her albums *Stories from the City, Stories from the Sea* (2000) and *Let England Shake* (2011). GA

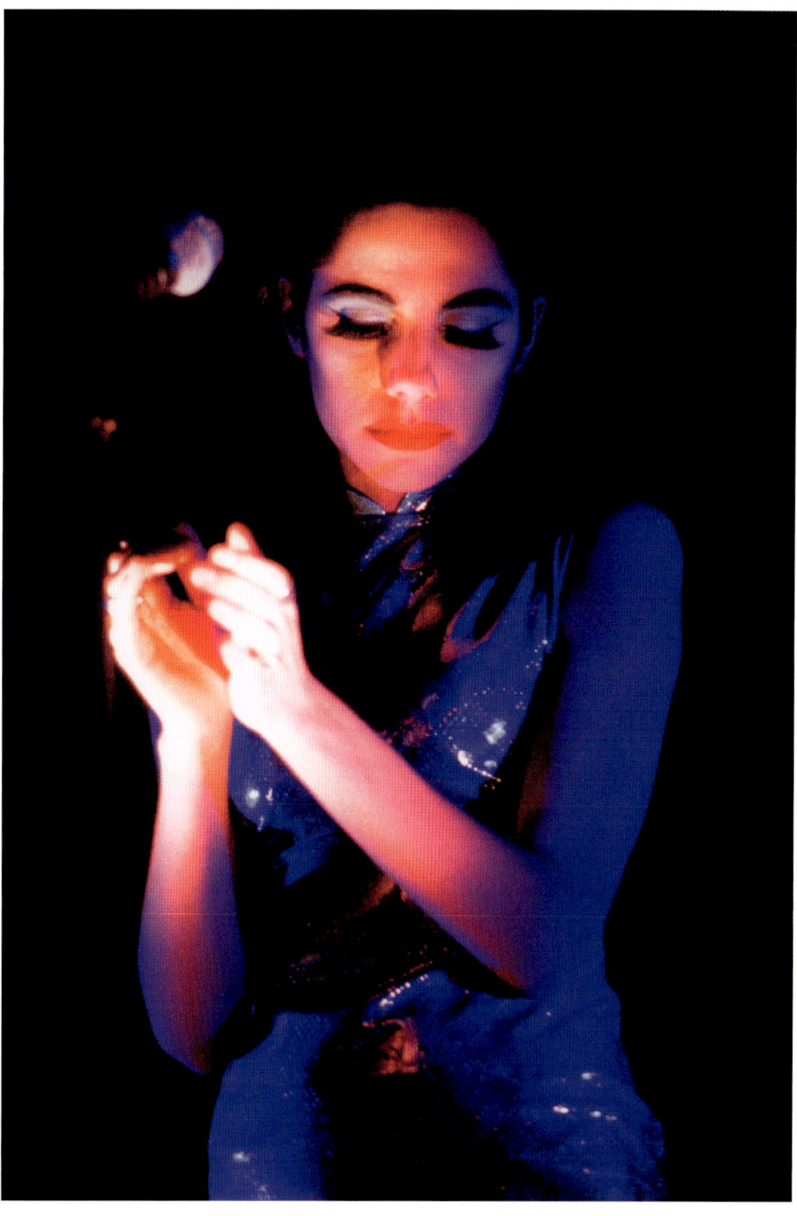

PJ Harvey (b.1969)
By Ian Dickson, 11 May 1995
Inkjet print, 378 × 254mm
National Portrait Gallery, London, x125367

Beryl Gilroy

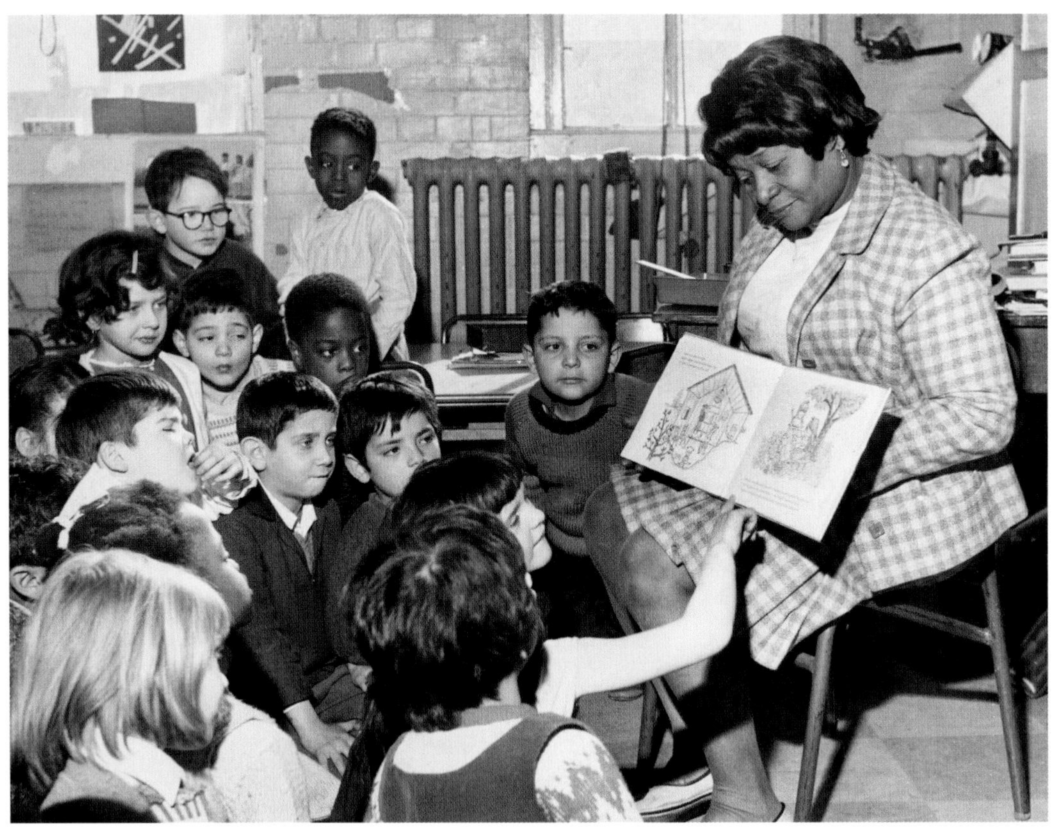

In the tradition of Black women who write to come to terms with their trauma, or alternatively to understand the nature of their elemental oppression, I wrote to redefine myself and put the record straight.[46]

Beryl Gilroy was a pioneering writer, one of the country's first black head teachers and an innovative psychologist. Her empowering memoir *Black Teacher* (1976), inspired by her own experiences in post-war Britain, provides an extraordinary account of the Windrush-era from the perspective of a woman writer and she is resolute in her depiction of racism in British society. Bernardine Evaristo (p.192), writing in the foreword for the newly reissued edition (2021), praises the prose as being 'full of wit, perceptiveness, humour and compassion' and recognises Gilroy's literary contribution as 'a hugely important memoir about the fifties and sixties from the rare perspective of a black woman transported to colonial motherland, leaving behind this brilliant first-person record.' Overlooked by literary historians of the period, whose focus spotlighted her male counterparts, Gilroy stands as the only woman writer to document the experience of post-war Caribbean migrants.

Born in British Guiana (now Guyana), Gilroy was raised by her grandparents and was encouraged to be independent and free-spirited. She trained as a teacher in Georgetown before migrating to Britain in 1952 to further her education and seek new opportunities. In *Black Teacher* she described her struggles in finding work due to racism and being forced to take on jobs for which she was overqualified. She was eventually employed as a class teacher and subsequently, with schools becoming more diverse, she thrived as an experimental educator with a focus on the child-centred approach; she was a trailblazer who believed in the power of education to transform people's lives. She wrote children's stories, collections of poetry, essays and went on to publish important works of fiction, including her award-winning *Frangipani House* (1986), establishing herself as a one of Britain's major Caribbean authors. In addition to her many achievements, in 1995 the University of North London conferred on her an honorary doctorate; she was honoured by the Association of Caribbean Women Writers and Scholars in 1996; and the Institute of Education made her a fellow in 2000, six months before her death. In 2020, the British Library acquired her literary archive. GA

Mo Mowlam

Immediately upon being appointed Secretary of State for Northern Ireland on 3 May 1997, following the Labour Party's General Election victory, Mo Mowlam left London to meet with shoppers in Belfast's town centre. Mowlam recalled the event in *Momentum* (2002), her memoir of her time in this role:

I wanted the first pictures after my arrival in Belfast to be of me talking to people on the streets rather than sitting behind a desk or meeting people on official business ... I wanted to say as clearly as I could to the people of

N. Ireland that they were what was going to be important to me in this job.

Her characteristic openness and warmth during this informal visit showed both the contrast between herself and her predecessors, as well as the reason she was already regarded as one of Britain's most popular politicians. Diagnosed with a brain tumour just months earlier and undergoing treatment, Mowlam revealed her illness following press jibes about her changing appearance, evoking immense public support for her honesty and courage. Now she was

taking on a notoriously challenging job, but which emerged as her greatest political triumph.

Mowlam had been elected Member of Parliament for Redcar in 1987, also serving as Junior Spokesperson and Shadow Minister for Northern Ireland during that time, which had given her an extensive grounding in the key issues and players. Tensions in Northern Ireland had resulted in decades of violence, known as the Troubles, between Unionists wishing to remain part of Britain and Nationalists wanting unification with the Republic of Ireland. Mowlam's most pressing priority was re-establishing the complex and fragile Irish peace talks, ongoing since the late 1980s, but with little progress made. Her renowned directness proved vital in drawing the opposing groups' leaders around the negotiating table. This notably included her controversial visit to HM Prison Maze to meet with paramilitary prisoners, which helped to secure the Ulster Loyalists' continued involvement. Meanwhile, her empathy and engagement with victims and survivors throughout also foregrounded formerly marginalised voices and ensured community support.

Mowlam's tireless efforts helped bring about the signing of the historic Good Friday Agreement on 10 April 1998, later endorsed via two public referendums. However, Mowlam understood it was only the starting point for peace, as was clear when talks went into crisis and violence escalated just as the artist John Keane proposed commemorating the deal with a painting of all its participants. Instead, this portrait of Mowlam was commissioned to recognise her personal contribution. She left politics the same year in which it was made, following a brief stint in the Cabinet Office. CN

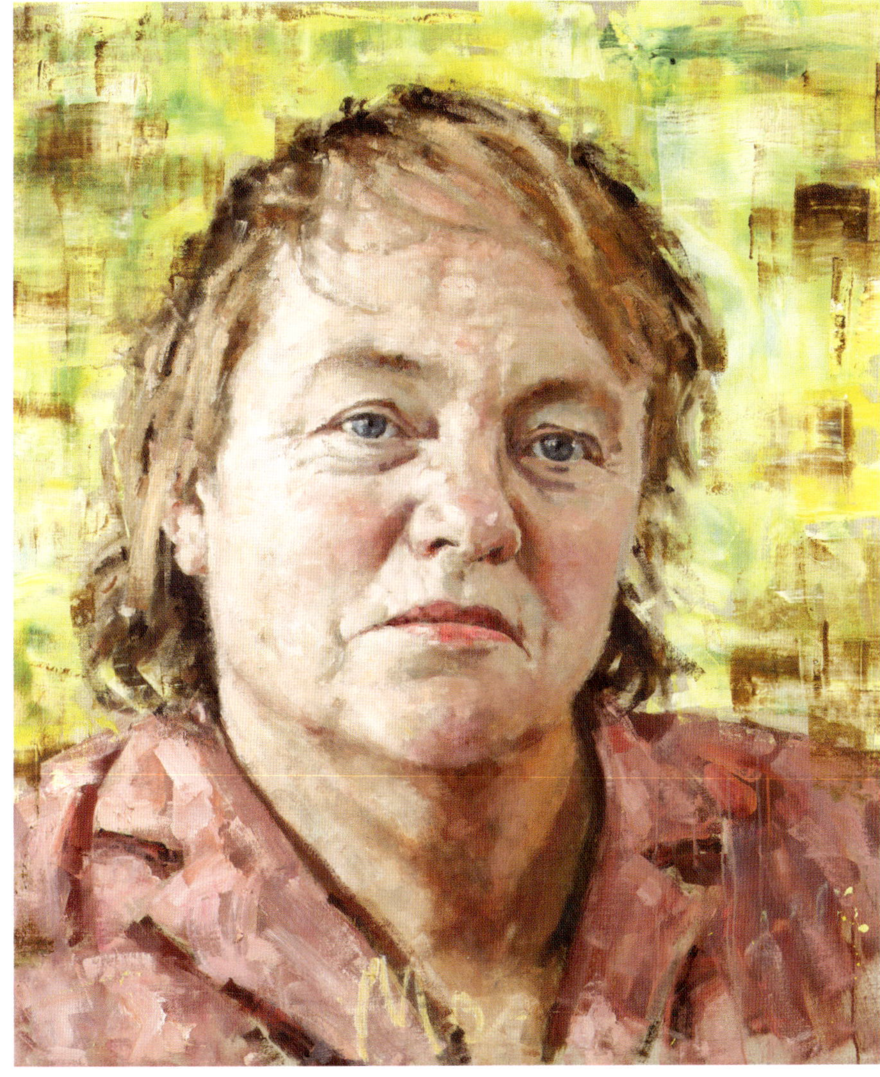

Mo Mowlam (1949–2005)
By John Keane, 2001
Oil on canvas, 1528 × 1224mm
National Portrait Gallery, London, 6468

1998   Doreen Lawrence

Born in Jamaica, Doreen Lawrence came to England aged nine, settling in London where she worked in a bank and, with her husband Neville, raised their three children. On the night of 22 April 1993, Lawrence's life changed beyond recognition when she received the devastating news that her eldest son, 18-year-old Stephen, had tragically died after being stabbed in an unprovoked, racially motivated attack while waiting for a bus in Eltham, south-east London. Despite numerous tip-offs, the ensuing police investigation proceeded slowly and opportunities for vital evidence were lost, leading to all five arrested suspects being released.

Frustrated by the lack of action, the Lawrences campaigned tirelessly for answers, embarking on an ultimately unsuccessful private prosecution and formally complaining against the police's mishandling of the case, which they believed stemmed from racism and incompetence. Amid intense public outcry and media attention, a judicial inquiry was launched in 1997, controversially concluding in 1999 that the Metropolitan Police was 'institutionally racist', sending shockwaves through British society. The resulting Macpherson Report suggested 70 reforms to policing and public institutions, paving the way for the Race Relations Amendment Act (2000) and the repeal of the 'double jeopardy' rule, which brought about the eventual conviction of two of the original suspects in 2012, 19 years after Stephen's death.

Despite continuing to deal with unimaginable grief, the Lawrences remained determined to also create a lasting, positive legacy in Stephen's memory. This began in 1998 with the Stephen Lawrence Charitable Trust (now called Blueprint for All) to provide disadvantaged young people with opportunities for advancing professional careers, particularly in architecture and urban design, inspired by Stephen's own unrealized dream of becoming an architect. An annual prize was also launched in Stephen's name to provide bursaries for aspiring architects. Since then, Doreen Lawrence has continued working towards social reforms through initiatives such as the Stephen Lawrence Day Foundation, started in 2020 to address societal inequalities and expand the prospects of marginalised communities through its services and resources.

Initially appointed OBE in 2003, Lawrence was made Baroness Lawrence of Clarendon in 2013 in recognition of the indelible mark she has made on British society and attitudes towards racism. Lawrence stated some years earlier:

I have not sought fame or notoriety. All I have ever wanted was justice for my son. I hope that as a result of what I have been through there will be a legacy for the nation. Stephen's legacy will be hope for the future.
CN

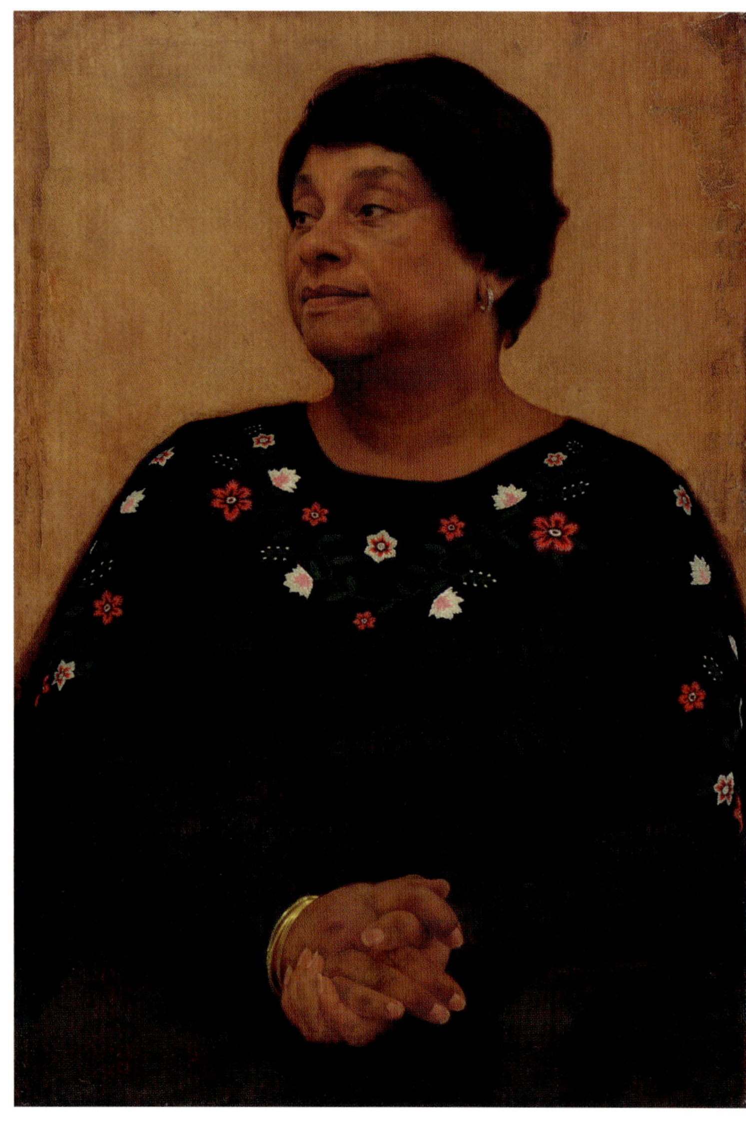

Doreen Lawrence (b.1952)
By Thomas Ganter, 2020
Oil on board, 660 × 440mm
National Portrait Gallery, London, 7113

Tracey Emin

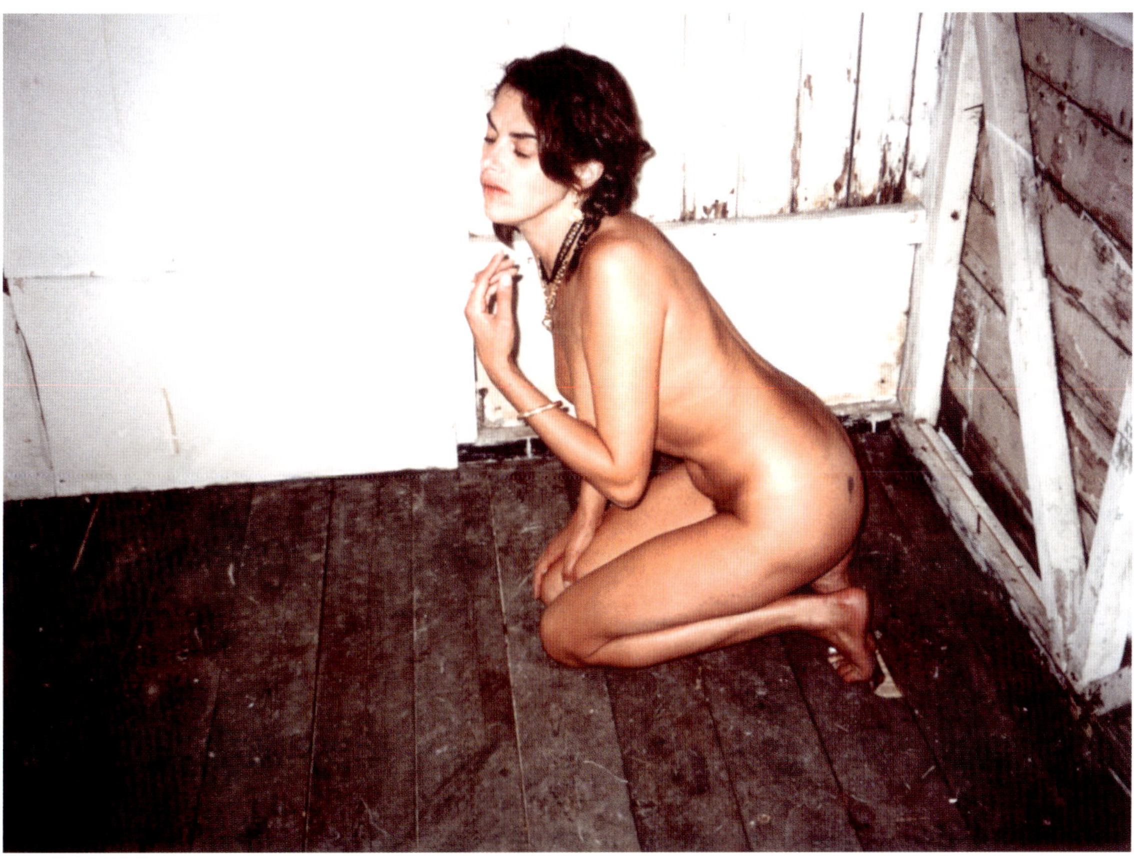

I love you, you hated me, you hated me, I wanted you, I need you, I care about you, you stopped loving me, you never loved me, you don't love me enough, I've got to have you, I need you, I miss you, I care about you, where are you, where are you, where are you …

These words cast light on the confessional nature of Tracey Emin's art. Since the early 1990s when Emin, as part of a sensational generation of young artists, took the London art world by storm, she has drawn on her unsettling inner worlds to make art. Her paintings, drawings, neon writings, installations and embroideries read like an explicit account of her life, erring between love, desire and pain.

In 1999, the artwork *My Bed* made Emin a household name in Britain when it was exhibited at the Tate Britain as one of the works shortlisted for the Turner Prize. The artwork – featuring the artist's own unmade bed surrounded by empty alcohol bottles, condoms, heaped ashtrays, medicines and cigarette packets – was a relic of Emin's own life. A portrait of sorts, it captured the turmoil of Emin's existence, made manifest by her most intimate physical surroundings. Viewers were shocked by the explicit nature of *My Bed* and questioned the legitimacy of it as an artwork. The outrage, which caused a media sensation, was not driven by the readymade nature of the work, but by its explicit reference to sex, desire and the unravelling of Emin's personal life. 'The carnal reality of life stains its sheets' is how art critic Jonathan Jones aptly described *My Bed*.

Like *My Bed*, most of Emin's works are an honest acknowledgement of her emotional life. In *The Last Thing I said to you is don't leave me here. 1* (2000) Emin uses herself once again as subject matter for her art. Her nudity is intentionally ambiguous and can be read as both provocative and vulnerable. All the while, the work hints at Emin's Margate origins, as the self-portrait was taken in a beach hut in the Kentish seaside town where the artist grew up and has recently moved back to. A champion of the town's recent renaissance, she has stated, 'I've come back to Margate as a different person, and I've come back to a different Margate. So it's like, we are both in tandem, in tune with each other.' Emin's life is her art and vice-versa.

In 2023 a new site-specific commission by Emin for the National Portrait Gallery was unveiled with the intention of paying tribute to pioneering British women. FF

'The Last Thing I said to you is don't leave me here. 1'
Tracey Emin (b.1963)
Self-portrait, 2000
Inkjet print, 813 × 1092mm
National Portrait Gallery, London, P879

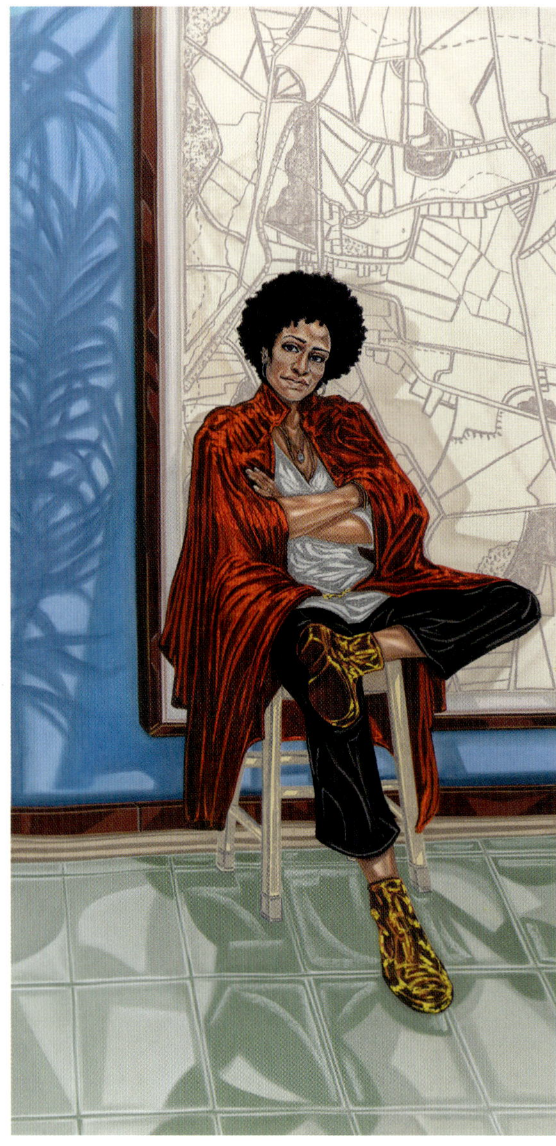

the Whitbread First Novel Award and James Tait Black Memorial Prize, establishing its status as a modern classic. Two years after its publication, Smith was elected a Fellow of the Royal Society of Literature, and a television adaptation was also filmed. A stage version in 2018 exemplified the book's continuing popularity.

Smith's subsequent writing additionally confirmed her as one of the most celebrated authors of her generation. Her other novels include *On Beauty* (2005) and *NW* (2012), centred on two girls growing up on the same north-west London estate and their diverging lives in adulthood. Smith has also published collections of her short stories and essays, along with her first play, *The Wife of Willesden*, in 2021, inspired by Geoffrey Chaucer's *Canterbury Tales*. That same year she demonstrated her versatility as a writer further with the first of several children's books co-authored with her husband, Nick Laird.

Toyin Ojih Odutola's portrait depicts Smith as an assured and established writer, looking directly at the artist in 'an exchange of energy' that Smith identifies as rare in the depiction of black sitters historically in painted portraiture. Using Smith's birth name (before she changed it to Zadie) as its title, it signifies the foundations of her life with shadows reminiscent of palm trees evoking her Jamaican heritage, appearing alongside her frequent inspiration, north-west London, represented by a map in the background. In response, Smith remarked:

I am very grateful [Odutola] chose to draw me as the person I would most like to be. Free of the projections of others, boldly at home in the world, connected to a beautiful heritage – and ready to make something new.
CN

The much-publicized circumstances surrounding the publication of Zadie Smith's debut novel, *White Teeth*, in 2000 are legendary in the history of contemporary fiction. Aged 21 and still studying for her undergraduate degree at Cambridge University, Smith reportedly received a six-figure sum from the publisher Hamish Hamilton to complete her first two books on the basis of an initial 80 pages of *White Teeth*'s manuscript. Mostly set from the 1970s to the 1990s in Willesden, north-west London,

where Smith grew up with a Jamaican mother and English father, the story centres on the lives and families of two long-term friends, Bangladeshi waiter Samad Iqbal and Englishman Archie Jones. The lively, multi-layered plot is rich with witty dialogue and humour as the main characters question and attempt to come to terms with their multicultural identities against a post-colonial backdrop.

White Teeth instantly became a critically acclaimed bestseller and numerous awards followed, including

'Sadie'
Zadie Smith (b.1975)
By Toyin Ojih Odutola, 2018–19
Pastel, charcoal, pencil and graphite on paper, 2235 × 1066mm
National Portrait Gallery, London, 7105

THE CHANGING ICONOGRAPHY OF THE WOMAN WRITER

By

Alison Smith

The enormous success and reputation of
authors such as Zadie Smith, Hilary Mantel
and Bernardine Evaristo in recent times
has presented artists with the dilemma of
finding a visual language for portraying
the female writer. It has rarely been easy
to identify a woman as a writer from a
portrait. Men are still far more likely to be
recognised as authors because artists have a
rich iconographic tradition to draw on when
representing male literary figures. Justin
Mortimer thus presents playwright Harold
Pinter as a man of letters, fronting a massive
pile of papers, while Peter Edwards shows
Kazuo Ishiguro deep in thought surrounded
by books. Although today women rank equal
to men as authors, and have greater control
of their own personae than ever before,
their paths to success and recognition have
not been straightforward. We have only
to delve a little into the past to find women
marginalised from the public sphere and
consequently diffident about the prospect of
being immortalised through the elite form
of the painted or sculpted portrait.

For much of the nineteenth century,
women as writers were not conspicuous in
portraiture. It was unusual for a woman to
commission a portrait, and those paintings
and studies that exist tend to emphasise
a sitter's homely, feminine qualities rather
than project an intellectual role beyond
the domestic sphere. Jane Austen and the
Brontë sisters, probably the most famous
women novelists of the romantic period, are
known primarily through amateur portraits
by relatives: Austen through her sister
Cassandra's slight sketch, the Brontës by their
brother Branwell's group portrait that reveals
little about the sisters' individual appearances
(fig.1). As 'relative creatures', to quote
Françoise Basch, women's main role was seen
to support family members rather than forge
an independent path outside the home. This

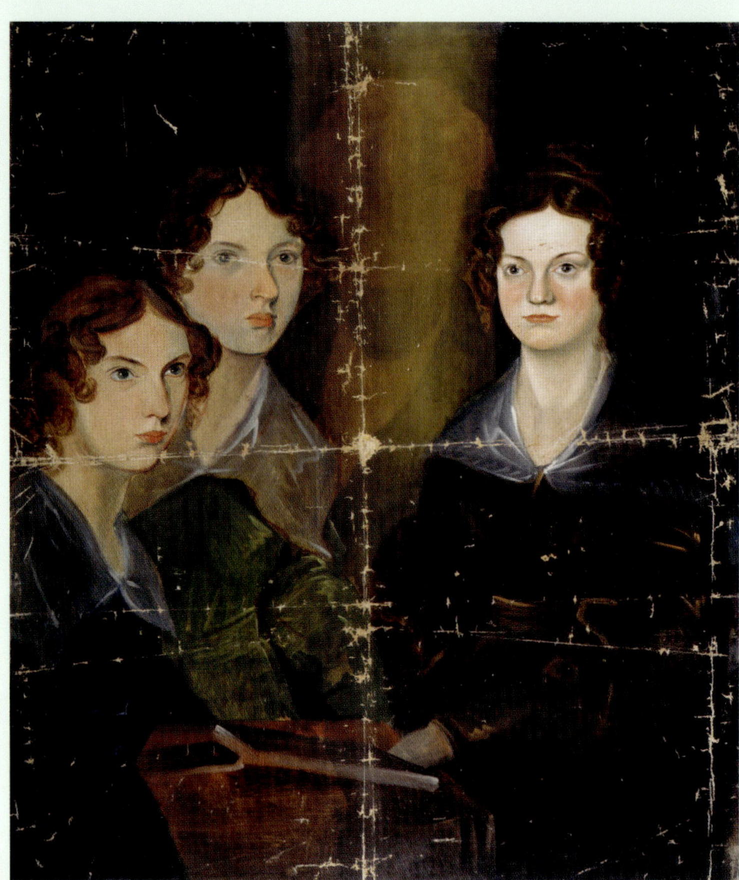

Fig.1: The Brontë sisters by Patrick Branwell Brontë

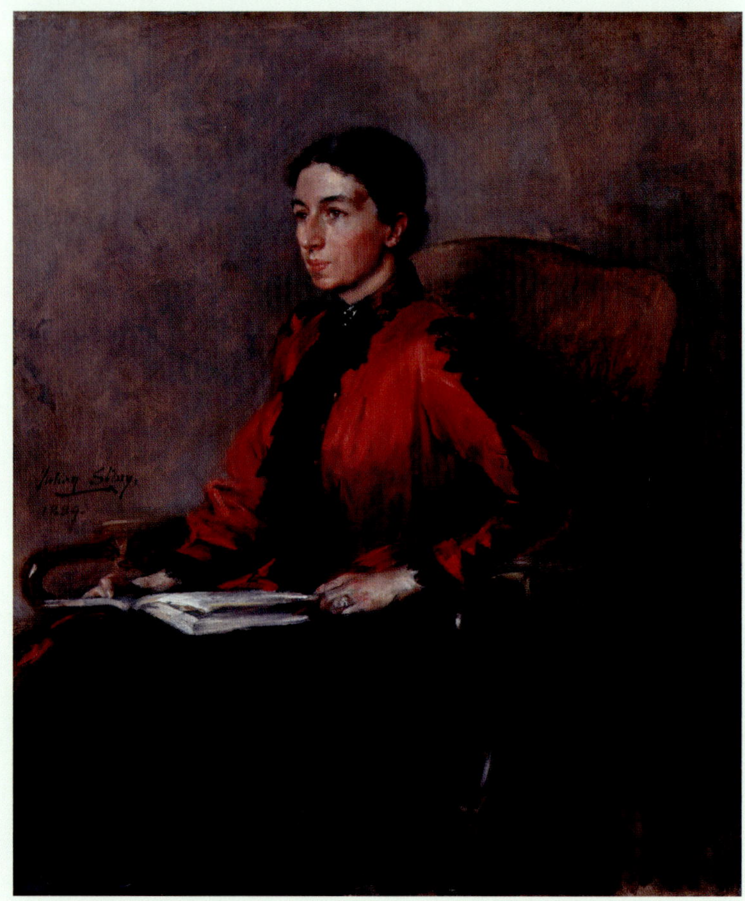

Fig.2: Mary Augusta Ward by Julian Russell Story

162

explains why so many portraits are demure and self-effacing. Women are sometimes depicted holding a book, as in Julian Russell Story's portrait of Mary Augusta Ward (fig.2), but are rarely, if ever, shown in a study or at a desk wielding a pen.

Unlike male literary portraits, there was no tradition of the inspired or suffering female genius – the very notion of a woman experiencing intellectual torment would have been found distasteful. This explains why images of the Brontës and Austen lack the intensity of expression seen in portraits of Blake, Wordsworth and Bryon for instance. The difficulties women faced in negotiating the boundary separating the home from the public realm encouraged some writers to adopt a male alias. The Brontës first published under the pseudonyms Currer, Ellis and Acton Bell while Mary Ann Evans chose to write under the *nom de plume* George Eliot. Women continue to use male or gender-ambiguous pseudonyms as one strategy to publish without prejudice. J.K. Rowling, who also publishes under the name Robert Galbraith, was apparently advised to use only her initials on the recommendation of her publisher, who thought the young male target audience for *Harry Potter* might be deterred by a series authored by a woman. Research indicates that men are still less likely to read books by women than vice versa.

The enduring association of female celebrity with beauty also presented problems for women deemed plain or unattractive. George Eliot, a household name in literary circles, was famously reticent about sitting for a portrait having internalised the perception that as a cerebral woman she was not conventionally good-looking (fig.3). It was for this reason she was omitted from G.F. Watts' Hall of Fame, a series of portraits made over an extended period that the artist gifted to the National Portrait Gallery as a permanent record of the great cultural personalities of the age. Watts' wife Mary recalled that 'he knew that the features belonged to a type he would have found most difficult and afraid of not doing the great mind justice, he did not venture to make the attempt.' Consequently, the Hall of Fame remained an exclusively male pantheon through to the early 1900s, although portraits of Eliot exist in other media, notably drawings and photographs, indicating that she was not totally averse to having her portrait made.

Photography became the most widespread and accessible form of portraiture from the middle of the nineteenth century. Its relative cheapness and potential for mass reproduction encouraged publicity and self-exposure for women working across a range of literary genres. Further recognition came with the emergence of the educated, independent

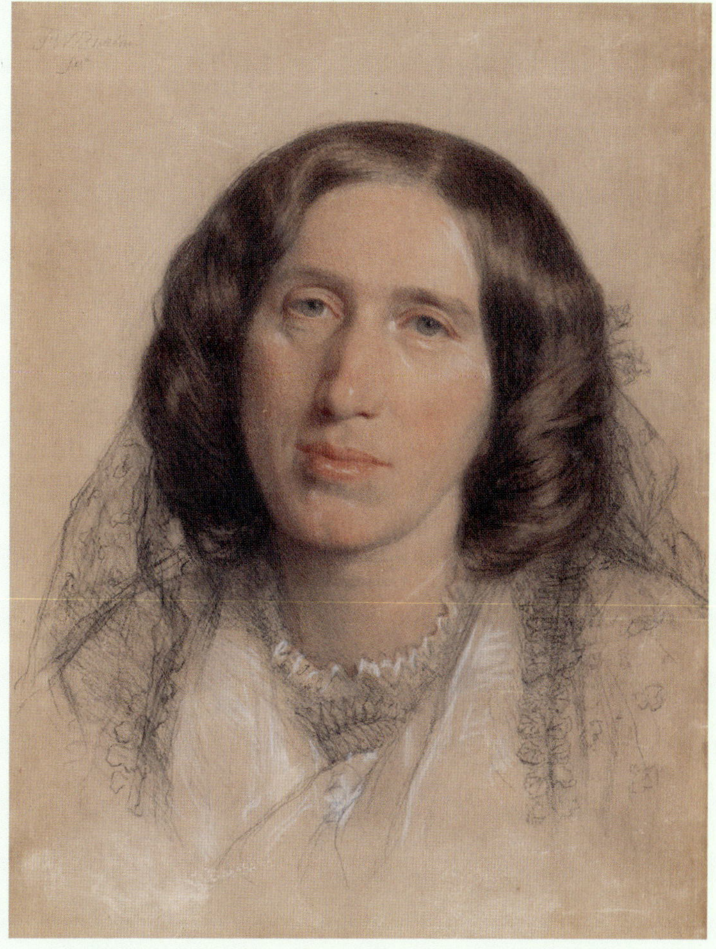

Fig.3: George Eliot by Sir Frederic William Burton

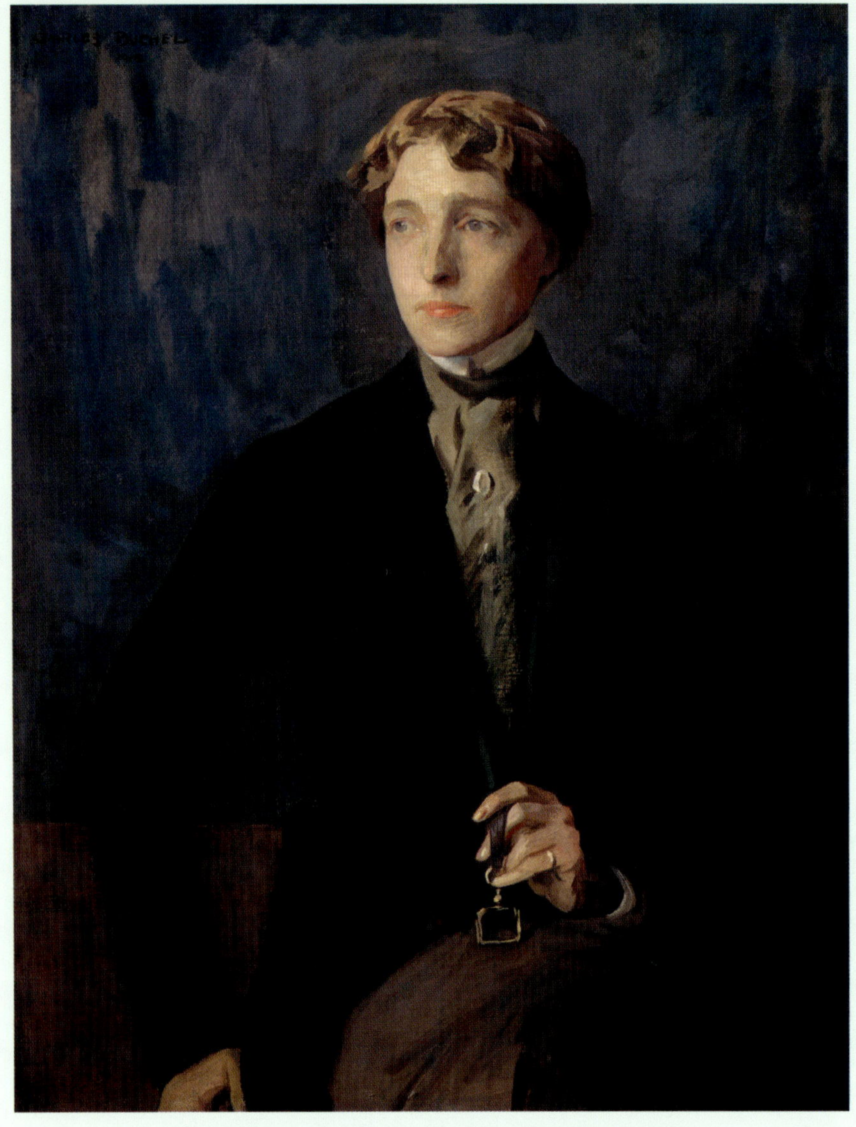

Fig.4: Radclyffe Hall by Charles Buchel

she wrote, 'I have just refused to sit for my portrait for the NPG ... why should I defile a whole day by sitting?' Woolf's self-consciousness about being observed comes across in her sister Vanessa Bell's psychologically astute 1912 portrait of her knitting (p.65). Woolf sinks back into the chair averting her gaze from the viewer; her blurred abstracted features suggest a need for privacy and serve as a kind of barrier against intrusion into her personal space, suggesting a need to preserve her identity.

However, as Woolf herself would have recognised, playing with identity could be both liberating and creative in enabling women to project themselves in public. Queering identity was one strategy through which women could assert themselves with confidence; appearing through an alter ego was another. Ray Strachey (p.37) and Radclyffe Hall (fig.4) thus chose to have themselves represented in dandified male attire, while Beatrix Potter is celebrated in Delmar Banner's portrait (p.24) as a respected breeder and judge of sheep rather than as a writer of children's books. The proliferation of literary genres allowed for greater diversity in representation, reflecting the fact that between 1920 and 1960 more women were publishing fiction in the United Kingdom than men. The rise of popular feminism during the 1960s had a great influence on both the commissioning and practice of portraiture. It was around this time that the National Portrait Gallery started to redress gender imbalance in a similar way to how it is now becoming more proactive in acquiring portraits of women of colour, as evidenced by recent commissions of the activist Malala Yousafzai (p.176) and writer Zadie Smith (p.160).

career woman towards the end of the century as more women secured financial and legal autonomy, culminating in the right to vote in 1918. Virginia Woolf's 1929 essay, *A Room of One's Own,* marked a turning point in exposing the social disadvantages women authors faced through history. Her famous declaration, 'a woman must have money and a room of her own if she is to write', became a rallying cry for women seeking to break the shackles of the past. As a member of the elite bohemian Bloomsbury group, Woolf could not claim to have suffered the same level of setback experienced by other women in British society but, even so, could not overcome a deep-seated anxiety about sitting for a portrait. In 1934

In 1969 the National Portrait Gallery changed its rules governing the acquisition of portraits to admit living sitters, a move that resulted in a striking number of portraits of female writers being commissioned for the Collection, particularly during the 1990s. Some of these are deliberately disruptive in challenging the idea that a woman should appear attractive rather than disclose any sign of her profession or intellect. In 1994, National Portrait Gallery Trustee Claire Tomalin proposed the commission of Sarah Raphael's *Women's Page Contributors to the Guardian* in response to the lack of women on the Gallery's walls (fig.5). Founded by Mary Stott, seated on the right, as an alternative to the predominantly domestic tone of women's journalism, the *Women's Page*

had been pioneering in being serious and feminist. In keeping with its spirit, the writers depicted in Raphael's literary salon are portrayed with unflinching realism, the lack of idealisation a deliberate homage to the individual achievement of each woman. Among the group is journalist Jill Tweedie, then dying of motor neurone disease.

Even more challenging is Paula Rego's 1995 large pastel of feminist writer Germaine Greer, author of the 1970 polemic *The Female Eunuch* (fig.6). In this deliberately unflattering portrait, Greer strikes a non-gendered pose with splayed legs and wearing old broken shoes. Described by critic Brian Sewell as a 'cruel combination of the immature nymphlet and the crumpled crone ... one of the ugliest and most unsatisfactory portraits

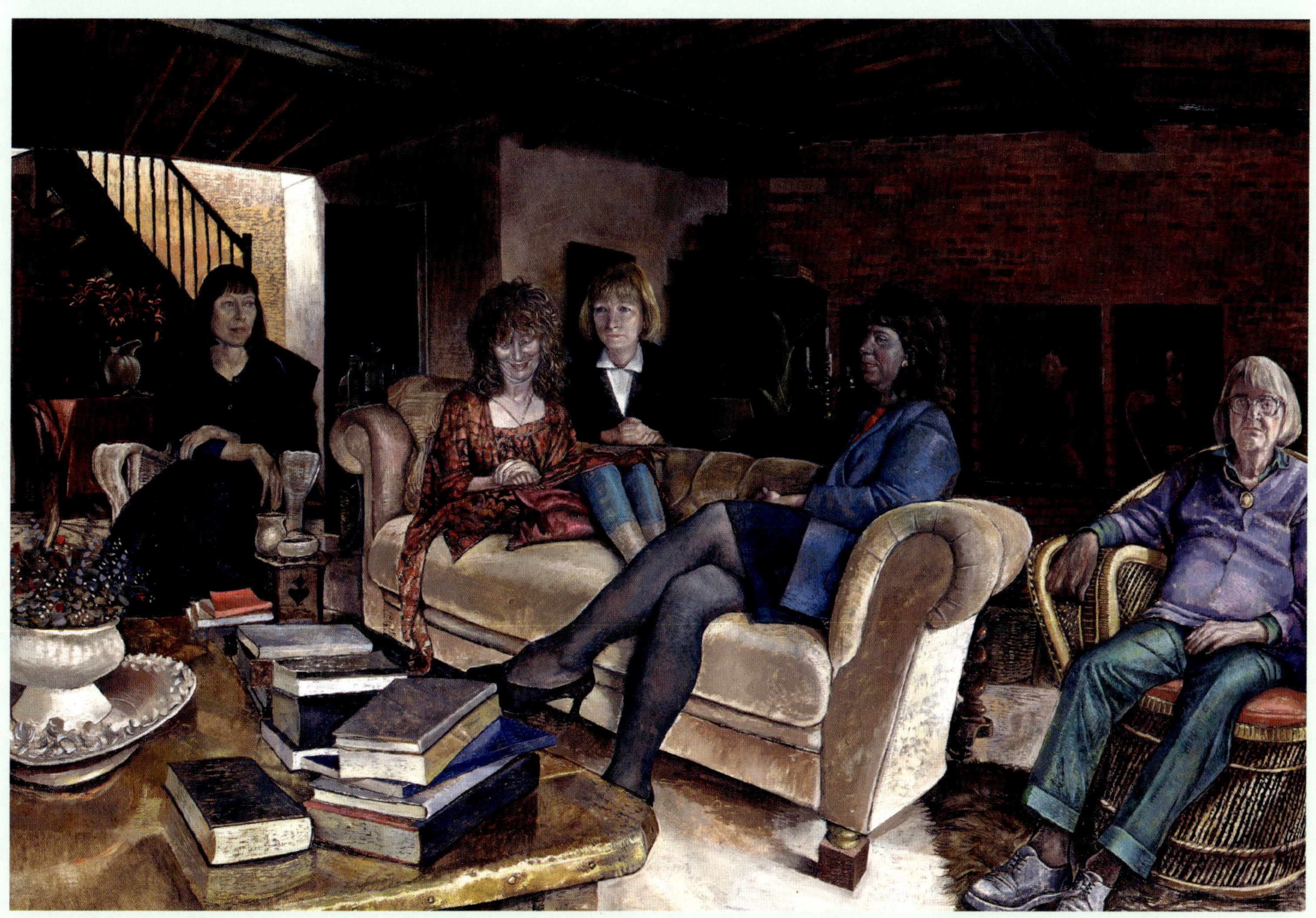

Fig.5: 'Women's Page contributors to the *Guardian*' by Sarah Raphael

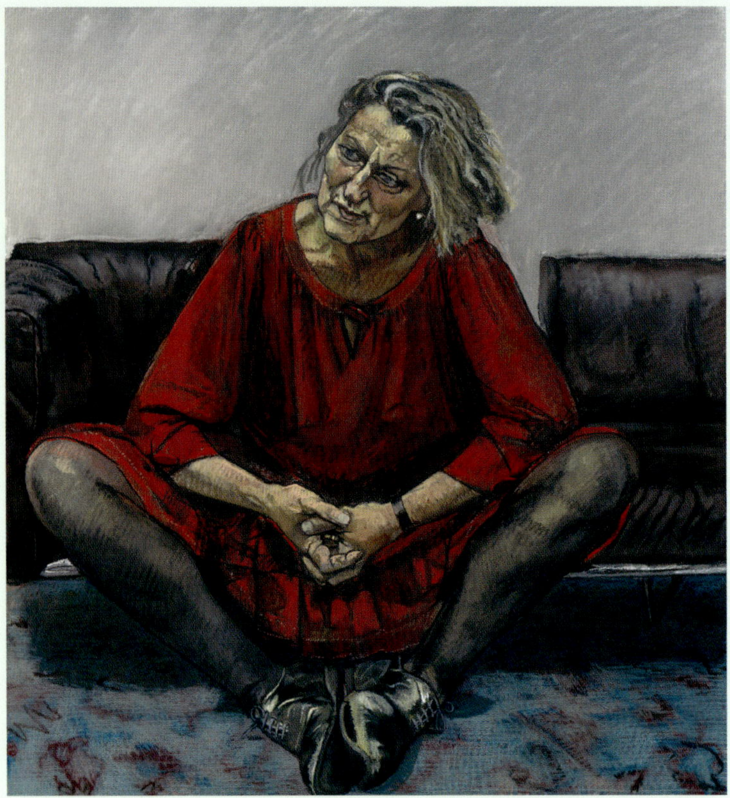

Fig.6: Germaine Greer by Paula Rego

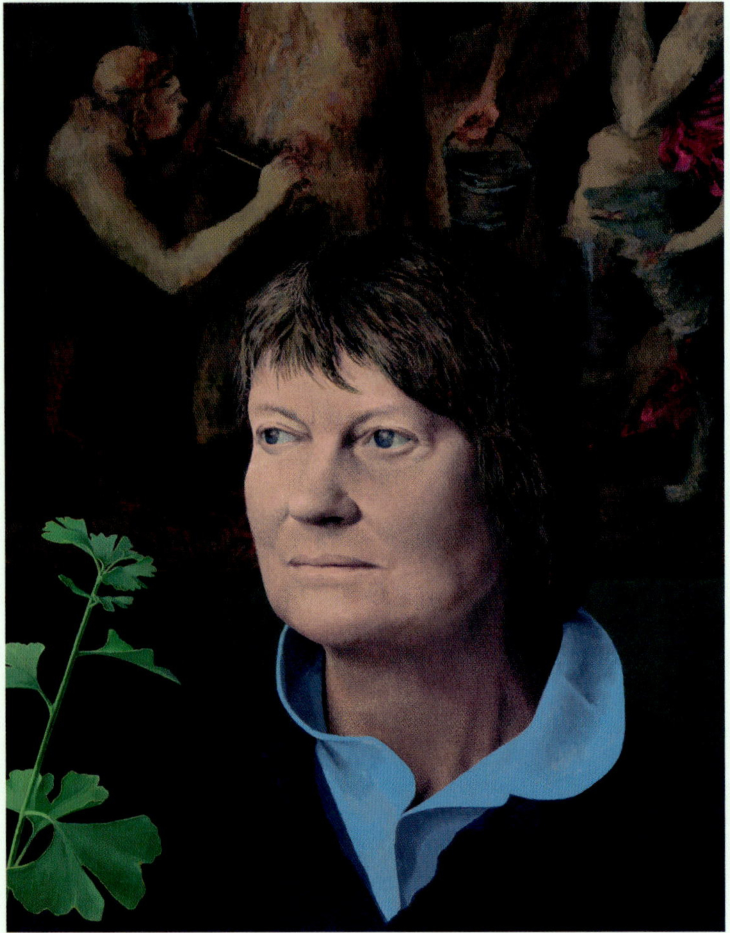

Fig.7: Iris Murdoch by Tom Phillips

in the gallery', it marks a landmark in the iconography of the female writer in its insistence on intelligence above any need to flatter the sitter or be condescending. To quote Greer herself: 'It's not usual to paint portraits of women in their past middle age, menopausal women, not to make some sort of obeisance to their beauty or their sexual relationships even.' The power of the portrait resides in its deliberate aggression, or as Greer puts it, 'two equal egos met in its making'.

Another, perhaps less confrontational, approach has been for artists to incorporate totems and emblems into portraits with the intention of reifying the internal imagination of the sitter. Tom Phillips's decision to present Iris Murdoch against a backdrop of Titian's *Flaying of Marsyas* in his 1984–6 portrait of the novelist has been seen to mirror the way her narratives scrape away at the surface of ordinary life to reveal underlying passions (fig.7). Likewise, the spatial distortion in Michael Taylor's 1996 portrait of crime writer P.D. James serves to underscore the dark nature of her writing (fig.8). The inclusion of a bust of the *Veiled Bride* after Raphaelle Monti on the table adds a sinister note, while the reflection of James's hand in the mahogany table reflects, in the artist's words, 'loathsome things lurking' in the depths of her imagination.

These portraits seem to position women writers as sibyls or savants transforming the world, rather than coolly assessing it in the male tradition. In so doing they also question the limitations of portraiture in asking if the face is enough to convey the complex inner world of the woman writer.

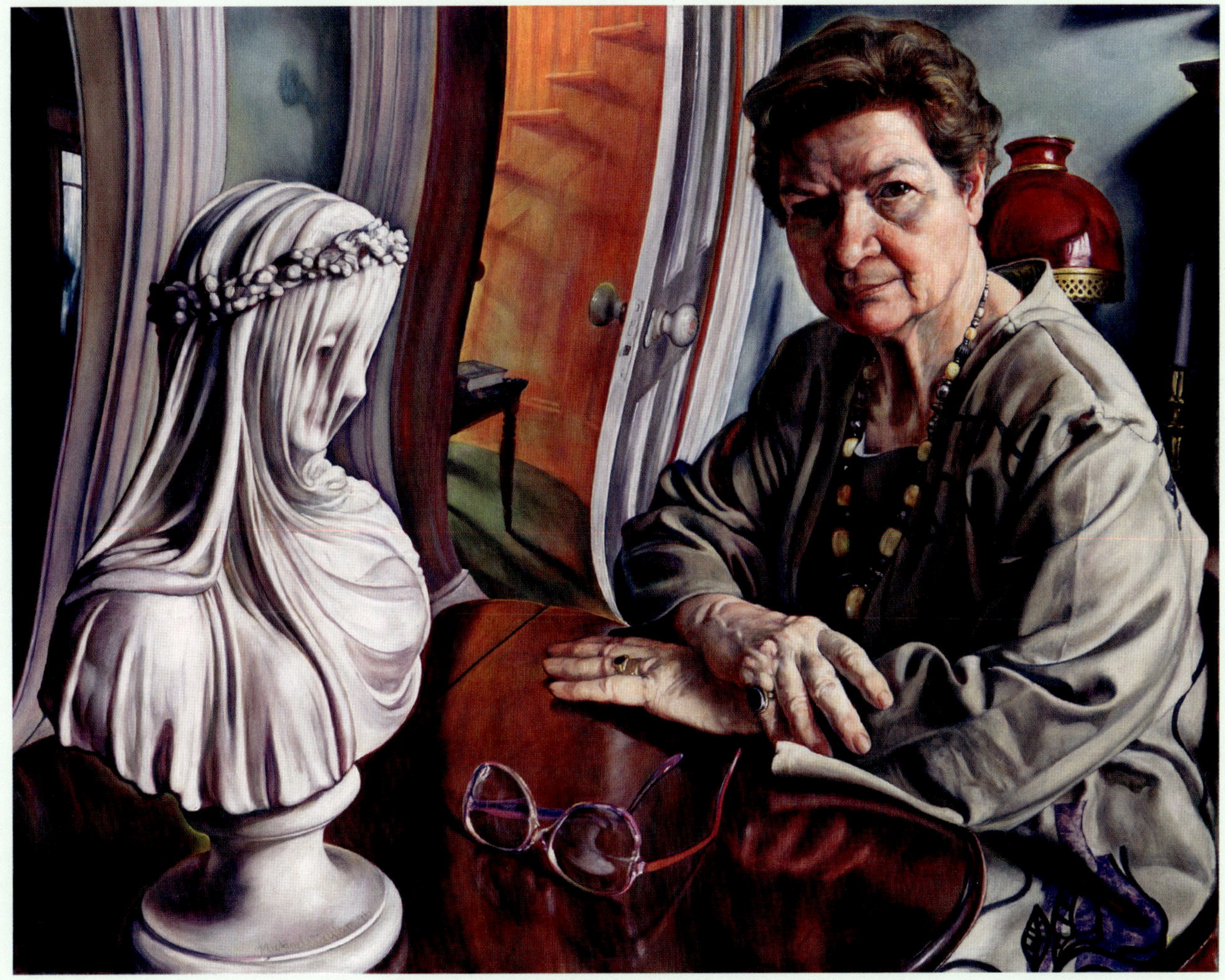

Fig.8: P.D. James by Michael Taylor

Fig.1
The Brontë Sisters
Anne Brontë (1820–1849), Charlotte Brontë (1816–1855)
and Emily Brontë (1818–1848)
By Patrick Branwell Brontë, *c*.1834
Oil on canvas, 902 × 746mm
National Portrait Gallery, London, 1725

Fig.2
Mary Augusta Ward (1851–1920)
By Julian Russell Story, 1889
Oil on mahogany panel, 445 × 356mm
National Portrait Gallery, London, 2650

Fig.3
George Eliot (1819–1880)
By Sir Frederic William Burton, 1865
Chalk drawing, 514 × 381mm
National Portrait Gallery, London, 669

Fig.4
Radclyffe Hall (1880–1943)
By Charles Buchel, 1918
Oil on canvas, 914 × 711mm
National Portrait Gallery, London, 4347

Fig.5
'Women's Page Contributors to the *Guardian*'
Posy Simmonds (b.1945), Jill Tweedie (1936–1993),
Polly Toynbee (b.1946), Elizabeth Forgan (b.1944)
and Mary Stott (1907–2002)
By Sarah Raphael, 1994
Oil on paper laid on board, 557 × 800mm
National Portrait Gallery, London, 6247

Fig.6
Germaine Greer (b.1939)
By Paula Rego, 1995
Pastel on paper laid on aluminium, 1200 × 1111mm
National Portrait Gallery, London, 6351

Fig.7
Iris Murdoch (1919–1999)
By Tom Phillips, 1984–6
Oil on canvas, 914 × 711mm
National Portrait Gallery, London, 5921

Fig.8
P.D. James (1920–2014)
By Michael Taylor, 1996
Oil on canvas, 860 × 1060mm
National Portrait Gallery, London, 6361

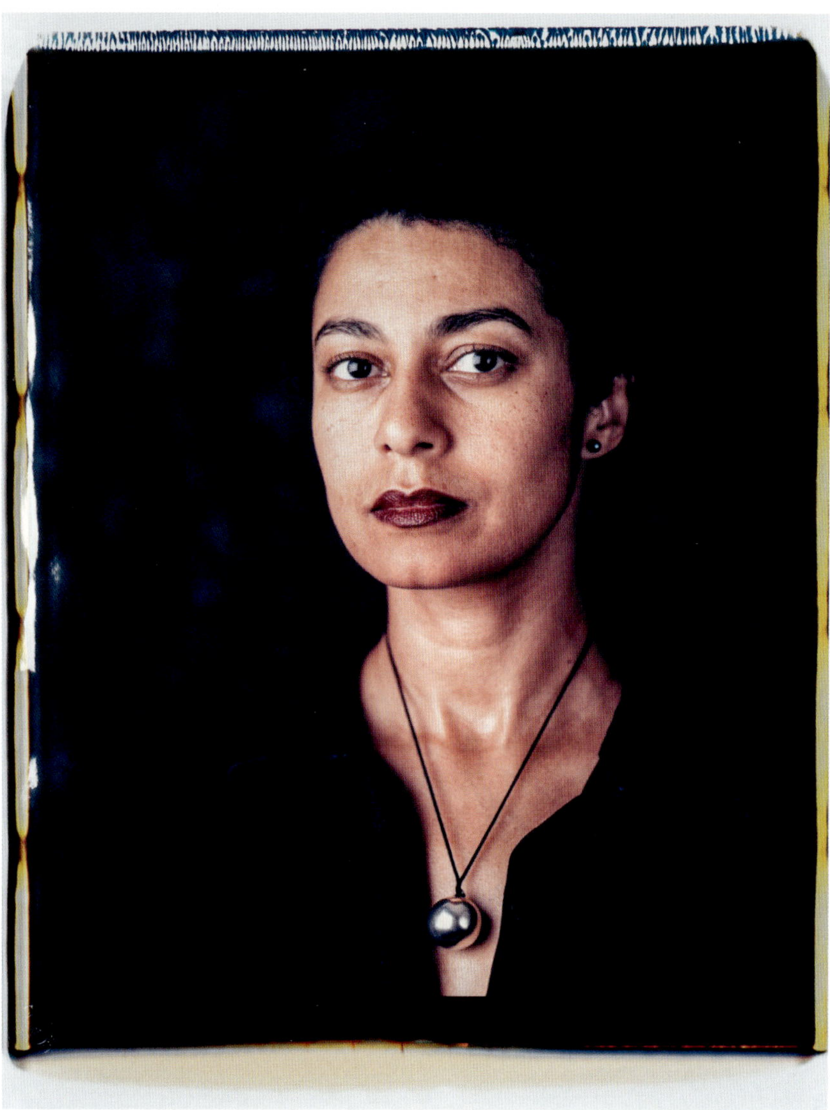

The National Portrait Gallery has a long history of commissioning portraits and has engaged in an active and sustained programme for doing so since 1980. In 2001 Maud Sulter became the first black woman to specially create portraits for the Gallery when she photographed six writers of children's fiction in connection with the exhibition 'Beatrix Potter to Harry Potter: Portraits of Children's Writers' (2002). Using a unique camera transported from Prague, the large-scale 20 x 24-inch Polaroid photographs significantly contributed to the diversity of writers represented in the Gallery's Collection, with portraits of John Agard, Malorie Blackman, Michael Bond, Jamila Gavin, Grace Nichols and Jacqueline Wilson added. A similar commission from the Scottish Poetry Library came the following year, which included Sulter's self-portrait among the ten Polaroids of contemporary poets that she made.

These commissions formed a small part of the many ways in which Sulter – an artist, writer, curator, cultural historian and university educator of Scottish and Ghanaian heritage – strived to 'put black women back in the centre of the frame – both literally within the photographic image, but also within the cultural institutions where our work operates' throughout her prolific and multifaceted career. With 'As a Blackwoman' (1985), the title poem from the first of her several poetry collections, Sulter won the Vera Bell Prize, one of numerous honours that she received. That same year, Sulter also contributed to 'The Thin Black Line', a groundbreaking exhibition at the Institute of Contemporary Arts showcasing works by contemporary black and Asian women. Closely involved with the black feminist and lesbian movements of the late twentieth century, Sulter's commitment to increasing the visibility and opportunities of black women artists led to her co-founding the Blackwomen's Creativity Project, publishing the pioneering *Passion: Discourses on Blackwomen's Creativity* (1990), setting up the Urban Fox Press and opening the Rich Women of Zurich gallery in London.

Sulter's ongoing preoccupation with 'the way that particularly black women's experience and black women's contribution to culture is so often erased and marginalized' in Western histories led to projects such as *Zabat* (1989), where she created photographic portraits of classical muses modelled by nine creative black women. *Hysteria* (1991) was inspired by the life of the nineteenth-century sculptor Edmonia Lewis, while Sulter's exhibition 'Jeanne Duval: A Melodrama' (2003) sought to give 'a name, an identity, a voice' to Charles Baudelaire's mixed heritage muse and partner, whom she first encountered through a photograph by Nadar considered to depict Duval. Years on since Sulter's untimely death from cancer at the age of 47, the themes in her work remain remarkably pertinent and her visual art continues to be exhibited and reappraised. CN

Maud Sulter (1960–2008) from her 'Scots Poets' series
Self-portrait, 2002
Large-format Polaroid print, 828 × 560mm uneven
Estate of Maud Sulter/DACS

Keira Knightley

I've never had an acting class. My plan was to go to drama school and I suddenly got all these jobs. I never went to drama school, I've never had a teacher. I knew that I didn't know what I was doing. I had my instincts, I knew sometimes I was good, I knew sometimes I was bad.[47]

Having had an agent from the age of six, Keira Knightley's breakthrough role came in 2002, in Gurinder Chadha's comedy, *Bend It Like Beckham*, in which she played a young footballer who struggles against social norms. She has since made her name with a series of period films, including *Pride & Prejudice* (2005) and *Atonement* (2007), and popular hits such as *Love Actually* (2003) and the *Pirates of the Caribbean* franchise (2003–7 and 2017).

In an interview after the launch of the biopic of the author Colette (2018), Knightley commented that she felt utterly inspired by the strong character and said of the film, 'It amazed me how current it was, what it's talking about with gender politics and sexual politics and feminism.' Knightley has become well known for being outspoken about women's rights and the objectification of women on the screen, pledging not to shoot nude scenes unless she is working with a woman director. Knightley is also vocal about gender imbalance in the business and has advocated for the visibility of women in front of and behind the camera, as well as highlighted the gender pay gap within modern society.

In 2018, she wrote a highly personal essay about childbirth and motherhood for the collection *Feminists Don't Wear Pink and Other Lies*. In her piece, entitled 'The Weaker Sex', she spoke about the birth of her daughter and the unrealistic pressures and expectations on new mothers as well as her experiences as a woman in the workplace. She has also been part of a campaign calling on governments to increase support and protection for

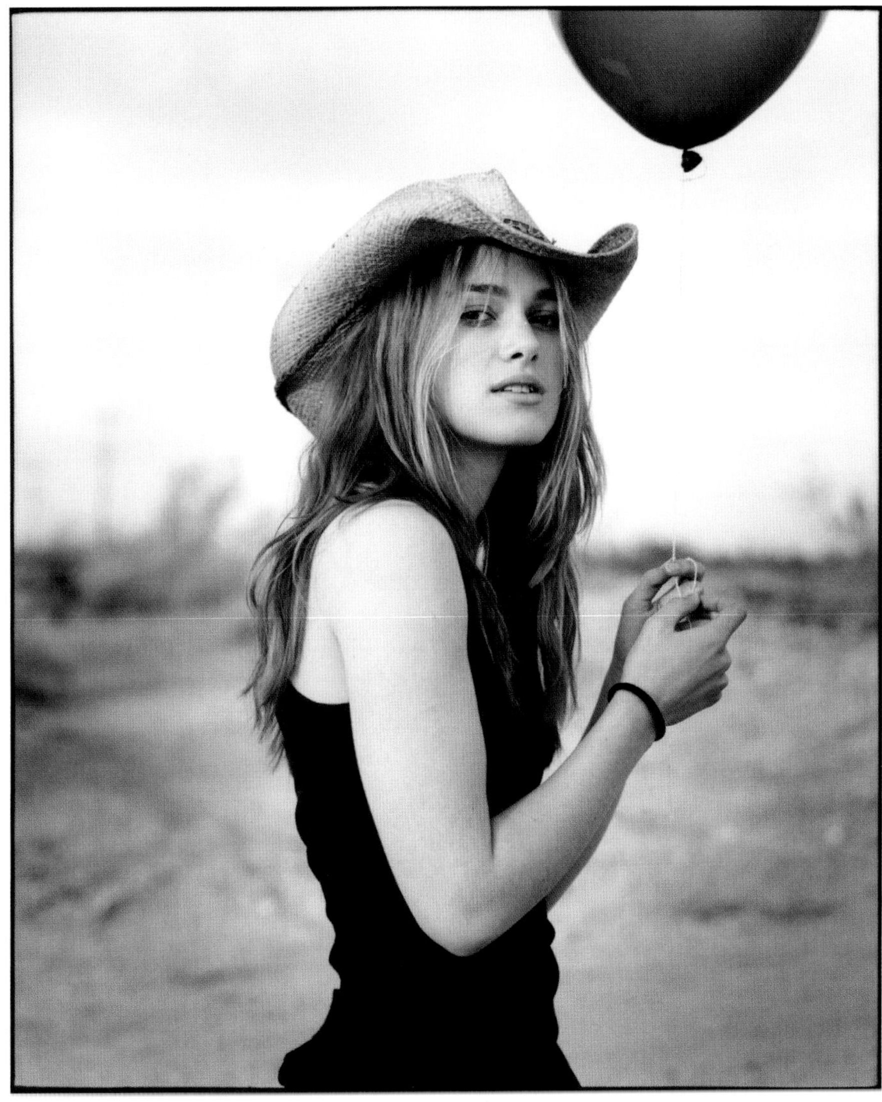

women fighting for their rights around the world.

Knightley has won numerous awards for her stage and film work and in 2018 she received an OBE for services to drama and charity. She has been a long-time CHANEL ambassador and over the years she has collaborated with a number of charitable organizations continuing to raise awareness on human and social rights. Knightley has also shared her experiences of dyslexia and in 2020 she backed Made By Dyslexia, a global campaign to train teachers and help

every workplace to spot, support and empower dyslexic minds.

Recent film work includes *Misbehaviour* (2020) about the infamous storming of the stage at the 1970 Miss World ceremony in protest at the objectification of women, in which Knightley played the historian and feminist activist Sally Alexander. She also voiced the lead role in the animated film *Charlotte* (2021), a true story about the German-Jewish painter Charlotte Salomon at the time of the Holocaust. GA

Keira Knightley (b.1985)
By Sarah Dunn, January 2003
Gelatin silver print, 354 × 282mm
National Portrait Gallery, London, x126719

Amy Winehouse

On 20 October 2003 Island Records released singer and songwriter Amy Winehouse's debut studio album *Frank*. The title is said to refer to Frank Sinatra, an early influence on Winehouse, whose smoky, evocative contralto vocals are now a matter of legend. In spite of the positive critical reception and the receipt of an Ivor Novello Award, the singer was disappointed with *Frank*; she voiced her frustration in an interview with music critic Garry Mulholland:

Some things on this album make me go to a little place that's fucking bitter. I've never heard the album from start to finish. I don't have it in my house. Well, the marketing was fucked, the promotion was terrible. Everything was a shambles.

Disarmingly honest in both her music and in person, Winehouse was prone to this kind of outburst. In fact, her songs became quickly embroiled with her erratic behaviour, making her a favourite subject of tabloid journalism. A tempestuous love life and an addiction to drugs informed her singing, but also tampered with

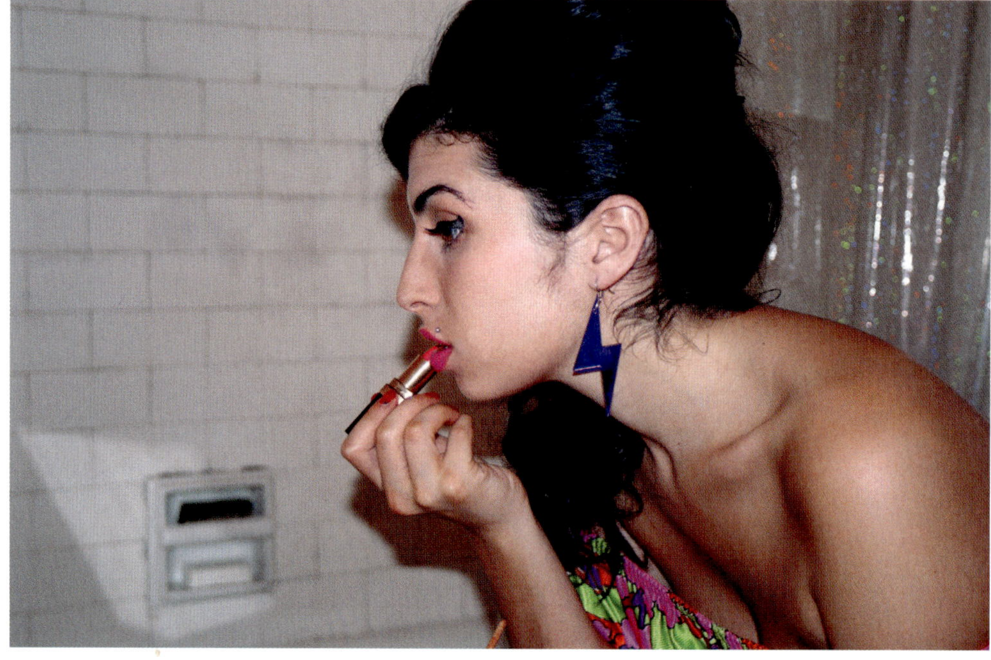

her career. Her on-off relationship with Blake Fielder-Civil, whom she eventually married in 2007, inspired many of the lyrics in *Back to Black* – an 11-track album benefitting from a compelling blend of jazz and soul. The reception of *Back to Black* was overwhelmingly positive; it was the bestselling album in the United Kingdom that year and *Time* magazine named 'Rehab' the best song of 2007. Winehouse had been safely launched into international stardom, a status confirmed by her receipt of five Grammy Awards in 2008. As music critic Cyril Cordor suggested, 'fans and critics alike embraced her rugged charm, brash sense of humour, and distinctively soulful and jazzy vocals.'

Despite her growing recognition, Winehouse's life was in constant turmoil, and on 23 July 2011 she was found dead in her London home. The cause of her premature death is largely believed to be accidental alcohol overdose. The portrait of Winehouse by Marlene Dumas in the National Portrait Gallery's Collection poignantly captures both the charm and shadow

of the singer's being. Dumas typically works from found images drawn from media outlets and, in this case, she based her commemorative portrait of Winehouse on one of the many photographs available in the public realm. The translucent blue colours refer to Winehouse's troubled life, and also her musical influences. FF

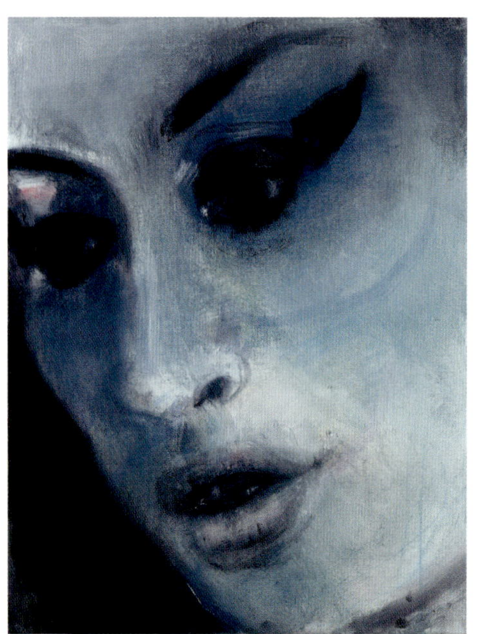

'Amy-Blue'
By Marlene Dumas, 2011
Oil on canvas, 400 × 300mm
National Portrait Gallery, London, 6948

Amy Winehouse (1983–2011)
By Charles Moriarty, July 2003
Chromogenic print, 406 × 608mm
National Portrait Gallery, London, x199205

2004 Zaha Hadid

Celebrating her unique vision and
talent for innovation, Zaha Hadid
received the Pritzker Architecture
Prize in 2004, becoming the first
woman architect to be awarded the
industry's most illustrious honour.
Mid-career and with a relatively
small existing portfolio of completed
projects, the jurors nonetheless
praised Hadid for having 'built
a career on defying convention'
and having 'shifted the geometry
of buildings'.

Born in Iraq, Hadid moved
to London in 1972 to attend the highly
regarded Architectural Association
School of Architecture. There, her
study of the work of Russian avant-
garde artist Kazimir Malevich became
an important influence, and she
began using abstract painting as
a means of conveying and exploring
multiple perspectives in her designs.
Three years after graduating, Hadid
established her own London-based
architectural practice, Zaha Hadid
Architects, but within the conservative
architectural climate of the 1980s
she focused her energies on academic
teaching and publishing her
designs in journals. Never feeling
part of the male-dominated British
architectural establishment,
competitions became an important
means for gaining commissions,
though her ambitious designs were
initially criticised as unbuildable.

With the emergence of computer-
aided technologies in the 1990s,
construction techniques caught up in
making her bold, sculptural, seemingly
weightless designs a reality. Embracing
asymmetry, fluidity and the suggestion
of motion, projects for housing
developments, a ski jump, bridges,
cultural centres, university buildings
and airports were completed. Her
most significant designs include the

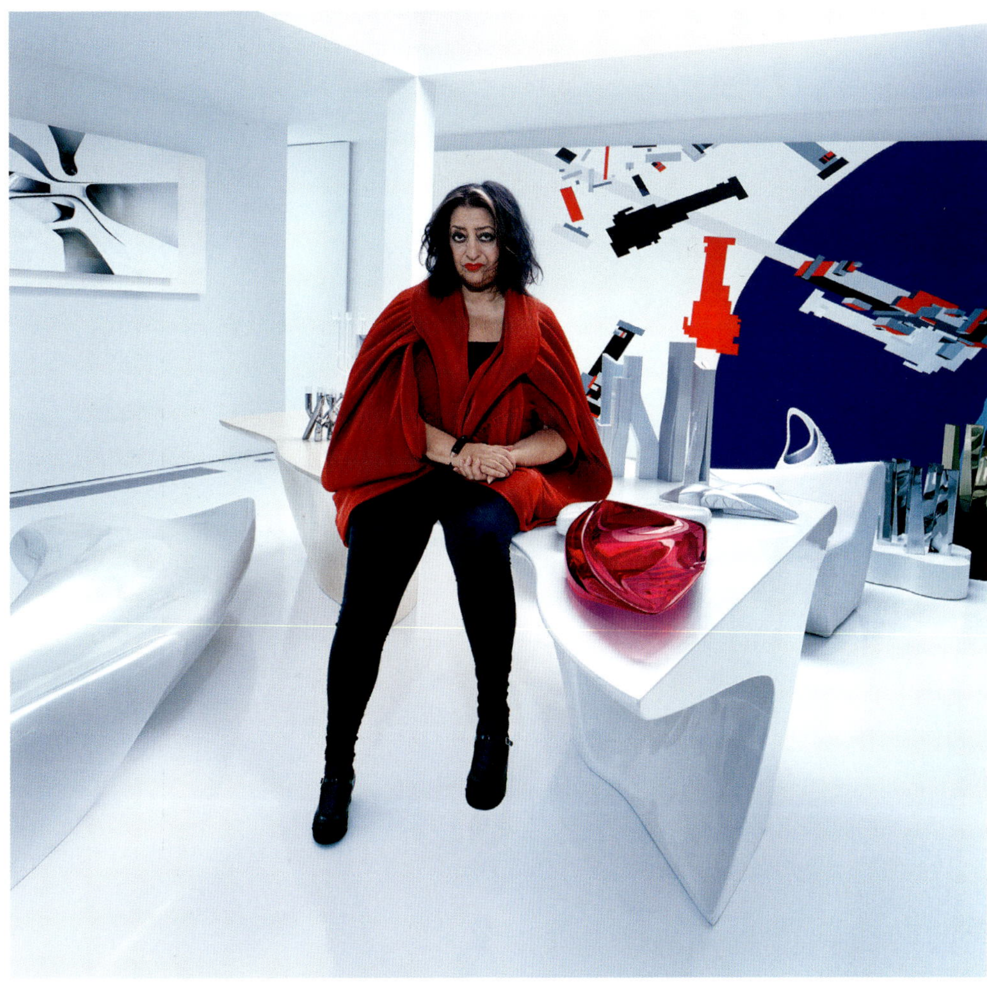

MAXXI contemporary art museum in
Rome – opening with no art on display,
the building served as an exhibit
in itself – and the Aquatics Centre for
the 2012 London Olympics. The latter
was inspired by the fluid motion
of water and mirroring its riverside
site it characterised Hadid's holistic
approach to environment. Hadid
also applied her design aesthetic to
furniture and product design, as can
be seen in the decor of her Clerkenwell
home in Miles Aldridge's photograph.
Her painted homage to Malevich covers
the wall behind her.

Among the other accolades Hadid
received during her lifetime were
Britain's most prestigious architecture
awards: the Royal Institute of British

Architects' Stirling Prize (2010 and
2011), and their Royal Gold Medal
(2016), for which Hadid was the first
woman in the award's 168-year
history to win the medal in her own
right. She was also made DBE in 2012.
Upon her death, Hadid was lauded for
inspiring a generation of architects
and capturing popular imagination
with her groundbreaking work.
Meanwhile, the modest business she
had established 36 years earlier had
expanded into the fastest growing
architectural firm in Britain, with 400
employees and a prolific portfolio of
54 completed projects in 16 countries
worldwide. CN

Zaha Hadid (1950–2016)
By Miles Aldridge, 2009
Chromogenic print, 508 × 508mm
National Portrait Gallery, London, x200101

Ellen MacArthur

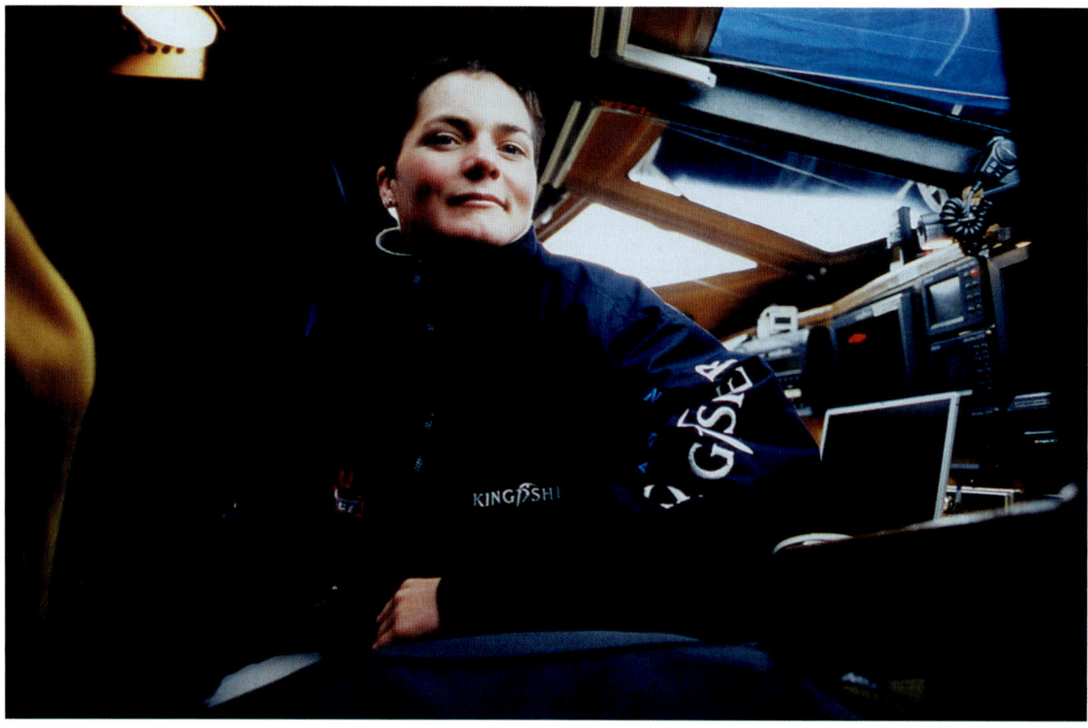

On 7 February 2005, solo long-distance yachtswoman Ellen MacArthur broke the world record for the fastest solo circumnavigation of the globe. This was not only an outstanding achievement for the sailing world as a whole, but it also quashed long-standing prejudices which questioned the ability of a woman to singlehandedly undertake such a monumental journey. The combination of these factors made MacArthur a national hero and the recipient of a DBE that same year.

It all began on 28 November 2004 when MacArthur and her B&Q trimaran set out on a voyage that was destined to make headlines and break numerous records along the way. She set records for the fastest solo voyage to the equator, past the Cape of Good Hope, past Cape Horn and back to the equator again. It took her a total of 71 days, 14 hours, 18 minutes and 33 seconds to sail non-stop around the world, beating the previous record set by French sailor Francis Joyon by 1 day, 8 hours, 35 minutes and 49 seconds. MacArthur covered 50,660 kilometres (27,354 nautical miles) at an average speed of 29.4 kilometres an hour (15.9 knots), before she crossed the finish line.

The journey was made all the more arduous by the extensive sleep deprivation endured by MacArthur along the way. On average MacArthur slept no more than three hours in every 24. Thanks to a device the size of a cigarette packet strapped to her right arm, scientific advisers – working closely with her team – were able to monitor MacArthur's sleeping pattern. One of the entries in her race log acknowledges the extreme nature of the circumstances under which she was racing. On 7 January 2005 she wrote: 'I am numb to tiredness as my veins are filled with adrenaline and fear. My brain is so active it cannot switch off at all.' In a similar vein, two days later she noted: 'We're in a boat that's getting tired, a skipper that's getting tired – mentally and emotionally zonked.' Echoing this sentiment, on 15 January 2005 MacArthur wrote: 'When the winds are changing so irregularly and the seas are very bad ... it's very hard to switch off and that little bit of grabbed sleep is never enough.'

Nutrition was also challenging for MacArthur, who had to eat more than 5,000 calories a day but could not weigh down her boat with too many reserves. This meant that she had to rely entirely on what she described as 'fuel rather than food' – dehydrated food made edible through the addition of boiling water. Despite the many challenges she faced, with physical and mental endurance and a phenomenal level of determination, MacArthur proved that a feat such as the solo circumnavigation of the globe was possible for a woman. Since retiring from sailing in 2010, MacArthur has launched the Ellen MacArthur Foundation. The Foundation promotes the idea of a circular economy across society and industry as a solution in the fight against climate change, pollution and waste. FF

Ellen MacArthur (b.1976)
By Andy Hall, 17 September 2001
Chromogenic print, 335 × 495mm
National Portrait Gallery, London, x125088

Alex Scott

My dream as a little girl playing in that football cage in the East End of London was to one day pull on the Three Lions shirt and represent my country. I am so proud and humbled that I managed to do just that.

With these words, in 2017 Alex Scott said farewell to international football to pursue a career as a broadcaster. One of modern women's football's early stars, she had originally started playing with Arsenal at the age of eight. Hardworking and determined, Scott built an illustrious career as a professional footballer, playing for Arsenal and England, as well as appearing for Team GB at the London Olympics in 2012.

One of her most unforgettable moments in football was with Arsenal when she scored the winning goal in the 2006–7 UEFA Women's Cup final. Arsenal became the first British side to win the competition, the pinnacle of club football, with Scott scoring the only goal. She also helped the club win the FA Women's Premier League (in which they won every game), the FA Women's Cup and the FA Women's Premier League Cup that year, a series of victories known as the Quadruple.

Over the course of her professional football career, Scott won 140 caps for England before retiring as the second most-capped England player of all time. She also represented her country in four European Championships and three World Cups. Scott was part of the Lionesses squad that finished as runners-up in the 2009 Euros and achieved a bronze medal at the 2015 World Cup.

Scott has continued to break the mould, becoming a leading sports broadcaster praised for her thoughtful and rigorous approach. She was the first woman pundit on BBC television at a World Cup, the first woman to host the BBC's *Football Focus* and the first woman football analyst on Sky Sports.

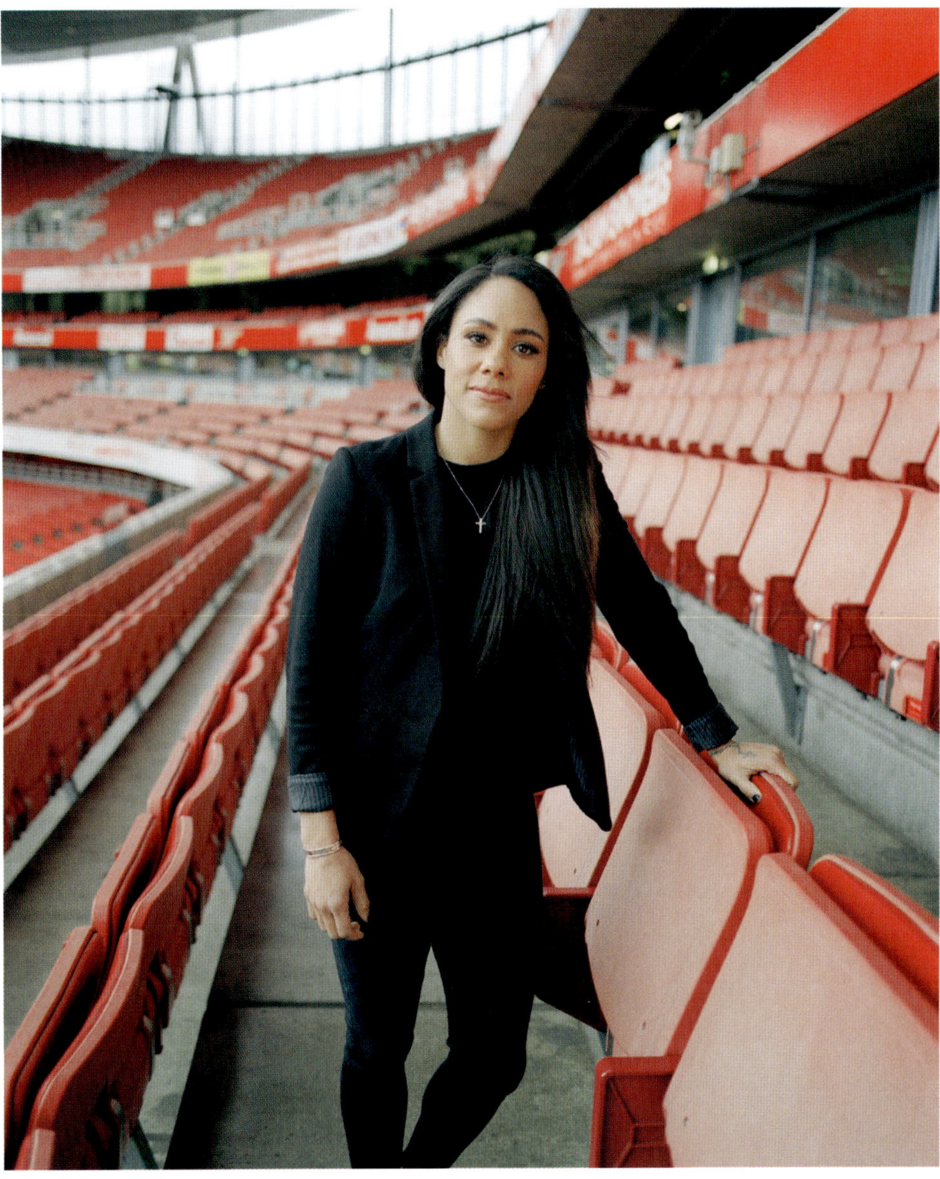

Of these achievements she has said: 'I want to get to that time where I'm not even regarded as the female pundit – I'm just a pundit.' An MBE recipient, Scott holds honorary doctorates from the University of East London and University of Hertfordshire in recognition of her contribution to sport. Throughout her career, Scott has had to navigate a male-dominated industry, paving the way for women coming into the profession. She declares, 'I've been part of the process, pushing for better contracts for women and sticking up for better standards', but acknowledges that there is much further to go. In 2022, Scott wrote about her life in the memoir *How (Not) To Be Strong*. GA

Alex Scott (b.1984)
By Nina Manandhar, 2018
Chromogenic print, 500 × 408mm
National Portrait Gallery, London, x201369

Doris Lessing

The storyteller is deep inside every one of us. The story-maker is always with us. Let us suppose our world is ravaged by war, by the horrors that we all of us easily imagine. Let us suppose floods wash through our cities, the seas rise. But the storyteller will be there, for it is our imaginations which shape us, keep us, create us – for good and for ill. It is our stories that will recreate us, when we are torn, hurt, even destroyed. It is the storyteller, the dream-maker, the myth-maker, that is our phoenix, that represents us at our best, and at our most creative.

This passage, eloquently investing each and every one of us with the power of storytelling, was penned by writer Doris Lessing for the lecture she gave to the Swedish Academy when accepting the Nobel Prize for Literature in 2007. The full text of her lecture was published the following year as *On Not Winning the Nobel Prize.*

Lessing's literary career began with her first novel, *The Grass is Singing* (1950), which was an immediate success. In it, Lessing offered a critical view of white colonial society in Southern Africa, portraying it as complacent and racist. The book was partially based on Lessing's first-hand experience of Southern Africa where she spent her childhood and early adulthood. After two unsuccessful marriages, Lessing moved to England where she quickly made her mark as a well-respected author. Her writing style was realist, reflecting various aspects of her life as well as her views on the politics of race and her early adoption of, and consequent disillusionment with, communism.

The publication of *The Golden Notebook* in 1962 established Lessing as a major writer of her time. The protagonist of the book is Anna Wulf, a writer torn between her various roles – woman, lover, writer and political activist. In an attempt to navigate these multiple and conflicting roles Anna keeps four notebooks, each corresponding to a different part of herself. As Anna comes to realize, public and private collide at any given time. Eventually, unable to cope with these competing pressures, the protagonist suffers a mental breakdown. The originality of Lessing's novel lies both in its topic and its style. To enable her to portray the modern divided self, Lessing experimented with structure, adopting a fragmented form. At the same time, her exploration of women's concerns firmly linked *The Golden Notebook* with the feminist movement, something that would always distress Lessing, who saw her book as a gender non-specific parable of individual fragmentation. FF

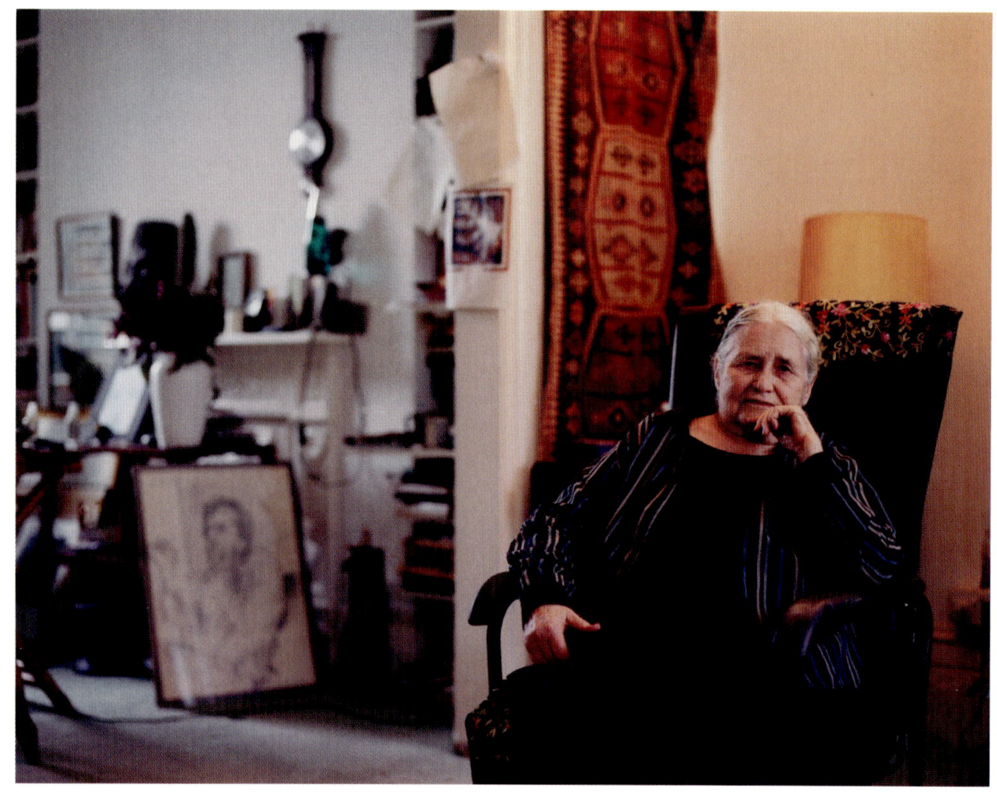

Doris Lessing (1919–2013)
By Reme Campos, published 20 April 2008
Chromogenic print, 387 × 485mm
National Portrait Gallery, London, x138156

Elif Shafak

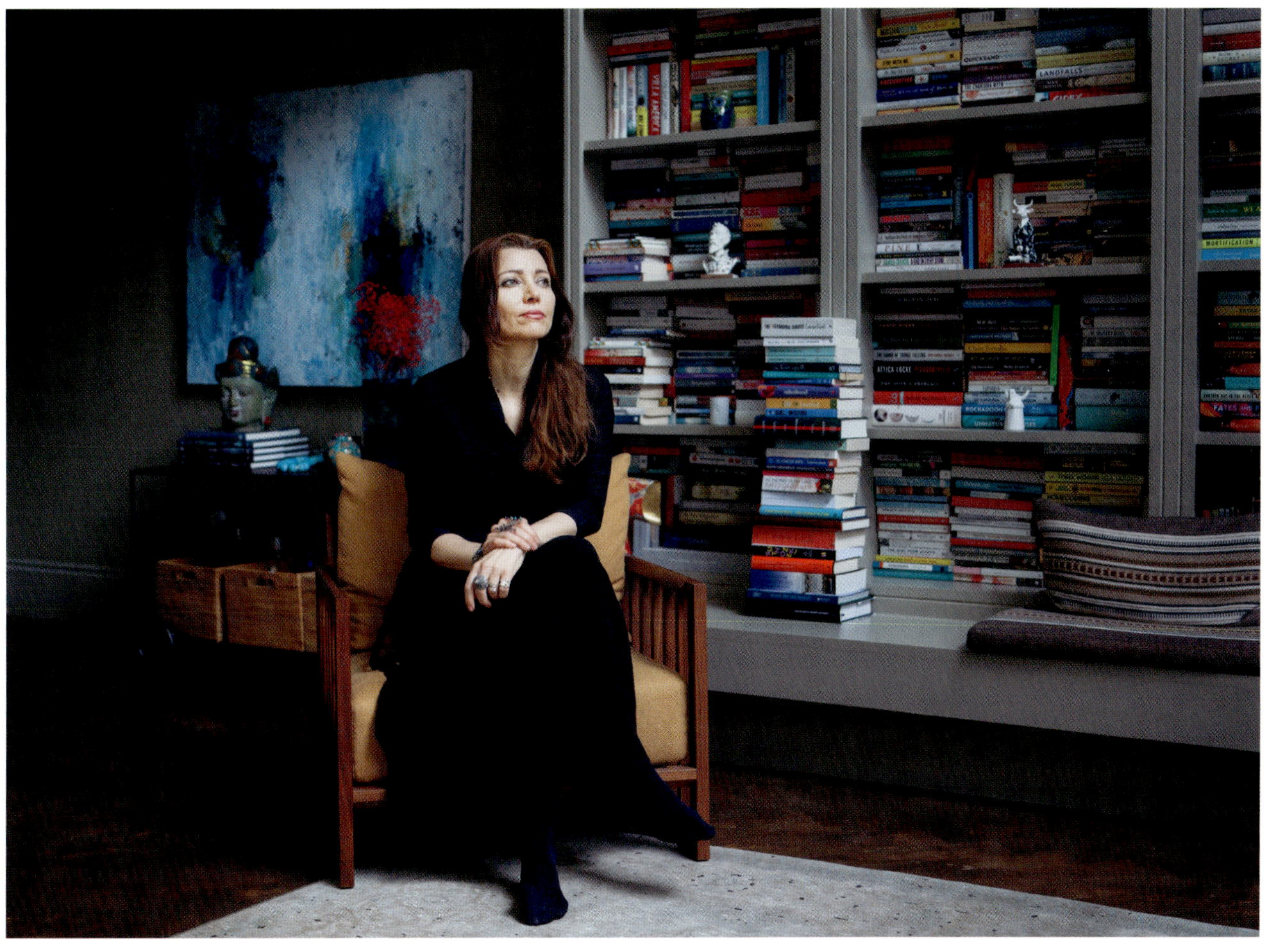

In 2008 Elif Shafak's second novel in English, *The Bastard of Istanbul* (2006), was longlisted for the prestigious Women's Prize for Fiction. After publication, Shafak was put on trial by the Turkish government for comments made by characters in the book. Although acquitted, her writing remains the subject of political debate in Turkey. She eventually moved to London in 2013 where she continues to live, championing the city for its diversity and multiculturalism.

Shafak is a crucial contemporary voice and her numerous accolades include being shortlisted for the Booker Prize for her 2019 novel *10 Minutes 38 Seconds in this Strange World*. As well as being a lauded storyteller she is also an advocate for equality and freedom of speech and a passionate activist for women's rights and those of the LGBTQ+ community. She says:

To be human means to embody at least several conflicting and co-existing selves within. It is the job of the novelist to peel off those layers and show the heart that beats underneath … I want to show the East within the West and the West within the East. I believe that as human beings we can have multiple belongings.

Shafak was born in France and raised in Ankara by her grandmother – who she describes as traditional, Eastern and spiritual – and her mother – an educated, urban, secularist and modern woman. She says of her family background, 'what was more unusual was that my grandmother, who was not educated herself, intervened so that my mother could return to university and have a career, she was later a diplomat.' This cultural diversity is often weaved into her stories and forms the basis of her belief in the enriching nature of social and cultural differences. Shafak lived in Istanbul, a city often featured in her novels, before moving to the US, where she worked as a professor, and then to England. She writes in both English and Turkish and is considered the most popular woman novelist in her homeland today. Her appeal goes much wider, with her books translated into more than 50 languages. Shafak's twelfth novel, *The Island of Missing Trees*, was published in 2021. GA

Elif Shafak (b.1971)
By Pål Hansen, 2021
Digital photograph

Malala Yousafzai

In early 2009, a series of blog posts were published on the BBC Urdu website written by an 11-year-old schoolgirl from Pakistan's Swat District, using the pseudonym Gul Makai (the name of a heroine from a Pashtun folktale) to protect her safety. Taliban militants had taken over Swat in 2007 and, in their strict interpretation of Sharia law, had already destroyed around 150 schools and issued an edict to ban girls' education from 15 January 2009.

The entries came about after the BBC approached Malala Yousafzai's father Ziauddin, an education activist running a chain of schools in Swat, who proposed his own daughter as their author. In contrast to news reports, Yousafzai's first-hand, honest account of how an ordinary girl experienced the military action and restrictions gave a personal voice to the human tragedy of events in the region. On 3 January, she wrote:

I had a terrible dream yesterday with military helicopters and the Taliban. I have had such dreams since the launch of the military operation in Swat. My mother made me breakfast and I went off to school.

Capturing the details of Yousafzai's daily life, alongside the fear and absurdity of war, her posts gained widespread attention with English translations and reproductions in the local Pakistani press also appearing.

By the end of the year Yousafzai's identity as the blogger was known. Despite death threats, she became an outspoken, high-profile advocate for female education. Then, on 9 October 2012, while travelling home from school on a bus in Swat, a Taliban gunman shot Yousafzai in the head as a reprisal, leaving her in a critical condition. While still in a coma, Yousafzai was transferred to Birmingham's Queen Elizabeth

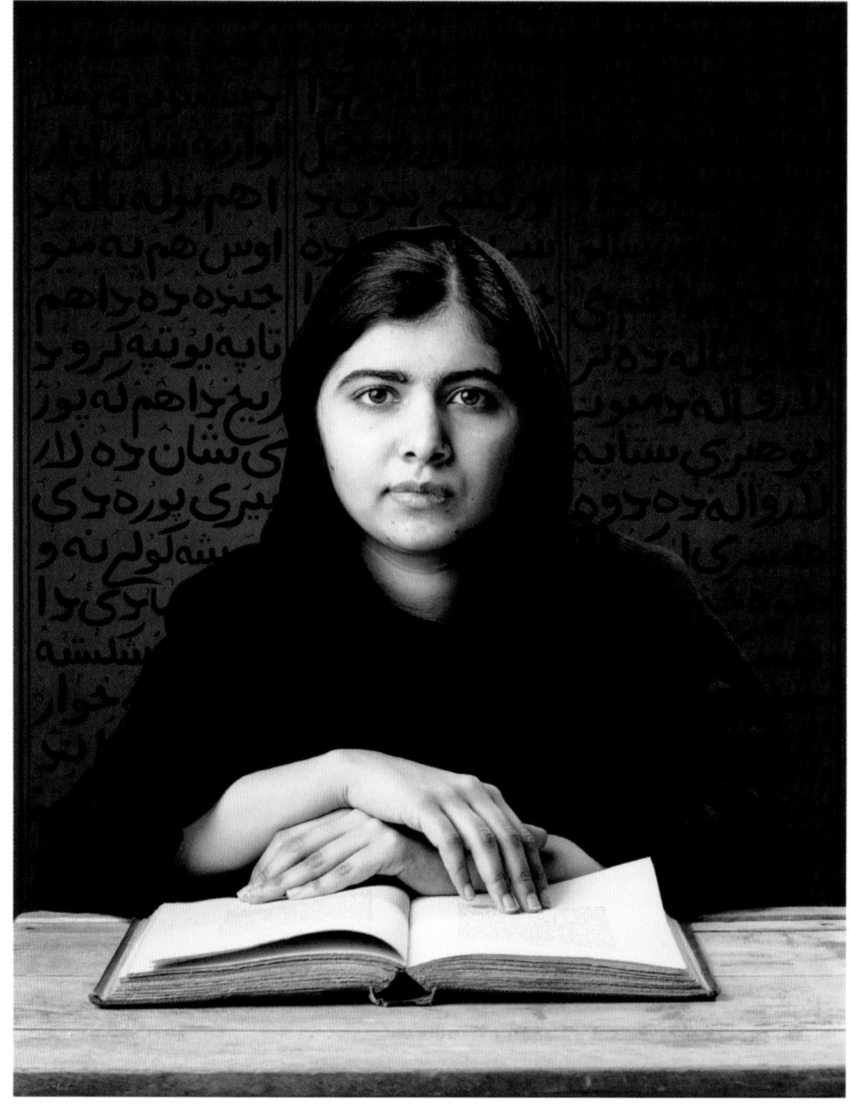

Hospital in the United Kingdom; she was eventually discharged on 3 January 2013. Amid an outpouring of international sympathy and condemnation over her attack, more than 2 million people signed a petition prompting the passage of Pakistan's Right to Free and Compulsory Education Bill. Undaunted by her experiences and on finding herself in an unfamiliar country, Yousafzai entered high school two months later, and graduated from Oxford University in 2020 while balancing her studies with her persistent activism.

On her sixteenth birthday in 2013, Yousafzai addressed the United Nations, powerfully underlining her belief in the importance of education in the 'struggle against illiteracy, poverty and terrorism'. That same year, with her father she co-founded the non-profit Malala Fund to champion girls' right to education, investing in projects and empowering activists globally to demand change. As a result, Yousafzai became the youngest recipient of the Nobel Peace Prize in 2014 and remains an inspirational voice and symbol for change. CN

Malala Yousafzai (b.1997)
By Shirin Neshat, 2018
Archival ink on gelatin silver print, 1524 × 1016mm
National Portrait Gallery, London, 7053

Leyla Hussein

A psychotherapist specialising in supporting survivors of sexual violence and a tireless activist, Leyla Hussein frequently speaks openly and movingly about the harrowing, life-changing experience of undergoing Female Genital Mutilation (FGM). Born in Somalia, where 97 per cent of girls aged 15 to 19 have undergone FGM, Hussein was 'cut' at the age of seven. FGM involves the removal of, or injury to, some or all of the external female genitalia for non-medical, cultural or religious reasons. It is usually practised on girls between infancy and the age of 15, often in countries across Africa, the Middle East and Asia, leaving survivors to endure a myriad of adverse physical, sexual and psychological repercussions. Pregnancy brought Hussein's trauma to the fore and after her daughter's birth, she resolved to safeguard her child and joined the campaign against FGM with full force.

Informed by her first-hand experiences, Hussein co-founded Daughters of Eve with fellow activist Nimco Ali in 2010, a non-profit organization working to raise awareness in Britain about FGM and available support services, while also pushing to urgently eliminate the abusive practice. Despite being illegal in the United Kingdom since 1985, there are many women living in Britain with FGM, with more girls at risk each year of undergoing the practice in secret or being taken abroad for it be carried out. A petition by Daughters of Eve in 2013 calling for the Home Office to devise and enforce a national strategy against FGM in Britain gained 110,561 signatures and attracted widespread media attention, prompting parliamentary debate and action.

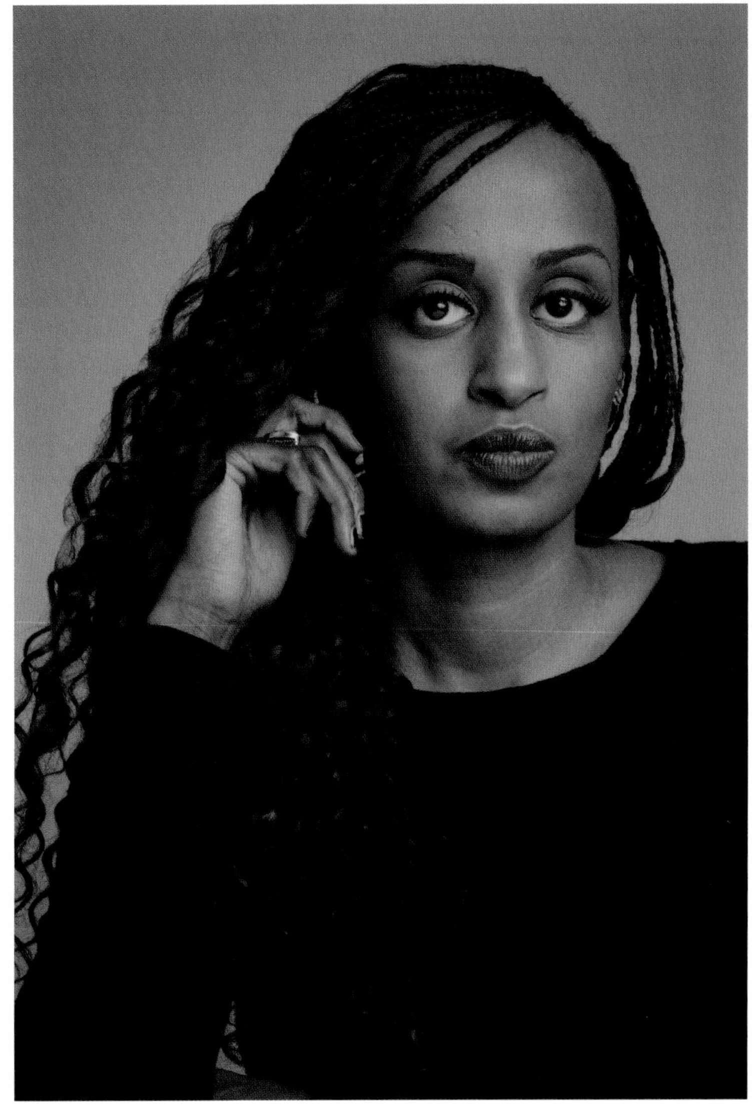

Hussein simultaneously presented and released a powerful, BAFTA-nominated Channel 4 documentary, *The Cruel Cut*, which increased public support, and challenged preconceptions and ignorance around the issue.

Daughters of Eve was the first of many groundbreaking initiatives begun by Hussein, including the Dahlia Project, established in 2014 to provide therapeutic services to FGM survivors, educate and empower communities, train professionals and work with policymakers. Through 'The Faces of Defiance' project, launched in 2015 with photographer Jason Ashwood and from which this portrait derives, Hussein challenged the way in which FGM survivors and campaigners are perceived by presenting them as empowered and beautiful, rather than as 'broken' women. Hussein also writes frequently in the press and serves as a consultant for bodies such as the World Health Organization and the United Nations, firmly establishing her place as a passionate and outspoken advocate at the forefront of the British and global movement against FGM. CN

Leyla Hussein (b.1980)
By Jason Ashwood, 2 May 2015
Gelatin silver print, 364 × 242mm
National Portrait Gallery, London, x199650

Farshid Moussavi

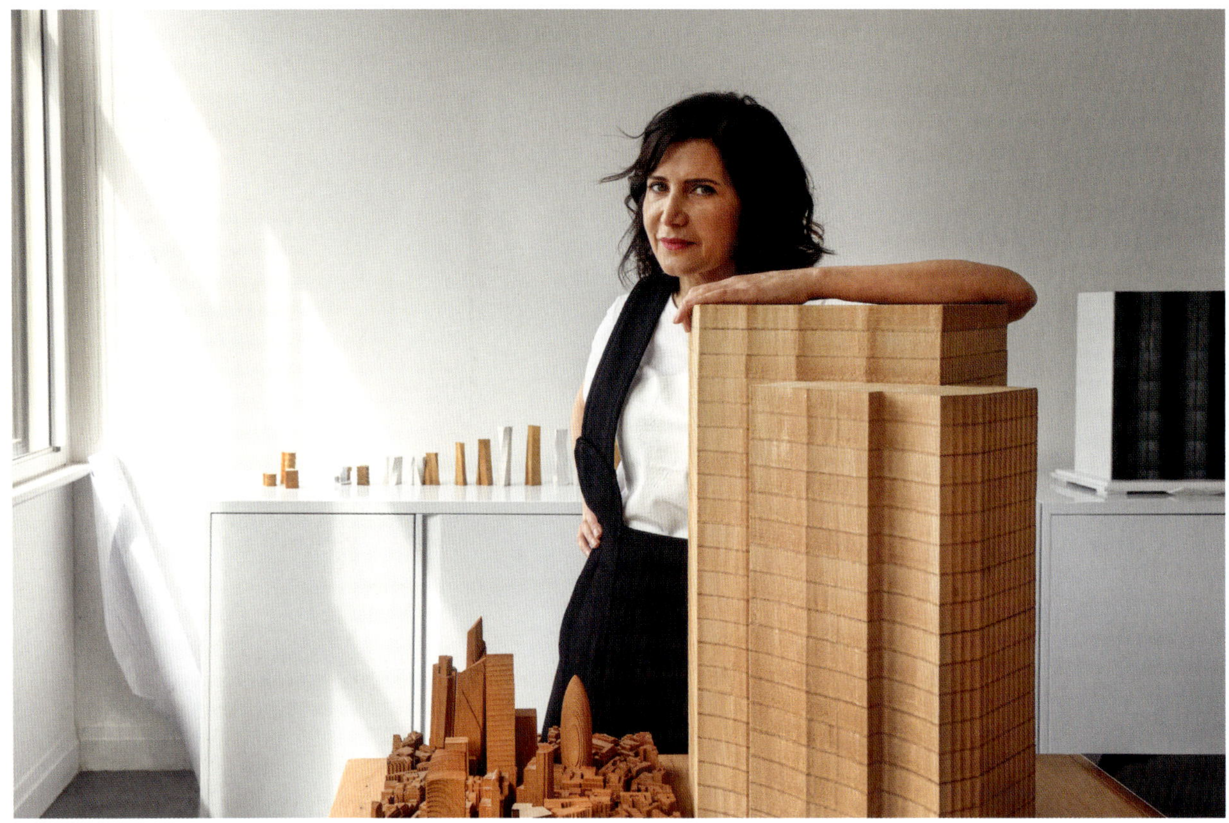

I was initially attracted to architecture because it brings humanities and technology together, it's at the intersection of so many subjects – from aesthetics to anthropology, economy, philosophy, politics, sociology, technology and craft; because it is embedded in the everyday.[50]

The London-based writer, educator and internationally renowned architect Farshid Moussavi founded Farshid Moussavi Architecture (FMA) in 2011. Throughout her career, she has consolidated a reputation as a leading female architect and she continues to play a key role in inspiring women as one of the most innovative practitioners and thinkers today.

The portfolio of her prestigious and pioneering architectural firm includes diverse projects across continents. Such designs include the Museum of Contemporary Art in Cleveland, USA; 'La Folie Divine',

a residential complex in Montpellier in the South of France; flagship stores for Victoria Beckham in London and Hong Kong; and the toy department at Harrods, London, among many others. Moussavi explains that FMA is a collaborative initiative that includes a network of specialists from different fields who work to create buildings that are functional in multiple ways, formally complex and surprising. Each project has a sense of being novel. Moussavi believes that architecture is not only a multi-faceted practice, which contributes to the culture of our rural and urban environment, but also that buildings influence our daily experiences and our emotional states.

Born in Iran, Moussavi trained at Dundee University and at The Bartlett School of Architecture, University College London before attending the Graduate School of Design at Harvard University. Prior to launching FMA,

she was co-founder of Foreign Office Architects (FOA), establishing their reputation with a competition-winning design for Yokohama Port Terminal in Japan. Alongside her professional practice, Moussavi teaches at Harvard's Graduate School of Design, and from her research interests, conducted through FMA's Function Lab, she has published the volumes *The Function of Ornament* (2006), *The Function of Form* (2009), *The Function of Style* (2014) and *Architecture and Micropolitics* (2022).

Among her many accolades she has been the winner of multiple RIBA International Awards, the Special Prize for best work in Topography at the Venice Architecture Biennale (2004) and the Kanagawa Prize for Architecture (2003). She also won the Jane Drew Prize in 2022 and received an OBE in 2018 for services to architecture. GA

Farshid Moussavi (b.1965)
By Anne-Katrin Purkiss, 2018
Digital photograph
Royal Academy of Arts, London

HIDDEN HEROINES OF DESIGN

By

Alice Rawsthorn

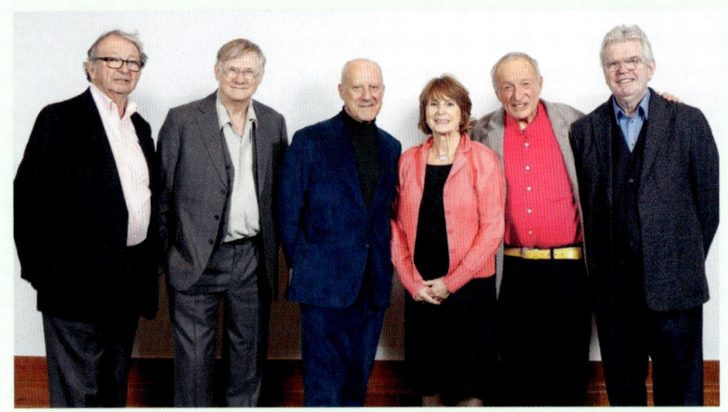

Fig.1: Six British architects

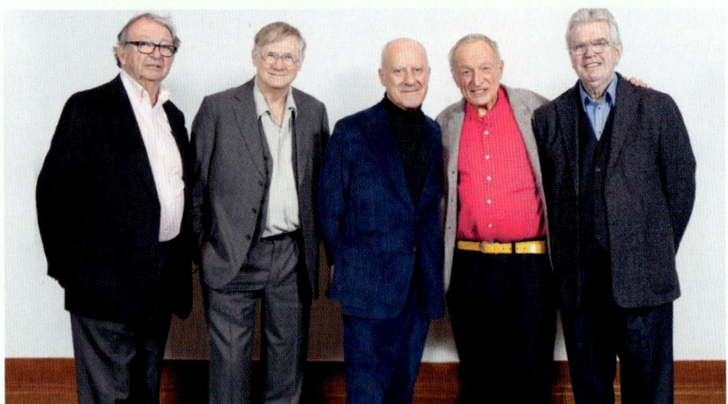

Fig.2: Five British architects

It was bad enough that there was only one woman among the six British architects who were photographed for a group portrait to promote the BBC's 2014 documentary series, *The Brits Who Built the Modern World* (fig.1). Patty Hopkins was the lone female alongside Norman Foster, Nicholas Grimshaw, Richard Rogers, Terry Farrell and her husband, Michael, with whom she co-founded their practice. But when it came to promoting the third episode of the series, the BBC used a different version of the image from which Patty Hopkins was deleted (fig.2). The lady vanished, leaving five white cis men to represent the BBC's choice of the nation's most influential architects.

This dispiriting saga tells us much about the misogyny that has long impeded the efforts of gifted and ambitious women to forge careers in design. Designers of colour have suffered discrimination too, as have those identifying as trans or queer, and anyone else differing from the archetype of the white cis men that dominate the design establishment. Not only did many educational institutions and professional bodies exclude all these groups until the post-war era, prospective employers and clients refused to hire them. Yet women also bore – and many continue to bear – the burden of juggling both work and a larger share of domestic responsibilities than their male contemporaries, and of being stereotyped as assistants or spouses, rather than professional equals. The mid-twentieth-century architect Jane Drew (fig.3), who, like Patty Hopkins, worked with her husband, Maxwell Fry, grew so infuriated at being introduced at lectures as 'Mrs Fry', that she would say: 'I'm sorry Mrs Fry can't be with us tonight, instead Miss Jane Drew has kindly accepted to replace her.'

Women in every sphere have confronted similar problems. One of the main barriers when it comes to careers in design is that it is an interdependent field, where the support of colleagues, in particular of those in senior positions, is required to secure entry, clinch commissions and to access research resources and production facilities. As almost all of the power brokers in the design world are men, it has remained a self-perpetuating

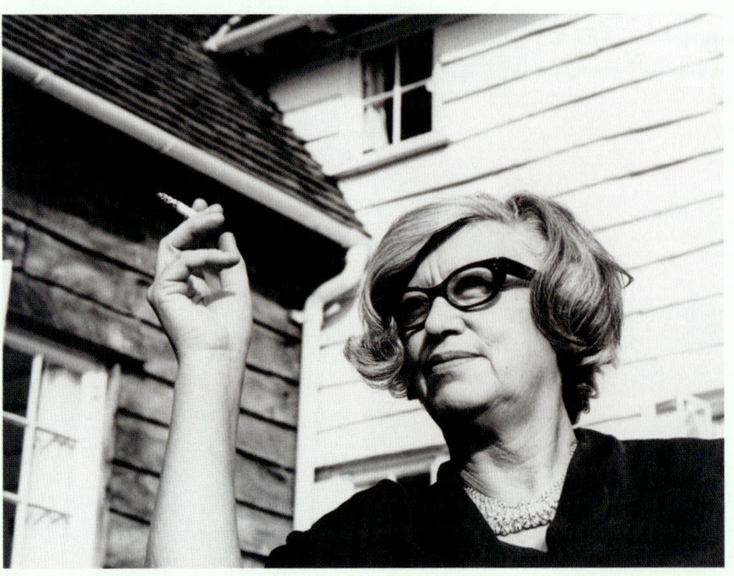

Fig.3: Jane Drew by Jorge Lewinski

male domain. Yet there have been historical exceptions of resourceful women who have managed to bypass the gatekeepers, and, in recent years, a new generation of female designers has flourished by doing the same.

One glorious anomaly was a group of women's suffrage campaigners during the late nineteenth and early twentieth centuries. Among them were the aspirant architects, Agnes Garrett (fig.4) and her cousin Rhoda, who spent much of their twenties struggling to secure apprenticeships. They finally persuaded an architect to employ them, only to be banned from visiting supposedly unladylike building sites. Hoping that interior design would be less repressive, they co-founded A & R Garrett House Decorators in 1874 as the UK's first firm of 'lady decorators'. Agnes and Rhoda defined what they described as a 'solid and unpretentious' style of interiors that they hoped would make it quicker and easier for women to clean their homes, liberating time for other activities. In 1877 they published a book, *Suggestions on House Decoration*, on their design philosophy and lectured on it across the country. They were lucky in securing early commissions from Agnes's two sisters, the pioneering female doctor, Elizabeth Garrett Anderson, and the suffrage campaigner, Millicent Fawcett, who then loyally recommended them to friends. After Rhoda's death in 1882, Agnes flung herself into the suffrage movement. She applied her professional skills to help other women by designing the interior of the New Hospital for Women, which was founded by Garrett Anderson, as well as establishing the Ladies' Residential Chambers to build apartments for single professional women in London. Among its investors were Garrett Anderson, Fawcett and a fellow female design pioneer, Fanny Wilkinson (p.25).

After completing a course (as the only woman student) at the Crystal Palace School of Landscape Gardening and Practical Horticulture in 1883, Wilkinson became the first woman to practise landscape design in the UK. She transformed graveyards, dumps and other unprepossessing sites in economically deprived areas of London into congenial green spaces where children could play, while designing beloved public parks including Myatt's Fields and Vauxhall Park, which was built on land donated by Millicent Fawcett and her husband. Whenever possible, she trained unemployed local people to

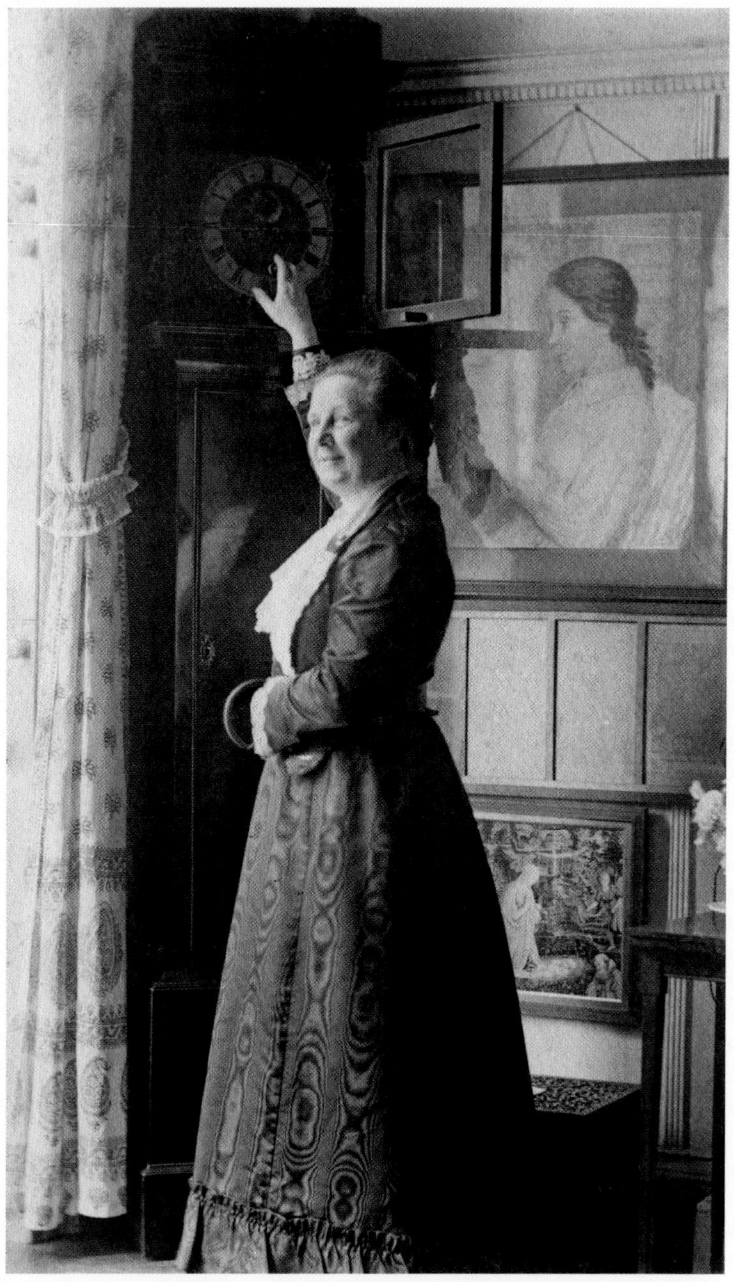

Fig.4: Agnes Garrett by Olive Edis

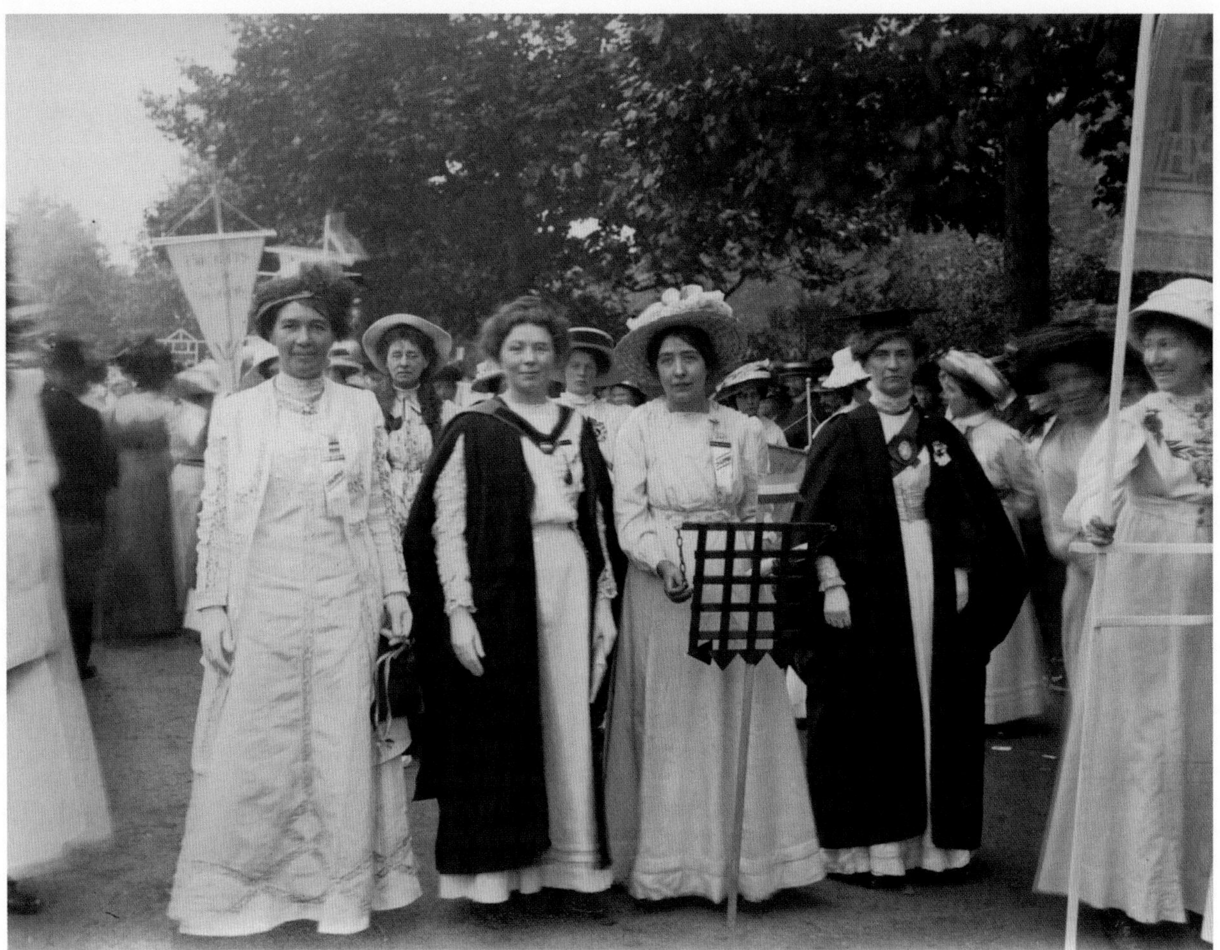

Fig.5: Suffragette march in Hyde Park by Christina Broom

work with her, hoping that their new skills would help them to find employment. After Wilkinson's appointment as the first female principal of Swanley Horticultural College in Kent, she turned it into a women-only school, where she empowered young women to pursue careers in garden and landscape design.

She and Agnes Garrett also participated in larger design endeavours through their involvement with the suffrage cause. Design was deployed as a strategic tool by the two leading organizations, the National Union of Women's Suffrage Societies (NUWSS) run by Fawcett and the militant Women's Social and Political Union (WSPU) led by Emmeline Pankhurst. Garrett and Wilkinson were involved with both factions. The NUWSS was renowned for staging spectacular pageants of its members dressed as Boudicca, Elizabeth I, and other historic heroines in costumes,

which they made themselves in splendid displays of improvisational design. The WSPU developed a dazzlingly effective visual identity, designed by Emmeline Pankhurst's daughter Sylvia and the journalist Emmeline Pethick-Lawrence to be instantly recognisable, yet capable of being customised to suit the needs of individual suffragettes.

The identity was launched at Women's Sunday, a WSPU rally in Hyde Park, London on 21 June 1908, attended by half a million people from across the country (fig.5). Sylvia Pankhurst and Emmeline Pethick-Lawrence chose three colours to represent the cause: purple for dignity, green for hope and white for purity. Suffragettes were told to wear white dresses – or white saris in the case of an Indian delegation – accessorised with purple and green sashes, hats, or jewellery. Specially designed accessories were sold to raise money for the WSPU, while impecunious suffragettes were encouraged to make their own from purple and green ribbons or scraps of fabric. Wilkinson arrived in Hyde Park accompanied by colour-coded Swanley students proudly carrying a 'Women Gardeners' banner. The identity was then adapted for future protests, notably by suffragettes who arrived at political meetings clad in deceptively 'feminine' white dresses before removing purple and green sashes from their bags and heckling the speakers. It was also used in new fundraising merchandise and badges of honour, including the Holloway Brooch, which was designed by Sylvia Pankhurst in 1909 to be awarded to militants upon their release from Holloway Prison. When she was expelled from the WSPU in 1914, after clashing with her mother and sister, she reinvented the identity for the newly formed East London Federation of Suffragettes, which supported working-class women, by adding a fourth colour, red, to symbolise socialism and freedom.

Agnes and Rhoda Garrett, Fanny Wilkinson, Sylvia Pankhurst, Emmeline Pethick-Lawrence and their collaborators were imaginative, ingenious and courageous designers. By constructing a circular economy of clients, funders and collaborators within the suffrage movement, they circumvented the male design establishment.

Few other women succeeded in doing the same during the twentieth century. Though a heartening exception was the group of textile designers who apprenticed with Ethel Mairet, a self-taught weaver, at her workshop in the East Sussex village of Ditchling from 1921 to 1952. Mairet had 130 apprentices, mostly women, several of whom went on to become influential designers. Among them were Elizabeth Peacock, who opened a workshop in a nearby village, and Marianne Straub

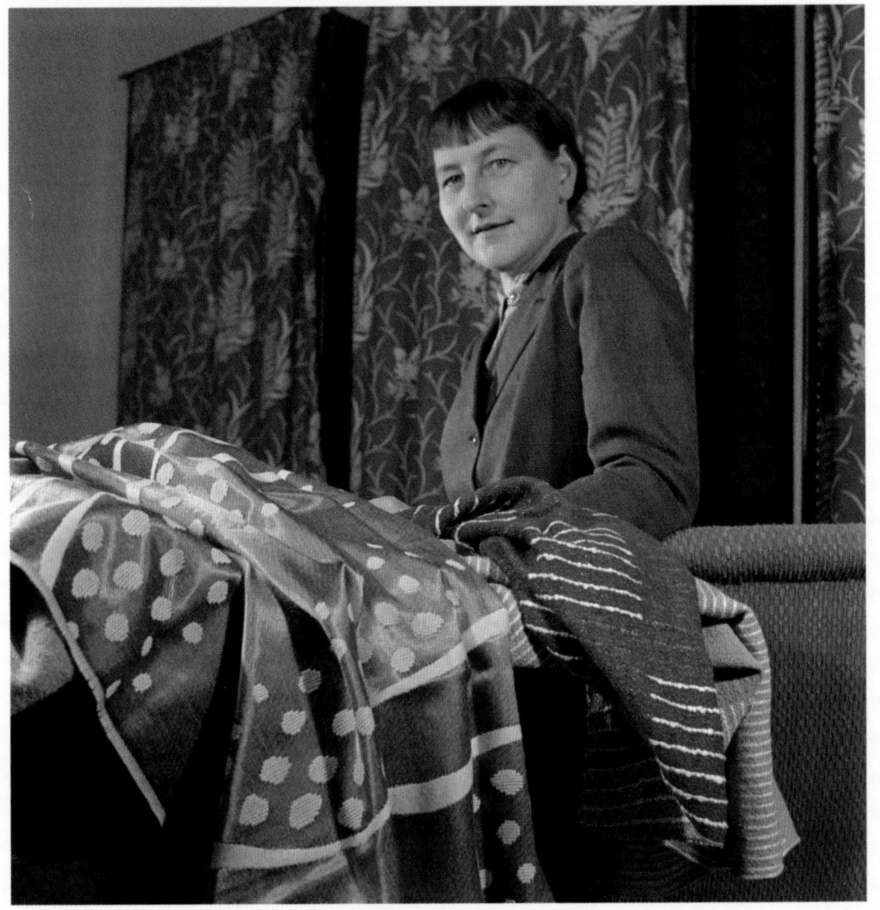

Fig.6: Marianne Straub by John Gay

(fig.6), who originally came to England from her native Switzerland to study industrial textiles at Bradford. (As the college wrote to Marianne as 'Mr Straub', it had clearly accepted her thinking she was a man.) They both continued Mairet's work in training and mentoring younger female designers, thereby creating a similar support network to that of the suffragists and suffragettes.

Decades later, there has been progress, though not enough. Even the most successful female designers of the mid- to late twentieth century were overshadowed by their male collaborators, as Jane Drew was by her husband and the graphic designer Margaret Calvert by her colleague, Jock Kinneir. Design remains a white cis male domain, particularly at senior levels of the design and architecture industries. Even so, the architects Amanda Levete, Lesley Lokko and Farshid Moussavi (p.178) have built successful practices, as did the late Zaha Hadid (p.171), who became the first woman to win the prestigious Pritzker Architecture Prize in 2004. Similarly, Ilse Crawford and Rose Uniacke are recognised as leaders in interior design, as are Nipa Doshi and Bethan Laura Wood in product design, and Frith Kerr in graphics. They all faced misogyny, especially early in their careers, but were better defended than their predecessors. Attitudinal changes towards gender equality helped, though a key catalyst was the availability of powerful, yet affordable, digital tools, which have transformed design culture. As well as using software to speed up the design process, designers can manage vast quantities of complex data on inexpensive computers,

use social media to raise awareness of their work and generate funding online.

Not only have these changes weakened the traditional male power structure, they have also expanded design practice by enabling designers to pursue their social, political and ecological concerns in new design disciplines devoid of traditional gender barriers. Hilary Cottam has emerged as a global pioneer in social design, as has Alison Killing in humanitarian architecture and Alexandra Daisy Ginsberg in design's intersection with science. We all benefit from their work, which, hopefully, will pave the way towards a more equitable and inclusive design community that will welcome the best possible designers based on merit, regardless of ethnicity, heritage, or gender.

Fig.1
'The Brits Who Built the Modern World'
Patty Hopkins (b.1942) (fourth from left)
By Jackie King, 2014

Fig.2
'The Brits Who Built the Modern World'
BBC press photo, 2014

Fig.3
Jane Drew (1911–1996)
By Jorge Lewinski, July 1965
Gelatin silver print, 296 × 376mm
National Portrait Gallery, London, x13714

Fig.4
Agnes Garrett (1845–1935)
By Olive Edis, 1900s
Platinum print, 150 × 89mm
National Portrait Gallery, London, x16323

Fig.5
Suffragette march in Hyde Park
Emmeline Pethick-Lawrence (1867–1954), Christabel Pankhurst (1880–1958), Sylvia Pankhurst (1882–1960) and Emily Wilding Davison (1872–1913)
By Christina Broom, 23 July 1910
Gelatin silver print, 113 × 144mm
National Portrait Gallery, London, x17396

Fig.6
Marianne Straub (1909–1994)
By John Gay, *c*.1947
Film negative
National Portrait Gallery, London, x200987

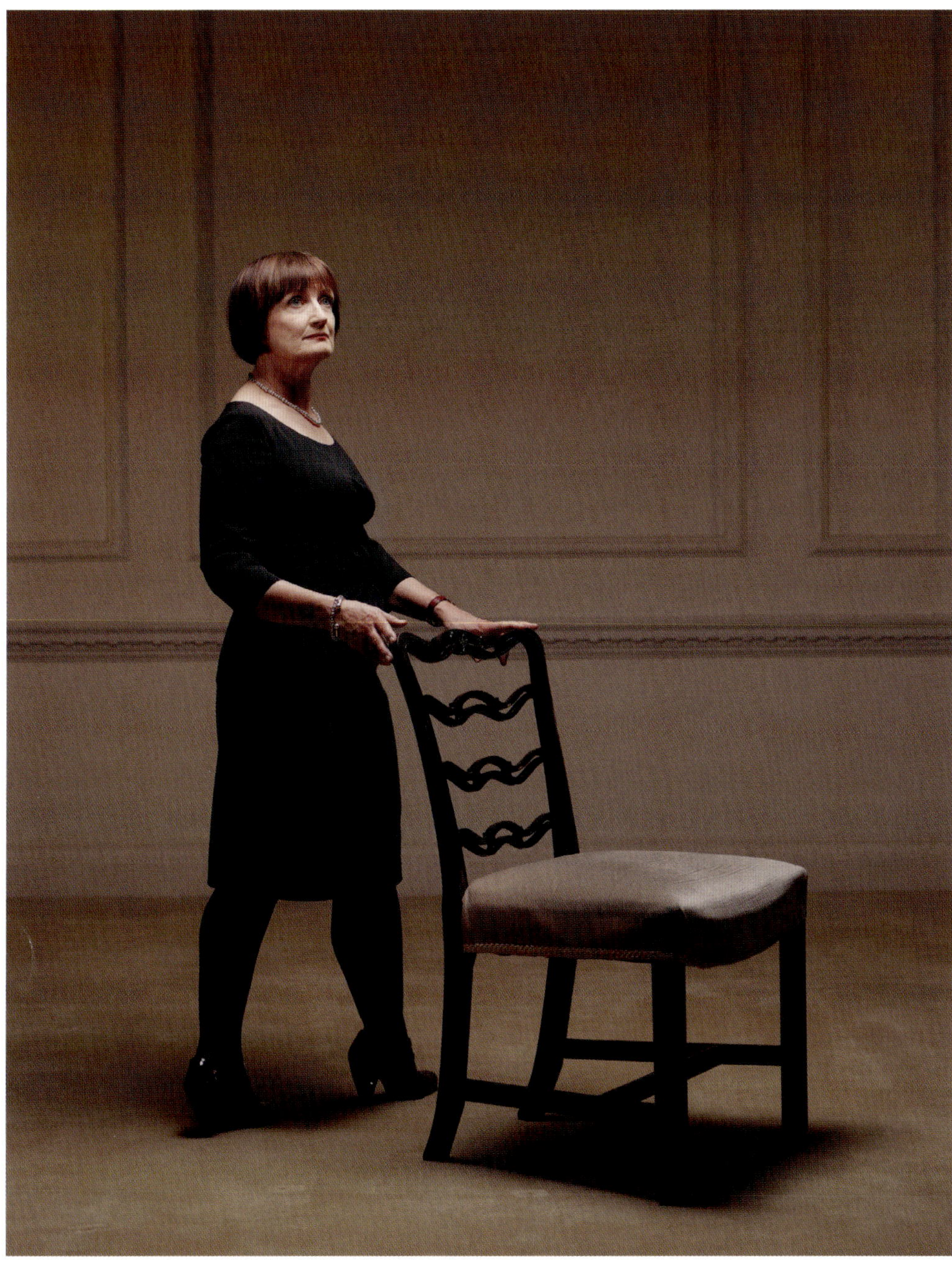

Tessa Jowell served as a Member of Parliament for 23 years, including 13 years as a Minister in the Labour government and 8 in the Cabinet. During her career, she was Minister of State for Public Health (1997–9), Minister of State for Employment, Welfare to Work and Equal Opportunities (1999–2001) and Secretary of State for Culture, Media and Sport (2001–7). Of her approach, Jowell stated, 'I hope always my politics are the politics of aspiration, ambition, possibility and the future.' She was a key figure in securing the 2012 Olympics and Paralympics for London, and was instrumental in its success. She truly believed in the opportunities and regeneration that the games would offer to the urban area of east London.

The idea of staging the games came to her when she was Culture Secretary, and she convinced her colleagues in government to support the 2005 bid. Jowell was appointed Olympics Minister and retained this position throughout Labour's time in office. Following the general election of May 2010, when Labour lost, she became Shadow Olympics Minister. Jowell continued on the 2012 Olympics Organising Committee, becoming an inseparable part of their ultimate success, and was later appointed Deputy Mayor of the Olympic Village.

Prior to becoming a Member of Parliament, Jowell worked as a childcare officer. She then qualified as a psychiatric social worker and went on to serve as assistant director of the mental health charity Mind. During her time in government, she worked towards gender equality and the Sure Start children's centre programme, championing early years education. Jowell was a trailblazer for women in politics and colleagues remember her as a campaigner who worked tirelessly to improve lives and promote social justice, with friends across political parties.

Jowell became a member of the Privy Council in 1998 and a Dame in 2012. She joined the House of Lords as a Baroness in 2015 and took up a number of academic appointments, including a senior fellowship at the School of Public Health at Harvard University.

After announcing she had brain cancer, she gave a moving speech in the House of Lords, in which she urged peers to support an international initiative to share resources, research and new treatments. GA

Tessa Jowell (1947–2018)
By Brian Griffin, 2 February 2010
Pigment print, 914 × 685mm
National Portrait Gallery, London, P1711

2013   Shirley Thompson

In 2013 Shirley Thompson was once again included in the *Evening Standard*'s 'Power List of Britain's Top 100 Most Influential Black People', an acknowledgment that she had received each year since 2010. As a pioneering composer, artistic director, filmmaker and academic she is renowned for creating her own unique sound in musical composition. Most notably, she has gained a reputation for her skill in using contemporary classical, popular and world music, as well as the spoken word, to deal with themes of social injustice and history, referencing the experiences of people of African heritage and her own Jamaican culture. She explains, 'For me, it's about creating a universal language of music; one that people can identify as classical music that speaks to them.'

Thompson is the first woman in Europe to have composed and conducted a symphony within the last 40 years. Commissioned in 2002 to celebrate Queen Elizabeth II's Golden Jubilee, the piece entitled *New Nation Rising, A 21st Century Symphony* debuted in 2004. It was performed and recorded by the Royal Philharmonic Orchestra, accompanied by two choirs, solo singers, a rapper and dhol drummers with nearly 200 performers. Thompson explains that the symphony was conceived as 'a story about London celebrating its legendary spirit of change, innovation, dynamism and cultural diversity'. This remarkable work exemplifies her originality and ability to fuse storytelling with different styles of music, making it accessible to new audiences worldwide.

Born in London to Jamaican parents, Thompson studied musicology at the University of Liverpool and then specialised in composition at Goldsmiths' College. She founded the Shirley Thompson Ensemble in 1994, which premiered many of her ground-breaking compositions. In addition, she has also composed for TV, film, theatre, ballet and opera. Important works include commissions for the Royal Ballet, most notably music for the award-winning ballet *PUSH* and for *Heroines of Opera*, in which she revealed hidden stories of women, challenging stereotypes and exploring themes such as the slave trade and Windrush. Most recently, Thompson was Composer-in-Residence of the UEFA Women's EURO 2022 Tournament and composed its Commemoration Anthem, *Beautiful Game*.

Thompson teaches composition and performance at the University of Westminster. As well as having held important appointments and received many awards during her career, in 2019 she was honoured with an OBE for services to music. GA

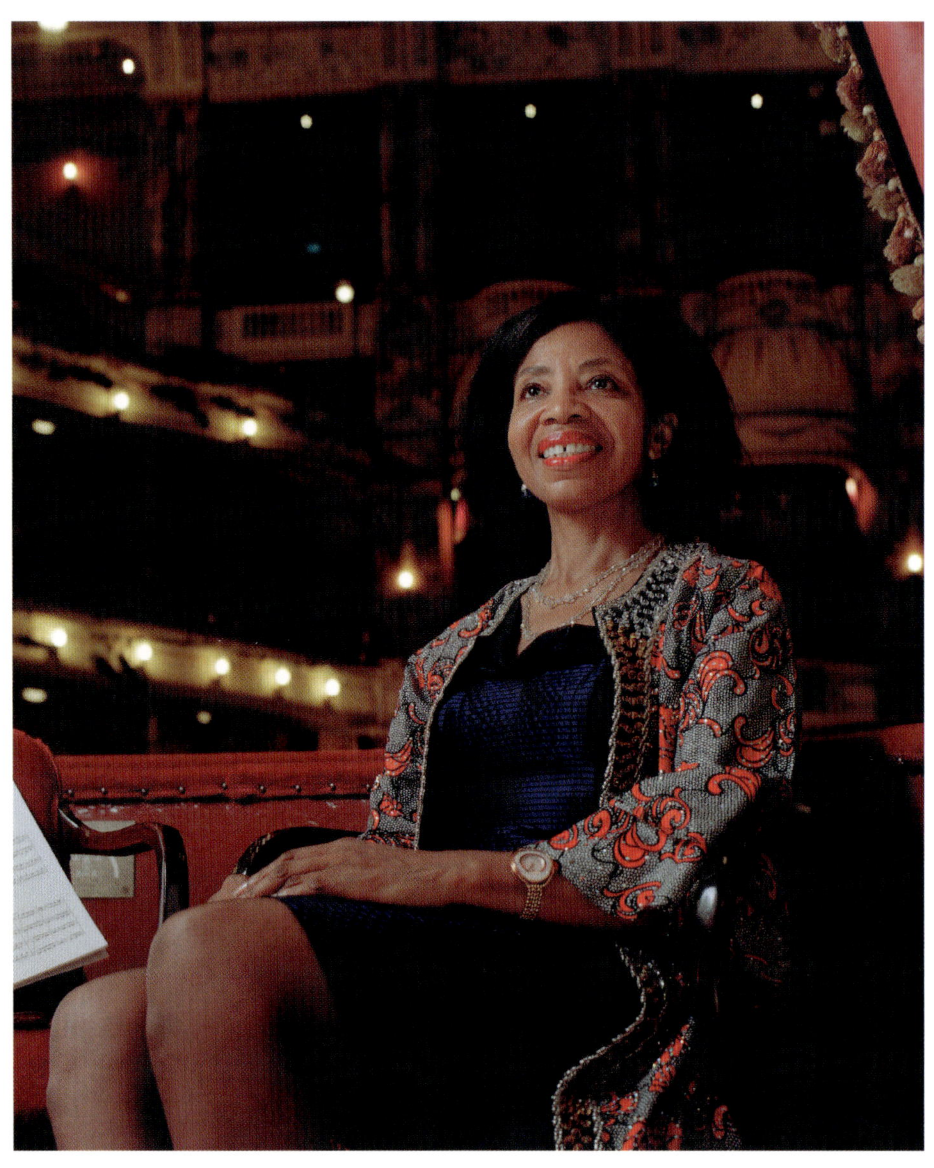

Shirley Thompson (b.1958)
From the series 'Breaking Barriers'
By Joy Gregory, 2019

We need to stop talking about climate change as a future problem, we really only have a short space of time to start making fundamental changes. The time for action really is now.[52]

Farhana Yamin is a leading international environmental lawyer and an expert on climate change and development policy. Born in Pakistan, Yamin grew up in England and read philosophy, politics and economics at Oxford University before qualifying as a solicitor in 1990. Her credentials are unrivalled; over the past 30 years she has worked on a number of international treaties, including the 2015 Paris Agreement on climate change. She has represented small island nations threatened by the effects of global warming and has taken part in the Extinction Rebellion protests. She comments, 'my life and work are a dance between an insider and an outsider.'

In 2014, Yamin set up Track 0, a not-for-profit initiative with the mission of supporting governments, businesses, communities and cities to undertake actions to help get global emissions to zero by the middle of the twenty-first century. This initiative was the precursor to her work as a key architect of the net-zero emissions by 2050 goal, set in the 2015 Paris Agreement. Through behind-the-scenes diplomacy, Yamin was instrumental in securing this legally binding international treaty on climate change. She came up with the concept of net-zero emissions, which means everyone commits to bringing emissions down to a safe level by reducing polluting gases and cutting out fossil fuels, the largest contributor to global warming. The goal has forced governments and corporations to create action plans for what they intend to deliver.

Disappointed by the failures of world leaders and fossil fuel polluters to act, and having spent years working with academics, civil society groups and lawyers to substantially reduce emissions, Yamin has also taken action by participating in protests demanding climate justice. As Coordinator of the Climate Justice and Just Transition Donor Collaborative, she is leading the fight within philanthropy to ensure power and resources go to those on the frontlines fighting for climate justice. She also leads the work of Climate Reframe, which seeks to platform UK-based climate experts and campaigners of colour.[53] GA

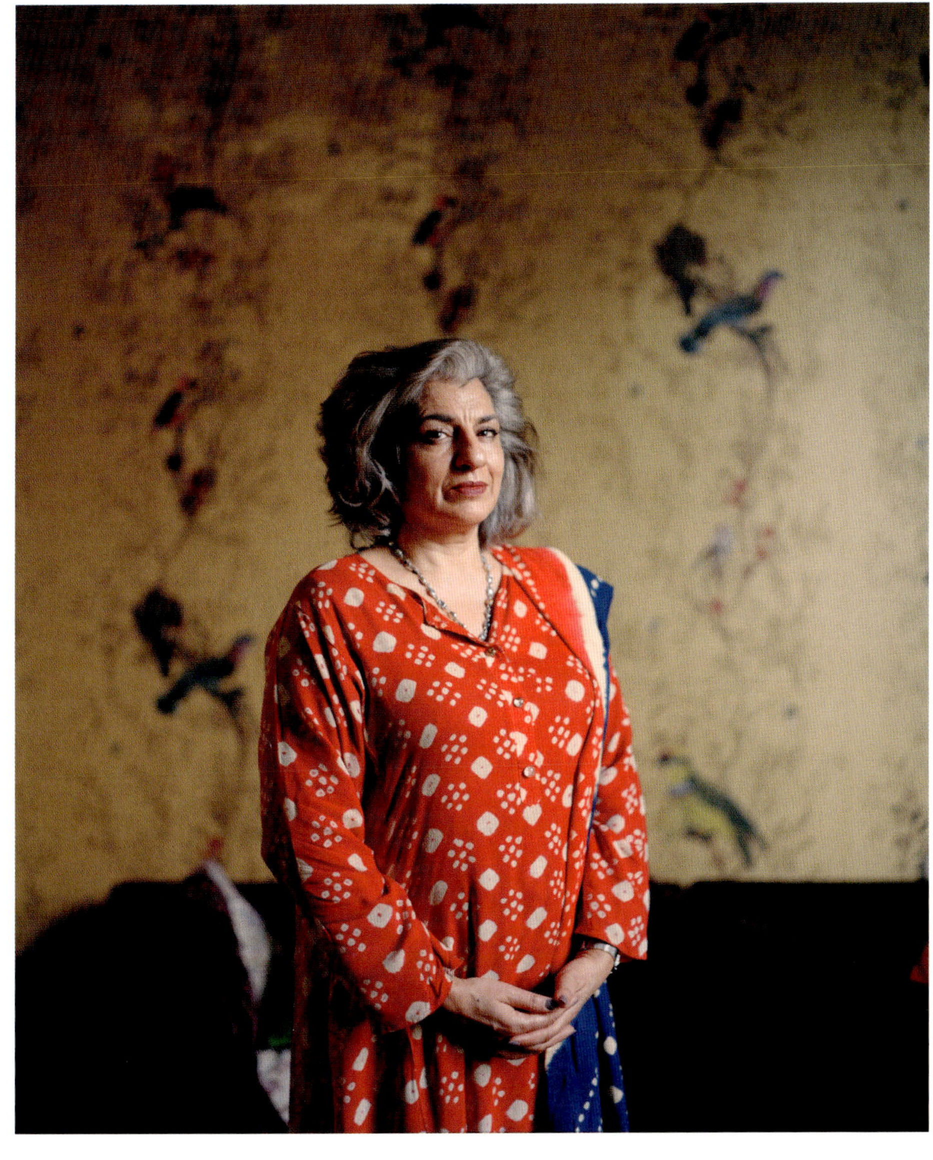

Farhana Yamin (b.1965)
By Olivia Arthur, 2023
Inkjet print, 535 × 430mm
National Portrait Gallery, London, x202543

2015   Evelyn Glennie

At a ceremony on 9 June 2015, Evelyn Glennie received the prestigious Polar Music Prize – akin to a Nobel Prize in music – in recognition of her wide-ranging musical achievements. Since the 1980s, Glennie has sustained a career as the first solo percussionist in history, with a diverse and prodigious musical output resulting from her constant endeavour to explore new avenues for percussion. Alongside more than 40 solo recordings, Glennie has collaborated with artists as varied as the singer Björk and banjo player Bela Fleck. Her notable performances include, in 1992, the first percussion concerto (a composition for a solo instrument, accompanied by an orchestra) in the history of the Royal Albert Hall's Proms, allowing for percussion to be regarded as a leading instrument. Meanwhile, at the London 2012 Olympic Games opening ceremony, she took centre-stage while leading an ensemble of 965 drummers performing 'And I Will Kiss', which she composed jointly with the electronic music duo Underworld.

Born in Aberdeen, Glennie was influenced by traditional Scottish music and was already a proficient pianist when she took up percussion at the age of 12, after being diagnosed as profoundly deaf. Supported by her school teacher, Ron Forbes, she began learning how to use the full range of her senses to listen: 'I would stand with my hands against the classroom wall while Ron played notes on the timpani … Eventually I managed to distinguish the rough pitch of notes by associating where on my body I felt sound with the sense of perfect pitch I had before losing my hearing.' Consequently, Glennie frequently performs barefoot, connecting with the music through the vibrations and using her body as a 'resonating chamber' in her dynamic performances.

As a teenager, Glennie's confidence in her ability led her to challenge the Royal Academy of Music's refusal to audition her, insisting that they judge her by her musical capabilities and not her disability. Her eventual acceptance into the school in 1982 paved the way for changes to the admission policies of British musical institutions. Glennie continues to challenge understandings of deafness and regularly advocates the importance of truly listening in all areas of our lives.

Glennie's wide support for future generations of musicians led her to co-found the Music in Education Consortium in the early 2000s to galvanise government spending in schools, while as the third President of Help Musicians since 2020 she supports musicians during hardship. For her broad range of contributions, Glennie was made DBE in 2007. CN

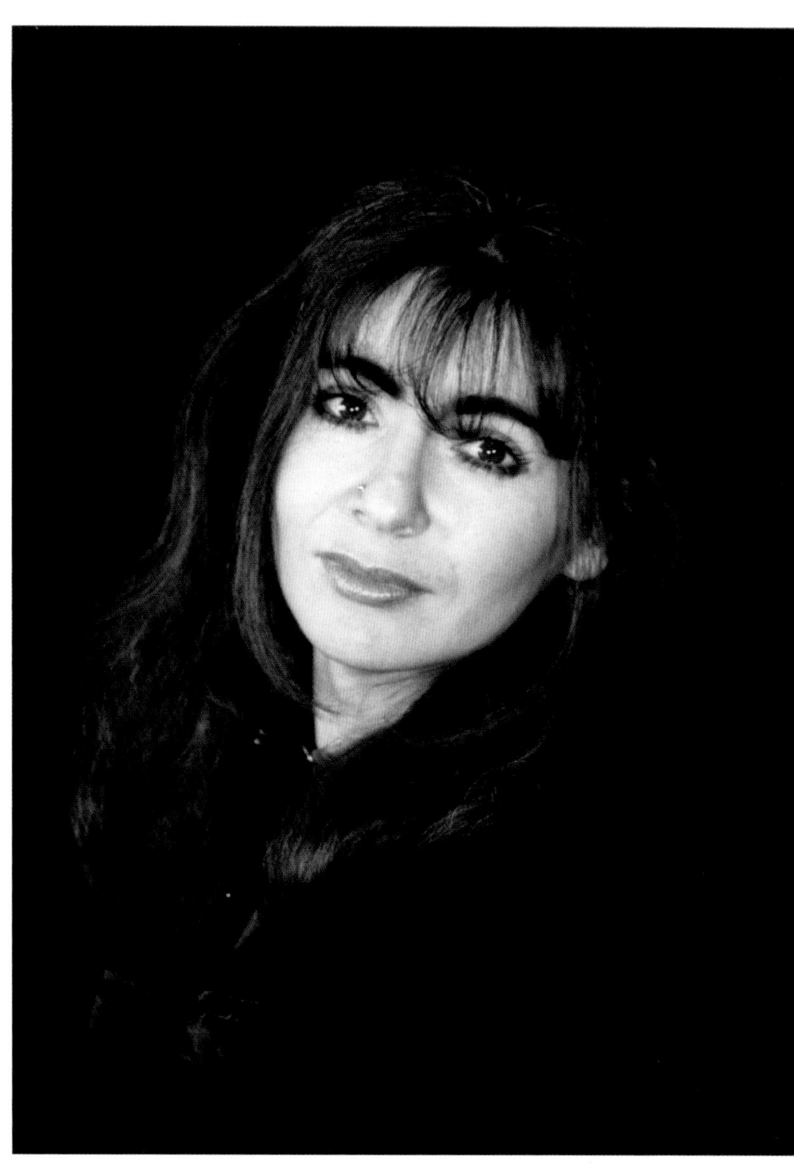

Evelyn Glennie (b.1965)
By Boo Beaumont, April 1998
Gelatin silver print, 255 × 177mm
National Portrait Gallery, London, x87575

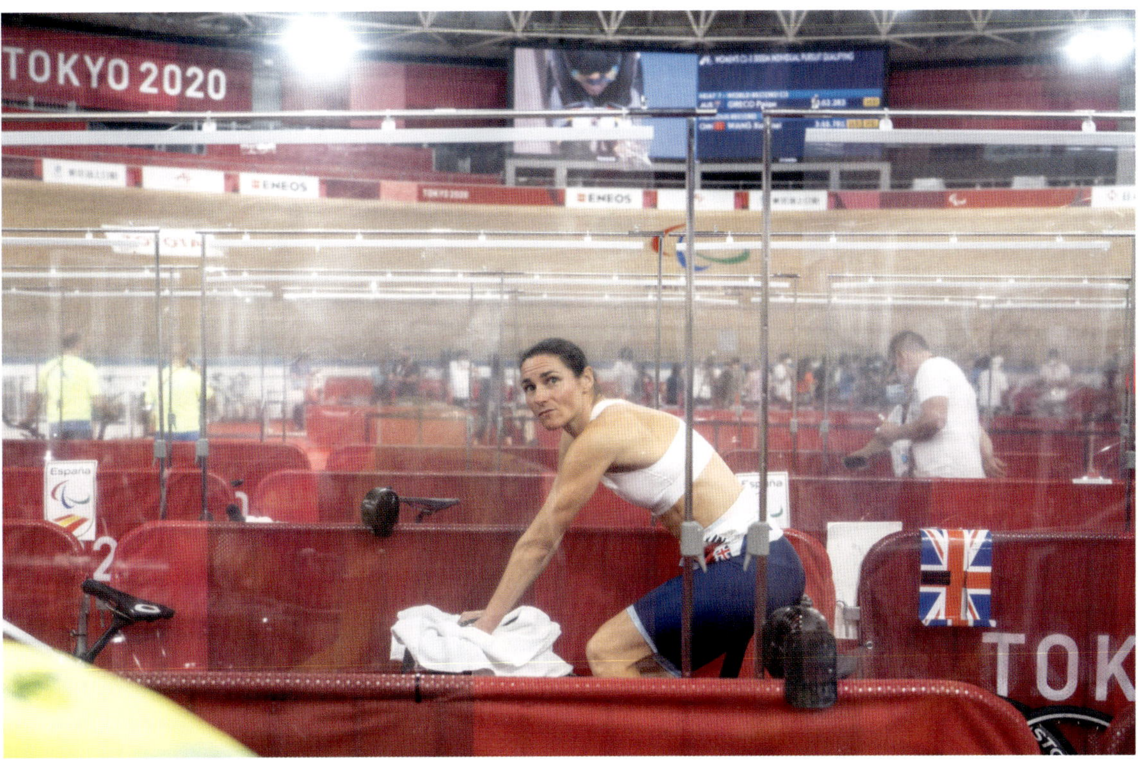

Don't measure success only by the outcome, but also by how you tackle the obstacles you might face on the journey to get there.[55]

Sarah Storey's remarkable sporting journey began over three decades ago as a 14-year-old swimmer at the 1992 Paralympic Games in Barcelona, returning home with an impressive six medals. Born in Manchester without a functioning left hand owing to complications in the womb, Storey learnt to adapt and also excel. She overcame bullying at school, an eating disorder, a coach disinterested in training a disabled athlete and the onset of chronic fatigue syndrome to go on to multiple medal wins in subsequent competitions. In 2005, repeated ear infections caused Storey to switch from swimming to cycling and her dominance on two wheels began.

From then on, Storey frequently topped the podium and set new world records both on the track and road during national, European and international para-cycling events. Appointed DBE following her victories at the 2012 London Paralympics, she returned in 2016 to compete in Rio. Here the demands of motherhood (she had her first child in 2013) did not prevent Storey from gaining three further gold medals and becoming Britain's most successful woman Paralympian.

Driven to achieve more, at her ninth Paralympic Games in Tokyo in 2020 Storey collected three more wins in the Individual Pursuit, Time Trial and Road Race, cycling through driving rain and fog along the foothills of Mount Fuji for the latter event. Thus, Storey secured her position as Britain's most successful Paralympian in history with a total of 28 Paralympic medals. Brian Facer, the Chief Executive of British Cycling, called her 'superhuman'. He stated:

To have had the mindset, the ability, and the body to be able to go on and do this, when others could give up and retire easily sooner than this, is just phenomenal. ... it's really hard to put into words what it means to the para-cycling community. It shows us all that if we go on and work hard then we can achieve great things in our own lives.

Indeed, Storey's achievements, including her success in non-disabled events, have contributed to breaking down barriers and preconceptions surrounding disability. Committed to promoting women's cycling, she started Storey Racing in 2017 with her husband, former Paralympic tandem pilot Barney Storey, to mentor young women cyclists in their careers. Storey continues to highlight the need for greater equality in sport and access to role models. As she has said, 'If you can't see it, you can't be it.' CN

Sarah Storey (b.1977)
By Charly Triballeau, 25 August 2021
AFP via Getty Images

Mary Beard

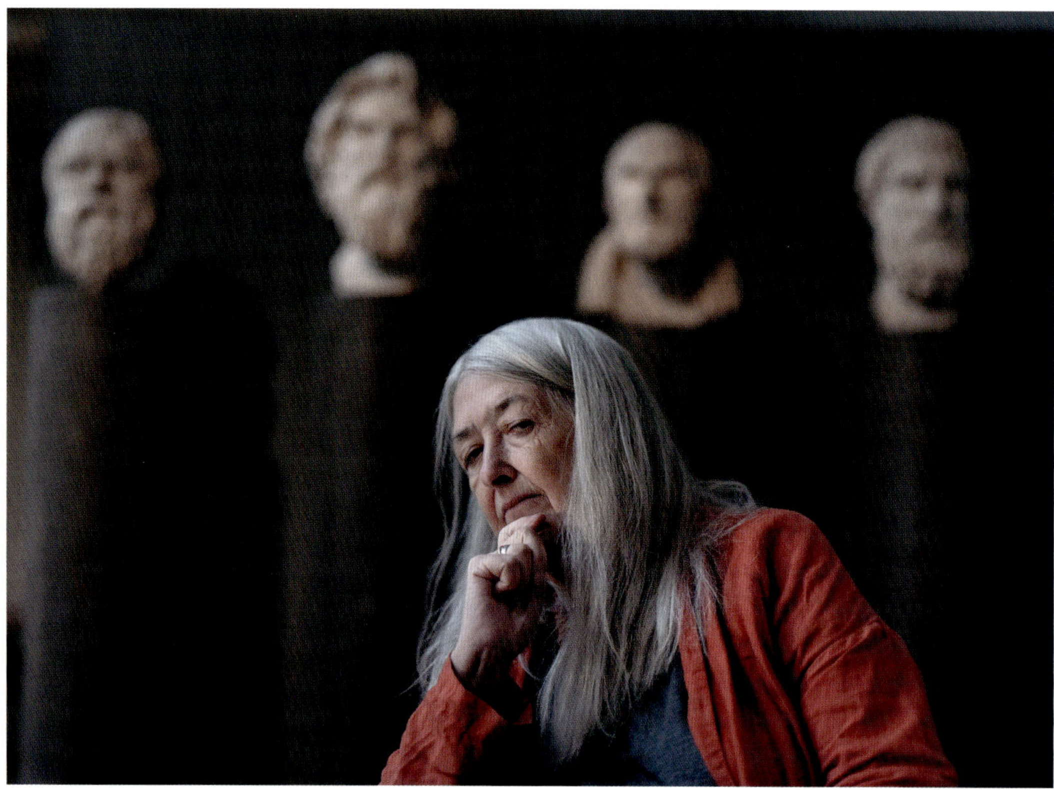

Women in the West have a lot to celebrate; let's not forget. My mother was born before women had the vote in parliamentary elections in Britain. She lived to see a female Prime Minister. Whatever her views of Margaret Thatcher, she was pleased that a woman had reached Number 10 and proud to have had a stake herself in some of those revolutionary changes of the twentieth century … But my mother also knew that it was not quite so simple, that real equality between women and men was still a thing of the future, and that there were causes for anger as well as for celebration.

Opening with these words, Beard sets the tone of her modern feminist classic *Women & Power: A Manifesto* (2017). Here, she explores gender issues, focusing on how history has regarded powerful women from the classical world to the modern age. Beard's main concern is women's silence, and she offers extraordinary insights, analysing misogyny within our cultural foundations, as well as discussing her own experiences of sexism. She argues that it is the structures of power that need to be redefined within our society. The book is adapted from two lectures that she gave in 2014 and 2017 and exposes radical ideas about how mechanisms embedded within Western society have contributed to women being silenced for centuries.

Beard's ability to weave her knowledge of the classical world into lessons on modern politics, culture and society has led to her becoming Britain's best-known classicist. This preoccupation with the relationship between the ancient and contemporary worlds underpins her unique and thought-provoking research as an academic, writer and presenter. Known for her informality and relaxed manner, she is passionate about our connections with the ancient world and the many ways in which we interpret and make associations with it. In 2018 she was made a Dame for services to classical scholarship, having previously been made an OBE in 2013.

Beard studied Classics at Newnham College and, after completing her PhD, taught at King's College, University of London, before returning to Cambridge where she has been a classics lecturer since 1984. She is a fellow of Newnham College and Professor of Ancient Literature at the Royal Academy of Arts. She is also the Classics editor of the *Times Literary Supplement*, which hosts her blog, 'A Don's Life'. Beard is the author of many books including most recently *SPQR: A History of Ancient Rome* (2015) and *Twelve Caesars: Images of Power from the Ancient World to the Modern* (2021). GA

Mary Beard (b.1955)
By Cristina de Middel, 2022
Inkjet print, 450 × 600mm
National Portrait Gallery, London, x202537

Bella Lack

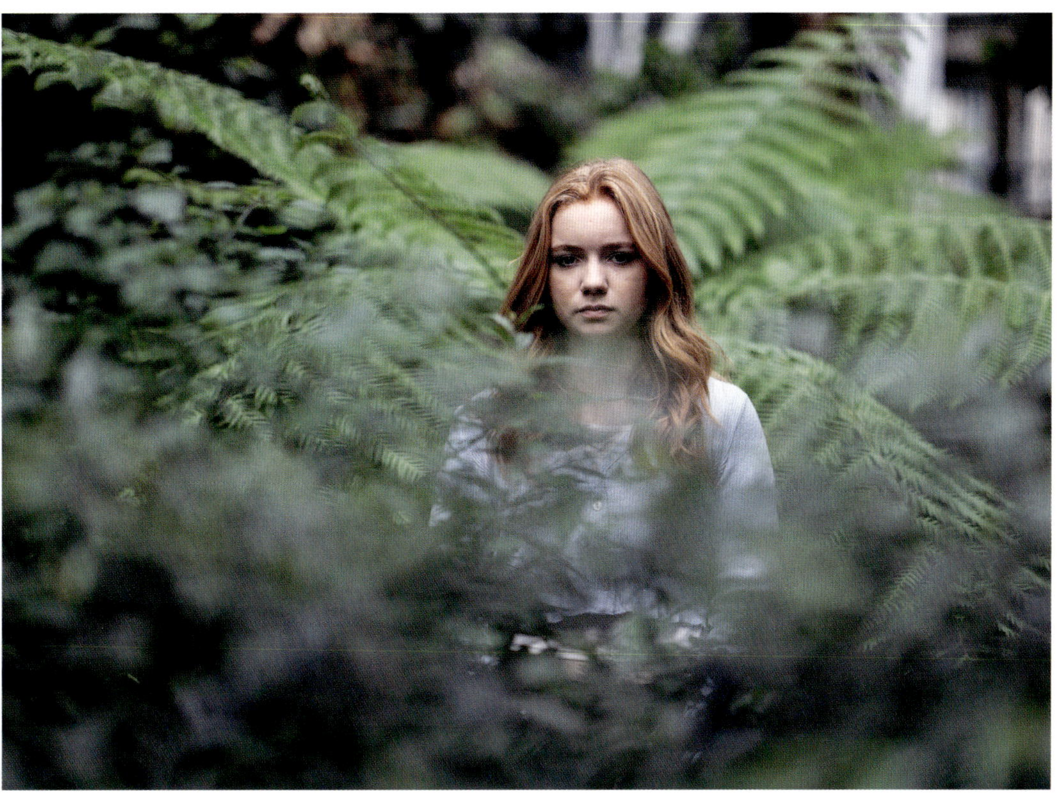

It's a recognition of the scale of the problem that makes you think: 'But what can I do?'[56]

Conservationist Bella Lack loved animals from a young age. She began campaigning at 12 years old after watching a documentary about the effects of unsustainable palm oil production on orangutans and the devastation that was occurring to their natural habitats. By 15 she was attending demonstrations and raising awareness of the consequences of deforestation and the need to take action to protect wildlife. Through social media and by delivering speeches, she has become a leading voice in the new generation of environmentalists, dedicated to engaging young people and making a stand on climate change.

In 2018, Lack successfully led a campaign to ban the use of wild animals in UK circuses. Her petition attracted nearly 200,000 signatures and the following year the Wild Animals in Circuses Bill was passed into law. In her efforts to protect animals, she has exposed the mistreatment of Asian elephants used in tourist rides and is a member of the group Ivory Alliance that works to combat the illegal wildlife trade. Lack is also an ambassador for the Born Free Foundation, Save the Asian Elephants, the RSPCA and the Jane Goodall Institute. She is a member of the board of directors of Reserva: The Youth Land Trust, the first international, youth-funded nature reserve, with a mission to conserve biodiversity.

Lack took part in the documentary *Animal* with ethologist Jane Goodall (p.150), which was selected for the Cannes Film Festival in 2021. Inspired by the young people that she met during filming, Lack decided to write about their stories in her debut book, *Children of the Anthropocene* (2022), which features a foreword by Greta Thunberg. In the book, Lack chronicles the lives of young people at the heart of the environmental crisis. She reflects:

Where many of us in the West are saying, 'we must protect elephants so our grandchildren won't have to live in a world without them', young people at the heart of the crisis around the world are saying, 'we must protect our planet so that I don't wake up unable to breathe because of air pollution, or riddled with cancer because of the plastic and chemicals in my water source, or displaced as the forest where I live has been cut down'.

Lack continues to be an inspiring voice in today's environmental movement. GA

Bella Lack (b.2003)
By Cristina de Middel, 2022
Inkjet print, 450 × 600mm
National Portrait Gallery, London, x202536

2019 Bernardine Evaristo

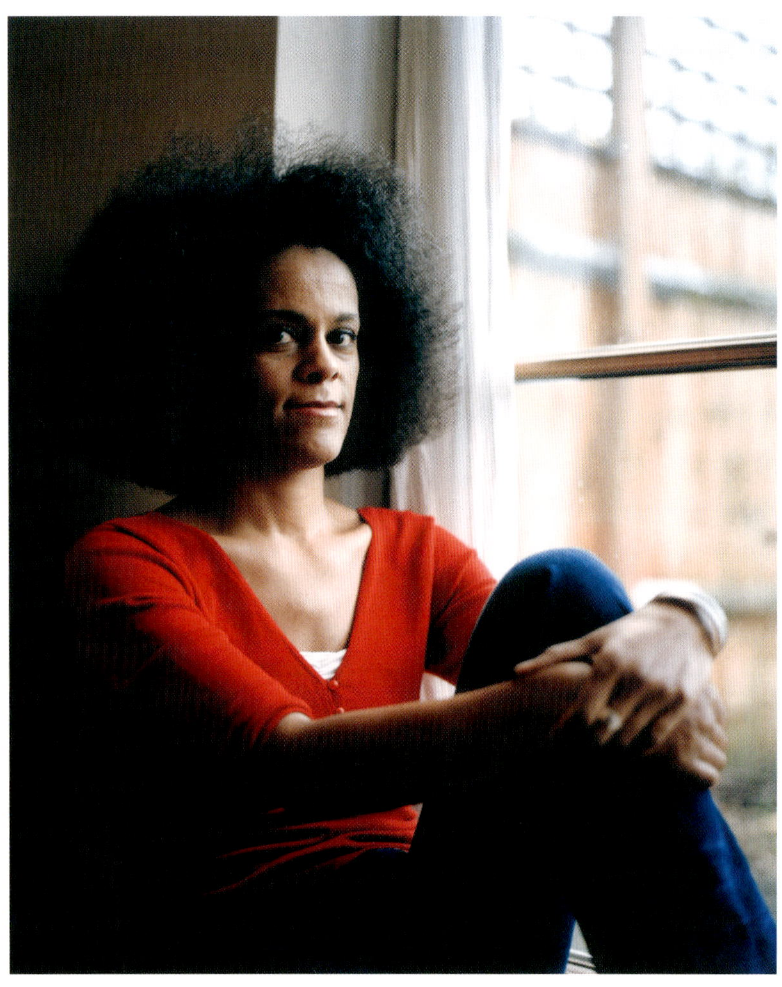

In 2019 Bernardine Evaristo was awarded the Man Booker Prize for her ninth novel, *Girl, Woman, Other*. The novel follows 12 interlinked characters – mostly black British women – through multiple stages of their lives. In Evaristo's words:

I wanted to create as many black British female protagonists as I could get away with. I decided that each woman would have her own section, but they are all kind of interdependent … I wanted to have a diversity of backgrounds, experiences and qualities, all of it!

The result is a choral narrative that traverses through time, encompassing broad societal shifts such as 1980s counterculture, the impact of Brexit and the booming age of Twitter.

Girl, Woman, Other treads new ground, both in terms of narrative scope and style. Evaristo was keen 'to put presence into absence', and succeeded in doing so by making the presence of black British women visible in the literary sphere. At the same time, she spotlighted intersectionality, giving visibility to the nuances of gender and sexual orientation. The cast of characters has at its centre Amma, a woman playwright in her sixties, who is premiering her latest provocation at London's National Theatre. Out of all the characters, Amma is the one most closely modelled after Evaristo herself, who in the 1980s co-founded the Theatre of Black Women.

From a stylistic perspective, *Girl, Woman, Other* benefits from a free-flowing prose poetry style described by Evaristo as 'fusion fiction'. Elaborating on this particular form of expression, Evaristo explains:

The form is very free-flowing and it allowed me to be inside the characters' heads and go all over the place – the past, the present. For me, there's always a level of experimentation – I'm not happy writing what we might call traditional novels.

Indeed, *Girl, Woman, Other* is not a traditional novel; that is its main strength.

Since winning the Man Booker Prize, Evaristo has published *Manifesto: On Never Giving Up* (2021) a memoir instigated by the many interviews she gave after the Booker win. In 2021 she was named President of the Royal Society of Literature, becoming the first person of colour to hold the position in the organization's 200-year history. Also that year, Penguin launched her curated book series of forgotten black authors, 'Black Britain: Writing Back', 'to correct historic bias in British publishing'. When asked in an interview if she had any advice for her younger self: 'Oh just carry on', she said, 'have fun, don't drink so much, stop smoking. Look after yourself. Not so many Chinese takeaways. And just go through it. It'll all be part of what you become in the future.' FF

Bernardine Evaristo (b.1959)
By Sal Idriss, 2004
Chromogenic print, 505 × 407mm
National Portrait Gallery, London, x126373

I wanted to make a movie feel like I think a lot of our lives feel, which is that they are beautiful and they are horrific.[57]

Emerald Fennell made her groundbreaking feature directorial debut with the dark comedy *Promising Young Woman*, which stars Carey Mulligan as Cassie, a woman seeking vengeance for a tragedy in her past. Written, directed and co-produced by Fennell, the film premiered at the Sundance Film Festival in January 2020 to critical acclaim. Talking about the ideas behind the script, Fennell explained:

You can't write a film like this unless you examine yourself and your own past. If this is a movie about forgiveness, it's important to say this is just a culture we've all grown up in. The incidents in this movie are in every romantic comedy, every TV show — we laugh at them.

With an undertone of feminist justice and subversiveness, the film delivers poignant messages about society, gender politics, consent and rape. Tensions are juxtaposed with humour and the use of a pastel palette, which challenges feminine stereotypes. Fennell said that, in writing the script, she too had to come to terms with her own passive role in toxic culture.

Promising Young Woman was shot in a brief 23 days in Los Angeles, when she was seven months pregnant; the editing was finished a few weeks after she gave birth to her son. Fennell received numerous accolades, winning Best Original Screenplay at the 2021 Academy Awards, the first time a British woman has won in this category, with additional nominations for Best Picture, Best Director, Best Actress (Mulligan) and Best Film Editing. The film also won Best Original Screenplay at the Critics' Choice Awards, Writers' Guild Awards, and at The British Academy Film Awards where it also won Outstanding British Film.

Known for her sense of humour and creativity in her acting, directing and writing, Fennell was previously best known as an actor, playing Camilla Parker Bowles in *The Crown*, and for working as head writer on the second series of *Killing Eve*, which earned her two Emmy nominations.

London-based photographer Violeta Sofia made this portrait of Fennell and Mulligan for *Deadline Hollywood* magazine in celebration of the Oscar nominations. She remembers watching the trailer for *Promising Young Woman* and immediately feeling inspired and empowered: 'I feel very lucky to have been part of the cover story of such an important, much needed film.' Her photograph encapsulates the unique collaboration between these creative women. GA

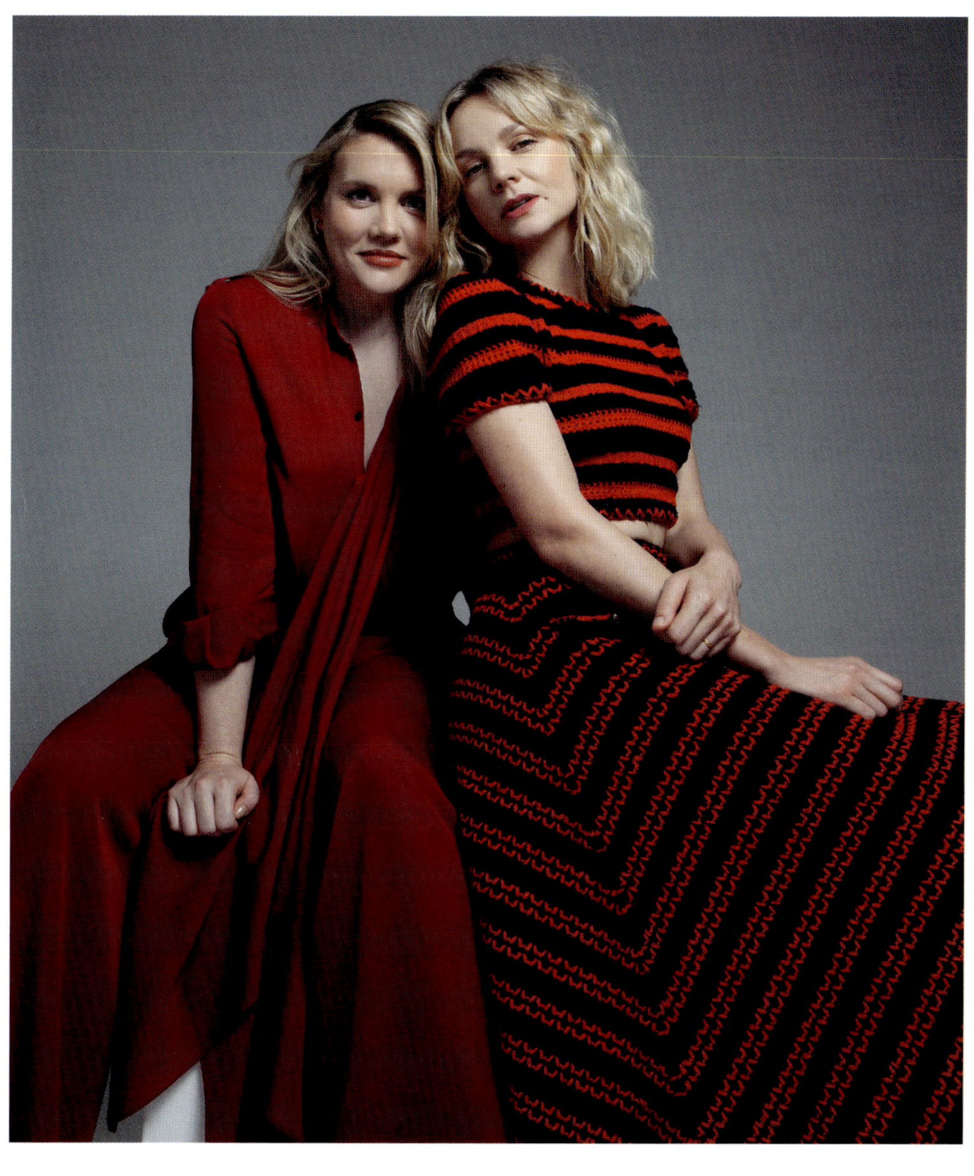

Emerald Fennell (b.1985) and Carey Mulligan (b.1985)
By Violeta Sofia Mbala Mbassa, 2020
Inkjet print, 610 × 510mm
National Portrait Gallery, London, x201395

Sarah Gilbert

In December 2019 the first known case of a severe acute respiratory syndrome, labelled as SARS-CoV-2, was identified in Wuhan, China. Within a few months the virus had spread across the world, resulting in the COVID-19 pandemic. After a normal start, 2020 soon morphed into a year when social distancing and lockdowns were implemented by most national governments; face masks became the norm for most people and international travel came to a sudden halt. The world as we knew it had taken a turn for the worst and the creation and fast distribution of a vaccine against

this new pathogen appeared to offer the only way out of the crisis. Sarah Gilbert, a Professor of Vaccinology at the University of Oxford, played no small role in the development of this vaccine against COVID-19.

A leading scientist at the University's Jenner Institute, Gilbert and her research team immediately set to work to create a vaccine. As she later recounted: 'We had recently started thinking about an appropriate response to Disease X; how could we mobilise and focus our resources and go more quickly than we had ever gone before. And then Disease

X arrived.' The team, led by Gilbert, were able to deploy their pre-existing knowledge around 'Disease X' in the creation of a vaccine against COVID-19. Aided by a £2.2 million grant from the UK's National Institute for Health Research and UK Research and Innovation, Gilbert and her team made fast progress and after the clinical trials involving 23,000 people in the United Kingdom, Brazil and South Africa, they were able to release the ChAdOx1nCoV-19 vaccine – more commonly known as the Oxford-AstraZeneca vaccine. Looking back on this highly ambitious timeframe Gilbert commented:

I have worked in the development of vaccines against infectious pathogens for many years and in the last two years have been able to draw on all that I have learned in order to respond to the SARS-CoV-2 pandemic. I have been so fortunate to work with a very talented and dedicated team who made it possible to develop a vaccine in less time than anyone thought possible.

The Oxford-AstraZeneca vaccine was indeed developed in record time and by the start of 2021 it was being administered to the wider population, both in the United Kingdom and abroad. Prevention through vaccination became a shared global goal and Gilbert, with the aid of her team, was responsible for making a vaccine against SARS-CoV-2 a reality for millions around the world. For her vital contribution, Gilbert was made a Dame in 2021. FF

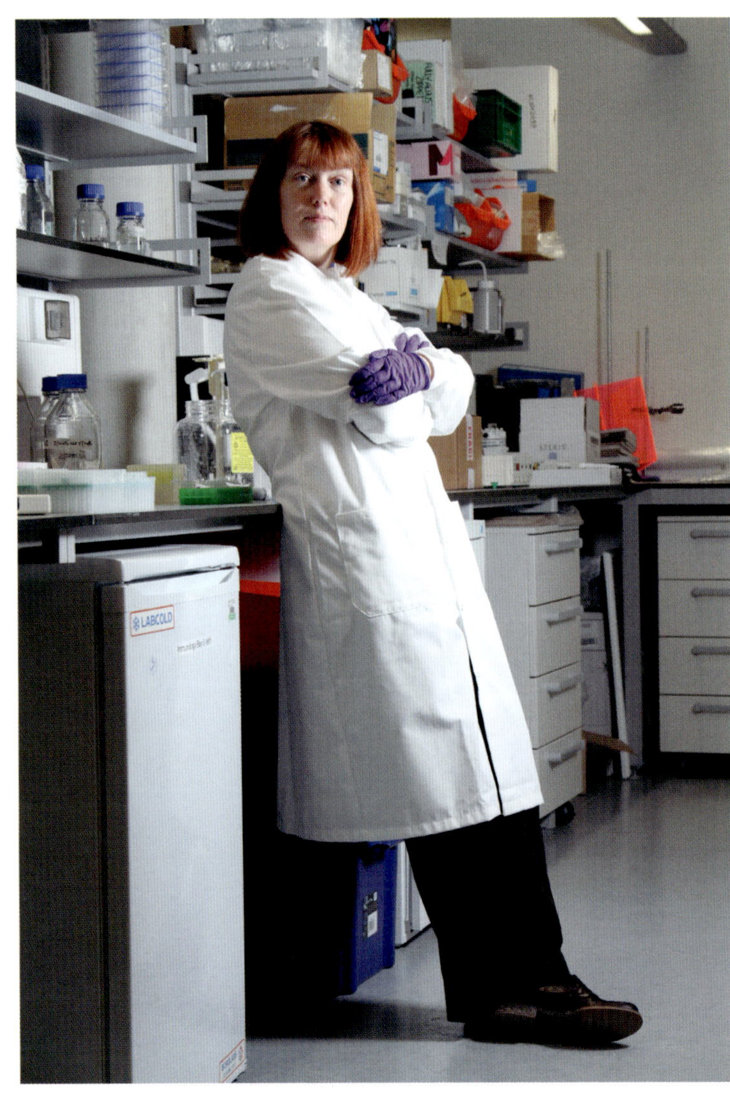

Sarah Gilbert (b.1962)
By John Lawrence, 2011
Shutterstock

The Lionesses

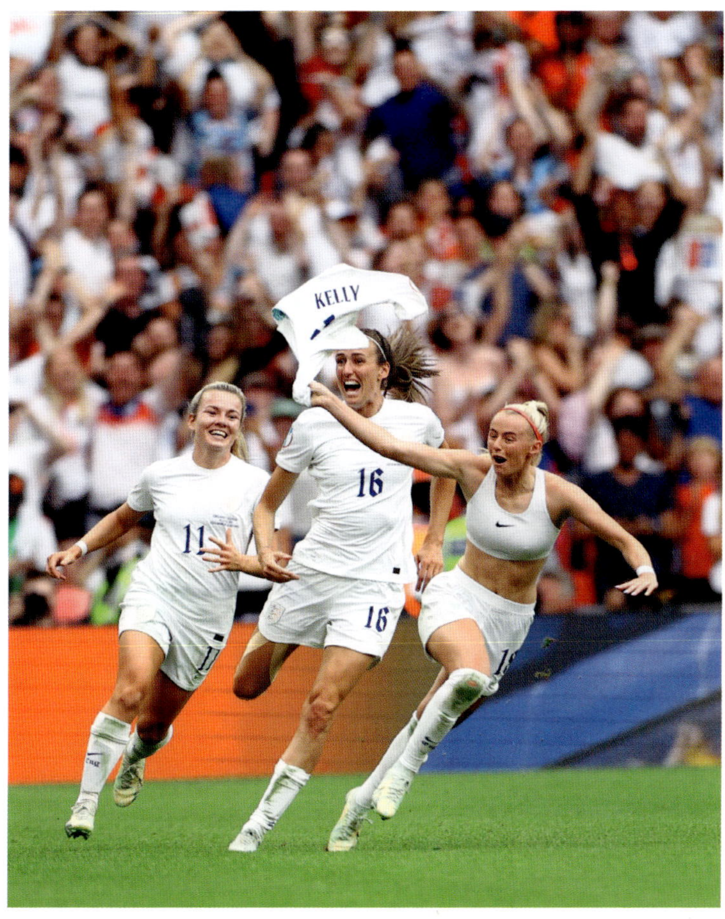

As a team we have just rewritten the history books.[58]

Winning the UEFA European Women's Championship in 2022 launched a new chapter in England women's football history.

Women have played football in England since the late nineteenth century. At first, it was considered shocking and matches were often abandoned. Despite the initial uproar, the popularity of the sport grew. During the First World War, women working in factories formed football teams, and, with the men's football league suspended, attendance at women's matches surged. On Boxing Day 1920, 53,000 people watched Dick Kerr's Ladies beat St Helen Ladies 4-0 at Goodison Park. However, by December 1921, the Football Association (FA) had imposed a ban that excluded women from playing on league pitches, from using club facilities and prohibited registered referees from officiating games. The ban was eventually overturned in 1971.

The quadrennial UEFA European Women's Championship tournament was due to kick off in the summer of 2021 but was postponed until 2022 due to the knock-on effects of the COVID-19 pandemic. With former Netherlands coach Sarina Wiegman now at the helm of England, she was able to lead the Lionesses to their first major tournament win, instead of defending the title as the head coach of her home nation. When Wiegman left the Netherlands, she was the country's most successful head coach and her leadership was instrumental in England's Euro 2022 victory. Keeping the same starting 11 for all six of England's matches brought consistency to the team and utilising her three 'super-subs' Alessia Russo, Ella Toone and Chloe Kelly in the latter stages of the game proved a winning strategy.

Alessia Russo scored four goals during the Championship, becoming the second highest goal scorer for England and the third highest in the tournament. She set up Ella Toone to score the equaliser in England's 2-1 quarter-final win over Spain and her bold back heel through the legs of the goalkeeper in England's 3-0 semi-final win over Sweden was voted UEFA's goal of the tournament.

Having made it to the final with just one goal conceded, England faced eight-time European champions Germany. A perfectly placed pass by Keira Walsh in the second half found Ella Toone and she put England ahead. Germany equalised but Chloe Kelly scored deep into extra time. Pulling off her shirt and swinging it around her head in celebration, Kelly channelled Brandi Chastain's iconic celebration after scoring the winning goal for the USA in the 1999 Women's World Cup Final. The photograph of Kelly celebrating is the tournament's defining image.

The final between England and Germany was held at Wembley in front of 87,192 fans, smashing the UEFA tournament record for attendance at both the men's and women's European championships. More than 17 million people watched the final on television, making it the most-watched women's football match in UK television history.

After the tournament, Wiegman declared: 'I think this tournament has done so much for the game but also for society and women in society in England but I also think across Europe and across the world.' SH

'Lionesses'
Lauren Hemp (b.2000), Jill Scott (b.1987) and Chloe Kelly (b.1998)
By Lisi Niesner, 31 July 2022
Chromogenic print, 390 × 305mm
National Portrait Gallery, London, x202501

Jann Haworth

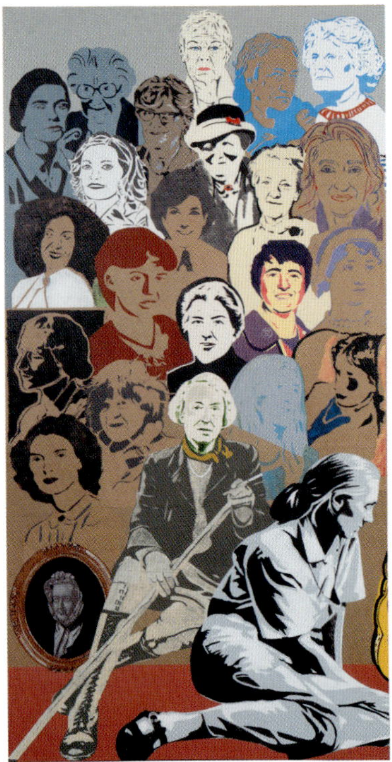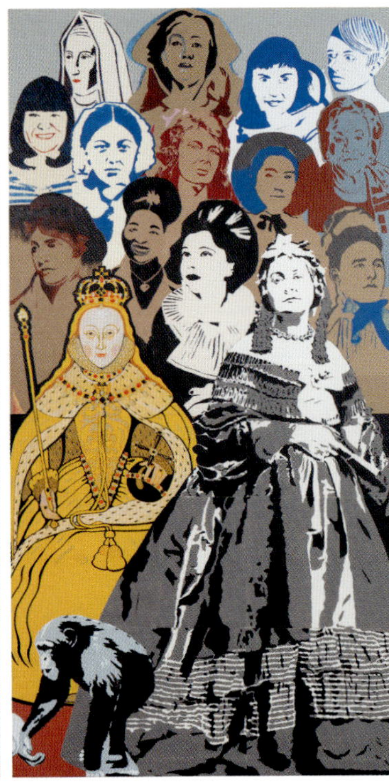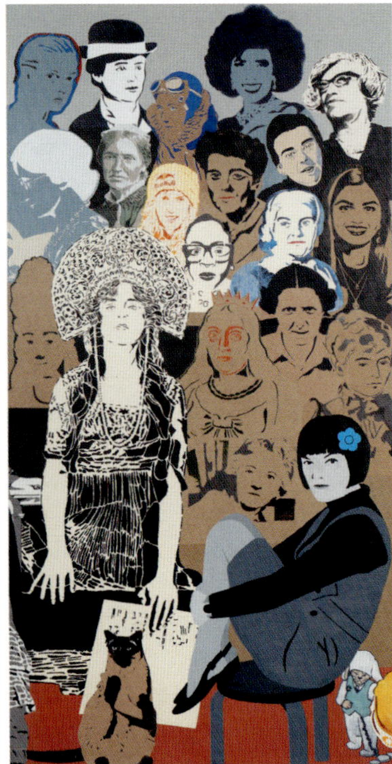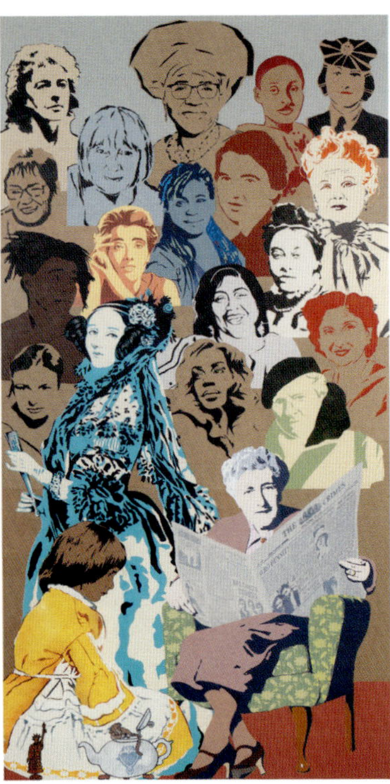

In 2023, the National Portrait Gallery unveiled *Work in Progress* (2021–2), a major seven-panel mural commissioned to showcase inspiring women, which was co-created by artists Jann Haworth and Liberty Blake in collaboration with communities across the United Kingdom. The mural celebrates historical and contemporary women who have paved the way for change across a range of disciplines, making a significant contribution to the course of British history and culture. 130 women are depicted, ranging from the ancient warrior queen Boudicca to mathematician and computer pioneer Ada Lovelace, and from physicist and radio astronomer Jocelyn Bell Burnell to Paralympic athlete Tanni Grey-Thompson.

While *Work in Progress* mostly draws on the depths of the National Portrait Gallery's vast Collection in order to shine a light on a broad range of both prominent and marginalised women, it also highlights 26 trailblazers who were previously unrepresented at the Gallery. They include painter and writer Ling Shuhua, football player Lily Parr, politician Maureen Colquhoun and nurse Elizabeth Anionwu. As the title suggests, such historical recovery should be considered a 'work in progress'; there are many more women deserving of attention and recognition beyond those shown. To acknowledge this visually, Haworth and Blake have included a silhouette of an unnamed woman on the seventh panel.

The featured portraits were produced during a series of workshops where Haworth and Blake guided participants through the process of stencilling on paper with acrylic paints, using an existing depiction of a woman of their choice. An additional 14 professional artists from the United Kingdom and the United States created full-length portraits for the mural's front row. Finally, Blake assembled and collaged the completed portraits on to the multiple panels to create the finished work, which forms

'Work in Progress'
By Jann Haworth and Liberty Blake, 2021–2
Acrylic on paper collaged on panels, 2440 × 8768mm
National Portrait Gallery, London, 7145

and   Liberty Blake

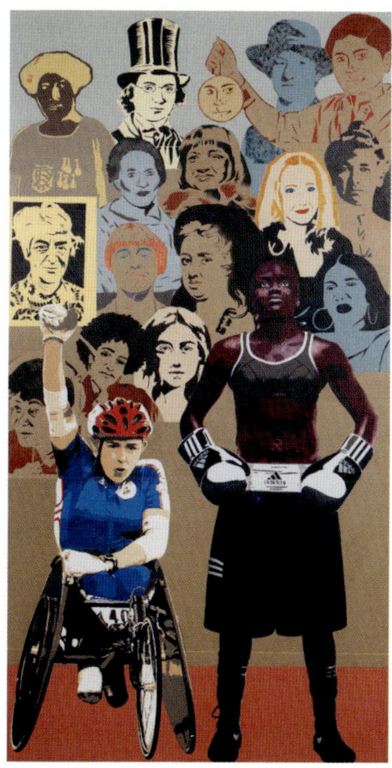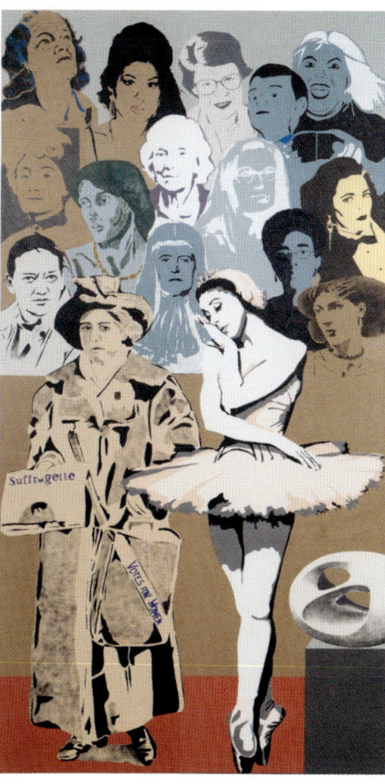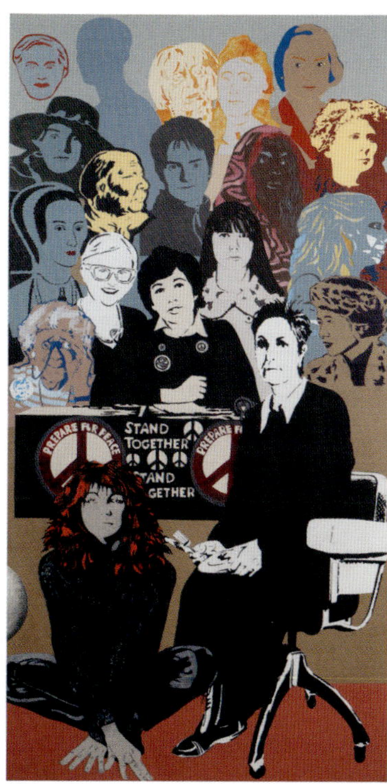

a vibrant, visual tribute to female achievement, and encompasses the diverse styles and aesthetic choices of its varied contributors.

This is not the first of Haworth and Blake's murals to foreground women pioneers. The first version of *Work in Progress* was begun in 2016 when the artists began conducting workshops in their local community in Salt Lake City, Utah, USA. It soon grew into an international project that is ongoing.

Beyond *Work in Progress*, Blake is a collage artist, whose abstract works are predominantly inspired by natural landscapes. Haworth is renowned as a pioneer of soft sculptures that she began making in the 1960s. Her works radically reimagined art, challenging gender stereotypes and the very idea of female identity. As a key member of the early British pop art scene, Haworth's contribution was long overlooked, but was instrumental in carving a place for women within the male-dominated movement. FF & CN

'Work in Progress'

List of Figures

Endnotes

1 Mary Wollstonecraft, *A Vindication of the Rights of Woman: With Strictures on Political and Moral Subjects* (printed by Peter Edes for Thomas and Andrews, Boston, 1792), p.322.

2 Veronica Jackson, 'Restructuring Respectability, Gender, and Power: Aida Overton Walker Performs a Black Feminist Resistance', *Journal of Transnational American Studies*, vol. 10, no.1, 2019, p.261.

3 Hertha Ayrton in 'Inventor of the Flapper Fan: Contrivance Which Saved Thousands of British Lives', *Daily News*, 16 July 1919, p.4.

4 Ray Strachey, *The Cause: A Short History of the Women's Movement in Great Britain* (Virago Press Ltd, London, 1978; reprint of 1928 edition), p.385.

5 Hilda Hewlett in Gail Hewlett, *Old Bird: The Irrepressible Mrs Hewlett* (Matador, Leicester, 2010), p.109.

6 'Ladies and Aviation', *Western Daily Press*, 7 March 1914, p.8.

7 Margaret Murray, *My First Hundred Years* (William Kimber & Co Ltd, London, 1963), p.115.

8 Mairi Chisholm in Diane Atkinson, *Elsie and Mairi Go To War: Two Extraordinary Women on the Western Front* (Pegasus Books, London, 2009), p.54.

9 Olive Edis to Agnes Conway, 20 October 1918, https://oliveedisproject.wordpress.com/2016/06/10/lots-of-letters/ [accessed 1 December 2022].

10 Caroline Haslett in Peggy Scott, *An Electrical Adventure* (James Truscott & Sons, London, 1934), p.108.

11 Pat Hitchcock, *Alma Hitchcock: The Woman Behind the Man* (Berkley Books, New York, 2003), p.33.

12 Sue Shephard, *The Surprising Life of Constance Spry* (Macmillan, London, 2010), ix.

13 Yevonde, 'Why Colour?', *Photographic Journal*, vol. 73, March 1933, pp.116–120.

14 Mercedes Gleitze in Doloranda Pember, *In the Wake of Mercedes Gleitze: Open Water Swimming Pioneer* (The History Press, Gloucestershire, 2019), p.209.

15 P.L. Travers in the *National Observer* (10 June 1972), cited in *Current Biography Yearbook 1996* (H.W. Wilson, New York, 1996), p.580.

16 'At the Hippodrome: Adelaide Hall's Success', *Eastbourne Chronicle*, 23 March 1946, p.5.

17 Betty D. Vernon, *Ellen Wilkinson: 1891–1947* (Croom Helm Ltd, London, 1982), p.204.

18 Lady Eve Balfour, *The Living Soil* (Faber and Faber Ltd, London, 1948), https://epdf.tips/the-living-soil.html [accessed 3 October 2022].

19 Cicely Saunders, 'Dame Albertine Winner', *Oxford Dictionary of National Biography* (2004), https://doi.org/10.1093/ref:odnb/39877.

20 Dorothy Crowfoot Hodgkin in Olivia Cox-Fill, *For Our Daughters: How Outstanding Women Worldwide Have Balanced Home and Career* (Praegar Publishers, Westport, Connecticut, 1996), p.176.

21 Comments by John Brett, RAS Fellow, as cited by Mandy Bailey in 'Women and the RAS: 100 years of Fellowship', *Astronomy & Geophysics*, vol. 57, 1, February 2016, pp. 1.19–1.21.

22 Jennian F. Geddes, 'Portrait of "The Lady": A Life of Dorothy Russell', *Journal of the Royal Society of Medicine*, vol. 90, 8, August 1997, p.460.

23 Elizabeth David in Lisa Chaney, *Elizabeth David: A Biography* (Pan Books, London, 1998), p.249.

24 Vera Brittain, *Envoy Extraordinary: A Study of Vijaya Lakshmi Pandit and her Contribution to Modern India* (George Allen & Unwin Ltd, London, 1965), p.113.

25 Ibid., p.116.

26 'Sheila van Damm', *The Times'* Obituary, 25 August 1987.

27 Roland Penrose, Foreword, *Dorothy Bohm: A World Observed*, (Hugh Evelyn, London, 1970).

28 Sheila Willcox, *Three Days Running* (Collins, London, 1958), p.168.

29 Claudia Jones in the first issue of the *West Indian Gazette*, March 1958, cited in Carole Boyce Davies, *Left of Karl Marx: The Political Life of Black Communist Claudia Jones* (Duke University Press, Durham and London, 2007), p.86.

30 Ida Kar, *Guardian*, 26 March 1960.

31 Vanessa Redgrave speaking about Michael Elliott (who directed her in *As You Like It* in 1963) in Michael Billington, 'Interview: Vanessa Redgrave: "I want to give people the jolliest time"', *Guardian*, 11 April 2012, https://www.theguardian.com/stage/2012/apr/11/vanessa-redgrave-brighton-festival [accessed 8 June 2023].

32 Peter Hogan, *Shirley Bassey: Diamond Diva* (André Deutsch, London, 2008), p.1.

33 Margaret Busby in 'The Margaret Busby Interview: A "Daughter of Africa"', *Alt Africa Review*, 2019, https://alt-africa.com/2020/01/04/the-margaret-busby-interview-a-daughter-of-africa-and-pioneering-force-in-publishing/ [accessed 5 November 2022].

34   Margaret Busby in Aida Edemariam, 'Margaret Busby: how Britain's first black female publisher revolutionised literature – and never gave up', *Guardian*, 22 October 2020, https://www.theguardian.com/society/2020/oct/22/margaret-busby-the-uks-first-black-female-publisher-everyone-assumed-i-was-there-to-make-the-tea [accessed 17 October 2022].

35   Hella Pick, *Invisible Walls: A Journalist in Search of Her Life* (Weidenfeld & Nicolson, London, 2021), p.147.

36   Carmen Callil, 'The stories of our lives', *Guardian*, 26 April 2008, https://www.theguardian.com/books/2008/apr/26/featuresreviews.guardianreview2 [accessed 30 October 2022].

37   Lennie Goodings, *A Bite of the Apple: A Life with Books, Writers and Virago* (Oxford University Press, Oxford, 2020), p.13.

38   Interview with the author, 2018.

39   Line Nyhagen Predelli, Beatrice Halsaa, Cecilie Thun, Kim Perren and Adriana Sandu, *Majority-Minority Relations in Contemporary Women's Movements: Strategic Sisterhood* (Palgrave Macmillan, London, 2012), p.55.

40   Angela Carter, *The Bloody Chamber and other Stories. With an Introduction by Helen Simpson*, 1995.

41   Linda Bellos in Katy Guest, 'Whatever happened to feminism's extreme sects?', *Independent*, 12 February, 2006, https://www.independent.co.uk/news/uk/this-britain/whatever-happened-to-feminism-s-extreme-sects-5335348.html [accessed 29 November 2022].

42   Charles McGrath, 'Her Magic Act: Transforming Herself Nightly', *New York Times*, 13 May 2009.

43   Richard York, 'Goodall's Light: Twenty Years With The Chimpanzees of Gombe', *Organization & Environment*, vol. 19, no.3, September 2006, p.371.

44   Averil Mansfield, *Imperial College Healthcare NHS Trust Blog*, https://www.imperial.nhs.uk/about-us/blog/first-uk-female-professor-of-surgery-averil-mansfield [accessed 8 June 2023].

45   Jo Salter, *Womanthology*, 22 February 2017, https://www.womanthology.co.uk/female-fast-jet-pilots-not-woman-best-you-can-be-jo-salter-director-people-organisation-pwc/ [accessed 11 May 2023].

46   Beryl Gilroy, *Leaves in the Wind: Collected Writings* (Mango Publishing, Florida, 1998), p.209.

47   Patrick Heidmann, 'Keira Knightley', *The Talks*, https://the-talks.com/interview/keira-knightley [accessed 11 May 2023].

48   Zaha Hadid in John Seabrook, 'The Abstractionist: Zaha Hadid's unfettered invention', *The New Yorker*, 13 December 2009, https://www.newyorker.com/magazine/2009/12/21/the-abstractionist [accessed 3 October 2022].

49   Leyla Hussein, 'My Pledge: "I'm a Woman, Hear Me Roar"', *Huffington Post*, 7 March 2014, https://www.huffingtonpost.co.uk/leyla-hussein/violence-against-women_b_4916912.html [accessed 15 October 2022].

50   'Interview: Farshid Moussavi, Architect, Author and Professor', *Something Curated*, 7 July 2016, https://somethingcurated.com/2016/07/07/interview-farshid-moussavi-architect-author-professor/ [accessed 11 May 2023].

51   https://blackbritishacademics.co.uk/2015/06/13/dr-shirley-thompsons-nanny-of-the-maroons-opera-continues-to-diversify-classical-music-performance/ [accessed 6 June 2023].

52   https://www.ucl.ac.uk/global-governance/podcast/4-farhana-yamin-journey-green-radicalism [accessed 23 May 2023].

53   https://climatereframe.co.uk/ [accessed 23 May 2023].

54   Evelyn Glennie, 'How to truly listen', TED Talk, 2003, https://www.ted.com/talks/evelyn_glennie_how_to_truly_listen [accessed 3 October 2022].

55   'Dame Sarah Storey following her 17th Paralympic gold medal at Tokyo 2020', *Storey Racing*, https://storeyracing.cc/news/ [accessed 6 November 2022].

56   Alex Moshakis, '"What's the alternative? To give up?": Bella Lack, the new queen of green', *Observer*, 14 August 2022.

57   Emerald Fennell in '"Promising Young Woman": How Carey Mulligan and Emerald Fennell Made the Most Audacious, Feminist Movie of the Year', *Variety*, https://variety.com/2020/film/news/promising-young-woman-carey-mulligan-emerald-fennell-1234848775/ [accessed 11 May 2023].

58   Leah Williamson, Captain of the Lionesses, https://www.tiktok.com/@womensfootball/video/7189277367263644934 [accessed 11 May 2023].

Further Reading

Note from the editors: This publication is indebted to the many in-depth studies carried out on individual figures by different authors over the years. Below is a list of books and articles that have informed our entries and essays. We would particularly like to acknowledge the importance of the Oxford Dictionary of National Biography in offering key biographical information.

Samira Ahmed, 'Introduction', Lydia Miller, *Inspirational Women: Rediscovering Stories in Art, Science and Social Reform* (National Portrait Gallery Publications, London, 2022)

Diane Atkinson, *Elsie and Mairi Go to War: Two Extraordinary Women on the Western Front* (Preface Publishing, London, 2009)

Diane Atkinson, *Rise Up Women: The Remarkable Lives of the Suffragettes* (Bloomsbury, London, 2018)

Judy Attfield and Pat Kirkham (eds), *A View from the Interior: Feminism, Women and Design* (The Women's Press, London, 1989)

Anne Barrett, *Women at Imperial College; Past, Present and Future* (World Scientific, London, 2016)

Paula Bartley, *Women's Activism in Twentieth-Century Britain: Making a Difference across the Political Spectrum* (Palgrave Macmillan, London, 2022)

Françoise Basch, *Relative Creatures: Victorian Women in Society and the Novel* (Schocken Books, New York, 1974)

Mary Beard, *Women & Power: A Manifesto* (Profile Books / The London Review of Books, London, 2017)

Simone de Beauvoir, *The Second Sex* (Cape, London, 1953)

Harriet Blodgett, 'Cicely Hamilton, Independent Feminist', *Frontiers: A Journal of Women Studies*, vol. 11, no.2/3, pp.99–104 (University of Nebraska Press, Lincoln, 1990)

Margaret Bondfield, *A Life's Work* (Hutchinson & Co. Ltd, London, 1948)

Frances Borzello, *Seeing Ourselves: Women's Self-Portraits* (Thames & Hudson, London, 2016)

Vera Brittain, *Envoy Extraordinary: A Study of Vijaya Lakshmi Pandit and her Contribution to Modern India* (George Allen & Unwin Ltd, London, 1965)

David Butler, *Delia Derbyshire*, https://www.bbc.com/historyofthebbc/100-voices/pioneering-women/women-of-the-workshop/delia-derbyshire

Nina Byers and Gary Williams (eds), *Out of the Shadows: Contributions of Twentieth-Century Women to Physics* (Cambridge University Press, Cambridge, 2006)

Angela Carter and Helen Simpson, 'Introduction', *The Bloody Chamber and Other Stories* (Vintage, London, 2006; first published by Victor Gollancz, 1979)

Lisa Chaney, *Elizabeth David: A Biography* (Macmillan, London, 1998)

Deborah Cherry (ed.), *Maud Sulter: Passion* (Altitude Editions, London, 2015)

Agatha Christie, *An Autobiography* (Collins, London, 1977)

Georgine Clarsen, '"A Fine University for Women Engineers": a Scottish munitions factory in World War I', *Women's History Review*, vol. 12, no.3, pp.333–56 (Taylor & Francis, Oxford, 2003)

Harriet Cohen, *A Bundle of Time: The Memoirs of Harriet Cohen* (Faber, London, 1969)

Rachel Cooke, *Her Brilliant Career: Ten Extraordinary Women of the Fifties* (Virago, London, 2014)

Elizabeth Crawford, *Enterprising Women: The Garretts and their Circle* (Francis Boutle Publishers, London, 2009)

Mary R.S. Creese, 'Martha Anne Whiteley (1866–1956): Chemist and Editor', *Bulletin History of Chemistry*, vol. 20, 1997, pp.42–5

Elena Crippa, *Paula Rego* (Tate, London, 2021)

Meredith Daneman, *Margot Fonteyn* (Penguin, London, 2005)

Carole Boyce Davies, *Left of Karl Marx: The Political Life of Black Communist Claudia Jones* (Duke University Press, Durham and London, 2007)

Hannah Dawson (ed.), *The Penguin Book of Feminist Writing* (Penguin, London, 2021)

Julia Dudkiewicz and Andrzej Szczerski (eds), *Young Poland: The Polish Arts and Crafts Movement, 1890–1918* (Lund Humphries, London, 2020)

Bernardine Evaristo, *Girl, Woman, Other* (Penguin, London, 2020)

Georgina Ferry, *Dorothy Hodgkin: A Life* (Bloomsbury Reader, London, 2014)

Jennian F. Geddes, 'A portrait of "The Lady": a life of Dorothy Russell', *Journal of the Royal Society of Medicine*, vol. 90, August 1997, pp.455–61

Jane Fletcher Geniesse, *Freya Stark: Passionate Nomad* (Chatto & Windus, London, 1999)

Midge Gillies, *Amy Johnson: Queen of the Air* (Weidenfeld & Nicolson, London, 2003)

Beryl Gilroy and Bernardine Evaristo, 'Introduction', *Black Teacher* (Faber & Faber, London, 2022; first published in 1976)

Edmund Gordon, *The Invention of Angela Carter: A Biography* (Vintage, London, 2017)

Juliet Hacking, *Lives of the Great Photographers* (Thames & Hudson, London, 2015)

Juliet Hacking and David Campany, *Photography: The Whole Story* (Thames & Hudson Ltd, London, 2012)

Cicely Hamilton, *Life Errant* (J.M. Dent & Sons Ltd, London, 1935)

Liz Heron and Val Williams (eds), *Illuminations: Women Writing on Photography from the 1850s to the Present* (Routledge, Abingdon, 1997)

Gail Hewlett, *Old Bird: The Irrepressible Mrs Hewlett* (Matador, Leicester, 2010)

Jennifer Higgie, *The Mirror and the Palette: Rebellion, Revolution and Resilience: 500 Years of Women's Self-Portraits* (Weidenfeld & Nicolson, London, 2021)

Peter Hogan, *Shirley Bassey: Diamond Diva* (André Deutsch, London, 2008)

Jennifer Holmes, *A Working Woman: The Remarkable Life of Ray Strachey* (Matador, Leicester, 2019)

bell hooks, *Ain't I a Woman: Black Women and Feminism* (Routledge, London, 2014)

Veronica Jackson, 'Restructuring Respectability, Gender, and Power: Aida Overton Walker Performs a Black Feminist Resistance', *Journal of Transnational American Studies*, vol. 10, no.1, p.261 (2019)

Selma James, *Sex, Race and Class: The Perspective of Winning: A Selection of Writings 1952–2011* (PM Press, Chicago, 2012)

Hilda Kean, 'Searching for the past in present defeat: the construction of historical and political identity in British feminism in the 1920s and 1930s', *Women's History Review*, vol. 3, no.1, pp.57–80 (1994)

Annie Kenney, *Memories of a Militant* (Edward Arnold & Co., London, 1924)

Pat Kirkham (ed.), *The Gendered Object* (Manchester University Press, Manchester, 1996)

Julie Laut, '"The Woman Who Swayed America": Vijaya Lakshmi Pandit, 1945', *Deportate, esuli, profughe*, no.37, pp.26–47 (2018)

Linda Lear, *Beatrix Potter: The Extraordinary Life of a Victorian Genius* (Penguin, London, 2008)

Luce Lebart and Marie Robert (eds), *A World History of Women Photographers* (Thames & Hudson, London, 2022)

Doris Lessing, *Walking in the Shade: Volume Two of My Autobiography, 1949–1962* (HarperCollins, London, 1997)

Jenny Lister (ed.), *Mary Quant* (V&A Publishing, London, 2019)

Ellen MacArthur, *Full Circle* (Michael Joseph, London, 2010)

Averil Mansfield, *Life in Her Hands: The Inspiring Story of a Pioneering Female Surgeon* (Ebury Spotlight, London, 2023)

Hilary Mantel, *Giving up the Ghost: A Memoir* (Fourth Estate, London, 2003)

Jane Marcus, *Nancy Cunard: Perfect Stranger* (Clemson University Press, Clemson, 2020)

Joan Mason, 'Hertha Ayrton (1854–1923) and the Admission of Women to the Royal Society of London', *Notes and Records of the Royal Society of London*, vol. 45, no.2, pp.201–20 (Royal Society, London, July 1991)

Hilda Matheson, *Broadcasting* (T. Butterworth, London, 1933)

George Mind, *Women and the Practice of Studio Portraiture in Britain 1888–1914: Politics, Commerce and Constructions of Femininity*, PhD thesis (University of Westminster in Collaboration with the National Portrait Gallery, London, October 2021)

Wendy Moore, *No Man's Land: The Trailblazing Women Who Ran Britain's Most Extraordinary Military Hospital During World War I* (Basic Books, New York, 2020)

Joanna Moorhead, *The Surreal Life of Leonora Carrington* (Virago, London, 2017)

Marjorie Mowlam, *Momentum* (Magna Large Print Books, Long Preston, 2002)

Clare Mulley, *The Woman Who Saved the Children: A Biography of Eglantyne Jebb* (Oneworld, Oxford, 2009)

Clare Mulley, *The Spy Who Loved: The Secrets and Lives of Christine Granville* (Pan Macmillan, London, 2013)

Jane Mulvagh, *Vivienne Westwood: An Unfashionable Life* (HarperCollins, London, 1998)

Billie Muraben, 'Elizabeth Friedlander: One of the first women to design a typeface', 8 March 2018, https://www.itsnicethat.com/features/elizabethfriedlander-graphicdesign-internationalwomensday-080318

Margaret Murray, *My First Hundred Years* (W. Kimber, London, 1963)

Andrea Nelson, *The New Woman Behind the Camera*, (National Gallery of Art, Washington D.C., 2020)

Linda Nochlin and Maura Reilly (eds), *Women Artists: the Linda Nochlin Reader* (Thames & Hudson, London, 2015)

Dennis Nordruft, Zandra Rhodes, Iris Apfel, Suzy Menkes and Marylou Luther, *ZANDRA RHODES: 50 Fabulous Years in Fashion* (Yale University Press, New Haven, 2019)

Pat Hitchcock O'Connell, *Alma Hitchcock: The Woman Behind the Man* (Berkley Publishing, New York, 2004)

Marilyn Bailey Ogilvie, 'Obligatory Amateurs: Annie Maunder (1868–1947) and British Women Astronomers at the Dawn of Professional Astronomy', *The British Journal for the History of Science*, vol. 33, no.1, pp.67–84 (Cambridge University Press on behalf of The British Society for the History of Science, March 2000)

Donald L. Opitz, '"A Triumph of Brains over Brute": Women and Science at the Horticultural College, Swanley, 1890–1910', *Isis*, vol. 104, no.1, pp.30–62 (The University of Chicago Press on behalf of The History of Science Society, March 2013)

Oxford Dictionary of National Biography (Oxford University Press, Oxford), online edition, https://www.oxforddnb.com

Rozsika Parker, *The Subversive Stitch: Embroidery and the Making of the Feminine* (The Women's Press, London, 1984)

Rozsika Parker and Griselda Pollock (eds), *Old Mistresses: Women, Art and Ideology* (Routledge, London, 1981)

Elliott Patrick, *Tracey Emin: 20 Years* (National Galleries of Scotland, Edinburgh, 2008)

Celia Paul, *Letters to Gwen John* (Jonathan Cape, London, 2022)

Cecilia Payne-Gaposchkin, *An Autobiography and Other Recollections* (Cambridge University Press, Cambridge, 1984)

Doloranda Pember, *In the Wake of Mercedes Gleitze: Open Water Swimming Pioneer* (The History Press, Cheltenham, 2019)

Caroline Criado Perez, *Invisible Women: Exposing Data Bias in a World Designed for Men* (Chatto & Windus, London, 2019)

Hella Pick, *Invisible Walls: A Journalist in Search of Her Life* (Weidenfeld & Nicolson, London, 2021)

Vanessa Redgrave, *Vanessa: An Autobiography* (Hutchinson, London, 1991)

Liz Rideal (ed.), *Mirror, Mirror: Self-Portraits by Women Artists* (National Portrait Gallery Publications, London, 2001)

Stella Rimington, *Open Secret: The Autobiography of the Former Director-General of MI5* (Hutchinson, London, 2001)

Naomi Rosenblum, *A History of Women Photographers* (Abbeville Press Publishers, New York, 2010)

Alex Scott, *How (Not) To Be Strong* (Century, London, 2022)

Lothar Schirmer (ed.), *Women Seeing Women: A Pictorial History of Women's Photography from Julia Margaret Cameron to Annie Leibovitz* (Haus Publishing, New York, 2003)

Sue Shepard, *The Surprising Life of Constance Spry* (Macmillan, London, 2010)

Marika Sherwood, *Claudia Jones: A Life in Exile* (Lawrence and Wishart, London, 1999)

Dame Stephanie Shirley, *Let It Go: My Extraordinary Story – From Refugee to Entrepreneur to Philanthropist* (Penguin, London, 2019)

Angela Smith, *Katherine Mansfield: A Literary Life* (Palgrave, Basingstoke, 2000)

Julie Sommers, *Dressed for War: The Story of Vogue Editor Audrey Withers, from the Blitz to the Swinging Sixties* (Simon & Schuster, London, 2020)

Frances Spalding, *John Piper, Myfanwy Piper: Lives in Art* (Oxford University Press, Oxford, 2009)

Jo Spence and Joan Solomon (eds), *What Can a Woman Do with a Camera? Photography for Women* (Scarlet Press, London, 1995)

Sue Tate, *Pauline Boty: Pop Artist and Woman* (Wolverhampton Art Gallery & Museums, Wolverhampton, 2013)

Virginia Trimble and David A. Weintraub (eds), *The Sky Is for Everyone: Stories of Women Astronomers in Their Own Words* (Princeton University Press, Princeton, 2022)

Libby Sellers, *Women Design: Pioneers in architecture, industrial, graphic and digital design from the twentieth century to the present day* (Frances Lincoln, London, 2017)

V&A, 'Althea McNish: An Introduction' https://www.vam.ac.uk/articles/althea-mcnish-an-introduction

Sheila Van Damm, *No Excuses* (Putnam, New York, 1957)

Betty D. Vernon, *Ellen Wilkinson: 1891–1947* (Croom Helm Ltd, London, 1982)

Dorothy Wilding, *The Pursuit of Perfection* (Robert Hale Ltd, London, 1958)

Sheila Willcox, *Three Days Running* (Collins, London, 1958)

Val Williams, *The Other Observers: Women Photographers in Britain 1900 to the Present* (Virago, London, 1991)

Virginia Woolf, *A Room of One's Own* (Hogarth Press, London, 1931)

Yevonde, *In Camera* (Women's Book Club, London, 1940 and John Gifford, London, 1940)

Yevonde, 'Photographic Portraiture from a Woman's Point of View', *British Journal of Photography*, 29 April 1921

Picture Credits

The National Portrait Gallery would like to thank the copyright holders for granting permission to reproduce works illustrated in this book. Every effort has been made to contact the holders of copyright material, and any omissions will be corrected in future editions if the publisher is notified in writing.

p.12 Given by the photographer's sister, Susan Morton, 1976. © William Hustler and Georgina Hustler / National Portrait Gallery, London. p.13 Purchased with help from the National Lottery Heritage Fund and Gallery supporters, 2008. © National Portrait Gallery, London. p.14 Purchased, 1996. © National Portrait Gallery, London. p.15 Bequeathed by Jane, Lady Shelley, 1899. © National Portrait Gallery, London. p.16 Purchased with kind support from the CHANEL Culture Fund for 'Reframing Narratives', 2022. © The Artist, Courtesy Richard Saltoun Gallery. p.19 Commissioned by the National Portrait Gallery in collaboration with Magnum Photos and kindly supported by the CHANEL Culture Fund. © Susan Meiselas / Magnum Photos. p.23 © Hulton-Deutsch Collection / CORBIS / Corbis via Getty Images. p.24 (left) Purchased, 2013. © National Portrait Gallery, London. p.24 (right) Given by Delmar Banner, 1948. © National Portrait Gallery, London. p.25 Image courtesy of Kenneth Northover. © Kenneth Northover. p.26 Given by the photographer's son, Cavendish Morton, 1991. © National Portrait Gallery, London. p.27 (left) Imperial College. © Archives, Imperial College. Photo courtesy of Anne Barrett, from *Women at Imperial College; Past, Present and Future* (World Scientific, London, 2016). p.27 (right) Purchased, 1996. © National Portrait Gallery, London. p.28 Purchased, 2019. © National Portrait Gallery, London. p.31 Acquired from Criminal Record Office, 1914. © National Portrait Gallery, London. p.32 Given by Memorial Committee, 1929. © National Portrait Gallery, London. p.33 (above) Purchased with kind support from the CHANEL Culture Fund for 'Reframing Narratives', 2022. © Sally Fraser. p.33 (below) Purchased as part of *Citizen UK: Tower Hamlets*, funded by The National Lottery Heritage Fund and Art Fund, 2021. © Paul Trevor. p.34 (left) Commissioned by the National Portrait Gallery in collaboration with Magnum Photos and kindly supported by the CHANEL Culture Fund. © Olivia Arthur / Magnum Photos. p.34 (right) Commissioned by the National Portrait Gallery in collaboration with Magnum Photos and kindly supported by the CHANEL Culture Fund. © Olivia Arthur / Magnum Photos. p.36 Courtesy of The Mistress and Fellows, Girton College, Cambridge. p.37 (above) Given by Barbara Strachey (Hultin, later Halpern), 1999. © National Portrait Gallery, London. p.37 (below) Given by Barbara Strachey (Hultin, later Halpern), 1999. © National Portrait Gallery, London. p.38 Given by Pinewood Studios via Victoria and Albert Museum, 1989. © National Portrait Gallery, London. p.39 Given by Arthur Myers Smith, 1976. © National Portrait Gallery, London. p.40 Courtesy of Le Couvey-Martin family archives. p.41 (above) Given by the artist's widow, 1945. © National Portrait Gallery, London. p.41 (below) Photo courtesy of the Hewlett family archive. p.42 (above) Purchased, 1996. © National Portrait Gallery, London. p.42 (below) Collection: Imperial War Museum © IWM Art.IWM ART 4084. p.43 (above) © Reach PLC. Image created courtesy of The British Library Board. p.43 (below) Given by Bassano & Vandyk Studios, 1974. © National Portrait Gallery, London. p.44 Given by Terence Pepper, 1997. © National Portrait Gallery, London. p.45 Courtesy of the Estate of Anne Acheson and the Royal Society of Sculptors. p.46 Bequeathed by executors of Marie Anita Gay (Mrs John Gay), 2003. © National Portrait Gallery, London. p.47 Purchased, 2004. © Lee Miller Archives, England 2023. All rights reserved. p.48 Given by Olive Edis, 1948. © National Portrait Gallery, London. p.50 (left) Given by Cordelia Curle (née Fisher), 1959. © National Portrait Gallery, London. p.50 (right) Purchased, 1991. © National Portrait Gallery, London. p.51 Given by Lallie Charles Cowell (née Martin), 1994. © National Portrait Gallery, London. p.52 Purchased, 2012. © National Portrait Gallery, London. p.53 (above) Given by Beatrice Johnson, 1991. © William Hustler and Georgina Hustler / National Portrait Gallery, London. p.53 (below) Given by Annette Ratuszniak on behalf of the Mary Spencer Watson Archive, 2010. © National Portrait Gallery, London. p.54 Given by Bauhaus Archive, 1995. © Estate of Lucia Moholy / DACS 2023. p.55 Given by Family of Eglantyne Jebb, 2019. © National Portrait Gallery, London. p.56 (left) Purchased, 1996. © National Portrait Gallery, London. p.56 (right) Photo courtesy of Rothamsted Research Library. p.57 (left) Purchased, 2014. © National Portrait Gallery, London. p.57 (right) Purchased, 1996. © National Portrait Gallery, London. p.58 Given by Martin Tomlinson, 2021. © National Portrait Gallery, London. p.59 (above) Purchased, 1955. © Estate of W. Milner Knight. p.59 (below) Given by Terence Pepper, 2014. © National Portrait Gallery, London. p.60 Lent by RSA, 1998. © reserved; collection National Portrait Gallery, London. p.61 (left) Purchased, 1976. © Ishbel McWhirter. p.61 (right) Given by Eileen Klein, 1999. © Eileen Klein / National Portrait Gallery, London. p.62 Purchased with kind support from the CHANEL Culture Fund for 'Reframing Narratives', 2022. © reserved; collection National Portrait Gallery, London. p.63 Given by Adam Nicolson, 5th Baron Carnock, 2011. © National Portrait Gallery, London. p.64 Photo by Paul Popper / Popperfoto via Getty Images. p.65 (left) Purchased, 1990. © Estate Gisèle Freund / IMEC Images. p.65 (right) Purchased with help from the Art Fund, 1987. © National Portrait Gallery, London. p.66 Given by L.C. Sedon-Thompson, 1961. © National Portrait Gallery, London.

p.67 Purchased, 1984. © National Portrait Gallery, London. p.68 Purchased with support from The Portrait Fund, 2021. © National Portrait Gallery, London. p.70 Given by Cordelia Curle (née Fisher), 1959. © National Portrait Gallery, London. p.71 (above) Purchased, 1983. © Carole J Cutner. p.71 (below) Given by Terence Pepper, 2014. © National Portrait Gallery, London. p.72 Purchased, 2017. © The Estate of Deborah Turbeville. p.73 Purchased with help from Jane and Michael Wilson and Ellen Shapiro, 2017. © Rineke Dijkstra. p.74 (above) Given by Annie Leibovitz, 2022. *Adele, London, 2015.* © Annie Leibovitz. p.74 (below) Given by the photographer, Annie Leibovitz, 1995. © Annie Leibovitz. p.75 Commissioned, 2007. © Estate of Corinne Day / Commissioned by the National Portrait Gallery, London / trunkarchive.com. p.76 Purchased, 2021. Photo © Janette Beckman. p.77 Given by Doloranda H. Pember, 2001. © National Portrait Gallery, London. p.78 Given by Adrian House on behalf of the sitter, 1986. Photograph © National Portrait Gallery, London. p.79 Reproduced with permission of Clive Duncan. © National Portrait Gallery, London. p.80 Given by Walter Stoneman, before 1951. © National Portrait Gallery, London. p.81 Accepted in lieu of tax by H.M. Government and allocated to the Gallery, 1991. Cecil Beaton Studio Archive. © Cecil Beaton Archive / Condé Nast. p.82 Given by BBC, 2006. © BBC. p.83 (left) Purchased, 1989. Photograph © National Portrait Gallery, London. p.83 (right) Purchased, 2001. Angus McBean Photograph. © Harvard Theatre Collection, Houghton Library, Harvard University. p.84 Given by Dame Freya Madeline Stark, 1981. © Estate of Herbert Olivier. p.85 Given by the Estate of William Stanley Moss, 2021. © National Portrait Gallery, London. p.86 Purchased with kind support from the CHANEL Culture Fund for 'Reframing Narratives', 2023. © Anna Pawlikowska. p.87 British Geological Survey. © UKRI (permit no. CP23/024). p.88 Purchased, 1994. © Lida Moser. p.89 © National Portrait Gallery, London. p.90 Purchased, 1996. © National Portrait Gallery, London. p.91 Given by Dame Albertine Louise Winner, 1981. © National Portrait Gallery, London. p.92 Commissioned, 1985. © National Portrait Gallery, London. p.94 Bequeathed by the sitter's daughter, Miss Martha Somerville, 1883. © National Portrait Gallery, London. p.95 Courtesy of the President and Fellows of Harvard College, gift of Dudley and Georgene Herschbach. © Patricia Watwood. p.96 Purchased, 1999. © Julia Hedgecoe / National Portrait Gallery, London. p.97 Purchased with help from the Friends of the National Libraries and the Pilgrim Trust, 1966. © National Portrait Gallery, London. p.98 Purchased, 1970. © Estate of J.S. Lewinski / National Portrait Gallery, London. p.99 Given by the artist's widow, Ruth Rosen, 2002. Photograph © National Portrait Gallery, London. p.100 Given by Cecil Beaton, 1971. © Cecil Beaton Archive / Condé Nast. p.101 © Elizabeth Friedländer Collection, Special Collections & Archives, UCC Library, University College Cork, Ireland. p.102 Given by Caroline Michie and Jonathan Michie and Susan Michie,

Director's Acknowledgements

In addition to Yana Peel, I am also most grateful to Hélène Fulgence, Directrice du Patrimoine at CHANEL, for her dedication in shaping this unique endeavour in its early stages. The team at the CHANEL Culture Fund have worked closely with my colleagues and provided invaluable support throughout the development of 'Reframing Narratives', and our particular and personal thanks must go to Diane Solway, Emily Hallie, Michael Nazaraly, Róisín McQueirns and Julia Kagelmann, who have helped at all times along the way.

Heartfelt thanks, as ever, go to my colleagues Georgia Smith and Amber Speed from the Development team, who were instrumental in ensuring the smooth running of this exciting partnership. Over the course of the development of 'Reframing Narratives' many individuals at the National Portrait Gallery kindly contributed key assistance related to collections, conservation, research, communications and press; I would like to thank all my colleagues for the effort and care they put into each and every detail. Special thanks goes to Chief Curator Alison Smith who provided essential assistance throughout.

This book has been conceived by Flavia Frigeri in close collaboration with Georgia Atienza and Constantia Nicolaides. In addition to their extensive contributions, my thanks go to Emma Chapman, Magdalene Keaney, Alice Rawsthorn and Alison Smith for their perceptive essays and to Clare Freestone and Sarah Holdaway for their insightful entries. The book has been designed with great skill by Nina Jua Klein and John Philip Sage. As always, the Gallery's Publications team have provided vital assistance in bringing this publication to fruition, and I am particularly grateful to Kara Green, Publishing Manager; Priti Kothary, Production Controller; Mark Lynch and Katie Anderson in the Rights and Images team; and Anna Starling, Director of Commercial. I would also like to thank Project Editor Laura Cherry, Publishing Assistant Jemma Jacobs and freelancers Lizzy Silverton and Nina Chang-Smith from First Pages for their editorial support.

Nicholas Cullinan
Director
National Portrait Gallery

Curator's Acknowledgements

Over the course of 'Reframing Narratives: Women in Portraiture' many individuals kindly contributed key assistance. A special note of gratitude goes to the artists and their relatives and representatives, who have enabled us to enhance our representation of women artists and sitters in the Collection: Richard Ansett, Tony Barrett, Dorothy Bohm, Monica Bohm-Duchen, Stephen Bourne, Zoë Buckman, Chila Kumari Singh Burman, Gabriella Bullock, Christine Isabelle Cole, Clare Coombes, Niamh Coghlan, Andrée Cooke, Gabriel Coxhead, Julia Donat, Clive Duncan, Sue Elliott, Chandan Fraser, Julia Griffin, Amanda Hopkinson, Lucy Howarth, Teddy Karatz, Andreas Leventis, Georgia Lurie, Neville Madden, Mayotte Magnus, Caroline Michie, Jonathan Michie, Susan Michie, Nadya Murdoch, Everlyn Nicodemus, Celia Paul, Julia Rank, Richard Saltoun, Violeta Sofia, Mark Szaszy, Kathryn and Robin Wroe-Brown and The Estate of Maeve Gilmore.

One of the most ambitious outputs of this project has been the commission of *Work in Progress*, led by the exceptional artists Jann Haworth and Liberty Blake; my thanks go to them and the many people who have joined forces with the National Portrait Gallery to bring this wonderful mural to life. Among the partner institutions, I am indebted to the following: National Portrait Gallery Youth Forum (Juno Rae); The Courtauld Institute (Jo Applin and Leyla Bumbra); Murray Edwards College, Cambridge (Harriet Loffler and Naomi Polonsky); Pallant House Gallery (Lucy Padley and Emily Robson) and The Holburne Museum (Dr Chris Stephens, Louise Campion and Anna-Louise Highley). I am extremely grateful to the artists who contributed front row figures to *Work in Progress*: Nicky Ackland-Snow, David Atkinson, Kent Christensen, Al Denyer, Emma Finch, Courtney Giles, Liz Jewett, Vincent Johnson, Alex Johnstone, Les Jones, Zoe Johnstone, Laura Leach, Tristan Manco and Jean Richardson. The team at Gazelli Art House – Mila Askarova, Tina Maskalova and George Lionel Barker – have provided support throughout. At the National Portrait Gallery, colleagues in Collections, Communications, Conservation and Framing worked diligently to accomplish the successful realization of this work; in particular I would like to thank Stuart Ager, Poppy Andrews, Florence Berridge, Jessica Daley, Rosie Macdonald, Cate Pennington, Jen Richards and Perry Stewart.

As part of 'Reframing Narratives', I was lucky to work in close collaboration with Magnum Photos on the commission of new photographic portraits by Olivia Arthur, Susan Meiselas and Cristina de Middel of Rose Ayling-Ellis, Mary Beard, Caroline Criado Perez, Amika George, Bella Lack, Elif Shafak and Farhana Yamin. At Magnum Photos Emily Graham has tirelessly worked to coordinate the making of these wonderful portraits. I would also like to thank her colleagues Marine Merindol and Francesca Filippini Pinto for their additional support.

The reach of 'Reframing Narratives' was greatly enhanced by digital features and a series of literary talks. My thanks go to all those who were involved in this rich constellation of activities.

I am also indebted to numerous colleagues at the National Portrait Gallery who have lent their assistance at different junctures, especially the curatorial team. I must single out the individuals who have been most intimately involved with this project – Georgia Atienza, Assistant Curator and Constantia Nicolaides, Assistant Curator. They have brought great organizational skills and enormous enthusiasm to this monumental project. Their calm and cheerful nature made them the perfect companions on this journey of rediscovery and their contributions to this book are invaluable. Lydia Miller, Assistant Curator, has provided critical support in the early stages of 'Reframing Narratives'. Throughout the project, I have benefitted from the steadfast support and encouragement of Nicholas Cullinan, Director and Alison Smith, Chief Curator.

Finally, I echo our institution's Director, Nicholas Cullinan, in expressing my profound gratitude to Yana Peel and Hélène Fulgence for believing in the importance of this project. This has been a felicitous partnership and I am grateful for the dedication, creativity and incisive observations of the entire CHANEL Culture Fund team.

To conclude, 'Reframing Narratives' proves that a new way of thinking is not just possible; it is already here.

Flavia Frigeri
CHANEL Curator for the Collection
National Portrait Gallery

Published in Great Britain by
National Portrait Gallery Publications

National Portrait Gallery
St Martin's Place
London WC2H 0HE

This publication is part of 'Reframing Narratives:
Women in Portraiture' – a three-year research
partnership with the CHANEL Culture Fund.

Every purchase supports the
National Portrait Gallery, London.
For a complete catalogue of current publications,
please visit our website at
www.npg.org.uk/publications

The following authors have contributed
to the entries:
[GA] Georgia Atienza
[CF] Clare Freestone
[FF] Flavia Frigeri
[SH] Sarah Holdaway
[CN] Constantia Nicolaides

Text pp.93–98 by Emma Chapman
Text pp.179–184 © Alice Rawsthorn

ISBN 9781855145689

A catalogue record for this book is available
from the British Library

10 9 8 7 6 5 4 3 2 1

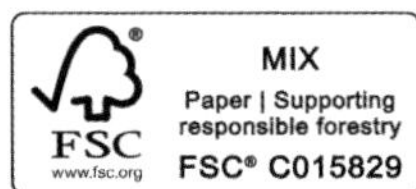

Director of Commercial: Anna Starling
Publishing Manager: Kara Green
Project Editor: Laura Cherry
Copy editing and proofreading: Nina Chang-Smith
and Lizzy Silverton, First Pages Ltd
Picture Rights Clearance: Katie Anderson
Production Controller: Priti Kothary
Publishing Assistant: Jemma Jacobs
Design: Nina Jua Klein and John Philip Sage

Printed in Italy by Printer Trento
Reproductions by DL Imaging, London

Front cover: *Work in Progress*
By Jann Haworth and Liberty Blake, 2021–2
National Portrait Gallery, London, 7145